THE ORIGINS OF THE MODERN STATE IN EUROPE

13th to 18th Centuries

General Editors: Wim Blockmans and Jean-Philippe Genet

THE ORIGINS OF THE MODERN STATE IN EUROPE

13th to 18th Centuries

General Editors: Wim Blockmans and Jean-Philippe Genet

Theme A. War and Competition between States
EDITED BY Philippe Contamine

Theme B. Economic Systems and State Finance
EDITED BY Richard Bonney

Theme C. The Legal Instruments of Power
EDITED BY Antonio Padoa Schioppa

Theme D. Power Elites and State Building
EDITED BY Wolfgang Reinhard

Theme E. Resistance, Representation, and Community
EDITED BY Peter Blickle

Theme F. The Individual in Political Theory and Practice
EDITED BY Janet Coleman

Theme G. Iconography, Propaganda, and Legitimation
EDITED BY Allan Ellenius

Economic Systems and State Finance

Edited by

Richard Bonney

European Science Foundation
CLARENDON PRESS
1995

Oxford University Press, Walton Street, Oxford OX2 6DP

Oxford New York
Athens Auckland Bangkok Bombay
Calcutta Cape Town Dar es Salaam Delhi
Florence Hong Kong Istanbul Karachi
Kuala Lumpur Madras Madrid Melbourne
Mexico City Nairobi Paris Singapore
Taipei Tokyo Toronto

and associated companies in
Berlin Ibadan

Oxford is a trade mark of Oxford University Press

Published in the United States
by Oxford University Press Inc., New York

British Library Cataloguing in Publication Data
Data available

Library of Congress Cataloging in Publication Data
Economic systems and state finance / edited by Richard Bonney.
p. cm.—(The Origins of the modern state in Europe)
Includes bibliographical references and index.
1. Finance, Public—Europe—History. 2. Taxation—Europe—History. 3. Europe—Economic policy. 4. Comparative economics. 5. Economic history. I. Bonney, Richard. II. Series.
HJ1000.E25 1995
336.4—dc20 92-34883
ISBN 0-19-820545-7

10 9 8 7 6 5 4 3 2 1

Typeset by Create
Printed in Great Britain
on acid-free paper by
Bookcraft Ltd., Midsomer Norton, Bath

GENERAL EDITORS' PREFACE

The seven books in this series are the proceedings of the seven working groups which together constituted the four-year-long programme, 'The Origins of the Modern State in Europe, 13th to 18th Centuries', sponsored by the European Science Foundation (ESF). From the outset, the aim was to bring together specialists from different countries, who accepted the challenge of developing a new vision of fundamental aspects of European state formation. Some of the seven themes were more original than others but, taken together, they reflected essential aspects of this far-reaching process. The choice of themes was also determined by what we, as the programme's initiators, saw as pre-eminent in terms of current research. Most themes, moreover, combined problems (and in some cases disciplines) rarely tackled in conjunction, and it was hoped that this would produce additional stimuli. No group could aim at comprehensiveness—whether thematic, geographical, or chronological. Rather, the volumes they have produced offer coherently chosen examples and approaches to fundamental aspects of state formation, in different contexts, so that at least the wide range of developments was covered.

The themes of the seven working groups were chosen in order to deal with key issues in the process of European state formation, while their goals were defined in somewhat broader terms than those often found in current historical research. This was mainly attempted through the combination of different disciplinary or thematic approaches in each group.

Theme A, *War and Competition between States,* focuses on various forms of competition between states, including both war and diplomacy. It starts from the assumption that interstate rivalries and conflicts were at the heart not only of the demarcation of territories, but also of the ever-growing need to mobilize resources for warfare. Institutionalization was consequently highly dependent on such competition. Fiscality—*pecunia nervus belli*—was of course another indispensable topic, and one which is considered here (Theme B: *Economic Systems and State Finance*) not only in terms of the comparative tax-generative capacities of different states, but also in relation to the economic systems on which it was based.

Law (that is, both legislation and justice), as a primary attribute of princes (whose legitimacy was founded on their effective guaranteeing of the rule of law and internal peace, later defined as public order), is treated from both an institutional and a legal viewpoint in Theme C, *The Legal Instruments of Power.* It was felt in this group that sociological theories of state formation tended to underestimate this fundamental factor. Case studies for several countries converge towards the conclusion that justice was a more effective factor in establishing the authority of the state, and in rendering it effective, than was legislation.

Prosopographical methods have been increasingly applied by historians of the medieval and early modern periods in the last twenty years or so, and the scope of their investigations has been considerably widened, thanks to the expansion of electronic databases. It was on the basis of these still fragmentary and selective materials that Team D attempted to formulate generalizations focusing on the themes of social foundations, recruitment, social reproduction, and political functions of power elites in Theme D, *Power Elites and State Building.*

It was felt that processes of state formation should be viewed from the periphery, as well as the centre. Small-scale public authorities, such as rural and urban communes, lordships, confederations, leagues and territories, established and institutionalized before the expansion of territorial monarchies into larger states in which many of them were incorporated, continued to hold real power until the end of the *ancien régime*, with or without a (semi-)sovereign status. Their political role was studied in Theme E, *Resistance, Representation, and Community*, in order to observe in what way, through various forms of representation and resistance, they contributed to the shaping of specific forms of states. The view 'from below' helps to diversify the picture of the early modern state and to include more of the great variety of European experiences of public authority. Several groups felt that general historical works at present largely overestimate both the level of centralization and the homogeneity of the larger dynastic states in early modern Europe.

The way in which the role of the state contributed to the concept of the individual was studied in Theme F, *The Individual in Political Theory and Practice*, in various areas of social and political life and on different levels of the theory and practice of philosophy and politics, while the uses made by states of the visual and performing arts for the purposes of political propaganda and the legitimation of power were studied through the fruitful interaction of both art historians in Theme G, *Iconography, Propaganda, and Legitimation.*

During the years 1988–92, the groups met six times in order to discuss common questionnaires, the data which had been assembled, and preliminary papers, some of which were produced collectively. Over one hundred scholars from eighteen countries examined sources (largely relating to the history of their own nations), as well as interpretations and explanatory models. Often they had to explain to their colleagues the terms in current use in the fields in which they worked. Inevitably, this all led to integrated volumes, reflecting the efforts of each group to come to terms with the variety of information and approaches.

When the programme was formally presented in 1987, we stressed some of its innovative aspects: it would be interdisciplinary, it would group together both medievalists and early modernists and, self-evidently, it would be international. During the course of the programme, we observed how the study of the *ancien régime* was accepted as a most fruitful and relevant means for the discovery of real continuities or disjunctions. The international nature of our enterprise is elaborated further below, while interdisciplinarity produced some creative confrontations, without ever raising obstacles. These three premises were fully accepted by all participants. Not only did they adopt them as a working scheme, but they also clearly had considerable influence on our collective work. This should be stressed, since it is not typical of most research in this field.

The international character of our research programme is far more meaningful in the context of the study of European state formation than it normally is in ESF activities. Unlike those who explore themes in molecular biology or oceanography, we are dealing with a subject which deeply influenced the organization and content of our research itself. Since the Middle Ages, states have stimulated their own national historiographies, whose effects continued to be experienced in our collaboration. We believe that the programme has played a considerable part in overcoming the predominant fallacy of studying states mainly, or exclusively, from within their twentieth-century borders, leading to the teleological view of state formation which we subjected to critical scrutiny in our First Plenary Conference at Rome.[1]

Not only did this research programme help us adopt a more open-minded attitude to the variability of developments from any given moment in history onwards: it also demonstrated clearly that the development of a few states in western Europe into centralized bureaucratic and absolutist monarchies is inadequate as a standard of reference for developments throughout Europe. Not only were more variegated models brought to the fore, we also learned that in practice the level of centralization, bureaucratization, and absolutism remained far below that assumed by earlier historians.

The working groups' international and long-term approach meant that their analysis could not be in terms of geographical borders. Close collaboration around specific themes offered the opportunity of complementing the information provided by each individual researcher. At this stage, however, it became apparent how deeply the states themselves interfere with our research. Many of us were hampered by linguistic shortcomings which obviously reduced access to

[1] Blockmans and Genet (1993).

material published in unfamiliar languages. Some groups largely overcame this difficulty by joining forces. We have to face up to this fact, which plays a greater role in our disciplines than in, for example, natural science and medicine. Beyond this first, and elementary, obstacle, we found two more in differences of terminology and conceptualization. These essential tools for communication proved largely dependent on specific historical context and languages, and thus inadequate for our more general and comparative analysis. However, we hope the publication of our results in several unilingual series will contribute to the introduction of a more generally consistent terminology.

Having tackled these obstacles of sources, conceptualization, and vision, we may hope that the wider scale of our analysis will lead us to further wide-ranging explanatory models, no longer reducing the broad phenomenon of state formation to mainly internal factors.

W. B.
J.-P. G.

PREFACE

*B*etween 1989 and 1992, the group of scholars who wrote this book met on six occasions as part of a wider 'scientific programme' co-ordinated by the European Science Foundation on the origins of the modern state ('The Origins of the Modern State in Europe, 13th–18th centuries', theme B). Conferences were organized at Netherlands Institute for Advanced Study, Wassenaar, in 1989 (organized by Wim Blockmans); at the Historisches Kolleg at Munich in 1990 (organized by Winfried Schulze); at the Fondation Ledoux at Arc-et-Senans in 1991 (organized by Jean-Claude Hocquet); and at the Casa de Velázquez at Madrid in 1991 (organized by Miguel Angel Ladero Quesada). The organizers of these meetings are thanked for their efforts, as also are the additional guest speakers who were invited to participate at each session. The group also met in the afternoon sessions at the plenary conferences organized by the European Science Foundation at the École Française de Rome in 1990 and at the Arquivo Nacional da Torre do Tombo in Lisbon in 1992.

The following scholars participated in the discussions of the group and contributed to the book: Professor János Barta (Debrecen, Hungary); Professor Richard Bonney (Leicester, UK, 'Team Leader'); Professor Carlo Capra (Milan, Italy); Professor Juan Gelabert (Santander, Spain); Dr Marjolein 't Hart (Amsterdam, Netherlands); Monsieur Jean-Claude Hocquet (Lille III, France); Professor Eberhard Isenmann (Bochum, Germany); Professor Martin Körner (Berne, Switzerland); Professor Giovanni Muto (Milan, Italy); Dr W. M. Ormrod (York, UK); Dr Bjørn Poulsen (Copenhagen, Denmark) and Professor Winfried Schulze (Munich, Germany). Professor Patrick O'Brien (Director, Institute of Historical Research, London, UK) participated in the earlier meetings of the group but had to withdraw, although his data was made available. Professors Miguel Angel Ladero Quesada and Wim Blockmans attended meetings of the group but did not contribute to the final volume. The Team would like to express its gratitude to the European Science Foundation for having facilitated this project and assisting it with a number of small research grants. We thank the programme's chairman, Wim Blockmans, and its scientific co-ordinator, Jean-Philippe Genet, for instigating the project in the first place.

Finally, a personal acknowledgement is due from the Editor. He thanks all members of the group for their support and enthusiasm over a relatively long period, when everyone has had competing demands for their time and other responsibilities. Particular thanks are due to Dr W. M. Ormrod, who kindly read the Editor's revisions of chapters, helping to avoid errors and to improve matters stylistic, and to Dr Juliet Vale who copy-edited the text, checked much of the bibliography and continued work on the Team's prose style in English. The Editor also thanks Dr Graham Smith for his computing advice and Dr Margaret Bonney for the statistical work and preparation of the charts for this book. Research assistance from the British Academy and from the Economic and Social Research Council (award no. R000231968) for the E[uropean] S[tate] F[inance] D[ata]b[ase], an international project in data collection, is gratefully acknowledged by the Editor. The ESFDB datasets cited in this book may be consulted via JANET at the ESRC Data Archive in the University of Essex (ARCHIVE @ UK.AC.Essex; generic code 33250). The Editor undertook most of the research for his own contributions between 1989 and 1991 while in Paris as Leverhulme Research Fellow and Professeur associé, Université de Paris-Sorbonne (Paris-IV). The book was set from disks prepared by the Editor, who integrated the bibliography and also compiled the index.

CONTENTS

LIST OF FIGURES

INTRODUCTION

Economic Systems and State Finance

Richard Bonney

The title of this book in itself introduces a substantial historiographical debate. If the term 'systems' alludes to the modern concept of systems theory with its own methodology, which may have some useful applications for the financial historian,[1] the phrase 'economic systems' refers to the observable fact that at no stage was the European economy a single economic system before the end of the *ancien régime*. France, for example, was a kingdom with several regional economies which were radically different one from another, and poorly integrated with each other; attempts to remove internal customs barriers before 1789 largely failed.[2] These regional economic systems were in turn related to other regional economies in Europe. To speak of a west European economy or economic 'system', let alone a world economy, is therefore to misrepresent the historical reality. Before *c*.1800 there could only be European economic systems and world economic systems with a tenuous relationship between them.

This is not to deny that before about 1350 there was little or no relationship between the European sub-systems and those of the rest of the world, while after that date these systems came into increasing contact with one another.[3] Thus the really powerful states came to be those which were not only capable, in economic and financial terms, of sustaining both armies and navies, but those which were able to exploit the possibilities offered by what in west European parlance is usually referred to as the 'New World'. The New World might more appropriately be termed the 'less advanced economic systems', those which were distant from western Europe and incapable of being exploited before the

[1] The applicability of the methodology of systems theory for financial history is usefully summarized for the non-specialist in Waquet (1990), 197–211.

[2] Bosher (1964).

[3] Abu-Lughod (1989); Wallerstein (1974, 1980); Braudel (1981–4), esp. vol. iii; also Viljoen (1974); Tracy (1990, 1991).

advance of technology (chiefly shipbuilding and armaments) in western Europe in the late Middle Ages and early modern period. By the eighteenth century, what was the proper form of government, administration and fiscal exploitation of overseas colonies had become matters for public debate in a way that was inconceivable in 1500.

The second part of the title, 'state finance', similarly opens up a whole area of conceptual and historiographical debate. Five broad general theories, or perhaps more properly taxonomies, of state finance—the classical and neo-classical, Keynesian, Marxist and Wagnerian—have recently been discerned; in addition one particular model, that of Gabriel Ardant (schematized by Charles Tilly), has been discussed in detail in the same essay, while a new theory has been proposed by its author, Waquet.[4] To these particular theories we should add three more (doubtless among several others) which Waquet does not introduce: Schumpeter's 'fiscal sociology',[5] the Peacock–Wiseman 'displacement effect' theory[6] and the Brennan–Buchanan concept of a 'fiscal constitution'.[7] The variety of views suggests that the subject of state finance remains in its relative methodological infancy and that earlier discussion of 'fiscal systems' will become outmoded. However, it seems unlikely that the full range of conceptual possibilities will ever be integrated successfully into an overarching theory, any more than for an overarching political theory of the state.[8] It is premature to propose a synthesis here, and in any case it is not the purpose of this volume, which is to analyse observable historical change, the evolution of pre-modern fiscal systems, in a comparative European framework. Our purpose is thus fundamentally different from that of Goldsmith, who advanced an essentially static depiction of distinct fiscal systems: 'A comparative dynamics remains the goal, but is as yet beyond reach.'[9] It is also important to discern the seminal aspects of the various general and particular theories which *contemporaries* proposed. These elements will be rearranged for the convenience of discussion and as an introduction to the two chronological sections of this volume (Chapters 1 and 6): all the ramifications of the various theories will not necessarily be explored. We need a better understanding of the long-term impact of ideas in the adoption of fiscal solutions. Enlightenment ideas, for example, had a practical relevance to the fiscal debate in

[4] Waquet (1990), 137–95, discusses and interprets previous theories. Note that some of Waquet's ideas had been anticipated by W. H. Beik in an article published in 1984 (cited by Waquet) and in Beik (1985), 245–78 ('tax flows and society').

[5] Schumpeter (1954*b*), 6, 19. Reappraisals in Seidl (1984), 89–109; Swedberg (1991), 58–61, 94–8.

[6] Peacock and Wiseman (1967).

[7] Brennan and Buchanan (1980).

[8] Musgrave (1969) still has material of interest for the historian apart from the economist.

[9] Goldsmith (1987), 8.

France between 1789 and 1794.[10] Finance and taxation, like politics, are 'linguistically constituted' activities and the role of tax structures is, or should be, inherent in any discussion of property rights.[11]

Two generations ago, this book would doubtless have adopted as its central theme the transition from feudalism to capitalism. The intellectual primacy of Marxist economic historians had already dimmed long before the events of 1989 swept away its residual east European vestiges and began the process of dismantling the profusion of chairs of Marxist history. Whatever the undeniable importance of Marxism to the early development of economic history as a discipline, its approach has two central problems for the historian of state finance. The first is the concept of the state as mere 'superstructure', with the economic 'base' providing the driving force of history. This has meant that, in practice, Marxist historians have almost invariably lacked any real interest in state finance because in their eyes the state was not autonomous but determined by specific forms of economic relations (Perry Anderson is a rare exception to this rule).[12] Marx did, it is true, concede that at times government policies might clash with the interests of the propertied classes; but such apparent social reform would, he thought, merely result in strengthening the underlying order of production relations and thus sustain capitalist domination. For Marxists, the fiscal system had to be interpreted within a framework of social, economic and political change in which the class struggle (defined as the dichotomy between capital and wage labour) was the key; fiscal control was, at least in later periods of history, basically in the hands of the capitalist class.[13] The assumption was that in earlier periods the economic 'base' had developed somehow of its own accord in an inevitable progression towards capitalism.

This approach denies the observable relationship between the state and the economy in European historical experience. The crucial objection to the Marxist interpretation is that the state has always, and at every stage, intervened either negatively or positively in the development of what a non-Marxist would call the 'tax base'. The rulers of Ming China (1368–1644), it is true, differed from almost all their west European counterparts in that they positively discouraged economic growth on the grounds that it accentuated regional imbalance which might threaten the empire's political unity. Since they were ultimately unsuccessful in this (they could not prevent the emergence of a money economy, with payment

[10] Gross (1993), 125.

[11] Ball, Farr and Hanson (1989), ix; Skinner, ibid. 6; though Ryan, ibid. 309–32, does not discuss the way in which taxation interrelates with the concept of property.

[12] Anderson (1974*b*; 1977). Cf. Bottomore (1983), 42.

[13] For a useful critique of Marxist fiscal sociology: Musgrave (1986), 177–9.

of taxes in silver, not in kind, or with statutory labour requirements),[14] it might seem that the tax base could sometimes be transformed without a clear power relationship between ruler and ruled or between the state and the economy. In reality, however, even in the case of Ming China the inadequacy of the Marxist formulation is fully revealed: if the ruler lacked any capacity to halt regional economic transformation, it was because there was no central authority administering the empire's finances other than the emperor himself; deviations from the fiscal regulations at a local level thus became the norm, and imperial control over the financial affairs of China slackened in the course of the Ming dynasty.[15] Regional power structures and the corruption of officials thus developed apace, and became the decisive influence in the relationship between the state and its tax base: local officials took from the taxpayers what they did not receive from the redistribution of an insufficient tax income at the level of the empire itself. In western European historical experience, in contrast to China, it is quite difficult to find rulers who were overtly anti-commercial or who did not show some wish to see the tax base develop, even if they lacked 'modern' ideas of such notions. Even in Muscovy, visited by Giles Fletcher in 1588–9, Ivan IV used to compare his people to a beard or to sheep, in that like them, to grow well, they required frequent clipping.[16] This relatively crude, exploitative, attitude nevertheless recognized the desirability of growth. Elsewhere in western Europe, the positive wish to intervene in what came to be termed the 'political economy' marked virtually all theories of state finance from the late Renaissance period to the age of Adam Smith and beyond (Chapter 6.8). The state neither was, nor did its theoreticians wish it to be, the passive captive of blind economic forces.

A second inadequacy of the Marxist formulation is its basic characterization of government—or the relationship between base and superstructure (glossed under the various levels of 'forces of production', 'relations of production' and 'mode of production')—as a form of class rule. Thus royal taxation has been referred to by Marxist historians as 'centralized feudal rent', with the state apparatus assisting the nobility (or seized by the nobility); the alliance of state and nobility has been seen as expropriating surplus peasant wealth and redistributing its proceeds in the form of noble pensions and appointments.[17] It is thus possible to conceive of a 'feudo-absolutist' order or system, and to depict absolutism (in Perry Anderson's phrase) as 'a redeployed and recharged apparatus of feudal

[14] Huang (1974), 1–4. [15] Ibid. 4–5. [16] Pipes (1974), 71.

[17] Cf. Genet and Le Mené (1987), 9–11. See below, Chapter 5.10, for a nuanced discussion of the alliance between crown and nobility.

domination'.[18] Even distinguished recent commentators of eighteenth-century Russia have come close to this viewpoint, arguing for the primacy of a ruling class which perceived a personal loyalty to the ruler and his or her financial needs, but none to the 'state' which consequently had only a shadowy existence.[19] The social composition and attitudes of royal or 'state' servants is not our concern,[20] but we would wish to question the Marxist concept of taxation as centralized feudal rent. This assumes that there was a clear concept of class interest at an earlier date in European history than is probably valid; it is too broad a categorization to be helpful in precise historical analysis; and, finally, it attributes a class motivation to a process which may in reality have served the interests of a dynasty, a republican state, or, in Waquet's formulation, the interrelated interests of the state and its individual members.[21]

If the Marxist model denies a symbiotic relationship between government fiscal policies and the economy, Gabriel Ardant's theories[22] as conceptualized by Charles Tilly[23] provide an alternative which accounts for the impact of financial policy on the economic infrastructure. In simple terms, Ardant defined the government as possessing goals which implied costs: the most obvious goal was warfare, which though not our primary concern pervades all the chapters concerned with the comparative development of the European states.[24] The '"military revolution" of the sixteenth and seventeenth centuries', it has been said, 'led to the strengthening of monarchical power in countries relying on *domestic* resources to finance modern armies.'[25] The objectives of governments were made achievable by a set of financial policies designed to extract sufficient resources from the population under the ruler's (or the state's) control.[26] The pre-existing economic infrastructure permitted (but also served to restrict) the extraction of resources and this in turn interacted with the government's policies. The result was the fiscal or financial consequences of applying a particular set of policies to a particular sort of infrastructure. Finally, the political and social

18 Anderson (1974), 18; Beik (1985), 30. Beik provides an overview of recent Marxist theoreticians.

19 LeDonne (1984), 16–17.

20 Reinhard (forthcoming), in this series.

21 Waquet (1990), 192: '... les finances sont à l'intersection de deux stratégies: celle, d'une part, suivant laquelle l'État acquiert et emploie ses revenus; celle, d'autre part, que les individus mettent en place pour satisfaire leurs propres fins.'

22 Ardant (1971–2). This in large part reorders and restates the material in Ardant (1965). See also Ardant in Tilly (1975), 164–242.

23 Tilly in Tilly (1975), 52–5.

24 Contamine (forthcoming), in this series.

25 Downing (1992), 3; cf. Parker (1988), 61–4; Tallett (1992), 207–16. For the role of internal coercion in the state, see Chapter 13.1.

26 Cf. Schumpeter, who postulated that economic policy up to the end of the 19th cent. had been 'motivated primarily by fiscal considerations': Schumpeter (1954*b*), 7.

consequences[27] of the policies worked their way through the system and may in turn have influenced the government's goals—though the biggest single stimulus to the increase in the fiscal burden in European states was the need to build up larger armed forces. Schumpeter emphasized the limits on the growth of a fiscal state: these were in essence limits on what we would call the pace of development of the tax base ('the tax state must not demand from the people so much that they lose financial interest in production or at any rate cease to use their best energies for it').[28]

This leads us to consider two further elements in an analysis of state finance, fiscal constitutions and crisis theory. The assumption underlying a fiscal constitution, as developed by Brennan and Buchanan in the context of states in the twentieth century, is that governments have a natural tendency to spend excessively and thus in effect to generate a budget deficit (although whether it was known at the time depends on accounting practice). Revenue maximization has thus been the essential aim of all states which could operate in this way, that is to say states unconstrained by broad political or specific electoral considerations or by a precise fiscal constitution. The government's ability to borrow (or to issue debt) amounted to a separate revenue source: it was tantamount to creating current assets which carried obligations for government in the future to pay to the holders of the assets (government bonds, loan contracts, and so on) designated sums, which were presumed capable of being financed from the tax revenues collected in the future. The total amount that a government could borrow was constrained by its ability to service and redeem the debt (itself largely determined by the future revenue capacity); by the relative preference of individuals in a given state for government bonds as against other assets; and by the general extent to which individuals either were prepared, or were able, to postpone current consumption and acquire assets. Since government access to large revenue resources (and, potentially, resources stretching years into the future) was, on the whole, undesirable (or in earlier periods, it might be added, difficult to achieve), it tended to be reserved for periods of fiscal 'emergency'. The precise definition of an emergency situation was problematic, but (one might add to the Brennan and Buchanan analysis) it tended to be equated with times of war. What mechanisms were in place to prevent the diversion of revenues from their intended purpose? What procedural constraints limited the

27 Ardant (1965), i, 16: '. . . c'est la *structure sociale* elle-même qui peut être déterminée, modifiée, construite en quelque sorte par les préoccupations fiscales . . .'

28 Schumpeter (1954*b*), 20: '. . . the state has . . . definite limits . . . to its fiscal potential.' Ibid. 23: '. . . the possible tax yield is limited not only by the size of the taxable object less the subsistence minimum of the taxable subject, but also by the nature of the driving forces of the free economy.' See most recently Collins (1988).

government's fiscal powers? Did tax reform operate for the purposes of the minimization of excess burden on individuals or for the maximization of net tax revenues? Above all, were the tax rules settled by the dominant political ruling group in their own short-term interests or did fiscal uncertainty prevail? Was there a set of quasi-permanent arrangements which allowed individuals to plan to restrict their contributions?[29] Such elements from the modern theory of a fiscal constitution, and no doubt others as well, can be applied by the historian to a given state, and the result is likely to reveal something of the diversity of the European experience (Chapter 13).[30]

The second consideration arising from modern analytical models is the historical contribution made by a sudden acceleration in the pace of change, or the absence of such change due to a structural crisis. Schumpeter's 'crisis of the tax state' was one of the first statements of this idea.[31] This debate, which now centres on the argument that there was a 'general crisis' in the relations between the state and society in a number of European countries—originally postulated by Hobsbawm for the 1640s, but now also asserted for the 1590s and (more tentatively) for the 1560s—has attracted much attention.[32] Its weakness is that the argument tends to be generalized and differently perceived by its protagonists. Ultimately, if states were undergoing crises in both the 1590s and the 1640s, then perhaps the term 'crisis' itself has been so devalued that it is no longer useful for the historian. The general crisis of the seventeenth century has also been found to have certain features in common with the great depression of the late Middle Ages: in particular both were preceded by a period of monetary abundance, rising prices and a credit boom, while both coincided with a decline in the production of precious metals and in the amount of bullion imported.[33] Yet the 'general crisis' argument has to be used with caution by the financial historian, because there were also specific financial crises which did not necessarily coincide with periods of so-called 'general crisis'. We might cite the crash of Law's System and the South Sea Bubble in 1720 to illustrate the point, although earlier crises in the sixteenth and seventeenth centuries would also serve (Chapter 6.3). A distinction therefore needs to be made between a general crisis and a specific crisis. Though Jean-Baptiste Say claimed in his *Traité d'économie politique* (1803) that general economic crises were impossible while specific crises were

29 Brennan and Buchanan (1980), 8–9, 26, 83–4, 103–5, 135–6, 190–3, 202–3.

30 For the full range of European diversity, see the various national chapters in the companion volume to this one: Bonney (1995).

31 Schumpeter, (1954*b*), 8: 'The modern tax state whose "crisis" is debated today grew out of the crisis of its predecessor, the feudal relationship . . .'

32 Aston (1965); Clark (1985); Parker and Smith (1985). For a recent restatement of the general crisis of the 17th cent. by a French regional specialist: Lemarchand (1989), 77–84.

33 Day (1991).

largely accidental, this view did not prevail subsequently. Economic historians tended to distinguish between crises of the *ancien régime* and more 'modern' crises, the first tending to be agrarian in origin, with a fall in rural consumption acting as the chief cause of any industrial crisis.[34] Yet more recent research has demonstrated that this model, too, is simplistic, and that there were other specific crises, such as those in France in 1715–16 and 1729–31, which were commercial in origin, and were marked by a significant number of commercial bankruptcies.[35] There is thus now a tendency to distinguish specific agrarian and commercial crises from fiscal crises. From the point of view of the state, a fiscal crisis might be termed a rise 'in expenses beyond both revenues and the ability to borrow'. If a ruler cannot 'borrow enough, or if he is forced to default on old loans, then a crisis has erupted'.[36]

This concept of a fiscal crisis is thus more precise than that of a 'general crisis'. General crisis theory has suffered from a methodological weakness, in that the precise mechanism by which it leads to significant economic transformations has never been properly explained. The concept of the 'displacement effect', originally proposed by Peacock and Wiseman in the context of the relatively recent history of UK public expenditure, served to bridge the gap between crisis theory and observable economic transformation. These two economists observed that Wagner's law of the 'expanding scale of state activity', which postulated a rising share of the public sector in the economy, although an allegedly empirical observation, was in reality true only in the very long term. Short-term change, or the actual process of change, could not be explained by the theory; and though based upon historical evidence, its acceptance as anything more than a statistical observation required acceptance of Wagner's own view of the nature of the state as a political entity. Peacock and Wiseman concluded that there were no permanent influences upon government spending capable of sustaining the assertion contained in Wagner's law, or general hypotheses which explained the behaviour of government expenditure in any state over a long period of time:

> The most definite general statement that it might be possible to make on the basis of our examination of these permanent influences is that government expenditures are perhaps more likely than not to increase in real volume as a country develops economically. Also, it is quite possible that the rise of expenditures will be at least as fast as the secular rate of increase of national product.

However, they concluded, 'there is nothing inevitable about this', and much was subject to the political structure of society and prevailing views on the role of

[34] The supreme exponent of this idea was Labrousse: Braudel and Labrousse (1970), 529–63. Boisguilbert was a contemporary theoretician of agrarian crisis: Perrot (1992), 275–7.

[35] Antonetti (1990), 35–44, 159–60.

[36] Hoffman and Norberg (1994), 2.

government. Instead of Wagnerian universal secular laws, they sought instead to draw out the implications of short-term change. 'Typically, the time chart of government money expenditures', in their view, 'describes a series of mountain ranges, with peaks of increasing height separated by plateaus ... There is, of course, obvious reason to expect the share of the community output taken by the government to rise in wartime ...' But more than this, 'the share of government expenditure in national product remains much greater after the wars than it was immediately before them ...' They postulated a reason for this phenomenon (which we might add is only observable in European history after *c.*1660, but not to the same extent before that date): 'people will accept, in a period of crisis, tax levels and methods of raising revenue that in quieter times they would have thought intolerable, and this acceptance remains when the disturbance itself has disappeared.'[37] We may suggest that, for example, the experience of certain German principalities during the Thirty Years' War amounted to a 'displacement effect': tax revenues after the war never returned to their low pre-war levels, while the prince emerged permanently strengthened with regard to the estates, or representative institutions, of his principality. Peacock and Wiseman postulated that what they called the 'concentration process' was a subsidiary characteristic of the displacement effect: 'the process of economic growth carries with it certain influences tending to change the size of the government unit upon which responsibility for public economic activities rests.' Thus, for example, improved transport and communications may have generated pressures for improved and uniform standards of public services; they may also have made larger areas of control not only possible, but economically efficient. However, Peacock and Wiseman also recognized that there were pressures operating in a different direction, so that the concentration process was not unilinear as Wagner's law might have suggested. The whole issue of transition from one fiscal regime to another is much more complicated than Peacock and Wiseman's thesis might suggest, though the terms 'regime' and 'transition' in themselves require definition. Moreover, shocks such as war did not necessarily have permanent effects.[38]

Such specific explanation of the impact of crisis on any particular economy and society must be placed within more general theories of fiscal development; these in turn must of necessity give full weight to the importance of monetary,

[37] Peacock and Wiseman (1967), 26–7; Tilly (1992), 89, suggests that the 'ratchet effect' does not occur universally but does occur frequently 'because the wartime increase in state power gives officials new capacity to extract resources ...; because wars either cause or reveal new problems that call for state attention; and because the wartime accumulation of debt places new burdens on the state'.

[38] Bordo and Capie (1994), 2–6.

demographic and technological change. Expenditure and revenue policies were a consequence of the interplay between social, cultural and political factors and the economy.[39] The phenomenon of urbanization was crucial in accelerating and concentrating economic growth, at least in some centres (urbanization being of course a relative phenomenon with its own history),[40] and permitting the taxation of a wider range of commodities, both of production and consumption, than that which was possible in a purely agrarian economy. Trade between regions, and within regions between town and countryside, was something which developed over time, with 'proto-industrialization' acting as the mediator between urban and rural sectors of the economy, and profits from the handling of tax receipts providing the main stimulus to the growth of urban capital.[41] The pace of monetary development over time, and vast differences between the extent of monetization between different regions even in the same kingdom, such as France, must be given due allowance. The transition from one 'monetary regime' to another, that is to say from one 'set of arrangements governing the monetary system' to another, may be considered of critical importance.[42] It has been argued that there is a distinction between monetization and monetarization, the latter process incorporating the widespread use of fiduciary instruments and thus representing a higher form of development. Can 'hyperinflation' caused by excessive emissions of paper money, such as occurred in France in 1795–6, be considered sufficiently stable to qualify for definition as a monetary regime?[43] It may be contended that before the later eighteenth century the state's issues of paper comprised relatively small proportions of the specie money stock, while one of the great imponderables for most states remains the economic significance of the prevalence in society at large of barter and offsetting arrangements as well as petty credit and tokens.[44] Yet it was usually not paper that mattered in most European states before the end of the eighteenth century, but bullion and coin. The 'bimetallic ratio' (the relationship between gold and silver in terms of precious metals) remained a central issue, even in the eighteenth and early nineteenth centuries.[45]

In general, it seems (Figure 1), Europe had a net balance in the difference between the arrivals of precious metals (mostly from the New World after the

[39] Musgrave (1969), chs. 3, 5; Musgrave (1986), 127–48.

[40] See the important synthesis by de Vries (1984).

[41] For profits on the handling of tax receipts: Dessert (1984); Bayard (1988).

[42] Bordo and Capie (1994), 3–4.

[43] Crouzet (1993), 328, 430, 563; cf. Bordo and Capie (1994), 3.

[44] Morineau (1990) advocates a distinction between 'monetization' and 'monetarization'. The most systematic discussion of the growth of the money supply is Riley and McCusker (1983). Challis (1989) discusses barter, offsetting, petty credit and tokens, and the increased demand for money.

[45] Tucci in Day (1984), 335–51; Crouzet (1993), 555–9.

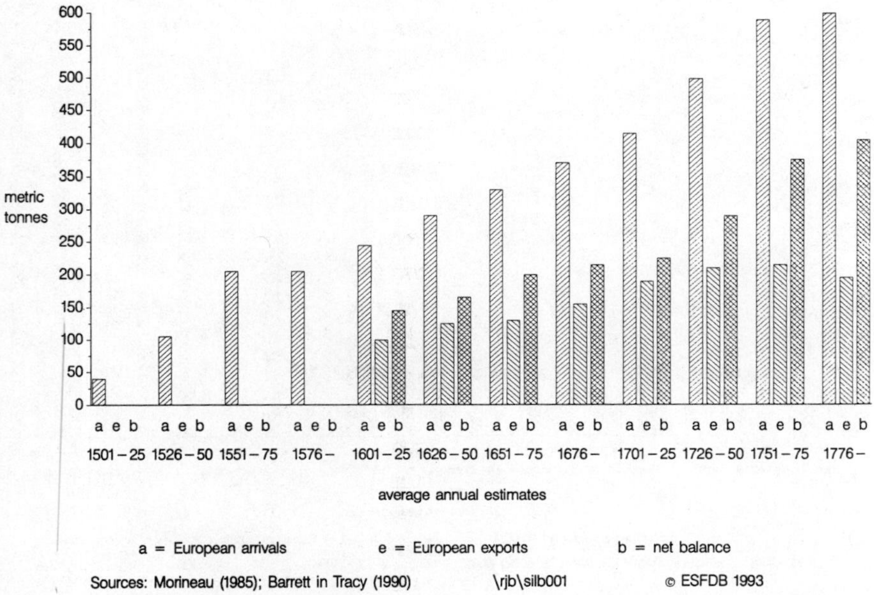

FIG. 1. American and European bullion flows, 1501–1800 (expressed in metric tonnes)

sixteenth century) and the export of the same (mostly to the Far East for the purchase of luxury commodities).[46] Finally, the relationship of taxation to the monetary stock, although difficult to quantify, was clearly of fundamental importance in all states. Thus, for example in France, it has been estimated that taxation represented perhaps 8 per cent of the monetary stock of the kingdom in 1683 (114 million out of 1,500 million *livres*, though the second figure may be an overestimate), 16 per cent in 1754, rising to 22 per cent by 1788 (respectively 250 out of 1,500 million and 472 million out of 2,200 million *livres*).[47] Such calculations depend crucially on accurate figures for the emission of coin, which are known for England and France in an almost unbroken run of statistics, from 1220 and 1308 respectively (Figure 2).[48] They also depend on estimates of the rate of renewal of coin in circulation, which is unknown: was there, for example, a

[46] ESFDB \rjb\silb001 based on \rjb\sild001; Barrett in Tracy (1990), 242–3; Morineau (1985), 40, 250, 483–4.

[47] See the table of Morineau in Genet and Le Mené (1987), 125. However, there is a contradiction between the table and Véron de Forbonnais's figures cited in the text. Since the revenue figure for 1683 was *c.*114 million, to reach a proportion of 16 per cent the monetary stock would have to have fallen to 700 million, which is surely too low. Crouzet (1993), 28, 143, accepts the figure of 2,200 million for 1789.

[48] ESFDB \rjb\frb005 based on \engindic\eind004 and \frindic\indd002. Figure 2 is expressed in nominal values which make no allowance for the decline in the precious metal content of the £ sterling or the *livre tournois*. For France: sources in Bonney (1992*a*), 154 n. 20; Miskimin (1963, 1984); Spooner (1972); Morineau in Day (1984). For England: Challis (1992), 676–93.

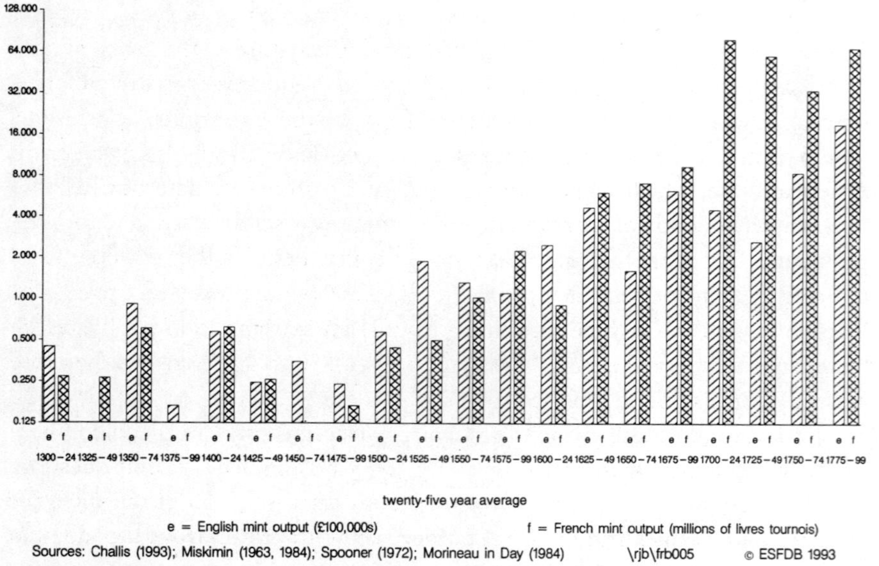

FIG. 2. English and French mint output, 1300–1799 (expressed in money of account)

thirty- or a sixty-year rate of renewal?[49] And what of the crucial aspect of the export of coin from countries which suffered an endemic insufficiency in monetary stocks, or where there were great regional disparities in the level of monetization? Poland, for example, could hardly raise a very substantial tax revenue (only 38–45 metric tonnes of silver at the high point of fiscal pressure in the mid-seventeenth century, as against a figure for ordinary revenues in France which rose from 191 to 1,135 metric tonnes),[50] since there were insufficient monetary stocks in the Polish–Lithuanian Commonwealth, even assuming the nobility (*szlachta*) had been willing to support the crown's ambitions and needs.[51] Before the mid-fourteenth century, Russia had no mint output of its own, and only foreign coins circulated there; the supplies of silver seem to have come from furs purchased by westerners at Novgorod.[52]

An introduction should not anticipate the conclusions of this book, which are presented in the form of four thematic chapters on expenditure, revenues, public

[49] Spooner (1972), 306–7.

[50] ESFDB \rjb\malet\malmo45: Malet's figures for ordinary revenues in 1600 and 1689. The maximum rises much higher if extraordinary revenues are included (to 2,287 tonnes in 1635). These figures serve only to highlight the contrast made by Mączak in the publications cited in the following note (he suggested a minimum of 225 and a maximum of 425 metric tonnes for France). Cf. Bayard (1988), 29, for slightly different figures; also Chaunu in Chaunu and Gascon (1977), 178–91.

[51] Mączak (1976) and (1982), 131–2.

[52] Hellie in Bonney (1995).

credit and the fiscal burden (Chapters 12–15). A number of questions suggest themselves for very brief comment. The first is the nature of the fiscal imperative: was the enlargement of the fiscal system a consequence primarily of forces for change which were revenue- or expenditure-driven? The group's conclusions would seem to confirm other studies, for example on the fiscal crisis of the Latin American state, which suggest that 'expenditure patterns are determined more or less independently of tax revenue (except in cases of severe crisis) and thus the problem is one of raising sufficient funds to cover them—rather than the fiscal revenue in any one year determining the extent of such expenditure'.[53] The Russian case in the eighteenth century is only an extreme example of the lag between revenues and expenditure (Chapter 11.6). Within reason, it is therefore perfectly permissible to look at expenditure trends to discern the growth of the fiscal state, since these were the *primum mobile* creating the need for new resources, whether in the form of tax or loan income. The second question, raised in the chapters on different periods and discussed also in the thematic chapters on revenues and the fiscal burden, is the transition from the 'domain state' to the 'tax state'. This is fiscal history's equivalent to the transition from feudalism to capitalism for economic history in general, and at times it has threatened to become the overarching theme of the book. The definition of what constitutes a 'domain state' as against a 'tax state' is not easy, since tax revenue could be, and was in certain circumstances regarded as, part of the domain: writing in 1760, Mirabeau took it for granted that tax revenue could be included within domainal receipts in France ('qui ne doivent point entrer dans le revirement de parties du fisc').[54] Moreover, as with the case of tax revenue, the nature of the domain evolved over a period of time (Chapter 13.3). The problems posed by the transition from the 'domain state' to the 'tax state' are thus particularly complex and, as with that other great transition, from feudalism to capitalism, it is not the case that all the issues can be resolved satisfactorily within a convenient theory.

A further question raised by various chapters of the book, and again by the thematic chapter on public credit, is the extent to which a revenue system needs to have been developed before an adequate structure of long-term borrowing could arise. Russia had no clearly developed tax structure before the seventeenth century and no significant public borrowing until the 1770s. Even in countries where there was extensive public credit, there were significant differences between states with high interest rates and those with low ones, and between states in terms of the size of the long-term debt. The difference in interest rates

[53] Fitzgerald in Toye (1978), 131.

[54] Mirabeau (1760, repr. 1972), 225. The most detailed study is Massaloux (1989); Naquet in *État, finances et économie* (1991), 105–6.

prompted contemporaries to ask whether the state should intervene to reduce the rate of interest by legislation. John Locke argued in 1691 (though an earlier version of his text had been drafted in 1668) that no law could restrict the rate of interest to 4 per cent if the free-market rate of interest exceeded that rate; but to the extent that the restriction could be enforced, it would be harmful.[55] Since state loans sometimes failed because the rate of interest was set too low—Necker ruefully accepted the National Assembly's decision to reduce the rate of interest on a loan of 30 million *livres* from 5 to 4.5 per cent, with the result that the loan failed[56]—it was evident that both the demand for loans and the supply for loans were highly sensitive to price. Locke's theory was thus incorrect, although it was the most advanced interest rate discussion in the period under review in this book.

Contemporaries were also aware of the increasing size of the public debt towards the end of the eighteenth century, and uncertain about its viability. By the seventeenth and eighteenth centuries, wars could not be financed by tax income alone. Jean-François Melon argued in 1736 that the debts of a nation were 'debts of the right hand to the left' which therefore had no tendency either to increase or diminish national wealth;[57] Isaac de Pinto, writing in 1771, argued on the contrary that they increased public wealth (Chapter 6.5). Hume attacked Melon's argument, and advocated the creation of budgetary surpluses to finance war, while later Ricardo stressed the need for tax revenue for the same purpose. It was not until 1823 that McCulloch argued that Melon was wrong because the payment of debt interest involved a tax burden on future generations; the costs of any debt reduction, as Alexander Hamilton had pointed out in the United States, also had to come from taxation.[58] Contemporary theorists were divided on this point,[59] but there is some measure of consensus among contemporary economists that loan income must be regarded as a deferred tax: loans have to be repaid, and in the long term only a growing economy permits borrowing to repay borrowing.[60] 'Mountains of debt' are a phenomenon of the 'modern' state, and

55 Locke, ed. Kelly (1991), i, 218–21; Letwin (1963), 156–61, and in *Times Literary Supplement*, 28 Feb. 1992, 8.

56 Necker (1791), 127.

57 Meysonnier (1989), 111; McCulloch, ed. O'Brien (1975), lix, 403 n. 5 (quoted from 1736 edn.).

58 McCulloch, ed. O'Brien (1975), lix–lxiv. McCulloch stated his view on the debt well before the publication of his *Treatise* of 1845.

59 Thus Mirabeau (1766, repr. 1972), 121: '... la dette & l'Impôt ne doivent avoir rien de commun'. Pinto however argued (trans. Baggs, 1774, repr. 1969), 21, that 'when once a fund is created, the numerary remains, and the contributive faculty increases as well as circulation, and without too great an increase of specie ... A light tax is drawn from the nation, into whose hands it returns again, with a general benefit to the whole'.

60 The issues are usefully debated by Modigliani (1961) and Barro (1974).

one definition of 'fiscal crisis' is 'a condition in which the fact of growing public debt and the problem of managing it becomes the overwhelming concern of public policy'.[61] As a broad generalization, we may suggest that in the Middle Ages the revenue base of the European monarchies (although in this respect the Italian city-states were in advance) was neither sufficiently secure nor sufficiently large to permit large-scale permanent debts to be established. This was a phenomenon of the sixteenth, seventeenth and eighteenth centuries and thereafter. By the eighteenth century, indeed, the test of a state's capacity to modernize was not simply its ability to accumulate debt, but its capacity to restructure it so that the combined effects of inflation and economic growth came near to permitting borrowing to repay borrowing. If Britain came close to Melon's happy state of affairs of a neutral debt ('debts of the right hand to the left'), or even to Pinto's New World where a large public debt was a source of national wealth, then this was because of a growing population and a revenue base that was enlarged because of economic growth. The United Provinces had accumulated permanent debts at an earlier date, but found it much more difficult to sustain the burden of debt servicing costs in the eighteenth century with a static population, little or no growth in revenues, a higher per capita rate of taxation than in England, and above all a decline in the rate of economic growth: 'such has been the pernicious influence of the too great increase of debts and objectionable taxes in Holland'.[62] The Dutch experience would thus tend to disprove Pinto's theory, and even Melon's neutral debt would be questionable but for the continuing international importance of Dutch finance capital in the eighteenth century.[63]

Such comparisons between countries and over time lead the fiscal historian ineluctably to the thorny issue of indexation. In the writings of certain Spanish economists of the School of Salamanca, and also in those of Bodin, there was an awareness of the importance of inflation by the second half of the sixteenth century; at the beginning of the eighteenth century, Boisguilbert was perhaps the first theoretician to argue that the revenues of the state might actually have fallen in real terms despite a nominal increase (Chapter 6.5). Not surprisingly, given their predisposition to regard land as the source of all wealth, the Physiocrats followed Boisguilbert and argued that the state's resources in real terms should be measured in grain equivalent. Thus Le Trosne contended in 1778 that Louis XVI two years earlier had had an income equivalent to 12.5 million *sétiers* of

[61] Veseth (1990), 14; Fitzgerald in Toye (1978), 125–6; O'Connor (1973).

[62] McCulloch, ed. O'Brien (1975), 394.

[63] Riley (1980).

grain[64] compared to Louis XII (1498–1515) who had had one equivalent to 15 million, but which had been less encumbered by fixed outgoings.[65] Though it is possible to use a grain conversion, there are disadvantages in doing so to measure the growth of the fiscal power of the state. Grain prices frequently rose more than the prices of other commodities, but no general index of commodity prices has won acceptance, while a local basic commodity which was less prone to harvest fluctuations (such as indexing Dutch revenues against butter prices) is too specific; moreover, though the state might be a large purchaser of grain or other commodities, it cannot be said that it was primarily concerned in this form of activity in normal circumstances. A more critical item, from the point of view of all states over time, was the cost of the armed forces. It is certainly possible to calculate the value of a state's revenues in terms of its capacity to purchase soldiers for specific periods[66] and, given the importance of the comparative cost of troops in one part of Europe as against another and the preference of Britain to purchase troops abroad (Chapter 11.1), it would be desirable to be able to do so generally. There are difficulties in using the cost of hiring soldiers to measure the growth of the fiscal power of the state: such costs were not recorded sufficiently systematically by most states for a series of 'prices' to be available comparable, for example, to grain prices; secondly, the nature of the 'military revolution' and the differences in military organization between states were such that there is no standard 'unit of account' over time. A knight, who served with his horse and armour, is not the same unit of measurement as a mercenary infantryman for whom a uniform and arms were provided by the captain. An alternative method is to recalculate the fiscal power of the state in terms of the predominant exchange rate of the time. The Dutch guilder is particularly seductive in this respect, since it was stable for most of the seventeenth and eighteenth centuries: a third, 'neutral', currency is helpful in making comparisons between two other states.[67] But, of course, the importance of a particular exchange rate varies over time. For the Middle Ages, the Florentine florin would provide an equivalent

[64] A *sétier* is taken to be 1.56 hectolitres. It is thus possible to convert into millions of hectolitres of wheat: Guéry (1978), 229; Bonney (1991*a*), 224. This methodology was also used by Mathias and O'Brien (1976), 618, 620. Alternative methodologies for prices are discussed by Riley (1987), 228–36; Fritschy (1990), 72–3.

[65] Clere in *État, finances et économie* (1991), 86 n. 21.

[66] Ormrod (1995) for 13th-cent. England. *Pace* Tilly (1992), 74, it is not useful to compare hours worked by an 'ordinary labourer' to measure taxation over long periods of time: such measurement lacks precision because of intervening changes in the economy and social structure. Over the short term, say a century or two, the method may have validity as an indication of the real fiscal burden.

[67] Riley (1980), 102–3. Riley's calculations use the data in Posthumus (1946) as a converter. Neither the *livre tournois* nor the £ sterling, for example, is a 'neutral' currency when making comparisons between England and France. Compare Figure 40 (Chapter 11.3) with Figure 30 in Bonney and Bonney (1993), 96.

base line for exchange rates, but the paucity of evidence for Castile rules this out as a basis for comparison (Chapter 5.6).[68] Nor, for the early modern period, is there an acceptable handbook of exchange rates much before the mid-seventeenth century.[69] We thus, perforce, return to silver as the unit of measurement over time and between countries in the chapters on the west European monarchies in the Middle Ages (Chapter 5) and on expenditure (Chapter 12), though we should note that the conversion into silver values, too, is open to question in periods when the supply of silver increased, as it did for much of the early modern period.[70]

We thus arrive at some notion of an evolution in the fiscal capacity of states over time: the most that they could afford to do was, on the whole, probably what they did,[71] bearing in mind that expenditure on war was the driving force. It has been argued that there was a 'fiscal limit' of some 30–35 million *livres* for the levy of the *taille* in seventeenth-century France, and that this restriction was imposed by the nature of the tax and the productive wealth upon which it rested.[72] As a general rule, it may be asserted that contemporary notions of taxable capacity were always associated with the amount of tax which could be justly or fairly imposed. As Pitt the Younger stated in 1795,

> The smallest burthen on a poor country was to be considered, when compared with those of a rich one, by no means in proportion with their several abilities; for, if one country exceeded another in wealth, population, and established commerce in a proportion of two to one, he was nearly convinced that that country would be able to bear near ten times the burthen that the other would be equal to.[73]

If taxable capacity is taken to mean the fiscal limit, or the maximum possible tax level, it is difficult to envisage any clear empirical test for contemporary fiscal systems, let alone for those of the past,[74] though there may well be a phenomenon of 'fiscal crisis', which may include a limit to taxable capacity as one of its features.[75] However, there may equally well be a phenomenon of 'undertaxation', exemplified in the eighteenth century by France in comparison with

[68] Cipolla (1982); Spufford (1986); Guenée (1985), 109, used the florin as a converter for his comparison of certain financial estimates across the 14th and 15th cents.

[69] McCusker (1978) has relatively few entries before *c.*1660.

[70] Riley (1987), 230: 'Because the supply of silver increased, deflating the *livre tournois* to constant silver weights incorporates a distortion.' Cf. Guéry (1978), 227; Bonney (1991*a*), 225.

[71] Tanzi (1991), 99 and esp. 102: '*Ex ante*, a country can plan to have, for a given fiscal year, any level of public expenditure and fiscal deficit. However, *ex post*, the maximum deficit it can have (expressed as a proportion of GDP) will be limited by the sources of financing.'

[72] Collins (1988), 219; Bonney (1992*b*), 120 n. 53.

[73] Prest in Toye (1978), 19.

[74] Ibid. 29.

[75] Fitzgerald in Toye (1978), 125–58.

Britain.[76] For some countries, it is possible to estimate the gross national product (GNP) at certain dates, and to guess at the relationship between the fiscal burden or debt burden and the GNP.[77] For most European states, however, this is not possible and, since the agrarian sector was predominant in most countries, the level of agricultural output is the nearest approximation to GNP. And when, as in the case of Russia in 1710, we learn that the real value of the tax burden was equivalent to 64 per cent of the grain harvest,[78] we may conclude that a limit to taxable capacity had indeed been reached. As is pointed out elsewhere in this volume (Chapter 15.5), it was the interaction of the state's demands with harvest fluctuations which determined the real fiscal burden carried by the majority of taxpayers.

Economic Systems and State Finance thus asks broad questions and seeks a fundamental reappraisal of the more important issues underlying European economic and state development. Necessarily, selection is the order of the day. No attempt is made to rewrite the economic history of Europe from the thirteenth to the eighteenth centuries in its entirety. If this book ends a little later than others in the series, in 1815 rather than in 1789, this is because in fiscal history the year 1789 marked a new beginning for only one country in Europe—France—though most European states were affected by the Revolutionary and Napoleonic crisis. By 1815, only one state—Britain—had emerged with economic hegemony largely because unlike many of its Continental rivals it had not been defeated and overrun, while its global maritime and colonial hegemony was confirmed when Spain and Portugal lost their South American empires (Chapters 11.6 and 11.7). This volume cannot claim to study the 'national' development of every European country or the full multiplicity of fiscal constitutions which developed in the Middle Ages and the *ancien régime*. We do, however, draw upon a range of such case studies which formed our starting-point.[79] We also allude to a database of statistics, which is available for consultation and which has helped inform our work as it developed.[80] Collective research is not easy to manage; nor is a book such as this easy to edit. If the overall interpretation of this volume is greater than the sum of its parts, then the group which wrote it will rest content.

[76] Matthias and O'Brien (1975); Bonney (1992*a*), 174; Wrigley in Stone (1994), 74–5.

[77] O'Brien and Hunt (1993), 158–60, 172–5.

[78] Hellie in Bonney (1995).

[79] These, with additions, are in Bonney (1995).

[80] The datasets developed by the European State Finance Database and deposited in the Economic and Social Research Council Data Archive at the University of Essex in 1993 may be consulted via JANET (e-mail: ARCHIVE@UK.AC.Essex, generic code 33250).

PART I

The Middle Ages: Developments and Continuities

CHAPTER I

Medieval and Renaissance Theories of State Finance

Eberhard Isenmann

The Middle Ages witnessed both the development of more differentiated and varied forms of taxation and—at least in most states—a more sophisticated financial administration. Contemporary theories of state finance comprise a broad spectrum of views, from legal and moral statements, maxims and principles to relatively simple ideas. Yet the Middle Ages also saw the emergence of comprehensive and far-reaching theories relating to the legal foundation and justification for imposing taxes; the classification of the various types of revenue and taxes; the techniques of assessment; the question of fiscal equity and fairness of both the tax assessments and the tax burden; and finally the interrelationship between taxation and the economy, the social order and the political system.

1.1 *Theories and Theoreticians*

The relatively rudimentary methods of levying taxes in the Middle Ages in comparison with the early modern period (except in the medieval city-states) do not necessarily imply that fiscal theories were equally undeveloped. On the contrary, definitions, maxims, theories and systems of thought were strengthened by theological commentary on the Scriptures and the writings of the early church fathers; by the study of Roman and canon law after the twelfth century; and, later on, by the rediscovery of Aristotle's *Politics* and *Nicomachean Ethics*, which opened up for contemporaries the philosophy of antiquity; finally, the law and practice of the fiscal state of the late Roman empire was also an object of study. Scholarship was thus in some measure in advance of fiscal policy in practice, and made a significant contribution to discussion of the issues of tax sovereignty (or the power to tax) and the requirement for formal consent to taxes and fiscal legislation by corporations or parliamentary assemblies. It also addressed the question of the conditions under which a liability existed to pay taxes, and whether or not the interest on government bonds (the *prestiti*, *prestanze* or *luoghi* of such states as Venice, Florence, Siena and Genoa) constituted usury.[1] Furthermore, contemporary theorists also discussed concepts of the nature of society and the economy (including the definition of money), the legal basis of the fisc (*fiscus*) and various aspects of a theory of the state including notions of public law, of the common good (*utilitas publica* or *bonum commune*) and *necessitas*.[2]

Of course, these ideas were not confined to the Middle Ages, but continued to develop (albeit partially transformed) into the early modern period, chiefly through the medium of canon and Roman law. The Aristotelian and Thomistic views of society and the state, or commonwealth (*respublica*), sometimes blended with Augustinianism: the late scholastic doctrine of legitimate and just taxation (as well as the concept of money and its circulation) was elaborated by Italian, Spanish, French, English and German theologians in the fourteenth and fifteenth centuries and was continued in the work of the famous School of Salamanca in the sixteenth and seventeenth centuries.[3] Since in the Middle Ages positive law always had to conform to divine and natural law and had to aim at human welfare (*bonum*) in general, contemporary theologians had the right, through their *Summae*, *Summae confessorum*, commentaries on the Scriptures and other expert opinions and tracts (*Sententiae*, *Quodlibeta*, *Quaestiones* and so on), to pass judgement on secular law. Philosophers, too, might claim authority to examine or verify the conformity of human positive law with morality and with natural law, including the *ius gentium*, rights common to all peoples and nations.[4] The scholastics amalgamated theology and philosophy, including moral science and doctrine. Many theologians had also studied law. Jurists passed opinion on what was legitimate with regard to courts of law (the *forum contentiosum*), while theologians concentrated on matters of sin and the dictates of conscience (*ratione peccati*); their teaching laid obligations on individuals *in foro conscientiae*. The principles of Roman and canon law and moral theology did not remain a matter of mere scholarship and theory, but were increasingly transferred into practice. The agents of this process of transmission were the lawyers of the ecclesiastical and secular courts, the councillors of princes, preachers and confessors.

Financial matters were discussed in the didactic and pedagogic literary works

[1] The author and the editor thank Dr A. K. B. Evans (Leicester) for her assistance in the editing of this text. Kirshner (1970); de Roover (1953*b*).

[2] Kantorowicz (1957); Ullmann (1961); Post (1964).

[3] It is not possible to specify here all the relevant writings of the jurists and theologians. Cf. esp. the surveys and lists of Kehl (1927); Wachenhausen (1972).

[4] Cf. Trusen (1961), 23–7.

written for princes (the literature known in various languages as 'Mirrors for Princes', *Specula regis*, *Miroirs au prince*, *Fürstenspiegel*) and in other politico-legal or politico-religious tracts of the later Middle Ages. The medieval theoretical and normative viewpoint was supplemented in the fifteenth century by the more analytical and empirical interests of jurists and historical and political writers. During the second half of the fifteenth century and the first half of the sixteenth, a strong empirical aspect became evident in the general reflections on government and the state of the *respublica*, in politics, in early historical writing and in other analytical tracts, which sometimes had a reforming purpose. Thus we find comments on finance and taxation in the very different writings of such figures as Philippe de Commynes, Sir John Fortescue, Francesco Patrizi, Matteo Palmieri, Francesco Guicciardini, Niccolò Machiavelli and Diomede Carafa. Other theories seem to have arisen almost irrespective of sophisticated ideas. This alternative, more pragmatic, body of theory might result from an immediate fiscal need or from a dispute between the ruler and the estates over the legal basis of tax power and taxation; the political necessity of taxation; fair tax assessments; or the economic and social consequences of a heavy tax burden especially with regard to the poorer classes of society. In many cases, it is difficult to establish whether such theories were based on an understanding of fiscal realities gained empirically, or whether they were an echo of other, more learned, maxims. Expert opinions concerning the tax laws, which might seek to analyse the interrelationship between taxation and economics, were a relatively rare phenomenon.

1.2 *Early Church Fathers, Jurists, Scholastics and Moral Theologians on Taxation*

There were two main biblical texts which taught Christians about the obligation to pay taxes. The first was Christ's answer to the Pharisees—'Render unto Caesar the things that are Caesar's' (Matt. 22: 21). The second was St Paul's Epistle to the Romans, where he stated that all civil powers were legitimized by God—'Discharge your obligations to all men; pay tax (*tributum*) and toll (*vectigal*)' (Rom. 13: 7). The early theologians were not, of course, concerned with contributing to a science of finance, but cared only about the spiritual welfare of their flock. The principal need was to inculcate the injunction of Christ and his apostles, which affirmed the unquestionable duty of subjects to pay taxes.[5] In a spiritual sense, the payment of taxes was an opportunity to part with some transitory and corrupting temporal property for the sake of eternal reward in heaven. Nevertheless, the early theologians deplored excessive taxation, for

[5] Hamm (1908), 125–83; Kehl (1927), 1–22.

example within the Roman empire, and any unequal distribution of the tax burden to the disadvantage of the poor. They demonstrated that adverse economic and social consequences would inevitably result from a policy of fiscal depredation and an unjust tax burden. The poor would be ruined and enslaved under the arbitrary domination of the rich, while 'barbarian' rule would appear much more attractive in terms of its likely fiscal policy (Salvian of Marseille, 395–490);[6] in agrarian areas, the productive power of the peasantry would decline, while there would be a desertion of estates and reafforestation of arable land (Lactantius, 250–340).[7]

St Paul had briefly justified the payment of taxes (*tributa*) to the sovereign as a consequence of the latter's services in maintaining order as a *minister Dei* for the benefit of his subjects (Rom. 13: 4–7). Commenting upon and interpreting the writing of St Paul, several early church fathers, particularly the patriarch and bishop of Constantinople, St John Chrysostom (344–407),[8] specified the many benefits which were granted by the sovereign: he secured peace, order and tranquillity; he thus preserved the temporal existence of people and cities, villages, houses and markets; he protected the weak against the strong; he provided services, whether those of his soldiers or his officials; he quelled revolts in the cities, rendered harmless political factions, and kept foreign enemies safely beyond the borders. Though taxes might seem merely burdensome, they were the inevitable quid pro quo for the sovereign's innumerable benefits. Therefore taxes were paid essentially as a compensation for the sovereign's providence and diligence. They were also needed to support his subsistence, since by taking care of public affairs and preserving his subjects' existence he neglected his own interests.[9]

The early theological view of a strict, unquestioning, duty to pay taxes to the sovereign was stressed, for example, by St Augustine (353–430), who stated that all commands of the Emperor must be endured.[10] This view did not change until the thirteenth century, when St Thomas Aquinas (1225–74) formulated the fundamental doctrine that human laws were morally binding only if they were just, and that unjust laws did not bind at all and did not therefore have to be observed.[11] When this was applied to taxes, which fell within the definition of burdensome laws (*leges onerosae*), only just taxes imposed a moral obligation; unjust taxes ought not to be paid. In contrast, the early fathers had defined only

[6] Kehl (1927), 10–14; *Patrologiae ... latinae* (1844–65), liii, cols. 97ff.
[7] Kehl (1927), 8.
[8] Ibid. 1–4.
[9] *Patrologiae ... graecae* (1857–66), lx, cols. 613 ff.
[10] *Patrologiae ... latinae* (1844–65), xxxix, col. 1905.
[11] Aquinas, ed. Caramello (1952–6), (1a.IIae.96.4); Kehl (1927), 22–5.

one restriction with regard to liability, which was whether human laws infringed divine law. The scholastic and moral theologians added the idea of justice in virtually all discussion of taxes—with the sole exception of Henry of Ghent (1217–93), who denied any right of subjects to examine or verify whether or not taxes were just, requiring strict obedience instead. Subjects who refused the payment of just taxes, or evaded full payment, violated commutative justice (*iustitia commutativa*) and committed theft; moreover, they committed a mortal sin and were obliged to make restitution for the sake of their salvation. But the same applied to the sovereign who levied unjust taxes: he had a duty to repay them.

Justice, however, was only relative and not always self-evident. Criteria in casuistry had to be established which enabled an identification of what could be considered just in the sense of Aristotelian distributive justice (*iustitia distributiva*). Thus, based on the Aristotelian doctrine of the final cause and purpose of all things, Aquinas and others elaborated a system of just causes (*iustae causae*) concerning taxes and a catalogue of typical expenditure. Whether taxes were just could now be determined by syllogistic conclusions (subsumptions), and writing by theologians on the subject of taxation became more and more extensive, parallelling its development, particularly in the cities. Classifications and definitions of different types of taxes were produced by canonists, particularly with the aim of clarifying ecclesiastical and clerical immunities. Among these writers were Innocent IV (Sinibaldus Fliscus, d. 1254), and the most important canonist of the fifteenth century, Nicolaus de Tudeschis (Panormitanus, 1386–1453), who followed the teachers of civil law. The concept of public charges and taxes was *munus*: according to civil law, in Panormitanus' definition, this was an obligation to be performed by virtue of the coercive power of law, custom or the authority of a sovereign with public power.[12] The payment or service need not necessarily be made immediately for the benefit of the commonwealth (*respublica*), but could be for the benefit of a private individual; such private rights, however, had to originate with the public authority.

Distinctions and classifications were made between *munera honesta* and *munera sordida*, primarily from a legal viewpoint without close reference to economic considerations. Ordinary and extraordinary *munera* were first of all distinguished by whether the legislative procedure was ordinary or extraordinary. Innocent IV distinguished between ordinary and extraordinary *munera*, but did not explain this distinction further.[13] But the scholastic Richard of Middleton (Richardus de Mediavilla, d. *c.*1300) in his *Quodlibeta* specified a reason for the distinction. Ordinary *munera* were payments which were predictable, certain and linked to

[12] Innocent IV (1570), (3.49.4.1); Kehl (1927), 53.

[13] Innocent IV (1570), (3.49.4), fo. 459[b].

periodic dates; extraordinary ones were not regular, but collected on the occasion of unforeseen events, for example, when the prince gave his daughter in marriage.[14] Periodicity and regularity in the payment of taxes may be taken to be key concepts in any modern discussion of finance, but many medieval theologians accepted the obligation of church and clergy to render ordinary *munera* merely in the legal sense of the term. However, ordinary *munera* defined by economic criteria such as periodicity, certainty and predictability were rare in the Middle Ages, much rarer than those defined by legal conditions; any inclusion of economic criteria therefore restricted still further the obligation to pay taxes.[15] In terms not dissimilar to those of other authors (and, later, of Panormitanus), Petrus Antibolus Allobrogis in his tract *De muneribus* (*c.*1360) classed as ordinary or canon *munera* those *munera* imposed by law, by a decision of the Senate or a *constitutio* of the Emperor; in contrast, extraordinary *munera* were those which were not imposed in an ordinary manner but on specific occasions, for instance when a prince married, knighted his son, bought land or visited the Pope.[16] Johannes Bertachinus (d. 1497), in his monograph *De gabellis* (*c.*1490),[17] defined as ordinary *munera* or *indicta* those established by an earlier law or general ordinance, and particularly by fixed and continuous payments over standard intervals of time for ordinary and continuing reasons. It did not matter whether the payment was sometimes increased by adding a multiplier, in the form of a *superindictum*, for reasons of necessity. Such a tax was regarded as essentially an ordinary *indictum* or *collecta*, that is, one which was announced to the people in advance so that they could prepare for it. Extraordinary *munera* had no such ordinary legal basis and were imposed on an extraordinary, transitory, occasion, such as a sudden hostile attack or military action against bandits.

Ordinary *munera*, according to Innocent IV and Hostiensis (Henry of Susa, d. 1271), could be subdivided into personal, property and mixed ones.[18] Personal *munera* (or *angaria*) were those which required the service of body or mind, but at no cost to the individual: for example, one might be obliged to fight in the king's war, but only at his expense. Subsequent authors (such as Antibolus) instanced administrative functions and services for the benefit of the *respublica* or private persons, such as that of guardianship. Property *munera* (*munera realia* or *munera patrimonalia*) were rendered at the sole expense and risk of the individual. Richard of Middleton explained and defined the *munus reale* (or *munus ordinarium*) as a payment resulting from a property right. He further distinguished

[14] Kehl (1927), 54. [15] Ibid. 74–5.

[16] *Tractatus universi iuris* (1584), fos. 19^a–51^b; Kehl (1927), 60–71.

[17] *Tractatus universi iuris* (1584), fos. 51^b–76^a; Kehl (1927), 47–9, 71–3.

[18] For the following cf. Amberg (1909), 1–13; Kehl (1927), 52–78.

between *munera realia*, which were imposed on the objects themselves (irrespective of the person) as taxes on property, and those which were imposed on individuals by reason of the property, and in proportion to it, as property-holding taxes (*collectae*). Mixed *munera* (*munera mixta* or *perangaria mixta*) were those charges which needed the service of body or mind, but at the individual's own expense and risk. Extraordinary *munera* were divided by Innocent IV and Hostiensis into those which concerned the commonweal (such as the defence of the *respublica* or the Christian faith); those which were a matter of duty (payments such as those for the reconstruction of bridges and roads; for the support of the sovereign when captured; payments to the sovereign who wanted to buy land or knight his son, or assistance to him in cases of high expenditure, impoverishment or heavy debts); and those which originated in the mere whim of the sovereign. Richard of Middleton differentiated between *munera extraordinaria*, which were for the benefit of the prince, and those which concerned the commonweal and duty (*pietas*).

Panormitanus made a fundamental distinction between *munera personalia*, *munera patrimonialia* and *munera mixta* (called *munera publica et civilia* by Antibolus), and discussed only secondarily the distinction between ordinary and extraordinary *munera*. *Munera patrimonialia* were payments in kind or in money which were further subdivided into those imposed on property irrespective of the person (*munera mere patrimonialia*); on the person irrespective of the property, that is the poll tax (*capitatio*); and on the person in proportion to the property held, that is the property tax properly so called (*collecta*). In the case of the *munera mere patrimonialia*, only the property was liable; this was a levy on the yield (*tributum* or *vectigalia*). Many varied distinctions and subdivisions were proposed, which differed in detail, and were demonstrated by casuistic examples: Antibolus used the example of the Roman empire in antiquity, the Italian or French cities and various regional examples. The distinction between *munera personalia* and *munera realia* (*patrimonialia*) was of great importance, since theologians generally accepted that church and clergy were obliged to pay taxes on property, but were exempt from personal taxes. This is why Bertachinus, for instance, ranked the *vectigalia* among the *munera personalia*, though they were undoubtedly taxes on property. Apart from this, it became more and more difficult to subsume new taxes under the classification of *munera personalia* and *patrimonialia* with the expansion of the money economy and the commutation of payments in kind into money payments. Subsequent theologians, such as Gabriel Biel (*c.*1410–95) and Sylvester de Prierio (Prierias, 1456–1523), contented themselves with definitions of the various types of taxes instead. These distinctions had started with glosses upon the terms mentioned in the Scriptures—*census*, *tributum*, *vectigal* and *teoloneum*—and the classical terms of the Roman empire;[19] but these explanations did not sit happily with the new taxes required by contemporary economic and legal conditions. New definitions, which explained terms current in the vernacular, were necessary.

1.3 *The Justification of Taxation*

The justification of taxation was related to the legitimacy of authority (*potestas*), as well as to questions such as the origin and nature of the state and society. An authoritative early statement was made by St Paul in his Letter to the Romans (Rom. 13) and in his First Letter to Timothy (1 Tim. 2: 2). The ruler obtained his power from God, and it was his main task to protect the internal legal order of the state, and further to defend the country against external enemies, so that his subjects might live in peace and tranquillity. For the ruler to be able to perform his task for the benefit of the public, his subjects had to place the necessary means at his disposal in the form of taxes. The relation between means and ends was also to be found in the context of Roman and canon law as well as in more pragmatic political thought. Commentaries on St Paul and the words of Christ (Matt. 17: 23–5; 22: 21) stressed that taxes had to be paid as a sign of subjection to the sovereign's authority. This position was further developed, with variations, by a great number of scholastics, moral theologians and canonists throughout the Middle Ages and into the early modern period. Apart from this mainstream within European political thought, there was another basis for the justification of taxation. This was by stressing the necessary utility (*necessaria utilitas*) of the *respublica* itself as a community, starting from a corporative concept of the *respublica* and not primarily related to subjection to the prince. In his *Quaestio* concerning the tax aspects of voluntary or forced loans (*prestiti*) to the public debt (the *Monte vecchio* of Venice), Nicolaus de Anglia, a fourteenth-century thinker, started from the concept of the *respublica* as a collective entity, of which the citizens compose the parts, and from the Aristotelian–Thomist maxim, that the good of the whole (*bonum commune*) or the people is better than that of the part. Therefore the part had voluntarily to sacrifice itself and its goods to the whole: in a case of 'imminent necessity' the goods of every citizen belonged to the community.[20]

The authoritative medieval justification of taxation was to be found principally in the statements of St Thomas Aquinas, in his commentaries on the Gospel of St Matthew (Matt. 17: 24ff.) and on St Paul's Letter to the Romans, in his own letter to the duchess of Lothringen and Brabant (*De regimine Judaeorum*), and in

[19] Kehl (1927), 78–85. [20] Kirshner (1970), 54, 68, 70–1.

his *Summa theologiae*.[21] According to his commentaries, princes received taxes from their subjects because they served God in their government. However, such payment was not a reward; it was for their maintenance and the costs they incurred ruling the *patria* in peace and tranquillity. Customs duties were paid at specific locations for the safe pursuit of trade, the repair and security of roads, the maintenance of the prince in his travels round his lands, and other legitimate purposes. The central section, the sixth question, of *De regimine Judaeorum* asked whether the taxing of Christian subjects by their rulers was permitted. Aquinas answered that princes should enjoy revenues from property and land, so that they should have enough income for their maintenance and thus refrain from plundering their subjects. Yet it might happen occasionally that the prince lacked sufficient revenue to protect his lands or carry out other tasks which he might reasonably wish to perform, and in such cases it was right for the subjects to provide sufficient means to defray the expenses of their commonweal. In some states, rulers therefore imposed *collectae* on their subjects in accordance with long-established custom; such taxes could be imposed without committing a sin, provided they were not excessive. According to the words of St Paul, nobody was expected to serve at his own cost. Therefore the prince, who served on behalf of the commonweal as a whole, could legitimately receive his maintenance from the public. His expenses might be discharged by revenues assigned for this purpose or, if these proved insufficient, by additional taxes collected from individuals. The same argument applied when there was a sudden increase in expenditure for the commonweal or for the honourable maintenance of the prince, and when revenues or customary taxes proved insufficient: for example, if an enemy suddenly attacked the state. In such cases, the prince might be permitted to levy taxes from his subjects over and above the more customary ones, provided that it was for the benefit of the commonweal. This passage of Aquinas was cited by a number of later theologians such as Johannes of Freiburg, Heinrich of Oyta, Antonino of Florence and Sylvester de Prierio. It seemed to justify the later medieval political maxim that the king was supposed to 'live of his own',[22] as well as providing a political justification for extraordinary taxes in times of national necessity and danger.[23] Aquinas himself treated this topic again in his *Summa theologiae*, where he discussed whether robbery, in certain circumstances, can be committed without sin.[24] His argument was that the collection by princes from their subjects, even by force, of what was owed them for the cost of

[21] Kehl (1927), 87–92.

[22] Dietz (1920), 16–17; Wolffe (1971), 40–51, *passim*; Coville (1888), 37; Rey (1965), 41; Wolfe (1972), 9.

[23] Mitchell (1914); Strayer and Taylor (1972); Harriss (1978); Elton in Winter (1975); Alsop (1982); Ormrod (1991*c*).

[24] Aquinas, ed. Caramello (1952–6), (IIa.IIae.66.8, cf. 87.1).

preserving the commonweal did not constitute robbery. Natural reason required that the public at large should pay the wages of those, such as princes and soldiers, who served the commonweal.

Tolomeo de Lucca, who completed St Thomas's *De regimine principum*, followed his master's thesis and stressed, in addition to the arguments adduced from the Gospels and St Paul, reason and natural law.[25] Since nobody served at his own cost,[26] and since it was in accordance with natural law that everybody should be paid for his labour,[27] the ruler was permitted to levy tribute and annual taxes from his subjects; but he must rest content with that payment and not burden their property unreasonably. Only the defence of the state, or a similar case which reasonably concerned the commonweal, could justly necessitate a higher burden. Provided that the king's government was legal, and the king thus acted for the common good (*utilitas publica*) and did not aim at personal gain (*utilitas privata*) like a tyrant, then he was entitled to collect taxes from his subjects in so far as this was dictated by the need to safeguard their welfare, but no more than that. The necessities of state served for the preservation of human society. The ruler was in effect the cornerstone of society, and must not be weakened: his every loss must be compensated for by levies and taxes paid by the society he protected. Richard of Middleton, followed by Gabriel Biel and others,[28] considered it also necessary to amass a surplus, and replenish it, by taxes, so that the king would be able to defend the kingdom against repeated attacks. If his adversaries knew him to be well supplied with treasure, they would fear him and the kingdom would as a consequence come to no harm.

The principal arguments justifying the levy of taxes thus tended to oscillate between the necessities and claims of the prince on the one hand, and the necessities of the commonweal on the other. They were mediated by the princely authority vested by God, the expenses and services rendered by the prince, the payments required of the subjects he ruled, and the benefits of princely government received by society at large. Comparing rulers with judges, soldiers, bishops, priests, professors and preachers, Heinrich of Hesse (or Langenstein, 1325–97) deemed it reasonable to maintain them at public expense, by a *census* on property or other suitable fiscal measures: such servants and administrators should not have to worry about their maintenance, since their labour was necessary for both temporary and eternal happiness.[29] The argument based on biblical texts and natural law, which maintained that levies and taxes compen-

[25] Innocent IV (1570) (3.11); Kehl (1927), 91–3.
[26] 1 Cor. 9: 7.
[27] Matt. 10: 10; Luke 10: 7; 1 Tim. 5: 18.
[28] Kehl (1927), 95–101.
[29] *De contractibus* (2.2) in Gerson (1484), iv, fo. 206^{b}; Kehl (1927), 96.

sated the prince for his labour, was transformed into another, that of the benefit received by taxpayers. Anselm of Laon (Anselmus Laudunensis, d. 1117),[30] later followed by Henry of Ghent,[31] was of the opinion that taxes in effect reimbursed the costs incurred by the ruler when he fought for his country and acted as judge. Gabriel Biel emphasized that an emergency, and the protection and defence of the state, were justifications for taxation, and he stated that in cases of necessity the sovereign was allowed to demand that which he could not at other times.[32] Already in the twelfth and thirteenth centuries, jurists had developed legal maxims from Roman and canon law, which allowed the prince to levy extraordinary taxes in cases of evident necessity in order to preserve the *status regni* and the *bonum commune*, notwithstanding special rights and privileges.[33] With regard to the Emperor, however, this was not a mere emergency power but a regalian right.[34] Jean Bodin in 1576 quoted the maxim of a 'Roman senator': 'Nothing is more just than that which is necessary' ('Il n'y a rien plus juste, que ce qui est nécessaire').[35] Tax-paying subjects had an equivalent gain from their outlay in the benefits resulting from the defence of the state and the protection of property, law, justice, truth and peace. Established peace allowed inhabitants to travel throughout the land and to carry on their business (St Albertus Magnus, 1193–1280),[36] and generally lead their lives in tranquillity and security. According to Heinrich of Oyta (d. 1397), much of the happiness of the body politic lay in peace, and he referred to St Augustine, who had remarked in *De civitate Dei* that there was no greater and better transient good than peace.[37]

1.4 *The System of 'Causae' with Regard to 'Just' Taxation*

Linked to this question of the justification of taxes was a second one: under what conditions were levies and taxes just, thus imposing a moral obligation on the ruler's subjects? The fundamental answers were given by St Albertus Magnus and, primarily, St Thomas Aquinas, who established formal and casuistic categories to ascertain the justice of human laws in general; these categories were

30 Anselm (1533), 91; Kehl (1927), 87.

31 [Henry of Ghent] (1518), fo. 393 (9.31); Kehl (1927), 93.

32 Biel (1508) (4.15.5, Lit. A, B); Kehl (1927), 98–101.

33 Post (1964), 18–19, 258–9; Harriss (1975), 16–17, 21–2, *passim*; Henneman (1971), 22–3, 303–4; Wachenhausen (1972), 81–90. Cf. also Leyden, ed. Fruin and Molhuijsen (1900), casus VI, 36–40, *passim*.

34 Cf. the 15th-cent. jurist, Jacobus Alvarotus, in his commentary on feudal law: Alvarotus (1522), fo. 173[r].

35 Bodin (6.2) (1583, repr. 1961), 878.

36 *Commentarius in IV sententiarum* (4.16.46) in Albertus Magnus (1890–9), xxix, 637–8; Kehl (1927), 87.

37 *De contractibus* in Gerson (1484), iv, fo. 227[a]; Kehl (1927), 96–8.

thought to be derived from divine law. Human laws were considered just (a) *ex fine*; (b) *ex auctore*; and (c) *ex forma*. From these a scheme of three *causae* developed, which were the premises of just laws and just fiscal laws and levies in particular: (a) *causa finalis*; (b) *causa efficiens*; (c) *causa formalis*. Gabriel Biel extended this scheme to make it even more comprehensive, by adding (d) *causa materialis*.[38] A fifth category, introduced by Thomas de Vio (Cajetan, 1469–1534), concerned the correct use of the tax yield, but this was already included in the *causa finalis*.

The *causa finalis* covered the cause and purpose of the tax.[39] Unlike modern taxes, which are required to meet a general financial need, medieval and early modern taxes, at least in their origins, could only be justified in terms of the general good or for more specific, and on the whole exceptional, purposes. *Collectae* (*talliae*, *tributa*) and *pedagia*, *vectigalia* and *gabellae*—taxes, road tolls, customs and excise duties—were only of just cause, if they served necessity (*necessitas*) and the commonweal (*utilitas communis*, *utilitas publica*, *bonum commune*) or the conservation of society (*communis conservatio societatis*, a phrase used by Aquinas). Tax receipts which were collected *sine causa* had to be returned. The argument of necessity and *utilitas publica* was made clear by a catalogue of the just purposes of expenditure, such as the protection and maintenance of roads and bridges, particularly by *pedagia* and customs duties; the protection of the legal order and peace within the state; the defence of the territory against external threats; and the defence of faith and fatherland against infidels and heretics, particularly by *collectae*. Just taxation and just war were interrelated. With regard to extraordinary taxes, the maxim was 'when the necessity ceases, that required by necessity ceases' (*cessante causa, cessat effectus*).[40] A further group of just causes referred to typical feudal aids—in such circumstances as the capture of the prince, the marriage of his daughter, the knighting of his son—but which might also include the purchase of fiefs. These feudal aids were considered beneficial to a ruler's subjects in the last analysis, since the suzerain gained new friends by the marriage of his daughter and more power to defend the territory by the knighting of his son; he might become richer by the addition of new fiefs and therefore be less likely to tax his subjects (as Guilielmus Redonensis stated). In Gabriel Biel's view, the ruler might impose moderate *collectae* in all matters yielding immediately or even indirectly a profit to the commonweal, or if he was not able to finance the government from his own resources: in these circumstances, the profit of the subjects was preserved in that they gained a greater good.

[38] Amberg (1909), 71–2; Kehl (1927), 104–9; Wachenhausen (1972), 68–70.

[39] Kehl (1927), 133–84; Wachenhausen (1972), 73–90.

[40] Wachenhausen (1972), 73–4; Henneman (1971), 24–5, 323–4.

The *causa efficiens* was the 'effecting cause' and covered the question of tax sovereignty. According to the modern notion of sovereignty, the power to tax (*potestas imponendi sive collectandi*) is a right of sovereignty belonging to the sovereign ruler or to the sovereign state. The situation in the Middle Ages, however, was more complicated and controversial. According to the jurists of Roman and canon law, the power to levy taxes was an attribute of supreme power (*suprema potestas*). Therefore, the Emperor (*princeps*) as the 'sole ruler of the world' (*monarcha orbis*) was permitted to levy all categories of taxes. More controversial was the question as to whether the kings and other subordinate powers, such as territorial lords, barons and cities, possessed the same right. The question was complicated by making a distinction between *vectigalia* or *gabellae* on the one hand and *collectae* on the other. Roman law knew only the Emperor's power to tax, though the Emperor could vest this right in others, whether communities or private persons, as a privilege: once granted, according to Bertachinus, this privilege should not be revoked, since it had assumed the character of an agreement or a contract.

In canon law, however, two canons[41] restricted the right to impose road tolls (*pedagia*), charges for providing safe-conduct and salt taxes (*pedagia*, *guidagia* and *salinaria*) to those authorized by Emperors, kings, the Lateran Council or immemorial custom. Unlike later theologians, the canonist Hostiensis meant by 'kings' only the Kings of the Romans, the Emperors-elect; he did not mean kings in general. The French king, for example, had no right to levy or to concede *pedagia*, because the Pope had not vested in him the same power as in the Emperor. Innocent IV, on the other hand, meant all kings, since in his view they had full jurisdiction in this area. Johannes Andreae, following Hostiensis, nevertheless had to acknowledge the fact that kings and also cities levied *pedagia* from their subjects and even from foreigners. Two hundred years after the commentary of Hostiensis on the *Decretalia*, Panormitanus referred to the canon *Super quibusdam* and argued that kings of lower rank, princes and cities, especially the Italian cities, could acquire imperial rights and the right concerning *pedagia* by prescription. A number of different positions resulted from the debate about the fact that the west European monarchies and free cities acknowledged no overlord (*superiorem non recognoscentes*), whether *de jure* or only *de facto*; the plea of liberty and exemption and other detailed questions concerning prescription and immemorial custom also provoked discussion. That the cities and monarchies were free in fact, if not altogether in theory, is clear from the discussion below (Chapters 3 and 5).

The right to impose a *collecta*, an extraordinary property tax, was a regalian

[41] *Corpus juris canonici*, ed. Friedberg (1879–91), ii, 625 (Extra, 3.39.10), 923 (x, 5.40.26).

right (*ius regale*) belonging to the supreme power (*suprema potestas*) which could be conceded by grant of privilege. Nevertheless, subordinate lords and communities were allowed to impose *collectae* in the case of necessity and for their own welfare, but not for the commonweal as a whole or the fisc of the kingdom. According to Antibolus, urban authorities were permitted to impose *collectae* in order to establish a fund to defray public expenses, but only with the consent of the citizens and inhabitants. In cases of necessity, however, the tax was obligatory and subjects might be forced to pay. This was the position of a number of jurists and theologians who stressed the case of necessity, for example, where a city had fallen into debt. Innocent IV and Ludovicus Pontanus emphasized the nature of the necessity, which had to affect the whole community. Bertachinus clarified the distinction between *gabellae* and *collectae*, which was either neglected or not perceived by other theologians. In his view, whereas cities acknowledging an overlord (*superiorem recognoscentes*) were not allowed to introduce new excise duties (*gabellae*) without the consent of the superior authority, they could at least impose *collectae* in the case of necessity, but not at will (as Johannes de Imola and Baldus de Ubaldis maintained). The cities' power to impose *collectae* was sometimes seen as analogous to their power to make special statutes.

Through the interpretation of Roman law by the civil and canon lawyers of the Middle Ages, the model of a secular state enjoying a monopoly of tax power was obtained. This applied primarily to the Emperor as *monarchus orbis* but also to the kings of western Europe, who were considered *de facto* independent from the Emperor and claimed to have authority equivalent to that of the Emperor in their realms. Subordinate powers were in theory permitted to levy taxes only by virtue of delegation or privilege and concession, as Bartolus de Saxoferrato (1314–57) made clear.[42] However, the medieval reality in continental Europe was that taxation at a lower level originated on the legal basis of special seigneurial (or 'feudal') personal relationships and protection: the subject was obliged to render aid and counsel in view of the lord's necessity. The king participated in this system of special feudal and seigneurial relations as the suzerain and lord of his domain; he had no general sovereignty to impose universal taxes for the sake of the realm and for the benefit of the commonweal without the magnates' consent. He was thus in no position to delegate such power to subordinate lords, who imposed taxes in their own right. For his part, the Emperor did not establish

[42] 'No one can impose a tax except the Emperor or kings, or those to whom they have granted the right to do so. He who imposes a tax established by custom does not presume to impose it without the authority of the Emperor or of kings: but he claims and assumes that such a practice is founded on the authority of the Emperor or of kings.' Bartolus de Saxoferrato (1535), *De expensis publicis*, fo. 128^{v}. Hostiensis (1537; repr. 1962), fo. 183^{r}, stated: 'Taxes are to be condemned, except those permitted by the Emperor or a king . . .' (*Super titulis decretalium*, 3.10); Wachenhausen (1972), 145–6.

general taxes—and then only with the consent of the estates of the Empire—until 1427, 1471–4 and 1495. In any case, the taxes of the *de facto* autonomous cities were based on the citizens' oath of loyalty, which obliged them to carry jointly the burden of community and city. The strongest and earliest legal title (apart from aid and counsel) possessed by the Emperor and the west European monarchs was the regalian right to levy customs duties.

In contrast to this reality, theory derived from Roman law established a legal monopoly of tax power in the hands of the supreme power, the ruler who was considered best able to achieve the common good for the whole realm. Nevertheless, subordinate authorities, according to Bartolus, were legally allowed to impose taxes in order to remedy common necessities. Bartolus stated that without the permission of the prince taxes which fostered the common good became legal *in usum necessitatis*;[43] and those lower authorities which levied taxes by virtue of immemorial custom possessed legal title to do so (that is, custom had the effect of legal title).[44] Whereas a jurist such as Hostiensis was of the opinion that the cause and purpose of taxation were not decisive factors, and the reasons for taxation irrelevant to taxpayers, the canonist and moral theologian Raymundus de Pennaforte (d. 1275), in his instructions to father confessors, emphasized the *causa finalis*, as against the *causa efficiens*, and argued that rulers should be allowed to levy taxes for just cause without asking the prior permission of the Emperor.[45]

The *causa formalis* was the measure of taxation.[46] The scale of the taxes levied had to be judged in proportion to the commonweal, and the tax burden had to be distributed according to equity, that is in proportion to the individual's capacity to pay (*facultas*), evaluated according to his property and his overall wealth. The apportionment of taxes was considered an aspect of distributive justice (*iustitia distributiva*), which—according to Aristotle and Aquinas (Chapter 1.2)—could not result in an absolute equality as with commutative justice (*iustitia commutativa*), but fixed the proportion by which the various parts of the total burden were to be distributed to individuals.[47] Taxes ought to be moderate relative to the person and to the purpose. Subjects must not be overburdened; instead, the tax had to be bearable; it must not lead to their impoverishment but preserve a necessary subsistence. Above all, taxation should not be imposed too frequently. The burden of the tax must not be higher than necessity required. Any surplus

[43] Bartolus de Saxoferrato (1535), *De expensis publicis*, fo. 33^r; Wachenhausen (1972), 150.

[44] Cf. e.g. Sylvester de Prierio and Gabriel Biel: Wachenhausen (1972),150, nn. 245, 247.

[45] Kehl (1927), 144–6.

[46] Amberg (1909), 95–118; Kehl (1927), 184–237.

[47] Esp. Neumann (1880), 526–47.

should therefore be distributed to those communities which had suffered most from the tax itself.

The principles, techniques and methods of a just and equal repartition and assessment (*peraequatio*) of taxes were discussed in detail, sometimes with reference to urban practices (Antonino of Florence, 1389–1459). Proportional tax rates (*pro libra et solidis*) were favoured, but never progressive ones. In certain cases, less sophisticated forms of taxation such as poll taxes and hearth taxes (*foragia*) were allowed in theory. Other questions discussed were whether the property recorded in the tax register should be assessed according to the yield or to the sale price, and whether or not the *census* should be increased after the improvement of an estate. Double taxation, which was a great problem resulting from divided jurisdiction within the same territory or from an external jurisdiction, was altogether to be avoided.

The fourth *causa* was the *causa materialis*:[48] just taxes must be paid by the appropriate persons and must tax the appropriate objects. Apart from the exemption of the church and clerics personally, *personae miserabiles* (the blind, the sick, widows, orphans and the poor) should be totally or at least partially exempt from taxation. Merchants were considered to be exceptionally suitable taxpayers. Thomas de Vio regarded levies on the transport of necessities (*vectigalia*) as unjust, since the poor had to pay as much as the rich and not in proportion to their capacity to pay. Similarly, he found it unjust that indirect taxes bore down on families with numerous children, since they consumed more and therefore paid more in taxes, yet the number of children impaired the capacity to pay.[49] But the theologians did not dare denounce tax rights affecting salt (*salinaria*), because they were approved by law and custom. With regard to the objects of taxation, it was held that what was necessary for subsistence at a minimum level should be exempt from tax, including basic necessities. As a matter of principle, succession duties and taxes on legacies *ad pias causas* were rejected, except where local statutes permitted them: but even in such circumstances, duty was payable only on the net yield.

The most advanced principles of taxation, which seem to anticipate those of Adam Smith, were put forward by Nicolas Oresme (Oresmius, *c.*1320–82), who discussed in his tract *De moneta*[50]—with regard to just causes only—the advantages of a debasement of coinage undertaken by the community as a form of levy (*tallia* or *collecta*). Debasement brought in much profit in little time; it was easy to assess and to collect without employing a large staff or risking fraud in

48 Kehl (1927), 237–75.

49 Cf. the justification of excise taxes by Francisco Suarez against Thomas de Vio: Amberg (1909), 108–9.

50 Oresme, ed. Johnson (1956), 35–7 (ch. 22); cf. Kehl (1927), 283–7.

collection; it was cheap to collect; it was equitable, since those who could afford most, paid most; for the return it gave, it was less noticeable or perceived than other forms of taxation—and therefore more easily endured without the ruler risking the danger of rebellion and the people's ill will. It was a universal tax, because neither cleric nor noble could make himself exempt by privilege or otherwise, as they tried to do with other forms of contribution, thus causing envy, discord, litigation, scandal and other evils within the body politic.[51] It is interesting to compare these principles, which were elaborated in a theoretical context, with others, which were enunciated later against an immediate political background. The most sophisticated Imperial tax law or ordinance, that of 1474, clearly laid down five principles for just taxation. The tax had to be 'universal'; it had to fall equally on all social and corporate groups; it had to be proportionate to the individual's capacity to pay; the tax had to be bearable; and finally, the predicted tax yield had to be sufficient with regard to the purpose of the tax.[52]

1.5 *'Specula Regis': Political and Reforming Tracts on Public Finance and Taxation*

Some of the political tracts of the later Middle Ages and the Renaissance searched more deeply into the political, administrative and economic problems of public finance. Maladministration and other abuses inspired writers with the desire to urge reforms. Italian writers[53] such as St Thomas Aquinas, Aegidius Romanus (Colonna, 1247–1316), Francesco Petrarch (1304–74), Giovanni Sercambi (1347–1424), Francesco Patrizi (1412–94) and Bartolomeo Platina (1421–81) all argued—though necessarily with some variations in detail—that the princely domain was the basis of public finance; moreover, the prince should provide the necessary means to support an army in peacetime. In principle, new levies were supposed to be an extraordinary expedient, and limited to certain clearly defined cases of pure and urgent necessity which were obvious to the public. The tax burden should be as moderate as possible (Petrarch), while the collection of taxes must be carried out in a simple and humane manner (Patrizi). Sercambi—without the benefit of modern psychological arguments in favour of indirect taxes—disapproved of direct taxes and recommended instead import and export duties, with especially high tariffs on the import of foreign wines.

In any case, new taxes had to be avoided as much as possible for political reasons, because, as Patrizi remarked, they always appear burdensome to the

[51] Cf. Smith, ed. Campbell, Skinner and Todd (1976) (5.2.2, 'Of Taxes'). For the reasons for the exemption of church and clergy: Kehl (1927), 344–401.

[52] Isenmann (1979), 71–7; Isenmann (1980), 161–82.

[53] Ricca-Salerno (1881), 17–41.

people and might lead to hatred of the government. Therefore, in order to obtain the necessary funds (*pecuniae*)—which Patrizi (quoting a classical phrase) called 'the nerves of the state' (*nervi civitatis* or *reipublicae*)[54]—the prince needed a large domain, and he had to preserve it for financial, political and even social and economic reasons. It was thought that the prince's domain administered by officials and (hereditary) tenants affected the rest of society and the economy: Patrizi seems to have assumed that a large princely domain restricted the capacity of private persons administering them to concentrate large landholdings in only a few hands, which was against the general good.[55] Sercambi advised the alienation to private individuals of those parts of the domain which were less fertile and without great advantage to the treasury.[56]

These fiscal and political aims could only be achieved by a diligent and strict administration. The prince therefore had to control and, if necessary, punish customs officials, tax collectors and leaseholders on his domain: he had to take action against fraud, abuse and extortion. A further requirement was that the prince himself should observe moderation in his expenditure policy. Petrarch stated that the prince must avoid useless and superfluous expenses so that he had sufficient money to spend on what was necessary and indispensable for the decorum and the benefit of the state (*civitas*).[57] Platina, like Petrarch, recommended useful public works, such as strengthening the embankments of rivers, draining marshes, or street repairs.[58] Aegidius Romanus gave similar advice, but also urged the prince to seek the consent of the citizens with regard to expenditure and the means of financing it, thus avoiding the risk of individuals' losing their property, and respecting the interests both of the treasury and of private individuals.[59]

As for the structure of expenditure, a French tract of 1347, which was translated into English in the middle of the fifteenth century,[60] considered that a prince or great lord must first estimate the likely annual total of his rents and revenues.[61] Ordinary rents and revenues were those which were of certain and annual return; extraordinary revenues were those which were not annual and which were 'casual' in the sense of being occasional and irregular. In order to organize

[54] Isenmann (1980), 144; cf. Stolleis (1983), 63–8. There were similar uses of the phrase by Aeneas Silvius Piccolomini and Platina.

[55] Ricca-Salerno (1881), 20.

[56] Ibid. 19–20.

[57] *De republica optime administranda* in Petrarch (1554), 426–7.

[58] Ricca-Salerno (1881), 20.

[59] Aegidius Romanus (1473); Ricca-Salerno (1881), 19.

[60] *The III Consideracions Right Necesserye to the Good Governaunce of a Prince* in Genet (1977), 174–219; 183–8 (financial matters).

[61] Cf. the tract *De regimine principum ad Regem Henricum Sextum* in Genet (1977), 141.

his expenditure, the ruler needed to divide his income into three parts. Firstly, he needed to ensure an honourable upkeep for himself, his family and his household including his servants and officials. Secondly, he needed to pay for his charitable giving, his daily alms,[62] and his rewards and gifts to men of virtue and merit according to their status and the quality of their service. Thirdly, he needed to establish a reserve, which would be at his disposal for the safety and defence of his person, his territory and his subjects or any other important matters. As for his purchases, the prince (in sharp contrast to the contemporary practice of royal purveyances) should pay the just price and pay promptly and in full, so that his subjects did not suffer as a result of his actions.[63]

Diomede Carafa (d. 1487), a supporter of the Aragonese King Alfonso V (Alfonso I of Naples and Sicily) and a close councillor of Alfonso II, similarly required that strict, reliable and frequent accounts be rendered of all the certain and legitimate revenues of the state.[64] Revenues should be divided into three categories with corresponding divisions of expenditure, firstly for troops, fortifications and other items necessary for the defence and the power of the state; secondly, for the maintenance of the prince and the royal family in proper dignity; and thirdly for unpredictable but inevitable extraordinary expenses. These three accounts should be balanced in such a way that a surplus would result, which could be spent on sudden and unforeseen contingencies.

A rather different allocation of revenues to expenses was that recommended by councillor Ritter Ludwig von Eyb the Elder (1417–1502) to the elector of Brandenburg in a memorandum of uncertain date (but before 26 February 1492).[65] One part of the revenues should be devoted to the expenses of the household, the court and the administration. A second part was reserved for debt redemption, while a third was intended to build up a reserve fund in order to cope with unforeseen events, such as wars. These measures were to ensure that the ruler, in cases of necessity, was not forced to sell property to usurers at half its value, or to alienate it. If the ruler was unwilling to establish a reserve and

[62] Cf. the alms of King John (occasionally 6 per cent of his revenue): Gilchrist (1969), 79.

[63] '. . . it be seyn and well considred that his officers take no thinge of the goodys of the subgites othir wise thanne at a just and convenable prys and with oute longe creaunce or delay of payment, ffor it is full good and grete honeure to every lord whan he paith truly and well that he dispendith, and whan he norysshith nat him self ne his meynee ne liveth upon the goodys of his pover subgites': Genet (1977), 184. The abuses of purveyance are bitterly attacked by two Latin tracts (*c.*1330): *De speculo regis Edwardi III* (1891), 115, 122. According to Wolffe (1971), 47–50, the earliest use of the maxim 'the king should live of his own', in 1311, is in connection with the abuse of the purveyance, which interferes with subjects' property rights.

[64] Carafa (1668) [written between 1469 and 1482], 53–4; Ricca-Salerno (1881), 22–3. Carafa's tract was not available to the present writer in Germany; references are therefore quoted according to Ricca-Salerno.

[65] Edited in Wagner (1885).

preferred to divide his expenditure between the costs of the court and debt redemption, then he would need to economize and act on the assumption that he had at his disposition only half his revenues; to be equipped to meet all eventualities, in normal circumstances he would have to manage with that half. These general financial maxims were reinforced by a set of detailed instructions for quite a sophisticated budget. Ludwig von Eyb drafted two lists, one of revenues and the other of expenditure, which specified all the various items within several separate categories; he also made some rough estimates of cost prices for goods and services. The ruler at the beginning of the financial year was to draw up an estimate of expenditure,[66] both ordinary (the costs of the household, court and administration) and extraordinary. These estimates were later to be compared with the actual totals of audited expenditure from the completed financial year. If the comparison revealed a deficit, there should be consideration as to how this might be reduced. The ruler was supposed to be well informed about the detail of his annual revenue which was to be ascertained from the accounts of the various officials. In this way, he would be able each year to observe the changes in revenue from different categories of income, and would be informed about the reasons for this by those councillors who had audited the annual accounts. Such measures were a first step towards active financial management by rulers, and similar procedures were to apply to expenditure. Revenue and expenditure were to be balanced in order to establish whether there was a surplus or deficit, which would be brought forward into the subsequent year's accounts. At the same time the ruler had to consider necessary measures to reduce the deficit or increase the surplus. He was supposed to control expenditure and, if irregularities were discovered, to take active measures against the officials responsible. Finally, the ruler and his councillors were to draw up an estimate (in effect, budget proposals) concerning the expenditure of the household for the next financial year. The four main court officials were to receive detailed instructions as to where and from whom they were to collect the revenues assigned to meet their expenditure. These revenues were to be paid out in four quarterly instalments. On the basis of weekly accounts, rough calculations were to be made every three months in order to establish whether the quarterly targets for income and expenditure in the budget proposals had been met. If there were no legitimate reasons for failing to meet these targets, and if it was likely to prove impossible to balance the account within the next quarter, the councillors were then required to take measures

[66] Cf. the estimates in England concerning revenue and expenditure of 1411, 1421 and 1433 in Fortescue, ed. Plummer (1885), nn. 210–15. Fortescue took the view that the personal expenditure of the king could be estimated by the officers of the household or the clerks of the exchequer: ibid. 122, ch. 6.

necessary to guarantee that the accounts were back on target by the time of the final annual audit.

Sir John Fortescue, Chief Justice of the King's Bench, expressed another viewpoint. In his treatise *On the Governance of England* (written 1471–6),[67] Fortescue stated as a fiscal principle that the king's revenues must be proportioned according to his charges and expenses. There should not be an absolute balance, for—with reference to a sentence of St Bernardino of Siena[68]—Fortescue thought that the accounts should show a surplus so that the king and his realm might meet the challenge of any unforeseen events. The king must always be rich, both for his own benefit and for that of his subjects. A poor king had to meet his expenses by borrowing and thereby lost the equivalent of a fifth or a quarter of his revenues to his creditors; moreover, in order to pay off his debts punctually he was forced to take out new loans and thus compound the loss. Thus he became impecunious and deeply in debt. A poor king was forced to grant gifts and rewards by assigning his revenue and by alienating crown lands to the detriment of his resources, when his servants would have been content with much lower payments made in cash. The worst consequence of the king's poverty was that he might be forced to resort to extreme fiscal expedients in order to obtain money, such as extorting fines unjustly, especially from the rich, and exhibiting severity where leniency should be shown and so on—all this risking the perversion of justice and disturbing the peace and quiet of the realm. Here Fortescue quoted the *Nicomachean Ethics* of Aristotle (1.8.15): 'it is impossible for the poor man to do good' (*impossibile est indigentem operari bona*).[69]

Fortescue accepted the traditional distinction between the king's ordinary and extraordinary expenses.[70] Since the ordinary expenses[71] were inevitable, it was necessary to assign revenues in order to meet them: these assignments should not be diverted for other purposes. Once this principle was firmly established, the expectation was that ordinary expenses could always be paid promptly in cash: this required liquid assets to the equivalent of a fifth or a quarter of total ordinary expenditure. Extraordinary expenses were those which occurred so unpredict-

67 Fortescue, ed. Plummer (1885).

68 'That if in your household expenditure and income are equal, an emergency could destroy its stability' (St Bernardino). Cf. Fortescue, ed. Plummer (1885), 216.

69 Ibid. ch. 5.

70 For the classification of revenues into ordinary (from the domain) and extraordinary (from taxation): Dupont-Ferrier (1933, repr. 1976), 2–22. With specific contemporary meanings: Wolffe (1971), 38–9; Henneman (1971), 18–19.

71 Fortescue, ed. Plummer (1885), ch. 6, lists the following expenses: (1) the king's household (and wardrobe); (2) wages and fees of the great officers, his courtiers and his council; (3) occupation ('keeping') of the marches; (4) occupation of Calais; and (5) maintenance of royal buildings. Naval expenditure ('the keeping of the sea') is not included in this category, since it could not be estimated and the king had for this purpose the subsidies of tonnage and poundage.

ably and 'casually' that nobody could ascertain in advance their annual total and the necessary assignment of revenues to meet them without difficulty;[72] but it might be possible to estimate the maximum expenditure which would not normally be exceeded except in extreme circumstances, and then it was reasonable and necessary that the whole realm should contribute towards a 'singular' levy. Fortescue maintained that the king certainly had sufficient revenues to meet his ordinary expenses. Any remaining surplus was at the disposal of the king, who might spend it at his pleasure on extraordinary needs. If the surplus did not cover extraordinary expenses, then the realm as a whole had to supply the deficit. Though Fortescue asserted in effect the principle that the king should live of his own, nevertheless he qualified this by another principle, that his realm 'is bounde by right to susteyne hym in euery thyng necessarie to his estate'.[73] As justification of this principle he referred, as the Scholastics had done, to the concept of kingship as an office, 'in wich he mynestrith to his reaume defence and justice'; since the king was thus a servant, he was owed sustenance from the one he served, that is the realm.[74] For political reasons—the need for a powerful and secure ruler—the revenue the king required to meet his extraordinary expenses should be greater than the total revenue of the greatest English lords, particularly since they had comparatively small households and therefore small ordinary expenses. A subordinate lord who was as powerful as the king, or even more powerful, might risk rebellion against his prince in order to obtain his lands and title. Worse still, other subjects might help him in his rebellion, because they would rather be subject to a prince who had twice the wealth of their former ruler, and who therefore might be expected to free them from taxes otherwise required for his maintenance.

Fortescue concluded that Edward IV, who at the beginning of his reign had almost one-fifth of the total yield from temporal property in the kingdom, had insufficient revenue a decade later. Comparing French indirect duties on essential goods, Fortescue considered a salt tax levied with the consent of the people not unreasonable, because all would be taxed equally; but it would have the disadvantage of being a new tax, which had not been imposed by the king's predecessors. Instead, he proposed a restoration of the royal domain. This might be achieved by inheritance, by the seizure of escheated (forfeited) fiefs including those lost through treason, and by a selective policy of purchase which made use

[72] Ibid. ch. 7. Fortescue listed among such costs: (1) embassies to foreign powers and the Pope; (2) entertainment, gifts and rewards for foreign legates and ambassadors; (3) rewards in money to persons who rendered services and favours; (4) new buildings, rich apparel appropriate to royal status, impressive furnishings, clothes and jewels; (5) formal visitation of seditious areas by commissioners and judges; and (6) defence of the country against attack on land or at sea.

[73] Ibid. 127, ch. 8.

[74] Quoting 1 Cor. 9: 7; Matt. 10: 10; Gal. 6: 6.

of the suzerain's right of first refusal. The most important measure would be a resumption of lands which had been granted away as undeserved or excessive rewards for services: this would be carried out on the basis of a general resumption by Parliament in connection with the grant of a subsidy.[75] Subsequently, services performed for the king were to be rewarded with money payments, with offices, marriages, franchises and privileges, or with revenues granted for the duration of one life only, which would revert to the crown after the death of the beneficiary. Like the church, the king should 'amortize' his revenue and property (that is, place it in mortmain), so that no part of it could be alienated without Parliament's consent. Fortescue called this a new foundation for the crown[76] and contended that this curtailment of the king's power of alienation would be no restraint of royal prerogative.[77]

Fortescue's concept of state finance, based on political experiences mainly from the Lancastrian period, was that of the royal domain supplemented by additional parliamentary grants in cases of urgent necessity. He sought to avoid regular taxation on the French model, which he thought led to the impoverishment of the common people, since the nobles were exempt from taxes. According to Fortescue, the French tax state was founded on the absolutist system of unrestricted royal power (the *dominium regale*), which allowed the king to rule his subjects by his own laws and to establish *tailles* and other levies without their consent. He favoured instead the alternative political system of England, where the *dominium politicum et regale* tied the royal government to laws to which the people had consented, and the king was not permitted to levy taxes without the people's consent. The oppressive government of the French king received much more revenue from taxation, but the wealth of his fertile realm was almost destroyed by the impoverishment of the common people: the French king thus committed a great sin and offence against the laws of nature.[78]

In France, Philippe de Commynes expressed a similar opinion on the constitutional and ethical aspects of the emergent tax state, when he wrote in his *Mémoires* that Louis XI, against his initial intentions, had levied more taxes than any previous king. But

> king Charles VII was the first ... to establish the principle of imposing *tailles* in his lands at his pleasure, and without the consent of the estates of his kingdom ... The French lords consented to this because of pensions they were promised in return for the sums levied on their lands ... But that this happened, and will continue to happen in the future, should

[75] Cf. the realization of such an idea by the redemption law of the *Cortes* of Castile in 1480: Merriman (1918–34), ii, 106.

[76] Fortescue, ed. Plummer (1885), ch. 19. Cf. chs. 11, 14, 17, 20.

[77] Ibid. 121, ch. 6.

[78] Ibid. chs. 1–4.

rest heavily on his conscience and that of his successors, since this cruelly wounded his kingdom, from which it will long bleed . . .[79]

On the other hand, Commynes described (under the year 1474) the habitual political manoeuvre or trick (*practicque*) of the English king to acquire extraordinary taxes granted by Parliament on the pretext of waging war against Scotland or France.[80]

1.6 *Empirical Analysis and Theoretical Insights towards the End of the Middle Ages*

Whereas Fortescue remained within traditional and almost feudal conceptions of state finance, the Italian Diomede Carafa, who possessed a penetrating theoretical mind, took up the modern question of economic analysis concerning the interrelationship between state, treasury and fiscal policy on the one hand and the economy and private business on the other. Justice and security guaranteed by the government were considered to be the prerequisites of economic prosperity: thus Carafa sharply criticized forced loans and the withdrawal and alteration of coin. His basic principle may be summed up in the maxim 'The resources of subjects should be regarded as the foundation of royal power' (*Subditorum facultates potentiae regiae fundamentum existimare oportet*).[81] This implied that the prince ought to restrict his activities to government and the administration of public affairs and to leave trade, industry and commerce to private individuals. Carafa disapproved of commercial transactions undertaken by the prince on his own behalf: the sovereign could not make the same profit as private individuals, since he could not undertake business on the same scale, or take the same care of it as private individuals; nor could he take advantage of favourable market conditions to the same extent. Therefore it was much more profitable to the prince to have an indirect share in the wealth of his citizens. Indeed, the extent of private wealth determined the scale on which public revenue could be extracted. This insight into the interrelationship between finance and national economy, between a good government and the wealth of the people, led Carafa on to more practical considerations. The prince had to go to great lengths in order to promote trade and commerce; but he also needed to reduce the taxes paid by peasant farmers and to abolish completely export duties.

[79] Commynes, ed. Calmette (1925), ii, 289–90 (6.6). Cf. Tocqueville, ed. Mayer (1967), 180. Also Commynes, ed. Calmette (1925), ii, 217 (5.19): '. . . y a-il roi ne seigneur sur terre qui ayt povoir, oultre son dommaine, de mectre ung denier sur ses subgectz sans octroy et consentement de ceulx qui le doyvent payer, sinon par tyrannie et violence?'

[80] Commynes, ed. Calmette (1925), ii, 8–9 (4.1).

[81] Carafa (1668), 66–7. In another figure of speech, ibid. 86: 'Nor can a king be poor when he has subjects who are very rich.' Ricca-Salerno (1881), 23.

The abolition or reduction of customs duties would be compensated for by greater economic growth (an enhancement of the gross national product, we might say), in which the prince could take a share. Carafa commented:

Nor will this involve you in any loss, when the tribute from those places is deducted and the unsought multitude of visitors and the abundance of all things is taken into account. It is wise to disregard immediate gain and have the foresight to perceive cause and effect and the connection between future developments and what has been done in the past.[82]

Though Carafa was to a remarkable extent ahead of his time, he was not entirely alone in his insights. The German humanist, Albrecht von Eyb (1420–75), similarly recommended to the prince a reduction of the customs duties and other taxes within the state payable by merchants; they would then visit his lands and trade there in greater numbers than before, and as a result the prince's revenues from customs duties, tribute (*Zinse*) and rents would increase.[83] But Carafa pursued the question of the relationship of fiscal affairs to private enterprise much further than his contemporaries. He took the view that most public revenues ought to be farmed out and not directly administered: the activity and diligence of those who worked on their own account was superior to the administration of salaried public officials, who damaged the interests of the treasury by their negligence. The system of leasing, which was thought to be the mark of every good administration, was advantageous to the state, since the leaseholders did not cause the state losses, and because of competition between themselves they guaranteed a regular increase in revenue to the ruler. Carafa developed his ideas and his reforming advice against the background of the lamentable economic and social consequences of Angevin rule in the kingdom of Naples. As an influential politician, he had the opportunity to inspire a series of reforming edicts from 1466 until 1482 under the rule of Aragonese kings, so that the nineteenth-century historian, Ricca-Salerno, can speak of a 'happy coincidence of theory and practice' ('accordo fortunato della teoria colla pratica'), which was not to recur in Naples until the days of the marchese Palmieri in the second half of the eighteenth century.[84]

In their analysis, Florentine authors turned to the practices of their municipal fiscal institutions, to the system of public loans, whether voluntary or forced (*prestanze* and *prestiti forzati*), the *Monte comune dei debiti* (1343) and *Monte delle doti* (1425); they also studied the *catasto* (1427), the system of direct and indirect taxes (*gabelle*) and customs duties (*dazi*). The two great Tuscan theologians and economists, St Bernardino of Siena (1380–1444) and Antonino of Florence (1389–

[82] Carafa (1668), 76–9; Ricca-Salerno (1881), 23.

[83] Von Eyb [1471] (1511), fo. xcv.

[84] Ricca-Salerno (1881), 26.

1458), as well as other moral theologians and canonists, approved of the right to resort to public loans and *prestanze* as fiscal expedients to meet urgent financial needs for the sake of the *comunità*. They also justified the payment of interest to the state's creditors, who had a right to demand compensation for their risks and potential losses; any reward they gained was legitimate and should not be open to the accusation of usury. According to Antonino, the government gave security to its creditors by assigning a source of public revenue as a pledge or guarantee of the payment of interest. Some authors accepted that creditors had the right to cede or to sell their claims, so that they became negotiable bonds and attracted prices which oscillated above or below the face value: Antonino remarked that this was an inevitable consequence of the risk, and was therefore justified.[85] The theological arguments on the acceptability of voluntary investments in public funds were a matter of contention between the various religious orders. Some Dominicans, Augustinians and Franciscans took the view that by purchasing interest-bearing *prestanze*, *prestiti* or *luoghi*, investors became voluntary lenders to the state and committed the sin of usury. However, others maintained that these investors were not lenders but had purchased a right (*ius*) to the debt and the annuity paid on it, and that the transaction was to be judged as a licit contract of sale.[86]

Florentine writers justified the power of the state to impose taxes, and the obligation of all citizens to pax taxes, by the argument of a balance or equivalence of benefits. According to Lodovico Ghetti,[87] the government guaranteed peace, justice and security to individuals and to their property; thus all citizens who enjoyed these benefits, including clerics, individuals who were not citizens and foreign nationals, had to meet the expenditure necessary for the defence of the Florentine state ('per salute della libertà e stato di Firenze') by the payment of taxation, which had to be equitable in its nature and method of levy, so that it could be borne without criticism or lament. Matteo Palmieri (1406–75) in his tract *Della vita civile* stated that there was an almost direct relationship between increases in citizens' property and the protection of the *patria*; as a result, such property could be taxed in the interest of public protection.[88] In order to meet the needs of the community, Ghetti suggested a general, direct and proportional tax in the form of a tenth (*decima*) imposed on the profit from agriculture, livestock, buildings, interest-bearing loans granted to the *Monte*, annuities, trade and commerce, and salaries. This proposed profit tax on landed and movable

[85] Ibid. 32; de Roover (1953*b*), 3–41; de Roover (1967), 38–40; Kirshner (1970); cf. Marks (1960); Molho (1971).

[86] Kirshner (1970), 53–4, *passim*.

[87] Ghetti in Roscoe (1825), 51–60 (appx 16); cf. Ricca-Salerno (1881), 34.

[88] Palmieri, ed. Battaglia (1944), 116–18. Most recent critical edn.: Palmieri, ed. Belloni (1982).

property, like the German *Decima* of 1471 and 1474,[89] is much more like a modern income tax than the usual medieval property tax.

The question of what were just and convenient objects of taxation, with regard to technical details, was taken up by Niccolò Machiavelli (1480–1540), who discussed the internal Florentine dispute over the new tax law of 1427, called the *catasto*, which was intended to lead to a greater equity in tax assessments, and which covered landed property as well as personal property, such as stock in the *Monte* and all business investments at home and abroad. The *catasto* was a property tax levied at half of 1 per cent of the total value of the property after certain allowable deductions; it had some characteristics of an income tax, since it was based on individual returns (*portate*), which were capitalized.[90] An earlier tax, called the *estimo*, was levied on landed and personal property, too, but it was ultimately a repartition tax and therefore subject to the arbitrary assessments of the tax commissions. When the *popolo* went a step further and demanded a retroactive application of the new fiscal law, the party of the patriciate (*potenti*) discredited the *catasto* on principle as an unjust tax, because it included movable wealth, which was subject to great changes and fluctuations from one day to the next, and was therefore uncertain and unsuitable for taxation. Furthermore, many persons were assumed to have money hoarded, which would not be declared, and could not be ascertained at the time of the assessment. The supporters of the *catasto*, which was to be revised every third year, argued that the individual tax burden could follow any changes in movable wealth, and frequent changes of the assessments would put everything right. Hidden money might be ignored, they argued, because it was infertile (in the sense of yielding no profits), and thus it was not taxable; if money was to become fertile, that is, produce profits, it would come to light and be taxed.[91]

Francesco Guicciardini (1483–1540) recognized that a tax imposed on the returns from landed possessions (*possessioni, beni sodi*) would be insufficient to meet public needs, because in Florence they constituted a relatively small proportion of the general wealth. But a tax on trade and commerce, and on movables, was considered by him to be virtually impossible to realize, because money circulated in various invisible ways; it would be difficult to levy, because it would be very laborious to take into account all the contracts, bills of exchange and business transactions which constituted the profitable operations of trade and commerce; it would also be injurious, since transactions were often based on credit, and the business situation of the parties concerned would be disclosed.

[89] Isenmann (1980), 161–82.

[90] Cf. the summary by de Roover (1963), 21–31; Herlihy and Klapisch-Zuber (1978), 17–106; Conti (1984), 119–80, 247–80.

[91] Machiavelli, ed. Gaeta (1962), 288–90 (4.14).

Guicciardini suggested a balanced system of taxes, which he considered the prerequisite of strong civil government: there should be a basic direct tax on immovable property, complemented by increased excise taxes and customs duties, especially on flour and salt.[92]

Machiavelli and Guicciardini discussed in some detail the political struggle between the Florentine patriciate and the *popolo minuto* for a more just distribution of taxation. The rich disliked direct taxes on principle and preferred indirect ones. According to Machiavelli, who drew on Giovanni Cavalcanti's *Istorie fiorentine*, the fiscal law establishing the *catasto*, which led to a heavier financial burden on the patriciate and which was established only by the authority of Giovanni de' Medici, partially checked the tyrannical actions of the tax commission, which had been run by the patriciate in their interests. The tax assessments and the collecting commissions remained a political instrument available to ruin rivals financially in the power struggle between the Florentine factions; it was, Guicciardini remarked, a weapon in the hands of Cosimo de' Medici.[93] Machiavelli furthermore commented that the supporters of the *catasto* argued that the patriciate objected on the grounds that they would be unable to wage war outside the state except at considerable personal loss, if they had to contribute to the expenses of the state like everyone else.[94] In his *Discorsi*, Machiavelli admired the system of self-assessment and tax payment safeguarded only by the tax oath, which he found still in operation in some German cities. This probity was explained by the relatively small-scale commercial relations of German cities without the allegedly corrupting influence of the French, Spanish and Italian nations. He thought that it was also to be explained by the free and uncorrupted constitution of the German cities, which was based on absolute civil equality and did not tolerate noblemen as citizens, since they considered the nobility to be the root of all corruption and political disorder.[95]

In contrast, Guicciardini was of the opinion that in the imposition of tax burdens the popular government (*governo popolare*) more habitually went to extremes than was the case with rule by a prince (*principato*)—it burdened the rich excessively to the general detriment of the state.[96] He and, earlier, Palmieri grappled with a new view of tax equity, that of progressive taxation, in contrast to the norm of medieval property taxes, which were generally proportional or regressive.[97] Firstly, in 1442 a progressive extraordinary tax called the *diecina*

92 Guicciardini, ed. Scarano (1970), i, 353–4.

93 Von Reumont (1883), 109–10.

94 Machiavelli, ed. Gaeta (1962), 289–90 (4.14); cf. Ricca-Salerno (1881), 34–6.

95 Machiavelli, ed. Crick (1979), 243–8 (1.55).

96 Guicciardini, ed. Scarano (1970), i, 349–53.

97 For Florentine tax laws of the 15th cent. and assessments of the Palmieri family: Palmieri, ed. Conti (1983), 132–5; Conti (1984), 197–245; Molho (1971), 22–59.

graziosa was imposed on the returns of landed property and the stock in the *Monte comune*; it started on a scale of fourteen tax brackets, from a rate of 4 per cent at the first level of under 50 florins in estimated income, and rose to 33.3 per cent in the last level at over 1,500 florins.[98] The *diecina nuova* of 1447 was a tax rising from 8 to 50 per cent on the same tax brackets.[99] In 1451, the *valsente*, a tax on the return from landed property, had only eight tax levels from 20 per cent (under 50 florins) to 60 per cent (over 600 florins).[100] On the occasion of the revision of the *catasto* in 1458, Cosimo de' Medici's faction in the *Signoria* established a progressively scaled income tax which divided the taxable citizens into fourteen progressive tax brackets up to the highest tax rate of 50 per cent (though the assessments themselves were arbitrary). In the end, the tax was not collected in this way. A progressive version of the *estimo* had been demanded during the regime of the *popolo* in 1378,[101] and in 1480 it was decided to extend progression to the *catasto*. This was carried out in 1481–2, and a scale of tax rates was established which rose from 7 per cent (under 50 florins) to 22 per cent (over 400 florins).[102] The yield on stock in the public debt was subject to a withholding tax, or taxation at source. In 1494–5, the *catasto* was abolished and replaced by another progressive tax, the *decima*, which in contrast was a tax on landed property only and excluded stock in the *Monte comune* and investments in trade and industry. The *decima scalata* was discussed once more during the war of Pisa in 1497 and rejected; but it was proposed again and established in 1499–1500.[103] Guicciardini composed two tracts on the *decima scalata*,[104] which remained in force into the eighteenth century.

Earlier, Palmieri had objected to progressive taxation. He took the view that, when necessary, every citizen should devote his fortune to his native country (*patria*), but this contribution should be proportionate. Private fortunes should be burdened by tax according to an equal, that is a proportionate, rate,[105] for the tax should not disturb the natural distribution of goods and wealth. The distribution of wealth according to the natural order was unequal, since it depended on such variables as personal virtue, individuals' capacity for activity, and their resources and patterns of consumption. Those who profited from honest trade and whose wealth and status rose as a result should not be the objects of envy—nor be taxed at a higher rate. Instead, their wealth and status as

[98] Conti (1984), 197–205. [99] Ibid. 211–21. [100] Ibid. 228–33.

[101] Von Reumont (1883), 108, 110, 113. [102] Conti (1984), 281–7. [103] Ibid. 297–302.

[104] Guicciardini, ed. Palmarocchi (1932), 196–217; cf. Ricca-Salerno (1881), 36–8; Marks (1954), 54–8.

[105] Palmieri, ed. Battaglia (1944), 117–18: 'La regola che fa ciascuno pagare la rata secondo gli altri, in modo che a ogni tempo le sostanzie di ciascuno privato sieno a un modo consumate, è ottima.'

citizens should be preserved and, if possible, increased since it was a reflection of superior ability (*virtù*) and good management. Palmieri thus stated the case of the wealthy and upper class against a progressive tax.

In his two short tracts, Guicciardini explained the arguments for and against the *decima scalata*, which he vehemently rejected for social and political reasons. The main question was whether the progressive *decima* was just, that is, equal, uniform and for the common benefit, or unjust, dishonest and detrimental to it, since it altered the economic conditions of the citizens by making the rich poorer. Every well-ordered body politic (*governo bene ordinato*) had to conserve each person in his *grado*, his status in society. The rich and powerful were those who honoured the city, gave it support and supplied in various ways the needs of the poor. In opening up this controversy, Guicciardini arrived at a modern discussion on tax equity and equality.

In favour of the *decima scalata*,[106] it was argued that equity (*giustizia*) and equality (*equalitá*) did not consist in a uniform proportional tax rate, but should correspond to an individual's income and standard of living and therefore to his 'faculty', that is, his ability to pay or the resulting strain on his finances (*incommoditá*), later called 'sacrifice' by John Stuart Mill and others.[107] It was right that a tenth of the earnings paid by the rich came to a higher amount of tax than a tenth paid by the poor. Even so, the poor suffered much more than the rich, as was shown by considering the effects of the scales of the *decima scalata*, from 1 *decima* (at 50 ducats or less), a *decima* and a quarter (at 100 ducats), a *decima* and a half (at 150 ducats), to a quarter of the income (at 250 ducats) or a third of the income (at 300 ducats). Citizens' expenses were considered to fall into three categories: those which were necessary, those which ensured comfort (*commoditá*) and those which were absolutely superfluous.[108] These expenses had to be considered—by a kind of marginal utility valuation—in relation to individual incomes, which were scaled according to those who were poor (with incomes of 50 ducats or less), in a middle band of neither rich nor poor (incomes of between 100 and 150 ducats) and rich (between 200 and 300 ducats). The lower a citizen's earning capacity, the less chance he had to buy anything other than necessities: he certainly could not afford comfort or superfluous expenses; indeed, the *decima* might adversely affect his capacity to buy necessities. Clearly, the higher an individual's income, the greater his surplus for comfort or even for superfluous

[106] Guicciardini, ed. Palmarocchi (1932), 196–206.

[107] Cf. Mann (1928), 112–40; Ricca-Salerno (1881), 33, 38.

[108] Similar categories of needs—'le nécessaire physique, l'utile et le superflu'—were later used by Montesquieu when explaining the progressive tax in Athens. Montesquieu, ed. Truc (1961), 226 (13.8).

expenses; his chances of accumulating a reserve were much greater, and the worst effect of the tax might be to reduce or prevent absolutely expenditure on comfort and on superfluous items.[109] Since the poor had insufficient earnings even to meet expenditure on necessities, the *decima scalata*, though a less unequal tax than others in terms of the sacrifice it imposed, nevertheless strained the poor more than the rich.

The beneficial effects of progressive taxation for the commonweal lay in its potential for a redistribution of property: the great disparities in fortunes were at least moderated and large accumulations of wealth and capital reduced. Excessive wealth and superfluous expenses were above all an affront to ethical standards and morality: the enormous wealth of the rich was (in a regime other than that of progressive taxation) detrimental to the poor since it denied them their 'honest portion' (*porzione onesta*), anything but a small share of the total wealth. The superfluous expenditure of those who lived on the returns from their properties conflicted with the ethical code that maintained it was virtuous to 'live honestly' (*vivere onestamente*) by effort and labour, and provided a ruinous example to those who could not afford to follow suit. Instead of sumptuary legislation, the *decima scalata*, by its redistribution of property, might create a middle class earning between 100 and 150 ducats and thereby establish economic and social equality, so that all citizens were of one and the same class (*grado*).[110]

The counterarguments[111] denied the validity of economic and social equality and asserted only legal equality, equality before the law and before the municipal authorities: 'equality in liberty'. Society was based on social hierarchies (*gradi e distinzione*) and distinct conditions of 'mine' and 'thine', according to divine law. God had created various levels (*gradi*) of men and things, and economic inequalities resulted from different activities as well as good or bad fortune. There were various ways to make profits, and everyone was entitled honestly to accumulate wealth and property by law and the universal custom of the whole world. Whosoever sought to overcome this inequality by law or tax systems, in effect sought to overthrow the world order and the political and social order of the city, which consisted in peace, unity, concord, wealth and liberty; he also would discourage economic activity. Thus at the end of the Middle Ages, Guicciardini confronted the two main principles of tax equality, while being aware that public finance had to be based on a whole system of direct and of

[109] Guicciardini, ed. Palmarocchi (1932), 198.

[110] Although not discussing progressive taxation, Aegidius Romanus remarked that the best city, the best kingdom and the best people were to be found where there were large numbers in the middle class as regards status and property, since this contributed to equality, justice and mutual love, and the elimination of the poor man's envy of the rich: Aegidius Romanus (1473) (3.2.32–3) derived from Aristotle, *Politics* (4.11).

[111] Guicciardini, ed. Palmarocchi (1932), 207–17.

indirect taxes, especially excise duties (*gabelle*), which weighed more heavily on the poor than on the well-to-do. The idea of tax equality now accepted is the equalization of sacrifice by tax progression, which tends to lead to a redistribution of property, as demanded by the Florentine *popolo*. The other concept is the conservation of the graduated social order by tax equality in the sense of a proportional tax rate. This is the old conservative medieval idea of tax equity. However, it reappeared later in the industrial and democratic society of the nineteenth century in the liberal 'leave-them-as-you-find-them' rule of taxation, which demanded that taxation should leave every individual in his relative economic and social position.[112]

[112] Walker (1887), 491; Mann (1928), 123, 134–5.

CHAPTER 2

The Feudal Structure and the Beginnings of State Finance

W. M. Ormrod and János Barta

There is no precise moment when the fiscal state can be said to have come into existence, and any attempt to define such a moment would be profoundly unsatisfactory. The chronological limits of the present project presuppose that something changed, or was changing, in the emergent states of Europe at the end of the twelfth and the beginning of the thirteenth centuries. In fiscal terms, there is indeed much to be said for that thesis, as later parts of this chapter will show. However, before discussing the more specific precedents for a 'modern' system of state finance, it is as well to emphasize the earlier structures out of which that system evolved. Such a discussion has perforce to be selective and general, with a bias towards those monarchical states for which at least some direct documentary evidence survives. This naturally gives a somewhat artificial prominence to the two major kingdoms of north-western Europe, England and France, while underrating the importance of other embryonic fiscal systems in central Europe, Spain, Italy, Scandinavia and elsewhere. It is hoped, however, that any resulting imbalance will be redressed by the discussion of the Empire and the eastern kingdoms appended to this chapter and the more detailed case studies that follow.

The parameters of the larger study of which this chapter is a part also preclude any wider discussion of state finance in the ancient world; this chapter therefore starts from the assumption that Roman fiscal practices were virtually obliterated by the collapse of the empire and the emergence of the kingdoms of the barbarian west.[1] A more viable starting-point is provided by the Germanic kingdoms that evolved in the west from the seventh to the ninth centuries. Although their fiscal systems were in turn overthrown by the second wave of barbarian attacks launched by the Vikings, Magyars and Saracens, there are many

[1] Schumpeter (1954*b*), 8.

signs that the fiscal practices established during this period were remembered and taken up again in the emergent states of the central Middle Ages. A sense of continuity is an essential factor in the search for 'origins' and provides the strongest justification for this choice of starting-point.

The intensive study of early Germanic society—and above all of Frankish institutions—has provided a reasonably coherent picture of the way in which the rulers of early medieval Europe raised the revenues needed to support them, their households, and the limited though increasing range of activities that came to be seen as the function and duty of kings. This is not to say that uncertainties have been eliminated in modern scholarship. The vagaries of terminology, for instance, can provide a real challenge: in an early medieval context, the word *census* can denote a whole range of revenue types from rent and tribute to toll and tax.[2] Even more problematic is the general absence of statistical material from which to draw a clearer picture of the dimensions and the range of royal revenue. The evidence that does remain can still be used to create an impression of fiscal structures and developments, but it has constantly to be borne in mind that impressions, by their very nature, are highly subjective.

2.1 *The Early Germanic Kingdoms*

It is natural to begin this survey in the expansionist Frankish kingdom of the late eighth century.[3] The heart of Charlemagne's financial machine was the *fiscus*, a word significantly used to describe both the Treasury (otherwise the *camera*) and an individual estate held immediately from the king (alternatively known as a *villa*). The totality of the royal estates made up a very extensive patrimony which in all probability provided the bulk of the king's revenues. But Charlemagne's fiscal rights were not confined within the geographical limits of the domain. The stewards who ran the *fisci* were also responsible for collecting revenues which fell to the king as the source of public authority rather than merely as landholder. Prominent among these were the profits of jurisdiction; the income from emergent royal monopolies over mineral resources, particularly salt and silver; and the revenue derived from another important, though as yet incomplete, monopoly over the production of silver coin. Even more interesting, perhaps, was the income received by Charlemagne from tolls on the movement of goods both within and outside the European mainland: in particular the 10 per cent *ad valorem* duty levied on the passage of merchandise through the Channel port of Quentovic, which provided a very effective means of exploiting the lively trade

[2] Maddicott (1989), 6.

[3] The following account depends largely on Ganshof (1968), 34–45.

between England and the Continent. Finally, Charlemagne may have depended for a considerable amount of his wealth on the plunder taken during military campaigns and the tribute paid by conquered and subject peoples: indeed, the predatory nature of all the successful fiscal systems in early medieval Europe needs particularly to be emphasized.[4] It is therefore clear that the Carolingian fiscal model, though heavily dependent on the royal lands, also provided important precedents for more general systems of state exploitation.

In those areas of Europe that remained outside the formal boundaries of the Carolingian empire and were only indirectly influenced by its customs and institutions, fiscal structures followed a broadly similar pattern, indicating not only the pervasive influence of Carolingian systems but also the fairly narrow range of options open to rulers of the Germanic kingdoms.[5] It is possible that Visigothic Spain maintained a sense of continuity with the Roman past: the land tax devised in the late Empire, as well as capitation taxes and tolls on the movement of goods, may have survived for several centuries.[6] In the multiple kingdoms of Anglo-Saxon England between the seventh and the ninth centuries, the key to wealth—and therefore to political hegemony—apparently lay in the control of cross-Channel trade. The flood of silver into England during this period, and the eagerness of kings to exploit their minting rights, meant an abundance of coin and an emphasis on the payment of royal dues in money rather than in kind.[7]

However, the development of more sophisticated forms of payment did not necessarily denote a radical change in types or classification of revenue. There were indications from the seventh century in Spain and the eighth century in England that kings and their great men drew a distinction between estates that formed part of an inalienable royal patrimony and newly acquired lands which could be disposed of at will.[8] But this idea does not appear to have translated into a fiscal theory distinguishing between the ruler's 'public' and 'private' revenues. Prior to the ninth century, what public obligations that did exist were measured in kind or in service, not in money. The common demand for food rent is one obvious example, evolving as it did from the requirement to supply the king's household with foodstuffs and other provisions. More significant was the theoretically universal liability to army service and to the building and maintenance of bridges and public fortifications which emerged into a properly organized system of defence in England and West Francia during the eighth and ninth centuries

[4] Reuter (1984); Searle (1988), 231–2.

[5] For discussion of Carolingian influences on other Germanic states: Campbell (1975), 43–51.

[6] O'Callaghan (1975), 68–9. This evidence is called into question by Collins (1983), 109.

[7] Maddicott (1989).

[8] O'Callaghan (1975), 68; John (1966), 40–3.

and in Germany in the tenth.[9] The absence of any real notion of an 'extraordinary' element in the actual fiscal structures of these early kingdoms is highlighted by the admittedly very schematic descriptions of royal expenditure provided by the contemporary biographers of Charlemagne and of the West Saxon King Alfred.[10] Here, royal spending was conceived almost exclusively in terms of the maintenance of the royal household (including its military arm) and the provision of ecclesiastical and secular patronage. The idea that a state of emergency translated into higher expenditure and necessitated new forms of revenue appears to have existed in only a very shadowy form. 'Royal revenues were determined by custom rather than by current need.'[11]

2.2 *Early Experiments in Taxation*

The internal divisions and external attacks that brought about the collapse of the Carolingian empire in the generations following the death of Charlemagne did not necessarily produce a complete breakdown of the fiscal system operating around 800. Indeed, the threat posed by external enemies in some ways strengthened the fiscal authority of the new Frankish kingdoms. This is most strikingly demonstrated by the levying of general subsidies in order to pay off the new Viking and Magyar raiders. Just as the Germanic kingdoms had extracted tribute from dependent territories, so now they found themselves having to buy off the threat of invasion. In 845 Charles the Bald, king of West Francia, is known to have paid 7,000 pounds of silver in order to win a respite from Viking attacks. There are no indications of how this earliest tribute was raised, but its sheer dimensions preclude the possibility that it came out of the king's existing resources. Furthermore, it is known that the subsequent series of West Frankish tribute payments beginning in 866 was raised as a general levy on the king's subjects and assessed on an elaborate sliding scale.[12] A similar public obligation was imposed for a short time by Henry I of Saxony as part of his defence system against the Magyars in the 920s.[13]

Although such levies did not endure in the Frankish kingdoms, they became a very important part of the fiscal structure of the late Anglo-Saxon state. In this case, *geld* or *danegeld* (as such tribute was known in England) survived beyond the first Scandinavian raids during the time of King Alfred and was reintroduced after

[9] Brooks (1971); Leyser (1982), 11–42.

[10] Thorpe (1969), 87–90; Keynes and Lapidge (1983), 105–7. For the possibility that the latter source drew directly on the former: Campbell (1986), 116–17.

[11] O'Callaghan (1975), 68.

[12] McKitterick (1983), 190, 233.

[13] Leyser (1982), 14, 48.

991, this time on a regular and systematic basis, to counter a new wave of Viking attacks. When England was itself taken over by the Scandinavian monarchy of King Cnut in the early eleventh century, the tribute was continued and translated into *heregeld*, a levy to pay for the military force maintained in the king's household. And although it appears to have been dropped during the reign of Edward the Confessor, *geld* was re-established by the early Norman kings on a more or less permanent basis.[14]

These tribute taxes—and above all the English *geld*—are clearly of great significance in the early history of state finance. They demonstrate the ability of kings in the ninth to the eleventh centuries to impose general, public taxation on their subjects for the declared purpose of defending the realm from outside attack. The English example also signifies a trend that was to be seen so often in the later history of taxation: namely the tendency for an 'extraordinary' tax to outlive its original context and become a regular or 'ordinary' levy. Above all, however, the Frankish and English material provides striking evidence of the way in which royal control over the production of silver coin could be used directly to increase the fiscal resources of the emergent state.

The survival of statistical material in contemporary chronicles provides the fiscal historian with a valuable opportunity to assess the value and the economic impact of these early tribute taxes. Despite the mid-twentieth-century reaction against the uncritical use of such evidence, the recent integration of numismatic and historical studies has given these figures new credibility.[15] Thus, for example, Charles the Bald's tax of 866 can be related directly to the major reissue of the coinage carried out two years earlier.[16] Likewise, the Anglo-Saxon data become a good deal more believable when we realize that the series of levies instigated in 991 followed the establishment in the 970s of a large number of new provincial mints and the implementation of a regular cycle of demonetization and recoinage (the system known as *renovatio monetae*).[17] In Figures 3 and 4, the totals supplied by the *Anglo-Saxon Chronicle* for the *gelds* levied between 991 and 1018 are set against estimates for the total amount of silver coin produced in the mint issues coinciding with the levies. Figure 3 gives the data in money of account, and Figure 4 converts them to their equivalent in tonnes of fine silver.[18] These graphs make it clear that the extraordinary leap in *geld* demands from £10,000 in 991 to £48,000 in 1012 and to an apparently impossible £82,500 in 1018 was in fact closely linked to the relative weights of the different mint issues and to

[14] Loyn (1984), 120–1.

[15] E.g. Stafford (1989), 142–3.

[16] Nelson (1990), 15–16.

[17] Dolley and Metcalf (1961).

[18] ESFDB \orm\engb010 based on \engm001; \orm\engb012 based on \engd032; Gillingham (1989), 373–4; Lawson (1989), 402–4; Metcalf in Hill (1978), 180–1.

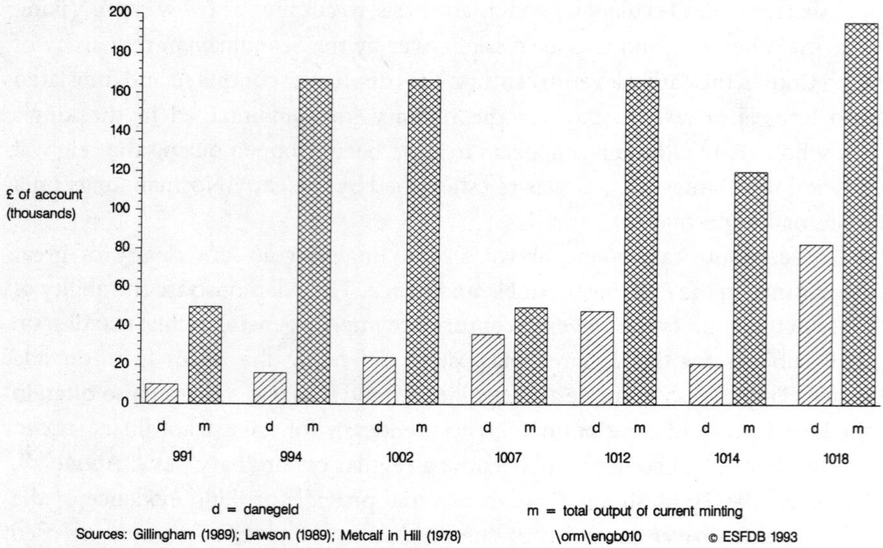

FIG. 3. *Danegeld* and the total money supply in England, 991–1018 (in £ of account)

the relative output from successive mintings. The only really problematic figure is that for 1007, when the tax (recorded as £36,000) would amount to 72 per cent of the total estimated currency: even in this case, however, it is quite possible that the mint output figure is too low and the tax figure itself may stand. Otherwise, the *gelds* represented anything between 10 per cent (in 994) and 42 per cent (in 1018) of the total currency. These figures do not seem unreasonable in the face of similar calculations for later periods: at the end of the thirteenth century, for example, the English crown was still capable of extracting anything up to a quarter of the silver coin in circulation.[19] It may not be strictly true to say that *danegeld* 'has no parallel in the Dark Ages', but the sheer longevity and apparent productivity of this tax do to some extent bear out the claim that it was 'the first system of national taxation to appear in Western Europe'.[20]

2.3 *Feudalism and State Finance*

The collapse of centralized authority and the increasing political fragmentation experienced in many parts of Europe during the later ninth, tenth and eleventh centuries inevitably had major fiscal repercussions: the relatively quick collapse of the system for collecting tribute in West Francia is in itself an indication of the

[19] Lawson (1989), 402–4; Prestwich (1982), 56.

[20] Stenton (1971), 645, 648, cited and criticized by Campbell (1975), 44.

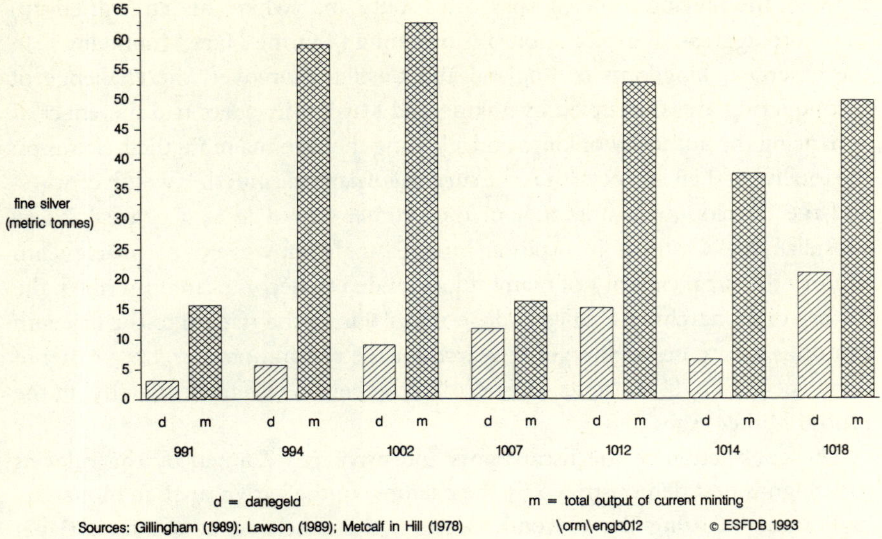

FIG. 4. *Danegeld* and the total money supply in England, 991–1018 (expressed in metric tonnes of fine silver)

contraction, if not complete collapse, of royal finances in that particularly obscure period that historians used to call the 'Dark Ages'. The biggest challenge to the fiscal authority of rulers and the principles of public obligation lay in the development of private jurisdiction by local noblemen, ecclesiastics and other powerful lords. The rise of seigneurial as against royal power is a principal feature of the 'feudal society' that emerged in the central Middle Ages: in the context of the present study, indeed, it is probably no exaggeration to argue that the feudalism of the tenth and eleventh centuries was the very opposite of the modern concept of the state.[21]

Under such circumstances, it is hardly surprising that most of the earlier fiscal manifestations of royal authority were lost, or at least went into abeyance, in many parts of Europe during this period. That is not to say that the process was uniform. The Ottonian regime in tenth-century Germany built up very considerable fiscal resources through traditional methods: the consolidation of the

[21] The terms 'feudal' and 'feudalism' are used here in the full knowledge that they are anachronistic and controversial: e.g. Brown (1974). In the present context, however, it matters little whether one adopts the all-embracing definition of feudalism as a medieval social force or the much more precise definition of feudalism as a kind of military and political organization, since the advocates of both interpretations are agreed that feudalism is characterized by 'fragmentation of authority' and 'the possession of public authority by private persons': Bloch (1962), 446; Strayer (1965), 11. For a further important contribution to the relationship between feudalism and the state: Bibó (1986).

domain, the levying of taxes, tolls and tribute and (when the latter dried up) the more aggressive exploitation of silver mining in the Harz Mountains.[22] In the emergent kingdoms of England and Castile, moreover, the challenge of reconquering areas occupied by Viking and Muslim invaders had the effect of enhancing the authority of kings and allowing them to maintain their claims on the totality of their subjects: thus the survival of *danegeld* into the twelfth century, and the development after 1091 of the *petitum* or *pedido* as a general tax to subsidize the Castilian *reconquista*.[23] Increasingly, however, in the eleventh century the fiscal capacity of many rulers tended to become circumscribed: the history of monarchy in France and Germany during the twelfth to the fifteenth centuries was to be very largely a search for the restoration of rights—many of them specifically fiscal rights—lost during the period of feudal 'anarchy' in the central Middle Ages.

The contraction of the fiscal rights and privileges claimed by the ruler as sovereign is best demonstrated by the example of the early Capetian monarchy in France.[24] During the eleventh century, the descendants of Hugh Capet continued to make certain general claims that were not in theory restricted to the royal estates: these included the right to free hospitality (*gîte*), the right to take foodstuffs and other provisions to support the royal household (*droit de prise*), the monopoly of mining and minting, and the levying of tolls on trade (*péage*). In practice, however, all these rights were often delegated to, or simply appropriated by, members of the feudal nobility. Consequently, the king found that his real fiscal authority was effectively limited to the royal domain. Here he could collect services in rent and kind, impose prerogative levies on dependent peasants, appropriate tithes, and exploit forests, hunting rights and other forms of special jurisdiction. In this sense, the king's revenues differed very little from those of other great lords. In only one major area, indeed, can the revenues of the early Capetians be distinguished from those of their greater subjects: namely, in the range of lands over which the king claimed immediate feudal and regalian rights and which reverted to him during the vacancies between the death of one holder and the admission of the next. Even here, however, the king's rights differed from those of the aristocracy only by degree: regalian rights in eleventh-century France were seigneurial, not sovereign. Indeed, it may be argued with some justification that it was not the monarchy but the main feudatories, such as the dukes of Normandy, who really kept alive the Carolingian principles of public authority and continued to translate them into fiscal resources during this

22 Leyser (1982), 84–92.

23 Green (1981); O'Callaghan (1975), 277–8; MacKay (1977), 102.

24 The following is based on Hallam (1980), 78–91.

period.[25] The French example therefore epitomizes the conceptual and practical limitations that feudalism imposed on the development of the state—and of the fiscal state in particular—during the central Middle Ages.

By the late eleventh and twelfth centuries, however, there were strong indications that certain other monarchies were able to transcend such limitations on their power and were beginning to harness the forces of feudalism in order to build up, or recreate, more centralized forms of authority.[26] One of the first and most striking cases is that of England. Recent scholarship has tended to play down the idea that the late Anglo-Saxon kingdom was a strong, unified state and has suggested that the forms of political and military organization emerging by the eleventh century had certain of the characteristics more usually associated with Continental feudalism.[27] This trend, however, was decisively and permanently reversed by the Norman Conquest of 1066. The new rulers of England were able to marry the administrative systems still operated by the English crown to the more advanced feudal structures found in contemporary Normandy and create a new kind of political organization which, under careful management, could considerably enhance the power of the monarchy. In itself, this union did not produce a leap forward in the fiscal capacity of the state. What really gave coherence and force to the new political and fiscal system emerging in England after 1066 was the revolution in landholding that accompanied the Norman Conquest. Not only was there a vast increase in the size of the royal domain, but the king was established as suzerain of the entire kingdom.[28] By carving out new lordships for his followers in England, William the Conqueror was able to drive a relatively hard bargain which allowed him and his successors to demand much more in the way of feudal services than was the case in the politically fragmented kingdom of France. This revealed itself in the large quotas of knights which tenants-in-chief were required to bring to the royal feudal host and in the very considerable sums which the king could make from the commutation of such service (the levy known in England as *scutage*) and from the levying of an aid (*auxilium*) from feudal tenants for the knighting of his eldest son, the marriage of his eldest daughter or the ransoming of his own person. Furthermore, there were large, if fluctuating, revenues to be had by controlling the estates of tenants-in-chief during vacancies or minorities, from the reliefs

[25] Musset (1960); Bates (1982), 152–4. This thesis has, however, been challenged by Searle (1988), 121–30.

[26] For the links between feudalism and state building in this period, see the recent discussion by Genet in Genet (1989), 261–81. The following discussion has benefited much from the comments of Mr Vincent Moss.

[27] Abels (1988); Fleming (1991).

[28] For the possibility that Domesday Book of 1086 was itself intended as a list of foedaries: Galbraith (1961, 1974); Holt (1987).

(entry fines) demanded from incoming tenants, and from selling royal rights over the remarriage of widows and the wardship of children of deceased tenants. As in France, this revenue may have derived from the king's seigneurial rather than his sovereign rights, but its sheer consistency and comprehensiveness made it quite unlike the privileges enjoyed by any other magnate in the kingdom of England.[29] England thus provides an important example of the new feudal monarchies that were to emerge in many other parts of Europe during the twelfth century.

This is not to say that England was the prototype from which all other feudal monarchies emerged. The English example was certainly influential: witness the adoption of Anglo-Norman institutions in Scotland and their rather less direct but arguably still considerable influence over the new kingdom created by another Norman dynasty, in Sicily and southern Italy, during the twelfth century.[30] The real interest of the English, as also of the Aragonese, example is that here, unusually, there also survived older principles of public obligation which remained unaffected by—and could even be enhanced by—the development of bonds of fealty.[31] The most striking example of this continuity is the collection of *danegeld* in England for almost a century after the Norman Conquest. It has to be stressed that the levy had now shrunk to much more modest proportions: having undergone no major revision or reassessment since the early eleventh century, the tax had inevitably become ossified.[32] But its survival until the 1160s ensured that the principle of public taxation was not dropped. Indeed, the principle was taken up again in a new series of taxes, known as *carucages*, collected between 1194 and 1220 and once again levied at a standard rate per unit of land.[33] A similar revival of public obligations in a specifically fiscal context can be seen in Catalonia, where a new levy, the *bovaticum*, was implemented after 1173, originally to subsidize a public peace policy and later to pay for external wars.[34] It was the particular combination of feudal profits and universal taxes which therefore offered the 'new' feudal monarchies of the twelfth century the potential for considerable fiscal development.

2.4 *Fiscal Institutions and Early Accounts*

The most obvious sign that the nascent states of the twelfth century appreciated the new importance attaching to their fiscal resources lies in the development of

[29] Waugh (1988).

[30] Frame (1990), 89–97; Matthew (1992), 207–53.

[31] Bisson (1989), 237–55.

[32] Green (1981). For the possibility that Domesday Book may have been intended to provide a new basis for taxation: Harvey (1975).

[33] Mitchell (1914), 8–9, 32–3, 122–3, 130, 134; Mitchell (1951), 127–31, 135, 136–7; Cazel (1961), 70.

[34] Bisson (1989), 215–36.

new systems of financial administration.[35] Until the end of the eleventh century, it would seem that all royal financial management was conducted within the household and co-ordinated by a chamber (*camera*) that itinerated with the court. The first significant signs of change came when the rulers of some of the larger territorial units began to set up separate treasuries, fixed points for the collection of royal revenues and the transfer of money to the chamber. In England, there was a Treasury at Winchester from at least the early eleventh century; in Sicily the Treasury became fixed at Palermo in the twelfth century; and in France the Templars are known to have been running the royal Treasury at Paris by 1146.[36] Much more important, however, was the decision not simply to collect but actually to account for income and, to a lesser extent, for expenditure: in other words, to make the officials of the state accountable for the money they collected and dispensed in its name.

Some of the earliest references to the auditing of accounts come, significantly enough, from smaller political units, such as Flanders in 1089 and Catalonia in the 1150s.[37] When the practice was adopted in the larger kingdoms, as in England from at least 1110 and in France from 1190, the intention was not to create a comprehensive statement of receipts and expenditure but to provide an effective means of supervising royal financial agents. It is therefore too easy to become infatuated by the earliest fiscal accounts: neither the English pipe rolls which exist in an imperfect series from 1130 nor the few precious early French accounts surviving after 1203 provide the medieval equivalent of a modern budget.[38] By the same token, the failure of the Norman kings of Sicily to develop a proper system of accounting certainly does not imply that they lacked a sophisticated and indeed highly productive system for realizing their revenue.[39] Despite these qualifications, however, it is still probably fair to say that the failure of the Capetians to establish anything like a permanent accounting body before the very end of the twelfth century does signify the relatively underdeveloped nature of French royal finances in comparison with the more advanced systems that had already emerged in such political units as England, Normandy or Flanders. Though it has nothing directly to say about the relative fiscal capacities of twelfth-century European states, the history of financial institutions can

[35] Lyon and Verhulst (1967) provide the best overview for north-western Europe; some of their conclusions are modified by more recent research cited in nn. 36–47 below. See also Bisson (1982).

[36] Hollister (1978); Takayama (1985); Baldwin (1986), 57.

[37] For Catalonia: Bisson (1984), i, 23–8.

[38] Nortier and Baldwin (1980), and Baldwin (1986), 240, argue that the Capetian account of 1221 can be more realistically labelled a 'budget' than can that of 1202–3.

[39] Systematic accounting was only instituted in the kingdom of Sicily in the 13th cent.: van Cleve (1972), 264–80. For the wealth of the Norman kings: Matthew (1992), 234–41.

therefore reveal a good deal about the relative sophistication of the mechanisms by which state revenues were realized.

Given the selective nature of the royal financial accounts, it is obviously extremely hazardous to use them for detailed comparisons across time or space. Most seriously, it is impossible to evaluate the proportion of royal revenue that circumvented the accounting agency and passed straight into the chamber. However, a brief review of the earliest statistical data surviving for England and France may at least furnish a rough guide to the fiscal regimes operating in these states during the twelfth and early thirteenth centuries.

The earliest English pipe roll has been meticulously studied by several generations of scholars and is the only such record so far to be thoroughly analysed by use of a computer program.[40] Figures 5 and 6 represent a summary of the data thus supplied, reorganized under seven different categories of revenue type.[41] The graphs reflect the advantages of an accounting system by showing that the pipe roll worked on two levels, not only auditing the revenues of the given financial year (in this case, Michaelmas 1129–Michaelmas 1130), but also continuing to make royal agents liable for debts carried over from previous years. They also demonstrate another phenomenon that was only revealed by the auditing process: namely the discrepancy that could exist between the amount charged and the amount actually collected. Not surprisingly, this was a particular problem with debts left over from previous years (Figure 6). When it came to the current year's charges, however, there were significant differences in the success rates for the various categories of receipts (Figure 5). The sums outstanding for income from justice were in fact sufficiently large to suggest that this form of revenue was more of a political than a fiscal weapon: it was the threat, rather than the collection, of the penalty that really mattered. The shortfall from *danegeld* may also be attributed to political factors, though it had clearly become an increasing administrative challenge to assess and collect this tax. The discrepancy between revenue demanded and revenue effected was however much smaller in the current year's demands from the domain. This can be explained by the fact that the profits of royal lands and associated rights were farmed by the king's local agents, the sheriffs. Once they had satisfied the Exchequer for the fixed sums owed, the sheriffs were free to take any excess profits for themselves and were therefore offered a powerful incentive to balance their accounts.[42] While revenue farming has often been seen as a symptom of the bureaucratic or political weakness of nascent states, this example serves to illustrate the positive

[40] Green (1982). We have used the revised data as set out in Green (1986), 220–5.

[41] ESFDB \orm\engb011 based on \engd033; \orm\engb013 based on \engd034. The category 'towns' is dropped from Figure 6 because there are no relevant entries in the 1129–30 pipe roll.

[42] Green (1986), 172–3.

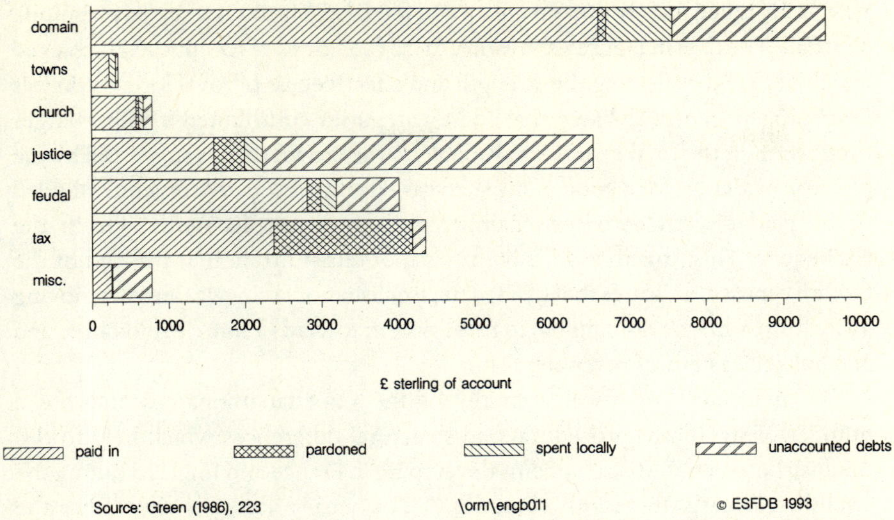

FIG. 5. Revenues of the English crown, 1129–1130 (in £ sterling of account)

advantages that could be had from a system that allowed the accounting agency to know in advance the approximate value of its gross and net yield from landed resources.

The main disadvantage of such a system, of course, was that it tended to fix revenues at a static level and made it difficult to adjust them to match fluctuations in expenditure. So far as can be ascertained, the twelfth-century English

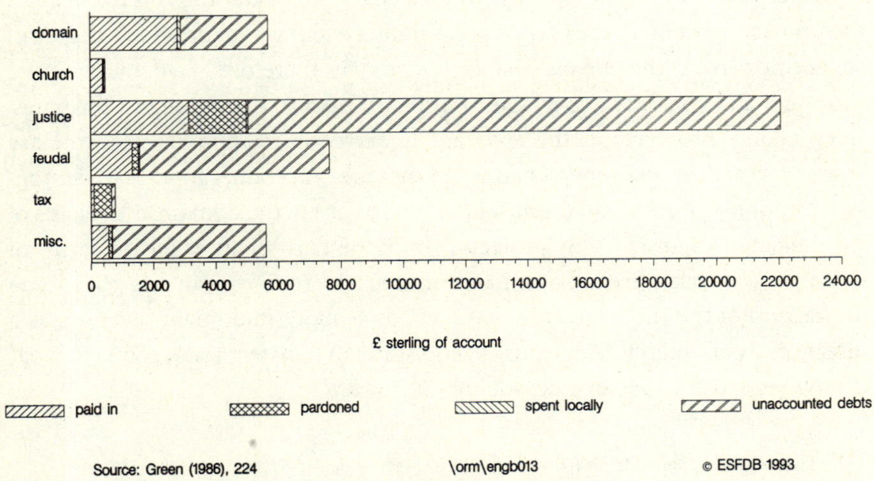

FIG. 6. Debts from earlier years accounted for in the English Exchequer in 1129–1130 (in £ sterling of account)

monarchy relied mostly on its regalian and feudal rights to make up any resulting shortfall. The data in Figure 5 show that these categories of revenue also achieved a high net yield, reflecting the strength and effectiveness of royal lordship in this kingdom. Indeed, it is likely that these categories contributed a rather larger proportion of the total resources available to the crown than is suggested by the pipe roll evidence, for a good many such casual and prerogative revenues tended to be paid directly into the chamber and were not accounted for in the Exchequer. This, together with the revival of direct taxation at the end of the twelfth century, indicates that by 1200 the English monarchy was already moving away from a strictly domain-based fiscal system towards a more exploitative and generalized system of revenue raising.

The first surviving fiscal accounts of the Capetian monarchy indicate a number of significant procedural and structural differences which help to distinguish between the fiscal systems developing in France and England during the twelfth and early thirteenth centuries.[43] The 1202–3 accounts show that the Capetians held audits not once a year (as was the English practice) but three times—a fact which, in itself, suggests something about the relative amounts of business dealt with in the two systems. Moreover, the French accounting system, possibly because it had been devised nearly a century later than the English, tended to draw a more coherent distinction between three types of receipt: ordinary revenues of a regular nature (chiefly the farms of the royal domain accounted for by the *prévôts*); ordinary revenues of an occasional nature (judicial, regalian and forest profits, accounted for by the *baillis*); and extraordinary revenues justified only by special circumstances. As in the English Exchequer, the primary function of the French accounting system was to provide a degree of supervision over the *prévôts and baillis*, and it therefore gave much more thorough and consistent coverage to ordinary than to extraordinary revenues. Even taking into account the apparent underrepresentation of extraordinary receipts, however, the general pattern of the 1202–3 accounts appears to demonstrate both the relative and the absolute importance of the domain as the basis of royal finance (Figure 7).[44] By projecting back the 1202–3 figures for the farms of those *prévôtés* that were in royal hands in 1179 and 1190, we can also gain some impression of the sheer increase that had come about in domain revenues as a direct result of Philip II (Augustus)'s acquisition of new territorial rights in what is now seen as the 'decisive decade' of the 1190s.[45]

[43] The following depends on Baldwin (1986), 144–75.

[44] ESFDB \orm\frmb003 based on \frmd005; Lot and Fawtier (1932); Nortier and Baldwin (1980); Baldwin (1986), 54, 154, 244.

[45] Baldwin (1981).

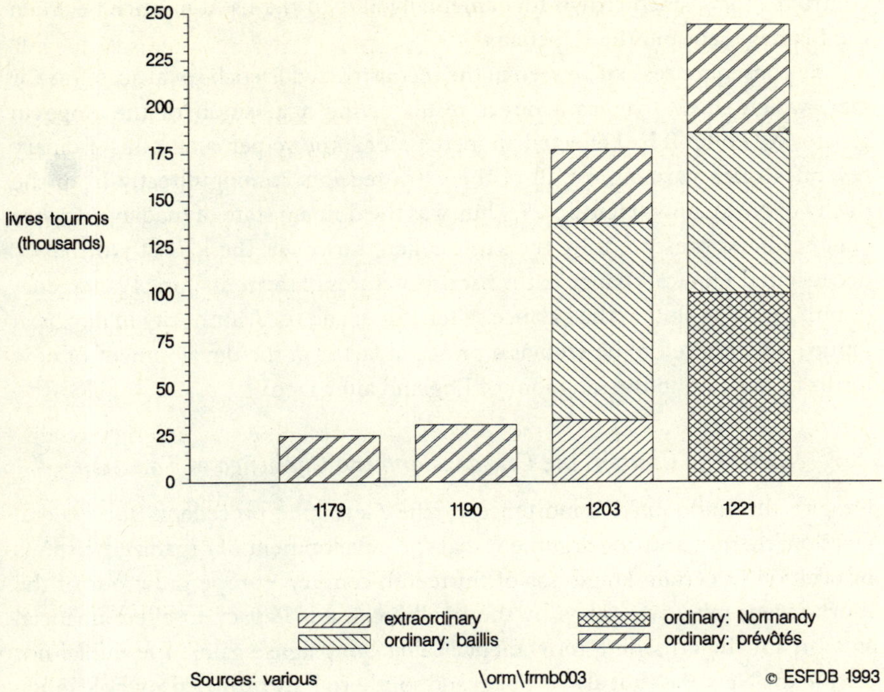

FIG. 7. Selected revenues of the French crown, 1179–1221 (in *livres tournois*)

The 1202–3 accounts take on still further historical importance when it is realized that they apply to the year immediately before Philip II's occupation of Normandy, a significant military enterprise which was to result in the collapse of most of the former Plantagenet possessions in northern and western France and a further very substantial growth in the Capetian domain. There has been much debate over the relative fiscal resources of Philip Augustus and King John in 1204, and whether or not the former's victory and the latter's defeat can actually be explained in terms of the contents of their respective treasuries.[46] For the present, it is sufficient to stress that the vital factor in the equation must be the revenues of the duchy of Normandy. In the 1190s these had provided Richard I of England with an annual income of somewhere between 56,000 *livres tournois* (in 1195) and 136,500 *livres tournois* (in 1198). If the latter was the more typical annual figure, then the revenues of Normandy were in fact almost as great as the total income recorded in the pipe rolls of the English Exchequer, which in 1202–3 stood at £34,600 (equivalent to 138,500 *livres tournois*). Whatever the precise situation in 1203, it is therefore clear that the transfer of the duchy of Normandy into the

[46] The following depends on Holt (1984), who summarizes earlier work on the subject.

control of the French crown fundamentally altered the fiscal balance between the Plantagenets and the Capetians.

The consequences can be seen in the reconstructed French royal accounts for 1221, which show that, as a direct result of the acquisition of the Angevin territories, Philip II had effected an increase of some 70 per cent in his ordinary revenues since 1203, almost all of the extra receipts coming directly from the duchy of Normandy (Figure 7).[47] Thus was the domain state of medieval France enhanced and preserved. By the same token, however, the loss of Normandy necessitated a radical change in the fiscal structures of the remaining Plantagenet dominions. The shift in the balance of territorial and fiscal authority in northern France must therefore be seen as a principal factor in the development of new forms of taxation in the kingdom of England after 1200.

2.5 *The Church, the Crusades and the Challenge of Taxation*

Despite the undoubted importance of the Germanic precedents for general taxation, there is a strong argument that the development of organized systems of taxation in certain kingdoms of thirteenth-century Europe grew out of the more recent initiatives taken by the twelfth-century Papacy to effect financial support for the crusading movement.[48] The campaigns against the infidel not only in the Near East but also in Spain and southern Italy provided a whole range of challenges and opportunities for the secular rulers of the west, not the least of which was the raising of money to support crusading armies. The ideological support which the Papacy gave to such initiatives provided precisely the kind of moral justification that kings needed to reinstate general direct taxation. One consequence was that, in the course of the twelfth century, the rulers of the west were able to add the crusade to the list of occasions on which they could legitimately demand aid from their feudal tenants. Much more importantly, they also began to argue that the crusades suspended normal political restraints and justified the levy of universal taxes on all their subjects, regardless of status.

The earliest known crusading taxes ordered in France and England in 1146 and 1166 were themselves initiated and effected by secular rulers. It was not until 1199 that the Papacy itself took on responsibility for such measures, and it is significant that this and subsequent Papal crusading taxes were restricted to the clergy. It was only under royal control that the normal functional and fiscal distinction between the laity and clergy could apparently be overridden and that

47 Baldwin (1986), 243–4. It should be stressed that the 1221 accounts only cover Normandy and Touraine; those for Anjou and Maine are lost. But *pace* Gillingham (1978), 303–4, it seems unlikely that the profits of these provinces were very large: Holt (1984), 104–5.

48 The following is based on Constable (1982); Cazel (1989). See also Green (1988), 606–7; Cazel (1955); Baldwin (1986), 52–4.

contribution to the crusade could be made a universal obligation on all adult Christians. It was on this basis, then, that in 1185 and 1188 Henry II of England and Philip Augustus of France ordered levies on movable wealth and revenues in preparation for the Third Crusade. The latter subsidy, collected at the rate of a tenth and popularly known as the 'Saladin tithe', was the most oppressive such levy to date. The financial success of these early crusading taxes should certainly not be exaggerated: although kings gave very specific instructions about the types of goods and revenues that were liable to assessment, it was not until the Saladin tithe that the state (and then only the English state) actually took some direct responsibility for collecting the levies and for proceeding against those who refused to contribute. It is also worth pointing out that the French royal injunctions carried no force in the main principalities, where the initiative was left to the dukes and counts. The true importance of these levies lies in their theoretical basis rather than their administration, for it is in such initiatives that we may discern some of the earliest practical applications of what would later turn into the key philosophical and political principle of urgent necessity, which justified the levy of extraordinary taxes for extraordinary purposes.[49]

It is therefore doubly interesting to note the contrasting responses of the French and English political communities to the Saladin tithe. In France there was a wave of protest, and Philip Augustus came under intense pressure not only to abandon the proposed levy but also to deny the principle that lay behind it. Movables, along with all other possessions and rights, would remain immune from royal taxation. In fact the successful defeat of the Saladin tithe can be seen as the first example of a consistent denial of obligation to non-feudal taxation pursued by the subjects of the king of France right up to the fourteenth century.[50] In England, by contrast, the levy proved a significant financial success: the chronicler who estimated that it raised £70,000 from the king's Christian subjects, and a further £60,000 in prerogative taxation of the Jews, was probably exaggerating, but his figures give a good impression of the scale of the exaction.[51] The most satisfactory explanation for the acquiescence of the political community in England must lie in the fact that the king's subjects were much more conditioned to extraordinary exactions by the state than were their counterparts in France. The survival of *danegeld* until the 1160s, coupled with the continued application of feudal taxes such as aid, scutage and tallage, had created the political environment in which a crusading tax, if not to be welcomed, could at least be countenanced.

The importance of the Saladin tithe as a turning-point in English state finance

[49] Kantorowicz (1957), 284–5.

[50] Henneman (1971), 1–39.

[51] Mitchell (1951), 119; Warren (1973), 378 and n. 1, thinks the estimate to be greatly exaggerated.

was demonstrated very forcefully in 1193 when the Emperor Henry VI imprisoned King Richard I and demanded the amazing sum of £100,000 for his release. This was the first in a series of ransom demands that punctuated later medieval European history, often provoking fundamental changes in the scope and scale of royal finance. Taking up the precedent of 1188, the regency government in England now imposed a further levy on movables and wealth, raising the rate from a tenth to a quarter. Although there are no surviving accounts, it is assumed that this was in fact the most profitable of a whole range of extraordinary taxes taken to realize the king's ransom.[52] The success of the levy is probably best illustrated by its subsequent adoption by King John, who collected a seventh on personal property in 1203 and a thirteenth on movables and revenues in 1207 to support his wars against Philip Augustus of France.[53] The evolution of the subsidy on personal property in England therefore represents the earliest clear example of another important theme that would emerge in the course of the thirteenth century: namely, the adaptation of crusading taxes to meet the exclusively secular needs of the state.

2.6 *The Exercise of Authority and the Purchase of Immunity*

Although the crusades were probably of greatest importance in shaping attitudes to public finance during the central Middle Ages, there were several other distinctly secular phenomena that also encouraged the development of general systems of taxation in twelfth- and thirteenth-century Europe. The revival of older traditions of public obligation within a specifically fiscal context provided the opportunity in at least some states for the emergence of a new political relationship between rulers and subjects, in which taxation became a medium through which to buy off the more intrusive and controversial aspects of royal government. The negotiation, rather than the simple imposition, of taxation obviously tells us much about both the political and the fiscal development of the state in this period and warrants brief discussion here.

One of the most significant trends to emerge in the twelfth century was the practice whereby rulers commuted their rights to take profits from minting into general 'money taxes' levied on all their subjects.[54] The system of *renovatio monetae*, although theoretically directed towards the preservation of a sound currency, was in practice open to a great deal of abuse, as it presented the ruler

[52] Mitchell (1951), 124–6.

[53] Mitchell (1914), 62–3, 87, 90–9; Mitchell (1951), 133. It is important to acknowledge that the seventh probably raised only a small amount, while the thirteenth, though it yielded the very considerable sum of £57,422, also aroused a great deal of opposition: Holt (1984), 102–3; Warren (1978), 149–50.

[54] For what follows: Bisson (1979).

with the opportunity to issue a larger number of lighter or debased coins and thus increase the profits he derived from the mints. The disruption that this caused within the economy was sufficient to persuade certain political communities that a general tax was preferable to a constantly uncertain currency. The result was the development of a levy often known by the same name as the royal prerogative it replaced—*monetagium*. Examples of such taxes can be found in twelfth-century Normandy, France and northern Spain. There is little or no evidence of formal consultation in these early taxes, but there was a clear sense in which the ruler was morally and politically bound to maintain the current standard of the coinage for a certain period after the payment of the tax. In 1205, when the first properly constituted *monedatge* was imposed in Aragon, the charge had clearly come to develop a conditional nature, being linked to a formal charter guaranteeing, among other things, the abandonment of currency mutations.

A similar trend can be discerned in England, though here the bargaining centred not on the currency but on the operation of royal justice. The precocious development of the English judicial system had provided the monarchy with a powerful political instrument which, in the hands of a ruler such as King John, could prove a fundamental threat to the perceived rights of his subjects. Not surprisingly, then, many of the clauses of the great charter of privilege, Magna Carta, extracted from John by his baronial opponents in 1215, were concerned with the jurisdiction and procedures of the royal courts. In 1225 John's son, Henry III, took a very important step when he confirmed Magna Carta as part of the political negotiation connected with the imposition of a tax of a fifteenth on movable property. This opened the way for a good deal of bargaining with local, and occasionally national, political communities throughout the thirteenth century.[55] In fact, the rulers of England, like their counterparts in Aragon, often proved less than scrupulous in upholding their side of such deals; the political structures of the thirteenth century were not sufficiently developed to provide effective guarantees that rulers would honour their promises. But a precedent had been set and was to prove of considerable significance in the more formal political structures that came into existence for the negotiation of taxation during the later thirteenth and fourteenth centuries.

2.7 *Europe in 1200: The Emerging Trends*

The cases highlighted in this chapter provide some conspicuous and quantifiable examples of two distinctive fiscal models that may be said to have emerged by the early thirteenth century: firstly (as in France) a system built around the successful extension and exploitation of a ruler's domainal and seigneurial rights;

[55] Maddicott (1984).

and secondly (as in England), a system that drew on a broader geographical and social base by emphasizing the ruler's rights to exact dues from the generality of his subjects. Although it may be convenient to use conventional terminology and label these models the 'domain state' and the emerging 'tax state', it must be remembered that these terms are anachronistic and tend to distort the very substantial similarities between the two models at this stage in their development. Even so, the distinction is sufficiently marked by the start of the thirteenth century to demand some further explanation.

The fundamental reason for the development of more advanced fiscal systems in this as in any other age was of course financial need: an increase in revenues usually reflects an equal—indeed, often a proportionately greater—increase in expenditure.[56] The factors that decided whether that development would follow the domain or the tax model were highly complex, reflecting not only the political but also the economic structure of the given state. But the preceding analysis strongly suggests that the fundamental reason for the divergence in fiscal structures that appeared towards 1200 lay in the nature of the tenurial, political and economic relationship between the ruler and his principal subjects. In areas of Europe where feudalism had grown up naturally, as in France, the aristocracy retained a high degree of autonomy even when faced with the more ambitious centralizing tendencies of the twelfth-century Capetian monarchy. In those kingdoms where feudalism was introduced primarily as a form of political organization, as in England, the monarchy was able to transcend the private rights of lords, retaining older general levies and devising new ones.

Again, it is important not to exaggerate the contrasts. By the early thirteenth century, it is clear that Philip Augustus had more than caught up with earlier Plantagenet practice and was making very large amounts of money from the exercise of lordship over his greater feudatories.[57] The main difference actually existed at a lower level, and emerged only when the crown attempted to draw directly on the resources of those people living within the jurisdictional and geographical orbit of a member of the high aristocracy. Where feudalism was primarily a political device, as in England, or where the tenurial and social features of feudalism never really took root, as in Castile or southern Italy, it was possible to identify a direct relationship between the king and all his subjects which transcended other forms of lordship and could, under special circumstances, be translated into a justification for universal taxation.[58] In those areas where the aristocracy enjoyed much greater jurisdictional rights, as in France, or absolute ownership, as in parts of eastern Europe, the king's direct fiscal

[56] E.g. the comments of Miller (1963), 305–6.
[57] Baldwin (1986), 277–9.
[58] MacKay (1977), 97; Kantorowicz (1957), 284–5.

authority was inevitably much more circumscribed. It is significant that even when systems of direct taxation were developed in states of the latter type, they were often not administered directly by the crown but operated as repartition taxes, with each province or lordship being given responsibility for organizing the collection of a prearranged or negotiated quota. Naturally, then, the medieval states in which the ruler's taxative authority was most restricted were those in which power had become almost completely devolved into the hands of private lords enjoying substantial control over their estates and extensive, quasi-regalian rights of jurisdiction and exploitation.

To emphasize the latter point and to indicate the restraints, as well as the opportunities, that medieval social and political structures imposed on the development of state finance, we may conclude this chapter with a brief review of the fiscal systems that emerged in some of the medieval states where aristocratic authority is often supposed to have been greatest: namely, the Empire and the kingdoms of east–central Europe. Here, the discussion will be carried beyond 1200 in order to demonstrate the enduring nature of certain medieval structures and the strong sense of continuity that characterized these state systems down at least to the fifteenth century.

2.8 *The Holy Roman Empire*

Any study of the fiscal structures of the Empire in the Middle Ages has of necessity to recognize the two levels at which finance operated: the Imperial administration itself, and the systems associated with the principalities and city-states of which the Empire was composed. The tendency towards dynastic continuity in the office of Emperor between the tenth and the thirteenth centuries had facilitated the creation and maintenance of a substantial Imperial domain (*Reichsgut*) including both a landed estate and extensive prerogatives over tolls, mining, minting and the Jews. The most important element in the Imperial revenues during the central Middle Ages, however, came from Italy: contemporary estimates of the wealth of Frederick I indicate that it was the north Italian towns that really made him the effective rival of the Angevins; and it was undoubtedly the profits derived from Henry VI's conquest of the kingdom of Sicily in 1196 that made Frederick II the richest ruler in thirteenth-century Europe. Above all, Frederick II's ruthless exploitation of the *collecta*, the universal tax levied on his lay and clerical subjects in Sicily, in order to finance his military and political ambitions in other parts of Europe, serves as a striking reminder of the conspicuous absence of any similar tradition of public taxation in Germany during this period.[59]

[59] Fuhrmann (1986), 162–8; van Cleve (1972), 264–80; Isenmann in Bonney (1995).

This deficiency became painfully apparent after the loss of Imperial control in Italy, the ending of dynastic continuity, and the increasing reliance of Frederick II's successors on the political goodwill of the German princes. By *c.*1440, the *Reichsgut* had all but vanished, and the late medieval Emperors had therefore to rely increasingly on their own ancestral lands (*Hausgut*) to pay for their administrations.[60] In the fifteenth century, some far-sighted individuals began to argue that the financial burden of government should be borne by general levies on all the Emperor's subjects. But the failure of all such schemes before the 'common penny' of 1495 illustrates in dramatic form the effective veto that the princes now enjoyed over imperial taxation. The only really significant developments of the fifteenth century lay in the evolution of extraordinary taxes to support quasi-crusades against the Hussite heretics and the Ottoman Turks. This was the first time that the doctrine of necessity was recognized as a legitimate political principle in Germany, and for a short time it seemed set to transform Imperial finances in the same way that it had earlier revolutionized the fiscal systems of the western monarchies. But despite some notable experiments with centrally administered direct taxes in the late 1420s, the only politically acceptable levy proved to be a negotiated repartition tax, the *Matrikel*, first devised in 1422. Meanwhile, the Imperial administration continued to lack both the political authority and the administrative apparatus which might have allowed for a more thorough and permanent reorganization of its ordinary revenue and expenditure. The Empire therefore provides an important example of the fiscal paralysis that could result from the fragmentation of political authority during the central Middle Ages.

It might be supposed that the devolution of power into the hands of the princes and free cities encouraged these subordinate states to move ahead of the Emperor and develop their own more sophisticated systems of public finance in the course of the later Middle Ages. The cities can certainly be said to have had fairly developed fiscal structures, including systems of direct and indirect taxation and, at least by the fourteenth century, forms of public credit. But it is significant that the principalities lagged behind, showing no greater sense of development than the Imperial administration itself. The reason may lie partly in the lack of a clear sense of territorial and jurisdictional sovereignty; but it also probably had something to do with the limited and very domestic nature of 'state' expenditure at this level. The princes may have developed fiscal rights beyond the domain and associated prerogatives by treating with representative assemblies for extraordinary taxes but, until the fifteenth century, the range of circumstances in which such taxes could be authorized appears to have been very

[60] For what follows: Isenmann (1980); Rowan (1980); Du Boulay (1983), 19–63.

limited: it is particularly interesting that taxation at this level was linked not to emergencies but, like earlier feudal aids, to ceremonial occasions such as the inauguration or marriage of the ruler and the birth of his first son. The absence of anything other than an itinerant *camera* for the administration of princely finances also serves to highlight the very restricted and private nature of financial administration in the territorial states of late medieval Germany.

2.9 *The East European Experience: Bohemia, Poland and Hungary*

Despite the apparently static nature of public finance in the German dynastic states, there were signs of significant, if not always permanent, fiscal development in certain parts of east–central Europe during the Middle Ages. In particular, the kingdoms of Bohemia, Poland and Hungary provide useful comparisons and contrasts with the changes that were effected in the west between the twelfth and the fifteenth centuries. All three states originally conformed very closely to the domain structure of fiscal organization. The kingdom of Bohemia, which actually fell within the Empire and itself provided three Emperors in the fourteenth and early fifteenth centuries, derived its political stability from a fiscal system based on a large landed estate, the profits of justice, commercial tolls, exploitation of the Jews and mining and minting. Here, in fact, there is comparatively little sign of a further extension of taxation during the later Middle Ages: rather than searching for new resources within their kingdom, the Luxemburg rulers preferred to adopt a policy of dynastic expansionism which brought Charles IV (1346–78) large domains in Silesia and Brandenburg and gave his son Sigismund the kingdom of Hungary.[61]

The rulers of Poland also relied heavily on territorial aggrandizement to maintain their financial and political strength: the union with Lithuania in 1385 marked the high point of this policy. It is interesting to notice, however, that the Piast dynasty which ruled Poland until 1370 not only drew on the profits of an extensive landed estate but also imposed certain public obligations, some of which were commuted into cash payments. The requirement on all the king's subjects to assist in the building of bridges and royal fortresses continued until the fourteenth century, while garrison duty within those fortresses was converted into a money payment known as *stroza*. Similarly, the obligation to provide hospitality for the prince seems early to have been evaluated and paid as a money tax (*stan*). Finally, a general levy in kind, the *narzaz*, appears to have been devised as early as the reign of Boleslav the Brave (992–1025) and was still being collected—in livestock and corn—during the thirteenth century. There are

[61] Palacký (1907), 170–1; Thomson (1949); Du Boulay (1983), 34–52.

obvious and important affinities here with the fiscal obligations developed in the later Germanic kingdoms and with the contemporaneous taxes devised in the kingdom of Denmark. In Poland, however, these early precedents seem to have died out as a result of the gradual alienation of royal rights to a virtually autonomous aristocracy and the granting of immunities from public obligations to more and more of these powerful political figures. The process reached its climax with the accession of Louis of Anjou to the throne in 1370 and the issuing of a formal contract—the privilege of Cassovia—which granted almost complete fiscal exemption to the nobility and the church. The kingdom of Poland therefore showed very much the same tendency as the later medieval Empire towards the devolution of fiscal initiative to the subordinate level.[62]

The case of Hungary is rather different and of considerable interest, not least because of the rare survival of certain semi-official summaries and estimates of royal revenue for various kings between the twelfth and the fifteenth centuries.[63] Used in a proper critical framework, the data supplied by these statements can help to illustrate changes both in the composition and in the overall size of royal income in medieval Hungary (Figure 8).[64] In conjunction with the Danish evidence, it can also provide a useful corrective to the assumptions of west European historians that the 'peripheral' states of eastern and northern Europe showed little fiscal sophistication and remained necessarily trapped in the confines of a feudal or domainal structure.

The estimates for the annual revenue of Béla III (1172–96) help to indicate the complexity and diversity that could exist within a domain state in the Middle Ages. Béla derived an impressive income from the royal estates themselves: the estimated figure of 45,000 marks (8.4 tonnes of pure silver) might seem impossibly large were it not for the evidence that St Stephen had earlier appropriated as much as two-thirds of all the land in Hungary. Nevertheless, profit from land represented little more than a quarter of the stated total. Tribute paid by immigrants and tolls (a complex category including some crown revenue from towns) actually brought in the same amount as the landed domain. It is probable that Béla collected most of these revenues (except tolls) in kind. This obviously raises certain questions about the reliability of the cash estimates in the register, particularly when compared to the revenues of Béla's contemporary and brother-in-law, Philip II of France (the French figures for 1203 set out in Figure 7

[62] Hüppe (1894), 108, 432–3; Lönnroth (1963), 365–8; Kieniewicz (1968), 47–8, 56–9, 84–5, 128–9.

[63] For the sources: Hóman (1916), 424–6 (though note that Hóman's intepretation of the statistics is now challenged); Hóman (1921), 280–7; Engel and Kristó (1987), 139–44, drawing on Thallóczy (1879), 84–6; Fügedi (1990).

[64] ESFDB \orm\hunboo1 based on \hundoo1; Hóman (1916), 424–32 (revised); Hóman (1921), 25, 280–7; Engel and Kristó (1987), 139–44; Fügedi (1990).

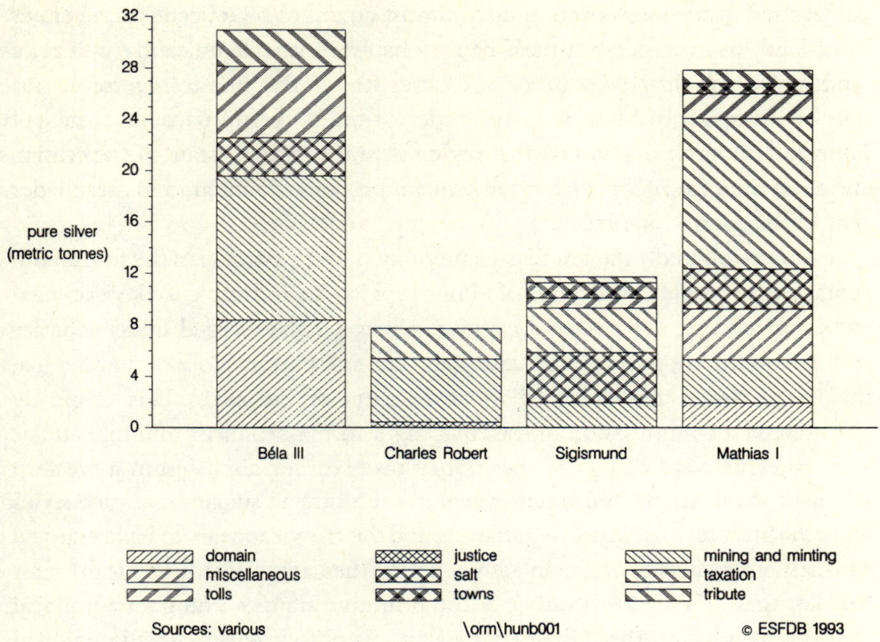

FIG. 8. Royal revenues in medieval Hungary at various periods (expressed in metric tonnes of pure silver)

represent a total of approximately 17.3 tonnes of fine silver).[65] But the estimates of revenue in kind may take on rather more credibility when they are set alongside the huge profits that Béla is reported to have made from the exploitation of mineral resources, including the royal monopoly over salt and, above all, the revenue from the mining and minting of gold and silver. That eastern Europe provided a substantial amount of the bullion circulating throughout the west in the central Middle Ages is of course well known; that the Hungarian crown was able to exploit this resource to such an extraordinary degree is surely a point that deserves much fuller recognition.[66]

The absence of data for the profits of the landed domain under Charles Robert (1308–42) and Sigismund (1387–1437) makes impossible a full statistical comparison of Hungarian state finance across time. Nevertheless, there is a strong argument that neither of these kings enjoyed the same traditional revenues as their twelfth-century predecessor. Not only was the general economic

[65] Béla's second wife was Margaret, sister of Philip Augustus and widow of Henry, eldest son of Henry II of England. Hóman (1916), 426, speculated that the statistical record of Béla's revenues arose directly as a result of Capetian and Angevin interest in the Hungarian king's finances.

[66] Hóman (1922). Spufford (1989) has little to say about Hungary before the 13th cent.

contraction of the fourteenth century almost bound to be reflected in revenues from land, but the domain itself had probably shrunk significantly in size, a tendency which the confiscations of Charles Robert did little to reverse. It was only the election of Mathias I, the leader of the powerful baronial family of Hunyadi, to the throne in 1457 that replenished the landed estate of the crown, and even then the income from the domain proper accounted for a mere 7 per cent of this king's total receipts.

It was undoubtedly the gradual disintegration of the domain in the fourteenth century that provided the kings of Hungary with the incentive to develop new forms of revenue. The most significant change that emerged under Charles Robert was the adoption of a general 'gate' tax, assessed and collected rather like the hearth taxes that operated in other parts of Europe.[67] This originally represented a commutation of the royal right to the profits of minting, and as such takes its place alongside the money taxes earlier discussed in a western European context. In Hungary, however, there is little to suggest that such levies were the product of political negotiation, and the crown appears to have enjoyed substantial freedom of action in administering the gate tax throughout the later Middle Ages. This reflects not only the primitive state of Hungarian political institutions but also the indifference of an aristocracy which already enjoyed complete immunity from such exactions. The same freedom of action also allowed Mathias I to carry through a radical reform of the tax system in 1462, introducing a hearth tax and creating mechanisms to ensure much greater central control over revenue.[68] The effect was to make general taxes by far the most important single element in the royal revenues (Figure 8).

This remarkable shift in the balance of Hungarian state finance between the twelfth and the fifteenth centuries does not in itself indicate a fiscal revolution of the type that can be demonstrated for the larger kingdoms of the west in the later Middle Ages. Indeed, when measured as tonnes of silver, Mathias I's total income in the 1470s was still slightly lower than that of Béla III in the late twelfth century (Figure 8). Even after further development in the 1480s, Mathias's revenues still only just equalled the twelfth-century level, reaching some 31.3 tonnes of pure silver.[69] Consequently, it is hardly surprising that estimates compiled at the very end of the fifteenth and beginning of the sixteenth centuries showed Hungarian state finance to be running at a deficit.[70] The Hungarian example therefore has a twofold significance. On the one hand, it provides an important example of the way in which royal prerogatives could be turned into productive systems of taxation by aspiring medieval state builders. On the other hand, it indicates that

[67] Hóman (1921), 280–1; Engel and Kristó (1987), 139.
[68] Fügedi (1990), 45–6.
[69] Ibid. 54.
[70] Thallóczy (1879), 109, 113–14.

the adoption of such tax systems—a development to which modern historians give such prominence—was not so much a grand policy of advancing state control as an *ad hoc* (and sometimes rather inadequate) response to the shortfall resulting from a decline in domain revenues. The domain and/or the feudal models remained the ideal for most European rulers until the very end of the Middle Ages, and it was financial necessity, rather than political ideology, that led to the adoption of new, more distinctively 'modern', fiscal structures.

2.10 *Conclusion*

The discussion of the Empire and the eastern kingdoms has taken us far beyond the year 1200 and provided valuable examples of the survival of early fiscal structures down to the very end of the Middle Ages. It has also indicated that continuity can be accounted for in two contrasting ways: a system endured either because it was productive and fulfilled the needs of the ruler or, ironically, because it became ossified and was preserved by subordinate political figures eager to prevent the extension of state control. As such, these examples reinforce the thesis that the development of state finance up to, and indeed well beyond, the thirteenth century was largely dictated by the attitudes of the aristocracy. Whether they held their land by conditional tenure in the formal feudal sense, as in France, or by allodial tenure, as in Poland, the nobility clearly acted as a conditioning, and usually limiting, factor in the development of state finance. Above all, this point is reflected in the considerable proportion of total economic output that was controlled by the aristocracy and was therefore unavailable to the state. If feudal society is simply defined in terms of seigneurial exploitation of dependent peasants, then all parts of Europe discussed in this chapter can indeed be said to have conformed to the 'feudal structure' of its title. The real sea change in state building, and the real beginnings of 'modern' state finance can only be discerned at that moment in time when private, feudal rights became subordinate to the public authority of the state and a fuller range of economic activity was rendered liable to state taxation. Among other things, the following chapters will help to identify such a moment—or rather, series of moments—in the history of the emergent states of later medieval and early modern Europe.

CHAPTER 3

City-State and Market Economy

Jean-Claude Hocquet

The city-state was the political creation of a commercial metropolis which, through war, diplomacy or purchase, succeeded in enlarging the territorial framework of the original urban commune and in dominating its hinterland of small and middling towns and villages. The geographical extent of the city-state depended on the size of the metropolis as well as its demographic and economic power; it was clearly also related to the importance of the surrounding towns and territorial principalities. Thus, in the fifteenth century, the commune of Venice, which had emerged from the buffer duchy between the Byzantine empire in the east and the Carolingian empire in the west, conquered an extensive territorial state in Italy at the expense of other urban lordships and continued to expand until it came up against other powerful cities such as Milan and Florence.

The city-state developed above all around primary maritime ports, at the intersection of rivers and leading maritime commercial routes (or, less frequently, at the base of Alpine passes); in regions of high- or middle-density urbanization; and always beyond the reach of powerful monarchical states. In other words, this type of state emerged on the periphery of the weakest of Europe's great political entities, the Holy Roman Empire. It is significant that the cities of Flanders and Holland failed to turn themselves into city-states, despite attempts during the fifteenth century (for example, at Ghent); the Burgundian inheritance of the Habsburgs ensured the failure of such attempts. Cities which were incorporated into ducal or monarchical states often fought hard but in vain to preserve their autonomy, and the Dutch revolt after 1572 was in certain respects a continuation of this centuries-old conflict between leading cities and the 'state'.[1] Subject cities might also seek to set themselves up as a counter-

[1] The Editor and the author acknowledge the assistance of Dr J. A. Bergin (Manchester) in preparing this translation. Blockmans in Bulst and Genet (1988), 171–3.

authority to the state. The Habsburgs, who promoted Antwerp and its financial market against the restless Flemish towns, ended up by placing excessive fiscal pressure on it, thus precipitating its bankruptcy in 1557. The leading towns of Flanders, Brabant and Holland signed the Union of Utrecht of 1579 which contributed towards the deposition of Philip II two years later. The Spanish reconquest helped to push a good part of the population, capital and the decision-making centres of the new 'world economy' towards Amsterdam, and thus beyond the reach of Habsburg control.

3.1 *The Characteristics of the City-State*

The Hanseatic League was born on the northern fringes of the Empire as a union of associations whose object was to protect the trade routes and activities of merchants, and which came together in 1282 at a time of serious Imperial weakness. The move towards a league of cities took place in 1356 during a general assembly of the Hanseatic cities held for the purpose of deciding to send ambassadors to foreign princes, a significant prerogative of states. But should the Hansa in general, or each of its constituent great cities, be regarded as the 'state'? Cologne, Lübeck, Danzig, Bremen and Hamburg could each aspire to the stature of a city-state, more so even than the Hansa as a whole, which always depended on the goodwill of its various members, and which only succeeded in harmonizing convergent interests by consistently ignoring those member-cities whose interests conflicted with, or which refused to discharge, the military or fiscal burdens required by the assembly of the Hansa. Of course, these conceptions of autonomy and independence are somewhat vague in relation to our contemporary concepts of national sovereignty and international recognition. The leading Hanseatic cities—the 'free' Imperial cities which had for so long conducted as sovereign powers their own economic policies—negotiated international agreements on a prince-to-prince basis and engaged in wars against the rulers of northern Europe. However, during the sixteenth and seventeenth centuries they found themselves increasingly subordinated to the Emperor who imposed various taxes on them; this was often because of the weakness of their public finances and their liquidity problems.[2] According to Eberhard Isenmann, Nuremberg's public receipts had amounted to 51,000 Rhenish florins in 1493, Hamburg's to 16,000 florins between 1491 and 1496, and Venice's to 1,285,700 florins in 1492—this last perhaps twice those of the French monarchy at that time (that is, reflecting fiscal concessions in the aftermath of Louis XI's death).[3]

[2] Pelus in Bulst and Genet (1988), 243–62.

[3] Isenmann in Bonney (1995).

Fifteenth-century Italian city-states clearly enjoyed a higher level of resources than even important German cities such as Nuremberg and Lübeck.

City-states preserved the republican institutions from their earlier history, in particular government through a council or councils. These institutions were maintained and even enhanced when cities became territorial principalities, regional states whose sovereignty was personified either in a non-hereditary elective monarchy (the doges of Venice and Genoa, for example) or in a dynastic principality (Florence under the Medici). Yet the territorial aspect of the state, an indispensable constituent of the city-state, was the creation of the capital city and not of the prince. City-states had to manage the complex relations between a form of political power which was urban in origin and in essence, and subject territories which encompassed peasant populations, feudal powers and a network of middling cities which had lost their political status but whose economic prosperity contributed to the state's power. The concept of a city-state does not have a single meaning, nor is it especially clear. It might indeed be preferable to replace it with the term 'mercantile republic', where 'republic' retains its medieval meaning of *respublica*. In other words, the 'state' (*respublica*), which was dominated by the city, directed most of its activities during the later Middle Ages towards trade, which in turn involved active participation in international commerce and commercial exploitation of the manufactures produced by a numerous and socially differentiated urban class of artisans. It is useful to note that the city-state was able to adapt to the profound economic change of the sixteenth and seventeenth centuries, and to direct its efforts at fiscal extraction towards faster developing sectors of the economy, the international world of finance and investment in landed property in the countryside.

How many attempts to create strong city-states, notably in fourteenth-century Flanders, failed or aborted in the face of counter-attack from princes? Likewise, if a powerful city such as Florence found itself subjected to permanent control by a princely family which had emerged from the ruling group of merchant bankers, and even if the old mercantile republic gave way to monarchical institutions, can it be said to have lost its status as a city-state? In reality, whatever the form taken by the government of the state, its basic organizing principle, that of the economic and fiscal domination of a hinterland by the capital city and its ruling oligarchy, remained unchanged. But did powerful merchant cities such as Barcelona or Marseille ever rise to the rank of a mercantile republic? Their rulers, respectively the counts of Barcelona and of Provence, held on to power and closely supervised the fiscal system. In the case of towns situated in the most powerful of western Europe's monarchies, France, England and Castile, the crown never tolerated the existence of autonomous urban power: cities such as

London and Paris never aimed to become city-states, but they could legitimately claim the status of capital cities of monarchical states. The situation becomes more confused in countries where central power appears extremely feeble in the face of powerful cities which had become rich from the profits of international maritime trade, and which were capable of conducting an active, even a warlike, foreign policy independently of any central monarchical or Imperial control. In short, were Amsterdam, Lübeck and Hamburg city-states? It would be tempting to add Cologne to the list, were it not for the fact that this powerful Rhineland city was governed by an archbishop who was also a prince of the Empire. And what of Danzig or Augsburg? Further south, the Swiss Cantons which bore the same names as the cities of Basle, Berne and Zurich (all of which resemble closely the classic communal pattern of the city dominating its *contado* in full autonomy) clearly better fitted the model of a city-state. Yet the struggle between the city, considered as a single entity, and the feudal structures of the *contado* from which it was liberating itself, belongs much more to the communal period of urban history, while the succeeding period was characterized by two contrasting patterns of development. One pattern was that of the city surrendering control to a lordship such as that of the Scala at Verona, the Carrare at Padua, the Este at Ferrara, the Gonzaga at Mantua or the Visconti at Milan, all of whom confiscated for their own purposes urban liberties and institutions so that their power came to be regarded as 'tyrannical'. The other pattern was that of the city which conquered a territory and then governed it without any fundamental alteration of its political structures. Instead, it simply established a political relationship between the *dominante* and the *dominio*, between master and subjects. The former urban ruling groups and vanquished lordships thus became part of the *dominio*, and formed a closely knit network of towns and rural areas. In the strict sense, the city-state corresponds to a territorial state in which sovereignty was exercised by the founding city and its governing class which had merely extended their power beyond the walls of the capital city. Its historical model was the prestigious example of Athens in the fifth century BC, but arguably only Venice, Genoa and Ragusa succeeded in emulating that model between the thirteenth and the eighteenth centuries.[4] If this definition is rejected, we risk ultimately analysing the finances of the city rather than those of the state.[5]

[4] It has been difficult to include Ragusa in the present study, given the lack of an accessible study of its finances for the late Middle Ages. The analysis in di Vittorio (1983) commences with the 17th cent.

[5] Körner (1980) appeared not to regard the Swiss cities as city-states, despite the existence of the Confederation. Körner in Bonney (1995) nevertheless refers to sovereign urban republics (*républiques urbaines* in French, *Stadtrepubliken* in German).

3.2 *The Fiscal System of the Italian City-States*

The mercantile republics were governed by a social class whose power and prosperity were founded in trade and the related activities of banking and shipbuilding, as well as export-led industries such as textiles, glass-making and metallurgy. Even today, these republics (whether Venice or Florence, Zurich or Amsterdam, or numerous German cities) retain a certain family likeness, thanks to the number and beauty of their patrician residences, both town palaces and rural villas. The dispersion of these buildings contrasted sharply with the monumental character of monarchical capitals, where majestic royal palaces situated close to opulent aristocratic residences proclaimed the pre-eminence of the sovereign.

In these city-states, the fiscal apparatus had long been in existence, as a result of taxes levied on the exchange of goods and wealth, and it operated chiefly by requiring indirect taxes, customs duties, tolls or *dazi* wherever commercial transactions were conducted. This fiscal practice confirmed the mercantile nature of the cities. The alternative would have been to levy direct taxes on property or on income. Apart from the fact that this might have taxed directly the rich merchant class, the raising of such taxes implied a problematic assessment of property-ownership and the singling out of those liable to pay taxes.[6] There was a twofold advantage in indirect taxes, even if they affected merchandise which constituted a part of merchants' working capital. Firstly, they were paid by consumers, that is to say by the population at large, both rich and poor; secondly, where they were carefully graduated, they proved to be an instrument in the service of the local merchant class against external competition.

Taxes on items of consumption were legion, and in order to ensure that they provided a worthwhile profit for the Treasury, they were levied especially on items of basic necessity—essential foodstuffs, grain brought for milling (and thus on bread), meat, salt, oil, and wine or beer in northern cities.[7] To increase the efficiency and yield of these taxes, certain forms of merchandise—salt in particular—were handled as monopolies. Since states did not themselves have the machinery needed to sell and distribute the products in question, due to a lack of personnel, they turned over control to tax-farmers who granted the state credit through the purchase of the taxes in question at public auction.[8]

Customs taxes operated more subtly, and in a way that was closely connected to the social structure of power which drew a distinction between 'citizens' and 'outsiders', that is, all those who were not born in the capital city. In Venice, two

[6] Felloni (1988), 767. [7] Körner (1980), 88–93. [8] Hocquet (1985), 307–14.

rates of taxation were paid on merchandise, 2.5 and 20 per cent, depending on whether goods moved by road or by sea, and the two rates were added together if merchandise which arrived by sea was re-exported by river or overland. But only foreigners were subject to this rate of taxation: in both cases the tax payable by Venetian merchants was reduced to 1.25 per cent—half of the lower of the two rates. This was a considerable advantage, crowning a virtual legal monopoly that existed purely for the benefit of Venetians, to whom foreigners were obliged to sell goods destined for the Levant. Customs privileges thus gave considerable substance to the *de jure* monopoly of maritime commerce enjoyed exclusively by Venetian merchants.[9]

During the fifteenth century, direct taxes began to be introduced and then to proliferate in the Italian city-states. At Genoa, they included the *avaria ordinaria* established in 1403, the tax on oil payable from 1582 onwards by the communities of Genoa's *dominio* producing oil for the city's needs, the milling tax established in 1610, the standing tax on galleys introduced at the end of the seventeenth century, and the taxes on hoteliers and tavern-keepers. Despite their names (such as 'oil tax' and 'milling tax'), all were direct taxes levied according to the same discriminatory principle: they only applied to the *dominio diretto*, that is the old subject communities, since the others which had been conquered more recently had taken the precaution of including in their acts of submission to Genoa a clause allowing them total exemption from, or the option of a buyout from, these taxes. The tax was simply returned by the local administrators in proportion to the value of real property in their areas as assessed in the *catasto*, since property belonging to Genoese in the areas was exempt from the *avaria* and the oil tax, a privilege which was respected until the fall of the republic in 1797. If a community could not pay the sums required of it by the central treasury, the balance was divided out, with two-thirds paid by the proceeds from property taxes on local inhabitants, and one-third by residents personally.[10] Church property was taxed when held on perpetual lease. The property of charitable institutions was exempt, which illustrates the fact that city-states were happy to delegate tasks such as assistance to the old, the sick, orphans and young female sinners (rather coyly called 'penitent girls'). In the city of Genoa itself, direct taxation, the *avaria mobili*, was levied on movable income, but the city exempted from it two corporations which were the pillars of its economic power, the silk-weavers' and the sailors' guilds. Direct taxes were slow to produce returns, and the commune often turned over unpaid taxes as payment to its creditors or to officials taking up office for the first time.[11] In 1490, the merchant patriciate,

[9] Hocquet in Bonney (1995). [10] Felloni (1988), 768–73. [11] Heers (1961).

which mainly paid this direct tax but preferred indirect taxes, secured the abolition of the *avaria*. For the levy of extraordinary taxes or the apportioning of forced loans, taxable wealth was calculated as the entire patrimony which made up the *azienda* of the taxpayer—the value of movables and immovables, credit notes, cash, merchandise, dowries, and all property situated in the *dominio* and even abroad. It is tempting to regard this as an equitable solution, but the assessment was left to commissioners who were susceptible to considerations of kinship and friendship, or simply open to corruption. They thus undervalued quite considerably the actual levels of wealth by allowing rates of evasion which have been calculated at half or two-thirds of the real taxable wealth.[12]

Venice, too, was reluctant to raise direct taxes. In fact, it had recourse to forced loans, known as *impositiones*, payable by those who did not subscribe to its ordinary loans (*prestiti*), and after 1382 it did this by holding back a proportion of the interest they were paid on bonds which had been purchased. Between 1382 and 1386, and again in 1452, it also raised impositions called *gravezze* on the houses and property of Venetians not subject to the *prestiti*. In fact, property-owners were subject to a differentiated tax, and direct taxes were a substitute for the forced loan which was raised from those who did not contribute to the *prestiti*. Following the suggestions of Wittmann,[13] Martin Körner reminds us that the classic distinction between 'ordinary' and 'extraordinary' finances is an outdated and largely unusable concept: extraordinary receipts were constantly being integrated and assimilated into ordinary receipts. Every new tax began life as an extraordinary one (*pro una vice tantum*), but this provisional characteristic was quickly subsumed into ordinary finance. Consequently, 'extraordinary' and 'ordinary' need to be replaced with a functional scheme of classification between 'profit and loss accounts' (*Verbrauchsrechnung* or *compte de consommation*) and 'investment accounts' (*Investitionsrechnung* or *compte de capital*). This formulation seeks to explain the relationship between expenditure, consumption and investment, as well as revenues—that is, taxes without capital repayment, or forms of borrowing accompanied by the establishment of capital funds and annuities.[14] It goes without saying that taxpayers preferred to lend their money against the promise of an interest payment and the return of their capital than to surrender it for no return at all.

Borrowing usually preceded direct taxation. It appeared in Venice by 1187 in order to finance the costs involved in recovering Zara. During the thirteenth century, debt servicing led to a wholesale reorganization of the city's finances: officials were entrusted with the receipt of loans and the allocation of the

[12] Felloni (1988), 780. [13] Wittmann (1975). [14] Körner (1981), 389–92.

revenues of the salt office, which were turned over to the procurators of St Mark for the payment of interest and debt redemption. Each new loan was accompanied by a rise in the *dazi*, which especially affected the price of salt. But the frequency of war obliged the state to halt capital repayments in 1363, a move which endangered the financial system because it increased the interest-payment burden and triggered a devaluation of the bonds. In 1375, the state decided to redeem the bonds at their market value. A new war with Genoa between 1377 and 1381 led to the levy of *prestiti* valued at 107 per cent of the capital of the *estimo*, or 30 per cent of the actual wealth of those taxed in this way. Such massive recourse to borrowing had serious economic and social consequences. The poorest taxpayers frequently sold their old bonds in order to buy new ones. The wealthy, who could afford to buy them at a substantial discount of up to 80 per cent, drew interest at 4 per cent of the bonds' nominal value (20 per cent in real terms). Such interest rates diverted them from investing in maritime business which had fallen off considerably because of war at sea, and the purchase of *prestiti* provided them with a temporary source of alternative investment. Moreover, as the *estimo* was not revised regularly and as it took greater account of immovable than movable wealth (which was easier to conceal), some people were taxed on wealth which they already had been forced to sell. The system encouraged the rapid circulation of wealth, which was to the advantage of the most energetic patrician families engaged in commercial transactions. Yet the permanence of war during the first half of the fifteenth century in the end threatened the entire edifice of public credit, since the city-state, which had previously given up repaying capital, now also suspended interest payments. By the time of the Peace of Lodi (1454), interest payments on a debt capitalized at 8.27 million ducats were twenty years in arrears.

It was in these circumstances that Venice had to take the decision to raise a direct tax in 1463 with the levy of a *decima*, a general tax that required the preparation of a *catastico* which listed all the property held by Venetians, the clergy included. Despite raising 40 *decimas* during the interminable war with the Turks from 1463 to 1479, the financial position was such as to require renewed recourse to borrowing, by raising repayable *decimas*, for which the *Monte nuovo* was established (whose capital stood at 3 million ducats in 1509). Previously, individual Venetians had been asked to bring their precious metals to the Mint which, in return for their deposit, opened a credit account for them. In 1509, the *Monte nuovissimo*, a third debt, was established and was managed directly by the salt office, which collected the repayable *decimas* on the understanding that it would repay them with revenues from the sale of salt. The system was highly dangerous for two reasons. Firstly, the state floated new *decimas* in order to clear the credit accounts registered at the Mint, and the salt office did not take in receipts; secondly, the salt office could no longer sell salt on the *Terraferma* which was occupied by foreign armies.[15]

As a result, Venice was tempted to abandon responsibility for the public debt by ceasing interest payments to private citizens so that it could continue to give preferential treatment to shipbuilding through the grant of bonuses, gifts and loans (even to merchant ships). In contrast, Genoa's policy after 1430 systematically supported the bond-holders and defended the structure of public finance. In Genoa, too, direct taxation had for a long time taken the form of compulsory interest-bearing loans. Even when the commune wished to borrow, it pledged its revenues, and during the twelfth century it entrusted its creditors with raising them. In short, the state's creditors purchased its taxes, which it awarded to the highest bidder by means of an auction (*appalto*). This purchase (*compera*) turned the creditors into 'tax-purchasers' (*comperisti*). In the thirteenth century, the state reclaimed the collection of taxes, the yield of which it then distributed to its creditors. In 1235, it established the *maone*, first at Ceuta, then in Chio and Cyprus. This was a further step in the privatization of public revenue, a path which Venice always refused to follow. When the Genoese Treasury was empty and the city-state was considering military action which might produce a profit, it did not merely turn over its revenues to its creditors; instead it entrusted the execution of the military enterprise to them and their ships, and repaid their costs out of the ensuing plunder. In 1259, the captain of the people, Guglielmo Boccanegra, consolidated all the loans and annuities in the same *compere*, without setting any term for repayment, though a fixed interest was paid annually. The state debt thereafter took the name of *compera salis*, as the interest on this permanent debt was payable from the salt receipts.

The *comperisti* banded together to form associations capable of buying loan bonds jointly. Each one of them held shares or *loca* which, being negotiable, possessed a market value and experienced considerable fluctuations resulting from the government's ability to pay interest on time. These shares were inscribed in the registers (*cartolari*) which the officials of the *compera* kept up to date. The government undertook to keep the value of the shares high by recognizing them as legal tender for the payment of taxes or fines to the public treasury. In 1323, the state's creditors secured permanent representation and elected *protectores comperarum* to look after their interests. These 'protectors' became Genoa's most important financial institution, and Sieveking correctly argued that the main aim of public finance was to protect the state's creditors. The costs of this protection fell principally on consumers of salt: in 1380, the state purchased the *mina* (the standard measure of salt) at 4*s*. 6*d*. and sold it for 60*s*. 1*d*.,

[15] Hocquet in Bonney (1995).

that is, at a profit of 56*s*. 1*d*. (or 1,246 per cent) which, even after allowing for the running costs of the salt monopoly, was a colossal profit.

In 1405, Marshal Boucicaut occupied Genoa for the king of France, after the nobility had requested his intervention. He installed four officials responsible for the reduction of the debt, who converted all the old debts ranging from 10 to 8 per cent to a new debt bearing 7 per cent interest. The new *compera* was called the *compera nuova regiminis Sancti Georgii* from the name of the city's patron saint. It was both a new debt consolidation and a simplification of the administration of the existing debt. The creditors, who suffered from this conversion, were exempted from the payment of subsequent taxes. The *Casa di San Giorgio* became the most powerful institution in Genoa which, torn by factional struggles during the fifteenth century, was frequently under the political control of representatives of foreign powers, whether Milan or France. The 'protectors of St George', advised by a council of fifty-two members chosen from among the main shareholders, were left in charge of the entire conduct of business and finance: their responsibilities included the administration of the public debt, the management of the revenues mortgaged to the *compere*, and control of the sinking fund. Successive governments of every ilk had to swear to respect the privileges of St George, which formed a strong and tightly knit body which Machiavelli regarded as 'la conservatione della patria e della republica'. The *Casa di San Giorgio* was not a trading company, but the state bank (Chapters 13.2 and 14.1).

In 1408, indeed, the 'protectors of St George' obtained the right to act as a bank, with the profits being used to amortize the debt. Limited to the role of a clearing bank for private customers, St George assumed the role played during the fourteenth century by private banks in the administration of public revenues. In both Genoa and Venice, the state had recourse to the services of numerous private bankers—frequently with more than twenty opening their counters in each of the markets—to pay interest or to collect the sums owed by tax-farmers, who often used the bankers as their surety when tax farms were being adjudicated. St George combined the two functions, collecting the credit payments of the tax-farmers and making interest payments (*luoghi*) to the state's creditors. It also provided current-account credit for the state with the risk of seriously weakening the state bank which, while being punctilious about paying the interest due to bond-holders, was frequently obliged to borrow in the money market. In 1444, after deciding to pay the creditors only 'sums strictly necessary for their daily needs', St George had to abandon banking. The 'protectors' then sought to strengthen the *Casa di San Giorgio* by bringing into it the *compere* which had remained independent, especially the *compera salis capituli*, with the result that its capital rose to 7.9 million *lire* in 1454. The result of this policy was that the state earmarked all its indirect revenues for the payment of its creditors, and could only count on direct taxes to balance its accounts. In this way, a transfer of wealth was effected from the *dominio* to the *dominante*, from the poorer classes who paid taxes to the richer classes who held shares in the public debt. Finally, in 1586 Genoa opened the Golden Book (*cartulario d'oro*), which registered the deposits of gold crowns that enabled individuals to obtain credit which they could then transfer to third parties. The St George bank thus added a deposit-banking dimension to its activities, increasing and speeding up the financial development which in the following century would turn Genoa into one of the great European financial markets.[16]

Florence also showed considerable concern for the state's creditors, and in the mid-fifteenth century even went as far as registering certain subscriptions to state loans at three times their nominal value in the *Monte* rolls, which had the effect of raising real interest returns to 15 per cent. Matteo Villani, the well-known chronicler who was active as an official of the *Monte*, warned that at such rates—which would nowadays be called 'first rates'—there was a risk of commercial investments completely drying up. In 1378, the Ciompi demanded the abolition of the *Monte*, the suspension of interest payments and the replacement of loans by direct taxes. In 1427, during the war with Milan, Florence abandoned forced loans levied on the basis of the *estimo* in favour of direct taxes on revenue inscribed on the *catasto*.[17]

3.3 *The Fiscal System of the German City-States*

Most of the leading German cities freed themselves in the second half of the thirteenth century from all forms of subordination to territorial princes, though without gaining the total independence enjoyed by the Italian republics. At the end of the Middle Ages, neither Imperial nor princely taxes did much to disrupt urban budgets which had to cope with the unpredictable demands of government, the threat of private war, and the hostility of local nobles and princes. Cities therefore kept their own armies and pursued distinctive foreign policies, which were also designed to protect them against commercial competition, reprisals and customs wars. The Imperial cities enjoyed very considerable autonomy. Many episcopal or princely cities were self-governing, having either bought from their lord or acquired by revolt regalian and domainal rights which fell to the town—rights which involved administration, coinage, customs and taxation. This movement towards autonomy was facilitated by princes' urgent financial needs. The great episcopal cities of Cologne, Augsburg and Mainz became free cities. In the struggle for autonomy, possession of financial

[16] Sieveking (1906). [17] Day (1983), 337–60.

resources was a decisive factor in victory, while impoverishment facilitated the return of the lords. Thus, the collapse of Mainz's finances prepared the way for the triumphant return of the archbishop. Cities where the patriciate refused to pay direct taxes willingly turned to borrowing, even on a permanent basis. They experienced extremely heavy indebtedness, which in turn led to a heavy tax burden on the townspeople with, as a consequence, a succession of urban revolts led by the guilds, as at Nuremberg in 1348, Cologne in 1364, 1370 and 1396, at Frankfurt in 1355 and 1364–5, at Augsburg in 1370 and at Lübeck in 1383.

The popularity of municipal borrowing was closely related to the sale of annuities.[18] Life annuities were sought after by people as a form of insurance providing a sort of pension for their old age. Lenders did not turn over their money to their own town; there was a market for public loans and, in order to reduce risk, people made loans to several cities. In 1408, the *Bürgermeister* of Rothenburg obtained loans from 120 different localities, something which clearly distinguishes borrowing from direct taxation, though in this case what we are witnessing is a *mutuum* or a voluntary loan, and not a *prestitum* (which was a forced loan). Short-term borrowing was gradually replaced by the sale of annuities. Life annuities were also favoured by governments, as they presented possibilities of profit should bond-holders die. This type of non-redeemable bond entailed a high rate of interest of 10 per cent. Certain cities preferred to replace them with perpetual bonds which meant lower interest rates of between 3 and 5 per cent and which, being redeemable, could easily become a form of short-term credit.

Cologne secured its independence in 1288: by 1275 it had contracted a short-term debt of 2,074 marks held by nine citizens. Before the revolt of 1396, it was governed by an oligarchy of rich patricians which financed the government's activities through indirect taxation and, in case of necessity, by borrowing. From 1351 to 1370, the sale of life annuities at 10 per cent interest was the main feature, reaching a total of 102,560 marks in 1370. At that point, it was necessary to turn to less expensive forms of borrowing, through short-term credit measures imposed on the wealthy. From 1370 to 1392, borrowing amounted to 768,948 marks, of which 76 per cent was provided in Cologne itself. Foreign subscribers lived mainly in Lübeck, Mainz and Augsburg. These foreign investors were offered perpetual, but redeemable, annuities at a rate of 5 to 5.5 per cent. Cologne's finances were healthy, but the burden of indirect taxes fell heavily on the mass of the population. The overthrow of the patrician regime profoundly changed its credit policies. Life annuities were encouraged. People of modest means, artisans and even domestic servants, appeared for the first time in 1418 among the lenders,

[18] Boone (1991–2).

purchasing annuities for small sums of money ranging from 1 to 5 *gulden*. The city's Treasury become a kind of savings and pensions bank. Cologne sought ways of keeping its credit high. In 1416 it introduced redeemable life annuities, speculating on the depreciation of silver currency in which interest was calculated and paid out. The rate for perpetual annuities was lowered from 5 to 4 and then to 3 per cent after 1450. Cologne's debt fell from 35,000 marks in 1432 to less than 29,000 marks in 1462. The war with Charles the Bold for the defence of Neuss in 1474–5 shattered its finances, and Cologne had to borrow more in two years than in the preceding four decades: 1.3 million marks in 1474–6 against 0.8 million between 1432 and 1473. Higher rates of interest had to be offered, and the annual cost of debt servicing rose to 121,000 marks. The rich merchants who held power wanted to increase indirect taxes in order to finance the growing cost of the debt, but in 1481 the artisans protested and demanded the suspension of annuity payments. This grievance divided the movement, with the moderate groups who had invested their modest savings in the city's finances siding with the rich. The revolt was defeated in 1482. The debt continued to rise, and in 1512 it stood at 3.24 million marks. Revolt broke out again, leading to a change in the form of government of the city and the execution of a number of magistrates; a tax on property and a reduction in the rate of interest payable on annuities was forced through; it was furthermore declared that in future municipal borrowing would require the consent of the whole community.

Nuremberg's accounts show how the great German cities' need for credit expanded regularly. From 1377 to 1385, direct taxation provided most revenue; the floating debt, which consisted of life annuities yielding 10 per cent interest, remained modest; and few new loans were contracted. The confiscation of Jewish property in 1385 enabled the city to abandon direct taxation and to sell redeemable perpetual annuities which in a few years doubled the initial floating debt. In the second quarter of the fifteenth century, Nuremberg acquired full control over its urban territory by purchasing the castle with its rights and revenue from Frederick of Hohenzollern. Between 1426 and 1429, the annual cost of the floating debt more than doubled, and it would have grown even more rapidly had Nuremberg not reduced to 5 or even 4 per cent the interest payable on the perpetual annuities (life annuities yielded 10 per cent). From 1431 to 1440, Nuremberg spent on average 37.5 per cent of its annual expenditure on annuity payments, and the city could only satisfy its creditors by floating new loans each year. Borrowing provided 33.9 per cent of revenue, direct taxes 20.2 per cent, and the excise tax on drink 21.2 per cent. From 1427 to 1442 the floating debt quadrupled, and then doubled again by 1458. Yet during the first half of the sixteenth century, the city amassed sufficient reserves—over a million pounds, or twice the annual revenue—to do without loans altogether in normal times.

Mainz provides an example of political decline caused by excessive debt and bad management of public finances. Financial difficulties had led to the guilds being involved in the government of the city from 1332 onwards, and serious conflict was thus avoided until 1411. But in 1411 the payment of debt annuities accounted for 48 per cent of total expenditure. The new city government established by popular uprising forbade the sale of any more annuities without the consent of the trade guilds. Despite this, the city's financial situation continued to worsen and, in 1436–7, 75 per cent of its expenditure went to creditors, whose interest payments continued to increase. Mainz had increasing difficulty in finding subscribers to its loans, and was forced to offer high interest rates. During the 1430s, it offered 5 per cent for the perpetual annuities instead of the previous 3 or 4 per cent. In 1444, its debt totalled 373,184 *gulden*, and in 1448, having failed to obtain a loan of 21,000 *gulden* from the archbishop and the clergy, the city declared itself bankrupt. Since 60 per cent of the debt was invested outside Mainz, the city was placed under Imperial ban, excommunicated by the Pope and placed under an interdict by the archbishop. Finally, deserted by its richest bourgeois and impoverished, Mainz was captured and set on fire by its archbishop; hundreds of its citizens were exiled; it lost its independence, and it was incorporated into the princely electorate.[19]

The Hanseatic cities of Hamburg and Bremen pursued a much wiser course of action. In Hamburg, debt servicing costs absorbed no more than 16 per cent of total expenditure during the period 1461 to 1496, despite a tripling of the debt in real terms between 1350 and 1500. Up to 1370, loans had been sought exclusively from the bourgeoisie and the ecclesiastical institutions of the city. However, after 1426 and the expensive war with Denmark, there was an influx of capital from Lübeck, which may be explained in terms of a shift of interest on the part of Lübeck's merchants away from active trade and into the safer waters of investment in municipal loans. From 1426 to 1453, they lent 47,000 marks to Hamburg, investing them mainly in perpetual annuities. By then they controlled over half of Hamburg's debt.

In Basle, the finances were based on a well-organized tax system. The city borrowed regularly each year, and its wars were financed through borrowing, but the municipal budget was not allowed to remain in deficit for long periods of time. To keep debt within acceptable bounds, Basle resorted to extraordinary taxation in the form of direct taxes on persons and on property. Periods of peace and prosperity were used to reduce the debt. All forms of municipal credit were used, especially the sale of annuities. As a supplement to taxation, rather than a substitute for it, borrowing may on occasion be viewed as a sign of strength, not

[19] Fryde and Fryde (1965).

of weakness. From an early date at Basle borrowing took the form of international loans.[20] In 1504, Basle created a public bank (initially an exchange bank acting as a central bank) which alone was entitled to withdraw from circulation and remint poor-quality coin. It also enjoyed a monopoly on the issue of new specie, for which it was empowered to buy and sell bars of gold and silver. It was also a deposit bank, in which the city invested large sums in order to increase the bank's own capital. Neighbouring cities like Strasbourg and Berne placed their deposits there. As a credit bank, it served merchants, artisans, nobles and clergy, as well as Swiss and German cities. Loans were initially made against pledges, and after 1533 against surety, mortgages or letters of exchange. It was in addition a clearing bank serving government agencies, merchants and artisans. It was a loan-issuing bank for the city of Basle, the Swiss cities and those of the Rhine valley, for the local nobility and those of Baden, Savoy, and France, as well as for the king of France and the Emperor. Basle's public bank offered its clients the stability of a venture guaranteed by the state, security for deposits, loans at reasonable interest rates, and professional secrecy. In the sphere of borrowing, it attracted the capital of individuals and religious houses from a radius of 150 kilometres. It became the main credit institution for much of the Swiss Confederation. During the sixteenth century, Basle made about sixty loans with funds drawn from its own treasury. In fact, anyone wishing to raise a loan had recourse to the bank which, as a consequence, was involved in all of the country's principal financial transactions. From 1560 onwards, the investment of capital in public borrowing became the prerogative of cities and the countryside took its place among the ranks of the debtors. From the end of the Middle Ages, Basle was the leading Swiss financial market, attracting nearly two-thirds of the capital lent by Swiss cities—a minimum of 1.62 million gold crowns. It strengthened its role during the sixteenth century with the introduction of a public exchange; the bank's entire range of clients were engaged in lending money.[21]

3.4 *Later Fiscal Developments in the Italian City-States*

Venice proved to be more reticent when it came to establishing a public bank, since it only decided in 1587 to set up the bank on the Rialto and the *Banco giro* in 1619—it was as though the city-state was unable to transform its fiscal revenues into financial assets which could yield profits. But Venice was expert in making its taxpayers produce returns. In the subject towns of the *dominio* on the

[20] Rosen and Sprandel in Kellenbenz (1971).

[21] Hallauer (1904); Körner (1980). Another city, Genoa, played a principal role in international lending: Felloni (1971).

Terraferma, the most significant revenues usually came from the *dazi* levied on economic transactions. The poor rural areas were subject to a permanent direct tax introduced in 1417. This was a 'war subsidy' earmarked for military expenditure, paid in cash, and channelled through the fiscal offices of the chief towns of each locality. There were also specific taxes on poor peasants who were subject to taxes on such property as they held and on other personal obligations, such as deliveries of straw and provender, the surrender of pasture rights, the requisitioning of lodgings for troops, and compulsory labour services for work on fortifications and for the transport of raw material. In short, each person contributed a share in accordance with the view formed by the city government of the available resources and way of life of the various categories of its subject populations. Indirect taxes were to be paid by urban groups who were consumers of goods, while more was demanded by way of direct taxation from the peasant classes living largely in a state of subsistence. Those who were unable to pay at all found themselves requisitioned as manpower for the large-scale deliveries of goods which were of little commercial value but indispensable for the army. Most of these revenues were spent on the spot.[22]

In the early sixteenth century, it was necessary to reform this obsolete system of taxation and troop quartering so as to house cavalrymen in towns and castles. To increase the number of soldiers, the Venetian Senate established territorial militias which involved its subjects in defending Venetian territory. The evolution of military techniques led to new forms of service and to profound changes in the fiscal system, the aim of which was to reduce the costs of maintaining a professional, mercenary army. Efforts to associate the inhabitants of the *Terraferma* with the future of the state went further still. Venice also proved successful in relying on its subjects' loyalty to create a new tax, initially in the form of a voluntary loan or 'subsidy', then as a forced loan, and finally as a regular, ordinary tax to be paid by all except the clergy and those who lived solely 'by working in the fields and by their manual labour'. This new tax, which was common to the *Terraferma* and which was levied on property and not on persons, was an important step towards the creation of a regional state.

The republic of Venice also tried to introduce a property tax, the *compatico*, which provoked opposition from the nobilities of the *Terraferma* and the urban councils which feared a questioning of their privileges by the assessors (*distrettuali*) arising from any new census of property ownership. This *catasto* would have revealed the property, including that belonging to Venetians, which had hitherto escaped all valuation. What was at stake was the overall relationship between the Venetian patriciate, the various urban patriciates, the peasantry and

[22] Hocquet in Bonney (1995).

the rural communities. On the one hand, Venetians were not included, while nobles paid their taxes in the towns, including taxes on lands which they owned in the countryside, with the effect that the entire fiscal burden for the countryside fell solely on the peasantry. This burden was becoming all the more unbearable in that urban groups acquired from the population of the *contado* of Verona alone between 1575 and 1627 landed property to the value of nearly 1.76 million ducats. After May 1617, the *compatico* was finally levied on the property of Venetians themselves. The tax took account of the growth of properties and the utilization of land—arable, meadow and marshland were subject to different rates of taxation. The *Terraferma*, which benefited from economic change and agricultural development, found itself increasingly subject to taxation, which corresponded to the fall in the returns from customs and commercial taxes at Venice following the decline in trade there.

Venice found another way of extracting money from the lands of the *Terraferma* at a time when investment in agriculture proved more profitable than putting capital into commercial or industrial activities. From the time of the conquest onwards, it confiscated the properties of defeated lordships which then became 'properties of the commune of Venice' (*bona communis Veneciarum*), placed at the disposal of rural communities. During the Italian wars, the Council of Ten considered putting a part of these properties up for sale. The peasantry, which had occasionally usurped some of the lands, was hostile and obtained the support of the local nobility: the latter knew from experience that the sale would benefit mainly the Venetian patriciate. It was only in 1603 that the Senate ordered a general census of such lands, and in 1637 the Veneto alone was recognized as possessing 209,000 hectares of commons, or 11 per cent of total agricultural land. In 1647, a few months after the Turkish attack on Candia, the first sales took place. Between 1647 and 1727, 89,000 hectares, 42 per cent of the total surface area, were sold, half to Venetian nobles. The sales yielded 3.3 million ducats. This impressive financial return had a number of serious repercussions: it had social consequences because it removed from the poor rights to graze their few cattle; it also had more general economic consequences because the deficit in provender provision led to a reduction in farm animals and fertilizers, which in turn had an impact on cereal yields.

In Tuscany, the republic of Florence had in the early fifteenth century launched an attempt to overcome the fragmentation of the commune-state, and to entrust to the *dominante* direct control over the subject cities around it. Yet in 1750, 70 per cent of the taxes collected for the servicing of the public debt were raised in Florence, its *contado*, and at Livorno which was highly dependent on Florence. Siena, Pisa, Arezzo, Pistoia and Volterra contributed only 30 per cent. The real power of the *dominante* did not consist therefore in paying fewer taxes, but in being the main beneficiary of public expenditure. The urban aristocracies answered three questions in a manner favourable to their interests: how to take advantage of opportunities to invest money in public funds; how to avoid any contribution to the fiscal exigencies of the grand duke; and how to control the management of the sums of money raised by taxation and public credit. In fact, the imperatives of political stability obliged the grand dukes to compromise with the aristocracy which tended to become co-proprietor of the financial system. These two constraints maintained a fiscal balance that was favourable to the provinces and entrenched the power of the traditional elites whose interests converged henceforth with those of the monarchy. Given the presence of such privileges, the burden of taxation fell on the peasantry of the *contado*, the artisans of the *dominante* and the international trade of Livorno.[23]

Not all the communities of the grand duchy were subject to the same fiscal regime (direct taxation based on the *estimi*). An anonymous commentator of the eighteenth century wrote:

> the *estimi* of each locality were drawn up by communities at various times and according to different rules from one place to the next, using different prices for foodstuffs or different coinages. The *lira d'estimo* was based on capital of 100 crowns in one place, on 500 crowns in another, and still elsewhere on 1,000 crowns. In some cases it is not calculated in terms of capital, but of revenue; on net revenue in one place, on gross revenue somewhere else; in some instances on all sources of revenue, in others on those of grain or wine only. One may suppose that such *estimi* are useful for the internal, local apportionment of a community's taxation, but they provide no evidence of the relations between different communities, and do not allow one to establish an equitable allocation of taxation.[24]

The system of *estimi* prepared by governing groups at various times, using different methods and coinages, provided a poor picture of the economic and financial state of communities, and indeed they were the most serious obstacle to any attempt at fiscal standardization. But since the beginning of the fourteenth century, the *catasto* registered 'all goods, possessions, substances, trade, merchandise and cattle' (that is, all immovables and capital), shares in the public debt, income from crafts or trade, and merchandise, from which negative assets (such as private or commercial debts, and the rent of a house) were then subtracted, before the share of the *estimo* (*rata d'estimo*) of each taxpayer was fixed. The operation was known as the *allirazione*, and the results were inscribed in a book called the *lira*. Mechanisms for differential assessment altered the *rata d'estimo*. Older or recent merchandise, as well as immovables acquired from tax-exempt persons, were taxed at 12 *deniers* per 100 florins, while immovables already

[23] Waquet in Genet and Le Mené (1985), 111–14.

[24] Quoted by Benigni (1980), 52.

subject to tax continued to be assessed at the old rate of 40 *deniers* per 100 florins. It was difficult to establish the value of such goods, except where they were rented out, in which case the annual rent was capitalized at 7 per cent.

In October 1545, Cosimo I, who was engaged in an administrative and financial reorganization of the *dominio*, issued a law on 'universal expenses' to which each community was obliged to contribute in accordance with the capital of its *estimo*. This was for the purpose of paying for soldiers, fortifications and public works. All sums required and collected were paid to the *dominante*. In 1546, a new *estimo* was produced in order to obtain a more equitable extension of the fiscal burden to those groups which had hitherto been exempt. Merchants and artisans protested and opposed the revision of the *lira de' trafici* because it was inappropriate to tax goods which were 'not themselves perpetual'. The owners of immovable property, who saw real property constantly rise in value at a time of change in the Italian economy and of commercial crises, attempted to secure exemption and succeeded in having land classified as 'good', 'mediocre' and 'bad', and even to diversify their income depending on the lands and the localities involved. They also ensured that the *rata d'estimo* was lowered from 40 to 20 *deniers* per 100 florins. These measures also played a part in keeping the *estimo* at a very low rate: in Arezzo, the officials of the *catasto* found a device for registering land at two-fifths of its value. Fiscal pressure, which was tightened on property-owners in the towns, brought about the resistance of the wealthiest social groups who bore a less heavy burden than was their due, while for local communities it led to a substantial deficit in the accounts, a significant increase in indirect taxes, and resulted in the impoverishment of the weakest social groups.

3.5 *Conclusion*

The city-state, viewed from the vantage point of the Renaissance of the fifteenth and sixteenth centuries, had undergone a profound change. This resulted less from the political evolution of state formation at the end of the Middle Ages than from the profound economic changes which were felt in both Italy and Germany, and which favoured non-urban activities and a 'return to the land'. The members of the same class benefited from this, as from previous trends, provided they had taken the precaution of diversifying their investments by taking capital out of commerce and placing it in agriculture. But public revenues changed in character, with indirect taxes and customs tolls levied in the city—and especially in the capital city which exercised a monopoly on trade—giving way henceforth to direct taxes and a property tax levied throughout the length and breadth of the state. The largest proportion of public revenues continued to service the public debt and borrowing, and for this reason went into the coffers of privileged groups living on unearned incomes. From this perspective, too, the lifestyle and financial resources of the urban nobility or patriciate came increasingly to resemble those of the court- and urban-based upper nobility. They owed less than the latter to the favour of rulers, since they were, with rare exceptions like Florence, themselves the rulers and directly wielded power through the councils. There has been very little discussion here of expenditure, to avoid repetition of what is said elsewhere (Chapter 12). There is a certain logic to this. War was the engine of expenditure and thus of revenue: but behind the mercenary soldier who collected a meagre wage, there was the *rentier* and the speculator who benefited from the advice given by lawyers to the ruling councils that the state's credit system must be expanded. It is thus in the evolution and operation of the system of public credit that the modernity of the city-state may best be perceived (Chapter 14).

CHAPTER 4

Kingdoms on the Periphery of Europe: The Case of Medieval and Early Modern Scandinavia

Bjørn Poulsen

How did the relatively backward areas of Europe narrow the gap, in terms of economic and fiscal development, with the 'more advanced' areas? This chapter seeks to explain what might be called the 'early harmonization' of the European economy, which was the product of a long period of state formation in Scandinavia. During this process, three kingdoms came into being, namely Denmark, Norway and Sweden (with Finland). Other types of governmental structure formed on the periphery of these kingdoms. The Danish and German social and fiscal systems fused in Schleswig and Holstein, while peasant republics existed in Iceland and Ditmarschen on the west coast of Holstein. This chapter attempts to demonstrate how and why these early states moved towards the European level of fiscal development.[1] The main emphasis will be on the majority of the population in these areas, the peasants, and on the mechanisms by which their economic surplus was transferred to the nascent state structure.

4.1 *Domains and Taxes*

In the large west European monarchies of France, England and Castile, taxation increased to such an extent in the late Middle Ages, that in fiscal terms they may be regarded almost as 'modern' states (Chapter 5). In northern Europe, it is certainly true that there was a development in the many forms of taxation. Brunner remarked of Germany that there were as many types of taxes as there were forms of lordship,[2] but this remark is equally valid for Scandinavia. Taxation must thus necessarily become a central concern for us. On the other

[1] There has been no general study of Scandinavian medieval state finances to date. Lönnroth (1940) is the most useful account. A number of articles in Danstrup and Karker (1956–78) constitute the basic introduction to a number of topics.

[2] Brunner (1965), 273: 'So viele Herrschaftsverhältnisse bestehen, so viele Steuerarten wird man underscheiden können.'

hand, it also becomes clear that the earlier development of the Scandinavian and the other north European states was more closely related to another form of revenue, that from domains.

The domain economy is a relatively unfamiliar subject to modern economists, so that a clarification of the concept in its Scandinavian form is useful at the outset, taking the specific example of the Danish duchy of Schleswig, which was united with Holstein during the fifteenth century. By the beginning of the sixteenth century, Schleswig consisted of nine administrative areas, the *Ämter* (as they are referred to in German) or *len* (in Danish), and it is these areas which historians term the 'domains'.[3] Every area had its own castle. In the case of Aabenraa *Amt*, the accounts for the years 1535, 1538 and 1539 have been preserved, which permits an analysis of the local domain economy (Figures 9 and 10).[4]

The centre of the *Amt* was the modest castle of Brundlund, outside the town of Aabenraa. Here the noble royal official, the *Amtmand*, lived with his family, his scribe and fourteen soldiers and servants. The revenues which he collected

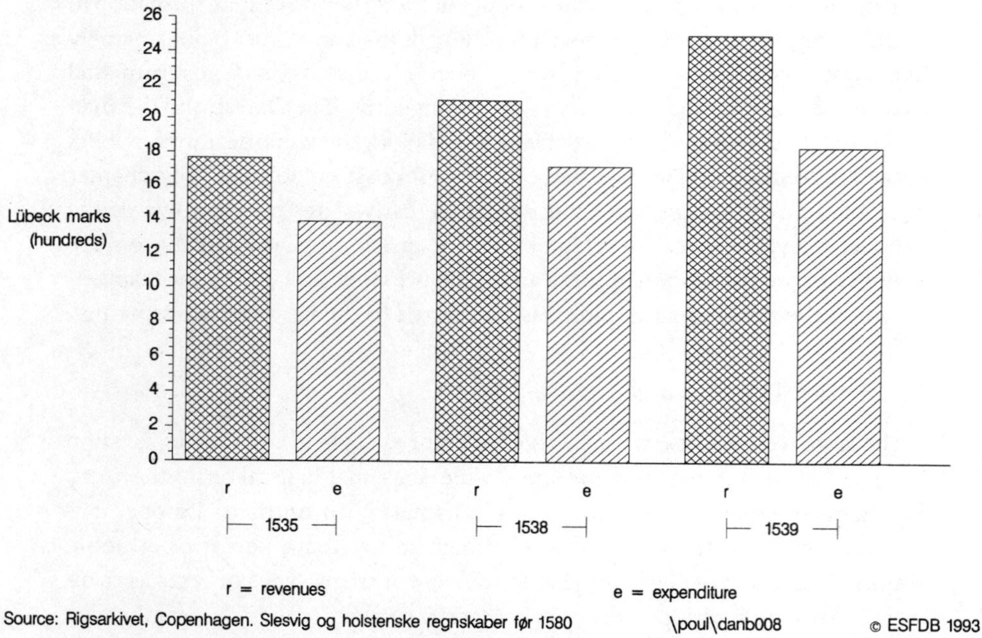

FIG. 9. Revenues and expenditure of the Aabenraa *Amt*, duchy of Schleswig, 1535–1539 (in Lübeck marks)

[3] Poulsen (1990*a*).

[4] ESFDB \poul\danb008 based on \dand023 and \danb007 based on \dand023; Rigsarkivet, København, Slesvig og holstenske regnskaber før 1580.

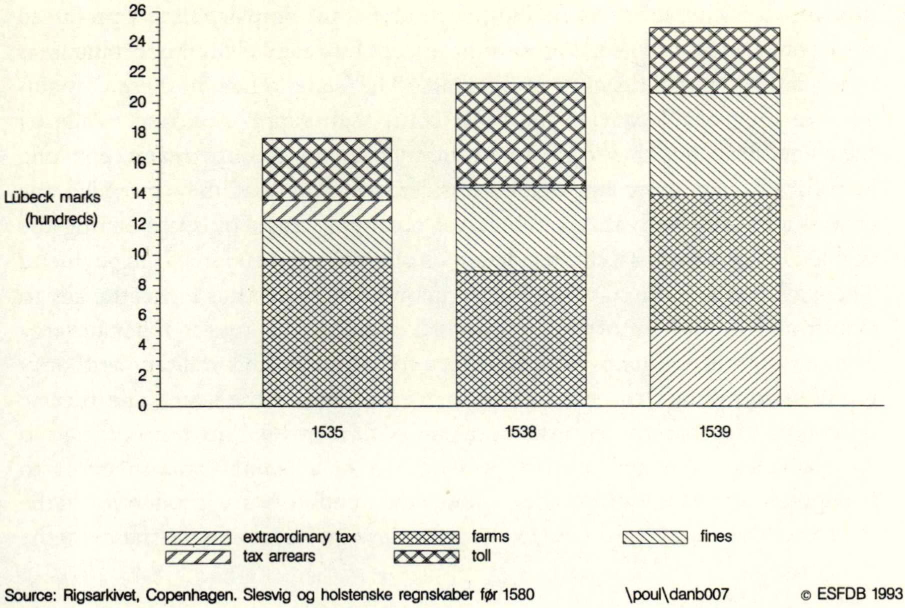

FIG. 10. Categories of revenues of the Aabenraa *Amt*, duchy of Schleswig, 1535–1539 (in Lübeck marks)

mainly came from the 318 farms belonging to the *Amt*. The area also included five mills which every year paid the *Amt* a quantity of grain; the farms also paid their levies and taxes partly in grain and partly in money. The money paid over included both tenants' rents and fixed amounts from the freeholders, which originated in taxes first levied in the thirteenth century; revenues were also drawn from fines and certain other levies. In 1539, these revenues were further supplemented by an extraordinary tax (Figure 9). A number of local administrative duties rested with the *Amtmand* who, for example, had to maintain his lord, Christian III of Denmark, when he travelled through the area. He had to defray the expenses of any military campaign and make purchases to cover the daily requirements of the garrison. In reality, all the revenues in kind were consumed at the castle, but there remained a disposable surplus from the revenues received in cash (Figure 10). These cash sums were not insignificant, but it is clear from the annual accounts presented in the chamber at the castle of Gottorf that the *Amtmand* was only able to hand over to the king a small proportion of the total revenues. This was true even in 1539, when the area paid an extraordinary tax. Most of the money collected was spent locally within the *Amt*. True, the surplus from the domains increased somewhat during the sixteenth century, but this example is not untypical of a relatively advanced domain economy. In earlier periods, we find that the domains simply produced no accounts at all or yielded no surplus, except for relatively unimportant areas reserved for the maintenance of the king.[5] The 'state' relied on these domains because they could provide the royal court with supplies in kind, while by their very existence they constituted the military force of the realm. For long periods an even more important consideration was that they provided the central authority with the possibility of obtaining credit by surrendering the domains to noble officials for fixed periods of time in return for a fixed payment. The way in which the state capitalized upon its domains thus forms the key to Danish and Swedish history for long periods in the Middle Ages. To alienate large numbers of the domains was in effect to fragment the military authority represented by their castles, and decisively to weaken the state. The reverse process, a strict control over the domains, with relatively low-born officials in command of them and a strict presentation of accounts, was in effect to strengthen central authority. Thus some of the trends towards 'modernity' in the state are to be found in the development of a firm and clear administration of the domains.[6]

4.2 *Trends in the Early Royal Economy of Scandinavia*

Decentralized structures remained in Iceland until the thirteenth century, with leaders (*goder*) exercising religious and legislative power; but elsewhere in Scandinavia, the different tribal areas were gradually united under a central authority in the years before 1150.[7] It was a complicated process and for a long time great differences between the provinces remained. It is appropriate after *c.*1000 to talk of Denmark and Norway as realms defined by borders, but a consolidated kingdom of Sweden did not exist before the mid-twelfth century.[8] At the outset, the three Nordic kingdoms were dominated by a peripatetic form of government. The kings ruled while they were travelling the country with their retinues; on such visits to the fortified strongholds of the realm, the king and his court consumed the stocks of produce accumulated in the crown lands. The stores were derived partly from gifts or duties owed by the inhabitants of the area visited, and partly from the king's own lands. The 'royal economy' was also to a substantial degree based on the control of trade, on the profits from raids against neighbours and on tribute.

The collection of taxes in a modern sense was rendered very difficult, if not impossible, in the Scandinavian lands throughout the Middle Ages, since the

[5] Cf. Christensen (1983).
[6] Cf. Erslev (1879).
[7] Cf. Mortensen and Rasmussen (1988–91).
[8] Sawyer (1991).

liability to pay taxes was considered to be irreconcilable with personal freedom. The king, however, had certain residual rights of lordship, and with the contributions received by an itinerant king from his population we are close to the origins of Scandinavian taxation, that is, the king's ceremonial journeys through the country.[9] Originally the costs of such journeys were met informally, but in the twelfth century these 'gifts' were transformed into a fixed system of levies. The increased formalization of revenues becomes evident from a list of the revenues of the Danish King Valdemar (*c.*1231), in which the royal demands are listed under the names of *apparatus*, *procuratio* and *servitium*.[10] In spite of this increasing formalization, the linguistic illusion of the 'hospitality' owed by the population at large was preserved. The Swedish word *gästning* and the Danish *gæsteri*, which were used to describe the duty to give sustenance to the king during his visits, in origin meant to enjoy food and accommodation in someone's house. The payment in kind made to the king during his visits in Sweden was called *gengärd*, or a collection of provisions, while in Norway it was called *veitsle* or 'contribution'.[11]

The tendency to fix the amount of the contributions paralleled the increased formalization of the duty of hospitality. Only in Norway did the peasants insist on their rights and maintain the principle that *veitslene* were given as free gifts and could not be fixed by law. In contrast, in Denmark the king stipulated their size. In the Danish list of revenues from *c.*1231 the contribution to two nights of royal *gæsteri* was specified in amounts of grain, malt, meat, butter, cheese, poultry, fish, honey and so on. The list also contained the amounts to be paid to officials and the staff of the kitchen and prescribed that 100 plates and 400 dishes should be supplied. The right to enjoy these supplies gradually also spread from the king in person to his officials when they were travelling on their own. The administrative centres on the crown lands were the usual places for the contributions to be paid or collected. For example, the central farms of the Norwegian crown lands had special barns, *veitslehaller*, where the revenues from the peasants of the area and the rents of the tenants were stored; the king had also acquired the right of *gæsteri* at monasteries and bishops' palaces.

The distribution of land in the kingdom, and the amount of royal land in particular, was a consequence of the evolutionary process by which the three kingdoms were formed. In Denmark it is possible to distinguish between an older, western style, *patrimonium*, concentrated in Jutland and Funen, and more recent additions to the crown lands mostly situated in Zealand and Scania. It is likely that this distribution was created in the years around 1000 when a new

[9] Cf. Gurevich (1985), 227–31. [10] Aakjær (1926–45). [11] Cf. Hertzberg (1893).

dynasty came to power.[12] In Sweden, the central group of crown lands (*bona coronae*) was known as *Uppsala öd*: significant numbers of farms were attached to the administrative centres (*husabyer*) in the area which had formed the nucleus of the Swedish kingdom. Similarly, in Norway it is possible to discern concentrations of crown lands which date back to the days of the formation of the kingdom around 1000 and to the later period of consolidation, when the king confiscated the lands of defeated opponents.

The Nordic countries shared a common characteristic in that the officials of the crown lands changed from the status of dependent bailiffs (*bryder*, or in Latin, *villici*) towards more professional administrators. The original task of the royal servants was to ensure the delivery of goods from the royal lands and the payment of rents by tenants: the produce was then stored until required by the king. However, the crown lands increasingly became the basis of territorial organization. In twelfth-century Denmark one finds the royal *ombudsmænd* at the head of a territorial area called a *herred*; in Norway in the same century the *sysselmannen* appears with a territorial area (called *syssel*) under his control. In Sweden, it was not until the thirteenth century that the old *husabyer* were abolished and new divisions called *län* introduced.

There can be little doubt that these increasingly sophisticated territorial divisions were introduced for fiscal reasons but, before we consider this development, we should reflect on the earlier origins of taxation. We have seen that in the Scandinavian lands, taxation was considered to be irreconcilable with personal freedom. Therefore only defeated rebels, conquered territories and outlying regions were liable to taxation. From the time of the earliest kings, and throughout the Middle Ages, we find periods when tributes were paid by outlying regions:[13] thus, for example, the English payment of *danegeld* fundamentally strengthened the power of Danish kings (Chapter 2.2). The element of coercion which underpinned such levies of tribute is vividly depicted in the words of the Slavonic *Chronicle of Helmod* (II, 13) concerning the conquest of Rügen by the Danish king in 1168. This states that the people of Rügen had to serve the Danish king and to pay him tax; he also received the sons of the aristocrats as hostages and took them away to his country. The relationship between the coercive force and those forced to pay tribute gradually evolved into that of ruler and subject, as is evident in the northernmost regions of Scandinavia. In this area, north from Bodö and in Finland, from the River Luleälv and northwards, a mainly nomadic population gained experience of taxation at an early date. Long before Norway was united into one kingdom, the reindeer-hunting nomads of this area became the subjects of chieftains in northern

[12] Andrén (1983). [13] Cf. Corbier in Genet (1990), 95–107.

Norway and paid levies to them in the form of valuable pelts. In the twelfth and thirteenth centuries, the population became less nomadic, and the area changed in character from a peripheral area paying tribute to an integrated part of a kingdom (either Norway or Sweden). Gradually, borders and rights of taxation were established as a result of warfare involving Russians, Norwegians and Swedes; but the border zones of authority and tax power remained unclear. The Peace of Novgorod of 1326 between Norway and Russia, for instance, determined that the peninsula of Kola should be a shared fiscal district open to both Norwegians and Russians. As late as the fifteenth century, Swedish *birkarlar* seem to have been collecting taxes along the northern Norwegian coast.

Iceland and Greenland provide a variation on the theme of inhabitants of outlying areas becoming integrated into the body of taxpayers.[14] These islands, which had long been self-governing, were forced to accept the rule of the Norwegian king in the mid-thirteenth century. In 1261, the Greenlanders agreed to pay taxes to the Norwegian king, while the proud oligarchy of the Icelandic 'free state' collapsed at about the same time: the following year, the Icelanders promised to pay the king of Norway an annual tax of homespun cloth for every man attending the public court, the *ting*, and to honour the agreement as long as it was not violated by the king. In return, the king was to allow the Icelanders to live in peace, and undertook not to change their laws. The king agreed to send six ships from Norway in the next two years; subsequently, as many ships would be sent as the king and the men of Iceland considered beneficial for the country. The transformation of tribute into taxes was undoubtedly an important factor in the development of taxation, but it was not the decisive aspect: in Scandinavia at least, commutation was more important.

4.3 *Commutation Taxes in the Twelfth and Thirteenth Centuries*

During the twelfth and thirteenth centuries, a general process of commuting duties into taxes took place in the Scandinavian kingdoms. In Denmark and Sweden, these taxes were in turn transformed into ordinary taxes.[15] It may be argued that extraordinary taxes and ordinary taxes arise from the same legal basis, and furthermore that extraordinary taxes tend almost ineluctably to become ordinary ones. The origin of the Scandinavian ordinary taxes appears to lie in the commutation of supplies and services in cases of necessity, both for the royal household and military services. However, as we have seen, the taxes themselves did not arise from the emergency itself, but from more normal conditions and customary obligations which were already fixed and regulated.

[14] Cf. Holmsen (1977), 303–30; Hastrup (1985), 223–37.

[15] Cf. Arup (1914–15), 141–237; Lindkvist in Genet and Le Mené (1987), 53–64.

In the case of Denmark and Norway, the first 'state' taxes took the form of the commutation of military service. The Swedish situation is more complicated, since three types of levy are encountered: commutation of military service; commutation of maintenance for the peripatetic king and his court; and a third category of levies of uncertain origin, which were collectively assessed on the province. In all three kingdoms, however, there was the possibility of commuting military service into levies which could then be used for the payment of professional soldiers. The social structure facilitated generalized military service: during the period when the kingdoms were formed, and thereafter, all free men were required to perform military service according to laws known as the *leding*. The new ordinary taxes were based on this system.

Already in Denmark before 1100, the peasants had to pay fines when not fulfilling their military duties. Settlements which grew up after the military system had been established were required to pay a fixed levy called *kværsæde* (literally, 'the right to remain at home'). In 1204, a new tax payable in oats was introduced, called the *stud*: this reflected the increasing use of horses and professional warriors. About the year 1213, a fixed military tax was established, the *ledingsskat* (or, in Latin, *denarii expeditionales*), which was assessed on all Danish lands and was usually paid in money. In Sweden, both the *gengärd* (or, in Latin, *procuratio*) and the *leding* (or *expeditio*) were in place as ordinary taxes by the 1260s. Thus, in both Denmark and Sweden the military service of peasants was converted into contributions. In Norway, the military duty of the peasants remained, but even so the *leding* was turned into a periodic tax from the middle of the twelfth century, and around the year 1200 there were several rebellions against the new tax demands. In 1270, it was finally accepted that Norwegian peasants would pay an annual tax in peacetime equivalent to half the amount they paid in times of war.

There were several reasons for the process that changed peasants from soldiers to taxpayers. Historians have attributed the transformation in both Denmark and Sweden to the growth of cavalry-based armies drawn from the tax-exempt landowning aristocrats. The process of aristocratization may have been more important than the dynamic of military change; it should in turn be connected with fundamental changes in the revenues of the three kingdoms. By the eleventh and twelfth centuries, the fiscal balance in all three kingdoms shifted from the control of trade and plunder (or external forms of revenue) to internal forms of revenue.[16] Bagge pointed out that the crisis of resources arising from the cessation of the Viking raids led in the eleventh century to prolonged conflict in all three kingdoms which did not cease until the aristocrats formed an alliance

16 Lindkvist (1990).

with the monarchy and thus gained the ability to extract larger revenues from their peasants.[17] On the other hand, it is clear that the emergence of a formalized nobility in Denmark and Sweden was partially a consequence of the new taxes, since a nobleman was defined precisely by the fact that he did not pay taxes but served in the army. In a wider sense, the transformation represents an adjustment to the more general European economic and social structure: large parts of northern Europe were becoming increasingly integrated with the rest of Europe.

This first real 'state' economy was made possible by increased monetarization in the twelfth and thirteenth centuries.[18] To a greater extent than previously, levies and tolls could be extracted from towns, and taxes could now be collected in money. As a result, it becomes possible for the historian to estimate the size of revenues after this date. In the list of the Danish king's revenues from 1231, for instance, we are told that one night's support of the king could be paid with 15 silver marks; but we can also start to calculate total state revenues. Erslev calculated that around the year 1230 the Danish king enjoyed about 20,000–40,000 silver marks (*c*.3·84–7·68 tonnes) from the revenues of the *leding* alone. Figure 11 shows the overall balance between types of revenue at this date.[19] For Norway around 1300, it has been estimated that, in the years when *ledingsskat* was collected, the total revenue would have been no higher than 3,000 silver marks (*c*.0.576 tonnes).[20] The figures are open to doubt, but the evidence indicates that

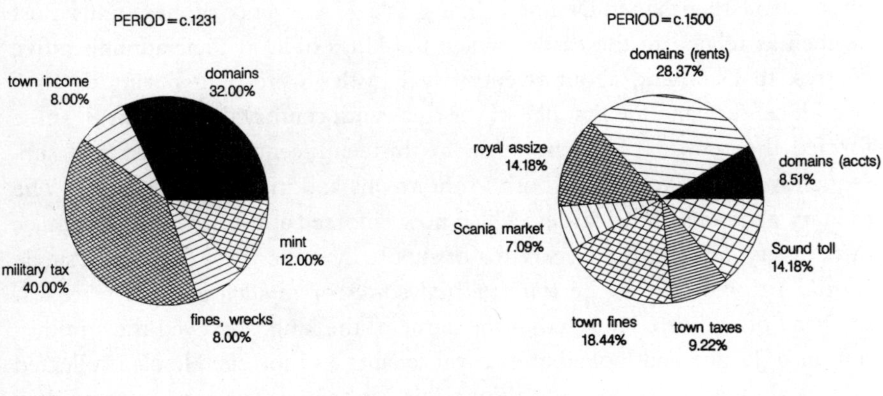

Sources: Erslev (1898); Danske Magazin (1843), 136–8 \poul\dani001 © ESFDB 1993

FIG. 11. Categories of estimated Danish royal revenues in *c*.1231 and in *c*.1500

[17] Bagge (1986).
[18] Poulsen (1990*b*); Klackenberg (1992).
[19] Erslev (1898); ESFDB \poul\dani001 based on \dand018.
[20] Steinnes (1933), ii, 207.

the revenue of the Norwegian king was the lowest in Scandinavia. This, however, was a consequence not only of natural conditions, but also of the absence of ordinary taxes. In Norway, a fleet manned by peasants remained the chief force, and a professional cavalry was out of the question because of the terrain. This structure of small state revenues and expenditure could still prove effective as late as the 1290s, when the Norwegian fleet attacked and seriously weakened the Danish kingdom.[21]

4.4 *The Victory of Extraordinary Taxes*

In 1281, the Swedish king informed the inhabitants of the island of Öland that new taxes were needed to cover the costs of those to whom he had entrusted his castles. This was a radical new linkage between castles and taxes. As a consequence of the aristocratization of Sweden and Denmark, the thirteenth century witnessed the creation of a fiscal system based on the link between extraordinary taxes, castles and new territorial units (*len* in Danish, *län* in Swedish and *Ämter* in German). The many small administrative areas in Denmark, the 200 or so *herreder*, were gradually gathered into larger administrative units, the *len*. Certain Danish *len* consisted of only one *herred*, but often they were composed of more; in the administrative area of Aalborg for instance there were eight *herreder*. Sweden experienced a corresponding process, except that the size of the *län* was often even larger than in Denmark. The gradual emergence of these units must be seen as related to the castles which the kings built as their administrative centres. In Denmark, about twenty royal castles were built during the late twelfth century and the first half of the thirteenth century (before 1241);[22] these formed the centres of the new *len*. In thirteenth-century Sweden and subsequently, castles were built both in the towns and in the countryside.[23] The military garrisons of the castles, which now enforced authority in the localities, of necessity demanded a larger area of supply than the royal farms of a single *herred*. A noble officer, the *lensmand* (*advocatus* or *capitaneus*), was placed at the head of each *len*. He acted in the name of the king, surveyed the administration of justice and looked after royal tenants and forests. He also collected long-established taxes and was responsible for the levy of new extraordinary taxes.

The first attempt by the Danish king to collect an extraordinary tax was the establishment of a plough tax in *c.*1231, the purpose of which was to replace the older system of coinage renewal (*renovatio monetæ*), which had been introduced

[21] Cf. Bagge (1986). [22] Jaubert (1988). [23] Fritz (1988).

in *c.*1075.[24] The peasants of Jutland paid a fixed levy for every plough in 1231; in the next decade it was also collected in Zealand and Funen; and in 1249 the Scania peasants were made to pay the tax. At least in parts of Jutland, the tariff was 18 *penninge* (*denarii*) on every plough. Presumably the taxes were not paid exclusively in money, at least not at the beginning of the fourteenth century when the burden of taxation per plough became significantly heavier: a Danish tax of the year 1325 was collected according to the tariff of 'one mark of silver per plough or the corresponding in meat or butter'. At that time, plough taxes were levied more or less biennially on the land in general. We know the rates of levy for certain extraordinary taxes levied in 1311 and 1316 (both 1 silver mark for every plough), in 1318 (half a silver mark for every plough) and in 1325 (1 silver mark for every plough). We do not know the rates at which extraordinary taxes were levied in the years 1328 and 1332 in Scania (even the levy itself is not certain in this case), and 1340 in Jutland. In addition to these taxes, a heavy *guldkorn* was demanded from the peasants in Jutland after the defeat of their rebellion in 1313 (this amounted to a levy of 3 marks for every plough, and a levy in kind of one horse from every parish). Furthermore, a tenth of all income was demanded from peasants, churchmen and nobility in Denmark in 1317. In Sweden, the fixed taxes remained important for a longer period, since the process of defining who were to be the taxpayers within the population at large proceeded less rapidly than in Denmark. By *c.*1300, the ordinary taxes proved to be insufficient for the needs of the Swedish crown, and extraordinary taxes were collected, at first with the name of *markgälder*. In 1318, a *subsidium generale* had to be paid; in 1323, the nobility was also taxed; and by the mid-fourteenth century, the number of extraordinary taxes was on the increase, as in Denmark.

These extraordinary taxes were collected despite popular opposition and the prevailing ideology. In 1249, when King Erik of Denmark tried to collect a plough tax in Scania, the peasants forced him to retreat, both literally and metaphorically. In 1340, Count Gerhard of Holstein tried to impose a tax on the peasants of Zealand: this required him to march against them, and to defeat their 'dirty and rusty weapons' in open battle. In the same year, a rebellion in Jutland was probably sparked off by the count's levy of a silver tax; the count himself was murdered, which provided new opportunities for exploitation by the Danish king. The support of the aristocracy was necessary in order to force through the new taxes. However, for its own reasons, the nobility sought to restrict the burden of royal taxation. Characteristically, during the reign of King Christopher II the Danish state council (*rigsrådet*) tried in 1320 to halt the imposition of further taxes. Taxes, the council argued, should remain at the level 'they were in King Valdemar's days', that is, before the emergence of extraordinary taxes. The

[24] Cf. Bolin (1954); Bisson (1979).

Danish coronation charters (*håndfæstninger*) of 1326 and 1376 also prohibited new taxes and promised the abolition of those which had recently been imposed. In Sweden, King Magnus I (1275–96) had to declare that 'extraordinary and unjust levies' were paid by the people *de gracia*, not *de jure*. In the so-called 'great letter of liberty' (8 July 1319) the Swedish king gave the magnates a guarantee that taxes would not be imposed arbitrarily by the crown. The document noted that previous kings and princes had not observed old privileges and freedoms, but instead had imposed taxes illegally. It was decided that if taxes were necessary 'for the defence and common use of the entire kingdom' (*pro defensione et communi utilitate tocius regni*) they should be examined by the state council (*riksråd*), and thereafter proclaimed to the communities in all the provinces in order to secure their approval. In 1346, the Swedish King Magnus II (Eriksson) nevertheless had to apologize to his subjects for taxes that had been levied; he had to promise that he would stop them being collected. If taxes became absolutely necessary, committees in each diocese were to be established in which the local bishop, six noblemen and six non-nobles would determine the amount to be levied. In the royal law issued the same year, the popular demands were summarized, and it was specified that the king should live off the *len*, the domains:

> The king shall sustain his castles and lands from their annual revenues.
>
> The king shall live off the revenues of *Uppsala öd*, the crown lands, and the ordinary annual levies of his realm and he shall not impose any new levy or duty, except under certain conditions: if a foreign or heathen army ravages his country; in case of rebellion against the crown and the inability of the king to defend himself without recourse to taxation; in case of the coronation or coronation circuit in the kingdom (*Eriksgata*); when the king marries off his children, whether boys or girls; and when the king incurs expenses for the building of castles. In such cases, the bishop and the men of law will consider the amount to be paid to the king by the people. (*Kong Magnus Erikssons landslag, Konungsbalken V*, caps. 4, 5.)

Magnus Eriksson's land law left a paradoxical legacy: extraordinary taxes seemed to be ruled out as a result of the prevailing ideology that the king should live of his own; yet assemblies of magnates, in reality, created the possibility that royal taxes might nevertheless be levied.

The connection beween the *len* and increasing taxation borne by the peasantry was a consequence of the increasing resources required by the new professional army. The collection of extraordinary taxes was made much easier by the new castles and their professional forces. These military expenses, however, were followed by what Schumpeter might have termed changes in fiscal sociology, that is, changes which occur when a fiscal system so burdens the population that it cannot function without friction, which in turn has social and economic consequences.[25] While the ordinary taxes of the thirteenth century were paid by most of the peasants, the number of taxpayers undoubtedly declined during the next century. There was also a process of increasing aristocratization, which led peasants to seek protection (*værn*) as the servants of armed lords: the lord could be the king, a prominent churchman or a member of the nobility. In Denmark, only the 'free' peasants of the royal *len* continued to pay the ordinary taxes. In this way, the ordinary taxes declined rapidly and in effect were transformed into protection money for the service of the soldiers of the royal castle. The individual freeholder had to consider whether the tenancy of a noble or ecclesiastical estate offered a cheaper and safer form of protection than the (taxed) royal domains. The number of transfers is difficult to estimate, but there seems little doubt that many peasants found it profitable to become tenants of lords other than the king. Therefore, it became inevitable that if the king needed to extract larger sums of taxation he had to turn to the country as a whole and to ask the noble and ecclesiastical landlords to tax their tenants.

Despite the maxim that the king should live of his own, a connection was established between the domain economy and the system of taxation, two forms of fiscal system which seem contradictory. The fiscal system which comprised these two elements was not unique to Scandinavia but emerged at about the same time elsewhere. In the *Ämter* of the German territorial states and similar forms elsewhere in the Baltic region (such as the *Reichsvogteien* and the structure of the Teutonic Order)[26] we observe the same connection between the territorial area, the castle and extraordinary taxes (*Landsteuer*, *Bede* in German, *petitio* in Latin). Fiscal developments in Denmark and Sweden thus roughly corresponded to those of other areas in northern Europe. Seen in a wider European perspective, this fiscal system represents the north and central European counterpart to the developments in taxation in the main west European monarchies during the period from 1250 to 1400. The different response to the military challenge was a consequence of the different level of commercial development. In northern Europe and Scandinavia, still characterized by a peasant economy, the royal domains were always likely to be of central importance to the development of the fiscal system.

4.5 *Crisis and Consolidation of the Domain State, 1350–1500*

The period between 1350 and 1500 was not one of great fiscal innovation in Scandinavia, but one in which both the weakness and the strength of the domain

[25] Schumpeter (1954*b*). [26] Jeserich, Pohl and von Unruh (1983), i, 96.

system became apparent. The increased reliance on borrowing, itself a consequence of growing war expenditure, became characteristic of the central European states from the early thirteenth century, and was also evident in Scandinavia. The newly created territorial organizations of the *len* either produced an inadequate surplus or none at all. The accounts of the Mecklenburg knight Rafn von Barnekow of Nyköping *län* and Dalarna in Sweden for the years 1365–7, for example, characteristically show a large deficit. Such deficits could not easily be met by the grant of new taxation since, as has been seen, magnates participated in the decision as to whether or not to grant taxes and often used their influence to block new fiscal measures. As a result, the king was forced into the loan market.

In Denmark and Sweden, state credit was necessarily connected with the system of the *len*. There were few or no burghers or bankers available with ready capital, and in order to obtain cash sums the king was forced to alienate or pawn the *len* for fixed periods of time to noble lords (such alienations were called *pantelen*, or *Pfandlehn* in German). The system of *len* which initially had buttressed royal power now substantially weakened the kingdoms. This first became evident in Denmark. By 1325, about half the total Danish *len* had been alienated as *pantelen*, with officials other than those of the king collecting their revenues. By *c.*1340 the entire kingdom was under Holstein or Swedish rule as a consequence of this practice; as late as 1365–8, considerable tracts of the land were pledged to the counts of Holstein and other noblemen.

After 1319, important parts of the Swedish *län* were similarly given away as *pant*, while by the mid-fourteenth century the financial crisis became acute. Paradoxically, King Magnus Eriksson's attempt to strengthen royal power was financed by extensive pledging of the *län* and, as a result of this policy, German princes (especially those of Mecklenburg) became lords of this country. Like Denmark, Sweden now experienced a process of decentralization, and the area governed directly by the king was reduced to the size of a county. However, the dissatisfaction of the magnates was growing and the trend towards a new Scandinavian unity followed in its wake. In Denmark after 1340, a new kingdom under King Valdemar Atterdag rose from the ashes, enforcing royal power, developing central and local administration and re-establishing and extending the royal domains. While the Swedish kingdom in the following decade became weaker, Danish royal power was strengthened under Valdemar and his daughter Queen Margrete (1387–97) by dynastic alliances in the 1370s and 1380s with Norway (and Iceland) and Sweden (with Finland). In 1397, the Union of Kalmar formally joined the three Scandinavian realms in a single union.

The formal union did not, however, lead to any unification in the area of state finance. In Norway, the old *leding* was still the base of ordinary taxes. The military system of the country did not at first lead to the building of castles, and it was not until the fifteenth century that *len* (*hovedsysler*) with castles as centres were established in Norway. There were certain extraordinary taxes: in the 1290s, a new tax had been introduced under the name of *visøre*, and after 1370 the Norwegian king several times tried to collect a heavy war tax (*utfareleidang*) even in peacetime, but fundamentally the old order continued. In Denmark, the system based on extraordinary taxes continued to predominate. In 1349, King Valdemar enumerated the extraordinary taxes levied in Zealand during the preceding eight and a half years—he had collected a total of 30,000 marks of silver. The yield of taxes imposed in 1352 and 1355 is not known, though the second tax was levied at the rate of 6 *gros tournois* for every cow, but an extraordinary tax collected for Queen Margrete in 1396 probably amounted to more than 50,000 Lübeck marks.

It was thus only in Sweden that new forms of taxation emerged in the period of the union. By the statute of Nyköping in 1403, Queen Margrete converted the Swedish extraordinary taxes into ordinary taxes, which were to be paid in money or in kind (which might be cattle, sheep, chickens, wood or butter). The king's peasants, and those of the noble and clerical landlords, were divided into groups of four, 'two rich and two poor', and ten years later a tax register covering the whole country was established. Foreign officials holding the royal castles seem to have implemented this tax reform, the beneficiary of which was the crown of Denmark: extraordinary taxes were almost unknown there in the first fifty years of the Union of Kalmar, yet, as has been seen, taxes had certainly been demanded in Denmark before the union. The Swedes seem to have been correct in 1434 when, during the rebellion against the Danish regime, they maintained that money and goods had been taken out of their country and had been transported to the royal court in Denmark.

During the second half of the fifteenth century there was a change in the fiscal policies of Denmark and Sweden. It was now Denmark which often collected extraordinary taxes, partly in money, partly in kind, in order to finance the attempts to recover political control in Sweden, which had established a *de facto* independence without formally ending the Union of Kalmar. From the mid-fifteenth century, taxes paid in money became very frequent in Denmark, indeed they were an almost biennial occurrence. In Sweden, in contrast, ordinary taxes were lowered by one-third, and during the periods of independence collection of extraordinary taxes ceased altogether. Admittedly, the native regent of the realm, Karl Knutsson, tried in the 1450s to impose a number of taxes, but this led to rebellion and his deposition. The extraordinary taxes which Sweden experienced were mainly collected by Danish kings, such as King Christian I after 1461. However, even the Danish kings recognized that taxation in Sweden met with almost insuperable opposition. In 1463, there was open rebellion when Christian I tried to collect a *skeppskatt*. There was little place for a dominant monarchy in a country ruled by a strong aristocracy and whose peasantry enjoyed considerable independence: in the years 1471–1512, the Swedes organized their state as an aristocratic government of noble regents (*rigsforstandere*). The *län* with their castles were given over to the magnates in return for service, and the regents in Stockholm only maintained direct fiscal control over a very limited area, the *fatabur*, to meet their financial needs.[27]

During the later fifteenth century there was thus a growing polarization between Sweden, which became marginalized under a decentralized government of *län*, and the Danish state which, although in principle with the same structure, in reality exploited a more centralized and monetarized state economy. Danish superiority increased with the development of levies on goods passing through the (Danish) Sound (Sund), and other taxes on the towns and on the sale of beer (the excise or *cise*). In the long term, the economy was further strengthened by the unification of Schleswig–Holstein in 1460, which gave the Danish king access to the money market in Kiel (*Kieler Umschlag*).[28] The structure of Danish state revenues of the late fifteenth century is revealed by a survey of royal revenues 'in the times of King Hans' (1481–1513). This was drawn up by the administration of Frederick I in about 1524 and though its total for revenues (between 70,500 and 80,500 marks) is probably exaggerated, the one item which can be checked, the Sound dues, is fairly accurate (Figure 11). Revenues from the domains, the *len*, constitute more than a third of the total; revenues from the towns were somewhat lower; while the revenues from the Scania market and Sound dues only amount to one-seventh of the total. A last but not unimportant item was the revenue from the royal assizes, the *kongelige retterting*. In other words, only the revenues from the domains and royal prerogatives were listed: the survey can be regarded as a practical example of the notion that the king should 'live of his own'. Extraordinary taxes were not included in a 'normal' or average budget. Yet the figures in the survey, which were given gross and not net, were far larger than the amounts which actually reached the king's treasury.

4.6 *State Finance in Scandinavia on the Threshold of Modernity*

At the beginning of the sixteenth century Denmark (with Norway and Schleswig–Holstein) was superior in fiscal terms to Sweden (with Finland). This is clearly revealed by the terms of the Peace of Copenhagen in 1509, when the

[27] Hammarström (1956). [28] Arup (1902–4).

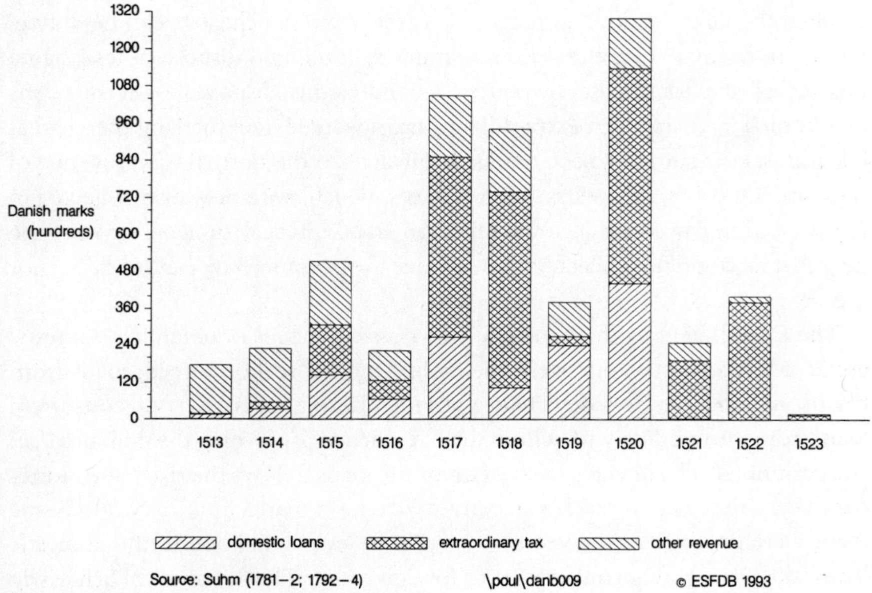

FIG. 12. Revenue of the Danish central administration, 1513–1523 (in Danish marks)

Swedish council recognized the right of the Danish King Hans to the Swedish throne and agreed to pay an annual tribute of 13,000 Stockholm marks until either Hans or his son Christian was received as Swedish king. However, King Christian II failed in his attempt to conquer Sweden in the years 1517–20. The Danish fiscal system is the point of departure in this analysis of the reasons for his failure. During the reign of Christian II, the receipts of payments from the administration were registered in the books of the royal Chancery, and even if smaller amounts passed unnoticed, a summing-up of individual entries no doubt gives a realistic picture of the revenue actually reaching the king. A subdivision of the amounts in extraordinary taxes and other revenues shows us that it was mainly the taxes which caused the fluctuations (Figure 12).[29]

Figure 12 shows that normal revenues of the central administration in the years up to 1520 moved somewhere between only 10,000 and 20,000 Danish marks (here we should leave the ailing revenues of the 1520s out of consideration). Totally different sums, however, reached the central administration in the years when extraordinary taxes flowed in (1515, 1517, 1518, 1520, 1521 and 1522), taxes which were levied in order to finance war with Sweden. If we accept the reliability of the estimate of royal revenues under King Hans (Figure 11) and that the totals of receipts in Figure 12 give a realistic picture of the amounts which

[29] ESFDB \poul\danb009 based on \dand024; Suhm (1792).

reached the king's central administration, then two conclusions can be drawn. Firstly, in normal years the central administration could dispose of less than a quarter of the total state revenues. Secondly, this disposable revenue was quadrupled in years when extraordinary taxes were levied: the king then had at his disposal the sum of 80,000 marks, equivalent to the normal total revenue of the state. Of course, the extraordinary taxes, which were now also collected in Norway, caused tax resistance and rebellion. In 1522, a local *lensmand* wrote to the king that he could not collect the taxes 'since the peasants have neither silver nor money'.

The Danish king by this time had two possible means of obtaining domestic credit. Most advantageous were the 'voluntary' (in reality, forced) loans from towns and the clergy—often paid without interest. Less advantageous were loans from the nobility, with whom the old practice of pawning the domains (*len*) still continued. The development of domestic loans follows the rise in extraordinary taxes after 1517 to reach a maximum of 44,445 marks in 1520. No domestic loans were obtained in the years 1522–3 (Figure 12). In addition to the domestic loans, the Danish king could resort to foreign credit. The revenues of Schleswig and Holstein, where the king reigned as a duke, in principle were to be used only in the duchies. The finances of Denmark and the duchies were linked, in reality, by means of a money market, the so-called *Kieler Umschlag*. This took place every year in February in the town of Kiel, near the southern border, close to the rich towns of Lübeck and Hamburg. To this market the king directed money from the Schleswig–Holstein domains (*Ämter*) in order to pay off loans, interest on payments and money owed to merchants. Impressive sums of money passed through this mechanism of financial exchange. A surviving account of 1518 shows that the royal agent of the *Umschlag* disposed of 21,000 Lübeck marks (corresponding to twice the amount in Danish marks), which had been paid by four Schleswig–Holstein officers of the domains and from the town of Lübeck.[30] Nearly the whole amount was paid out again to creditors, who included the king's uncle, Duke Frederick of Schleswig–Holstein, clergy and rich magnates of Schleswig and Holstein, plus some merchants of Lübeck. On his way home from Kiel, the royal agent brought 3,200 Lübeck marks with him, which were personally delivered to the king in the monastery of Sorø on Zealand. As the expenses of the war rose, less and less revenue could be extracted by the central administration from the surplus of the duchies. In 1521, after payments to Lübeck merchants for cannon, nothing was left of the 17,692 Lübeck marks which the royal secretary Anders Glob had at his disposal in Kiel. Under such circumstances new loans were necessary. In 1520, the secretary had to borrow 5,957 Lübeck

[30] Galster (1944–53), 148–56.

marks on the *Umschlag* directly for the king's central administration.[31] A loan of 22,335 Danish marks raised in 1522 from Danish and German merchants in Stockholm was quite exceptional. Normally the only road to foreign credit went through Kiel.

The effort of Christian II was in vain, but his war economy may be regarded as the shock treatment from which the early modern state emerged in Scandinavia. Two separate monarchies grew out of the former union of three states, and in the years *c.*1523–40 important financial reforms were carried through both in Denmark and in Sweden; these reforms made it possible to transfer much larger resources to the central administration. At first, the developments took place in parallel. Both in Sweden and in Denmark the kings succeeded, in the name of Lutheranism, in taking over the lands of the church and decisively increasing the size of the royal domains, in the years 1527 and 1536 respectively.[32] Initially, both Denmark and Sweden tried to organize their armies after the Continental practice, that is, using mercenaries: they therefore had to raise the money to pay these troops. In both countries during the 1520s a number of extraordinary taxes were collected and the mint was severely exploited. From around 1530 there was

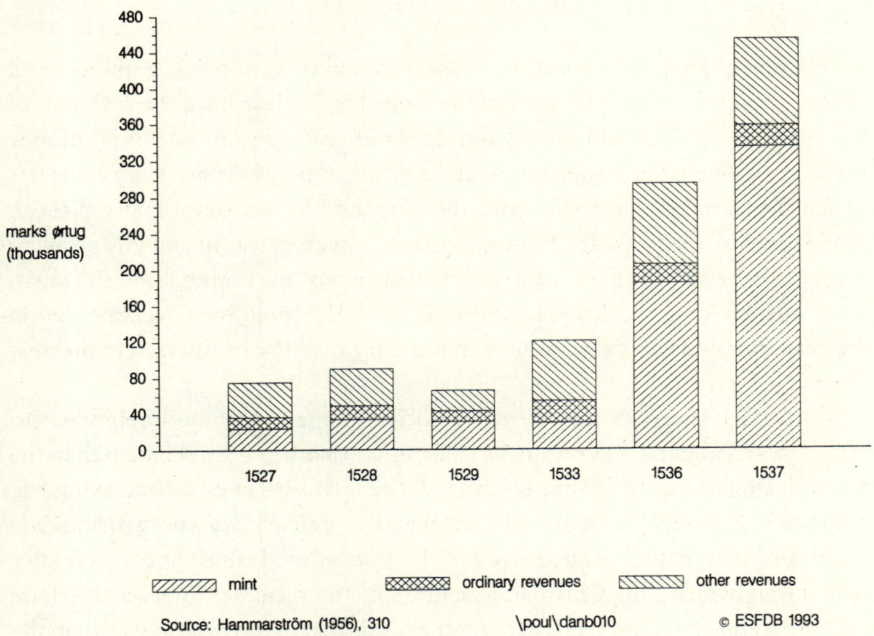

FIG. 13. Revenues of the Swedish royal chamber, 1527–1537 (in *ørtug* marks)

[31] Suhm (1792), 361. [32] Cf. Petersen and Jespersen (1987).

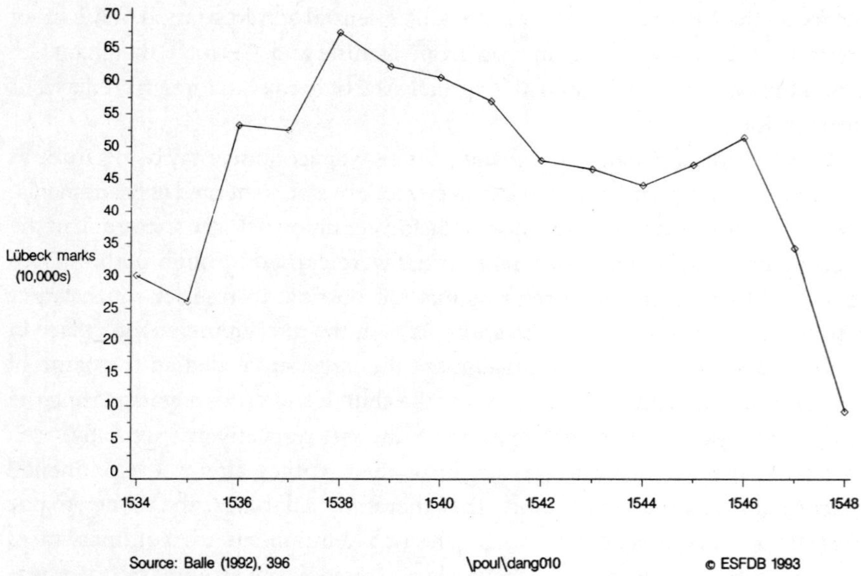

FIG. 14. Total debt of the Danish king, 1534–1548 (in Lübeck marks)

a tendency in Sweden towards the concentration of all income in money and silver within the central chamber of the king. This is clear from the revenues of the chamber in silver and money during these years (Figure 13).[33] The money was derived from goods sold locally in the domains (*fogederierne*), from contracts which the local officials made with the king, and from extraordinary taxes in money paid by the peasants. Most important, however, was the rapidly growing revenue of the silver mine of Sala, which made it possible for the Swedish king to accumulate a large surplus. The revenues from the mine were so large that in 1538 a surplus of more than a million marks *ørtug* could be transferred to the next year.

The Danish king, too, tried to raise sufficient money to pay his foreign troops, but he lacked mineral deposits in his lands, and to a much greater extent than the Swedish king he had to finance his expenditure by means of credit and extraordinary taxes. The movement of credit and the extraordinary taxes used to liquidate it can be documented for the period of the War of the Danish Succession after 1534, during which King Christian III had to buy mercenaries in order to secure the Danish throne (Figure 14).[34] It becomes clear that in the 1530s and even in the 1540s substantial loans were a heavy burden on the Danish fiscal system; but with

33 ESFDB \poul\danb010 based on \dand025; Hammarström (1956), 310.

34 ESFDB\poul\dang010 based on \dand026; Balle (1992), 396.

the help of extraordinary taxes, they were largely paid off by the end of the 1540s. With the debt thus paid off the king could theoretically live as the magnates still wished, that is, from his ordinary revenues. This structure became characteristic of the Danish financial system until the early years of the seventeenth century. Only occasionally did the state become a tax state; in normal circumstances, it remained a domain state. This was the Danish solution to the military challenge of the sixteenth century. The Swedish solution was very different. At the beginning of the 1540s, Sweden experienced a dramatic shift in its financial policy. Taxes in kind were reintroduced, the recourse to mining was intensified, and warehouses were organized to store and to sell goods accumulated as revenues paid in kind on the domains. The revenues from the domains were in effect commercialized. Sweden turned away from a money economy because the government recognized that the nature of peasant society blocked the transformation to ordinary taxes in money.[35] Sweden, it seemed, in the long run would not be able to pay for its foreign mercenaries. Instead, the Swedish army was built upon native recruitment and with a form of payment adjusted to the finances of a natural economy: the soldiers were supported in kind and received only a relatively small salary; in times of war, they received larger monthly payments. The revenues of the Swedish state from the sale of natural products from the domains increased during the late sixteenth century and in the seventeenth century, and the military system of domestic recruitment was preserved.

Sweden and Denmark thus followed very different forms of military mobilization. Although the largest item of expenditure in both states was war, the development of the two fiscal systems was dissimilar.[36] In Denmark the military forces until 1600 and beyond consisted of expensive professional armies, which could only be paid for by extraordinary taxes. In Sweden, the country's own conscripts were used, and such men were cheap. Furthermore, the Swedish financial system used the resources of the domain economy more effectively so that by the year 1630 the state revenues amounted to the equivalent of 1.2 million *Reichstaler*, or twice the level of those of Denmark.[37] The advantage gained by the more effective use of the state's natural resources became evident in the seventeenth century, when Swedish armies were victorious on the European battlefields, while the structural crisis which showed up in the Danish fiscal system resulted in defeat, first in Germany in 1629 and then against Sweden in 1645, 1658 and 1660. The result was that the whole domain structure was overthrown with the introduction of the new system of absolute monarchy in

[35] Odén (1966, 1967). [36] Krüger in Repgen (1988). [37] Krüger (1988).

1660.[38] If the fiscal development leading to the establishment of the early modern kingdoms of Scandinavia can be summarized in a few words, it may be argued that some adjustment towards the model of central European states became decisive for their survival. However, the success of the Swedish model demonstrates that great gains were to be made by a state following its own path, and turning the shortcomings of a natural economy to its own advantage.

[38] Petersen (1975).

CHAPTER 5

The West European Monarchies in the Later Middle Ages

W. M. Ormrod

It is widely acknowledged that 'modern' fiscal systems can be said to have emerged at the point when the 'private' resources of the ruling power were exceeded in value by the 'public' revenues derived from a system of general taxation. In the European context, this is normally expressed as the transition from the 'domain state' (*fiscalité féodale*) to the 'tax state' (*fiscalité d'État*). Several generations of scholars have identified the first signs of the transition in thirteenth- and fourteenth-century England and France; indeed, Jean-Philippe Genet has used the example of these two realms between 1290 and 1360 to create a model not only for the fiscal, but also the political, juridical and cultural development of the early modern state.[1] In a specifically fiscal context, it must be emphasized that the example of the centralizing monarchy extending its range and developing new modes of extraction provided only one of the possible avenues for state development in late medieval Europe: some of the alternatives are discussed in other chapters of this volume. However, the present contribution aims not so much to challenge the model developed by Genet and others, but to test its validity over a rather wider geographical range and in a more precise statistical context than has hitherto been attempted. For this purpose the kingdom of Castile has been chosen to act as a third example alongside those of England and France, and the chronological scope has been extended to cover the period from *c.*1250 to *c.*1500.

5.1 *The Forces for Change*

Between the mid-thirteenth and the late fourteenth centuries there were distinct signs of change in the fiscal systems of England, France and Castile. The dynamic forces behind such change were many and various. The economic and demo-

[1] Genet (1990), 261–81.

graphic expansion of the central Middle Ages reached its high point around 1250 and created unprecedented sources of wealth, while the commercial revolution of the thirteenth century made it easier to tap that wealth by transforming a predominantly agrarian economy into one based on markets, money and credit. The dissemination of Aristotelian ideas greatly altered perceptions of political power, stressing the legitimacy and authority of rulers and creating new concepts of consent which found tangible expression in universal taxes granted by newly evolving representative institutions. The growth of administration, represented by a significant increase in record-keeping throughout west and southern Europe, also created important new opportunities for the implementation of royal authority and the effective management of the resources of the state. In an age of growth, the growth of fiscal resources was almost inevitable.

Above all, fiscal systems owed their development to the financial pressures arising from a policy of dynastic and territorial aggrandizement. In 1255, Henry III of England made a deal with the Papacy to secure the succession of his younger son, Edmund, to the kingdom of Sicily. In 1257, Henry's brother, Richard of Cornwall, was elected King of the Romans and thus became prospective Emperor. Edmund and Richard had no chance of establishing themselves in their new titles unless Henry was prepared to divert large sums out of his own revenues to support their enterprises. Richard's election was contested by Alfonso X of Castile, who, notwithstanding his already considerable military involvement against the Moors, promptly embarked on a twenty-year programme of expensive diplomacy and war in an attempt to secure the Imperial title for himself. In the 1290s, trouble also flared between France and England over the feudal status of the Plantagenet-held duchy of Aquitaine. By this stage, Edward I was already involved in a series of disputes in the British Isles arising out of his contested suzerainty over Wales and Scotland. In the early fourteenth century, the scale of this military activity extended still further. The Anglo-Scottish wars rumbled on more or less continuously for the first fifty years of the century, and the renewed conflict between Edward III of England and Philip VI of France precipitated the outbreak of the so-called Hundred Years' War in 1337. Under Alfonso XI, the kingdom of Castile become involved in heavy military commitments against the Moors of Granada and Morocco. No sooner had these campaigns begun to bear fruit than a devastating civil war broke out between Pedro I and his eventual usurper, Enrique II. Indeed, the Castilian succession crisis proved the real centre of west European military activity in the third quarter of the fourteenth century, as the two sides vied for support from the major powers of England and France. Meanwhile, the application of crusading conditions to wars not merely against the infidel but also against pagans, heretics and schismatic Christians provided moral justification and spiritual inducements for an increasing number of military enterprises launched by, and sometimes between, the kingdoms and principalities of western Europe. If medieval society was organized primarily for war, then it was from the late thirteenth century that it surely found the greatest opportunities for expressing its militaristic ethos.

War was expensive. The decline of feudal military organization meant the rise first of conscript forces and then of contract armies, whose members had to be paid, fed, clothed and armed by the state.[2] This change was already under way in France and England when Louis IX and the future Edward I drew up plans for their projected crusade in 1269, and it was fully instated by the time Edward III launched his multiple campaigns against Philip VI through Aquitaine, Brittany and Normandy in the 1340s. The Castilian military system underwent a fundamental change when many mercenary soldiers previously engaged in the Anglo-French dispute offered their services in the war of succession. Furthermore, the kings of Castile had already extended the range of their military obligations by enlarging their naval forces in the late thirteenth and early fourteenth centuries. All this necessitated a huge increase in spending. The cost of wages and compensation for lost horses during Edward I's war against Philip IV in 1294–8 was some £249,000, or over £62,000 a year; yet just a decade before the start of this war Edward's ordinary revenue had been calculated at not more than £27,000.[3] In 1315, the Castilian *Cortes* estimated the king's revenues, minus certain frontier profits, at 1.6 million *maravedís*, but calculated that an additional 8 million *maravedís* was needed to cover all his expenses.[4]

Confronted with such huge demands for cash, the states of western Europe had two options: to exploit their existing fiscal systems more fully, or to develop fundamentally new forms of revenue. Inevitably, the result was usually a compromise between the two. A large-scale military enterprise was not always the best context in which to carry through a radical fiscal reform: indeed, the administrative burdens of war, coupled with the need for political support at home, could in the short term at least act as a real disincentive to fiscal development.[5] Throughout the first half of the fourteenth century as much effort was often put into the revival and extension of traditional revenues as into the evolution of new ones: witness the resurrection of fiscal feudalism in England during the first half of the fourteenth century and the periodic attempts made in both England and France to increase the profits of justice by encouraging individuals and communities to buy their release from royal commissions

[2] Contamine (1984), 90–101, 150–65; Housley (1992), 421–56.

[3] Vale (1990), 281–2; Mills (1925).

[4] MacKay (1977), 103–4.

[5] Ormrod (1991*b*).

of inquiry.[6] In England and Castile, the representative assemblies tried to buy off some of the more controversial royal prerogatives by offering substitute taxes.[7] In other cases, however, traditional rights could still account for a very significant proportion of royal revenue. The most obvious example is the manipulation of the coinage, which in 1349 accounted for a remarkable 70 per cent of the receipts of the French royal Treasury.[8] If the western monarchies did indeed undergo a fiscal revolution in the late thirteenth and fourteenth centuries, then it was a revolution characterized by a high degree of continuity.

Although war was the continuum in which this revolution occurred, the actual catalyst of more radical change was sometimes—and rather ironically—the making of peace. International diplomacy was a highly expensive affair in the later Middle Ages. Alliances very often depended on the payment of large subsidies: in 1255, Henry III of England had to promise the Pope over £90,000 to have his son recognized as king of Sicily, and Edward I paid out over £142,000 in subsidies to his allies in the Low Countries during the Anglo-French war of 1294–8.[9] Above all, the indemnities and ransoms charged as condition of peace grew to prodigious proportions: witness, for instance, the compensation demanded by Charles IV of France as the price of peace with England in 1327 and the large sums extracted in turn by the English crown from the kingdom of Scotland and the duchy of Burgundy in 1328 and 1359.[10] In particular, the ransom charged for the release of Richard I of England in 1193–4 clearly set a trend taken up again during the period of the Hundred Years' War: in the treaties of Berwick (1357) and Brétigny (1360), Edward III of England set ransoms of £66,700 and £500,000 for the release of David II of Scotland and John II of France respectively; and, in 1388, Edward's younger son, John of Gaunt, was able to extract compensation of £100,000 and a life pension on agreeing to abandon his claim to the Castilian throne.[11] Not all royal ransoms created fiscal emergencies: the 200,000 *livres tournois* required for the release of Louis IX and his crusading army after their defeat at Mansourah in 1250 represented only a modest part of the total cost of the campaign; and the economic impact even of a large ransom demand such as that for David II of Scotland could be cushioned by an agreement that it would be paid in instalments and by the fact that later payments were often remitted or fell into abeyance.[12] But in some cases the combined psychological and financial

[6] Harriss (1975), 401–16; Crook (1982); Hadwin (1981); Henneman (1968*b*).
[7] Harriss (1975), 356–419; Ladero Quesada (1973), 220; MacKay (1988), 381–2.
[8] Miskimin (1963), 43.
[9] Fryde (1962), 1170; Powicke (1947), i, 371.
[10] Sumption (1990), 102; Grant (1984), 17; Harriss (1975), 491.
[11] Harriss (1975), 490, 493; Russell (1955), 505–6.
[12] Jordan (1979), 65–104; Grant (1984), 37–8.

shock of losing and ransoming a king was sufficient to move the state to radical action. Just as the ransom of Richard I had allowed the English government to adopt new and unprecedentedly burdensome fiscal measures at the end of the twelfth century, so too did the ransom of John II help precipitate fundamental changes in the theory and practice of public taxation in the kingdom of France.[13]

5.2 *The Symptoms of Change*

The first sign of real change in the fiscal structures of the western monarchies was a notable increase in borrowing. Prior to the end of the thirteenth century, the credit systems of all three states under discussion here were fairly primitive, based largely around dealings with the Jews. But in the second half of the thirteenth century the Italian merchant bankers began to establish themselves in the principal economic centres of western and northern Europe.[14] The Franzesi brothers, 'Biche' and 'Mouche', began working for Philip IV of France in 1289 and by the early 1290s had become the single most important lenders to the French state. In 1294, they raised and lent about 200,000 *livres tournois* to the Capetian monarchy.[15] In Castile, too, there was a substantial increase in royal borrowing during the reigns of Ferdinand IV and Alfonso XI: in 1309, a group of Genoese merchants lent the crown the equivalent of 239,000 *maravedís* in money and merchandise.[16] But the development of credit was probably most marked in England.[17] In 1275, Edward I institutionalized his relationship with the Ricciardi of Florence by granting them the profits of a new customs duty as security for loans, and between 1272 and 1294 this company lent the English crown a remarkable total of £307,000. In the first decade of the fourteenth century, the Frescobaldi of Florence took the place of the Ricciardi, and by the 1330s Edward III's principal financiers were the Bardi and Peruzzi. Unfortunately, the Plantagenets had a strong tendency to borrow beyond their means, and the enormous debts built up during the early stages of the Hundred Years' War led to the collapse of the Peruzzi in 1343 and the Bardi in 1346. Thereafter, Italian bankers had little part to play in royal credit dealings until the Medici began lending to Edward IV in the later fifteenth century; even then, the scale of such transactions was a good deal more modest than in the time of Edward III. In France, too, the Italian ascendancy was brief: Philip VI concentrated less on courting the Italian merchants trading in his realm and more on taxing them.[18]

[13] Henneman (1976). [14] Fryde and Fryde (1963). [15] Strayer (1980), 150.
[16] Menjot (1987), 165. [17] For a convenient summary: Kaeuper (1988), 42–52.
[18] Henneman (1969).

So long as war continued, however, so did borrowing; and the second half of the fourteenth century witnessed an interesting change as the crowns of England and France turned increasingly to their own wealthy subjects—prelates, nobles and merchants—for supplies of cash.[19] Most of these loans were voluntary, and lenders were persuaded to co-operate with the crown out of a mixture of personal loyalty to the king and the hope of commercial profit: thus the large-scale lending of the earls of Arundel and of Cardinal Beaufort in fourteenth- and fifteenth-century England.[20] Forced loans were more controversial: one of the accusations made against Richard II of England at his deposition in 1399 was that he had forcibly extracted loans from his subjects with no intention of reimbursing them; and the political crises of Charles VI's reign in France arose in part from frequent demands for this type of substitute taxation.[21] In theory, almost all loans were short-term: that is, they had to be repaid in full, with or without interest, within a fairly short period of time. This put tremendous pressure on resources: the dismembering of the crown jewels by Edward III of England and later by Charles VI of France in order to provide security or repayment for loans is a dramatic indication of the desperate financial situation into which late medieval governments could be driven by the demands of their creditors. In the absence of long-term credit structures, then, medieval states could only continue to raise loans if they had large, reliable and easily realizable assets out of which their creditors could be repaid. This challenge proved to be one of the most important factors in stimulating the development of taxation.

5.3 *The Evolution of Direct Taxation*

In an attempt to explain the origins of direct taxation, historians have divided into two exclusive and sometimes hostile camps: those who see universal taxation as a natural extension of the feudal rights of medieval monarchs, and those who argue that general levies arose out of the new application of the Roman and canon law principle of 'urgent necessity' which obliged all subjects to assist their rulers in times of emergency.[22] In fact, it is reasonably easy to reconcile these two competing interpretations. Viewed in a pragmatic way, the ability of later medieval kings to extract general levies from their subjects can be said to have

[19] Fryde and Fryde (1963), 465, 485.

[20] Given-Wilson (1991); Harriss (1988), 401–6.

[21] Fryde and Fryde (1963), 465–6, 485–6.

[22] Compare Mitchell (1951), 156–325, with Post (1964), 241–309. For a more recent debate in the English context compare Harriss (1975), 3–26, and Prestwich (1990), 109–28. Henneman (1971), 17–27; Henneman (1976), 10–17, 283–90, notes the gap between political theory and political institutions in France at least prior to the 1350s. That is not to say that other philosophical maxims and political ideas were not present in the fiscal procedures of the French monarchy: e.g. Brown (1972, 1973).

depended on two main factors. Firstly, there was the degree of political and jurisdictional power wielded by the monarchy over the classes of society beyond its immediate feudal tenants, the geographical areas outside the royal domain, and the principal sources of wealth within the national economy. Secondly, there was the question of whether or not the polity enjoyed a tradition of consultation and consent and whether or not there existed an assembly, preferably containing a representative element, which could judge the king's appeals for money and authorize general taxes. Irrespective of its philosophical basis, the concept of necessity was obviously a great deal easier to implement if the state had a strong central authority and a single powerful institution capable of making decisions binding on the whole realm: the problems of imposing and collecting taxes in the later medieval Empire, discussed in an earlier chapter (Chapter 2.8), provide an obvious illustration of this point. In this context, too, it becomes easy to understand why direct taxation should have occurred earlier and developed faster in the kingdoms of Castile and England than it did in France.

As early as 1188, the *Cortes* of Castile had included not only members of the ecclesiastical hierarchy and the secular nobility but also elected representatives of the towns, and in the later thirteenth century this body emerged as the sole authorizing agency for extraordinary taxes paid to the king.[23] It was in the *Cortes* of 1269 that the nobility first agreed to the imposition of royal taxation on their dependents by authorizing six *monedas* to support Alfonso X's wars against the Moors. Five year later, the representatives of the towns consented to a similar subsidy of two *monedas*, and in 1277 the *Cortes* granted Alfonso X one *moneda* every year for the rest of his life. These levies operated as repartition taxes: the king and council decided the amount of money needed, and, after securing the consent of the *Cortes*, imposed quotas on each region of the country. Statistics are generally lacking in these early years, but it is known that a special levy made by the regent, Maria of Molina, in 1297, raised 1.5 million *maravedís*. Direct taxes of this kind continued to be an important source of income for the Castilian state throughout the later Middle Ages.

The chronology of English taxation is similar, though the details are markedly different.[24] The exact nature of the assemblies that authorized direct taxes before 1290 is obscure, but from that date onwards there is no doubt that every subsidy on movable property was granted in a Parliament containing at least some elected representatives of the community. Although direct taxation became a great deal more frequent after 1290, each subsidy taken until 1332 continued to be followed by a new, centrally administered, assessment of taxable goods: the idea of a repartition tax was not taken up in England at this stage. The categories of

[23] The following depends largely on O'Callaghan (1971); Menjot (1987).

[24] The standard work is Willard (1934).

property that were assessed remained broadly the same in each successive levy (chiefly livestock and grain in the countryside and merchandise and domestic goods in the towns), but the resulting tax base could vary dramatically. It was partly to counteract an alarming downward spiral in valuations that the crown adopted a new method of assessment in 1334, negotiating block payments with each town and village and leaving the task of assessment and collection to each community. This experiment proved politically and administratively successful, and the quotas were reused, with modifications, for every subsequent 'fifteenth and tenth' (as these taxes were known) between the fourteenth and the seventeenth centuries. Because the value of the tax was fixed, the crown could calculate income with some confidence and assign a considerable proportion of the subsidy to its creditors in advance of payment. But the system adopted after 1334 also exposed a weakness in the late medieval English state. Every attempt in the later fourteenth and fifteenth centuries to carry out a new assessment or to create a broader tax base was treated as an exceptional case, and no supplementary or alternative system of regular taxation was devised to reflect the redistribution of wealth that occurred in the generations after the Black Death.

It was the political and administrative problem of assessing the tax base, compounded by the absence of a central representative assembly capable of voting subsidies on the whole realm, that undoubtedly explained the early problems experienced by the French state in its attempts to set up a tax system comparable to those emerging in Castile and England. To some extent also, the slow development of universal taxation was a reflection of the existing wealth of the French monarchy. The geographical expansion and more intensive management of the royal domain which had been such a feature of the reign of Philip II continued during the thirteenth century so that by 1290 the annual ordinary revenues of the crown stood at approximately 450,000 *livres tournois*.[25] Admittedly, the crusade of Louis IX in 1248–54 was a considerable financial burden, costing an estimated 1.5 million *livres tournois*, and necessitating not only the fuller exploitation of occasional ordinary revenues from the Jews and the towns but also the imposition of extraordinary levies on certain categories of persons and occupations.[26] The special and temporary nature of Louis's crusade and subsequent ransom, however, meant that these tentative steps towards a more organized system of direct taxation were not yet recognized as powerful precedents. In the 1290s, Philip IV seemed about to institute a more ambitious and coherent system of public taxation by imposing taxes on personal property at the

[25] Favier (1978), 185. [26] Jordan (1979), 65–104.

rate of a hundredth in 1295, a fiftieth in 1296 and another fiftieth in 1297. An estimate of *c.*1296 put the profits of the hundredth in Languedoc alone at 315,000 *livres tournois*; and a similar subsidy in 1304 has been estimated to have raised a remarkable 735,000 *livres tournois*.[27] Nevertheless, it is striking that Philip and his immediate successors found it very difficult to repeat these general levies. The failure of the central representative institution, the Estates General, to develop into a taxative body proved a serious setback, and there was still no properly co-ordinated system for the authorization of taxes at the start of the Hundred Years' War. It is significant that the one notable financial intervention by the Estates General—the attempt in 1347 to impose fixed quotas for the payment of armed forces and to allow localities to develop their own system of raising the money—collapsed in the administrative chaos brought on by the Black Death of 1347–50. The ability of the English state to ride out that particular emergency and maintain its fiscal system virtually intact provides a revealing insight into the relative strengths and weaknesses of the two systems.[28]

The significant breakthrough in French taxation came only after 1357, when the security of the state was threatened first by the capture of the king, John II, at the battle of Poitiers, and then by the bands of brigands demobilized from French and English armies after the Treaties of Brétigny and Calais of 1360.[29] For the first time, *fouages* (repartition taxes calculated on the basis of mostly outdated lists of hearths and apportioned and collected as best suited the locality) began to be levied annually for the purposes of defence. This inevitably aroused a good deal of opposition, and Charles V officially abolished such levies on his deathbed in 1380. In the mid-1380s, however, direct taxation was revived in the form of the *taille*, originally an indirect levy but soon applied on the same basis as the former *fouages*. After various flirtations with the Estates General in the early fifteenth century, Charles VII finally assumed the right to impose the *taille* on his own authority and levied it as a permanent charge after 1440, using the profits to build up the first French standing army. The high degree of provincial autonomy and the deeply ingrained nature of local custom and privilege had delayed the development of a general form of direct taxation in France until roughly a century after its emergence in the kingdoms of Castile and England; but once established, the *taille* was to be one of the mightiest instruments of royal power known in fifteenth-century Europe.

27 Strayer (1980), 149–50.

28 Compare Henneman (1968*a*) and Ormrod (1986).

29 Henneman (1976), 84–311.

5.4 *The Church and Taxation*

The history of royal taxation of the clergy follows a rather more even course in the three realms under discussion here.[30] In each case, levies on the church grew out of the periodic crusading taxes ordered from the clergy by the Papacy since the late twelfth century. The extension of the concept of the crusade to cover a number of religious, racial and political wars within Europe during the thirteenth and fourteenth centuries encouraged successive Popes to allocate the profits of these clerical taxes for the use of secular rulers: indeed, the appropriation of crusading tenths was merely part of the larger process by which later medieval states came to control the recruitment, organization and leadership of crusading armies. There were particularly important developments in the pontificate of Innocent IV (1243–54). In 1247, Innocent granted the *tercias*, representing two-ninths of the ecclesiastical tithe, to the Castilian crown for the purpose of fighting the Muslims of southern Spain. It was with Innocent's consent that Louis IX also raised the remarkable sum of 950,000 *livres tournois* from the French clergy for the costs of his crusade. Finally, in 1254, Innocent promised the profits of three crusading tenths on clerical income to Henry III of England in order to pay for the latter's campaigns in Sicily. In Castile, the *tercias* was at first seen as an alternative to the appropriation of crusading taxes, but in 1265 Clement IV followed his predecessor's example and granted Alfonso X a crusading tax to run in conjunction with the *tercias*.

It was a short but highly significant step from this practice to the direct negotiation between kings and their clerical subjects for financial assistance. This naturally occurred first in the crusading state of Castile: in 1255, Alfonso X asked the clergy for a *servicio*, and in 1291 Sancho IV raised a forced 'gift' of 1,400,000 *maravedis* from the church in his realm. Already in 1280, 1283, 1286 and 1290, however, Edward I of England had managed to extract subsidies directly from the English clergy with no reference to the crusade but on the very different and more contentious grounds that the clergy should contribute directly to the defence of the realm. The really decisive turning point in this respect came during the Anglo-French hostilities of 1294–8, when both Edward I and Philip IV attempted to impose direct taxes on the clergy of their realms specifically to pay for their war over Gascony. Philip contented himself with the conventional tenth part of clerical incomes, but Edward increased the rate to an unprecedented half ('moiety') in 1294, raising about £80,000 by such means. The Fourth Lateran Council had specifically forbidden the clergy to pay any tax or gift to the secular power without Papal permission, and in 1296 Boniface VIII tried to enforce this

[30] The large bibliography on England and France is usefully summarized in Green (1988). For Castile: Linehan (1971); Menjot (1987), 164–5. For a wider discussion: Housley (1992), 427–50.

decree through the bull *Clericis laicos*. But Boniface's stand against the power of the state proved a fiasco, and under his successor Clement V (1305–14) the Papacy not only allowed direct royal taxation of the clergy but also conceded crusading taxes which were themselves channelled into paying for the escalating warfare in western Europe. The Avignon Papacy continued to co-operate with the Valois monarchy after the opening of hostilities with England, and from 1337 clerical tenths became virtually annual exactions in France, the crusading ideal now being little more than a sham. In England, all such pretence was dropped after the quadrennial crusading tenth of 1330; thereafter all taxes were negotiated directly with the clergy meeting in their own representative institutions and judging the king's requests for money purely on the basis of national security.

The fact that the clergy paid their own regular state taxes in each of the three western monarchies inevitably conditioned their attitude to other exactions and led to concerted (and sometimes successful) campaigns for clerical immunity from direct and indirect levies such as the subsidy on movables in England, the *taille* in France, and the *alcabala* in Castile.[31] Nevertheless, the formal or *de facto* assumption of secular control over the taxation of the clergy represents one of the most remarkable and significant steps towards the decline of the church and the primacy of the state in the political life of later medieval Europe.

5.5 *Indirect Taxation*

It was the crown of Castile that seems to have led the way in the development of indirect taxation during the later thirteenth and fourteenth centuries.[32] Customs duties formed a long-standing element in the permanent ordinary revenue of the Castilian state, but it was in 1268 that Alfonso X regularized the system and established an *ad valorem* tax of 10 per cent on a wide range of exports. This was originally designed as a protectionist measure, and the customs provided a comparatively small part of royal revenues, standing at about 10 per cent of ordinary receipts by the first half of the fifteenth century. Other minor levies included the profits of the royal monopoly on salt, formally established by Alfonso XI in 1338, and the *servicio y montazgo*, a combination of older tolls on the movement and grazing of animals instituted from 1347. What really transformed the political economy of Castile, however, were the internal sales taxes imposed from the later thirteenth century. Picking up a precedent from municipal taxation, Alfonso X began to exact a 5 per cent sales tax in the towns. In 1294, Sancho IV imposed a levy of 1 per cent on all business and commercial transactions

[31] Denton (1980), 55–268; Lewis (1968), 171, 312; Ladero Quesada (1973), 65–6.

[32] Ladero Quesada (1973), 61–182.

called the *sisa*, and although this was dropped by the government during the minority of Ferdinand IV, it was subsequently revived.

It should be stressed that these early Castilian sales taxes were levied without the consent of the *Cortes*: here, as indeed in France and England, indirect taxation did not originally fall within the scope of representative institutions. On the other hand, the co-operation of the political community was of obvious importance in the establishment of any fiscal novelty, and it was perhaps with this practical consideration in mind that Alfonso XI appealed to the *Cortes* in 1342 to authorize a new sales tax—the *alcabala*—at a rate of 3.33 per cent for three successive years. This was successively renewed for fixed periods by a number of subsequent assemblies, and by the later fourteenth century the rate had risen to 10 per cent. But the period of parliamentary control proved fairly brief: from *c*.1400, the Castilian crown no longer considered consent to be necessary and thereafter collected the *alcabala* on its own authority as a permanent and integral part of state revenue. In theory, everyone was liable to pay the *alcabala*, including the nobility and clergy, but in practice the tax undoubtedly bore most heavily on townspeople. In this respect, it reflected the importance of the urban centres in the economy of later medieval Castile and provides an important example of the ability of the late medieval state to identify and exploit available sources of wealth.

In France, the story of indirect taxation really begins with the establishment of the customs system in 1277.[33] The original intention behind this was to protect the internal economy by banning exports of certain commodities; but the sale of export licences proved profitable to the crown, and in 1324 a new *ad valorem* tax of 4 *deniers* per *livre* (known as the *droit de rève*) was introduced alongside the older tolls based around the licensing system (the *haut-passage*). This two-tiered structure was simplified as part of the administrative campaign to raise the ransom of John II, and a single *imposition foraine*, an *ad valorem* tax of 5 per cent, was established on exports. Nevertheless, the absence of duties on imports, and the fact that France had no particularly valuable export commodities, meant that the customs were of little financial significance.

Much more important in France, as in Castile, were internal sales taxes. In the first half of the fourteenth century, direct subsidies were often commuted into excise duties in northern France, and in 1360 it was decided to extend this practice into a general imposition, the *aide*, to help pay the ransom of John II. Levied at the rate of 8 per cent (later rising to 25 per cent) on wine sales, and 5 per cent on all other commodities, the *aides* were collected almost continuously until 1417 and again after 1436. Although Languedoc still preferred to pay direct taxes, the

[33] Strayer (1971), 232–8; Henneman (1988).

southern estates finally agreed in 1443 to replace the *aide* with an *équivalent*, a lump sum of 83,000 *livres tournois* per annum to be raised at least in part by sales taxes. The final and most famous of the French indirect levies was the *gabelle*. In 1341, Philip VI established a royal monopoly on salt throughout the realm: anyone wishing to deal in salt would in future have to buy it from the king. This assertion of royal power proved controversial, and the monopoly was withdrawn in 1346–7; but it was reinstated in 1358 and was used to raise money for the release of John II after 1362. Thereafter its history runs in parallel with the *aides*.

The kingdom of England came rather slowly to a full appreciation of its capacity to raise indirect taxation. Although there were experiments with a centrally co-ordinated customs system in the early years of the thirteenth century, the crown continued to rely heavily on the system of direct taxation at least until the middle of Edward III's reign. Internal sales taxes never developed in medieval England, and it was on the basis of England's great export commodity, wool, that the monarchy eventually came to base its system of indirect taxation.[34] In 1275, Edward I negotiated the so-called 'ancient custom' with a group of merchants: this was a levy of 6*s*. 8*d*. on every sack of wool exported from the country. In 1303 and 1347, the range of goods was extended to include cloth, wine and general merchandise, with an additional levy of 3*s*. 4*d*. per sack being paid by all aliens on the export of English wool. As in Castile and France, these customs duties were permanent levies collected on the king's authority: although they were originally negotiated with groups of merchants and magnates, they required no further authorization, even on the accession of a new monarch.

A clear distinction needs to be drawn between these comparatively modest charges and the much heavier subsidies imposed on English overseas trade specifically to support wartime expenditure. In 1294, Edward I imposed a surcharge of £1 13*s*. 4*d*. on each sack of wool exported from England in order to pay for his war against Philip IV. The combined customs and subsidies represented approximately 40 per cent of the sale price of wool on the domestic market and not surprisingly raised a storm of protest which forced Edward to rescind the levy in 1297. The experiment was not fully revived until the opening stages of the Hundred Years' War, when a series of extraordinary subsidies on wool exports was negotiated by Edward III, first with the merchant community and then with Parliament itself. In 1342, the subsidy was set at £2 per sack, and was collected at this rate in a series of interlocking grants for the following twenty years. Finally, in 1362 Parliament agreed to the continuation of the wool subsidy

[34] The large bibliography is summarized, with statistical apparatus, in Ormrod (1991*a*), 167–75.

during peacetime, albeit at a reduced rate. Whereas the Castilian *Cortes* lost control of the *alcabala*, the English Parliament retained formal control over the authorization of the wool subsidy.[35] The contrast should not perhaps be exaggerated, since the subsidy was never actually refused. Nevertheless, the continued control exercised by the representative institution is of great importance when we realize that the customs and subsidies on overseas trade formed the most valuable single source of royal revenue for every English king from Edward III to Henry VII.

5.6 *Towards a Quantitative Comparison*

Having surveyed the development of direct and indirect taxation in each of the three western monarchies that provide the focus for this chapter, we may now attempt to make some statistical comparisons of the fiscal structures of England, France and Castile at various points during the later Middle Ages. The nature of the surviving data means that a quantitative comparison has to be restricted largely to the revenue side of royal budgets: expenditure was never subject to the same types or degrees of accounting, and is extremely difficult to reconstruct in reliable detail for most of the states of later medieval Europe. Examining only one side of the budget inevitably raises certain problems, particularly since there is a strong temptation to use fluctuations in revenue as an index of the relative strength or weakness of a monarchy. In fact, the only true index is to be found in the relationship between revenue and expenditure. To what degree could the state realize the resources necessary to match its ambitions, and did it function in profit or deficit? Such questions can sometimes be answered impressionistically, but even in the case of England, where the fiscal data are the fullest, it is agonizingly difficult to produce an accurate guide to the supply and demand sides of royal finance.

Even if we restrict ourselves to revenue, there are still a large number of technical problems to be encountered in the interpretation of the fiscal records, and three particular qualifications need to be made about these records before proceeding to an analysis of the figures. Firstly, there is the discrepancy between the 'total' or gross revenue collected at the point of extraction and the 'realized' or net revenue that actually reached the central Treasury. In England, accounting techniques were developed in the first half of the fourteenth century to ensure that almost all income, whether or not expended locally, was recorded in the Exchequer; but in France, no such mechanisms were devised and the

[35] Harriss (1975), 420–49, 466–71; Edwards (1979), 19–23.

surviving Treasury records of the fourteenth century suggest an increasing—though by its very nature unquantifiable—degree of local expenditure.[36]

Secondly, we have to encounter the problem of expressing money of account in real terms. Dramatic and erratic inflation, and more occasionally deflation, was a regular phenomenon in the later Middle Ages, sometimes indeed provoked by the state's manipulation of the coinage.[37] While price and wage data exist for all three realms under discussion here, it is extremely difficult to create compatible or reliable indexes through which to express figures given in money of account. A similar problem emerges when one tries to construct a detailed index for all three kingdoms based on medieval exchange rates.[38] Consequently, the following discussion relies on the use of only one economic indicator, namely the expression of money of account in terms of its silver content. This provides the opportunity for rough-and-ready comparisons across time and space, but it should always be borne in mind that the conversion is a notional one, and that even quite significant changes in the weight of so-called 'heavy' currencies like English sterling tended to have less effect on the real value of the coin than did the debasement of 'light' currencies such as that of Castile.[39]

Thirdly, we face the considerable problem of categorizing receipts. In an earlier chapter, a distinction was made between ordinary revenues of a regular nature, ordinary revenues of an occasional nature, and extraordinary revenues (Chapter 2.4). In the west European states of the later Middle Ages, these three categories generally resolved into a binary system of ordinary and extraordinary revenues. However, the classification of particular receipts under these heads does not necessarily coincide perfectly with the conventional ideas of 'domain' and 'tax' revenues. On the one hand, there were certain taxes—such as the English customs and the Castilian *alcabala*—which became regular impositions collected on the authority of the king alone and which can therefore be comfortably accommodated into the ordinary revenues of the given state. On

[36] Ormrod (1991*b*); Henneman (1967), 295–6; Radding (1976). In the following statistical analyses relating to England, it should be particularly noted that voluntary loans are considered as a separate, independent form of revenue. In fact, of course, they had to be guaranteed against, and repaid out of, other forms of crown revenue, most usually taxation; as a result, certain incomes are technically counted twice. The justification for this methodology is that the data are intended to demonstrate total income on a year-to-year basis; the repayment of loans was a matter of expenditure, and is not discussed in detail here.

[37] Miskimin (1963); Miskimin (1984); MacKay (1981); Hatcher (1977), 52–4.

[38] For such an attempt, and the problems it raises: Spufford (1989), 291–3. The figures collected in Spufford (1986) would allow for the creation of an index expressing English and French fiscal data in Florentine florins, but equivalent figures for Castile are conspicuously lacking.

[39] Spufford (1989), 289–300. A further consideration to be borne in mind is that the standard of fineness itself varied between states: Munro (1972), 14 n. 10; MacKay (1981), 147; Spufford (1989), 218–24.

the other hand, there were certain occasional ordinary revenues imposed on the king's own authority which, if they grew to sufficient proportions and imposed sufficient burden, could be identified as forms of taxation. The outstanding example here is the exploitation of the king's monopoly over the mints. Thus in England, the crown made little out of this right, and the profits of minting can therefore be regarded as part of the domain receipts; whereas in France, seigniorage could be an important and often controversial form of income considered even by contemporaries as a form of taxation and is therefore categorized in the ensuing discussions as extraordinary revenue. Any system of classification is likely to be unsatisfactory in an era that generally lacked clear fiscal typologies of its own; and it seems much more appropriate to respond to the problem flexibly by treating each state, in each period, as a separate case.

5.7 *The Early Fourteenth Century*

Between 1322 and *c.*1340 a range of Treasury records relieves the usual poverty of the French data and allows us to reconstruct the fiscal system of the late Capetian and early Valois regimes with more than usual precision. Fortunately, this material coincides with the preliminary stages of the Hundred Years' War and, when set against the English evidence for the same years, provides a fairly solid foundation for a comparison of the two states on the eve of their greatest medieval power struggle.

Historians usually contrast the financial capabilities of these two states in the early fourteenth century, estimating English revenues at between a fifth and a third of French royal income.[40] The ordinary income of the French crown was certainly impressive, reflecting the size and wealth of the royal domain and the extensive feudal and regalian rights built up over some two centuries of Capetian growth. That strength was further enhanced by the Valois regime, as the data in Figure 15 make clear: ordinary revenue rose from a yearly average of 18 tonnes of fine silver in 1322–5 to over 26 tonnes in 1328–32, and the improvement was sustained, so far as the figures allow for precise analysis, throughout the 1330s.[41] In England, by contrast, crown lands and associated rights on their own yielded a gross income of only £15,000, or 5 tonnes of fine silver, per annum. Although the domain was swollen by the profits of a large number of confiscated estates in the 1320s, it is significant that the single most important element in the ordinary revenue of the crown during this period derived not from land or the profits of

[40] E.g. Kaeuper (1988), 62–3. Kaeuper, following the scheme in Henneman (1971), 350, includes the French crown's income from clerical tenths as ordinary revenue; in the present discussion it is taken as extraordinary revenue, using the alternative classifications in Henneman (1971), 348.

[41] ESFDB \orm\frmg004 based on \frmd001; Henneman (1971), 348, 350; for the multiplier: Munro (1972), 14 n. 10.

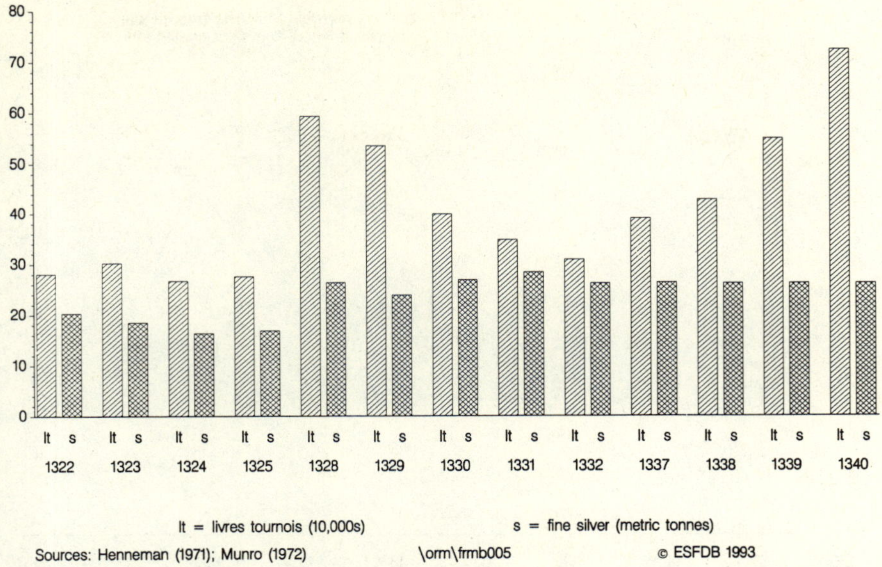

FIG. 15. Total French Treasury receipts from ordinary revenue, 1322–1340 (expressed in *livres tournois* and in metric tonnes of fine silver)

jurisdiction but from the customs duties levied on overseas trade. The notional totals expressed in Figure 16, representing an annual average of some 10 tonnes of fine silver, place England in a more favourable position *vis-à-vis* France than is usually calculated, but it should be stressed that a considerable proportion of the Plantagenets' ordinary revenue was taken up in standing charges and other incidental expenses and never reached the central Treasury.[42] So far, then, the traditional contrast is largely sustained.

This picture might be modified to some extent if we were to take into account the revenue which the English crown derived from its wider dominions in the British Isles and France. In the 1320s, these still yielded a gross total somewhere in excess of £20,000 (7 tonnes of fine silver) per annum, though a large, and increasing, proportion of this was again spent at source.[43] Given that the lion's share of that sum, and almost all the cash actually reaching the English Exchequer from the dependent territories, came from the holdings in southern France, the fiscal implications of the Anglo-French hostilities are also thrown into sharper relief. Indeed, the principal reason for the increase in the French crown's

[42] ESFDB \orm\engg029 based on \engd027, based on numerous sources cited there.

[43] This is a rough estimate based on the known data for the three largest parts of the remaining Plantagenet possessions, Wales, Ireland and Aquitaine, for which respectively: Fryde (1974); Richardson and Sayles (1962); Vale (1990), 142. Contemporaries classified the revenues from these colonies as ordinary receipts: Harriss (1975), 523–4.

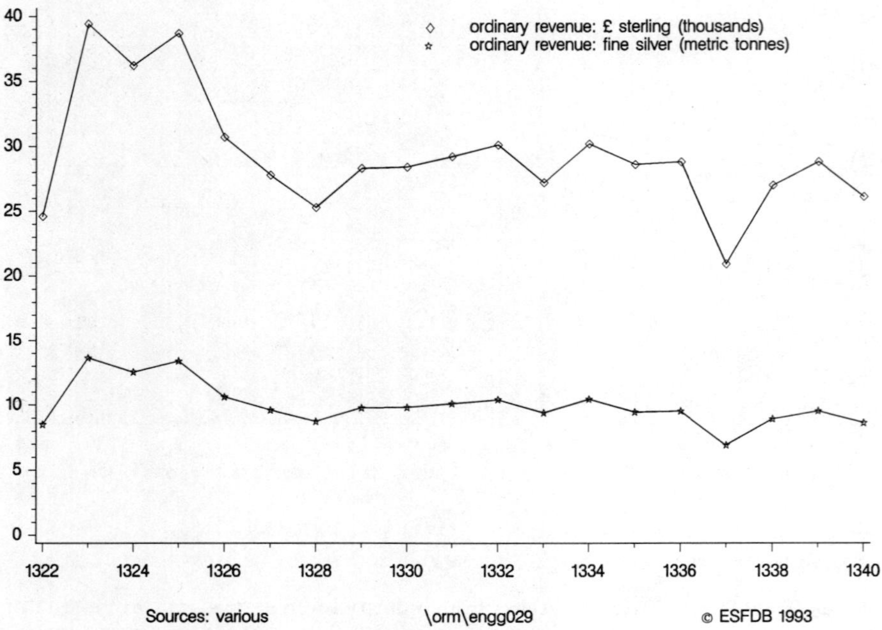

FIG. 16. Ordinary revenue of the English crown, 1322–1340 (expressed in £ sterling and in metric tonnes of fine silver)

ordinary revenue after the mid-1320s was the acquisition of large parts of greater Aquitaine by forfeiture from Edward II and III.[44] England's loss had thus become France's gain.

The principal difference between early fourteenth-century England and France, however, lay in the composition and relative importance of their extraordinary revenues. Figure 17 demonstrates the relative stability and equality in the relationship between ordinary and extraordinary receipts at the French Treasury between 1322 and 1340.[45] Across these years, indeed, ordinary receipts accounted for an average of 49.2 per cent, and extraordinary receipts for 50.8 per cent, of total income. The breakdown of extraordinary revenue for the years 1322–30, presented in Figure 18, demonstrates how this relative stability came about.[46] The majority of extraordinary receipts came not from general subsidies but from the raising of clerical tenths and from the full exercise of the royal prerogative demonstrated through the levying of communal and individual

[44] Henneman (1971), 308–9.

[45] ESFDB \orm\frmb004 based on \frmd002; Henneman (1971), 348, 350.

[46] ESFDB \orm\frmb001 based on \frmd003; Henneman (1971), 348.

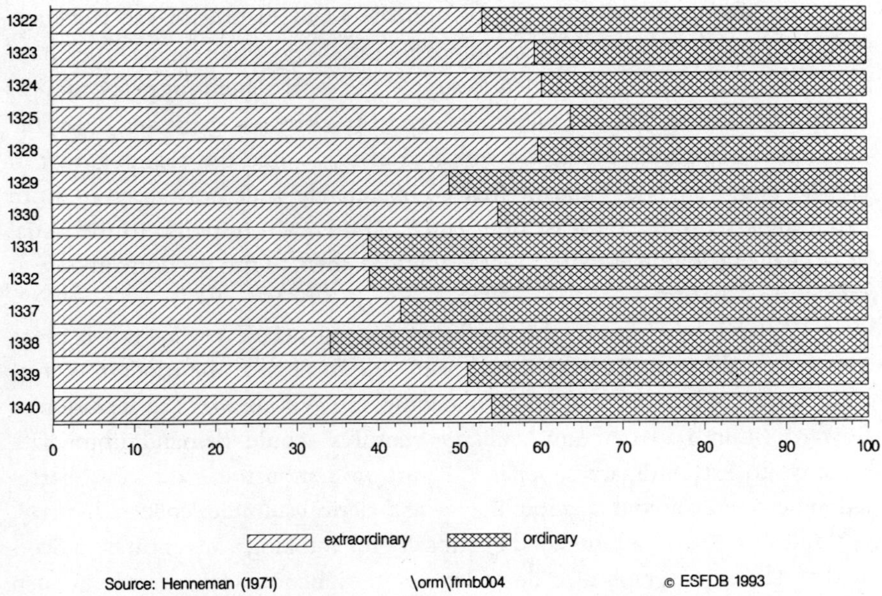

FIG. 17. Ordinary and extraordinary receipts as percentages of total French Treasury receipts, 1322–1340

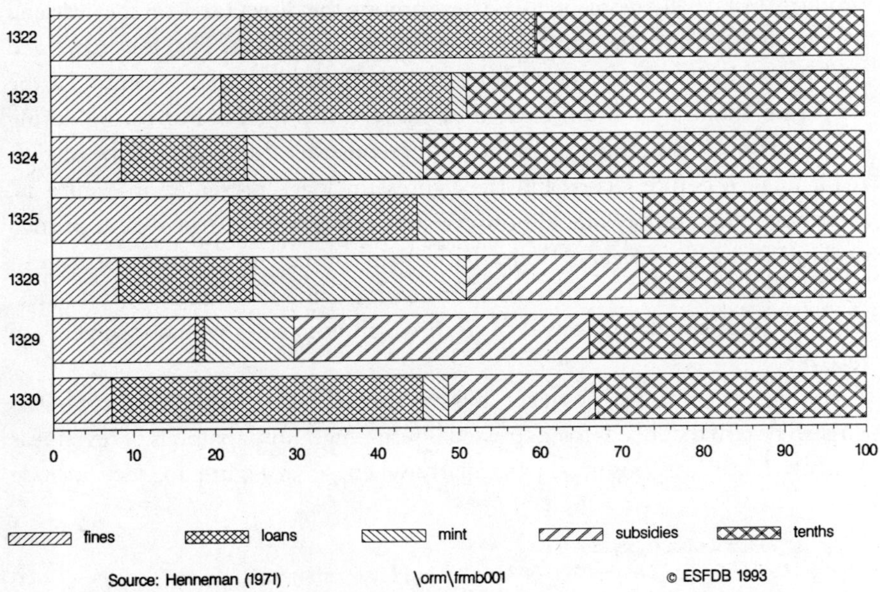

FIG. 18. Categories of extraordinary revenue to the French Treasury, 1322–1330

fines, the extraction of forced loans and the manipulation of the currency. Although detailed breakdowns are impossible after 1330, there can be little doubt that ordinary revenues continued to supply the most significant proportion of Philip VI's income. The cancellation of export taxes between 1333 and *c*.1337, the decision to return the feudal aid collected in 1333–5, and the abandonment of clerical tenths in 1336–7 meant that comparatively little was received from extraordinary taxation at least until 1339.[47] The French response to the initial fiscal challenge of the Hundred Years' War was, then, to run the domain state at maximum capacity.

In England, by contrast, the profits of general taxation were much more important. Although Edward II had been able to finance the modest War of Saint-Sardos of 1324–5 out of his own income, it was clear after the accession of Edward III in 1327 that any military ventures would demand immediate recourse to extraordinary supplies.[48] Figure 19 demonstrates the close correlation between war and taxation: the lay and clerical subsidies collected in 1328, 1333 and 1335–7 were all intended specifically for the king's adventures in Scotland.[49] The same graph also demonstrates the phenomenal increase in such subsidies after the opening of the Anglo-French war in 1337. For the first time, large amounts of money were now made from extra subsidies imposed over and above the existing customs duties on overseas trade. Still more important was a series of direct levies between 1338 and 1342 raised not in cash but in agricultural produce, principally wool, included here among the direct taxes on the laity and expressed in terms of the equivalent domestic market prices. That the crown and Parliament had to resort to such exceptional measures is a reflection of the desperate financial situation created by Edward III's rush of borrowing during the late 1330s. It is notoriously difficult to reconstruct the credit side of English royal finance before *c*.1350, and the figures for loans presented in Figure 19, enormous though they are, almost certainly underrate the true extent of such dealings during these years.[50] Indeed, the main consequences of the first stage of the Hundred Years' War were to be much the same in England as in France: namely, a potentially ruinous debt from which both sides would take years to recover.[51]

For present purposes, however, it is the success rather than the failure of the English system that needs to be stressed. Presenting summary totals of revenue is a highly hazardous business, particularly when, as in Figure 20, they include

[47] Henneman (1971), 80–114.
[48] For the costs of the War of Saint-Sardos: Fryde (1979), 94.
[49] ESFDB \orm\engb008 based on \engd028 and numerous sources cited there.
[50] Fryde (1949–50). [51] Henneman (1971), 116–90; Harriss (1975), 231–355.

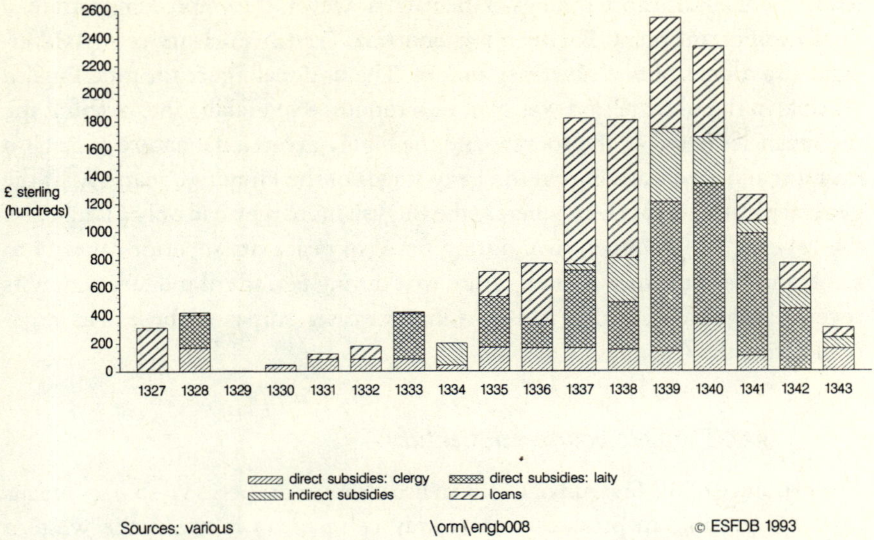

FIG. 19. Extraordinary revenues of the English crown, 1327–1343 (in £ sterling)

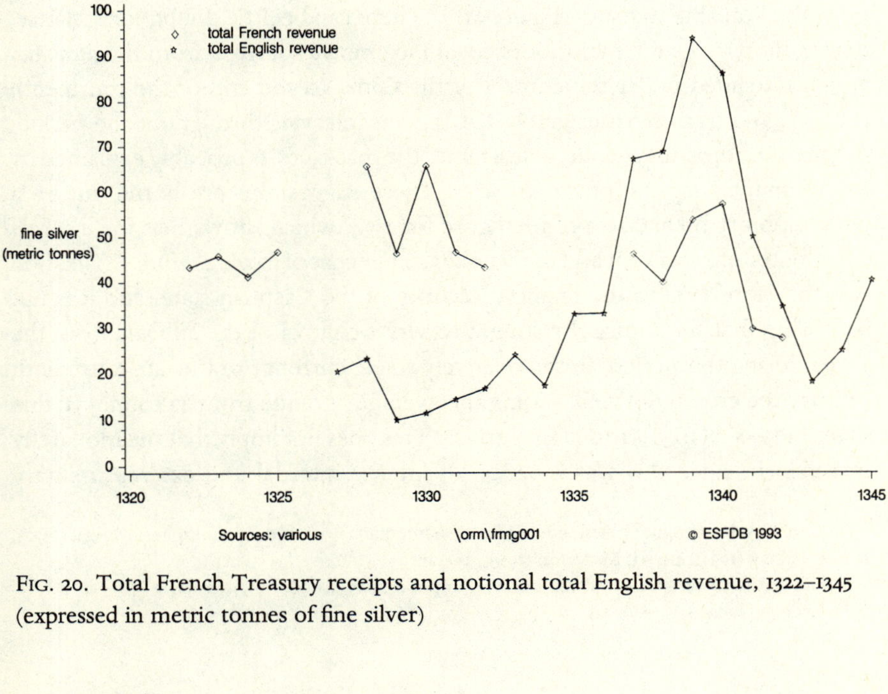

FIG. 20. Total French Treasury receipts and notional total English revenue, 1322–1345 (expressed in metric tonnes of fine silver)

loans.[52] For all the shortcomings of the data, however, the graph demonstrates a vitally important point. Between 1337 and 1342, French Treasury receipts averaged 42.5 tonnes of fine silver per annum. The notional figure for total English receipts in the same period was over 66.5 tonnes. Even taking into account the discrepancies between the sources and the highly exceptional nature of English taxation and credit dealings in the early stages of the Hundred Years' War, the general picture seems clear: whereas the English monarchy had only a fraction of the revenue of its French rival during times of peace, its superior capacity to transform itself into a war state meant that during periods of military action its revenues may have equalled and even, in some cases, surpassed those of its larger rival across the Channel.

5.8 *The Late Fourteenth Century*

The existence of the first run of Castilian fiscal data in the period 1369–1401 means that it is possible to produce a three-way comparison between the western monarchical states in the late fourteenth century. The Castilian material consists of summary totals of revenue computed by the *Cortes* on the basis of royal accounts. The absence of those accounts makes it impossible to test the accuracy of the estimates or to break the totals down into their constituent parts. However, if we assume that the *Cortes* achieved some degree of consistency, if not full accuracy, in its calculations, then some trends can certainly be discerned from the available statistics (Figure 21).[53] There can be little doubt, for instance, that in most years the majority of royal income was derived from the *alcabala*, which remained under the control of the *Cortes* to the end of the fourteenth century, and from *servicios* granted at regular intervals throughout the period. Any marked drop in revenue, at least until the mid-1390s, is probably explained by the temporary lapsing of the *servicios*. These suggestions are borne out by a contemporary breakdown of the figure for 1394, which shows that the *alcabala* contributed 42.9 per cent and the *servicio* 32.1 per cent of total revenue.[54] Taxation was therefore vital to the financial security of the Castilian state, and it is not surprising that the monarchy sought to wrest control of the *alcabala* from the *Cortes* during this period. In the relatively stable currency of the late fourteenth century the crown did well, raising the average revenue from 42 tonnes of fine silver in 1369–78 to 51.5 tonnes in 1379–88. This does not imply that the monarchy waxed rich, since this was a period of intense internal and external military

[52] ESFDB \orm\frmg001 based on \engd029; Henneman (1971); for the multiplier: Munro (1972), 14 n. 10; Craig (1953), 410–13; Miskimin (1963), 137–40.

[53] ESFDB \orm\casg001 based on \casd001 (unpubd data of Ladero Quesada).

[54] Ladero Quesada (1988), 315–16.

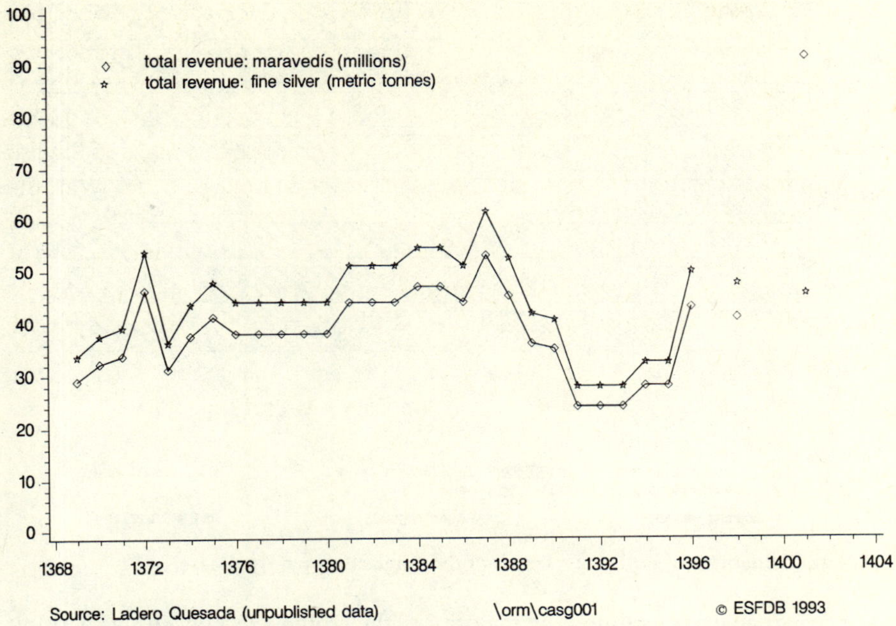

FIG. 21. Total notional revenue of the Castilian crown, 1369–1401 (expressed in *maravedís* and in metric tonnes of fine silver)

activity. Even after peace was established, the state was still faced with the challenge of paying off the large indemnity and pension offered to the erstwhile English pretender, John of Gaunt.[55] The resulting fiscal crisis was also exacerbated by the devaluation of the currency, which almost completely nullified the apparent increase in revenue as registered in money of account for the year 1401. Across the last decades of the fourteenth century, however, the picture that emerges is of a sophisticated and productive system which yielded an average yearly revenue equivalent to nearly 44 tonnes of fine silver.

The English material for the same period is fortunately susceptible of much more detailed analysis. Figure 22 indicates that the various constituent parts of the crown revenues now fluctuated a good deal less than they had in the early years of the century.[56] The contributions made by the domain and other traditional revenues along with ordinary revenues from the customs were considerably more stable, representing between a fifth and a third of total income, and even with the considerable swelling of the royal estates after the succession of Henry of Lancaster to the throne in 1399, the ordinary revenues of

[55] MacKay (1977), 121–5. For details of collection: Russell (1955), 508, 510–11, 536, 540 n. 2.

[56] ESFDB \orm\engb007 based on \engd030 and numerous sources cited there.

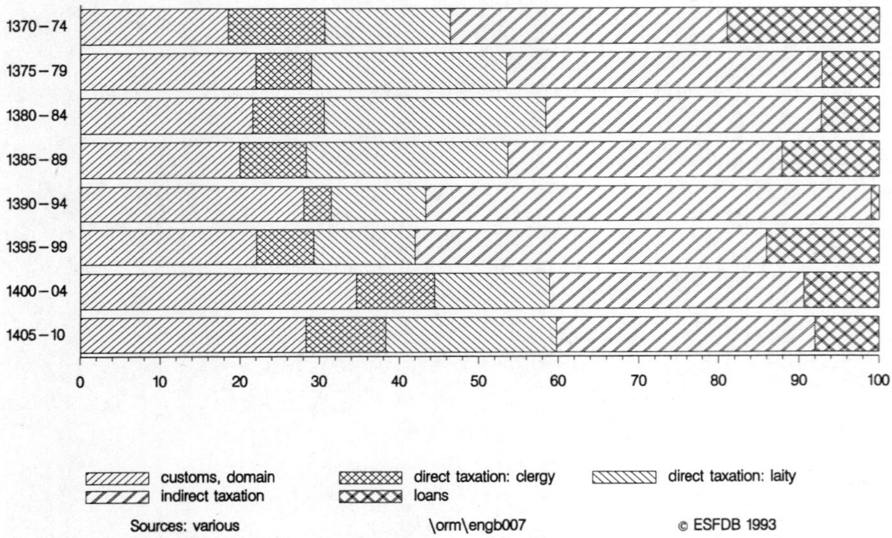

FIG. 22. Categories of notional receipts of the English crown, 1370–1410

the crown never constituted the majority of the crown's receipts in this period. The reduction in royal borrowing also marks a stark contrast with the situation in the early years of Edward III's reign: in only four out of these forty years did loans contribute more than 25 per cent of notional royal revenue. The most significant difference, however, lies in taxation. There were only five years between 1370 and 1410 when instalments of lay and/or clerical taxes did not fall due. This reflected the endemic nature of warfare with Scotland and France, though it also signified the crown's success in securing allocations of direct taxation to cover certain areas of ordinary expenditure hitherto not officially subsidized out of taxation. In general terms, however, the political community maintained the principle that direct taxes were payable only under extraordinary circumstances.[57] Indirect taxation, by contrast, had now definitely become a regular part of the fiscal structure requiring no special circumstances to justify its continuation. The permanent collection of the wool subsidy and the introduction of an additional levy on overseas trade known as the subsidy of tonnage and poundage meant that indirect taxation, although still theoretically extraordinary, now contributed a regular and indeed considerable proportion of the king's income. In the light of this evidence, and of the successful attempts by Juan I of Castile to wrest control of the *alcabala* from the *Cortes*, it is interesting that Richard II managed to manipulate the English Parliament into making him a life grant of the wool subsidy in 1398. Had Richard not been deposed a year later, it is

[57] Harriss (1982).

quite possible that parliamentary control over the principal tax in the English fiscal machine might have been virtually eradicated.[58]

England, then, had adapted to the long-term pressures of war and appeared, like Castile, to be an embryonic tax state. But it is worth noticing that these adjustments had also meant a scaling-down of fiscal activity. Since the start of the Hundred Years' War there had been only one significant reduction in the weight of English silver coin, so that inflation took little toll on crown revenues (Figure 23).[59] In the decade 1371–80, a period of exceptionally harsh taxation, the average annual revenue of the crown (including loans) represented some 40 tonnes of fine silver, an impressive sum when compared with all but the largest annual totals during the first half of the fourteenth century. The drop in the figures after *c.*1390 reflected a reduction in military activity following the truce with France, rather than a failure of the fiscal machine, and in any case the average annual total during the period 1391–1410 was still nearly 32 tonnes of fine silver. The potential profitability of the English system was to be highlighted once again during the 1410s, when massive amounts poured into the Treasury from taxes granted in the aftermath of the English victory at Agincourt.[60] It is not impossible, indeed, that

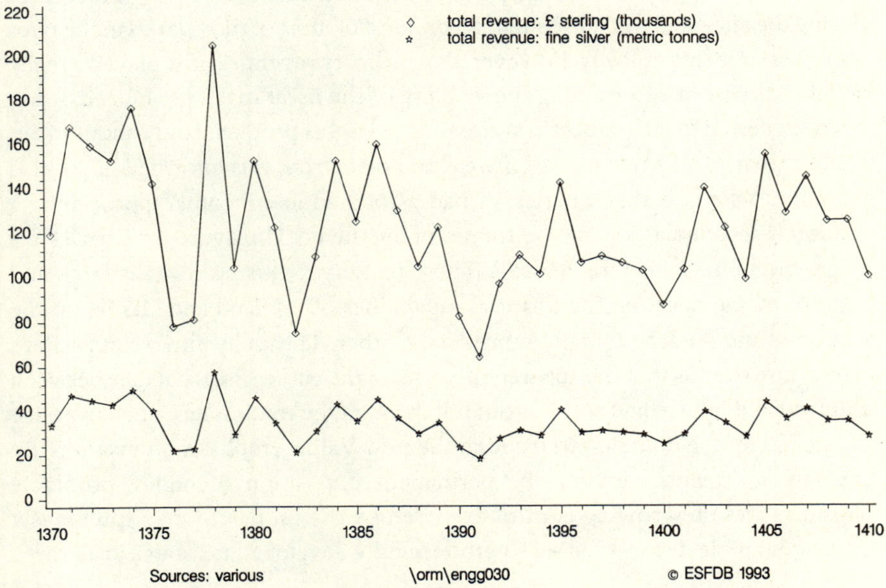

FIG. 23. Total notional revenue of the English crown, 1370–1410 (expressed in £ sterling and in metric tonnes of fine silver)

[58] Harriss (1988), 84.

[59] ESFDB \orm\engg030 based on \engd030 and numerous sources cited there.

[60] Steel (1954), 153–60.

Henry V hoped to capitalize on this generosity by establishing permanent direct taxation in England.[61] When the euphoria of the English political community subsided, however, it is significant that the state concentrated its attention on extracting resources from its newly won territories in northern France, and the level of direct taxation in England sank lower than at any point since the start of the Hundred Years' War.[62] The figures for the late fourteenth century may therefore represent something of a ceiling of sustainability beyond which the English state could no longer reach.

The situation in France is unfortunately much more difficult to judge. The few surviving Treasury registers from the reigns of Charles V and Charles VI apparently omit a large proportion of the receipts from taxation and do not provide a reliable index either of royal revenue or of the balance between ordinary and extraordinary income. In order to avoid further confusion, the figures are deliberately not reproduced here.[63] This is not to say, however, that some qualitative judgements cannot be made. The profits of the domain and associated rights seem to have declined under Charles V and then experienced at least partial recovery under Charles VI. This is precisely what would be expected given the handing over of large parts of southern France into English control during the 1360s and the subsequent reconquest of most of those lands in the 1370s and 1380s. It seems unlikely, however, that ordinary revenues now played a really significant part in determining the viability of the fiscal machine. Indeed, it has been suggested that the domain and associated rights produced only about 10 per cent of Charles VI's revenues.[64] If we extrapolate from this informed guess, it is possible to suggest that Charles VI had a total annual income approaching 2 million *livres tournois*, or over 70 tonnes of fine silver. The figure for Charles V's reign would have been higher still. These tentative statistics reveal a large and significant gap between the financial capabilities of England and Castile on the one hand and the kingdom of France on the other. The really important point to stress, however, is that the apparent reversal of the earlier fiscal balance between England and France had come about not through the traditional Capetian policy of expanding the domain but through the new Valois emphasis on taxation. By the late fourteenth century the permanent imposition of highly profitable subsidies and the growing control exercised by the monarchy over previously extraordinary levies seemed set to produce fully developed tax states in all three

[61] Harriss (1988), 84.

[62] Doucet (1926).

[63] The treasury figures for isolated years between 1384 and 1409 are printed in *Comptes du Trésor* (1930), lxv–lxvii, and Rey (1965), 81–90, 97–9. For critical comment on Rey's interpretation of the data: Radding (1976).

[64] Henneman (1976), 295–6.

of the principal western European kingdoms. It was left to the fifteenth century to reveal whether such trends would continue or collapse.

5.9 *The Later Fifteenth Century*

The obvious point at which to recommence this quantitative comparison of fiscal structures is the period immediately following the end of the Hundred Years' War in 1453. After 1461, the English state experienced a change not only of dynasty but also of financial management, and it seems most appropriate to take the period of the Yorkist kings (1461–85) as the base for this discussion. Unfortunately, administrative reorganization meant that a large proportion of the king's ordinary revenues fell out of the scope of the Exchequer and can only be reconstructed with some degree of guesswork.[65] Extraordinary revenue, however, can still be calculated with some precision, and the figures presented in Figure 24 provide a reasonably reliable guide to the relative importance of the various constituent elements of English state finance in this period.[66] The graph reveals a significant increase in the importance of ordinary revenues, which may have yielded an average of about 50 per cent of total receipts across the period 1461–85. This has something to do with the swelling of the royal domain and the

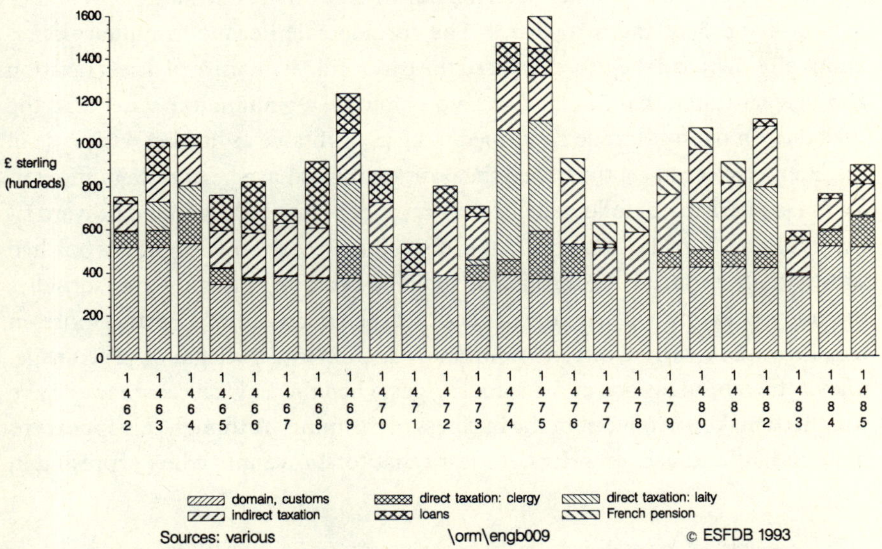

FIG. 24. Notional receipts of the English crown, 1462–1485 (expressed in £ sterling)

[65] Wolffe (1970).

[66] ESFDB \orm\engb009 based on \engd031 and numerous sources cited there.

increase in the yield from traditional sources during the Yorkist experiment with land revenues; but it also reflects the considerable scaling down of the crown's total financial operations after the close of the Hundred Years' War. Since revenues from the customs and subsidies on overseas trade had fallen significantly by the later fifteenth century, the total ordinary income was less impressive than is often suggested, and in real terms was probably smaller than the revenue from similar sources in the 1320s and 1330s. Indeed, despite the conventional thesis that the Yorkist financial administration signified the arrival of the principles of 'new monarchy' in England, this was in many ways a simple reversion to the older household organization of royal finance that had existed in the twelfth and thirteenth centuries.[67]

That the Yorkist regime lacked the full fiscal armoury properly associated with the new monarchies of the late fifteenth century is forcefully demonstrated by the restrictions imposed on its exploitation of extraordinary taxation. Not only had the English Parliament successfully maintained control over the authorization of direct levies, but it had also been able in broad terms to uphold the principle that direct subsidies were payable only in times of war. Much has been made of Edward IV's attempts to circumvent Parliament and collect so-called 'benevolences' (mandatory gifts); but it is important to note that these were also restricted to periods of military activity during short-lived hostilities with France in 1474–5 and Scotland in 1481–2.[68] The considerable decline in military operations after 1453 had therefore exposed the extraordinary nature of direct taxation and demonstrated that England was not, after all, a genuine tax state. Had the subsidies on overseas trade continued to be as profitable as had been the case in the later fourteenth century, then the position might have been rather different, for in 1464 Parliament followed fifteenth-century practice and granted Edward IV the subsidies for life. However, the decline in exports of English wool had substantially reduced the profits of indirect taxation, bringing the subsidies themselves down to an average of about £20,000 per annum.[69] Furthermore, in 1464 Edward IV carried out an important reduction in the weight of the coinage, one of the rare occasions in the Middle Ages when the English crown may have sought to make a profit out of the business of the mints. Although this appears to have had little impact on prices, it meant that total revenue, when expressed in

[67] For a survey of recent thought on the 'new monarchy' in England: Pollard (1992).

[68] Virgoe (1989).

[69] For the data used in estimating this figure for the wool subsidy and tonnage and poundage, as also for the profits of the customs (included among ordinary revenues): ESFDB \orm\engm009 and its source files. It should be noted that the author's calculations for the revenue from the customs and subsidies are in fact a good deal lower than those of Ramsay (1892), ii, 461–2, 470.

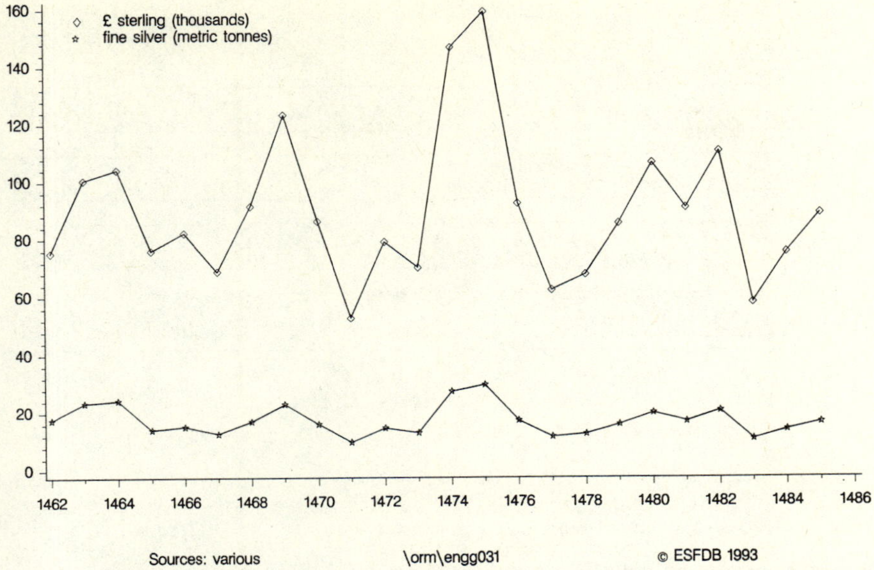

FIG. 25. Total notional revenue of the English crown, 1462–1485 (expressed in £ sterling and in metric tonnes of fine silver)

fine silver, fell still further to an annual average of just over 17 tonnes per annum (Figure 25).[70]

It is important to stress that this dramatic fall in revenues reflects an equally dramatic drop in expenditure. The financial position of the Yorkist monarchy was in fact a good deal stronger than that of the Lancastrian regime it replaced: indeed, whereas Henry VI's debts had been computed at a disastrous £372,000 in 1449, Edward IV died at least technically solvent.[71] Nevertheless, the comparative inability of the English monarchy to transcend the link between taxation and war deserves to be stressed in the context of what was happening in other fifteenth-century states. In England, at least, the apparent potential that had existed during the late fourteenth and early fifteenth centuries had not been fulfilled, and a tax state had failed to emerge. Whatever else the Tudor regime was able to accomplish during the sixteenth century, it could not reverse this basic truth.[72]

The broad trends in Castilian state finance in the fifteenth century are also fairly easy to discern, though the statistical material is rather patchy. Because the regime of the 'Catholic Monarchs' introduced a number of important changes in

70 ESFDB \orm\engg031 based on \engd031 and numerous sources cited there.

71 Ross (1974), 371–87; the picture of Edward's wealth is revised by Horrox (1987).

72 Schofield (1988).

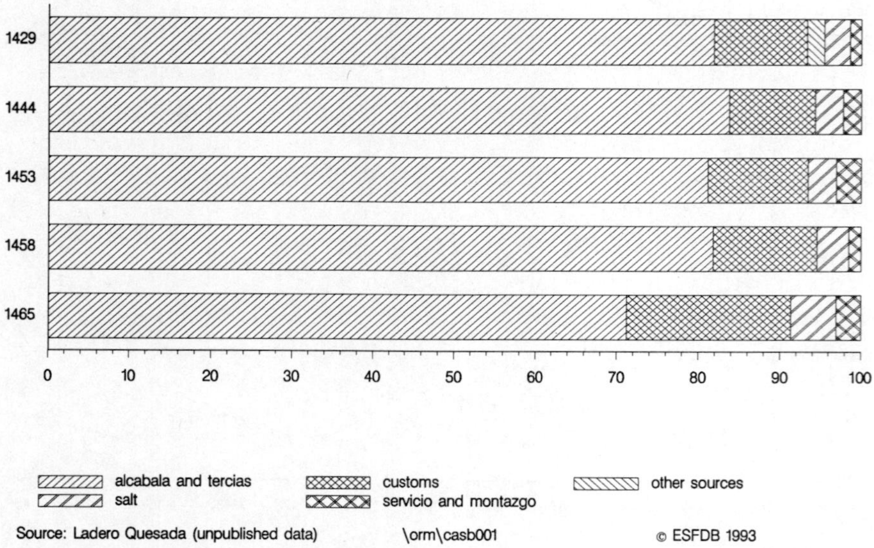

FIG. 26. Categories of ordinary revenues of the Castilian crown, 1429–1465

the system which were to have a significant impact on sixteenth-century Spanish finance, it seems appropriate to restrict this late medieval survey to the period before 1474. It is possible to break down ordinary revenues in a number of years between 1429 and 1465, and the results, shown in Figure 26, demonstrate a high degree of consistency across the period.[73] The *alcabala*, now collected permanently on the sole authority of the king and therefore classified as ordinary revenue, contributed, in conjunction with the much less productive *tercias*, an average of about 80 per cent of ordinary receipts. Unfortunately, this consistency was not matched by increasing productivity: the inflationary process caused by the regular devaluation of the *maravedí* bit deep into ordinary revenue, reducing it to the equivalent of less than 10 tonnes of fine silver by 1474. Much the same fate befell the *servicios* sanctioned by the *Cortes*. Contributions to the *servicios* were collected in forty-six out of sixty-eight years between 1407 and 1474, with a particularly long period of almost continuous direct taxation from 1429 to 1458 (Figure 27).[74] The quotas fluctuated, but they too were subject to a serious reduction in value: not even the apparently impressive 71 million *maravedís* imposed in 1455 could in the end counteract the impact of the devaluation of the currency. In the second half of the 1460s, civil war compounded such problems

[73] ESFDB \orm\casb001 based on \casd002; unpubd data of Ladero Quesada.

[74] ESFDB \orm\casg004 based on \casd004; unpubd data of Ladero Quesada; MacKay (1981).

and actually prevented the collection of the subsidies granted in the *Cortes* of 1465.[75] The simple addition of ordinary receipts with *servicios* suggests a particularly serious situation (Figure 28).[76] It was mitigated to some extent by the tribute paid by Granada and by the revenue from the sale of indulgences which the crown was allowed to appropriate for the continuing war against the Moors. Nevertheless, Castilian revenues were clearly in overall decline by the 1470s, and it was to take all the ingenuity of the regime of Ferdinand and Isabella to reverse this trend by developing new forms of taxation.[77]

By contrast with the downturn in English and Castilian revenues, the income of the French crown increased considerably during the later fifteenth century. Although precise fiscal data are almost wholly lacking, the general state of royal finances at the start and the end of the reign of Louis XI (1461–83) can be reconstructed with some degree of assurance from the statistics recorded in the

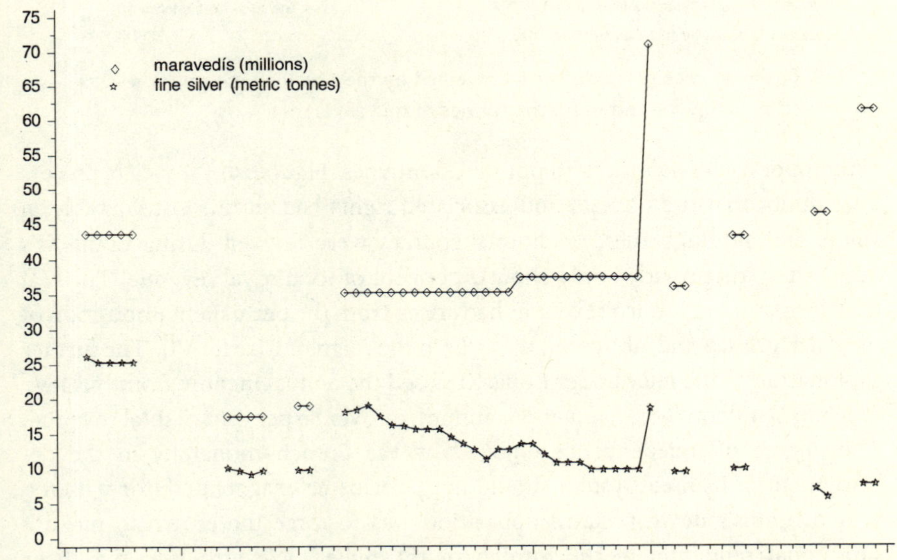

FIG. 27. *Servicios* granted by the *Cortes* of Castile, 1407–1474 (expressed in *maravedís* and in metric tonnes of fine silver)

[75] MacKay (1981), 74.

[76] ESFDB \orm\casb002 based on \casd003; unpubd data of Ladero Quesada; MacKay (1981).

[77] Phillips (1978), 102–3.

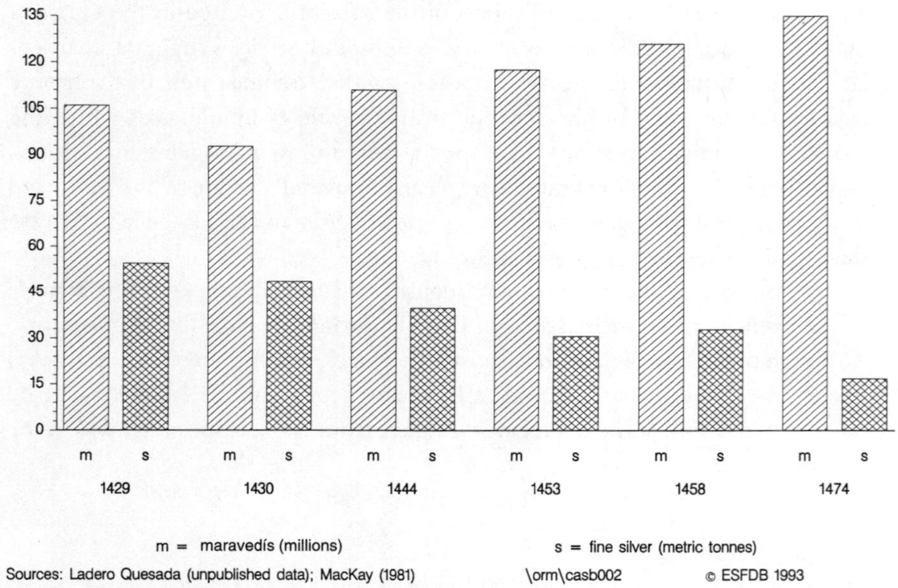

FIG. 28. Ordinary receipts and *servicios* received by the Castilian crown, 1429–1474 (expressed in *maravedís* and in metric tonnes of fine silver)

contemporary *Mémoires* of Philippe de Commynes (Figure 29).[78] By 1460, there is little doubt that the domain and associated rights had shrunk considerably in value, and although these traditional sources were revived during Louis XI's reign, they still provided only about 2 per cent of total royal revenue. The real transformation in French revenues had arisen from the permanent imposition of the *aides*, *gabelles* and, above all, the *taille* in the reign of Charles VII. The further exploitation of the *taille* under Louis XI raised the annual income from this levy to nearly 4 million *livres tournois* per annum, or over 80 per cent of total revenue. The degree of independence enjoyed by the French monarchy in the development of its fiscal system should not perhaps be exaggerated, for within a year of Louis's death political opposition was to force the crown to make a substantial reduction in the burden of the *taille*.[79] Nevertheless, the sheer expansion of royal resources under Louis remains extremely impressive, representing as it did a twofold increase in real terms from about 49 tonnes of fine silver per annum in 1460 to an astonishing 95 tonnes by 1483. If these statistics are indeed reliable, they represent a truly remarkable divergence in patterns of state

[78] ESFDB \orm\frmb002 based on \frmd004; Commynes, ed. Calmette (1925), ii, 200 n. 2, 290 n. 2. For discussion of these figures: Lot and Fawtier (1958), ii, 270, 272; Lewis (1985), 8; Henneman (1988), 624. Compare the Treasury figures for 1477 printed in *Comptes du Trésor* (1930), lxx–lxxi.

[79] Wolfe (1972), 60–1.

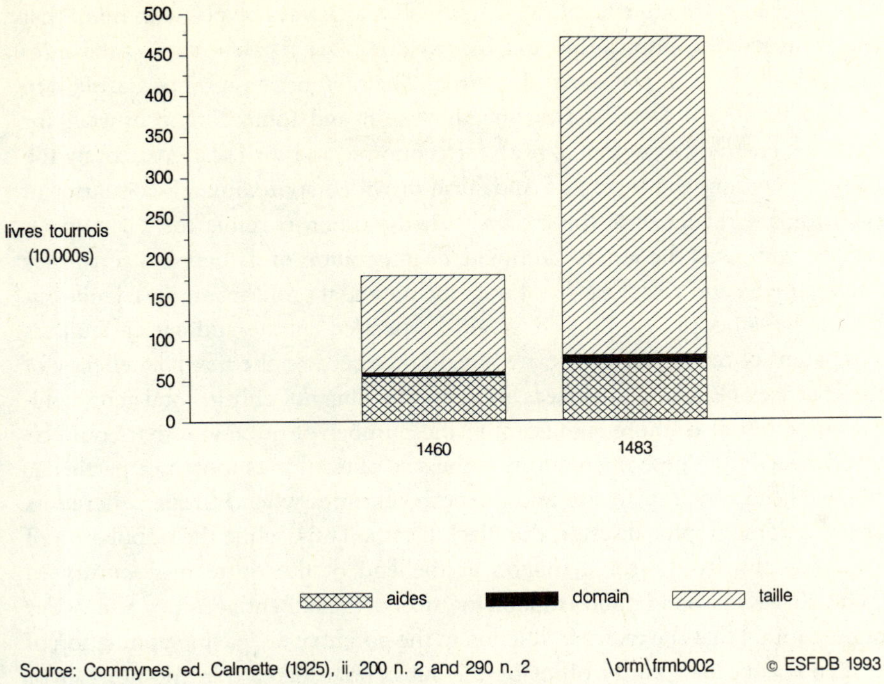

FIG. 29. Notional revenue of the French crown, 1460 and 1483 (in *livres tournois*)

finance in fifteenth-century Europe. Alone of the three examples studied here, France had capitalized on the precedents of the fourteenth century to create a permanent system of taxation whose sheer productivity was able to shield the state from the adverse effects of inflation and render it vastly more wealthy than its neighbours and rivals.

5.10 *The Late Middle Ages in Context*

This analysis of the fiscal systems of later medieval England, Castile and France represents a highly selective and condensed interpretation of a much larger subject whose ramifications are picked up and developed elsewhere in this and other volumes. In order to place the developments of this period into some perspective, however, this chapter concludes with a broad assessment of the factors that conditioned levels of extraction in different areas at different times and a discussion of the degree of modernity demonstrated by the fiscal systems of the three largest western kingdoms in this period.

In examining relative fiscal capacities it should always be borne in mind that the frontiers, the population and the wealth of any given state could alter dramatically over a given period of time. The final penetration of Castile into Moslem southern Spain during the thirteenth and fourteenth centuries, for instance, created the potential both for economic and for fiscal growth: by the fifteenth century the region of Andalucía provided approximately a quarter of the ordinary revenues of the crown.[80] At the other extreme, the Plantagenet regime witnessed the almost complete disintegration of its overseas territories between 1200 and 1450, losing not only the potential profit from those lands but also large amounts of English wealth expended in the ultimately fruitless campaigns of reconquest.[81] Meanwhile, France became the main beneficiary of the collapse of England's overseas empire, extending not only its total geographical range but also, more significantly, the number of provinces that could be taxed directly.[82] These fluctuations in the size of territories took on a particular significance in the fourteenth and fifteenth centuries when Europe suffered its greatest demographic disaster, the Black Death. Thus, while the population of England sank from over 6 million at the end of the thirteenth century to somewhere between 2.5 and 3 million for most of the fifteenth century, the Valois regime found that the radical reduction in the potential tax-paying population of France was at least partly offset by the substantial increase in the number of regions where it was able to establish, or re-establish, direct rule.[83] Finally, the economic effects of war and plague could have a dramatic impact on fiscal structures, as witnessed by the serious decline in English profits from overseas trade during the recession of the mid-fifteenth century.

It would be unwise, however, to suggest that the demographic and economic base was the sole or even the chief factor determining the success of the state in the collection of taxes. The extension of territorial sovereignty did not always guarantee a concomitant increase in revenues, since peripheral areas were often taxed much more lightly than the traditional heart lands of a medieval state.[84] Nor did the Black Death mean an immediate or automatic reduction in revenue: for some time, rulers continued to assess direct taxes on the basis of pre-plague valuations, and simply broadened the liability to taxation or increased the per capita burden to compensate for the decline in the population.[85] It must also be stressed that fluctuations in medieval state revenues are a very uncertain guide to

[80] Ladero Quesada (1982), 88–113.

[81] Postan (1964).

[82] e.g. Brittany, which became subject to royal taxation after 1491: Kerhervé (1992).

[83] Recent demographic research is summarized by Hatcher (1977); Le Roy Ladurie (1987).

[84] e.g. the case of the Plantagenet territories: Frame (1990), 169–224. Fiscal densities in Castile are discussed in detail by Ladero Quesada (1982), 88–107.

[85] Strayer (1970), 70–1; Henneman (1976), 290–6; Ormrod (1986), 182–5.

the real economic situation: the appreciable decline in the fiscal capacity of the kings of Castile, for example, certainly cannot be attributed to economic misfortune, for the Black Death had little impact in this part of the Iberian peninsula and the economy of the region remained remarkably resilient for most of the fifteenth century.[86] In fact, fluctuations in the revenue of the state seem to have depended a good deal more on a number of political factors which in their turn conditioned the range of economic activities open to state exploitation.

Undoubtedly the most important of these political factors was the relationship between the ruler and the power groups that made up the political society of the day. Given a finite and relatively static economic base, the search for fiscal resources in medieval realms inevitably turned into a competition between kings on the one hand and nobles, ecclesiastics and merchants on the other. The point was made very forcefully in the early stages of the English political crisis of 1297, when a number of members of the high aristocracy opposed royal military policy on the grounds that the long series of direct taxes exacted by Edward I had impoverished both them and their servile tenants: in other words, that royal taxes effectively struck twice at private seigneurial incomes.[87] The incompatibility between traditional feudal lordship and the demands of the state has been highlighted by Guy Bois, who has demonstrated how the extension of royal taxation in late medieval Normandy was made possible only by the collapse of traditional forms of seigneurial exploitation.[88] It is natural, then, to link the development of more organized and regular systems of state taxation with the 'crisis' and ultimate decline of feudalism in much of western Europe during the fourteenth and fifteenth centuries. Indeed, it is possible to build on this idea by suggesting that the later Middle Ages witnessed precisely that shift away from the private and towards the public exploitation of economic resources which is often identified as one of the key characteristics of the emergent 'modern' state.

This thesis has obvious attractions, and in the light of the foregoing analysis does indeed appear to be sustainable when applied to the principal western kingdoms in the later Middle Ages. The main difficulty arises if we see the state as an impersonal institution with a coherent, aggressive and coercive policy. In reality, it is clear that the fiscal 'policies' of later medieval governments developed in a rather haphazard fashion and that novel exactions could only be authorized and implemented with the consent and active co-operation of the elite. By the same token, it is clear that state taxation could only be successful if it

[86] MacKay (1977), 168–9.

[87] Denton (1978), 576.

[88] Bois (1984). Bois, 288, comments of the period immediately before the Black Death that 'the introduction of an excessive levy effected by the state . . . would have been inconceivable without the previous failure of the direct seigneurial levy'.

offered the politically powerful some positive advantages. Limiting personal liability or offering complete immunity from direct and/or indirect taxation was one obvious and common means by which to gain the goodwill of the king's natural supporters. For example, the long campaign of the French nobility to secure exemption from the *taille* finally achieved victory in the royal ordinance of 1445; within a short time, Louis XI also began a conscious policy of tax concessions for the towns.[89] A second means of persuading the elites to co-operate in the implementation of royal taxes was to offer them an active part in administering the system: the continued and widespread practice of farming certain state revenues in the late Middle Ages demonstrates the importance attached to profit, as well as honour, in the service of the king. Finally, the nobility in particular could benefit appreciably from royal expenditure. The general effect of royal fiscal systems in the later Middle Ages seems to have been the withdrawal of resources from the lower end of the socio-economic scale and their redistribution among the higher levels of society: to express it at its most basic, taxes paid by peasants found their way directly into the pockets of nobles and knights in the form of war wages, fief rents, salaries, perquisites of office and a host of other payments. The degree to which the aristocracy was dependent on such patronage obviously varied, and the extent to which royal money compensated for the decline in seigneurial incomes after the Black Death is a matter of some dispute.[90] But the vested interests bound up in the mechanisms of the state—and the mechanisms of state finance in particular—were undoubtedly to be of paramount importance in determining public fiscal systems for several centuries after 1500.

For the historian of the state, this alliance of king and nobility has two possible implications. On the one hand, it suggests that the interests of the elite became more and more bound up in the preservation and prosecution of royal governmental systems and therefore encouraged the movement towards a more modern form of state supremacy. On the other hand, it may have been a highly pragmatic alliance intended to preserve private privileges and therefore acted against, rather than in favour of, the expansion of public authority. In the very nature of the debate, neither interpretation holds the monopoly of the truth.[91] In the specific context of this chapter, it may be more satisfactory to suggest a middle way, by seeing the later Middle Ages as a period of transition between the 'domain' and the 'tax' states during which the resources of the ruling power were realized neither by the direct exploitation of prerogative rights nor by the

[89] Henneman (1978, 1983). For the situation in Castile: MacKay (1986), 161.

[90] Miller in Winter (1975); Maddicott (1975); Strayer (1977); Cazelles in Genet and Le Mené (1987); Hocquet in Genet and Le Mené (1987).

[91] For some suggestive comment in a late medieval context: Guenée (1985), 188–91, 198–205.

coercive powers of sophisticated bureaucratic machines but by formal and informal negotiation with the social, economic and political elite. Such a conclusion strongly implies that, for all their undoubted advances and sophisticated developments, late medieval fiscal systems still had some way to go before they became genuinely 'modern' both in their ethos and in their structures.

In a fiscal sense, the most obvious and important reflection of this lack of modernity is the absence of a concept of long-term borrowing in the larger kingdoms of the later Middle Ages. The only properly co-ordinated system of public credit to develop in the medieval monarchical states during this period was the scheme launched in fifteenth-century Catalonia under which long-term investors were guaranteed regular dividends paid at fixed rates of interest out of certain royal revenues kept in a special reserve fund and managed by a standing commission known as the *generalitat*.[92] It was not until the very end of the fifteenth century that a similar system began to operate in Castile with the selling of *juros* (annuities) which gradually took on the characteristics of government bonds.[93] To some extent, the economic and financial infrastructures may simply have been too primitive to allow the Catalan system to be adopted on a wider scale. But it was the implied loss of control resulting from the allocation of large amounts of royal revenue to the service of an ongoing debt that probably did most to prevent its adoption in the other monarchical states. Credit transactions continued to be seen as personal arrangements: when a king died, his creditors often stood little chance of satisfaction.[94] The receipts from a particular tax might be earmarked for the repayment of short-term loans and possibly even managed by a committee of notables; but any real notion of public finance and permanent accountability was anathema to the principal monarchies of late medieval western Europe.[95] In 1500, the kings of England, France and Castile were still in many ways running their fiscal systems as an extension of the early medieval domain, and it is no accident that the great leap forward in public credit during the sixteenth century had its origins outside the unified monarchies in the very different context of Italy and the Low Countries (Chapter 14.1).[96]

Modernity, however, is both a subjective and a relative concept. There can be little doubt that the policies and precedents established in royal finance during the thirteenth, fourteenth and fifteenth centuries coloured, conditioned and in some cases created the fiscal systems of early modern France, England and Spain.

92 MacKay (1977), 162–3. 93 Elliott (1963), 81, 197–9.

94 Fryde and Fryde (1963), 465–6; Harriss (1955–6), 194.

95 Rogers (1969); McFarlane (1972), 78–101; Ladero Quesada (1988), 304–25; Ladero Quesada (1989), 42.

96 Tracy (1985).

In particular, a closer study of developments in these three kingdoms between *c.*1250 and *c.*1500 has sustained the broad thesis that the systems of direct and indirect taxation developed in later medieval Europe had an important part to play in the evolution of a more coherent and distinct concept of the state. When the history of state finance in Europe achieves the prominence that it truly deserves, then what may be labelled the 'fiscal revolution' of the late Middle Ages may indeed become a term with as wide a currency as the 'commercial revolution' of the thirteenth century or the 'financial revolution' of the sixteenth and seventeenth centuries. If this chapter provides a convincing argument for the adoption of that term, then its purpose is fulfilled.

PART II

The Evolution of the State System after 1500

CHAPTER 6

Early Modern Theories of State Finance

Richard Bonney

It has already been seen that the theoreticians of the Middle Ages and the Renaissance had developed sophisticated theories with regard to the nature of taxation, and that in some measure they had anticipated 'modern' debates on the 'progressive' or 'regressive' aspects of a fiscal system in terms of its economic and social consequences (Chapter 1). This chapter concentrates largely on what was new in the arguments of early modern theoreticians, on new disciplines such as the study of monetary circulation and its impact on the economy; on population growth and its implications for society, the economy and the state; and on the development of credit instruments and their relevance to the long-term growth of state finance. The aim of this chapter therefore is not to rewrite in entirety the history of those parts of political theory which relate to state finance; nor even to select certain particularly influential theorists and cover the entire corpus of their works. Instead, its purpose is to demonstrate the evolution of ideas in as brief a survey as possible so as to provide a context for the discussion which follows. A number of obvious questions present themselves: what did the authors actually say? What did they mean by their statements? Why did they hold these views? Were their statements internally consistent? There are also some more important questions which involve a greater degree of qualitative judgement: were their statements based on correct observation? What was the influence of their views on their own and on subsequent generations? What was the quality of their intellectual response, as judged by the standards of later times?[1]

Whether or not the theoreticians in question were also theoreticians of the state in a more general sense is of importance, and we cannot altogether ignore

[1] Coats (1973), 486. The author wishes to thank Professors Murray Forsyth and Patrick O'Brien for commenting upon a draft of this chapter.

other dimensions of their thought. For example, early modern theoreticians often emphasized the moral aspects of the ordering of a state which had little or nothing to do with our subject in detail, but which represented a significant constraint on a state's capacity for action. In this respect, there is some resemblance between the moral philosophy of Bodin (with his emphasis on the harmonious ordering of a commonwealth) and that of Adam Smith: Smith's idea of an 'invisible hand' (which leads men while intending only their own good to further social ends) may be considered an offshoot of his moral philosophy which was also illustrated by his history of astronomy.[2] Ultimately, however, these important moral constraints on a state's action, or on the actions of individuals within the state, have to be considered subordinate to our central preoccupation, which is the changing perceptions of state finance and of the state itself.

A bewildering number of conceptual theories are encountered in the period under review—Mercantilism, Cameralism, Physiocracy, Anti-Physiocracy to name a few—as well as linking themes such as populationism. Three points need to be borne in mind when these concepts are addressed. The first is that all discussion depends to a lesser or greater extent on a retrospective placing of a selection of writers within a given school of thought or ideology, which carries with it a danger of anachronism: Adam Smith formulated the concept of the 'mercantile system' (hence Mercantilism) in order to denigrate the views of earlier proponents of ideas which he contested. Secondly, these schools of thought or ideologies overlap to a considerable extent; the relationship between Mercantilism and Cameralism is a good example, since in the view of some commentators Cameralism was no more than an Austrian and German version of Mercantilism. A third point is the importance of printing in creating a wider audience for such theories. Authors became more aware of their audience: the erudite speculations of the canon lawyers and scholastics were replaced by more practical (and sometimes self-interested) theories advanced by laymen in the course of the seventeenth century:[3] the School of Salamanca in the mid-sixteenth century represented the last great example of the medieval tradition[4] and one of the last systematic expressions of scholastic argument was Juan de Mariana's

[2] Rose (1980), 42–51; Smith, ed. Wightman and Bryce (1980), 45, 49, 67, 104–5; Ahmad (1990); Davis (1990). Galiani's 'Supreme Hand' is akin to Smith's 'invisible hand': Cesarano (1976), 383.

[3] Thus de Roover in Spengler and Allen (1960), 92, who contrasts 'scholastic economics' (which enjoyed 'the unquestioned superiority of being an integral part of a coherent philosophical system') with Mercantilism (which was 'never more than a conglomerate of uncoordinated prescriptions by which the authors of the Mercantilist tracts sought to influence economic policy, usually in a sense favourable to their private interests').

[4] Grice-Hutchinson (1952).

treatise against the introduction of debased *vellón* currency in Castile (*De mutatione monetae*, which was published at Cologne in 1609).[5]

At the risk of oversimplification, we must distinguish between different levels of theory and speculation on state finance. At the base of society, there was at most times a consensus about the nature of the fiscal system and its abuses; there was a contemporary concept of the 'just tax' in the same way that there was a popular idea of the 'just price', although it is the latter which has been much better studied.[6] The 'just tax' of one state was not necessarily what was regarded as 'just' in another; but it tended to be a tax which was sanctioned by tradition; one which was moderate, allowing the taxpayer to maintain subsistence for his family; and one which was levied at a convenient moment and in a convenient way without undue coercion. (Thus in certain crucial respects, the 'moral tax economy' anticipated Adam Smith's four canons of taxation.) In some states, it was a tax which required some degree of consent or ratification by a public body, but this was an area rife with popular mythology: had the French Estates General ever consented to regular taxation, let alone voted upon tax increases 'since time immemorial', as the rebellious peasants of Saintonge and Angoumois claimed in 1636?[7] There is a double significance in the attitude of the 'moral economy' regarding just taxation: it tended to provide a breeding ground for relatively simple arguments that could justify tax rebellion, one in which rumours of tax remissions (often apparently justified by an interpretation of contemporary events) could play a decisive role;[8] it also severely constrained the capacity of states to innovate in the fiscal process, yet continued to emphasize the duties of the government towards the people.[9]

At the next level (from a conceptual viewpoint, in ascending theoretical importance), there were practical decisions of government to be taken, which might have theoretical aspects or implications. These might concern, for example, the establishment of a new tax proposed by a 'projector' or *donneur d'avis*, whose views then had to be discussed by royal councillors or the relevant officials of the state. In Castile under Philip III and Philip IV, laymen who were essentially 'outsiders' gave advice on a whole range of political and economic

[5] Grice-Hutchinson (1978), 149–51, 174 n. 57. Thompson views Mariana as a 'constitutionalist' in his denunciation of manipulation of the coinage: Thompson in Hoffman and Norberg (1994), 190. Sancho de Moncada was a professor of theology at the University of Toledo: Grice-Hutchinson (1978), 141; de Roover in Spengler and Allen (1960), 98 n. 19; but Moncada's work, which was published in 1619, is usually regarded as Mercantilist in argument.

[6] Thompson (1971); Root (1990).

[7] Bonney (1988), 208.

[8] Bonney (1978), 224–8, 234–6; Kamen (1969), 276, 278.

[9] Bush (1991), 396–7.

decisions of government. At a somewhat higher level, there were theoreticians whose task essentially was to comment upon existing practice: this was the role played, for example, by a clerk of the finance ministry in France, Jean-Roland Malet, who wrote down his views on the existing fiscal system but did not publish them in his lifetime.[10] Neither of these two levels of theorizing necessarily implied an audience, though at any moment publication might result (in most states, this was usually against the wishes of the government and in any case the opportunities for publication were conditioned by the prevailing rules of press censorship within the state). A final level of sophistication concerned those theoreticians who consciously wrote for an audience, whether or not their views were published in their lifetime. Ultimately, all theories of state finance, other than those within the popular 'moral economy', arose from the conceptual models imposed by such individuals, who may nevertheless have drawn upon arguments arising from the lower levels of theorizing. Even so, an individual's views were not necessarily consistent with the majority opinion of the school of thought in which he is categorized for the purposes of historical explanation.

6.1 *Sovereignty and the Fiscal Powers of the State*

We must start with Jean Bodin (1529/30–96) because of his central, pivotal, role both as a theoretician of the state and of the economy and economic change.[11] In *La Response . . . au paradoxe de Monsieur de Malestroit, touchant l'encherissement de toutes choses, & le moyen d'y remedier* (1568), Bodin asserted that the quantity of gold and silver in the French kingdom was much greater than four hundred years previously;[12] the amount of coin in circulation crucially influenced the level of prices, and both were thus affected by the imports of precious metals from Spanish America. Under Charles VII, the revenues of the French kingdom had stood at only 1.7 million *livres*; but Louis XI had levied 3 million more than his father in the form of the *taille*, and revenues had risen still further in the sixteenth century.[13] The growth of short-term royal borrowing at Lyon under Francis I and Henri II, and the extension of the consolidated debt in the form of *rentes* were further indications of the expansion of the money supply.[14] One remedy proposed by Bodin for inflation in France was to impose taxes on grain, wine and salt exports ('la traite foraine du blé, vin, sel . . .')[15] on the grounds that the supply of such primary commodities was inexhaustible within the kingdom, while

[10] Bonney (1991*a*); Bonney and Bonney (1993).
[11] Schumpeter (1954*a*), 164–5, 311–12.
[12] Hauser (1932), xliii, 9.
[13] Ibid. 11.
[14] Ibid. 14.
[15] Ibid. 36.

foreigners could not dispense with purchasing them. French inflation and the fiscal needs of the French crown could thus be remedied at one and the same time, he argued. In contrast, he denounced debasement of the coinage as a fiscal device ('c'est une imposture et une pure tromperie des courtizans, de dire que le roy et le peuple y gagne');[16] only a sound currency could prevent the ruin of the kingdom.

In the *Six Books of a Commonweal* (*Les six livres de la République*, 1576) Bodin not only formulated a concept of sovereignty which was to be extremely influential ('the principal point of sovereign majesty, and absolute power ... consist[s] principally in giving laws unto the subjects in general, without their consent')[17] but enunciated principles both with regard to a state's revenue and its expenditure. As a member of the third estate at the Estates General of Blois of 1576, he had been involved in the question of monetary reform, and it is hardly surprising that the text of Book 6, chapter 3 of the *République* ('Of coins, and the means to prevent that they be not altered, nor falsified') reflected this preoccupation.[18] The previous chapter ('Of treasure') demonstrated Bodin's concern for political stability. The state's treasure, in his view, was built on seven possible foundations. Firstly and most securely, on the income from the domain, which was inalienable (a common characteristic, he thought, of monarchies such as France, England, Spain, Poland and Hungary, as well as Venice and certain Swiss cantons such as Lucerne).[19] The inalienability of domainal revenues in France was well illustrated, in Bodin's view, by Francis I's repudiation of the Treaty of Madrid (1526);[20] but notwithstanding this juridical principle, the alienation of the king's revenues had occurred in fact, to the extent of nearly 15 million *livres* by 1569.[21] Bodin regarded conquest as a second means of increasing the king's revenues: the proof appeared to be the new fiefs (*timârs*) established in the conquered lands of the Ottoman state, and the captaincies (*encomiendas*) established in Spanish Mexico and Peru.[22] Free gifts (*dons gratuits*) by a ruler's subjects were a third source of revenue, though Bodin noted that the *servicios* in the Spanish monarchy had been 'almost converted' into an ordinary revenue.[23] Pensions from allies were a further source of revenue: the classic case was the profit drawn by the Swiss Confederation from its alliance with France.[24] The fifth source of revenue was a colonial trading empire, such as that of Portugal after the discovery of the

[16] Ibid. 46.

[17] Bodin (1583, repr. 1977), 142; Bodin, ed. McRae (1962), 98. For its influence: Bonney (1989).

[18] Bodin, ed. McRae (1962), 700.

[19] Ibid. 651.

[20] Ibid. 652; Knecht (1982), 207–8.

[21] Bodin, ed. McRae (1962), 654.

[22] Ibid. 656.

[23] Ibid. 657.

[24] Ibid. 658.

Gold Coast and later the East Indies.[25] The sixth source of revenue was import and export duties ('which is one of the ancienteth and most usual in every commonwealth, and grounded upon equity'): here Bodin reverted to his idea of taxing grain, salt and wine exports from France.[26] The seventh source of revenue was taxation of the king's own subjects, which in Bodin's view rulers 'must never use, unless all the rest fail, and that necessity forceth them to have a care of the commonweal, being suddenly oppressed by the enemy, or by some other unexpected accident...'[27]

Yet if Bodin denied the centrality of taxation in a state, he was clear that prudence dictated that rulers should have a financial reserve to avoid beginning a war by borrowing or relying on subsidies.[28] He denounced Francis I's dependence on short-term loans ('no well advised prince will ever take that course, for thereby he shall ruin the foundation of his treasure, if he will keep his faith and pay; but if he will not, or cannot pay, then he must break and lose his credit, which is the ruin of an estate').[29] He doubted (incorrectly) that Philip II would allow the Genoese to dominate the Spanish revenue farms and the tax and loan contracts as Italian financers had recently done in France.[30] In general, the fewer the financiers and tax officials in a state the better, in his view, 'for the king's treasure will still decrease when it passes through the hands of so many officers'.[31] If there had to be taxes, then those which were most pleasing to God and most profitable to the state were taxes on luxury goods.[32] In contrast, 'all good princes have abhorred that impost which they called *Capitatio*'. Those who encouraged fiscal innovation in princes were roundly denounced by Bodin, especially the 'projector' ('that multiplier') who advocated raising the French king's revenues to 30 million *livres* per annum by taxing fallow as well as fertile land, and undermining the fiscal exemption of clergy and nobility.[33] Taxation was a cause of sedition in states, as the example of the Dutch revolt had shown.

Bodin's equation of absolute power with undivided legislative sovereignty was a seminal concept for the development of the state. This, and other aspects of his theory, came to exercise a significant influence over institutional developments in France and elsewhere.[34] However, his legacy for the fiscal power of the ruler was more paradoxical. The Roman law maxim that 'the prince is freed from—absolved or above—the laws' (*Princeps legibus solutus est*), which Bodin specifically endorsed in Book 1, chapter 8 of the *République*, was not very far from 'necessity knows no law' (*necessitas legem non habet*), which he appeared to refute.

[25] Ibid. 660. [26] Ibid. 661–2. [27] Ibid. 663. [28] Ibid. 682.
[29] Ibid. 676; cf. Knecht (1982), 389. [30] Bodin, ed. McRae (1962), 675.
[31] Ibid. 685. [32] Ibid. 670. [33] Ibid. 671–2. [34] Lloyd (1980); Bonney (1990).

Thus, talking about the consent of Parliament to new taxation in England, Bodin commented that 'other kings have in this point no more power than the kings of England: for that it is not in the power of any prince in the world, at his pleasure to raise taxes upon the people, no more than to take another man's goods from him . . .'[35] There were cases of evident necessity which might brook no calling of a Parliament; but to use 'necessity', that is a national emergency, as the reason for the levying of increased taxes without consent and to continue them after the peace was to act tyrannically:[36] Bodin was thus an advocate of the contrary maxim, 'when necessity ceases what necessity requires should also cease' (*cessante causa, cessat effectus*). There was thus a 'sovereignty–taxes paradox'[37] bequeathed by Bodin. Natural law allowed the king's subjects to hold property and thus enshrined their right to consent to taxation. To a certain extent, the sovereign courts in France tended to share his viewpoint in the seventeenth century, that taxation retained something of its original voluntary character, even though Charles VII had made the *taille* permanent in the *pays d'élections*; moreover, fiscal innovation was something to be reversed with the return of peace and the end of the emergency.[38] In contrast, later political theorists such as Cardin Le Bret in *De la souveraineté du roy* (1632) cited *necessitas legem non habet* and thus effectively removed Bodin's principal limitation on the exercise of royal power.[39] As reinterpreted by Le Bret and others, it was precisely the king's undivided legislative sovereignty which subsumed his fiscal power and removed the necessity for any consent to taxation. The levying of taxes was akin to any other act of legislation, and could thus be enforced by coercion if necessary.[40] This coercive power of the state in defence of its fiscal interests is a decisive attribute of the modern state, and even if Bodin himself rejected this development, it was one which was encouraged by successors who followed up his ideas and drew out the logic of his argument.

Hobbes is particularly significant in this respect. Unlike Bodin, Thomas Hobbes (1588–1679) argued that the state was founded, in theory if not in reality, by a general compact between individuals. The compact established a sovereign authorized to carry out the basic task of providing for internal and external security. Property, for Hobbes, did not precede the formation of the state: it only came into existence when the sovereign was in place and able to provide security.

[35] Bodin, ed. McRae (1962), 97. [36] Ibid. 664.

[37] Wolfe (1968); Skinner (1978), ii, 296–7, esp. 297 n.1.

[38] Bonney (1978), 116 n. 6, 216 n. 1.

[39] That Bodin regarded it as a limitation is clear from his introduction to the 1578 edition of the *République*: Bodin, ed. McRae (1962), A 71–2.

[40] Bonney (1978), 115–16, 216 n. 1, 219; Guéry (1984), 1259.

Furthermore, it was illogical to authorize the sovereign to provide security without giving him the means to carry out his functions. Hobbes thus concluded that the sovereign must have the power to raise troops, and to levy taxes to maintain them, without any requirement for the consent of property-owners.[41] His preference was for taxation on expenditure, since this was the least easily evaded: '... when the Impositions are layd upon those things which men consume, every man payeth Equally for what he useth: Nor is the Common-wealth defrauded by the luxurious waste of private men.'[42] In this respect, Hobbes did no more than repeat the Parliamentary justification of the excise of 1643, which was that it was 'the most easy and indifferent levy that can be laid upon the people'.[43]

In most of the practical aspects of his political theory, Bodin was much more of a conservative than his successors such as Hobbes. His significance in terms of economics rests with his debate with Malestroit in 1568 and his formulation of the quantity theory of money. Bodin was less original than it is sometimes claimed, because Martín de Azpilcuetza Navarro, a theologian of the University of Salamanca, had anticipated the idea by some twelve years (*Comentario resolutorio de usuras*, 1556).[44] However, Bodin certainly publicized the argument much more widely than had his intellectual precursor in Spain; and it is generally thought that he had the better of the debate with Malestroit over the causes of the rise in European prices.[45] He did not, perhaps, arrive clearly at the conclusion that the revenues of the state would inevitably decline in a period of price inflation unless dramatic action was taken to reverse the trend—the 'achievement' of Louis XIII and Richelieu in France in the 1630s, for example.[46] On the other hand, as has been seen, he proposed that inflation in France and the fiscal needs of the French crown should be remedied at one and the same time by taxes on basic commodities such as grain, wine and salt exports: the idea was probably impracticable, but the rapid rate of price increase of basic commodities, especially foodstuffs, would have worked to the direct advantage of the crown.

[41] Hobbes, ed. Oakeshott (1960), 117. The author is indebted to Professor Forsyth for making this contrast with Bodin.

[42] Quoted in Seligman (1899), 12 n. 2.

[43] Quoted in Kennedy (1913), 55.

[44] Grice-Hutchinson (1952), 61, 95: 'And even in Spain, in times when money was scarcer, saleable goods and labour were given for very much less than after the discovery of the Indies, which flooded the country with gold and silver. The reason for this is that money is worth more where and when it is scarce than where and when it is abundant.' Grice-Hutchinson (1978), 106.

[45] Spooner (1972), 92; Bonney (1991*b*), 421–2.

[46] Bonney (1992*b*), 118–20.

6.2 *Mercantilism and the Spanish 'Arbitristas'*

The theologians of the University of Salamanca had developed ideas on the origin and functions of money; on the quantity theory of money; on the theory of value applied to both goods and money; and on the purchasing-power parity theory of exchange.[47] It is hardly surprising, given the prestige of the theologian-economists of the School of Salamanca, that Castile should have been the first country to produce advisers of rulers with a clear economic viewpoint which we might term 'Mercantilist':[48] there was no intellectual rift between the doctors of the universities and the lay economists and 'projectors'.[49] The term 'Mercantilism' is, of course, a neologism: it was Adam Smith who first publicized the alleged sins of the 'mercantile system' in 1776 and thus gave rise to what has come to be known as the concept of Mercantilism.[50] Yet already in 1558 we find Luis Ortiz, controller of the royal finances, denouncing to Philip II the consequences to Castile of an adverse balance of payments and linking the financial plight of the monarchy (which had been forced to reschedule its debts the previous year) to the economic situation. When kings were rich, he wrote, 'many good things come to their subjects'. But when they were in need, 'necessity knows no law, and less where princes are concerned'. He advocated many specific reforms, including reforms of the currency and tax system and the creation of a war chest.[51]

Yet Ortiz's proposals were not adopted, and by the last year of Philip II's reign it seems that there were already reform treatises (*arbitrios*) in circulation, because the king was warned to 'beware the reasoning and false presuppositions of the arbitristas' (that is, their authors).[52] At least 165 Spanish economic tracts have survived from the period between 1598 and 1665; the actual number written must

47 Grice-Hutchinson (1952), 60.

48 The contention of E. J. Hamilton that 17th-cent. Spanish writers can all be labelled broadly 'Mercantilist' was criticized by de Roover in Spengler and Allen (1960), 98 n. 19. Grice-Hutchinson (1978), 160, considered that the 'age of Mercantilism' closed in Spain around 1740: it must therefore have existed in the earlier period!

49 Grice-Hutchinson (1978), 135. This notwithstanding the argument of de Roover in Spengler and Allen (1960), 92, that 'the differences between Mercantilism and scholastic economics are striking and profound'.

50 Smith, ed. Campbell, Skinner and Todd (1976), i, 429 (Bk. 4, ch. 1, 'Of the principle of the commercial, or mercantile system'). Hecksher (1935) remains the fundamental synthesis, though see Hecksher in Seligman (1930–4), x, 333–9; cf. Coleman (1969).

51 Grice-Hutchinson (1978), 127–30.

52 Much depends on the reliability of the dating of a text by Baltasar Alamos de Barrientos: Elliott (1989), 243 n. 6. If his text is indeed from 1598, it antedates by some fifteen years the first appearance of the word *arbitrista* in literary usage (by Cervantes in 1613): Vilar Berrogain (1973), 48; Grice-Hutchinson (1978), 139.

have been much higher. The theorists advocated sensible practical reforms: royal expenditure must be regulated, the sale of offices halted, and the tax system overhauled.[53] While they differed in their economic doctrines—among them there were bullionists and anti-bullionists, proto-Physiocracts and protectionists—most were obsessed with the problem of Castilian decline.[54] Many of the theoreticians recognized the interrelationship between demographic circumstances and economic growth. In part, this reflected the tradition of economic debate in the Spanish universities; there was also an awareness of recent government enquiries, most notably the compilation of land surveys (*Relaciones topográficas*) under Philip II;[55] but Sancho de Moncada seems to have been unique in his use of parish registers to document the decline in marriage rates in his native Toledo.[56] Others seem to have recognized at a relatively early date the disastrous consequences of rampant inflation for the crown's revenues and the purchasing power of its taxpayers: Martín González de Cellorigo argued that

> the great quantity of money which has been coined has raised the poll tax, and the other taxes and contributions, to a point where they cannot be met unless such a flood of money is kept coursing through the kingdom that the price of goods corresponds to the sums which the taxpayers are obliged to provide and which are needed for the support of the monarchy and the honouring of its debts (*Memorial de la política necessaria y útil restauración a la República de España*, 1600).[57]

To what extent did the *arbitristas* succeed in influencing government policy? Philip IV and Olivares both commented that Columbus must have seemed almost as strange a 'projector' as the wild Sir Anthony Sherley.[58] Olivares was the great reformer; yet only three *arbitristas* appear in his library catalogue.[59] One of these, however, is extraordinarily significant, a work by Jerónimo de Ceballos (*Arte real para el buen gobierno de los reyes y princípes*, which was written in 1621, and published two years later). This text was dedicated to Olivares, and advocated a national banking system into which royal revenues would also be channelled. The proposed system would reduce the costs of tax collection, and the funds of the bank would be made available for royal expenditure on such necessary items as the maintenance of the fleet. Furthermore, Ceballos denounced existing taxes such as the *millones* and *alcabalas* and proposed their abolition and replacement by a single tax on flour. The two key aspects of his scheme—a national banking scheme and the replacement of the *millones* by a new fiscal system tied to the needs of defence—were embodied in a royal letter of

[53] Elliott (1989), 231.
[54] Elliott (1986), 89–94; Elliott (1989), 219, 244–5, 249.
[55] Salomon (1964).
[56] Elliott (1986), 94.
[57] Grice-Hutchinson (1952), 110.
[58] Elliott (1989), 244 n. 8.
[59] Elliott (1986), 121.

October 1622 and were an early version of Olivares's Union of Arms scheme.[60] Olivares's reforms embroiled him in immense political difficulties, and the net impact of the views of the *arbitristas* was disappointing. From the point of view of economic theory, however, Ceballos is an interesting precursor on the one hand of John Law, with his banking scheme, and the attempt to interrelate the state's revenues with the bank; and on the other hand, of the Physiocrats and their obsession with a single tax scheme.

Sancho de Moncada, writing in 1619, viewed government as a science (*ciencia*), whose laws should be learned by every administrator; for example, currency questions formed a demonstrable science (*ciencia demonstrativa*), the understanding of which was guided by 'universal scientific principles':[61] 'Government, or reason of state', he wrote, 'is the method of founding, conserving or expanding a kingdom . . .' The 'science of government' provided 'a fixed and infallible rule, standard and yardstick to guide and direct men along the right and certain path . . .'[62] Nevertheless, the vision of a 'restoration of Spain' brought about by administrators who were 'scientifically' (*científicamente*) trained[63] (a viewpoint shared by many of the *arbitristas*) remained remarkably elusive. The collapse of the *vellón* currency, predicted by Mariana in 1609, duly led to a reduction in the real value of the crown's revenues, as he had also warned.[64] Single tax schemes were proposed by Jacinto de Alcázar Arrizia in 1646[65] and Bautista Dávila in 1651 (who also proposed measures to reform the *vellón* currency):[66] both writers preferred a form of personal income tax. The Spanish government responded to such ideas by proposing a single tax scheme (*medio grande universal*) in 1655, but this was rejected by the *Cortes* of Castile.[67] Alvarez Osorio, writing in 1686, proposed a single tax scheme drawing upon essential foodstuffs such as grain, wine and meat.[68] Francisco Centani, writing in 1665, was the first to expound the doctrine so central to the Physiocrats, namely that land was the only true source of wealth. The single tax should therefore 'fall equally on those who hold the lands that produce the native fruits by which these Kingdoms are sustained and which constitute their physical and true wealth'. Centani claimed that the

[60] Ibid. 121–4.

[61] Grice-Hutchinson (1978), 141; Elliott (1986), 93 n. 32.

[62] Elliott (1984), 167.

[63] An expression used by Tomás Tamayo de Vargas in his introduction to Moncada's *Restauración de España* (1619): Grice-Hutchinson (1978), 141.

[64] Grice-Hutchinson (1978), 150.

[65] Ibid. 147, 173 n. 52

[66] Ibid. 147, 152, 173 n. 53. Schumpeter (1954*a*), 203 n. 4, noted that Dávila's tract 'was a milestone on the road to single-tax ideas'.

[67] Thompson in Hoffman and Norberg (1994), 194, 203.

[68] Grice-Hutchinson (1978), 147.

proposed tax was both more just than existing indirect taxes and easier to collect; it would also have the advantage of bringing down prices by freeing commodities from the sales tax.[69] It was in such ideas (a Spanish form of Physiocracy *avant le nom*?) that the *única contribución* reform of the mid-eighteenth century had its true origins.[70]

Although there were reforming ideas and reformers under Carlos II, the long delay before the implementation of radical tax schemes in Spain is notable: when fiscal reform was attempted, as in 1683, it was found that it led to a significant reduction in revenues.[71] Nevertheless, the views of one of the most important financial advisers to Philip V, Melchor de Macanaz, were formed during Carlos II's reign.[72] Macanaz was sent to Valencia in 1707 to reform its finances and administration; by his labours in the eastern provinces, and his literary output to defend his actions, he helped establish the new Bourbon dynasty on a path of reform that was essentially Spanish.[73] Macanaz was the theoretician, architect and apologist of the new regime in the crown of Aragon, which achieved what Olivares had so singularly failed to do in 1640. Philip V introduced fiscal reform in Aragon, Valencia and Catalonia after revoking the privileges of these areas, and this change is reflected in the writing of Jerónimo de Ustáriz (1670–1732), whose *Theorica y practica de comercio y de marina* (1724)[74] was later translated into both English and French; the English edition was cited by Adam Smith.[75] Ustáriz was a government official who had intimate knowledge of the way in which contemporary assessments of the population size were made; his figures provide the standard account of the population of Spain for this period, although there is reason to suppose that some of his figures were overestimated.[76] Ustáriz cited Vauban's *Dixme royal* in the context of the population size of a kingdom;[77] and his own population estimates (7.5 million inhabitants) were influential in the eighteenth century.[78] There is a double interest in Ustáriz's work: his awareness of the continuing need for internal reform to make the Spanish monarchy competitive with its rivals; and the relationship between the fiscal burden and economic

[69] Ibid. 147–8, 174 n. 54.

[70] Cf. Matilla Tascón (1947).

[71] Kamen (1980), 366–7.

[72] Ibid. 360.

[73] Kamen (1969), 48–9, 302, 310–12, 415–19. Though he was expelled from Spain, along with Orry, in February 1715, Macanaz had in fact disagreed with him: ibid. 53 n. 27, 54, 114.

[74] Ustáriz, trans. Kippax (1751); Wilson in Otazu (1978*a*), 189–96; Mounier (1919); Schumpeter (1954*a*), 170; Grice-Hutchinson (1978), 160–5.

[75] Smith, ed. Campbell, Skinner and Todd (1976) ii, 899: ('It is to the Alcavala . . . that Ustariz imputes the ruin of the manufactures of Spain').

[76] Kamen (1969), 272–3, 365–9.

[77] Ustáriz, trans. Kippax (1751), i, 50–1; Wilson in Otazu (1978*a*), 193.

[78] Ustáriz, trans. Kippax (1751), i, 73; cf. Herr (1989), 52, 757.

progress. He was a populationist, a bullionist[79] and a Mercantilist, and as such he was well aware of the gains made by England, France and the Dutch at the expense of the Spanish monarchy. The benefit to Spain of the imports of precious metals from the New World had been negligible, he concluded, since most of its proceeds had been immediately transferred to commercial competitors. Worse still, the payments mechanism in Spain had degenerated in the course of the seventeenth century so that transactions were paid for in copper (*vellón*), which put up transportation costs and was unknown in France, England and the Netherlands.[80]

Ustáriz advocated both a return to sound money and the imposition of tariffs against the principal commercial competitors of Spain (he praised the English Navigation Acts and Colbert's tariffs of 1664 and 1667 and proposed reforms of Spanish import and export duties); a strong navy was needed to resist the other Maritime Powers.[81] Even more important, however, was his sense of the per capita fiscal burden. He advocated the abolition of certain indirect taxes (the *alcabala* and *cientos*) on the first sale of goods in Castile for those involved in manufacturing, in order to boost production. He estimated the yield of the *catastro* in Catalonia in 1721 at almost 12.9 million *reales de vellón*[82] levied upon 103,360 families, or 13 *escudos* per family. In contrast, taxation in Valencia and Aragon was much less oppressive, representing a fiscal burden respectively of 9 and 5 *escudos* per family. Valencia was a smaller geographical area than Aragon, but had made considerable economic progress since the War of the Spanish Succession, especially in terms of silk manufacture. Aragon had less trade and fewer inhabitants, further proof (and here he echoed Botero) that 'the revenue and power of princes depend more upon the number and commerce of their subjects, than upon the extent of their dominions'.[83]

Thus a varied fiscal response was necessary to stimulate commerce:[84] in Aragon, it amounted to a reduction by one-third of the *real contribución*, that is, a tax of 4 instead of 6 per cent, equivalent to the exemption from the *alcabala* and *cientos* in Castile; in Catalonia, it was a reduction by half of the *catastro* on manufactures since a 10 per cent levy was considered by Ustáriz 'very oppressive, and a heavy clog (*sic*) upon' them; but for Valencia, the policy was essentially one of no change, since it had been fiscal incentives in the first place which had

[79] Though on this, see the strictures of Mounier (1919), 287, who argues that Ustáriz did not oppose the export of specie.

[80] Ustáriz, trans. Kippax (1751), ii, 352–3.

[81] Mounier (1919), 265–75; Brading in Bethell (1984), 394.

[82] Ustáriz, trans. Kippax (1751), ii, 297–8.

[83] Ibid. ii, 305 (Aragon); cf. ii, 294 (Catalonia) and ii, 310 (Valencia).

[84] Cf. Mounier (1919), 249–53.

promoted the development of the silk manufacture.[85] The expansion of manufacturing output was a consequence of a sound tax regime; and from the expansion of manufacturing output a higher level of population could be sustained.[86] Fiscal equity was clearly the aim, notwithstanding the differences between fiscal systems in the various kingdoms. It is therefore peculiarly fitting that it was Ustáriz's grandson and namesake who as intendant was charged with establishing the Physiocratic single tax (*única contribución*) in Extremadura; he, too, cited Vauban's *Dixme royal* when discussing the idea of fiscal reform in the interests of justice and equity.[87] Most of the subsequent writers in eighteenth-century Spain may be characterized as latter-day Mercantilists until the 1780s.[88] Then there was a growing demand for land reform and, above all, for economic liberalism on the model advocated by Adam Smith. Jovellanos's proposals for agrarian reform (1794, published the following year as the *Informe de la Sociedad Económica ... en el expediente de ley agraria*) were influenced both by the Physiocrats and by Smith.[89]

6.3 *Mercantilism and 'Political Arithmetic' in England*

An early English statement of Mercantilist views, but one which stands rather isolated in terms of its period, was John Hales's *A Discourse of the Common Weal of this Realm of England* (1549). A bullionist by nature, Hales asserted that 'the king cannot have treasure when his subjects have none'.[90] More influential (and quoted by Smith, if only by way of refutation) was Thomas Mun's *England's Treasure by Foreign Trade* (written *c.*1628, but published in 1664).[91] This was an unashamedly protectionist and bullionist tract. It proclaimed that 'the true form and worth of forraign Trade' was 'The great Revenue of the King ... The means of our Treasure, the Sinnews of our wars, The terror of our Enemies ...'[92] Naked commercial rivalry with the United Provinces was proclaimed for reasons of state (indeed the publication of the pamphlet was almost certainly part of the propaganda campaign against the Dutch which preceded the outbreak of war in 1665):

[85] Ustáriz, trans. Kippax (1751), ii, 245–6 (Castile); ii, 300, 304 (Catalonia); ii, 307–8 (Aragon); ii, 312 (Valencia).

[86] Mounier (1919), 255–9.

[87] Otazu (1978*b*), 71–2, 218.

[88] Herr (1969), 48–50; Herr (1989), 68, on Campomanes and Olavide.

[89] Herr (1969), 376–9; Herr (1989), 48–59, 70–7.

[90] Hecksher (1935), ii, 20 and ii, 45 n. (at ii, 46) on the frequent usage of 'treasure'; Grampp in Spengler and Allen (1960), 63–4.

[91] Smith, ed. Campbell, Skinner and Todd (1976), i, 431–2; Hecksher (1935), ii, 113; Hutchison (1988), 22–3; Mun (repr. 1933), 19.

[92] Mun (repr. 1933), 88.

> ... since they have cast off the yoke of *Spanish* slavery, how wonderfully are they improved in all humane policy ... are not their provinces the *Magazines* and *Store-houses of wares* for most places of Christendom, whereby their wealth, shipping, mariners, arts, people, and thereby the publique revenues and excizes are grown to a wonderful height? If we compare the times of their subjection, to the present estate, they seem not the same people ...[93]

Yet 'the endeavours of the industrious Dutch' were an achievement which redounded to the 'great shame, and no less peril' of the English.[94] The logic of Mun's argument was protectionism against the Dutch, and in some respects he may be seen as the intellectual progenitor of the Navigation Act of 1651.[95]

Attempts to compute the wealth of the nation derived primarily from the *Observations on the London Bills of Mortality*, published in 1662, the joint work of John Graunt and William Petty.[96] Both men were interested in the recurrence of plague and its impact on demographic growth: Petty commented that plagues in London 'do commonly kill one fifth part of the inhabitants'.[97] They were both concerned with other questions such as the resources of the state in manpower, revenues and trade; but of the two, Sir William Petty (1623–87), a founder member of the Royal Society,[98] was the one who better understood how medicine could serve the Mercantilist ambition of increased resources and power for the state, arising from a large population whose health was maintained because the ravages of disease would at last be checked.[99] In contrast to later writers such as Cantillon, he believed that a larger population would in itself lead to increased production.[100] Although his assumption that the English population would double every 320 years or so proved to be an underestimate of the actual growth rate in the eighteenth century, his was one of the first population projections.[101] Petty had been educated in France and the Netherlands, and had worked as Hobbes's assistant in France, where he had been influenced by the French school of mathematics; he sought to apply the Baconian method of the

93 Ibid. 73–4; Wilson (1953), 340.

94 Mun (repr. 1933), 72, 81. The 'cruel and unjust violence' of the Dutch (presumably in the Amboina incident) was also noted.

95 Wilson (1965), 60–2.

96 Ibid. 227. Riley (1985), xv, 10, who also links this to the emergence of life contingency valuations in the Dutch Republic. For the joint authorship: Aspromourgos (1988), 352. It is probable that the disputed authorship will never be resolved: Keynes (1971), 77; Hutchison (1988), 42–5. The work was translated into German in 1702. Graunt, Gregory King and the development of 'political arithmetic' are discussed by Laslett in Schürer and Arkell (1992).

97 Slack (1985), 151, 244.

98 Aspromourgos (1988), 342.

99 Riley (1985), 20, 35. For Petty as populationist, see also Brewer (1992*b*), 36.

100 Brewer (1992*a*), 715.

101 Ibid. 714.

Royal Society, marked by the use of 'number, weight and measure'; his analysis was inevitably built upon an accounting framework.[102] Petty's *Treatise of Taxes and Contributions* (1662) was written with a thoroughly practical purpose, justifying as it did the hearth tax; the book was published in the very month that Parliament published the hearth tax grant. Yet Petty also considered the general causation of increased taxes.[103] He noted the unwillingness of people to pay taxes and the problems caused by the requirement to pay them at a specific time in money, and not in commodities. When he came to reflect on 'the general causes of the unquiet bearing of taxes', Petty's first reason was that the sovereign sometimes asked for more in the way of taxation than was actually needed. The misappropriation of revenue by needless expenditure was clearly also a source of grievance. However, Petty's central theme was the lack of 'political arithmetic' on the part of statesmen:

> Ignorance of the number, trade, and wealth of the people, is often the reason why the said people are needlessly troubled, *viz.* with the double charge and vexation of two, or many levies, when one might be served...
>
> Besides, for not knowing the wealth of the people, the prince knows not what they can bear; and for not knowing the trade, he can make no judgement of the proper season when to demand his exhibitions.[104]

Petty was one of the few theoreticians to show a keen awareness of the relationship between the size of the fiscal burden, the taxable capacity of the state, and the political constitution. His papers reveal that he was well informed about the balance of regional expenditure in the Low Countries and about the French and Irish revenue systems.[105] He was thus in a position to make informed comparisons: as he wrote in *Political Arithmetick* (published posthumously in 1690, but written *c.*1671–6):

> It is said that the king of *France*, at present doth levy the fifth part of his people's wealth; and yet great ostentation is made of the present riches and strength of that kingdom. Now great care must be had in distinguishing between the wealth of the people, and that of an absolute monarch; who taketh from the people where, when and in what proportion he pleaseth. Moreover, the subjects of two monarchs may be equally rich, and yet one monarch may be double as rich as the other; *viz.* if one take the tenth part of the people's

[102] Ibid. 713; Endres (1985), 247; Letwin (1963), 115–16, 130; Keynes (1971), 86.

[103] Chandaman (1975), 78; Petty, ed. Hull (repr. 1963), i, 5–97, esp. i, 20–1. For Petty's significance: Schumpeter (1954*a*), 210–12; Letwin (1963), 140–6; Hutchison (1988), 27–41. In the Petty papers, the earliest treatise of a fiscal kind ('How all persons & Things may contribute proportionably to their Government & defence') concerned the excise: B[ritish] L[ibrary], London, Petty papers, box g, item 25.

[104] Petty, ed. Hull (repr. 1963), i, 34. For the term 'political arithmetic', first used in December 1672: ibid. i, 239 n. 2, 244; Keynes (1971), 31.

[105] BL Petty papers, box a, nos. 28, 30, 32 (fo. 3), 33, 34, 36, 49, 51–3.

substance to his own dispose, and the other but the *20th.* nay the monarch of a poorer people, may appear more splendid and glorious, than that of a richer; which perhaps may be somewhat the case of *France*...[106]

More than this, however, Petty was the epitome of the seventeenth-century 'projector', unifying in his fertile genius the varied aspirations of Mercantilists, populationists and proponents of cheap credit systems. The increase of trade, he declared, depended chiefly and naturally upon the increase of population and not upon interest rates alone.[107] If the population could be doubled in size, then the wealth of England, Scotland and Ireland would increase by £1,619 million in twenty-five years, while the fiscal burden (which he thought to be 5 per cent of gross national product) would fall to 1 per cent, and interest rates, too, would fall.[108] Yet how could the population increase rapidly? Anticipating the German Cameralists, Petty concluded that immigration should be encouraged, and as a 'question in politicall Arithmetick' proposed that a million Irish people should be transported to England; this would lead to growth in the gross national product and thus in crown revenue.[109] Petty's first famous work, the treatise on taxes, had publicized his ideas on the need for 'exact computation' so as to avoid fiscal fraud,[110] and shortly before his death in his *Accompts of the Lands and Hands of a Nation, Making a Paire of Spectacles through which Statesmen May Look upon their Business* (1686), Petty proposed an 'exact and universall knowledge of the lands, hands and goods' of the kingdom, so as to make possible a 'proportionable levy' and to halve collection costs.[111]

What has never been fully revealed, however, is the closeness of Petty to the fiscal concerns of the government on the eve of the outbreak of the Third Anglo-Dutch War. A letter from Petty to Arlington, secretary of state and a prominent member of the group of ministers known as the Cabal, in September 1671 reveals that at the king's 'command' he had considered how any new levy might be 'equally and proportionably taxed upon all persons and things' as well as 'speedily, safely and inexpensively collected'. A second consideration was not merely how the new fiscal system might be established for the current needs ('some single emergency') but subsequently, so that the crown could judge what

[106] Petty, ed. Hull (repr. 1963), i, 272–3. That manuscript copies were in circulation in October 1673 and April 1674 is indicated from letters to Petty: BL Petty papers, vol. vi, items 51, 52.

[107] *Petty Papers*, ed. Lansdowne (1927), i, 247–8; BL Petty papers, vol. i, item 49.

[108] *Petty Papers*, ed. Lansdowne (1927), ii, 55–7; BL Petty papers, vol. i, item 22. For one-twentieth 'of the people's expence': iv, items 21, 34, 36.

[109] *Petty Papers*, ed. Lansdowne (1927), i, 1; BL Petty papers, box c, item 13.

[110] Petty, ed. Hull (repr. 1963), i, 53–4.

[111] *Petty Papers*, ed. Lansdowne (1927), i, 193–8, does not print the final points from BL Petty papers, vol. iv, item 33 (arts. 33, 34).

'real effect and value' there might be in any tax proposals. The king must be in a position to know 'the wealth and other efficiencies of his subjects', as might be estimated by their expenditure and income from land, labour and personal estate: he would then be able to judge 'what part or proportion his subjects are able to spare in case of the greatest extremity and [that] which will suffice in the most serene and secure tymes'. 'An exact accompt' must be taken of the population 'in a conspic[u]ous and examinable man[n]er soe as to prevent all imaginary and arbitrary proceedings in this great poynt'. It was proposed that this investigation was to take place over a year between September 1671 and December 1672, and should comprise a census of the population, according to age, trade, office, title, religious status or other qualifications; the value of lands in each parish, their quantity, quality, situation, rentable value, and so on would be enumerated; so too would the external measurement of every house in the kingdom, its location whether in city, market town or village, and the rent and value of each building; a property valuation of each inhabitant (including furniture, clothes, and utensils as well as an estimate for 'ye ware and tare of ye same') would be carried; and finally other forms of wealth ('goods out of doors'), including shipping and exports, the cost of poor relief and so on, would be evaluated. The purpose of the investigation, declared Petty, was not to enable the king to 'take one pen[n]y more than is necessary but only to levy with ease, certainty and equality what ye reason of his affaires requires'. In one sense, Petty failed. He proposed to Arlington a scheme which was far too ambitious for the needs of the moment, and far too costly in its implementation, apart from risking re-creating the intrusive state which Englishmen felt had been laid to rest at the end of the Commonwealth. Yet even in their failure, the ideas were of seminal importance. Petty's confidential memorandum to Arlington enumerated a number of other advantages 'of these accompts', which together with his interest in encouraging population growth, encompassed virtually the whole spectrum of both Cameralism and the later cadastral reform movement of the eighteenth century:

1 The equall assessing of any sum as above mentioned.
2 Preventing ye exorbitant & irregular gayne of farmers & collectors.
3 Knowing ye wealth & power of ye whole kingdom.
4 The easy raising of any forces suitable to any designe whatsoever & ye most remediary raising of ye same.
5 The knowing of what number of forces are required & enough to keep the publicq peace.
6 Whether ye whole kingdome doth empoverish or emprove.
7 Whether ye people are able to undertake any other trade & manufacture than now ...[112]

[112] BL Petty papers, box c, item 23.

With Sir William Petty and his successors, Gregory King (1648–1712) and Charles Davenant (1656–1714),[113] we arrive at the age in which different states' resources were compared systematically (or at least were quoted and debated) as an aspect of state competition. In *Natural and Political Observations* (1696), King compared the per capita fiscal burden of England, France and Holland and concluded that Holland was taxed over twice as heavily as the two monarchies. However, his calculations were vitiated by a gross underestimate of the French population.[114] In *Discourses on the Public Revenues and on the Trade of England ...* (1698), Davenant similarly compared the tax burden of the three states,[115] but took the debate further than either Petty or King and elevated 'political arithmetic' into a virtual science of government:

> By Political Arithmetic, we mean the art of reasoning by figures, upon things relating to government. The art itself is undoubtedly very ancient; but the application of it to the particular objects of revenue and trade, is what Sir William Petty first began ... And he who knows what taxes and impositions one country can pay, by considering the different humours of the people, their stock and wealth, their territory, their soil and trade, shall be able, by comparison, to form a good conjecture, what revenues can be raised in another nation; and consequently he may make a near guess how long either kingdom can carry on a war ...[116]

Correctly or incorrectly, Davenant considered that during the War of the League of Augsburg, the Dutch had contributed a third of their national income in taxation (an excessive fiscal burden made possible only by 'the equal manner used in taxing the subjects of their dominion')[117] and about a quarter in time of peace.[118] France had paid a fifth, and England an eighth, of its national income during the war. In other words, as a proportion of its national income, England paid little more in time of war than France had paid in time of peace.[119] Hence the importance of the fiscal burden as a proportion of the 'annual income'

113 For their importance: Schumpeter (1954*a*), 210 n. 3 and 212–13; Hutchison (1988), 46–53.

114 The figures are presented in tabular form by Wilson [1969], 120. King's population calculations for France (14 million) were much too low: Le Roy Ladurie (1968), 1096.

115 Davenant, ed. Whitworth (repr. 1967), i, 250. These figures were later edited by Forbonnais with conversions from the £ sterling to the *livre tournois* at a rate of 13 to the £, which was the level in 1693 but not in 1698. A more realistic conversion would have been 15 to the £: Véron de Forbonnais (1758), ii, 296.

116 Davenant, ed. Whitworth (repr. 1967), i, 128, 134–6. Davenant also cited Gregory King's 'general knowledge in political arithmetic': ibid. i, 137. See also Hume (1974), 476, on Davenant's hope for rational decision- and policy-making.

117 Davenant, ed. Whitworth (repr. 1967), i, 268.

118 Ibid. i, 253.

119 Ibid. i, 142, 253.

or what we would call the relationship of the tax base to the gross national product:

By annual income, we mean the whole that arises in any country, from land and its product, from foreign trade and domestic business, as arts, manufactures, &c ... The revenue of the government is part of this annual income, as likewise a part of its expence [*sic*]; and where it bears too large a proportion with the whole, as in France, the common people must be miserable and burthened with heavy taxes.[120]

Political arithmetic had, in Davenant's view, revealed the reasons for the ending of the War of the League of Augsburg in 1697:

... time has now brought to light, that England had some millions more of money than was believed, and that France is indebted many more millions than was imagined ... Their annual income is not double to ours; and their debt, with what was contracted before the war, is above five times more than ours; the expenses of their government do much exceed that of England; we shall in all appearance sooner recover our trade than that kingdom possibly can; add to this, that during the war they have had a scarcity of corn, which almost amounted to a famine; want of nourishment must have destroyed a great number of their people; they had little exportation of their home product; the persecution of the [P]rotestants must have forced away more inhabitants than was first thought; and all this must have so impaired their annual income, that they could not raise the [necessary] 16 millions [sterling] within the year; by which the crown every year so increased its debt, as that the war could not be carried on much longer with any safety for their government ... Though our taxes were heavy, our national stock was great, and not exhausted as was that of France, by former impositions ...[121]

Though Adam Smith pronounced that he had 'no great faith in political arithmetic'[122] and was ideologically opposed to attempts to measure the tax base, there is little doubt that the work of Petty, Davenant, Sir Josiah Child and Gregory King prepared the way for the achievements of Anglo-Scottish liberal thought in the eighteenth century, and was highly influential on the Continent, particularly in France.[123] John Locke's contribution to monetary theory should not be forgotten either, for it was influential in the formulation of Cantillon's more advanced ideas. In *Some Considerations of the Consequences of the Lowering of Interest and Raising the Value of Money* (1691), Locke also argued half a century

[120] Ibid. i, 251–2. [121] Ibid. i, 265–6.

[122] Smith, ed. Campbell, Skinner and Todd (1976), i, 52, 534.

[123] Hecksher in Seligman (1930–4), x, 338, claimed that Mercantilist doctrine was 'elaborated principally by a host of English writers in the seventeenth century' while the German writers contributed 'little of an original character in this field'. This verdict diminishes the originality of Cameralism.

before the birth of Physiocracy that 'Taxes, however contriv'd, ... for the most part terminate upon Land'.[124]

6.4 *Populationism, Cameralism and the Fiscal implications of the State's Human Resources*

Bodin had discussed population levels, and believed that France could support a large number of inhabitants; but he did not advance a theory of population as such; nor did he relate it to other aspects of his fiscal theory.[125] This task was left to an author who had read Bodin's principal work on a visit to France in 1585:[126] in *The Greatness of Cities* (1588), the Piedmontese Jesuit Giovanni Botero, who had spent much of his career as secretary and councillor to the Borromeo archbishops of Milan, had noted (in almost Malthusian language)[127] that because of subsistence crises and plague the population of cities and kingdoms could not 'increase and grow immoderately'.[128] Reflecting no doubt upon recent Milanese history (where the plague of 1576–7 had carried off about 18 per cent of the population),[129] he remarked that plague affected cities 'more surely and more often, with great loss of people'.[130] In his various *Relazioni*, and above all in his *Reason of State* (1589), Botero produced an early version of the criteria for measuring and assessing the power of states, such as the revenues of the prince, the prosperity of agriculture and industry, and above all, the size of the population.[131] It was in Book 7 of *Reason of State* that he argued the case for a large population as a source of national wealth. In words that were frequently cited later, he considered 'the true strength of a ruler' to consist 'in his people: for upon them depend all his other resources'.[132] He considered that 'if Spain is accounted a barren land this is not due to any deficiency of the soil but to the sparseness of the inhabitants'.[133]

124 Locke, ed. Kelly (1991), 272; Brewer (1992*b*), 145; Hutchison (1988), 56–75. There is no evidence that Locke knew the writings of Francisco Centani: Locke, ed. Kelly (1991), 96–100.

125 Spengler (1942), 13–15.

126 Botero, ed. Waley and Waley (1956), x.

127 Cf. Schumpeter (1954*a*), 254: 'Divested of nonessentials, the "Malthusian" Principle of Population sprang fully developed from the brain of Botero in 1589.' There is in fact an inconsistency between Botero's pessimism (the association of population increase with actual or potential misery) and his populationism (that a state's strength was derived from its size of population).

128 Botero, ed. Waley and Waley (1956), 279.

129 Biraben (1975–6), i, 156. It was known as the plague 'di San Carlo' because of Borromeo's efforts on behalf of its victims: ibid. ii, 81.

130 Botero, ed. Waley and Waley (1956), 277.

131 Riley (1985), 40; Elliott (1986), 93; Hutchison (1988), 18–19.

132 Botero, ed. Waley and Waley (1956), 143.

133 Ibid. 145. Elliott (1986), 93 and Elliott (1989), 255, demonstrates that the Spanish *arbitristas* knew of Botero's argument.

Botero's *Reason of State* was translated into German in 1596 and was known to Ferdinand II's court at Graz before he became Emperor;[134] the role of Jesuits as confessors to the Emperors, the Italianate influence at the court of the Austrian Habsburgs, and the disastrous population losses during the Thirty Years' War all contributed to the propagation of populationist ideas. Cameralism (so called after the *Kammer* or chamber of the princely or territorial state in the Holy Roman Empire) was an Austrian and German form of Mercantilism. Though the economist Heckshar denied the originality of Cameralism,[135] it is clear that the early Cameralists had a much clearer emphasis upon fiscal policy,[136] with no sharp distinction between political and economic tasks, and a concept of the *Polizeistaat*, in which the good of the ruler was indistinguishable from the good of the populace. The historian Justus Christoph Dithmar (1677–1737), writing in 1731, considered that the purpose of Cameralist science was to study 'the means of raising revenues' for 'general improvement and utilization in the maintenance of the commonweal so that every year a surplus remains'.[137] The improved organization of the state and its proto-bureaucratic apparatus were clearly critical elements in the Cameralist argument, and provide a link from early thinkers such as Melchior von Osse (1506–57), through later writers such as Veit Ludwig von Seckendorff (1626–92)[138] to the Habsburg Cameralists under Leopold I.[139] The term 'Austrian' is avoided, since none of the three main theoreticians in the later seventeenth century was a native of the hereditary lands, and all had travelled abroad, either to England or the United Provinces; a clear separation from Mercantilist ideas in western European is therefore impossible to establish.[140] Johann Joachim Becher (1635–82) was heavily influenced by Dutch ideas and practice; in 1665 he was appointed Leopold I's economic adviser (*Commerzienrath*), a post which he held until 1677. His *Political Discourse* (1668) also showed him to be a populationist; he anticipated the Physiocrats by stressing that consumers' expenditure generates income, but failed to turn this concept into a

[134] Bireley in Evans and Thomas (1991), 232; Tribe (1988), 27–8.

[135] Heckshar (1935), ii, 262–3, thought that 'they had little in common with the writers of western Europe'. Contrast Sommer in Seligman (1930–4), ii, 158–61, and Sommer (1920–5), who characterized Cameralism as 'properly the German and Austrian variety of Mercantilism'. For Tribe (1988), 66, 'to label Justi or any other Cameralist writer as a "Mercantilist" would be grossly misleading. And yet ... there are features in Cameralistic discourse that fit quite naturally into Smith's conception of Mercantilism.' The author acknowledges generous assistance from Professor János Barta, who supplied a working paper on Cameralism.

[136] Meyer (1991), 31. However, this emerges less clearly from Raeff (1975) and Raeff (1983), 118.

[137] Tribe (1984), 264; Tribe (1988), 52.

[138] Tribe (1984), 271 n. 27, 272; Small (1909), 60–106.

[139] Johnson (1964).

[140] Bérenger (1975), 187–8, who also demonstrates that Becher, von Hörnigk and von Schröder were related by marriage; Kann (1973), 28–31.

principle of analysis.[141] Wilhelm von Schröder (1640–88), a salt tax administrator in Upper Austria, was a disciple of Thomas Mun and was also heavily influenced by the English school of 'political arithmetic'.[142] In his *Treasury Chamber and Prince's Income* (*Fürstliche Schatz und Rentkammer*, 1686), he proclaimed that 'a prince must first procure for his subjects a good livelihood if he will take anything from them'.[143] (The imagery of the prince as a sheep-shearer, taking the wool from his subjects, was drawn from Mun.) The management of a ruler's revenues, he thought, 'consists in the proper distribution of expenditures' and also the increase of his income.[144] Schröder's idea of establishing a public granary (*granarium publicum*), though not itself original, recognized the potential difficulties for the state resulting from sudden dearth. Schröder was hostile to the territorial estates, and it is significant that Count Friedrich Wilhelm Haugwitz, the proponent of far-reaching reform in the Austrian lands in the 1740s, was his disciple.[145] Schröder's writings, and above all his advocacy of the so-called 'Dutch tax', a percentage tax on the total fortune of the inhabitants which would enable the crown to share in the increase of wealth which would follow from a prosperous economy, were influential in Sweden, where the fiscal experimentation under Charles XII found its inspiration in his work.[146] The third writer, Philipp Wilhelm von Hörnigk (1638–1714), was in many respects a minor figure, except that his work (*Austria above All, when It so Wishes*) was the one which was republished most frequently in the eighteenth century (it went through sixteen editions between 1684 and 1784). It categorically asserted that the Austrian hereditary lands could support double their existing level of population.[147]

The first chairs of Cameralist policy were established in two of the Prussian universities in 1727[148] and thereafter the influence of the movement grew—though relatively slowly,[149] as the number of chairs in Cameralism or political economy expanded. The two best-studied authors in the German universities

[141] Schumpeter (1954*a*), 283–4, stressed his originality and called it 'Becher's Principle'; Braun (1975), 306–7; Small (1909), 107–34; Hutchison (1988), 91–3.

[142] Barta, unpubd working paper on Cameralism. Small (1909), 135–74; Bérenger (1975), 188; Hutchison (1988), 90, 95–6.

[143] Hecksher (1935), ii, 20–1; cf. Dithmar's definition of Cameralistic science in 1731 as 'the proper use of the domains and *Regalien* of the ruler, and how obligations of the subjects and other public funds of the ruler's income can be raised, improved and employed to maintain the common welfare': Tribe (1988), 52.

[144] Tribe (1984), 270. He used the term *menagie* for management.

[145] Dickson (1987), i, 225 n. 20 and ii, 8 n. 19; Scott in Scott (1990), 152; Schröder's work was republished in 1744 and 1752, but note the long delay in implementing the ideas in practice.

[146] Hatton (1968), 344.

[147] Sommer in Seligman (1930–4), ii, 160, emphasizes the populationist views of later writers such as von Justi and von Sonnenfels; Hutchison (1988), 93–5.

[148] Tribe (1988), 42–3. [149] Ibid. 46.

who also held posts in the Cameralistic sciences were Justi and Sonnenfels.[150] Johann Heinrich Gottlob von Justi (1720–71) published his most important work, *State Economy* ... (*Staatswirthschaft*) in 1755,[151] and though he dedicated it to Maria Theresa it was influenced by Prussian administrative practice (he entered Danish service in 1757 and then Prussian service in 1765). Justi considered Cameralism a 'science concerned with the economic collection of the property of the republic ... [and how] prudently [to] employ it for the common good of the ruler and subjects ...'[152] In Justi's view, the purpose of Cameralist science was to inculcate a proper understanding of how to increase the state's fiscal base and then of how to exploit it: 'the Cameralist is concerned to abstract from out of this total wealth of the state the most accessible part, without disadvantage to the whole, for the necessary expenses of government'.[153] The necessary skills included not merely domain administration and a knowledge of how to exploit the ruler's regalian rights, but a proper appreciation of the relationship of fiscal policy to economic development and the encouragement of population growth: the example of the Netherlands demonstrated that a country could never have too many inhabitants.[154] Justi pointed out that if some scheme similar to Vauban's royal tithe was to be adopted then its amount (10 per cent of revenues) would prove insufficient: by the second half of the eighteenth century, Justi thought that 'most governments collect a fourth of all earnings and profits from their subjects in contributions, some as much as a third of earnings'.[155] Justi enunciated six principles for a tax and contribution system[156] which foreshadowed Adam Smith's 'four canons' on taxation. Firstly, subjects had to be in a position to pay the taxes without 'depriving themselves of necessaries, and without trenching [*sic*] upon their capital'. Secondly, the 'contributions must be levied upon the subjects with complete equality and just proportions'—this idea was hardly new; its realization was the problem. Thirdly, 'the methods of raising the contributions must be of such a character that the welfare of the state and of the subjects and civil freedom suffer no harm'. 'The fourth fundamental rule', wrote Justi, 'is that contributions should be organized according to the nature of the state and of the form of government'—this was in embryonic form the idea of a fiscal constitution. Tax-farming, he contended, was unsuitable for republics and 'it was no wonder, therefore, that the masses rebelled against these tax-

[150] Ibid. 117–18.

[151] Schumpeter (1954*a*), 170, who gives his date of birth as 1717.

[152] Tribe (1984); Tribe (1988), 73.

[153] Walker (1971), 162.

[154] Justi (1758); Small (1909), 341–3, 421–2; Tribe (1988), 62–5; Hutchison (1988), 249–52.

[155] Monroe (1951), 387.

[156] Ibid. 379–99.

farmers in Holland about 16 years ago'—that is, in 1748.[157] 'The sixth and last rule', he concluded, 'is that contributions should be so arranged that they can be collected in the easiest and most convenient way, and with as little expense as possible, both on the part of the state and of the subjects.' Justi was a firm believer in the requirement upon the state to gather information: a statistical bureau should collect reports from the customs officials, and prepare an annual table (*Handlungsbilanz*) for the guidance of the ruler and his ministers.[158] Despite the king's commitment to the common good[159] there was an enormous gulf between the recommendations of the Cameralists and the actual practice of government in the (relatively advanced) Prussia of Frederick II,[160] where enlightened reform (*Aufklärung*) 'was born among us and has led to the prosperity of the entire state'.[161] A prominent critic of 'enlightened' reform, Justus Möser of Osnabrück (1720–94), argued that variety existed in nature and should be preserved in politics; '*idées simples et uniques*', in his view, 'marked the clear path to ... despotism'. Möser quoted Necker's maxim that 'the more general the principle adopted, the greater the distance between it and the objects to which it is to be applied'. He could thus act as a stern critic of despotism while advocating regional economic planning.[162]

If Justi anticipated some of the Physiocratic ideas, Joseph von Sonnenfels (1732–1817) was influenced by Véron de Forbonnais, one of their foremost critics.[163] Sonnenfels' *Principles of Police*,[164] *Commercial and Financial Science* (*Grundsätze aus der Polizey, Handlungs- und Finanzwissenschaft*) were published in three volumes at Vienna between 1765 and 1776. This work covered the principles of internal security, commercial science and financial science, the last including the preferred methods for raising state revenue. Both Justi and Sonnenfels were populationists;[165] and they clearly regarded a large and increasing population as a source of strength both to the state and its finances. For Sonnenfels, 'the augmentation of civil society' was the principal purpose of government. It was critical in all aspects of political affairs, for defence, for facilitating civil control,

157 Ibid. 397. For the looting of the houses of tax-farmers: Prak (1989), 171.

158 Johnson (1964), 389.

159 Hubatsch (1975), 70; cf. ibid. 71, where Frederick rejected the advice of de Launay which was ahead of its time, and if accepted would 'ruin everything'.

160 Johnson (1964); Johnson (1975), 105. Justi himself died in a Prussian prison in 1768, only three years after being appointed inspector of mines. Braun (1975), 308, emphasized the influence of the Prussian model on Justi; cf. also Small (1909), 312–13.

161 Quoted in Brunschwig (1974), 21.

162 Parry (1963), 187–8; Knudsen (1986), 120.

163 Tribe (1988), 79–82.

164 The word 'police' is used in the sense of 'administration'.

165 Kann (1973), 175; Tribe (1988), 65, 85–6.

for consumption and the circulation of goods, and for taxation; population increase, moreover, would result in a fall in the per capita tax burden:

The enlargement of society thus subsumes within itself all the subordinate separate means which, collectively, further the general welfare ... We take the increase of civil society through encouragement of population [growth] as the chief and general principle of statecraft and of the sciences contained within statecraft; and the test of every measure adopted to further the general welfare is: is it conducive to population [growth]; is it disadvantageous to population [growth]?[166]

The third volume of Sonnenfels' *Principles of Police* was entirely concerned with financial administration.[167] The distinction between the state and a household revealed a fundamental truth about the growth of the fiscal state in Europe. In a private household, income determined the need to reduce, or the capacity to increase, expenditure. A state, however, had no such opportunity: if a foreign army was poised to attack, it could not reduce its expenditure on defence simply because of insufficient revenue. Expenditure was capable of being known, within certain limits; income was much less certain; and a state's needs were expenditure-, not income-driven.[168] Sonnenfels enumerated the various elements of ordinary and extraordinary revenue, and though he showed some interest in the Physiocratic single tax on net income, he nevertheless considered (like Adam Smith) that it was a mistake to regard agriculture as the only source of wealth in a state.[169] Sonnenfels also revealed a hostility to revenue farming, while recognizing that it was desirable to increase the state's income by widening the tax base and reducing administrative costs. He recognized the growing importance of credit within the structure of state finance, but adhered to the traditional Cameralist viewpoint that the credit structure should remain a national one. Despite the growth of Dutch international financial investment in the second half of the eighteenth century, in Sonnenfels' view it was disadvantageous for the state to borrow abroad: at least with a national credit structure the advantages from the recirculation of wealth accrued to citizens of the same nationality.[170] At the same time, if the state relied on its internal credit structure, it was essential to avoid the mistakes of Law's System, which had seen the overvaluing of its own financial assets.

Though for a time Physiocratic ideas were fashionable in Germany, the

[166] Braun (1975), 304, 309; Bartlett (1979), 24, 273 n. 77 (for quotation). In other respects, Walker (1978), 246, views Sonnenfels as a decadent thinker. Kann (1973), 174–81; Hutchison (1988), 252–3.

[167] For Tribe (1988), 89, it held 'little of interest for our investigation'.

[168] Barta, unpubd working paper on Cameralism, citing Sonnenfels (1771–6), iii, 37–9.

[169] Barta, unpubd working paper on Cameralism, citing Sonnenfels (1771–6), iii, 296. Cf. Tribe (1988), 89, who considered that his discussion here drew upon Véron de Forbonnais; Small (1909), 583–4.

[170] Cf. Riley (1980); Small (1909), 54.

best-read foreign author before the last decade of the eighteenth century was not any of the Physiocrats, nor even Adam Smith, but Sir James Steuart, who had resided on the Continent. In 1782, Smith's *The Wealth of Nations* was regarded by von Pfeiffer as merely proposing 'a refined Physiocratic system', while as late as 1794, it could be said that Smith had enjoyed 'absolutely no influence on the alteration of the doctrine of state economy in our Fatherland . . .'[171] However, from the mid-1790s, Smith began to exercise a much greater posthumous influence in Germany: Sartorius (d. 1828), for example, claimed in 1796 that Smith had 'discovered the truth' and he sought to disseminate his findings.[172] Out of the resulting intellectual ferment, a new concept of *Nationalökonomie* gradually came to displace traditional Cameralism as taught in the universities. In the intervening period, Cameralist ideas had come to influence the practice of government in Russia, though the precise way in which this happened remains elusive, leaving aside the general 'rhetoric' of the Enlightenment.[173]

6.5 *France: The Search for Fiscal Reform, Physiocracy and the Tax on Net Income*

The fiscal pressure in France resulting from the long wars of Louis XIV's reign prompted a debate on fiscal reform. Three men dominated this debate: Sébastien Le Prestre, Maréchal de Vauban (1633–1707); Pierre Le Pesant, seigneur de Boisguilbert (1646–1714) and lieutenant-general of police at Rouen; and Charles-Irénée Castel, abbé de Saint-Pierre (1658–1743).[174] Vauban's contribution is the best known of the three. His *Projet d'une dixme royale* was published illegally in 1707; but it was less the circumstances of its publication which influenced the debate[175] than the fact that a draft of its text ('pour remedier aux desordres de la taille') had been read to the king seven years earlier, in June 1700. Vauban assumed that most of the existing taxes (the *taille*, *aides*, *douanes*, *décimes* on the clergy, and the *affaires extraordinaires*) could be abolished, and moreover that the sale price of salt under the system of the *gabelle* could be reduced by half. He denounced the abuses of the *taille* both as a personal and as a land tax. A new tax modelled on the ecclesiastical tithe should replace these revenues.[176] The system

171 Tribe (1988), 144–5. 172 Ibid. 165.

173 Raeff (1983) mentions reforming decrees, but is less clear on the movement of ideas. De Madariaga in Scott (1990), 306, comments that many of the ideas Catherine II considered useful 'had their origins in German Cameralism' but cites Raeff.

174 Schumpeter stressed Boisguilbert's importance as a precursor of the Physiocrats: Schumpeter (1954*a*), 203–4, 215–16; Vaggi (1987), 78; Gross (1993), 83–7.

175 Vauban, ed. Pernot (1988), ix–xiii. 176 Ibid. 7.

would be established after careful consultation between the provincial intendants.[177] Vauban provided calculations of a specimen conversion between the *taille* and the *dixme royale* for the *élections* of Rouen and Vézelay:[178] in both cases the new tax would be higher than the old one, simply because this was the case with the existing ecclesiastical tithe. Vauban's estimate of the likely yield of the royal tithe (116 million *livres*) was in itself hopelessly exaggerated,[179] and his methodology, which proposed the measurement of the kingdom so that the ruler would no longer have to visit distant provinces but could ascertain all the necessary details in an hour's private study,[180] was more influential than his specific proposals. The practical difficulties of the scheme were immense, and in those small areas of France where a version of his plan was introduced in 1718 (the *élection* of Niort and five *élections* of the *généralité* of La Rochelle), it was found to be unworkable and was abandoned in 1722–3.[181]

Boisguilbert denounced Vauban's scheme.[182] He was in agreement that the way in which the *taille* was levied was so corrupt that it would have to be replaced. He was equally insistent that one tax should replace a series of different levies. But he parted company with Vauban on three grounds. Firstly, the ecclesiastical tithe was frequently much lower than the levy of the *taille*: he cited the examples of the *élection* of Pont de l'Arche in Normandy, and the *élection* of Paris. Secondly, Boisguilbert considered that the exemption conferred by the *taille* was jealously guarded precisely because it conferred substantial financial benefits on the privileged classes: were all the other taxes to be abolished, the *dixme royale* would need to be set at four times the rate of the *capitation*; this could not be done without risking severe social discontent, particularly from the most politically important groups in society. Finally, the mechanism of local collection, which Vauban seemed to assume could continue under the *dixme royale* much as it had under the ecclesiastical tithe,[183] would prove unworkable in Boisguilbert's view: no peasant would be prepared to risk alienating his lord by accepting responsibility for it.

The devastating critique of Vauban prompted Boisguilbert to come up with his own proposals, and by October 1703 he had established a number of maxims

[177] Ibid. 78. [178] Ibid. 83–92. [179] Ibid. 66.

[180] Ibid. 151; Perrot (1992), 31–2. The scheme was proposed at about the same time that the provincial intendants provided their memoranda for the 'instruction' of the duc de Bourgogne: Perrot (1992), 24.

[181] Desaivre (1880).

[182] A[rchives] N[ationales], Paris, G[7] 721 no. 6, untitled memorandum of Boisguilbert against Vauban's *Projet d'une dixme royale*. This is reprinted in Boislisle (1874–9), ii, 524–6 and Boisguilbert, INED edn., (1966), i, 270–4; Spengler (1984); Hutchison (1988), 107–14.

[183] Vauban, ed. Pernot (1988), 32–3.

for the next tax: it was better to have a large tax which was equitably distributed than a series of smaller ones which were unfair ('la justice dans la repartition des imposts est absolument necessaire ou tout est perdu . . .'). The tax also needed to be fixed at the outset, since there was great resistance to arbitrary taxation. France should model itself on its principal rivals, particularly England with its land tax (he thought this tax was much more efficient than it was in reality: 'l'on donne le cinquieme sans murmure jusqu'aux grands seigneurs pour at[t]aquer la France').[184] He argued later in the *Factum de la France* (1707) that in England a tax equivalent to a fifth of revenues, and in Holland equivalent to a third of revenues, could be levied without coercion. In both these states the yield was the equivalent (he thought) to 100 million *livres*; the yield would be 300 million in France, bearing in mind the greater wealth and fiscal capacity of that country. The number of taxes should be reduced to three or four, and they should be administered with greater equity and efficiency as in Holland and England.[185] For Boisguilbert, Henri III with 32 million *livres* of revenue in 1582 was richer than Louis XIV in 1695 with 112 million.[186] An inefficient revenue-raising system had become more inefficient with the passing of time, so that France had lost out in the competition with England. What was needed was a completely new tax—the *dixième*—which would recreate 'la parité de la France avec l'Angleterre'.[187] When it was finally established in 1710, however, the *dixième* proved a disappointment to Boisguilbert, since it failed to meet a number of his criteria for such an important new fiscal measure.[188]

The abbé de Saint-Pierre is the least well known of the trio of French Mercantilists and agriculturalists.[189] His denunciation of Louis XIV's policies was if anything even more extreme than that of Vauban and Boisguilbert, with the conviction that financial, and especially tax, policy had been arbitrary in character. He was an admirer of the United Provinces; his *Discours sur la polysynodie* (1718) denounced the *vizirat*, his term for the excessive authority enjoyed by Louis XIV's ministers. As with Vauban's and Boisguilbert's publications, this work was castigated at the time, but the immediate governmental response gave it celebrity abroad. It was, however, his scheme for fiscal reform, the *taille tarifée*, which was most influential in terms of practical reforming measures: both this, and Vauban's *Dixme royale*, for example, were known to Pompeo Neri, the great

184 AN G^7 721 no. 17, 27 Oct. 1703; Boislisle (1874–9), ii, 534.

185 Boisguilbert (1707), 49–50; Boisguilbert, INED edn. (1966), ii, 900.

186 Boisguilbert, INED edn. (1966), i, 31 and ii, 587–8.

187 Ibid. ii, 669.

188 Bonney (1993*a*), 387.

189 On Saint-Pierre: Paultre (1903); Kaiser (1983); Perrot (1992), 38–59.

expert of the Milanese *censimento*.[190] Saint-Pierre proposed his scheme in 1717, and developed it further in 1723. He described seventeen sources of wealth for the taxpayer, on the basis of which he should make his voluntary declaration of wealth.[191] Specific procedures were adopted for the evaluation of wealth; landholdings should be measured in a common unit (he specified *arpents*); but the distinction between types of land (good, mediocre and poor, for example) was rejected as unsatisfactory as a guide to the yield. Saint-Pierre accepted that merchants' declarations of wealth could prejudice their businesses, but the alternative, fiscal injustice, was considered more dangerous.[192] The great weakness of the scheme, apart from the complexity of the 'tariff' or graduated tax bands and rates of tax,[193] was the falsification of the voluntary declarations: this was a general problem of direct taxes in France, which resulted in serious underassessment of individuals' tax liability, and on this Saint-Pierre had no real answer except to ask 'who is more likely to know the total income of a taxpayer than the taxpayer himself?'[194] At issue here was the question of the legitimacy of new forms of taxation, and above all the legitimacy of powers of coercion, especially concerning the verification of tax declarations. In March 1732, the government under Orry appeared to be committed to an implementation of Saint-Pierre's ideas;[195] but apart from Picardy and the *généralité* of Paris, the principal area where the *taille tarifée* was introduced was in the *généralité* of Limoges: Aubert de Tourny introduced it there in 1738, and Turgot refused an alternative intendancy so that he could remain in the Limousin to establish a justly proportioned tax which could be adopted elsewhere. He was relatively successful, but the scheme was not transferred to the other provinces.[196]

Charles Louis de Secondat, baron de Montesquieu (1689–1755) was a transitional figure between the abbé de Saint-Pierre and the Physiocrats. By the time of Montesquieu's *De l'esprit des lois* (1748), the difference between state systems had become expressed as a general rule on the relation between the amount of taxes paid and political liberty. Montesquieu's 'general rule' was that the freer the country in political terms the greater the public revenue that could be extracted. Thus England and Holland were heavily taxed. As political liberty declined, he

[190] Neri was of the opinion that the *dixme royale* and the *taille tarifée* were 'plus difficiles que le cadastre': AN K 880 no. 60, 'Extrait du journal envoyé à Monsieur d'Ormesson par le Sr Harvoin ...' The full journal is in AN 114 ap Dr. 2 [156 mi 72].

[191] Paultre (1903), 37.

[192] Ibid. 44–5.

[193] Ibid. 50–67. This was new only in so far as it was proposed to apply it to the *taille* in France: cf. Chapter 1.6 on the *decima scalata* at Florence.

[194] Ibid. 46–9; Gross (1993), 87. Fines were insufficient as a deterrent.

[195] Paultre (1903), 96; Marion (1901), 47–55; Marion (1910), 153–6.

[196] Paultre (1903), 256–7; Marion (1901), 40, notes an early implementation of the ideas at Lisieux in Dec. 1717; Noailles championed the idea at first: Marion (1910), 132–8.

postulated, so too did the fiscal burden, with Ottoman Turkey the least oppressively taxed of all. Moderate taxes were thus the compensation for a loss of political liberty. Poll taxes, or per capita direct taxes, were common to political regimes without political liberty, whereas taxes on commodities, which were less directly related to the person, were more common in states which enjoyed such freedom. But in any case fewer taxes were levied in so-called tyrannical states than in the western European states, and there was, according to Montesquieu, a preponderance of payment in kind (via the distribution of lands) rather than in money.[197] In England, Montesquieu wrote, because of the prevalence of indirect taxation, a merchant in effect lent the state £50 to £60 sterling for every barrel of wine he received. What merchant, he asked, would dare to do such a thing in a country governed like Turkey? And if he dared to do it, how would he be able to do so, with a suspect, uncertain and ruined fortune?

Montesquieu's views were representative of ideas of modernity in a fiscal system in the mid-eighteenth century and three of his theses bear careful examination. Firstly, on the relationship between indirect taxes and direct taxes: Montesquieu asserted the principle that the nature of taxation was relative to the government of the state; indirect taxes, or commodity taxes, were thus more natural than direct ones in free political states since they were related less directly to the person.[198] Secondly, Montesquieu was clear in his preference for direct administration (*régie*) rather than revenue farming, which he considered carried with it fatal abuses.[199] Thirdly, on the subject of the relationship between war finance and the consequent development of credit, Montesquieu showed himself to be studiously out of step with his times: he lamented the development of large standing armies and thus the permanent increase in taxes that resulted.[200] He knew of no advantages in a large public debt, except when (as in the case of England) a large amount of specie was simultaneously attracted into the kingdom by trade so that credit was not jeopardized and the just proportion between the state as creditor and state as debtor was maintained.[201] Montesquieu asserted the principle that there was no harm in some people paying insufficient tax since their plenty always reverted to the public; on the contrary, if individuals paid too much in taxes their ruin turned against the public interest. The desirable form of fiscal regime was therefore one which developed at the pace of the real economy,

[197] Hutchison (1988), 220–4; Montesquieu, ed. Cohler, Miller and Stone (1989), 220–2, extracts from Part 2, chs. 12 ('The relation of the size of taxes to liberty'), 13 ('In which government taxes are susceptible to increase'), 14 ('That the nature of taxes is relative to the government').

[198] Ibid. 222. [199] Ibid. 226. [200] Ibid. 224–5. [201] Ibid. 418–19.

but which left privilege intact.[202] He may thus be regarded as the theoretician *par excellence* of the endemic 'undertaxation' which was so detrimental to the French monarchy in the eighteenth century and which left such a perverse legacy in the period of the French Revolution.[203] Montesquieu was suspicious of direct taxation, since he regarded land taxes as inherently inequitable if they rested on the assessment of landed wealth; yet they were not necessarily oppressive if the amount levied was reasonable. Indirect taxes he considered to be least damaging, if two prior conditions were fulfilled: the tax should be levied at the point of production rather than consumption, since it was less noticeable there; and the balance between the price of the commodity and the amount of tax levied must be respected. A disproportionate levy on a particular item required a royal or governmental monopoly, which Montesquieu regarded as inherently disadvantageous.[204]

Writing shortly after the outbreak of the Seven Years' War (1756–63), which cut France's foreign trade significantly, and compromised her colonial future (Chapter 11.3), but left her agriculture intact, François Quesnay (1694–1774) took a quite different approach from his predecessors such as Montesquieu and Cantillon:[205] he was concerned with the dynamic process of income generation, primarily from the land, and its implications for fiscal policy: 'the wealth of the husbandman (*laboureur*)', he wrote, 'secures the revenue of the nation, the power of the sovereign and the prosperity of the state.'[206] Anne Robert Jacques Turgot (1727–81) later attributed to Quesnay the notion of revenue; it was he who had distinguished between the gross and net product, and excluded the profit of the cultivator from the net product.[207] Quesnay was the founder of a school known

202 Ibid. 217.

203 Cf. Crouzet (1993), 64; Norberg in Hoffman and Norberg (1994), 281–2.

204 Montesquieu, ed. Cohler, Miller and Stone (1989), 217–18.

205 Schumpeter (1954*a*), 223–5, 287. Brewer (1992*b*), 193, refers to 'Cantillon, and ... his disciples, the Physiocrats'. For the influence of Cantillon on Quesnay, ibid. 159–75. Brewer concludes (ibid. 174) that 'much of Quesnay's economics came almost direct from Cantillon'. Cf. ibid. 196: 'Cantillon's most direct and obvious influence was on the Physiocrats, but they misused his work, and made it into a dogmatic and cranky system.' Cantillon is viewed below (Chapter 6.6) chiefly in terms of his critique of Law, a viewpoint perhaps of the historian of state finance rather than economics.

206 *François Quesnay* (1958), ii, 566; Vaggi (1987), 38–9, 100; Weulersse in Seligman (1930–4), v, 348–51; Weulersse (1910, 1950, 1959); Meek (1962) provides some of the key texts, to which should be added Kuczynksi and Meek (1972); cf. also Spengler (1942), 170–211, who notes (183) Quesnay's (wildly inaccurate) figures for French population decline; Hutchison (1988), 273–85.

207 *François Quesnay* (1958), ii, 582; Meek (1962), 104; Groenewegen (1977), 102–3; Hutchison (1988), 308–21; Brewer (1992*b*), 159, 186, comments that Turgot himself 'was, in many ways, the first classical economist (though he is not always recognized as such)'. For Turgot's views on population: Spengler (1942), 282–90, who calls him a 'non-Physiocratic economist'.

to contemporaries as the *Économistes*[208] and to historians as the 'Physiocrats' after the publication of Quesnay's and Du Pont de Nemours's *Physiocratie* of 1767.[209] (The allusion was to the physiology of the social order: Quesnay himself was one of Louis XV's doctors and referred to the necessity of recourse to medical knowledge 'in the appalling crisis to come'.)[210] In his later writings, Quesnay elevated the study of the economy, and the relationship between the crown and agriculture to a science, the study of which was essential to avoid great disasters in policy-decisions: 'the great number of factors involved demands that they should be grouped together in comprehensive patterns, which form the foundation of a very far-reaching and self-evident science ...' ('la multiplicité des objets exige de grandes combinaisons qui forment le fond d'une science évidente fort étendue ...').[211] His theory was first propounded in three articles for the *Encyclopédie* of Diderot and d'Alembert, on *fermiers* (1756), *grains* (1757) and *impôt* (1757, but only published in 1902).[212]

Quesnay wanted the net income (*produit net*) in agriculture to be assessed effectively so that it would be able to support the full burden of taxation through the imposition of a single tax, the *impôt unique*. The purpose of this tax was to minimize collection costs by taxing directly those incomes that ultimately carried the burden of taxation: the proprietor would be compensated for his tax payment by increased revenue from land. This in turn would assist the regeneration of agriculture.[213] Taxes on revenue were considered less burdensome to proprietors than indirect taxes, which required proprietors both to pay tax on their personal expenditure and to carry the collection costs of different items subject to taxation.[214] Taxes on industrial profits and enterprises were illusory and self-defeating because in the last resort the burden would be shifted on to the primary

[208] Adam Smith termed them this: Smith, ed. Campbell, Skinner and Todd (1976), ii, 678–9, 830; he referred to Quesnay: ibid. ii, 672–4.

[209] Weulersse (1910), i, 128. The abbé Baudeau had referred earlier in the same year to 'l'ordre naturel et social fondé sur la nécessité physique et sur la force irrésistible de l'évidence': loc. cit. Cf. Einaudi in *François Quesnay* (1958), i, 6. McClain (1977), 220, comments that 'Quesnay's *Physiocratie* ... probably would not have seen the light of day without Du Pont's editorial efforts'; cf. Hutchison (1988), 290–2.

[210] Meek (1962), 18, 108. Quesnay was *premier médecin ordinaire du roi*: Antoine (1989), 867. Adam Smith referred to the fact that he was 'a physician, and a very speculative physician': Smith, ed. Campbell, Skinner and Todd (1976), ii, 674. For the influence of his medical views on his economic ideas: Foley (1973), 121–2, 143, 145. Foley also notes the influence of Cantillon (and thus indirectly Petty): ibid. 140–1.

[211] Meek (1962), 154 n. 1.

[212] *François Quesnay* (1958), i, 307; Vaggi (1987), 218 n. 35.

[213] Meek (1962), 25, 106; Vaggi (1987), 21. For Du Pont de Nemours's adherence to the idea throughout his long career: McLain (1977), 26–7, 88, 168, 181, 205.

[214] Meek (1962), 106–7; Vaggi (1987), 54–5, 210 n. 48 ('indirect taxes weigh upon the prices received in sales at first hand').

producer, the agriculturalist. In the *Tableau Économique*, Quesnay provided a vivid graphic illustration of the economic system as three interacting sectors, with capital regarded as a series of 'advances' (respectively of seed and expenses for cultivation; land and buildings; and livestock and agricultural improvements). Mirabeau called the depiction one of the three greatest inventions in the history of mankind (the others being writing and money).[215] The base calculation varied between the first and the third editions of the *Tableau Économique*, but by the third edition, an annual revenue of 600 million *livres* for the productive expenditure class of proprietors was said to generate 300 million for state taxation.[216] Simple arithmetical progression would ensure increased prosperity both for the state and for the agricultural producers.[217]

However, first certain conditions had to be fulfilled, which were expressed essentially in terms of negative requirements in the *Tableau Économique*, allegedly based on the maxims of Henri IV's finance minister, the duc de Sully. Thus the administration of finance had to ensure that monetary fortunes were not created which would remove revenue from circulation; taxes must not be destructive, or disproportionate to the revenue of the nation; taxes must follow upon increases in revenue, rather than anticipating them; taxes also should be levied upon the net product of landed property and not on its produce which would serve only to increase the cost of collection. Taxation should not be taken from capital advances of the farmers of landed property, which should be regarded as the nation's wealth, to be preserved with great care to ensure the future revenue of the nation. Arbitrary assessments on farmers must cease. The precedent of England ('a flourishing nation ... confined to a territory which is not very

[215] Vaggi (1987), 195 n. 20; Smith, ed. Campbell, Skinner and Todd (1976), ii, 679.

[216] The base figure had been 400 in the first edition. Kuczynksi and Meek (1972), v: 'Les *richesses de la classe des Dépenses productives* d'une nation ... Un revenu de 600 millions pour les Propriétaires suppose en outre 300 millions d'impôts & 150 millions pour la dixme du produit annuel, total frais compris ...' Both here and at Meek (1962), 131, the passage is translated as 'an extra 300 millions for taxes'. However, comparison with the *Philosophie rurale* of 1764 shows that the figure can only have been 300 million (in this case reduced to 262 or 264 million): ibid. 141. Only after the progressive increase in the proprietors' revenue would the revenue of the state rise to 493 million by means of the *impôt unique*, but this only on the assumption that all indirect taxes had been abolished: ibid. 144, 146. Total ordinary revenues in 1758 were in the region of 236 million, with a total of 300 million if loan revenue is included: Riley (1987), 225, 227. The figure of 300 million for the *impôt unique* before the abolition of indirect taxes is also accepted by Weulersse (1910), ii, 378. On the differences between the *tableaux*: Vaggi (1987), 25–7.

[217] Though Quesnay demonstrated this in the later *Philosophie rurale* (1766), and not in the *Tableau Économique* (1758–9). The *Analyse* of 1766 postulated further advances for the crown, to 572 million: Meek (1962), 153. The *Problème Économique* of 1766 placed indirect taxes at 450 million (ibid. 170), which should then be abolished progressively; the revenue of proprietors would treble as a result; this increased revenue would then be taxable by the crown, which would regain 400 million in revenue, rather less than what it had lost under the old system: ibid. 184.

extensive') must instead be followed, where temporary land taxes in wartime were dispensed with in time of peace so that agricultural revenues were safeguarded. Any failure to observe these rules would result in taxation degenerating into the ruin of the state.[218] The Physiocrats themselves were divided on what sort of fiscal system was desirable, and on the practicality of their *impôt unique*.[219] Quesnay clearly believed that the *cadastre*, a national land register which would ensure a more equitable distribution of taxation, had to follow upon, and not precede, agricultural prosperity or the crown would be the loser.[220] But the inability of the Physiocrats to advise the ruler of Baden–Durlach on precisely how to implement the single-tax system suggests that there was an abstract, if not utopian, aspect to their thinking on this central fiscal issue,[221] while even in French-controlled Corsica the implantation of a new administrative structure did not in the end lead to the introduction of the single tax on land.[222] The Physiocrats were in general agreement that the single tax was not to exceed one-third of the net product or pure rent, and that its implementation should be a gradual process. There were overwhelming arguments in favour of gradualism: land values would tend to fall to about 70 per cent of their preceding levels following upon the implementation of the tax. The measure was therefore likely to be desperately unpopular with landowners, unless it could be seen that general prosperity had increased as a result of the introduction of the scheme.[223]

Free trade for the Physiocrats was tantamount to the freedom for the agriculturalist to produce whatever he pleased and to dispose of his produce without restriction. It was predicated on a high price for grain (*le bon prix des grains*),[224] and on the free export of agricultural surpluses from one province to another. The excesses of such complete freedom (*liberté plenière*)[225] were not the sole difficulty with the theories of the *Économistes*. They were accused of favouring a form of legal despotism.[226] The disarray of the Physiocratic movement in France was most evident in the circumstances following Terray's appointment as controller-general in 1769. The change of ministerial policy encouraged the abbé Ferdinando Galiani (1728–87) to publish his *Dialogues sur le commerce des blés*, which attacked Physiocracy at its most unpopular and

218 Kuczynksi and Meek (1972), 4–6 and nn.

219 Weulersse (1950), 155, 282–5.

220 Meek (1962), 185; *François Quesnay* (1958), ii, 613.

221 Tribe (1988), 124–6; Liebel (1965), 47–51.

222 Hall (1969), 885, 893–4, 901–2 for the contrast between reforming ideas and actual achievement. Other experiments with the *impôt unique* were planned by Peter Leopold of Tuscany: Schumpeter (1954*a*), 232; and by a succession of reforming ministers in Spain: Matilla Tascón (1947).

223 Buurman (1991), 492–4; Vaggi (1987), 140, 143.

224 Weulersse (1910), i, 474–5.

225 Weulersse (1950), 212–13.

226 Weulersse (1910), ii, 48–52, 657–9; Vaggi (1987), 187–8.

vulnerable point on the policy of grain liberalization. Galiani maintained that famine was an inevitable consequence of their system, which he denounced with vehemence ('un enthousiasme, une mode, un caprice littéraire, un Mississipi, un Jansénisme, une Fronde, une croisade, enfin une de ces maladies épidémiques d'esprit dont la nation française est parfois attaquée, et qui causent de cruels ravages jusqu'à ce que le calme de la raison revienne').[227] Faced with this assault, the government itself was divided. Choiseul was one of the sponsors of a refutation of Galiani's *Dialogues* by the abbé André Morellet; but Terray ordered the suppression of Morellet's work almost immediately after publication.[228] Crucially, however, Diderot wrote his *Apologie de l'abbé Galiani*, a refutation of Morellet's defence of the Physiocrats. One of the greatest of the *Philosophes* thus turned against the *Économistes*, representing a split within the Enlightenment on the issue of grain liberalization.[229]

Adam Smith later denounced 'the capital error' of the Physiocratic system, which in his view was to represent the 'the class of artificers, manufacturers and merchants, as altogether barren and unproductive'.[230] It is true that Quesnay urged that the policy of *laissez-faire* or *laissez-aller*[231] should be applied to 'sterile expenditure'; but his aim was to remove the favour and protection traditionally afforded to manufactures and commerce since the time of Colbert, privileges which he thought had been gained essentially at the expense of agriculture.[232] The Physiocrats were not overwhelming supporters of free trade, however: Quesnay confined freedom of export to grain and agricultural products when the domestic market could no longer guarantee enough outlets. Foreign trade was an evil to be avoided as much as possible; nevertheless, where it took place, it had to operate in the interests of France alone.[233]

Though still limited in vision, Mirabeau's *Théorie de l'impôt* (1760) was one of

[227] Weulersse (1910), i, 212; ibid. ii, 662 for Galiani's accusation that the system rewarded only proprietors. Kaplan (1976), ii, 602; Vaggi (1987), 97–8.

[228] Kaplan (1976), ii, 607. For Morellet's earlier views: Meysonnier (1989), 309–25.

[229] Kaplan (1976), ii, 608–10, 687: 'Grain liberalism was too radical for one of the most radical of *Philosophes*.'

[230] Smith, ed. Campbell, Skinner and Todd (1976), ii, 674.

[231] The formula originates with Boisguilbert in 1702: Gross (1993), 83 n. 9. It is usually attributed to Vincent de Gournay: Weulersse (1910), i, 77; Antoine (1989), 867. In his *Éloge de M. de Gournay* (1759), Turgot attributed to Gournay the view that agriculture was the source of all revenues and that all taxes were in the final analysis paid by the landowner: Groenewegen (1977), 30–1. The term had also been used earlier by the marquis d'Argenson: Meyssonnier (1989), 59, 178, 189. Gournay was a protectionist, if his unpublished comments on the work of Josiah Child are to be believed (he published a translation of Child in 1754): Cantillon, ed. Tsuda (1979), 423–4; cf Hutchison (1988), 224–5. Quesnay used the expression *laissez-faire* only once: Vaggi (1987), 214 n. 21.

[232] Meek (1962), 244–6, 396. Definition of 'sterile expenditure' in Kuczynksi and Meek (1972), i.

[233] Vaggi (1987), 102–3, 110–14, 173–4; Perrotta (1991), 308.

the earliest studies of a fiscal system in its entirety. It has been little read since,[234] though other Physiocratic writers such as Le Trosne, who published a treatise entitled *De l'administration provinciale et de l'impôt* in 1778, were clearly influenced by it.[235] Mirabeau's treatise remains of interest as a precursor of Smith's 'four canons' on taxation, and for its emphasis that 'taxes should be levied directly on the annual reproduction' (or income) and 'on the source of all revenue', that is, the net product of land. He contrasted a 'blind' and 'fiscal' administration with a regime of good government, where the state's revenues grew or diminished in proportion to the subjects' increased or reduced wealth. All forms of intermediary in the levy of taxation, but especially the farmers of indirect taxes, were declared an anathema. For Mirabeau, 'the great secret of fiscal science' was to secure a burden of taxation restricted by considerations of justice and equity, while the 'great task of finance' was to ascertain how to tax only the net product which composed any individual's revenue.[236] Thus taxes should be established as near as possible to the source of the revenue taxed; they should be levied in proportion to such revenue; and the burden of taxation should not be increased by excessive collection costs. The mass of taxable revenue should determine the amount of taxation, not the other way round. Taxation should not 'extinguish the reproduction of revenues', that is to say, taxes should not be self-defeating and destroy the source of revenue they sought to tax. A tax of 150 million *livres* levied on a 'sterile revenue' would result in the destruction of that revenue. Subject to his rules, there was no objection to an increase in taxation; on the contrary, Mirabeau argued that Louis XV was poorer in real terms than his predecessors and enjoyed insufficient tax revenue in comparison with his needs. Since land was the basis of wealth, Mirabeau distinguished four main categories of land which produced a different level of revenue (meadows; forest; vineyards; and agricultural land), but which taken together constituted 'the sum total of revenues' of the nation.[237] In his *Supplément à la théorie de l'impôt* (1766), Mirabeau argued the case for a 'fiscal limit' on the power of the state: a tenth of the net wealth of his subjects was 'reasonable and sufficient' for a ruler's needs, and this principle should be enshrined in a 'fiscal law'. The immunity of noble and clerical lands would be abolished.[238]

That France needed an 'agricultural revolution' comparable to that of England was unexceptionable; but it was unfortunate that Quesnay tried to demonstrate

234 Seligmann (1899), 102, devoted a mere page to it when discussing Physiocratic theory; Schumpeter (1954*a*), 231; Hutchison (1988), 285–7.

235 Clere in *État, finances et économie* (1991), 81–101.

236 Mirabeau (1760, repr. 1972), 64–5, 70, 121, 146–7, 151.

237 Ibid. 161–2, 164, 189, 270, 378, 383.

238 Mirabeau (1766, repr. 1972), 118–19, 142–3, 205; cf. Gross (1993), 96–7.

this need by arguing that manufacturing was sterile, while both he and Mirabeau postulated that taxation could be based on the net product of land alone. It was Turgot who made substantial inroads into the 'stillborn paradox' of the sterility of industry and trade by arguing in his *Reflections on the Formation and Distribution of Wealth* (*Réflexions sur la formation et la distribution des richesses*, 1766) that a sort of equilibrium established itself between different uses of capital:[239] 'The different uses of the capital produce, therefore, very unequal products; but this inequality does not prevent them from having a reciprocal influence on each other, nor from establishing a kind of equilibrium amongst themselves . . .'[240] Turgot's period as controller-general of finance (1774–6) was in part the failure of the application of reforming ideas to an intractable political problem, above all the inability to produce fiscal reform ('améliorer les revenus de l'État et de rétablir les finances'). He left his successor, Necker, a clear statement of the need for change: 'taxes must be (re)partitioned among the contributors in proportion to their revenue.'[241] By this date, the Physiocratic idea of a tax on net income had been vigorously refuted by David Hume (1711–76) in his essay *Of Taxes*, which appeared in the edition of his *Essays and Treatises* in 1770. He denounced the Physiocratic argument that all taxes fell ultimately upon land.[242] This could not be sustained, in his view, because fiscal evasion was common to all: a landowner would seek to avoid taxation just as would an artisan. Moreover, the Physiocratic idea denied the central proposition that it was human endeavour, rather than land, that was the essential source of productive wealth. In his essay *Of Commerce*, Hume commented that 'the arts of agriculture employ *at first* the most numerous part of the society'.[243] However, he postulated that 'the more labour . . . is employed beyond mere necessaries, the more powerful is any state . . . the greatness of the sovereign and the happiness of the state are, in a great measure, united with regard to trade and manufactures.'[244] Hume condemned all arbitrary taxes, including the *capitation*; 'on the other hand, a duty upon commodities checks itself; and a prince will soon find, that an encrease [*sic*] of the impost is no encrease of his revenue'.[245] His praise of indirect taxes was little short of an encomium:

> The best taxes are such as are levied upon consumptions, especially those of luxury; because such taxes are least felt by the people. They seem, in some measure voluntary;

[239] Meek (1962), 310; Meek (1973*a*), 173. For the importance of Turgot as a theoretician of capital: Meyssonnier (1989), 325–31; Schumpeter (1954*a*), 243–9, 332–3; Brewer (1992*b*), 190–1.

[240] Groenewegen (1977), 87.

[241] Gross (1993), 88 n. 23, 97; Weulersse (1950), 151; cf. Faure (1961), 525.

[242] Hume, ed. Rotwein (1955), 87. See also Hume to Turgot, late Sept. 1766: ibid. 208–9. On Hume's fiscal ideas: Deleule (1979), 230–41; Hutchison (1988), 210–11.

[243] Hume, ed. Rotwein (1955), 6.

[244] Ibid. 11–12. [245] Ibid. 86.

since a man may chuse how far he will use the commodity which is taxed; they are paid gradually and insensibly; they produce sobriety and frugality, if judiciously imposed; and being confounded with the natural price of the commodity, they are scarcely perceived by the consumers. Their only disadvantage is, that they are expensive in the levying.[246]

Although other commentators, especially Montesquieu, had viewed the method of levying indirect taxes by means of farming as a crucial disadvantage, Hume was prepared to justify the revenue farmers' self-interest as a fiscal advantage to the state. He commented to Montesquieu that there were 'a hundred thousand tricks and devices for dealing with fraud on the part of individuals, which are suggested to the fermiers by self-interest, and which the government collectors would never have dreamed of...'[247]

Though Hume visited France, and his writings were read avidly there, his thinking clearly reflected conditions in England. In contrast, François Véron de Forbonnais (1722–1800) was a specialist in French financial structures and adviser during the short-lived ministry of Silhouette, who was controller-general for a few months in 1759.[248] Forbonnais was also a critic of Quesnay, whose originality he denied: had Boisguilbert written in a less polemical style, he would have been regarded as the originator of the circular system later described in Quesnay's *Tableau Économique*. Forbonnais shared some of Hume's criticisms of Physiocratic fiscal ideas, and also asserted the need for a much greater reliance in France on differential indirect taxes upon consumption (instead of the *gabelles* and *aides*).[249] These were to be levied in such a way that urban wealth would have been taxed effectively.[250] However, the size of the agrarian sector of the economy in France precluded an exclusive reliance on consumption taxes. Instead, Forbonnais proposed that direct taxes should continue to be used until such time as levels of prosperity and consumption rose in the countryside. It is significant that during his time as adviser to Silhouette a second *vingtième* was introduced: Forbonnais regarded the *dixième* of 1710, and its successor the *vingtième*, as the least objectionable of direct taxes.[251]

The Physiocrats shared some of the central Mercantilist doctrines, but their view of the relationship between the state and society, and the functions of wealth, was more supple and dynamic. In their view, the path to modernization

[246] Ibid. 85. [247] Ibid. 187.

[248] Morrisson (1967), 3, 52–3; Schumpeter (1954*a*), 174; Hutchison (1988), 225–7; Perrot (1992), 278–80. Crouzet (1993), 37, 119–20, notes his long career.

[249] Morrisson (1967), 46, 55.

[250] Ibid. 33, 81.

[251] Ibid. 52; Véron de Forbonnais (1758), i, 511 (denunciation of the *taille* and the *gabelles*); i, 526 (criticism of the *capitation*) and ii, 221–2 (praise of the *dixième*).

lay through economic (and especially agricultural) expansion, and for this to occur the restrictions imposed by *ancien régime* governments had to be removed.[252] Much of the reforming endeavour of enlightened absolute monarchs and their ministers in the later eighteenth century reflected Physiocratic ideas and preoccupations (Chapters 10 and 11). The Physiocrats also succeeded in influencing even those, like Sir James Steuart (or Steuart-Denham, 1713–80), who formally opposed them. A precursor of Adam Smith, if only by a few years,[253] Steuart's *Inquiry into the Principles of Political Oeconomy* (1767), was written in a long period of exile (almost twenty years) after the failed Jacobite rebellion of 1745. He was well informed on European affairs (though less so on England) and his analysis was strong precisely in those areas where Smith was weak, in the discussion of the role of banking, public credit and paper money.[254] Steuart denounced the French Physiocratic practice of devising 'systems' as 'mere conceits; they mislead the understanding, and efface the path to truth'.[255] If he laid claim to no system,[256] it was perhaps a weakness of his scheme that, unlike Quesnay, Steuart did not emphasize the importance of capital, or clearly distinguish between categories of return such as wages and profits. In effect, Steuart's was a two-sector economy, with agriculture and manufacturing each dependent on the other for its products. Steuart was something of an eclectic: among statesmen, he referred with approval to Colbert, Law and Walpole; he cited Vauban's *Dixme royale* as an 'excellent performance' and Montesquieu as a 'great man' who 'reasoned from fact and from experience';[257] but his greatest debt was probably to Cantillon and the Physiocrats, despite his criticisms of the latter.[258] His notion was one of community.[259] Notwithstanding this sense of community, the principle of self-interest served as 'a general key'[260] to Steuart's enquiry: 'It is the combination of every private interest which forms the public good . . .'[261] Here Steuart sought to distinguish between self-regarding actions of the individual and objective actions of statesmen, who were required to act not

[252] Here the rejection of a clear antithesis between Mercantilism and liberalism by Kaplan (1976), ii, 688–9, is more satisfactory than the more traditional viewpoint advanced by Deyon that Cantillon and Hume 'ont porté ce coup mortel au mercantilisme' before Smith: Deyon (1969), 70.

[253] He is regarded as such in Meek (1973*b*); cf. Hutchison (1988), 335–51, and esp. 5 for the importance of the period 1662–1776 for the formation of political economy as a subject.

[254] This is the verdict of Skinner in the introduction to Steuart, ed. Skinner (1966), i, p. lxxxiv. Steuart acknowledged that he had divested himself of English notions and may have written the original version in French: ibid. i, 5, 6 n. 7.

[255] Ibid. i, 8. Though on the relationship with them, cf. Vaggi (1987), 128–9, 216 n. 15.

[256] Steuart, ed. Skinner (1966), i, 19.

[257] Ibid. i, 79, 238; he also cited Hume: ibid. ii, 339, 343. On the statesmen: ibid. i, 74.

[258] Brewer (1992*b*), 175–83.

[259] Steuart, ed. Skinner (1966), i, 88.

[260] Ibid. i. 142. [261] Ibid. i, 143.

for themselves but for the people they governed.[262] The abilities of statesmen were fully revealed 'in directing and conducting what I call the delicacy of national competition'.[263] For Steuart, the power of princes derived 'from other circumstances, which do not necessarily follow in consequence of their elevation to the throne'.[264]

How far were particular forms of government favourable or unfavourable to nations in competition with each other? Republican states, he thought, had historically allowed more liberty to their subjects and this had enabled foreign trade to flourish. In contrast, the disadvantage of monarchical government did not proceed from the inequality it established among citizens 'but from the consequences of this inequality, which is very often accompanied with an arbitrary and undeterminate subordination between the individuals of higher classes, and those of the lower; or between those vested with the execution of the laws, and the body of the people': it was 'the irregularity of the exactions more than the extent of them' which served to ruin industry.[265] On this point, Steuart's words were prophetic:

In countries where the government is vested in the hands of the great lords, as is the case in all aristocracies, as was the case under the feudal government, and as it still is the case in many countries in Europe, where trade, however, and industry are daily gaining ground; the statesman who sets the new system of political oeconomy on foot, may depend upon it, that either his attempt will fail, or the constitution of the government will change. If he destroys all arbitrary dependence between individuals, the wealth of the industrious will share, if not totally root out the power of the grandees. If he allows such a dependence to subsist, his project will fail ... *Trade* and *industry* are in vogue; and their establishment is occasioning a wonderful fermentation with the remaining fierceness of the feudal constitution.[266]

The link between the economic and political spheres of interest observed by Steuart applied also to government servants:

Trade and industry ... owed their establishment to the ambition of princes who supported and favoured the plan in the beginning, and principally with a view to enrich themselves, and thereby to become formidable to their neighbours ... The money gatherers are become more useful to princes, than the great lords; and those who are fertile in expedients for establishing public credit, and for drawing money from the coffers of the rich, by the imposition of taxes, have been preferred to the most wise and learned counsellors.[267]

Doubtless here Steuart was thinking of John Law, whose System he analysed in great detail in Book 4 of the *Inquiry into the Principles of Political Oeconomy.* Steuart

[262] Ibid. i, 145 n. 3. [263] Ibid. i, 203. [264] Ibid. i, 210.
[265] Ibid. i, 211–12. [266] Ibid. i, 214–15. [267] Ibid. i, 215–16.

considered that taxation vested in statesmen 'an authority ... which in former ages, even under the most absolute governments, was utterly unknown';[268] however, 'modern' political economy was in his view 'the most effective bridle ... against the folly of depotism'.[269]

Even Adam Smith was prepared to acknowledge that, though never fully implemented anywhere in Europe, the Physiocratic system 'with all its imperfections' was 'perhaps the nearest approximation to truth that has yet been published on the subject of political oeconomy'.[270] It was left to others to condemn the Physiocratic system in entirety. Most notable of these critics was Isaac de Pinto, whose *Traité de la circulation et du crédit* (*Essay on Circulation and Credit*) was published at Amsterdam in 1771 and translated into English three years later. Part 3 of this treatise (entitled 'Of Finances, Taxes and Agriculture, considered principally with respect to France: Refutation of the Principle which reduces everything to the Territorial Produce')[271] was a critique of Mirabeau's *Théorie de l'impôt*. Holland was cited as a demonstration that Mirabeau's argument (that 'a state like France, whose riches belong to the soil, has no real revenue but its territorial produce') was false: 'if nothing were to be exacted but a portion of the territorial produce, Holland long ago must have ceased to exist ... yet the republic pays troops, maintains a marine, and has often figured on a level with the first powers of Europe.'[272] Instead, de Pinto argued that 'though the landed revenue forms an important article, it is still the smallest part of the faculties of the subject'; and that 'manufactories should be considered as one of the principal arteries of the public revenue'; thus to make agriculture the sole base of taxation was 'a mere whim, or madness', which would destroy 'the true principle of finance'.[273]

> It is not credit that has ruined the finances of France, as Monsieur de Mirabeau pretends. On the contrary, it was the failure of credit in time of need that did the mischief, and probably was the chief cause of the late disasters [in the Seven Years' War]. If the credit had been supported as it might have been, France would have been less in debt. At the beginning of the year 1715, the king was obliged to negotiate thirty-two millions in bills, in order to raise eight in specie.[274]

In Part 4 of his work, which was largely directed against the writings of Boisguilbert, de Pinto emphasized the centrality of credit:[275]

268 Ibid. i, 278.

269 Ibid. i, 279.

270 Smith, ed. Campbell, Skinner and Todd (1976), ii, 678. Though at ii, 664, Smith implies that the Physiocrats were too extreme in their reaction to Mercantilism, and at ii, 663, he insisted that the system had 'never been adopted by any nation, and it at present exists only in the speculations of a few men of great learning and ingenuity in France ...'

271 Pinto, trans. Baggs (1774, repr. 1969), 109.

272 Ibid. 110, 115.

273 Ibid. 133, 137, 139–40.

274 Ibid. 144–5.

275 Ibid. 174.

The application of it [the theory applicable to a private person's debts] to the state is absolutely false. That which ruins an individual does not always ruin the state. The money a man lays out for his subsistence, or in articles of luxury, does not return again into his family; whereas the internal expenses of a monarch, or of the state, return into the nation, encourage and improve it. The nation in a body pays these expenses, or rather lends the money for its own advantage. With the assistance of loans a war may be supported by moderate taxes, in comparison with what the nation would otherwise be obliged to pay, at the same time that the numerary wealth and circulation increase with the debt . . .[276]

De Pinto argued that indirect taxation should form the basis of the revenue system, since the 'collection is insensible, successive and gradual, and thereby gives time for the money to issue out of the public treasury, and circulate again through the public'.[277] In contrast, a *capitation* he thought no more than 'a supplementary measure', since 'such a tax would take too great a quantity of money out of circulation at once, and make specie extremely scarce at every period of collection . . .'[278]

Such was the general hostility to the French revenue farmers, and the Physiocrats' rejection of indirect taxes, that virtually all reformers in the last quarter of the eighteenth century concentrated on the system of direct taxes. The abbé Emmanuel Joseph Sieyès (1748–1836) may be taken as representative of this, as in so much else that was central to the movement of ideas that produced the early period of consensus in the French Revolution. He had worked in the provincial assembly of Orléans on the reform of the *vingtièmes* and the *capitation*; he wanted to end the arbitrary and unpredictable incidence of the former by introducing a fixed annual subscription (*abonnement*) to be paid by the province, while he sought to remodel the latter into a graduated, progressive tax, based solely on the level of income.[279] The tax changes introduced during the Revolution demonstrated that Physiocratic ideas were no longer predominant, because only one of the three new taxes—there was a land tax (*contribution foncière*), a tax on movables (*contribution mobilière*) and a commercial profits tax (*patente*)—was based exclusively on land (though it was by far the most important of the three);[280] subsequently, indirect taxes made a reappearance under Napoleon. The concept of a single tax was decisively rejected, while an administrator and theoretician such as Pierre-Louis Roederer (1754–1835) used his

[276] Cf. ibid. 20–1, 30; cf. ibid. 104–5, his critique of Hume (and of Law's System).

[277] Ibid. 120; cf. his comments on the French revenue farmers: ibid. 120–1.

[278] Ibid. 118, 141.

[279] AN 284 ap 7, dossier 7, 'Échelle de gradation sur la capitation', 20 Dec. 1787, and draft decree 'pour l'abonnement des vingtièmes', 22 Apr. 1788. The author is grateful to Professor Murray Forsyth for access to unpublished material of his on this point. For Sieyès generally: Forsyth (1987).

[280] Crouzet (1993), 120–1.

memoirs to refute the Physiocratic claim that the entire economic surplus arose from the profits of agriculture. He argued on the contrary that industry was responsible for most of the cultivation of land which had taken place, since it was the opportunities for increasing consumption provided by industry that gave landowners an incentive to produce a surplus with which they could purchase the products of industry. Jean-Baptiste Say (1767–1832) went further, and used the term *industrie* to refer to productive activity as such in whichever sector of the economy it arose (agriculture, manufacture or commerce).[281] Say argued that no matter how tax revenue was spent by the government, its value and potential were permanently removed from the economy: 'However the money levied by taxation is refunded to the nation, its value is never refunded; because it is never returned gratuitously, or refunded by the public functionaries, without receiving an equivalent in the way of barter or exchange.'[282] Not surprisingly, ageing Physiocrats such as Du Pont de Nemours tried to argue that the essential elements of their system had to be retained: 'we have not written and governed for fifty years in countries with widely differing laws and customs without learning anything.'[283] The whole climate had shifted against them, however. There was a brief adoption of Enlightenment ideas on progressive taxation in 1793–4 (Chapter 13.5). Once this experiment was rejected, the pragmatic implementation of existing tax legislation and above all the gradual introduction of the *cadastre* under Napoleon made Physiocratic ideas seem irrelevant. Napoleonic administrators relied on tables of statistics, 'facts' about the real world which they contrasted with the 'theories' and 'speculations' of the dogmatic 'sect', that is the Physiocrats.[284]

6.6 *'Paper Money Mercantilism' and Its Critics*

The intractability of the fiscal problems of the French monarchy, and the large legacy of debt resulting from the wars of Louis XIV, encouraged other solutions of a more adventurous kind than those proposed by Vauban, Boisguilbert and Saint-Pierre. The economist Heckshser called John Law (1671–1729) an exponent of 'paper money Mercantilism'. He argued that Law's views did not differ from earlier exponents of paper money; 'all he did was to express the doctrines of the new school with particular clarity, and he becomes of special interest because he later was able to translate his ideas into action'.[285] This view minimizes Law's

[281] James (1977), 464–6.

[282] Say (repr. 1841), 503–4; McLain (1977), 204; Staum (1987), 540–2.

[283] McLain (1977), 205.

[284] Woolf in Perrot and Woolf (1984), 86.

[285] Heckshser in Seligman (1930–4), x, 338; Heckshser (1935), ii, 234. Schumpeter (1954*a*), 294–5, 321–2, considered Law to be 'in the front rank of monetary theorists of all times'; Blaug (1978), 20, also called Law a 'paper money Mercantilist'; Hutchison (1988), 134–9.

originality, but it is true that he was uniquely well placed: at the height of his influence over the Regent, Philippe d'Orléans, he was appointed controller-general of finance (5 January–27 May 1720).[286] He was the clearest example of an economic theorist being appointed to the highest charge of a nation's affairs in the early modern period, and the extent of the disaster which followed discredited systems and system builders, and the idea of appointing economic theoreticians to posts in the government.[287] The impact of Law's System in France was so enormous that it is difficult to view Law as little more than a latter-day Mercantilist. He might cite Thomas Mun in his early writings,[288] and even seem a bullionist;[289] but by 1707 he was advocating the total replacement of gold and silver by paper convertible for the purposes of land transfers, basing his argument on French rather than Scots experience as he had done in *Money and Trade* . . . (1705).[290] Law presented Louis XIV and Desmaretz with a proposal for the redemption of public debt in May 1715 and a memorandum for the establishment of a bank (not dissimilar to the later System) in July 1715. State competition for resources was transmuted by Law into state competition for credit instruments.[291] Law rejected the argument that absolute monarchy in France was compelled to act as an irresponsible power, seizing the assets of the proposed bank in time of need. All banks had moments of crisis in time of civil and foreign war; but the Bank of Amsterdam had survived the mass withdrawal of deposits during the crisis of the French invasion in 1672.[292] There was every reason to suppose the king of France would have an interest in conserving the credit of his bank rather than in diverting its assets. It was not the constitution of the state which had led to the failure to establish a bank in France, but false principles.[293] Law maintained that the effect of establishing his bank would be comparable to a substantial increase in the money supply. It would act as a general stimulus to economic recovery. He considered the French national product to be three times that of England and that it would be further increased by the establishment of the bank.[294] Law's System was thus intended to deal simultaneously with a chronic financial problem, namely the burden of debt carried over from the War of the Spanish Succession; with a lack of confidence resulting from the emission of

[286] Lévy (1980), 246, 265. The Regent even resuscitated the *surintendance des finances* for Law, which had been in abeyance since the arrest of Foucquet in 1661: Faure (1977), 316.

[287] By comparison with Law, even Turgot had practical experience as a provincial intendant.

[288] Law, ed. Harsin (1934), i, 28.

[289] Ibid. i, 32.

[290] Ibid. i, 210, 212–13.

[291] Ibid. ii, 45–6.

[292] Ibid. ii, 37; cf. Israel (1989), 293.

[293] Law, ed. Harsin (1934), ii, 48; cf. ii, 274.

[294] Ibid. ii, 51; Bonney (1992*a*), 166 n. 68, and acknowledgement there to Antoin Murphy.

worthless paper during the war; and with the need to stimulate the economy during a short-term commercial crisis in 1715–16.

The collapse of Law's System in France in 1720 sent shock waves through the west European financial structures and prompted comment from theoreticians. The most important early critic of Law was Richard Cantillon (*c.*1680/90–1734).[295] Cantillon's *Essai sur la nature du commerce en général*, though not published until 1755, was written in 1728–30.[296] The book was primarily an attempt to encompass the whole of the economic system. It dealt with market behaviour and the role of the entrepreneur; the interrelationship and interdependence of markets; with the linkage between monetary theory and the real economy; and with the monetary economy. Cantillon was no populationist. Though he conceded that 'Men multiply like mice in a barn if they have unlimited means of subsistence',[297] the population expanded to take up the economic opportunities that presented themselves: population increase was the result of other economic changes, not a cause of economic growth in its own right; through insufficient evidence at his disposal, he failed to perceive the European growth in population in the eighteenth century and its implications for the state and its finances. Cantillon provided the first picture of the overall working of the economy, demonstrating the circular interaction between output, income and economy. One person's expenditure formed another's income, which was derived from the creation of goods and services. Though Quesnay later gave visual presentation to this circular flow in his 'economic picture' (*Tableau Économique*) of 1758–9, it was Cantillon who was the first to demonstrate the argument.[298]

From the point of view of its influence on theories of state finance, the most significant aspect of Cantillon's writing was the critique of financial innovation in Book 3 of the *Essai*. Cantillon had already postulated in Book 1 that the efficient working of the economy required the use of money, which was not something to be expanded artificially at the whim of monarchs or governments: '. . . when

[295] For Cantillon: Schumpeter (1954*a*), 217–23, 318–21; Spengler in Spengler and Allen (1960), 105–40; Murphy (1986); Hutchison (1988), 163–78; Brewer (1992*b*); Perrot (1992), 162–5.

[296] Murphy (1986), 247. Murphy demonstrates (309) that the work was published by the intervention of Vincent de Gournay's group. He also notes that the English version of the *Essai* was modernized by Higgs, its 20th-cent. editor: Cantillon, ed. Higgs (1931). A more recent edition, based on a manuscript version at Rouen, is Cantillon, ed. Tsuda (1979).

[297] Cantillon, ed. Higgs (1931), 83; Brewer (1992*b*), 36, 47, concludes that 'Cantillon's population theory was perfectly reasonable, given the evidence available to him'.

[298] Murphy (1986), 260–1 (quoting Schumpeter); Meek (1962), 268, notes the significance for Quesnay of Cantillon's remark that 'all the classes and inhabitants of a State live at the expense of the Proprietors of Land'. The influence of Cantillon is also stressed by Meyssonnier (1989), 249; she stresses that Cantillon was in turn influenced on this point by Sir William Petty: ibid. 284. However, Brewer (1992*b*), 15, 126, rejects the influence of Petty: Cantillon 'completely remade the little that he did take'.

princes have debased their money, keeping it at the same nominal value, all raw produce and manufactures have gone up in price in proportion to the debasement of the coinage.'[299] He considered earlier theoreticians such as Locke to have been simplistic in their analysis of the mechanism by which this price inflation occurred as a result of debasement.[300] Instead, Cantillon enunciated what has been termed the 'specie flow mechanism', by which excess money balances spilled out of the economy through a balance of payments deficit.[301] No nation could indefinitely maintain excess money balances: thus, Spain and Portugal had not received any permanent advantage from the gold and silver mining revenues from the New World, the benefit largely going to foreign merchants and privateers instead.[302]

This analysis was in some respects similar to that in David Hume's essay *Of the Balance of Trade* (1752),[303] but with a significant difference. Whereas Hume emphasized the relative price effect in the self-adjusting balance of payments process, Cantillon incorporated both a relative price effect and a cash balance effect.[304] Cantillon's theory of economic development encompassed a full account of the evolution of society from landlord-dominated control to an entrepreneurial market economy, with corresponding transitions from barter to money and from a closed to an open economy. Finally, there had been a transition from a simple specie system to a more complex foreign exchange system, with paper money being added to the specie system. In fiscal policy, he was a critic of Vauban, whose *dixme royale* he judged to be neither advantageous nor practicable: instead, taxes on land should be levied in money in proportion to the rents enjoyed by proprietors (akin to the *dixième* tax in France: Chapter 13.5).[305]

It was above all in his condemnation of Law that Cantillon, a profiteer from the System, revealed both his conservatism and the limitation of his vision of the way in which paper money and the banking system might evolve in the future. He was prepared to admit that banks were useful in a state to prevent hoarding of

299 Murphy (1986), 263; Cantillon, ed. Higgs (1931), 112–13.

300 Murphy (1986), 265; Cantillon, ed. Higgs (1931), 160–1. For Locke's views: Leigh (1974); Brewer (1992*b*), 137–46, for the influence of Locke on Cantillon.

301 Locke had already anticipated the modern phrase 'velocity of circulation' with the expression 'quickness of its circulation' to describe the movement of money: Locke, ed. Kelly (1991), i, 77, 235; Meyssonnier (1989), 129; Hutchison (1988), 65; Cantillon called it *vitesse de circulation*: Cantillon, ed. Higgs (1931), 130, 134; Brewer (1992*b*), 80; Brewer (1992*a*), 722.

302 Murphy (1986), 267, 270; Cantillon, ed. Higgs (1931), 166–7.

303 Schumpeter (1954*a*), 366.

304 Murphy (1986), 271. David Hume, according to Murphy (1986), did not base his essay on a manuscript version of Cantillon's *Essai* in circulation prior to publication in 1755.

305 Cantillon, ed. Higgs (1931), 158–9.

specie.[306] But what he would not do was to concede the point that in a large state (he specifically referred to France) a bank could bring good rather than harm: 'an abundance of fictitious and imaginary money causes the same disadvantages as an increase of real money in circulation . . .' More money had been in circulation in France than in neighbouring states during the middle period of Louis XIV's reign, Cantillon asserted, and this had easily been levied without recourse to a public bank.[307] And (in an evident allusion to the collapse of Law's System) the risk of a bank was a sudden collapse of confidence so that the 'bomb would burst' ('on en viendroit à crever la bombe') in the vociferous public demand for the conversion of banknotes into silver.[308] There were advantages in a state having enough money in circulation: the power of the state would be great, because revenue would be easy to raise and 'munitions of war and food', as well as military personnel, could be paid for without difficulty. The terms of trade would be more favourable than if money had been less abundant and domestic prices lower. 'It is clear', Cantillon wrote,

> that every State which has more money in circulation than its neighbours has an advantage over them so long as it maintains this abundance of money . . . [T]he revenues of the State where money abounds are raised more easily and in comparatively much larger amount. This gives the State, in case of war or dispute, the means to gain all sorts of advantages over its adversaries with whom money is scarce.[309]

However, if there was excess money in circulation and the ruler did not withdraw it by creating a surplus for himself ('to withdraw money from circulation, keep it for emergencies . . .'), then the advantages would disappear, and an export surplus be turned into an import surplus. Money would flow abroad and the state would become weak: 'The too great abundance of money, which so long as it lasts forms the power of States, throws them back imperceptibly but naturally into poverty.'[310] Cantillon could not have foreseen the epoch of hyperinflation during the *assignat* period in the 1790s, but his words were prophetic.[311] Instead, drawing upon the evidence of French history from 1646 to 1684, Cantillon postulated that growth cycles were transitory, whereas decline might be more prolonged: 'one may say that the power of France . . . has done nothing but recede since this last date.'[312]

If Cantillon was an opponent of Law's views concerning the desirability of

306 Ibid. 146–7, 174–5, esp. 304–5; Brewer (1992*b*), 103–4.
307 Murphy (1986), 277; Cantillon, ed. Higgs (1931), 310–11.
308 Murphy (1986), 278; Cantillon, ed. Higgs (1931), 322–3.
309 Cantillon, ed. Higgs (1931), 189; Brewer (1992*b*), 115.
310 Cantillon, ed. Higgs (1931), 185; Spengler in Spengler and Allen (1960), 126–7; Brewer (1992*b*), 88, 116.
311 Crouzet (1993) is now the outstanding account, but he does not cite Cantillon.
312 Cantillon, ed. Higgs (1931), 187; Brewer (1992*b*), 117.

establishing a national bank, Ferdinando Galiani directly confronted his views on paper, or token, money. Galiani devoted a chapter of his book *Of Money* (*Della moneta*, 1751) to a consideration of French monetary events in 1718, and a critique of Law's System underlies his work. He regarded Law as 'a man of the rarest and most remarkable genius but one without virtue or religion';[313] his principal mistake had been to issue an excessive quantity of banknotes, 'mere images of money' as Galiani called them in a phrase which anticipated the term *signe* as a description of the later *assignats*.[314] He attempted to estimate the amount of banknotes in circulation which would have restricted the total stock of money to its level in 1698, a more prosperous year in his view than 1718. Above all, he criticized Law's attempt to use his System to assist the French monarchy in its bankruptcy:

> Law made this blunder: that he thought that all State debts could be extinguished with notes, and thus he created them in proportion to the mass of all the debt of the French crown. A very serious and inexcusable mistake for so great a man; because one thing has nothing to do with the other; because it is neither useful nor feasible to extinguish all State debts; and finally, because, if it could be done, justice requires that it be done with real money, and not with that imposture, namely paper, which represents nothing actually in existence and represents nothing certain in the future.[315]

Galiani argued that people could not long endure the use of representative money, but needed a metallic coinage. If the country was occupied by a hostile power, he speculated, would the conqueror be content with paper currency; would he not prefer a metallic coinage?[316] Few rulers would have been impressed by such arguments. Instead, there were positive revenue advantages to be gained from the debasement of a metallic currency. Unusually, Galiani was one of the few theoreticians in the eighteenth century to stress the adoption of alternative economic policies in different circumstances. He advocated the evaluation of the costs and benefits of particular policies to decide which to follow.[317] In a sense, he anticipated the resort to inflation under the French Revolution rather than the repudiation of the public debt (given that there was no political will to raise additional taxes to meet the needs of public expenditure).[318] Since he was convinced that there was an optimal money supply for states (he attempted to estimate the quantity of money and the velocity of

[313] Quoted in Cesarano (1976), 386; Cesarano (1990), 336.

[314] Crouzet (1993), 210, citing Saint-Just's denunciation in November 1792 of 'l'émission déréglée du signe...'

[315] Cesarano (1990), 337, n. 30 (translation amended).

[316] Ibid. 332, n. 21. For Galiani, cf. Schumpeter (1954*a*), 292–3, 300–2; Hutchison (1988), 255–70, 293–4.

[317] Cesarano (1976), 383.

[318] Crouzet (1993), 127–39.

circulation in the kingdom of Naples),[319] Galiani was an opponent of Mercantilist policies which sought continuous accumulation of precious metals. Higher prices, in his view, would cancel out all the beneficial effects of increases in the quantity of money within the state. His most important contribution was to what is now known as the 'rational expectations' hypothesis: expected inflation is completely useless to a ruler; people have to operate within an assumption of stable prices. The 'augmentation of money', he postulated, 'is a profit that the prince and the state make from the slowness with which the multitude changes the connection of ideas about the prices of goods and money.' '... A prince', he argued, who 'abusing augmentation, practised it every month, destroying every connection of ideas between prices and commodities, would render it quite useless and inefficacious ...'[320] Thus the ruler had to evaluate the costs and benefits of an inflationary policy to judge whether or not debasement should be practised. Inflation was a concealed way of levying taxes, which could nevertheless be used by states confronting an emergency when taxes could not be increased.[321] (Galiani was thus unwittingly a precursor of those who justified the *assignat* experiment in France in the 1790s, when for political reasons it was impossible to increase taxes yet there was open war against a foreign coalition; the difference was that paper was issued instead of money.)[322] Galiani's views on the desirability of the redistributive effects of inflation depended on whether it was the 'rich' and unproductive, rather than the rich in the sense of entrepreneurs, who bore the brunt of its consequences.[323] In reality, nothing could protect workers from the effects of inflation, as the *assignat* experiment was to demonstrate.[324]

6.7 *The Classical Theory: Smith, Ricardo and Malthus*

Adam Smith (1723–90) published *The Wealth of Nations* in 1776, and it is from this date (not 1766, when Turgot had anticipated many of the features of the classical theory in his *Reflections on the Formation and Distribution of Wealth*)[325] that

[319] Cesarano (1976), 390; Cesarano (1990), 328 n. 15.

[320] Cesarano (1976), 393–4.

[321] Ibid. 395.

[322] Aftalion (1990); Crouzet (1993). For the *assignat* experiment as a product of Enlightened, rational thought, cf. the views of Lavoisier and Cérutti: Olsen (1992), 313. Du Pont de Nemours, basing his views on American experience, wanted only a small *assignat* experiment, with the interest-bearing paper backed by land: McLain (1977), 150–2.

[323] Cesarano (1976), 396: 'Those who rent are not only well off but are idle and slothful, and should pay more because without increasing the wealth of the state they consume not only their own but also foreign goods.'

[324] Crouzet (1993), 279, 352, 566.

[325] Groenewegen (1977), 43–95; Brewer (1992*b*), 183, 187.

'classical' economics, which dominated thinking until the mid-nineteenth century, came into being. 'The great object of the political oeconomy of every country', Smith wrote

> is to encrease the riches and power of that country. It ought, therefore, to give no preference nor superior encouragement to the foreign trade of consumption above the home-trade, nor to the carrying trade above either of the other two. It ought neither to force nor to allure into either of these two channels, a greater share of the capital of the country than what would naturally flow into them of its own accord.[326]

There were historically different systems of political economy, of which the most important in Smith's view were the Mercantilist and Physiocratic systems (called by him respectively 'the commercial, or mercantile system' and 'agricultural systems, or . . . those systems of political oeconomy which represent the produce of land as either the sole or the principal source of the revenue and wealth of every country').[327] Because economists naturally emphasize the modernity of Smith's views (preceding theorists tending to be dismissed simply as his 'precursors') it is worth stressing the contemporary reception of *The Wealth of Nations* abroad. In Germany, as has been seen, Smith was at first regarded as a latter-day Physiocrat.[328] There is no doubt that he drew some of his key ideas (the theme of wealth as 'the consumable goods annually reproduced by the labour of society', the doctrine of productive labour, and the emphasis on the circular process of production and distribution) from the Physiocrats.[329] Yet Smith emphasized the economic role of profit on capital and capital accumulation; this theme, more than any other, provided unity and strength to the structure of *The Wealth of Nations*. To call him a Physiocrat is misleading, since as has been seen he sought to distinguish his own viewpoint and denounced the *Économistes'* conception of a sterile class as a 'capital error'.[330] Yet there were clear similarities. Smith implied that Physiocracy should be regarded as a reaction to the Mercantilist policies of Colbert and the other ministers during the reign of Louis XIV, just as he sought to overturn the accepted views of Mun and

[326] Smith, ed. Campbell, Skinner and Todd (1976), i, 372.

[327] The titles respectively to chs. 1 and 9 of Book 4.

[328] Thus von Pfeiffer in 1782: '. . . The only point at which the author differs from the orthodox Physiocrats is that he allows a tax on luxury goods, while however subjecting it to unmistakable difficulties; and that he lays upon everyone the duty of contributing proportionally to the expenses of the state, without providing usable rules concerning its purpose.' Tribe (1988), 145.

[329] Blaug (1978), 24.

[330] Ibid. 25. Blaug argues that Smith misrepresented the Physiocrats' position on this point, and that, 'apart from a quibble on words', he was forced to concede 'the whole of the Physiocratic argument'. Tribe (1978), 107–8, agrees that he misconstrued Physiocracy.

the English Mercantilists of the seventeenth century.[331] And Smith's characterization of Physiocracy in chapter 9 of Book 4 of *The Wealth of Nations* is deficient, since it contained no discussion of the most notorious of the Physiocratic ideas, the *impôt unique*,[332] while elsewhere he referred only obliquely to it when favouring the taxation of ground rent.[333]

In Book 4, chapter 9, of *The Wealth of Nations*, Smith defined 'three duties of great importance' for the state. These were the provision of military security; the administration of justice; and the

> duty of erecting and maintaining certain public works and certain public institutions, which it can never be for the interest of any individual, or small number of individuals, to erect and maintain; because the profit could never repay the expense to any individual or small number of individuals, though it may frequently do much more than repay it to a great society.[334]

This was a limited role for state intervention; services should only be provided where the market had failed to do so, but in principle they should be paid for by those who used them. In Book 5, chapter 3, devoted to public debts, Smith strongly criticized excessive public spending financed by taxes or the sale of government bonds as a process which necessarily diverted productive labour into unproductive employment. Nevertheless, some taxation was inevitable, and in the previous chapter he enunciated his four canons on the subject.[335] These were:

> I The subjects of every state ought to contribute towards the support of the government, as nearly as possible, in proportion to their respective abilities; that is, in

[331] Smith, ed. Campbell, Skinner and Todd (1976), ii, 467 (allusion to Colbert's 'great abilities' but imposed upon 'by the sophistry of merchants and manufacturers'); ii, 663–4 ('that minister had unfortunately embraced all the prejudices of the mercantile system'). After quoting Mun (ibid. i, 431–2), Smith commented (ii, 433) that 'those arguments were partly solid and partly sophistical'.

[332] For Smith's contacts with the Physiocrats: Smith, ed. Campbell, Skinner and Todd (1976), ii, 663 n. 1. At ii, 665–6, where Smith describes the Physiocratic system, there is, however, an allusion (ii, 666) to their idea of the tax on net agricultural income.

[333] Ibid. ii, 830: 'A tax upon the rent of land which varies with every variation of the rent, or which rises and falls according to the improvement or neglect of cultivation, is recommended by that sect of men of letters in France, who call themselves the oeconomists, as the most equitable of all taxes.' Smith preferred, however, not to enter into 'disagreeable discussion of the metaphysical arguments by which they support their very ingenious theory . . .', choosing instead to demonstrate his preferred tax solution.

[334] Ibid. i, 35 and ii, 687–8. Frequently quoted, e.g. by Blaug (1978), 59–60.

[335] Or as Blaug has it, ibid. 61, 'the ability-to-pay theory and three administrative canons'. Smith, ed. Campbell, Skinner and Todd (1976), ii, 825–6. Schumpeter (1954*a*), 186, argued that Smith's treatment of public expenditure, revenue and debts was primarily historical and that the theory was 'inadequate, and does not reach much below the surface. But what there is of it is admirably worked in with the reports on general developments as well as on individual facts'.

proportion to the revenue which they respectively enjoy under the protection of the state...

II The tax which each individual is bound to pay ought to be certain, and not arbitrary. The time of payment, the manner of payment, the quantity to be paid, ought all to be clear and plain to the contributor, and to every other person...

III Every tax ought to be levied at the time, or in the manner in which it is most likely to be convenient for the contributor to pay it...

IV Every tax ought to be so contrived as both to take out and to keep out of the pockets of the people as little as possible, over and above what it brings into the publick treasury of the state...

The four canons of taxation illustrate both Smith's attitude towards the state, and the weakness of his position. The two basic concerns of a minister are to ensure that the revenue system does not imperil the political support for the regime; and to ensure that the system yields sufficient revenue.[336] Implicitly taking David Hume to task, Smith commented that taxes on luxury goods, for example, were 'as agreeable ... as any other' to the first three maxims, but that they offended 'in every respect against the fourth'.[337]

Smith's maxims, it has been said, 'touched on aspects of a revenue system which are relevant to its productivity and acceptability ... but they form a wholly inadequate basis for judging individual taxes'.[338] Nevertheless, he was among other things an analyst of contemporary systems of taxation, and drew upon Moreau de Beaumont's printed edition of the French enquiry of 1763 into comparative revenue systems in Europe.[339] Smith commenced with a survey of what we would call the domainal or regalian rights of the monarch. These rights he defined as being drawn either 'first, from some fund which peculiarly belongs to the sovereign or commonwealth, and which is independent of the revenue of the people; or secondly from the revenue of the people'. Such funds or sources of revenue might consist of stock or in land. Smith illustrated his argument with the example of the republic of Hamburg, which was said to derive a considerable revenue from the profits of a public wine cellar and apothecary's shop.[340] 'The state cannot be very great', Smith commented, when the ruler had 'leisure to carry on the trade of a wine merchant or apothecary. The profit of a public bank has been a source of revenue to more considerable states' such as Venice and

[336] Stigler (1971), 272–3.

[337] Smith, ed. Campbell, Skinner and Todd (1976), ii, 896.

[338] Stigler (1971), 273.

[339] Smith, ed. Campbell, Skinner and Todd (1976), ii, 816 n.; Bonney (1994).

[340] Smith, ed. Campbell, Skinner and Todd (1976), ii, 817, 820; Hartmann (1979), 138; *Mémoires*, ed. Moreau de Beaumont (1768), 73.

Amsterdam. He calculated the net annual profit of the Bank of England at £592,900, but contrasted the 'orderly, vigilant and parsimonious administrations' of Venice and Amsterdam with the 'slothful and negligent profusion that is perhaps natural to monarchies' such as England. 'A state may sometime derive some part of its publick revenue from the interest of money, as well as from the profits of stock. If it has amassed a treasure, it may lend a part of that treasure, either to foreign states, or to its own subjects'; elsewhere, he mentioned Dutch holdings in English and French funds.[341] In Smith's view 'the unstable and perishable nature of stock and credit' made them unfit to be trusted as 'the principal funds of that sure, steady and permanent revenue, which can alone give security and dignity to government'. Land provided a fund of 'a more stable and permanent nature'. However, he judged that

> in the present state of the greater part of the civilized monarchies of Europe, the rent of all the lands in the country, managed as they probably would be if they all belonged to one proprietor, would scarce perhaps amount to the ordinary revenue which they levy upon the people even in peaceable times.

At the time of writing *The Wealth of Nations*, Smith did not consider that there was 'any civilized state' which derived 'the greater part of its publick revenue from the rent of lands which are the property of the state', the problem being that crown lands were invariably neglected in comparison with the revenue yielded from the same lands when placed under private ownership.[342]

Smith observed that the private revenue of individuals arose from rent, profit and wages, and that 'every tax must finally be paid from some one or other of those three different sources of revenue, or from all of them indifferently'. Many of the taxes he studied did not, in his view, fall on the source of revenue which had been the original target of the tax.[343] For Smith, the tithe and other land taxes of its type were 'very unequal taxes; a certain portion of the produce being, in different situations, equivalent to a very different portion of the rent'. Since its real burden could vary between a tax of a fifth or a half, the tithe was 'a great discouragement both to the improvement of the landlord and to the cultivation of the farmer'.[344] Smith contended that, had there been no tithe in England and Ireland, the landed classes could have paid an additional £6 or £7 million in land tax without significantly adding to their fiscal burden.[345] Smith distinguished

[341] Smith, ed. Campbell, Skinner and Todd (1976), i, 108: 'The great property which they possess both in the French and English funds, about forty millions, it is said, in the latter (in which I suspect, however, there is considerable exaggeration) . . .' The most modern estimate is in the region of £21 million: Riley (1980), 123.

[342] Smith, ed. Campbell, Skinner and Todd (1976), ii, 821–4.

[343] Ibid. ii, 825. [344] Ibid. ii, 837. [345] Ibid. ii, 934.

between building rent and ground rent, considering that the latter was 'a more proper subject of taxation'; though 'in many different countries of Europe, taxes have been imposed upon the rent of houses', he knew of none in which ground rents had been considered as 'a separate subject of taxation'.[346] Interest gained on the investment of money might have appeared as proper a subject for taxation as the rent of land. In reality, there were two great difficulties:

First, the quantity and value of the land which any man possesses can never be a secret, and can always be ascertained with great exactness. But the whole amount of the capital stock which he possesses is almost always a secret, and can scarce ever be ascertained with tolerable exactness. It is liable, besides, to almost continual variations . . . Secondly, land is a subject which cannot be removed; whereas stock easily may . . .[347]

Thus, Smith concluded, 'in all countries a severe inquisition into the circumstances of private persons has been carefully avoided'.[348] Smith then dealt with taxes 'upon every different species of revenue' including capitation taxes.[349] His verdict was that they had failed:

The impossibility of taxing the people, in proportion to their revenue, by any capitation, seems to have given occasion to the invention of taxes upon consumable commodities. The state not knowing how to tax, directly and proportionably [*sic*], the revenue of its subjects, endeavours to tax it indirectly by taxing their expence [*sic*], which, it is supposed, will in most cases be nearly in proportion to their revenue. Their expence is taxed by taxing the consumable commodities upon which it is laid out.

Smith postulated that taxes upon necessities of life operated exactly in the same way as a direct tax upon the wages of labour. Taxes upon luxuries, in contrast, had no tendency to raise the price of other commodities except that of the commodities taxed. Smith took the example of the tobacco monopoly in England and France (exaggerating as he did so the price in France):[350] 'Though [tobacco] is taxed in England at three times, and in France at fifteen its original price, those high duties seem to have no effect upon the wages of labour.' In Britain taxes upon necessities such as salt, leather, soap and candles were relatively moderate.[351] Of salt in Britain he commented that 'the quantity

[346] Ibid. ii, 844. [347] Ibid. ii, 848. [348] Ibid. ii, 850. [349] Ibid. ii, 867–9.

[350] Legitimate tobacco cost 60 per cent more in France than England after prices were raised in 1758: Price (1973), i, 448; ibid. i, 671–7 on the French position in the market at a later date.

[351] Smith, ed. Campbell, Skinner and Todd (1976), ii, 874; cf. Beckett and Turner (1990), 392–3, for candle, soap and hides (i.e. leather) consumption per head in the eighteenth century. They add tea to the list. Smith regarded taxes upon drink as taxes upon luxuries, although he noted that tea and sugar in Holland and England had 'become luxuries of the lowest ranks of people' as had chocolate in Spain.

annually consumed by any individual is so small, and may be purchased so gradually, that nobody, it seems to have been thought, could feel very sensibly even a pretty heavy tax upon it'. Elsewhere in Europe, however, he considered that taxes upon necessities were much more common:

Duties upon flour and meal when ground at the mill, and upon bread when baked at the oven, take place in many countries. In Holland the money price of the bread consumed in towns is supposed to be doubled by means of such taxes ... These, and some other taxes of the same kind, by raising the price of labour, are said to have ruined the greater part of the manufactures of Holland.[352]

Smith's verdict on taxes upon consumable commodities was that though there were 'inconveniencies [*sic*] ... in some degree inseparable' from them they were a relatively light burden in England. In contrast, he depicted the Spanish *alcabala* as an onerous tax since though reduced from 10 to 6 per cent 'upon the sale of every sort of property, whether moveable or immoveable' it was repeated 'every time the property is sold ...' It was to the *alcabala* that Ustáriz imputed 'the ruin of the manufactures of Spain'; but in Smith's view he might have added the decline of agriculture since the tax was also levied on agricultural produce. The Neapolitan equivalent, which was a tax of 3 per cent on all contracts including contracts of sale, was allowed to be partially bought out by the towns and parishes and was thus 'not near so ruinous' as its Spanish counterpart.[353]

One of the more evident weaknesses of *The Wealth of Nations* was Smith's inattention to that central preoccupation of the German Cameralists, population growth. This was the more surprising, since Steuart had highlighted the danger of overpopulation. It was not until the first edition of Thomas Malthus's *Essay on Population* in 1798 that this problem was properly addressed, and a (controversial) theory of population growth devised. Less well known is the relationship Malthus (1766–1834) attempted to establish between population increase, subsistence wages[354] and taxation, which was adumbrated in his *Principles of Political Economy* (1820).[355] In this work, he commented that 'an expenditure, which would have absolutely crushed the country in 1770, might be little more than what was necessary to call forth its prodigious powers of production in 1816'. However, there were great dangers in excessive fiscal concessions at the end of a long period of war:

... it is scarcely possible to doubt that, at the end of the war, when so large a mass of taxes

352 Smith, ed. Campbell, Skinner and Todd (1976), ii, 875–6, 905; *Mémoires*, ed. Moreau de Beaumont (1768), i, 202, 210–11, 233.

353 Smith, ed. Campbell, Skinner and Todd (1976), ii, 899–900.

354 Blaug (1978), 77, denies that the 'subsistence theory of wages' is a theory at all, and dismisses it as 'hopelessly ambiguous'.

355 Schumpeter (1954*a*), 480–3; Harvey-Phillips (1984); Hollander (1986).

would at once be restored to the payers of them, the just balance of produce and consumption would be completely destroyed ... The evil occasioned by imposing a tax is very rarely compensated by taking it off ... There is every reason to believe that the working classes of society would be severely injured by attaining the object which they seem so ardently to wish for.[356]

Malthus was a latter-day Physiocrat. Though he condemned the Physiocratic idea of the single tax on land as 'one of the[ir] principal errors', he agreed with them that 'all taxes certainly fall upon the land'.[357] Malthus's principal opponent was David Ricardo (1772–1823), who agreed with him on one point at least: 'notwithstanding the immense expenditure of the English government' since 1797, 'there can be little doubt but that the increased production on the part of the people has more than compensated for it'.[358] He thought that the annual revenue of the people, even after the payment of their taxes, was probably 'greater at the present time than at any former period of our history'.[359] The rate of growth would have been greater under a free system than under protection, however. Ricardo was also an opponent of the growth of the public debt, and would have preferred instead heavier wartime taxes. He accepted that individuals felt richer holding government bonds than paying taxes, even though the existence of such bonds implied future tax payments.[360] However, what he feared most was massive debt repudiation at the end of the war. A high public debt disturbed the price of commodities and thus disadvantaged British trade in foreign markets. He asserted that a large private debt would have been much less injurious in its economic effects than a large public debt, while heavier taxes during the war would, in contrast, have caused 'little permanent derangement ... to the industry of the country'.[361] Galiani's perception of the problem differed from the reality of the British experience during the Napoleonic Wars (Chapter 11.7).

Ricardo was in one sense a pure exponent of *laissez-faire*. 'Under a system of perfectly free commerce', he wrote, 'each country naturally devotes its capital and labour to such employments as are most beneficial to each. This pursuit of individual advantage is admirably connected with the universal good of the whole.'[362] In his view, agriculture, commerce and manufactures flourished best without government interference. But this ideal world was unattainable. Ricardo

[356] Malthus (1836), 423, 436–7.

[357] Semmel (1964–5), 534; Rashid (1981), 75; Hollander (1992), 380.

[358] Ricardo, ed. Sraffa and Dobb (1951–5), i, 151; Shoup (1960), 42; Tullio (1989), 728.

[359] Ricardo, ed. Sraffa and Dobb (1951–5), i, 151–2; Hollander (1977), 13.

[360] Ricardo, ed. Sraffa and Dobb (1951–5), i, 247 ('he deludes himself with the belief that he is as rich as before'); Shoup (1960), 153.

[361] Shoup (1960), 158.

[362] Ricardo, ed. Sraffa and Dobb (1951–5), i, 133–4.

was perfectly aware of the realities: 'the necessity which the state has for money to defray the expences [*sic*] of its functions, imposes on it the obligation to raise taxes, and thus interference becomes absolutely necessary. It is here that the most perfect knowledge of the science is required . . .'[363] Ricardo had been urged, both in 1819 and 1821, to write a study of 'the principles of taxation . . . and their application to our particular situation'; this should be a textbook 'to which Statesmen may refer, at once, to regulate their financial operations. Hitherto, Taxes have not been levied upon any settled principle . . . it is time to abandon this disgraceful, and ruinous mode of proceeding . . .'[364] Ricardo's reply was cynical but realistic: '. . . Ministers will always look more to the facility with which they can raise money by a tax, and the produce they can obtain from it, than to its consequences on the prosperity and future resources of the country . . .'[365] Ricardo's principal concerns in his *On the Principles of Political Economy and Taxation* (first edition, 1817) related to the question of what determines the taxable capacity of a country; he sought to demonstrate that a state might be able to pay additional taxes 'although the aggregate money value of the mass of its commodities should fall' as a result of technological improvements in agriculture, or by a removal of import restrictions on grain.[366] Even so, taxation was at best 'an obstacle to production', there being no tax which had not 'a tendency to diminish production'.[367]

Adam Smith had stated that 'the riches, and so far as power depends upon riches, the power of every country, must always be in proportion to the value of its annual produce, the fund from which all taxes must ultimately be paid'.[368] Though he owed much to Smith's ideas,[369] Ricardo criticized this concept, arguing that it was 'obvious, that the power of paying taxes, is in proportion to the net, and not in proportion to the gross, revenue'.[370] Ricardo's gross income was in modern parlance the net national income. His concept of the net income of a country was the sum of profits and rent only, for which modern national income accounting has no corresponding term.[371] Population size was relatively unimportant:

Provided its net real income, its rent and profits be the same, it is of no importance

363 Ibid. viii, 110; Shoup (1960), 8.

364 Shoup (1960), 16. This had been urged by his friend Hutches Trower.

365 Ricardo, ed. Sraffa and Dobb (1951–5), ix, 87–8.

366 This was the argument in the 'advertisement to the third edition' (Mar. 1821): Ricardo, ed. Sraffa and Dobb (1951–5), i, 8; Shoup (1960), 8.

367 Shoup (1960), 45.

368 Smith, ed. Campbell, Skinner and Todd (1976), i, 372.

369 Schumpeter (1954*a*), 474.

370 Ricardo, ed. Sraffa and Dobb (1951–5), i, 349; Shoup (1960), 191–2.

371 Shoup (1960), 86, 192; Ricardo, ed. Sraffa and Dobb (1951–5), i, 178, 347.

whether the nation consists of ten or twelve millions of inhabitants. Its power of supporting fleets and armies, and all species of unproductive labour, must be in proportion to its net, and not in proportion to its gross income.[372]

The definition of net revenue suggests that Ricardo was influenced by the Physiocrats, though there is no direct evidence that he studied them.[373] However, he had a much broader view of economic activity than the *Économistes*. Taxation was always paid from net income, whether in a growing or in a static economy; the difference was that in a growing economy 'the net produce of land is always diminishing in proportion to its gross produce ...'[374] Even so, a retrograde state was a distinct possibility (though the free entry of corn would prevent it arising in England):

Taxation has happily never yet in any free country been carried so far as constantly from year to year to diminish its capital. Such a state of taxation could not be long endured; or if endured, it would be constantly absorbing so much of the annual produce of the country as to occasion the most extensive scene of misery, famine, and depopulation.[375]

Ricardo finally arrived at something akin to the modern concept of a tax base (something which Smith had always eschewed),[376] without fully drawing out the implications that the tax base is more than simply the aggregate of the estimates for each tax, since the effect of each tax on the base has first to be taken into consideration:

If the revenue of the individuals of a country be 10 millions, they will have at least 10 millions worth of taxable commodities. If by taxing some, one million be transferred to the disposal of Government, their revenue will still be nominally 10 millions, but they will remain with only nine millions worth of taxable commodities...[377]

'Taxes', he considered, 'are a proportion of the produce of the land and labour of a country, placed at the disposal of the government; and are always ultimately paid, either from the capital, or from the revenue of the country.'[378] Ricardo continued:

All taxes must either fall on capital or revenue. If they encroach on capital, they must proportionately diminish that fund by whose extent the extent of the productive industry

[372] Ricardo, ed. Sraffa and Dobb (1951–5), i, 348; Shoup (1960), 192.

[373] Shoup (1960), 10.

[374] Ibid. 86–7; Ricardo, ed. Sraffa and Dobb (1951–5), i, 178.

[375] Shoup (1960), 42; Ricardo, ed. Sraffa and Dobb (1951–5), i, 185. Shoup (1960), 257, notes that J. S. Mill was much more pessimistic on the imminence of the stationary state.

[376] Sraffa notes that Ricardo's analysis of taxation closely followed the structure of Adam Smith: Ricardo, ed. Sraffa and Dobb (1951–5), i, pp. xxiii, xxv. Shoup (1960), 14, notes that 'Ricardo's analysis involves very little duplication of Smith's'. A similar approach could produce a rather different conclusion.

[377] Shoup (1960), 139; Ricardo, ed. Sraffa and Dobb (1951–5), i, 239.

[378] Ricardo, ed. Sraffa and Dobb (1951–5), i, 150.

of the country must always be regulated; and if they fall on revenue, they must either lessen accumulation, or force the contributors to save the amount of the tax, by making a corresponding diminution of their former unproductive consumption of the necessaries and luxuries of life. Some taxes will produce these effects in a much greater degree than others; but the great evil of taxation is to be found, not so much in any selection of its objects, as in the general amount of its effects taken collectively.[379]

Ricardo continued with an analysis of taxes on raw produce, or as we would say in modern parlance a specific tax per unit of agricultural produce.[380] Smith had stated that the burden of a special tax on farmers would be shifted; the farmer would seek to move his capital if he could not obtain a reasonable profit after tax, and he concluded that he would transfer the effects of taxation to his landlord, by a reduction in rent.[381] Ricardo agreed that the burden would be transferred, not in his view to the landlord but to the consumer: 'Any tax which may be imposed on the cultivator, whether in the shape of land-tax, tithes, or a tax on the produce when obtained, will increase the cost of production, and will therefore raise the price of raw produce' chiefly by the effect of a rise in wage rates.[382]

6.8 *Conclusion*

In 1771, Isaac de Pinto declared—in a rare moment of candour for a theoretician of state finance—'that the true and exact distribution of all the branches of finance is a science, all the principles of which are not yet understood'.[383] The preceding pages have demonstrated that in the years between *c*.1570 and 1820 the modern concept of economics emerged from the largely practical preoccupations of commentators who were much more concerned with the financing of the state than has sometimes been allowed. Schumpeter maintained that 'economic analysis has not been shaped at any time by the philosophical opinions that economists happened to have'.[384] By this he seems to have meant not that economic analysis was independent of political philosophy, but that the philosophical beliefs of economists were not relevant to the validity of the economic hypotheses they advanced.[385] Strictly speaking this may be true. But our concern

[379] Ibid. i, 152.

[380] Ibid. i, 156–72; Shoup (1960), 58–60.

[381] Smith, ed. Campbell, Skinner and Todd (1976), ii, 856.

[382] Ricardo, ed. Sraffa and Dobb (1951–5), i, 156. Shoup notes that 'any tax which may be imposed on the cultivator' needs to be understood to include only a tax that extends to the cultivator working at the margin, i.e. principally on wages.

[383] Pinto, trans. Baggs (1774, repr. 1969), 136.

[384] Schumpeter (1954*a*), 31.

[385] Blaug (1978), 5. Blaug points out that much of the text of Schumpeter's analysis concerns 'narrative history, political theory, and philosophical climates of opinion, presumably because of their relevance to economic theory'.

has been less with the validity of an economic theory in terms of the modern discipline of economics than its historical importance at a given period of time. The Physiocrats may have been utopian or misguided; but that does not diminish their fundamental influence on their contemporaries and on the evolution of subsequent economic theory. From this evolutionary standpoint, the debts left by Louis XIV, their influence on Law's ideas, and the subsequent failure of Law's System are of more relevance, perhaps of greater significance for modernity in terms of the development of the state, than any narrow preoccupation with whether Ricardo rather than Adam Smith should be regarded as the paradigm of the modern economist. Turgot and Cantillon may be regarded as the 'finest economic theorists of the eighteenth century'; but Smith had far greater influence over his immediate successors.[386]

Though this discussion has necessarily been selective—like Schumpeter, we have left on one side the agricultural treatises;[387] several of the distinguished Italian theorists[388] are given further treatment elsewhere in the context of eighteenth-century financial reform (Chapter 10); while the emerging debate in countries such as Portugal[389] and Sweden[390] with a less than determining role in economic affairs has had to be ignored—it is clear that some states responded much faster than others to conceptual arguments. In part, this was a consequence of intellectual endeavour and publishing possibilities. No other state apart from Britain[391] could match France, with 2,869 titles of political economy published between 1660 and 1789, of which 357, or 12 per cent, were devoted to the question of finance and taxation.[392] In part, the speed with which a state responded to conceptual arguments may have resulted from the openness or otherwise of the political system to debate and innovation. Yet an open political system did not necessarily breed a lively conceptual debate in the area of political economy, as the paucity of significant theoreticians in the United Provinces

[386] Brewer (1992*b*), 191.

[387] Schumpeter (1954*a*), 157; Tribe (1978), 53–79.

[388] Schumpeter (1954*a*), 176–9, 292–3, 300–4, 306–7.

[389] Caroso (1990).

[390] Magnusson (1987).

[391] A search of the *Eighteenth-Century Short Title Catalogue* on CD-Rom, covering the years 1701–1800, reveals 235,748 imprints for Britain and Ireland, of which some 2,478 were listed by a search on the key words 'bank$', 'expendit$', 'econom$', 'mercantil$', 'financ$', 'tax$', 'public credit', 'public debt', 'loan$', 'annuit$', where $ is the wildcard. There are no doubt other key words which would add to the total, and which would compensate for any incorrect inclusions and, since new titles are still being added to the ESTC, the figure may be considered an underestimate.

[392] Perrot (1992), 74–5. It should be noted that the great bulk of the titles (2,263 titles or 78.8 per cent of the total) dated from after 1750 and were therefore associated with the Physiocratic or anti-Physiocratic debate. The proportion of titles on finance and taxation was somewhat higher (306 titles or 85.7 per cent of the total of such titles).

demonstrates.[393] A distinction needs to made between practical men who wrote treatises on the basis of their administrative experience (Pompeo Neri in Milan and Tuscany, for example)[394] and theoreticians who later entered government and tried to implement some of their ideas during their period of office, usually with disastrous consequences (Law was the supreme example; Turgot and Necker were more flexible in their approach). Governments were also influenced by outsiders who conveyed technical innovations resulting from mathematical advances such as life-expectancy calculations, and in the United Provinces Johan de Witt indulged in such calculations in an effort to reduce Holland's public debt: the greater sophistication of governments is revealed by their capacity to calculate the probable cost of life annuity contracts and *tontines* in the second half of the seventeenth century.[395] 'Modern' visual devices for the presentation of statistical material such as graphs and maps with values to demonstrate the relative strength of states were produced by the end of the eighteenth century.[396] Algebraic formulae for calculations on life-expectancy information were not, however, accepted even in Napoleonic France.[397] Individuals—whether acting together as consortia or not—seem to have been able to outwit successive French finance ministers in the later eighteenth century in the serious business of calculating the risks for life rents. The government opted for what seemed to be a cheaper solution only if the capital market was relatively uneducated, which after the publication of Deparcieux's life-annuity cost tables in 1746 it certainly was not.[398] Individuals were no longer reliant on insider information to trade safely in negotiable assets: the financial market had been transformed since Richard Cantillon had made his fortune under Law's System.[399]

Freedom from prior censorship or subsequent harassment may have facilitated the spread of ideas: Petty, Davenant and the school of 'political arithmetic' in England could indulge freely in their speculations, unlike Boisguilbert, Vauban and even Mirabeau in the mid-eighteenth century, who were placed temporarily under arrest (though, it should be said, such arrests were in wartime and were

[393] Though de la Court, writing in 1662, calculated that for the production of half a Dutch cloth, 70 guilders were spent on wages, more than 20 guilders of which were due to excises: van Tijn in van Daal and Heertje (1992), 24. For the pressure on wage costs caused by excises: van Zanden (1993), 138.

[394] Klang (1977), 24–32, who notes, 29–30, that Neri himself was influenced by the views of Sallustio Bandini, 'the first Tuscan of the century proposing organic renewal guided by economic considerations'.

[395] Jennings and Trout (1982), 14–15, 19; Riley (1985), 11–15.

[396] Perrot (1977), 7 and n. 5.

[397] Staum (1987), 535.

[398] Velde and Weir (1992), 29, 31–3; Crouzet (1993), 67–71.

[399] Murphy (1986), 187–8.

always of short duration).[400] The freedom of debate resulting from a representative system of government may have speeded the pace of innovation. Walpole is said to have remarked that the English House of Commons took 'figures of arithmetic' more seriously than 'figures of rhetoric' when listening to speeches, though the validity of the remark is open to question given the self-interested nature of much Parliamentary debate.[401] Even so, there was a considerable delay between developments in the area of public credit in England between 1680 and 1790 and the broad public acceptance of innovation as evidenced by contemporary attitudes.[402] It was to open up the royal finances to public debate and scrutiny that Necker published his celebrated *Compte rendu* in 1781, but what is most noticeable about this event was just how late it occurred in the eighteenth century. How many other theoreticians, like Jean-Roland Malet, had not published their views because of the *secret des finances*? Once public opinion came into existence, however, it had to be taken seriously by governments. Louis XVI did not wish to repudiate the state debt in 1787 but, once a polemicist such as Brissot undertook a pamphlet campaign proclaiming *Point de banqueroute*, to have done so would have carried a heavy political price.[403]

Many of the theoreticians we have been considering were Mercantilists or crypto-Mercantilists. Were their arguments quite as misguided as Adam Smith contended?[404] It is insufficient to criticize them on the grounds, for example, that they did not anticipate fully, or explain sufficiently, the price–specie flow mechanism;[405] rather than expecting contemporaries to provide clear and consistent (let alone, modern) accounts of economic theories and depictions of economic systems, we should perhaps be seeking specific concepts which they recognized and which remain valid (supply and demand elasticity, some aspects of trade and money flow analysis, and so on).[406] In defence of the Mercantilist position, it has been stressed that their concept of international trade—one country's gain is another's loss—fulfilled the requirements of national economies at the time, and was therefore not a consequence of intellectual imprecision or

[400] Boisguilbert and Vauban: Bonney (1991*a*), 209. Mirabeau: McLain (1977), 30; Vaggi (1987), 143; Perrot (1992), 75. Sonnenfels commented on state secrecy: Small (1909), 528–9.

[401] Walpole cited by Burke (1992), 132. Contrast O'Brien in Dickinson (1989), 173–4: 'We should add that members of the House of Commons paid so little attention to the details of tax administration or the management of the public debt that the Prime Minister's authority was virtually unchallenged ... The parliamentary debates of the eighteenth century exemplify little more than deep ignorance, political animosity and ideological prejudice.'

[402] Hoppit (1990), 322.

[403] Crouzet (1993), 79; Root (1994), 223–5.

[404] Perrotta (1991) is a fundamental revision.

[405] Allen (1970), 387. Cf. Schumpeter (1954*a*), 345: 'Why then did [a theoretician such as] Malynes fail to draw this conclusion himself?'

[406] Coats (1973), 487–8.

theoretical error. The prevalence of colonial wars such as those between England and France for the control of the West Indies, Canada and India, and the struggle between monopoly companies such as the Dutch and English East India Companies tended to convince contemporaries that gaining wealth meant largely the pillaging of others (Chapter 11).[407] The ultimate purpose of the Mercantilist theoreticians (and statesmen who followed their views, starting perhaps with Colbert in France) was to increase domestic production, and thus particularly exports. Protectionism and government control of foreign trade were seen as indispensable for the take-off of an industrial economy and the shoring up of a weak economy against a stronger one;[408] once the advantage had been gained over trade rivals, they were seen as measures necessary to defend and maintain it, if not permanently (an impossibility, since all political or economic ascendancies were prone to dissolution,[409] a point well understood by contemporaries) then at least for as long as possible. Mercantilists were not ideologically opposed to free trade, but required a selective but active policy of encouraging trade and hindering damaging competition on the merits of each particular commodity or sector of the economy. This pragmatic approach did not prevent them developing a theory of economic development or general criteria as to how best to promote it. By the end of the period, theoreticians were questioning the legitimacy of fiscal exemptions, while noting that such exemptions had been granted by the crown whose fiscal power they sought to strengthen. In principle, the duty to contribute was the equal responsibility of all, argued Sonnenfels; if specific privileges endangered public welfare, it was the duty of rulers to revoke them.[410] The French government was not alone in finding that the practical obstacles to the establishment of an equitable fiscal system were greater than the theoreticians allowed.

What was their view of the state? It has been argued that many of the economists of the seventeenth and eighteenth centuries up to and including Sir James Steuart, writing in 1767, conceived of the state as a royal household to be managed by the sovereign or a statesman on his behalf according to the laws of a new science of 'political economy'.[411] Thus Antoine Montchrétien de Watteville (*c.*1575–1621), who publicized the term 'political economy' in his treatise of 1615 (*Traicté de l'Œconomie politique*),[412] derived it from the Greek *oikonomia*, which

[407] Perrotta (1991), 314, 324. [408] Ibid. 305, 324. [409] Cipolla (1970).

[410] Small (1909), 580–1. [411] Tribe (1978), 80–109; Small (1909), 588–9.

[412] Schumpeter (1954*a*), 167–8, denounced the quality of the work. More recent treatments are those of Lublinskaya (1968), 104–35; Parker (1971), 78–80; and Perrot (1992), 63–7, 145–6, who notes that Montchrétien was virtually unread in the 18th cent. King (1948), 231, and Letwin (1963), 217, noted that the first early modern author to use the term had been Louis Turquet de Mayerne, who wrote his treatise in 1591 although it was not published until 1611: Mousnier (1970*b*), 57–75; cf. Hutchison (1988), 17, 337, who repeats the old view that Montchrétien formulated the term.

distinguished the effective and thrifty ordering of a household from the business of money-making and trade.[413] Montchrétien argued, in contradiction to the Greek view, that 'economy' must not be separated from 'police', that is, administration, because 'the science of wealth acquisition is common to the state as well as the family'. He identified 'political economy' with public housekeeping (*mesnagerie politique*), which included not only government finance but also *la bonne police*, which might include the regulation of agriculture, trade and industry. *Œconomie politique*, it has been said, is 'therefore a body of knowledge concerned with the just and wise regulation of the royal household, in which economic activity cannot be conceived without the presence of the monarch's guiding presence to place this activity within some ordered framework'.[414] Thus Steuart argued that 'What oeconomy is in a family, political oeconomy is in a state'. Political oeconomy was concerned with specific duties and tasks such as 'population, agriculture, trade, industry, money, coin, interest, circulation, banks, exchanges, public credit and taxes'.[415] Smith's *The Wealth of Nations* was also avowedly a work of political economy and has an ambiguous place in the debate on the subject.[416] Book 4 had as its introduction a definition of the subject:

> Political oeconomy, considered as a branch of the science of a statesman or legislator, proposes two distinct objects; first, to provide a plentiful revenue or subsistence for the people, or more properly to enable them to provide such a revenue or subsistence for themselves; and secondly, to supply the state or commonwealth with a revenue sufficient for the publick services. It proposes to enrich both the people and the sovereign.[417]

Nevertheless, Smith's 'invisible hand' which ruled over the process of production and distribution in large measure displaced the guiding hand of the statesman. Indeed, the model of the state as a royal household to be managed by the sovereign or a statesman on his behalf is an inadequate depiction of the aim of Cantillon, Turgot and the classical economists, who showed that while rulers might be concerned with prestige and power, the 'statesman' need rarely intervene in the economy, and if intervene he did, his powers were fundamentally limited.[418] Smith's advocacy of the system of 'natural liberty' was a product of the Scottish Enlightenment. In his view, it was the force of commerce and capital accumulation, not the actions of any person or government, which had brought Europe to this state of 'natural liberty'; commerce was thus a force

413 Seligman in Seligman (1930–4), v, 345; Tribe (1978), 81–2.

414 Tribe (1978), 82.

415 Steuart, ed. Skinner (1966), i, 7, and also the definition at ibid. i, 16–17. Tribe (1978), 84.

416 Tribe (1978), 101–9.

417 Smith, ed. Campbell, Skinner and Todd (1976), i, 428; Evensky (1989).

418 Brewer (1992*b*), 183.

for rationalization which had eliminated arbitrary rule by monarchs and feudal lords.[419] Smith did not question the Mercantilists' goals, only their methods. If 'the great object of the political oeconomy of every country is to increase the riches and power of that country',[420] as Smith adduced, there was nevertheless a limit to growth. Mismanagement might arrest the development of nations below their full potential—the examples of ancient Egypt and China were dismissed because of their lack of foreign trade—but growth might cease when a country 'acquired its full complement of riches'. In principle, however, this should not be a problem for an economy regulated by the appropriate 'laws and institutions'.[421] The Smithian and Ricardian view of the long-term effects of the growth of government expenditure, taxation and debt may still have contemporary relevance.[422]

The title of this book, *Economic Systems and State Finance*, with its inclusion of the term 'economic systems', would have probably appeared fanciful to contemporaries even towards the end of the period under study. A contemporary of Wellington, Metternich and Talleyrand discussed the budget proposed by the restored monarchy in France in 1814 in these words:

> In France there has never been an economic system: Sully laid the foundations of an agrarian system, but Colbert gave greater importance to a commercial system. The contradictory ideas of these two great men has been an obstacle to the success of either doctrine ... Subsequently, 28 ministers have held office [in financial affairs], most of whom have operated without any system ... [423]

In contrast, Talleyrand justified what he called the 'financial system', that is to say the budget of 1814, on the grounds that it would 'establish the prosperity of France on the basis of a public credit proportionate to the extent of its resources'.[424] He argued that Frenchmen were somewhat less taxed than Americans and were considerably less taxed than the British: the figures he cited were of a respective per capita fiscal burden of 23, 25 and 120 francs.[425] Talleyrand had opposed Necker, and threw in his lot with those who argued that instead of

419 Prasch (1991), 347–8.

420 Smith, ed. Campbell, Skinner and Todd (1976), i, 372; Prasch (1991), 346.

421 Smith, ed. Campbell, Skinner and Todd (1976), i, 89, 495; Prasch (1991), 338–42.

422 Tullio (1989); Wrigley in Stone (1994), 90–1.

423 Bruguière (1969), 98.

424 Ibid. 131.

425 Ibid. 131 n. 2. In the case of Britain, £60 million in tax revenue was taken to be the equivalent of 1,440 million francs; tax revenue for France was placed at 600 million. The population was taken to be 12 million for Britain and 28 million for France. O'Brien estimates direct taxes in Britain in 1814 at 21.2 million and indirect taxes at 42.1 million, that is 63.3 million in total: ESFDB \obrien\engd010.

borrowing, the crown should seek to balance expenditure and revenue (another contemporary called this 'the great secret of finance').[426]

The French debates on the budget in 1814–15 thus led to the rehabilitation of the word 'system' in terms of its application to public finance. Before that date, the word had had a pejorative connotation:[427] Law had invented a system which had failed. The *Économistes*, or Physiocrats, had been motivated by a similar spirit and their ideas, too, had been discredited. Necker had rejected such plans with their stress on uniformity,[428] while even the Revolutionaries of 1789–90 rejected the *esprit du système*, that is to say the Physiocratic single tax on net income or its variants.[429] And yet, for all the arguments against systems and system builders, Law's ideas and those of the Physiocrats had deeply penetrated the attitudes of contemporaries and the practice of governments. Roederer, perhaps uniquely, was prepared to acknowledge this reality. He commented on his role in the National Assembly, drafting the laws on the stamp duty, patents, landed property and moveable property:

> It was I who expounded to the Assembly the general plan of the system of direct and indirect taxes, and who explained how each part interacted within the general system; who showed how they were linked to each other and to the whole, and how the whole was linked to the annual reproduction of national wealth.[430]

The emission of paper money in France and the growth of the public debt in Britain to finance the Revolutionary and Napoleonic wars, and the accompanying growth of a more modern system of direct (and later, indirect) taxation, amounted to a fiscal 'system' that was not far short of a revised scheme of Law and the Physiocrats, a fundamental and permanent change in the political economy of the two most powerful west European states before 1815. Contemporary perceptions of the role of the state in the economy had also developed, perhaps most rapidly during the long period of conflict between France and Britain between 1792 and 1815. The attempt to calculate the economic consequences of the French Revolution was an obsession of contemporaries, and required a much more sophisticated evaluation than hitherto of the gross national product (GNP), debt ratios to GNP, the per capita fiscal burden and the per capita debt burden. With such attempts at evaluation we arrive at something close to the fiscal theory of the modern state. Even if the calculations differed, the conclusion on the whole did not, that Britain had gained a substantial lead over France in matters financial as well as economic.[431]

426 Bruguière (1969), 133.

427 Rousselot de Surgy (1784–7), iii, 597.

428 Harris (1979), 91–2. For Necker as an opponent of the Physiocrats: Spengler (1942), 324–33.

429 Rapport de l'Assemblée Nationale (1790), 2.

430 Roederer, ed. Forsyth (1989), xxi.

431 Crouzet (1985, 1990); Thuillier (1983), 248–61; Perrot (1992), 454–62, 467–9; Crouzet (1993), 491–7.

CHAPTER 7

The Spanish System: Centre and Periphery

Giovanni Muto

There was a close connection between the process of state formation and the development of state finance in early modern Europe. This took different forms according to the nature of the state (whether it was a republic, a principality or a monarchy), its structure (whether it was a nation state, an empire or a confederation), and the political objectives that each state set itself. During the early years of the sixteenth century, monarchs and their advisers realized, if it had ever seriously been doubted, that territorial control and the assertion of their rule were impossible to achieve without adequate financial resources. Yet to obtain these resources was no easy task. The state met with numerous difficulties in finding the right solutions to ensure that money flowed into its coffers or to those places which most urgently required the payment or remittance of funds. Not all states succeeded in establishing the most suitable financial system for the requirements of their political development (this was the case with France, for example, in its mid-sixteenth-century crisis). Success or otherwise crucially affected the hierarchy of states, and the place of each state within the system of international relations.

Apart from the rank which each state occupied in the political and economic sphere, it may be argued that at least five conditions had to be met before a state achieved a high level of competitiveness and an efficient financial system. Firstly, the state needed to operate within a society able to produce wealth and in an economic system which was capable of satisfying demand. Secondly, the economy had to be open to international exchange and in itself possess a high rate of monetary exchange. Thirdly, the state itself had to be able to mobilize substantial monetary resources (reserves accumulated previously and private savings, as well as the exploitation and creation of new cash surpluses). Fourthly, there had to be an acceptable level of management of the state's bureaucracy capable of finding new forms of revenue and operating a reasonably efficient tax system. Finally, the public authorities had to be capable of entering the international financial market by means of connections with entrepreneurs, merchant bankers or other types of international financial expertise. In early modern Europe, it was first Spain, and then to a lesser degree France, which were able to achieve such conditions in the course of the sixteenth century. Subsequently, England, too, in the seventeenth century, developed a firm system of relations between the state and the world of finance.

Spain is a particularly interesting case, since it was arguably the most significant and complex European 'state'. The first distinctive aspect was territorial: what is improperly called the Spanish 'empire' was, in fact, a community of states with a well-defined political and institutional identity, each of which retained its own constitutional features, laws and governmental framework. The community had a political centre, the kingdom of Castile, from which developed a process of unification within the Iberian kingdoms (Aragon, Catalonia, Valencia) though these states retained their own administrative, fiscal and legal autonomy. Portugal was also united within the 'imperial' community between 1580 and 1640. Despite their internal differences, the Spanish kingdoms maintained a basic cultural identity. Beyond them lay the Italian provinces (the kingdom of Naples, the kingdom of Sicily and the duchy of Milan), Franche-Comté and the Netherlands which all largely maintained a separate institutional structure even if the crown could exert pressure on them to limit their independence. The conquests of the New World had a special status, since they depended directly on Castile. From the Castilian viewpoint, the other Iberian territories and the provinces outside the peninsula might equally be viewed as peripheral regions. However, in the Iberian kingdoms there was much greater political and administrative autonomy and fiscal pressure was, on the whole, modest, whereas in the other territories Spanish monarchs could intervene much more decisively in order to obtain taxation. This imperial community possessed a significantly greater money supply than other European countries.

The second distinguishing characteristic of the Spanish system was its access to an additional supply of money derived not from a direct taxation of the wealth produced by its subjects but from the precious metals sent from the Americas to Seville. The flow of precious metals was itself subject to a fixed tax of 20 per cent, the so-called *quinto real*, plus, in exceptional circumstances, compulsory confiscation often repaid with bonds from the public debt. Braudel and Spooner, among others, tried to estimate the order of magnitude of the European money supply in the sixteenth and seventeenth centuries and to what extent American gold and silver changed the position of Europe's precious metal stocks in comparison to the rest of the world (Figure 1).[1] Their conclusions give the impression that over a period of 150 years between 1500 and 1650, the European stock of gold increased by no more than 5 per cent, while stocks of silver rose by nearly 50 per cent.[2] These increases, however, turned out to be totally insufficient to guarantee a balanced mechanism of money supply in the private and public sectors, which in turn helps explain the expansion of the *moneta aerea*, the great spread all over the Continent of the instruments of commercial and banking credit. In this perspective, Morineau's researches are important, not so much for the correction of Hamilton's data as for the confirmation of imports of precious metals into Europe throughout the seventeenth century.[3]

Thirdly, it must be stressed that this enormous quantity of money, or rather its counterpart in the form of bills of exchange, moved within a circuit of financial markets (Seville, Medina del Campo, Antwerp, the fairs of Besançon) which were controlled by the Spanish crown and those financiers who were its close allies. Confidence in the creditworthiness of the Spanish crown in these as in the German markets, was considerable, and lasted for more than a century until the mid-seventeenth century. It underpinned the great sixteenth-century expansion, when a great flow of private capital seeking investment opportunities was followed by an abundance of precious metals from Spanish America.

Any analysis of the Spanish system must make some judgement concerning the efficiency and operational skill exercised by the financial 'bureaucracy'. There has been a scholarly tendency to criticize the bureaucratic machinery of both centre and periphery for its lack of efficiency in administering the territories of the empire.[4] Yet the financial management of the sixteenth century cannot be assessed according to our own criteria of efficiency and competence. The hierarchical framework of society and its division into orders did not allow, for example, any importance to be given to the criterion of equal taxation: in all countries of the *ancien régime*, privileges and exemptions were considered legitimate. Moreover, the extent of the fiscal burden was determined at a higher political level than that on which the bureaucrats operated. Expenditure derived from political decisions which were often taken without a serious assessment of the likely costs. In these circumstances, it was by no means easy for financial officials to carry out efficient tax measures.

The fact that there was no central co-ordinating body for the financial policy of the empire constituted a further check on the proper working of the system.

[1] Braudel and Spooner (1967). [2] Parker (1974). [3] Morineau (1985).

[4] Cf., most recently, Calabria (1991), 132: 'Through much of the sixteenth century, Naples, like Castile, was probably taxed beneath its capacity to contribute. But that was no doubt more than made up for by the rapacity and unscrupulousness of His Majesty's officials.' [Ed.]

Even the legislative powers of the *Consejo de Hacienda*, whose importance increased over the years, were limited to the kingdom of Castile. The decisions taken by the *Consejo de Estado*, for example, would undoubtedly have been more effective if they had been taken by a unified body endowed with greater powers than the various bodies that administered the peripheries. On the contrary, the latter often clashed with the rival jurisdiction of other councils. Thus, for example, in the course of the Thirty Years' War, if the *Consejo de Estado* indicated the means of payment for the troops stationed in Milan, the *Consejo de Italia* would immediately intervene, asserting its territorial competence in such matters and thus slowing down the pace at which problems might be solved. However, it must be pointed out that throughout the sixteenth century and, at least until the time of Olivares's ministry, the financial machinery was undoubtedly more efficient than the rest of the imperial bureaucracy. It was run by a nucleus of officials who on the whole were well capable of identifying problems and finding technical solutions. Of course, there were areas where such qualities were deficient (this was particularly true of Sicily) and some where a higher degree of financial management would have been desirable. In general, however, we may accept the assertion of Ruiz Martín that 'at no time was there disorder, nor did the officials fail to recognize the true financial position, with regard to income and expenditure and the extent of the consolidated and floating debt; and book-keeping in silver and copper equivalents was also diligent'.[5]

7.1 *The Financial Relations of Centre and Periphery*

Financial relations between the central state machinery of the empire and its provinces were regulated in a manner which had shortcomings as well as advantages. Each country retained its own financial administration and at no stage did the crown insist on unifying different financial practices and management into a single model. This necessitated respect for different norms and procedures and for the rights of the financial magistracies of the different territories. It often caused difficulties for the central government in following rules which differed from one country to another: every local official was eager to adhere to rules which were not necessarily rational but which were jealously guarded against the encroachments of central authority. The crown tended to respect these institutional arrangements, which inevitably caused problems in terms of the length of time required to solve urgent problems. When a decision had to be taken to increase a tax or conclude a loan contract (*asiento*) in one of the Italian provinces, the reports of the financial tribunals in Milan or Naples went

[5] Ruiz Martín (1990), 179.

twice or three times between these cities and the *Consejo de Italia* or the *Consejo de Hacienda*, wasting precious time and reducing the benefits of the operation.

There was also an intrinsic difficulty in following through a problem from the centre and assessing the effectiveness of the measures that were proposed. The authorities in the regions continually complained, perhaps rightly so, about the intolerable tax demands, price increases and widespread poverty in their kingdoms. Viceroys and governors tried to apply the directives of central government but were often forced to agree with the views expressed by local elites. The lack of exact information often precluded the adoption of suitable steps to solve important problems. Moreover, financial questions were complex and the best course of action was by no means obvious: we need only consider the difficulty involved in the circulation within the empire of different currencies (the Castilian ducat, the Aragonese *lira*, the *livre de gros* and the *stuiver* of the Netherlands, the imperial *lira* of Milan, the Neapolitan and Sicilian *tari*), plus an even greater number of royal coins cast in gold, silver and copper (*vellón*). All this required a highly qualified staff of officials who had to be expert at book-keeping and exchange, and who could check revenues and expenditure, calculate the rate of interest and advance payments, keep the Treasury accounts up to date and estimate the level of debt or surplus.

The lack of a clear chain of command among the various administrative bodies makes it necessary to examine financial organization at central and local government level separately. In the kingdom of Castile, financial organization was governed by two bodies until 1523: the *Contaduria Mayor de Hacienda* and the *Contaduria Mayor de Cuentas*. The former was the body involved in active administration: it was in charge of ordinary revenue, informed the monarch of the state of his finances, decided on the issue of bonds and reported on the balance between expenditure and income. The latter controlled all the book-keeping activities: it recorded all the incoming and outgoing items, established the amounts of revenue collected, issued payment mandates and basically acted as a centralized general accounting office. Estimates of cash flow, both in revenue and expenditure, were carried out by the Treasury, though this body did not have exclusive control. As elsewhere in Europe (Chapter 13), there were many management agencies outside the Treasury, where accounting took place at separate treasuries.

This, therefore, was the basic organization of the *Hacienda* when Charles V succeeded Ferdinand the Catholic in 1516. Various authors have stressed the importance of the education Charles received at the court of Burgundy and the influence of that political model. When he became king of Castile, Charles immediately concerned himself with the kingdom's finances and showed a clear tendency towards centralized financial management in July 1517 by granting

Francisco de Los Cobos wide controlling powers over the crown's income and expenditure and general cash flow; Cobos was at first assisted by the Burgundian Guillaume de Croy, lord of Chièvres. There is evidence that some figures at court pressed for a more far-reaching rationalization of financial management: Martin de Salinas argued that everything should be modelled on Flanders ('todo se quiere ordenar al modo de Flandes').[6] The *Consejo de Hacienda* established at the beginning of 1523 does indeed seem to have been taken from the Burgundian *Conseil des finances*, originally composed of only three members: Count Henry of Nassau, Don Juan Manuel and Jacques Laurin. With the adoption of this reform in Castile, the dual organization of the *Contadurias* was broken; while the *Contaduria Major de Hacienda* had its powers progressively reduced until it was finally absorbed by the *Consejo de Hacienda*, for its part, the *Contaduria Major de Cuentas* strengthened its techniques and became a fully fledged chamber of accounts. However, the problem of the lack of a unified treasury was not resolved. An initial attempt to create an *argentier* with the functions of a general collector for the kingdom came to nothing; and a second attempt in 1524 to create a receiver-general with a network of subordinate receivers likewise did not materialize.

These early attempts at financial centralization did not produce the improvements expected. The real problem, in the sixteenth and seventeenth centuries, was that the council never succeeded in becoming an effective co-ordinating body for the financial policy of the whole empire. Whenever it was a question of raising money, the matter was decided in the Netherlands, in northern Italy or in central Europe, where the distant *Consejo de Hacienda* had difficulty exerting its authority (even when its powers were strengthened, its jurisdiction continued to be limited to the territories of Castile). There was no shortage of reforming endeavour: the council was reformed in 1568, 1602, 1621, 1635, 1651 and 1658. By 1658, the council was organized in four sections: *Sala de Millones*, *Sala de Oidores*, *Contaduria Mayor de Cuentas* and *Sala de Gobierno*. This organization administered a vast amount of revenue and taxes. After 1590, the Castilian *Cortes* voted the *servicio de millones*, which was destined to become one of the principal sources of revenue. However, the administration of this *servicio* was carried out directly by the *Cortes* through its own body, the *commision de millones*, which was independent of the *Consejo de Hacienda*. In this way, at the beginning of the seventeenth century two separate financial administrations were established: the *Hacienda Real*, which was presided over and headed by the monarch and governed by his *Consejo de Hacienda*, and the *Hacienda del Reyno*, administered by the *Cortes* through the *commision de millones*.[7]

[6] Carande (1959), ii, 70.

[7] Gelabert in Bonney (1995). On the origin and development of this process: Fortea Pérez (1991).

It must be stressed that this organization was responsible for the financial management of the territories which were directly dependent on the crown of Castile, but certain areas were excluded from its jurisdiction, such as the kingdom of Navarre which, on being incorporated into Castile in 1512, retained its own *Cámara de Comptos* at Pamplona. The Castilian possessions in the New World were in a curious institutional position. After 1503, all economic activity in these territories came under the *Casa de Contratación* of Seville; yet after 1524 territorial jurisdiction passed to the *Consejo de Indias*. The *Hacienda* of Castile still kept its own officials (treasurer, *contador*, *factor* and *veedor*) in each district in order to control financial management.[8] Within the Iberian peninsula, the crown of Aragon long continued to maintain its own particular political and administrative identity. Each of its three component territories (Aragon proper, Catalonia and Valencia) retained its own financial organization which was the direct expression of the power of the three *Cortes*. The power of these parliamentary assemblies was significant and conditioned the monarch's attitude towards the kingdoms: the king and his representatives were obliged to observe the *fueros*, the sum of ancient privileges, which meant that no economic measure or tax levy could be implemented unless it had been previously approved by a unanimous vote of the three estates of the *Cortes*. Under these conditions, it is easy to understand why the monarch of Castile never managed to receive any substantial financial assistance from these territories. The *Consejo de Aragon*, which was founded in the fifteenth century, was very inefficient at linking these areas to the central authority and was never able to increase the flow of funds from the region to the empire as a whole.

Outside the Iberian kingdoms, the organization of public finance was inevitably much more heterogeneous. For the Netherlands the matter is complicated by the revolt in the 1560s and thereafter, which makes it impossible, at least until the end of the sixteenth century, to define what we call 'the Netherlands' in precise territorial terms. It is therefore necessary to determine an appropriate dividing-point: the year 1579 has been adopted, since after this date the various cities and territories gradually chose to remain within either the Union of Utrecht or the Union of Arras. Before 1579, we can refer to a formally united territory but subsequently it is possible to distinguish between the United Provinces, which left the Habsburg union, and the Spanish Netherlands which remained within it. At the beginning of the sixteenth century, these territories were a personal union of about seventeen states, cities and lordships which Charles had inherited from the dukes of Burgundy. Some areas, such as the Tournaisis, had been conquered with great difficulty in the 1520s. In general the provinces lacked a strong central

[8] Sanchez Bella (1968).

government, because of the important political role played by the cities and their urban elites. In 1487, the dukes of Burgundy had tried to reform the fiscal system by creating a *bureau des finances* with a *receveur général* and a treasurer. Ten years later, the new post of *surintendant chef des finances* was added above this hierarchy. After 1531, the new *Conseil des finances* was one of the three collateral councils (the others were the council of state and the privy council) and was responsible for managing the patrimonial revenue of the crown and levying taxes. A second body, the *Chambre des Comptes*, was in charge of book-keeping, with its responsibilities divided up into five separate sections at Dôle, Lille, Brussels, The Hague and Arnhem. In fact, this financial bureaucracy controlled a relatively small amount of state revenue. The greater part derived from ordinary and extraordinary subsidies (*aides* or *beden*) which were voted by the provincial states; each province shared a proportion of expenditure which it had to meet through taxes levied within its own area. These sums were collected by provincial receivers (*rentmeisters*) and administered by delegations and officials of the provincial states. Such bodies existed in Flanders from 1522, Zealand from 1544 and the Tournaisis from 1558,[9] while states-appointed officials were on the commissions set up by the chamber of accounts to check the sums collected as *aides*.[10]

This structure therefore left local administrators with great bargaining powers and tight control over public finance, which strengthened provincial autonomy and weakened central authority. It has been argued that 'this participation of the states in financial administration prepared them directly for the political role which they were called upon to play during the revolt of the Low Countries, and once the United Provinces had broken away from Spanish control'.[11] After 1567, when the Spanish government realized that it could no longer count on the *aides*, there was an increase in contributions arriving directly from Spain. These were managed by a separate administration under a *pagador general*; in 1578, the office of *superintende de Hacienda* was created; and finally, in 1595, a *Junta de Hacienda*.[12] Basically, from the 1570s, the flow of public money was channelled into two separate organizations, which never merged into a single administrative unit. The *Consejo de Flandes* set up on the abdication of Charles V came into its own only in 1588 and never succeeded in changing the situation.

In the provinces of Spanish Italy the question of financial management was easier because in those territories the organizational model of the *Hacienda* was based on some of the functions already existing in Milan, Naples and Sicily, where there tended to be a general management body, an accountancy body and

[9] De Schepper (1984), 12.
[10] Ibid. 19.
[11] Craeybeckx (1967), 345–6.
[12] Parker (1972, 1979).

a central treasury office. But the weak point in the relations between Castile and the Italian provinces was the lack of a proper co-ordinating body for financial policy. The *Consejo de Italia*, which was set up between 1557–8, could have taken on this function because it included in its personnel the *Conservador del Patrimonio de Italia*, whose task was to inspect the balances of the Italian territories. In reality, the financial competence of this council was always very limited and its jurisdiction mainly affected administrative work, in particular nominations to offices. In the duchy of Milan, which on the death of the last Sforza duke at the end of 1535 in effect became part of the empire, financial management depended on the *Magistrato Ordinario* who was in charge of the administration of tax and revenue; this official issued measures concerning economic and monetary policy and drew up the balance of revenue and expenditure. He was assisted by the *Magistrato Straordinario* who administered the prince's patrimony and had jurisdiction over fiefs, smuggling and confiscations. Both officials had a staff consisting of a president, six *questors* (councillors) and a varying number of officers with executive functions. Among the latter an important role was played by the two *ragionati* (accountants) of the *Magistrato Ordinario*, who acted as a sort of accountancy office and recorded cash income and expenditure. Tax collection, the payment and the movement of funds were the responsibility of the General Treasury: this had a civil and a military division, which were merged between 1570 and 1615 but subsequently separated.

However, it is important to recognize that a slow process of change was taking place outside this institution, which affected relations between the Milanese financial administration and the peripheral communities of the duchy. This process started in 1543, when Charles V ordered the drawing-up of a new general census including both landed property and other sources of income. While the operations of the land registry office were completed in 1564 the assessment of *mercimonio* (income from trade) lasted until 1594.[13] In the course of these decades, the *contado* (rural communities subject to urban jurisdiction) of the nine Lombard towns constituted their own representative body, the Congregation of the *contado*, which was in charge of the division and collection of taxes in the rural communities. In this way, the degree of political bargaining power between town and country was redefined and there began the process towards a fairer distribution of taxation, apparently unopposed by the Spanish authorities.

In the kingdom of Naples, the financial administration depended on three bodies. The *Camera della Sommaria*, the old chamber of accounts, was the

[13] Vigo (1979).

organization which administered the patrimony of the kingdom. It was presided over by a lieutenant, at whose side were at least six presidents who shared responsibility for fiscal matters. Below them operated a number of officers with specific functions. The *Scrivania di razione*, which was set up between 1505 and 1509, was an accounting office which noted all income and expenditure. The General Treasury exercised closer central scrutiny over money which had been collected and paid. After 1612, the *Cassa Militare* (Military Treasury) was detached from the civil treasury and its endowment, which was intended for the payment of necessities, could not be sold. Parallel to this central organization there operated in each of the twelve provinces of the kingdom a provincial collector who was directly responsible to the *Camera della Sommaria*. Interestingly, the officers of the Neapolitan financial administration were, in the seventeenth century, considered very good at checking accounts. They were often invited to other parts of the empire to review accounts or to seek out cases of administrative malpractice.[14]

Finally, in the kingdom of Sicily, the ancient *Magna Curia* was transformed in 1569 into the *Tribunale del real patrimonio* to which the administration of Sicilian finances was entrusted, with an organization and staff which closely resembled the Neapolitan model with a president, six *maestri razionali* (masters of accounts) and a small nucleus of executive officers. Accountancy functions were carried out by the *Conservatore del real patrimonio*, while the general treasurer was in charge of the cash flow. In this apparently straightforward organization an important role was played by the Sicilian Parliament through the *Deputazione del regno*, which was a commission of twelve deputies, elected by the assembly, which controlled the use of extraordinary subsidies. In fact, the delegation arranged for the payment of the seven subsidies, informing each community of its quota, and it directly administered at least three extraordinary subsidies. The role of this parliamentary commission seems to have been decisive until 1567, when a reform reduced its functions. Subsequently, in the 1612 Parliament, the concession of a special nine-year extraordinary subsidy was made dependent on a return to the control exercised by the *Deputazione del regno*. Financial control beyond the capital was less effective. It was not until 1570 that the island was divided into three tax areas under the control of a royal collector. This official proved unable to prevent widespread fraud, since public money was often entrusted to individual depositors.

[14] In 1573, Juan de Ovando, president of the *Consejo de Hacienda*, 'held up the Neapolitan Council of Finance as a model of how an Exchequer should be managed ... Not only were Neapolitan officials better trained but the Neapolitan system was far superior to that of Castile.' Lovett (1972), 12.

7.2 *The Organization and Structure of Public Finance*

The fiscal systems of early modern Europe were clearly very different from their modern counterparts. Unlike the states of today, the early modern state was a competitor for resources with other powers, such as the church, and social groups, such as the nobility. There was greater reliance on indirect, as opposed to direct, taxes in many European countries. A third difference was in the way that taxes were collected in the sixteenth and seventeenth centuries: the state was unable to collect impositions directly and had to rely on private entrepreneurs or contractors (Chapter 13.2). In the Iberian kingdoms, direct collection of tax by the *Hacienda Real* was unusual. Three other procedures were much more widespread. Firstly, the *ripartimients*, which applied particularly to the *servicios*, were the amounts stipulated by the *Cortes* or the *Hacienda* as due from the various communities and contributors, who were directly responsible for the collection of the prescribed sum. A second system, the *arrendamiento* or leasing, was common in Spain as well as in the Italian provinces: through a series of auctions an individual made an advance payment of the tax, which he then ensured was collected from others by his own officials. The third system, the *encabezamiento*, a fixed lease or fixed farm, operated in relation to the *alcabalas*: a specified sum was payable for a certain number of years, which the *Cortes* or particular municipalities agreed with the crown as to the value of a particular tax.

Revenues reached the various central treasuries net, after the expenses incurred in collection had been deducted, as well as those which had been assigned on the revenue (Chapter 13.1). A central treasury system existed only in theory, while a plethora of banks and autonomous treasuries was the order of the day in both Castile and the provinces.[15] These structural factors provide serious limits on our capacity to interpret the evidence of the accounts, and on the reliability of reconstructed figures based on balances, *sumarios*, *relaciones*, *tanteos* and so on. For the Spanish system, it is legitimate to accept the order of magnitude given by the documentation, provided that the source is an official one and the result of the work of the officials of the *Hacienda Real*. The reliability of the material is enhanced if we reconstruct a run of figures concerning specific items, such as taxes on consumer goods, military expenses or elements of the public debt.

Subject to these caveats, we may attempt an analysis of the items of the budget of the separate territories of the empire, distinguishing revenue from expenditure. In the kingdom of Castile, among the ordinary revenues were first and foremost the *alcabala*, the 10 per cent indirect tax which affected every kind of transaction whether in cash or property; the *tercias*, a direct tax which affected two-ninths of all crops and income; excise taxes, such as the *servicio y montazgo*,

[15] Ulloa (1986), 117.

diezmo del mar, almojarifazgo major of Seville, *almojarifazgo major de Indias* and *puertos secos*; taxes on the exportation of Castilian wool and Grenada silk; the *estancos*, or private right over salt marshes and coinage, and the income of the grand masterships (*maestrazgos*) of the three military orders of Santiago, Calatrava and Alcantara. Among the extraordinary revenues, the most important were the *servicios*, which in turn were either ordinary or extraordinary (these were voted by the *Cortes* and then divided among the contributors as a personal tax);[16] church revenues confiscated by the crown as a result of Papal concession (*cruzada, subsidio, excusado*, church benefits); and finally the remittances of precious American metals, whether those collected directly for the benefit of the crown or others on which it levied the *quinto real*.[17] This concise list is proof that throughout the sixteenth century the revenues of the Castilian *Hacienda* were largely based on two great items, remittances of precious metals and income from the *alcabala*, which alone provided between 40 and 45 per cent of the total, followed by the *servicios* and church revenues, which together contributed an average of 20 per cent. Between the early years of Charles's reign in 1522[18] and the first years of Philip II, in 1560,[19] total revenues rose fourfold, from about 1 to 4 million ducats. At the beginning of the reign of Philip III, in 1598, total revenues were about 10 million ducats[20] and in little more than fifty years, in 1654, 18 million[21] and finally, in 1674, about 30 million.[22]

It is also possible to distinguish between ordinary and extraordinary expenditure. The former includes the allowances of the royal households, not only the expenses of the court of the king but also those of the queen and princes. Added to this were the expenses for the running of the palaces and official residences. Although contemporary evidence gives us a picture of great pomp, these two items taken together represented only between 5 and 8 per cent of ordinary annual expenditure. The cost of the internal administration must have been much higher, given the total cost of salaries paid to royal officials, leading members of the judiciary and other royal administrators. This item is difficult to calculate, however, because apart from the official salary the king accorded his employees various types of subsidy, in the form of pensions, *mercedes, entretenimientos, ayudas de costa* or *ventajas*. Over a period of time, the subsidy greatly

[16] For the *servicios* during the reign of Charles V: Carande (1959), ii, 536–7. For those under Philip II: Ulloa (1986), 480.

[17] For the annual and quinquennial averages of the contributions from the Indies: Ulloa (1986), 694–7.

[18] Carande (1969), 122.

[19] Le Flem (1980), 88 (the source indicated is Ruiz Martín).

[20] Domínguez Ortiz (1960), 5.

[21] Sureda Carrion (1949), 87.

[22] Garzon Pereja (1980), 146.

exceeded the official salary and became a considerable burden on the country's budget. In contrast, expenditure on diplomats, other agents, special envoys and messengers was often charged to the provinces to which they were sent. The largest two items of expenditure were those which it proved difficult to contain. The first was the payment of annual interest on the public debt, which continued to increase in size. The second was the cost of maintaining the army, which was often engaged on a number of fronts from the Mediterranean to the Netherlands.

In the Italian provinces, the distinction between ordinary and extraordinary income was much less important because extraordinary new taxes became regarded as ordinary revenue over a period of time. Extraordinary revenues were always more important in terms of their size. In the duchy of Milan, the clearest example of this process can be seen in the *mensuale*, a direct tax introduced as an extraordinary measure in 1536 which became a regular tax. There were many direct taxes, including the salt tax, the *imbottato*, military taxes such as the *tasso dei cavalli*, *tasso d'ambo le cavallerie*, the *presidi forensi* and the *carico dei 14 reali*, besides taxes on income such as the *annata* and *mezz'annata*. Indirect taxes included numerous excises on property and goods, the most important of which was that on merchandise which may be considered a reasonable indicator of the scale of industrial and commercial activity.

Similarly, extraordinary taxes were gradually assimilated into ordinary ones in the kingdoms of Naples and Sicily. The basic rate of direct taxation in the earlier sixteenth century was fixed at 1 ducat and 52 *grana a fuoco*. The basic rate progressively increased, especially after 1566, when ordinary taxes were increased by a six-monthly subsidy of 1.2 million ducats, payable by three-quarters of the hearths of the communities in the kingdom. This was not the only form of direct tax. In addition to these ordinary taxes there were at least six other extraordinary levies paid by each hearth. Feudal lords had to pay a direct tax, the *adoa*, which consisted of the remaining quarter of the six-monthly subsidy. A pervasive system of customs duties affected the production of raw materials, especially silk, and all trade in goods. The taxes on consumer goods were especially widespread and significant. In Sicily, in addition to the ordinary subsidy which was fixed at 50,000 *scudos* throughout the sixteenth century, the people had eight more special subsidies to pay (for the costs of galleys, fortifications, bridges and royal palaces; there was also a tax on milling, and other contributions were levied for the costs of the cavalry, fortifications and even for the payment of tax collectors). These levies were all first introduced as exceptional measures, but became regular taxes with the passing of time. Except for the tax on milling, which was the most profitable to the crown and was payable by all the hearths, the taxes were repartitioned among the three estates of the Sicilian Parliament: one-sixth of the tax was payable by the church and the other five-sixths by the 'state' and 'military estates' in equal parts. The allocation of the taxes between areas was carried out by a parliamentary committee, the *Deputazione del regno*, according to the 'means' or 'faculties' possessed by the inhabitants of the individual communities. Parallel to the subsidies, there were a large number of indirect taxes in the form of customs rights, trading rights on grain exports and taxes on consumer goods. Revenues from church benefices (*spogli*) had their origin in Papal crusade bulls. Tax revenues in Spain's three Italian provinces were used for similar purposes: expenditure on the civil administration was usually quite moderate; in contrast, expenditure for defence rose drastically between 1550 and 1650; the other elements were cash contributions sent to meet the crown's military commitments elsewhere and interest payments on the public debt.

The tax system in the Netherlands was significantly different from that of the Mediterranean countries, because of the special position of the provinces themselves. The *aides* granted to the ruler by the States General were allocated between town and countryside on the basis of a sort of land register which in Flanders was called the *transport*. This system caused abuses, which Charles V tried to halt in 1517 by asserting the principle that each should be taxed according to his 'faculty and means' ('qu'un chacun soit imposé selon ses facultés et puissances').[23] In reality, it was only after 1536, in a serious financial emergency arising from the renewal of war with France, that the system was changed by the introduction into state finance of the system of indirect taxation which was already widely applied in the towns. After 1537, the method of collection for direct taxes was revised. An even more radical change took place in 1542–3, when the states of some provinces accepted the *nieuwe middelen*, a series of taxes which affected incomes from property as well as from capital. Some progress was thus made towards fiscal equity. The crown increased its revenue through a system which reduced exemptions and privileges and became characterized by its universality and differentiation. A system had gradually emerged in which 'each taxpayer found himself answerable to the central government for his individual quota; thus between the central government and the population there developed a link in the area of a public law, which bypassed local magistrates and the functionaries of the provincial states'.[24] Of course, all this carried quite a high political price, which was the demand of the provincial states to administer the collection of the new taxes:[25] this reduced the benefits which the central government could hope to obtain from its new tax policy. The level of expenditure and the costs of internal administration were lower in the Low Countries

[23] Craeybeckx (1947), 91. [24] Arnould (1967), 287. [25] Tracy (1985), 87.

than in other provinces of the empire, but military expenditure incurred there weighed heavily on the Castilian budget. The payment of interest on the public debt ended up as the largest item of expenditure.

7.3 *The Relationship between the Spanish Habsburg Empire and the International Financial Markets*

The use of the expression 'international financial markets' poses no problem for a historian of the twentieth century, but it is a difficult term to use for the early modern period. A series of questions arises if we try to construct a dynamic model of the financial sector. What does this sector produce? What transformation processes do producers and consumers carry out and what are the costs and prices? What are the variables that affect supply and demand? How may a balance sheet be calculated for this sector of the economy?[26] It is difficult to give precise answers to these questions but we can try to understand how different aspects of the problem interrelated. If we try to establish a chronology, then it is clear that different dates apply for the various European countries. The concept of crisis may be useful, since it indicates a period of disintegration of the system, when changes in the hierarchy of states and groups may have occurred. Crises do not only explain the 'pathology' of the economic system but also its 'physiological' symptoms. Just as a rise in temperature shows the ability of a human being to react to a bodily change, so the financial system reacts to the poor functioning of its structures by entering a period of crisis. In the first half of the sixteenth century, the European financial market as a whole was resilient enough not to be undermined by the difficulties faced by some of the individual operators on the market. The period was characterized by the continuing importance of the fairs of Lyon, while Antwerp played a central role. Substantial resources were deployed by German bankers, while Castilian revenues provided a general underpinning for the financial market (Figure 30).[27] Even so, there was clearly an internal dynamic within the period: Carande depicted four distinct phases in the Spain of Charles V: 1520–32, 1533–42, 1543–51 and 1552–6. In contrast, Ruiz Martín identified a centuries-long trend within which there are two distinct phases: an expansion from 1445 to 1586 and a decline between 1586 and 1690.[28]

For our analysis, it is necessary to start in the middle of the sixteenth century when the mature imperial financial system underwent its first crisis between 1556 and 1566, arising from excessive short-term debts in the larger west European

[26] Cf. Goldsmith (1987) [Ed.].

[27] ESFDB \rjb\spain\spag002 based on \spad001; Artola (1982), 86–7.

[28] Ruiz Martín (1970).

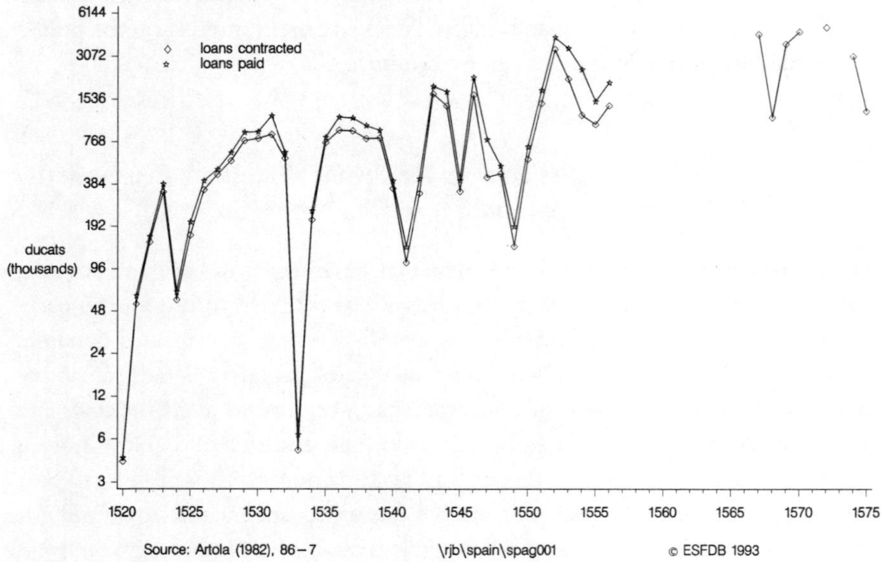

FIG. 30. Loans to the Spanish Treasury, 1520–1575 (in ducats)

monarchies. While France witnessed the collapse of the *grand parti*,[29] Spain, through the crises of 1557 and 1560, managed to consolidate her own debt even though this undermined the balance between the commercial and financial sectors.[30] The central role of Antwerp, the greatest European money market, and its links with the English market came to an end. The power of the German banks was finally reduced, while a new ascendancy, that of the Genoese, emerged.[31] Between the 1570s and the early 1620s, the financial situation was transformed. A phase of general economic expansion in the Mediterranean economies underpinned financial relations, which were increasingly regulated by the fairs of Besançon. This fifty-year period also saw changes in the private sector (with the decline of private banks and the rise of public ones), but the system seemed generally able to face the crises of public finance. Losses incurred as a result of the bankruptcies of the Spanish crown in 1575, 1596 and 1607 were reabsorbed by the international financial system, even if, as will be seen, they affected the economy at large as well as Castilian merchant and financial groups.

29 Doucet (1933).

30 After 1566, the Spanish crown freely granted *licencias de sacas* to foreign merchant bankers who were no longer obliged to pay compensation for their credits by drawing on Castilian goods and products: Ruiz Martín (1965).

31 Ruiz Martín in Kellenbenz (1970), 84–99.

The second crisis occurred between 1619 and the end of the 1620s. This was much more serious than that of the mid-sixteenth century because it coincided with crises in both the industrial and agricultural sectors. For some countries, in particular the Italian states, the crisis of the 1620s marked a decisive break in their development.[32] The Spanish bankruptcy of 1627, which arose in these circumstances, marked a change in the hierarchy of international finance: the Genoese *hombres de negocios* were replaced by Portuguese *marranos*, who drained capital away from Amsterdam to the advantage of the Castilian crown. This change moved the international financial centre towards northern Europe. In the view of Gentil da Silva, the Genoese and Portuguese represented two different models of economic organization. The Genoese epitomized a system totally concentrated on the Mediterranean, which was based on the re-distribution of precious metals from the New World. In contrast, the Portuguese were more involved in the distribution of goods from Atlantic and Far Eastern trade.[33] In reality, the money–goods contrast was not quite so clear-cut, since the Genoese also traded on a large scale and invested in production, just as Portuguese *émigrés* in Amsterdam sought to regulate the great flow of gold and silver from America. The change in their relative financial importance resulted from Portugal's greater access to abundant capital markets. Whereas in the sixteenth century the financial markets had tended to operate as a single market, after the 1630s the Mediterranean countries were gradually excluded. As Ruiz Martín remarked, the Spanish empire entered the final stage of its economic decline, from which it would not recover until the 1680s, and then only slowly.

Apart from these general, what we might term 'organizational', crises there were other short-term crises which affected individual countries or groups of financial operators. This second type of crisis tended to arise from the relationship of the money supply to the demand for credit, whether from public authorities (such as the 'state' or communities seeking credit to balance their budgets) or private individuals involved in agriculture, industrial production (peasants, craftsmen and guildsmen) and trade. The scale of credit transactions varied greatly between these different groups and in accordance with the extent of monetization: until the eighteenth century there were regions in every country where money was a rare commodity. Each regional economic subsystem retained some features of autarchy, being self-sufficient in some goods but not others: the commercialization of production thus advanced relatively slowly. The scale of monetary circulation tended to increase at the higher levels

[32] Romano in Parker and Smith (1985), 165. [The article was originally published in 1962.]

[33] Gentil da Silva (1956). Also of the same opinion was Braudel (1973).

of economic activity, where exchange transactions had to be paid in cash.[34] At this upper level of economic activity, the exchange transactions and the demand for credit were inevitably met by those who had capital assets in liquid funds, and who could, in certain circumstances, 'supply money'.

The money supply should be viewed as a network organized on hierarchical principles. The 'state', though in a special position because its monopoly of coinage fixed the actual amount of cash in circulation, was the most important supplier of money, followed by other corporations and groups (churches, religious houses, confraternities, privileged social groups and *rentiers*) whose liquidity exceeded their needs. Even among suppliers of funds there was an internal stratification: not all those who participated were the sole owners of large amounts of capital. The supply circuit, in fact, often had a rapid turnover as a result of social change, especially in urban societies. The professional dealers operated at a third level. Banks and bankers accumulated large capital sums on the various markets which were used in loan operations and other investment opportunities.[35]

Within this general scheme it is clear that our focus must be on the demand generated by the crown, and the way in which it was satisfied within the Spanish imperial community. The underlying reasons for the Spanish fiscal requirements have already been assessed. It is clear that in normal conditions the management and control of the territories of the empire could have been achieved with ordinary revenues. The problem was that the political system had never enjoyed 'normal' conditions, that is, long periods of peace and internal recuperation. Instead, the system was tested by one war after another, on different fronts and with frequently changing adversaries. Hence the resort to extraordinary financial measures and the need to obtain capital to invest in the fight for territorial control. Within fifty years, between 1548 and 1598, the annual cost of wars sustained by Spain outside its own territory rose at least fourfold.[36] Between 1567 and 1654 no less than 218 million ducats was sent from Castile to the Netherlands (Figure 31) in comparison with remittances from the Americas to Castile for a total of 121 million ducats.[37] In the outflow of 97 million ducats, the difference between these two totals, lies the key to understanding most of the Spanish Habsburg financial difficulties.

In this situation it was necessary to resort to the capital markets and to exploit the potential role of international bankers. Between the sixteenth and seventeenth centuries great private financiers were able to maintain a strong sense of

[34] Braudel (1981–4), i, 457 and (1973), 344–57.

[35] Ruiz Martín (1975).

[36] Parker (1972), 143 n. 2, 287; Parker in Winter (1975), 49–71; Parker (1979), 101, 188; Parker (1988), 61.

[37] Parker (1972), 293–6; ESFDB \rjb\spain\spb005 based on \spd008.

national identity, yet at the same time collaborated in the management of the machinery which regulated the international system of payments. This 'international republic of money' was stratified internally, with regard both to function and status. At the outset, financial specialization was by no means the rule. The figure of the merchant banker was very common, while exchange operators were even more numerous. This state of affairs seems to have lasted until the mid-sixteenth century, when the complex financial relations of the empire came to require distinctive professional services. In the decades between 1560 and 1580 the great international financier emerged: he was essentially someone who was able to move large sums of money across various countries, though the scale of activity varied according to the operator and the importance of the market. In Seville, the number of Genoese exchange merchants rose from 80 in the years 1494–1525 to 182 between 1537 and 1556; it fell back to 40 between 1557 and 1584. At Medina del Campo in the same years the same group rose from 19 to 79 but then fell back to 6.[38] In 1571, out of 183 foreigners operating on the Lyon market 27 were bankers (all of whom were Italians with the exception of one German).[39] Out of 207 *hombres de negocios* who, directly or indirectly, carried out credit operations for Charles V between 1520 and 1566, at least 109 were Italians.[40]

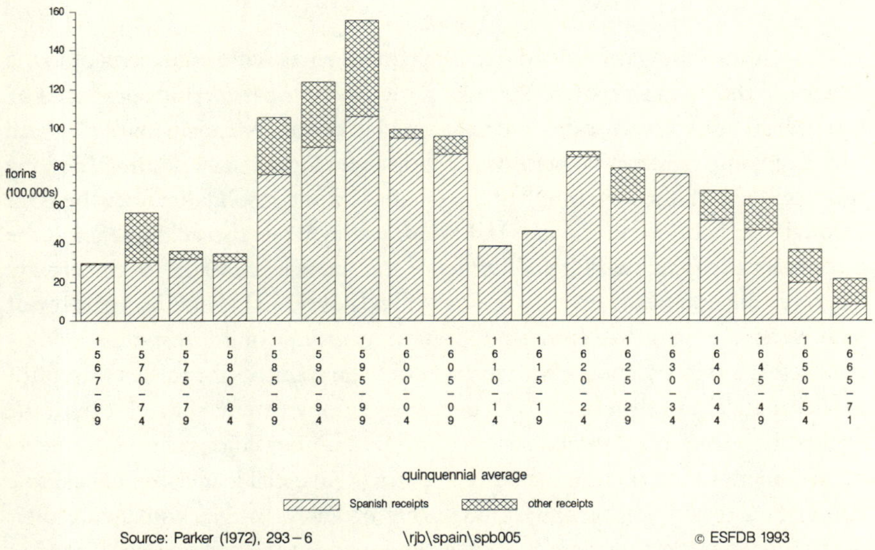

FIG. 31. Receipts of the military Treasury of the Spanish army in Flanders, 1567–1671 (in florins)

[38] Otte in de Maddalena and Kellenbenz (1986).

[39] Gascon (1971), ii, 908.

[40] Carande (1978), 73–6.

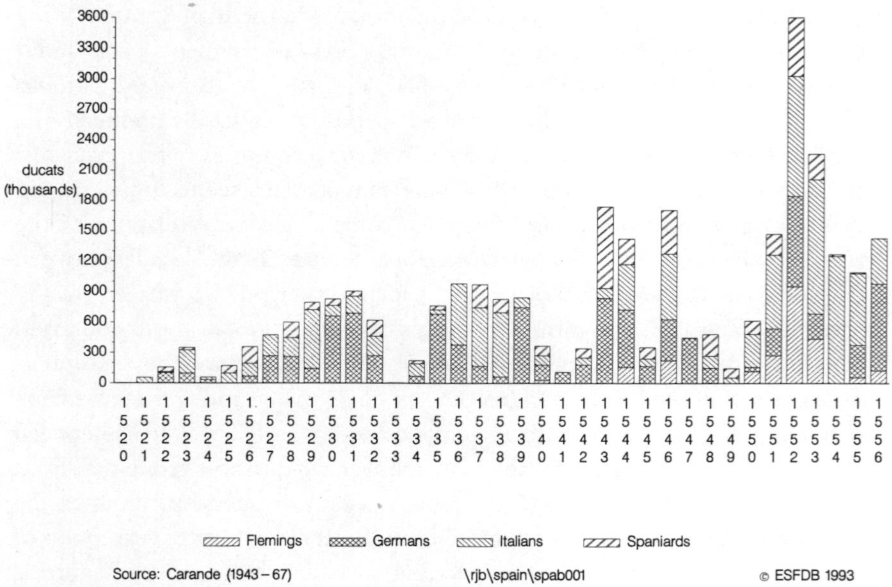

FIG. 32. Loans contracted by the Spanish Treasury, by national groups, 1520–1556 (in ducats)

In what chronological order did these financial elites achieve supremacy in the service of the Spanish crown? Following the division into periods proposed by Carande, four national groups alternated in loan contracts under Charles V, with each enjoying a distinctive period of importance (Figure 32).[41] During the long reign of Philip II, the hegemony of the Genoese was consolidated after the 1570s through their control of the fairs of Piacenza; they were also able to exploit the international capital market and influence the financial activities of the crown. Towards the end of the century, when Philip II ordered his final bankruptcy or debt rescheduling in November 1596, out of 29 groups of *asientistas* affected by the decree, 20 were Genoese who turned out to be creditors for at least four-fifths of the total debt of the crown.[42] Genoese hegemony extended at least until the end of the 1620s. With the bankruptcy in 1627 another change in the top level management of international finance occurred. Financial leadership passed to a tightly knit group of Portuguese financiers of Jewish origin who made their operational base in Amsterdam. This group, whose top level was composed of about 40 financiers, was already active in 1626 and operated in favour of the

[41] Carande (1967), iii, 33–5; ESFDB \rjb\spain\spab001 based on \spad002.

[42] Ruiz Martín (1968), 168–9.

Spanish crown until the middle of the century.[43] This change was much less drastic than is normally supposed. In reality, the Genoese remained engaged in operations for the crown yet managed simultaneously to convert their capital into industrial and commercial activities.[44] In the second half of the seventeenth century there seemed to be a greater harmony among the various groups, partly because the crown was borrowing on a smaller scale. As well as the Portuguese, who though not numerous remained the most important group in financial terms, there emerged a new generation of Genoese, while there was also a significant group of Spanish financiers.[45] Changes in the dominant financial elites did not exhaust the whole complex network of relations between public and private finance. The model that we have briefly outlined clarifies only the external aspects of these relations. The relations between public and private finance established on the internal money markets of each country in the imperial community were often quite different. The *Banco di San Ambrogio* in Milan, the eight public banks in Naples and the *Tavola* of Palermo, did not participate in the supply of international capital, but they certainly maintained control over the internal credit market of their own countries.

The last point to be clarified concerns the financial mechanisms used by private financial operators in their dealings with state finance. The great merchant bankers of the early sixteenth century initially had no difficulty in financing the needs of Charles V. The instrument through which they regulated loans to the monarch was the *asiento*. Legally, this was a contract in which both parties freely negotiated the conditions of an exchange. They could be negotiated directly at court by the *Consejo de Hacienda* with the monarch's approval or negotiated outside Spain by a governor or viceroy. There were two types of *asientos*: in coin of the realm or in other national currencies (*en metalico*); and in kind (*en especie*). The former were divided into internal and external. Internal *asientos* were negotiated and paid inside Spain and calculated in Castilian ducats of 375 *maravedís*. The external ones aimed at a transfer of foreign exchange outside Spanish territory and involved an exchange of foreign currency. The *asientos en especie* were usually intended for matters such as galley contracts, or the supply of food or munitions for the army. From a legal point of view, the *asiento* was a document underwritten by the parties which fixed the quantity and nature of the loan, the timing and location of payment, and the conditions of

[43] Boyajian (1983). According to Castillo Pintado, the Portuguese were 'agents of an extensive capitalism, of patrons and masters, who from their base in Amsterdam—the New Jerusalem—controlled European business arriving from places such as Leghorn, Rome and Venice': Castillo Pintado (1982), 234.

[44] A good example of this is the monopoly of the Idria mercury mines which in 1631 passed to Bartolomeo Balbi: Pickl in de Maddalena and Kellenbenz (1986), 171.

[45] Sanz Ayan (1988).

refund. The latter included the *consignaciones*, the indication of the revenue of the *Hacienda* on which any refund was to be made; the rate of interest; the *conducciones*, or the costs of transporting the sum of money in question; the *adehalas*, the supplementary cash which acted as a guarantee against risk; and the *facultades*, privileges which might be conceded by the crown, such as permits for exporting precious metals or goods. The interest rate on these *asientos*, according to Carande, rose progressively under Charles V, from 17.6 per cent in 1520–32 to 21.3 per cent in 1533–42; 27.9 per cent in 1543–51; and finally, to 48.8 per cent in 1552–6. The *consignaciones* preferred by the *asientistas* were obviously American precious metals, but they did not mind the safer revenues of Castilian taxation, such as the *alcabalas*, *tercias* and, later on, the *millones*. Until 1557 they refused to be paid in *juros*, except for some *juros de caución* which acted as a form of subsidiary guarantee in case the Treasury did not honour the debt. Throughout the sixteenth and seventeenth centuries, the Spanish Habsburgs negotiated about 1,500 *asientos* with the *hombres de negocios* of various countries;[46] about a third of these were negotiated during the reign of Charles V.

Indeed, under Charles V the *asientos* constituted the backbone of financial policy and, as a form of short-term debt carrying a high interest rate, they represented the bulk of the Castilian public debt. There were, however, other forms of debt for which the crown contracted with third parties: these included so-called 'free' loans, which were in effect compulsory payments extracted from the nobility and the clergy; sums paid in gold and silver which were confiscated from the private owners of shipments from the Americas; and forms of treasury debt converted by means of bills of exchange. The most important element, in terms of their impact on public finance, were the *juros*, long-term national debt bonds carrying a low rate of interest, which were registered securities, with no fixed terms of settlement. Legally a *juro* was

> a mixed contract established between the king as king, and a personage, either an individual or a collectivity, by virtue of which the latter handed over, as a general rule, a certain sum in cash to the sovereign, who in recompense (*contrapestación*) granted him an annual pension in specie or in coin assigned on the revenues of the crown.[47]

They were already in use before the reign of Charles V but only Castilians had been allowed to buy them; by the 1560s, they were not only allowed to transfer them but also to negotiate them with third parties. *Juros de caución* became widespread in the first half of the sixteenth century and provided an additional guarantee for the *asientista*. The same function was also extended to the *juros de resguardo*. They were further differentiated by the time for which they

[46] Ruiz Martín (1990), 118. [47] Barthe Porcel (1948–9), 228.

were valid from the *juros de heredad* (which were perpetual), *juros de merced* and *juros de por vida* (which were limited to the lifetime of their holder) and the *juros al quitar* (which were redeemable). The interest received by the holder of a *juro* depended, in any case, on the kind of bond he possessed and on the revenue on which it was assigned. In the financial jargon of the time the term 10,000 *al millar* expressed the interest rate on a *juro*: for a capital of 10,000 *maravedís*, the holder received an annual income of 1,000 *maravedís*, that is 10 per cent. Similarly, 8,000 *al millar* equalled 12.5 per cent, 14,000 *al millar* 7.14 per cent, 18,000 *al millar* 5.55 per cent, 20,000 *al millar* 5 per cent and 25,000 *al millar* 4 per cent. *Asientos* and *juros* were the two structural elements on which the Spanish public debt system was based and it was a model which seemed compatible with the very similar systems which later developed in other provinces of the empire. The real problem would be how to transform the floating debt into a consolidated one by applying techniques which penalized neither operators nor savers.

7.4 *The Financial Policy of the Spanish Habsburgs*

Although lacking a specific plan for economic policy there is no doubt that both the court and the central bureaucratic machinery tended towards a consistent policy under Charles V which relied on increasing the patrimony of the crown, intensifying production and enhancing trade, and using savings to meet any financial shortfall.[48] The constitutional organization of the imperial community did not allow this policy to be applied uniformly throughout the empire, because of the strong political tensions in countries outside Castile which rendered territorial control precarious. In these conditions, it was necessary to insist on Castilian resources, especially tax revenues. However, these were not always exploited effectively. The most striking example can be seen in the *encabezamiento general* of the *alcabalas* in 1536, under the terms of which the Castilian *Hacienda* would receive for ten years a fixed sum equal to 317 million *maravedís* a year. In fact, it turned out to be bad business for the *Hacienda*, which lost out in real terms because of the rapid rise in prices during the decade. The *servicios* provided some compensation, but at the price of extensive exemptions and immunities. Income from the *servicios* rose from index 100 in the quinquennium 1526–30 to index 123 in the quinquennium 1551–5. Over the same period, income from the *alcabalas* fell from index 112 to index 82.[49] This tendency was confirmed by a reduction in the relative importance of the *alcabalas* to the total of ordinary revenue. In 1536, they formed 79.4 per cent of the *rentas ordinarias*, but by 1553 this

[48] Carande (1969), 117. [49] Gelabert in Bonney (1995), quoting Hendricks (1976).

proportion had declined to 66.6 per cent of the total.[50] The expenditure figures for the period demonstrate the increasing burden of the *juros*, which absorbed 36.6 per cent of the *rentas ordinarias* in 1522, 65.4 per cent in 1543 and 58 per cent in 1553.[51]

The 1540s opened a new phase in the crown's financial policy which required the other Habsburg territories to shoulder a greater proportion of the financial burden resulting from renewal of war with France. In 1542, the provincial states in the Netherlands had to accept the *nieuwe middelen*, that is, province-wide excise and land taxes paid to the central government as extraordinary subsidies; and also a new series of annuities (*renten*) funded by these revenues, which for this purpose were collected and disbursed by the provincial states themselves.[52] The early 1540s also marked a critical turning-point in the fiscal history of the duchy of Milan. In 1542, extraordinary revenue was three and a half times that of ordinary revenue, reflecting the extensive use of taxation. In 1543, a new general census was established which included landed property as well as *mercimonio*, or wealth deriving from industrial and commercial business.[53] It is interesting to note that after the *nieuwe middelen* were introduced in the Netherlands, the *dixième denier* on the income from property and trading profits was established in December 1542, a tax to be applied on the basis of a land survey, the rules of which required definition.[54] This measure came out only three months before the new Milanese census and suggests that some aspects of tax policy probably had a basis in common planning, perhaps at the imperial court itself, to which bureaucrats and politicians referred when exchanging different opinions and experiences. There were also considerable increases in the kingdom of Naples, both in the rates of direct taxes (especially between May 1542 and August 1544) and indirect taxes, notably the tax on silk.[55]

The 1550s were the crisis of Charles V's reign. The *asientos* contracted with bankers between 1552 and 1556 amounted to almost half (48.8 per cent) of all the short-term loans during his reign, while the *situado*, or total sum in *juros*, rose in 1556 to 68 per cent of total expenditure. Yet the other provinces of the empire were unable to help the Castilian *Hacienda*. In spite of some 22 million florins remitted by Spain in the years 1551–6 to help finance the costs of the war against France, the government of the Netherlands was in no position to help, since it, too, was overwhelmed by a debt which was no less serious than that of Castile. Between 1551 and 1555 the floating debt rose from 1.3 million to 7 million florins, while the consolidated debt doubled over the same period.[56] Milan, too, was

[50] Carande (1969), 125.
[51] Ibid. 131.
[52] Tracy (1985), 73.
[53] Vigo (1979), 55.
[54] Arnould (1967), 286–7.
[55] Galasso (1965), 176.
[56] Braudel (1972), 191–200; Rodríguez-Salgado (1988), 54–60.

unable to help; the chronic balance deficit had forced the government to decide in 1546 and 1554 on a partial suspension of payments.[57] In an extreme attempt to tackle the serious debt of the whole imperial system, the new king, Philip II, considered a plan in October 1555 which aimed 'to reform the financial structure of the empire and introduce new management'.[58] The essential element in the plan was to nominate a 'factor general' or general agent who, aided by other 'factors' operating on the major financial markets, would have had autonomous powers to transfer funds and negotiate more favourable conditions with the *hombres de negocios*. The plan was strongly opposed by political and economic interest groups in Castile and it was only in 1556 that the king was able to nominate Lopez del Campo as factor in Spain, Lopez Gallo as factor in the Netherlands and Silvestro Cattaneo as factor in Italy.[59] Various plans were put forward, but it was impossible to tackle simultaneously the expiry dates of the floating debt, the payment of the *situado* and the requirements of current expenditure: thus, on 17 April 1557, Philip II was forced to order the suspension of all payments. The monarch fully recognized the commitments made with the bankers and the floating debt was converted into *juros al quitar* at 5 per cent. This did not resolve the problem, because a more accurate inspection of the books found the total debts of the Castilian *Hacienda* to be about 25 million ducats, of which about one-third were in either short- or medium-term loans.[60] The cash position was particularly serious: by 1560, the *situado* had risen to an equivalent of 103.9 per cent of ordinary revenue. A new suspension of payments was decreed on 14 November 1560, and this time the monarch acknowledged his debts in full. The solution on this occasion was more ingenious: the short-term debt was again converted into a long-term debt, in *juros* at 5 per cent, but these were to be guaranteed by the *Casa de Contratación* of Seville which, having its own funds, would act as the sinking fund of the Spanish national debt. To the great satisfaction of the Genoese, whose interests would have been most adversely affected, the operation was a total failure.[61] This in turn influenced the king's decision of 31 October 1563 to reduce the rate of interest on all the *juros al quitar* to 7.14 per cent.[62]

With the 1560s there began a long hegemony of the Genoese bankers over the finances of Spain and the Italian provinces. However, it was not only speculation that fostered the interplay of supply and demand of capital on the Spanish market. According to Ruiz Martín, between 1560 and 1580 'Castile had the decisive moment in its history', and not only for political reasons. In these decades the population increase reached its peak, the great industrial and

[57] Chabod (1971), iii pt. ii, 300–22.
[58] Rodríguez-Salgado (1988), 235.
[59] Ulloa (1986), 137.
[60] Ibid. 150.
[61] Castillo Pintado (1963*a*), 52.
[62] Ruiz Martín (1968), 118–21.

merchant cities, like Segovia, Granada and Toledo, maintained a very high productivity rate and agriculture had not yet been affected by the crises that would shortly follow: 'a wave of euphoria, which was more or less artificial, swept over everything'.[63] The situation in Italy was also improving and the second half of the sixteenth century shows a clear expansion both in agricultural and manufacturing sectors. This expansion assisted the finances of the three Italian provinces whose financial position depended less on political and military considerations than did that of the Netherlands. The real problem was the high costs of defending the Low Countries, which were largely borne by Spain with only a modest contribution from the seventeen provinces themselves. This situation prompted the duke of Alba, sent as governor in August 1567, to suggest that the States General in March 1569 should adopt three tax measures. These were firstly the *centième denier*, a 1 per cent tax on the value of property and other sources of income; secondly, the *vingtième denier*, a permanent 5 per cent tax to be paid by the seller on all property sales; and thirdly, the *dixième denier*, a permanent 10 per cent tax which was similar to the Spanish *alcabala*, to be paid by the seller on the prices of goods. There was strong resistance to these measures and Alba succeeded in imposing only the first of them, the *centième denier*, while in 1571 he was prevented from levying the other two. Recent historians—Arnould, Baelde and Craeybeckx—have assessed these measures more positively, in that they introduced an element of rationalization into the organization of public finance, allowing the state to reduce its debt and freeing the central authority from restrictions on tax revenue imposed by the provincial states. The aim was to guarantee constant, regular and homogeneous revenues in all provinces.[64] This interpretation seems to be confirmed by the fact that Alba reversed the trend, creating a surplus for the first time which doubled its value between 1569 and 1571,[65] before tax resistance really began to bite in 1572, which coincided with the invasion of the Sea Beggars.

The failure of Alba's policy, in addition to the further costs of war with the Turks in the Mediterranean, in particular the equipping of the armada which fought at Lepanto, stressed the dependence of the imperial *Hacienda* on the Genoese *hombres de negocios*. The increasing debt and the growing role of the Genoese was the subject of long discussions which took place at the Castilian *Cortes* in 1573–5. There the prevalent opinion was that the financial crisis was due to the onerous terms imposed by the Genoese in their contracts, and the king was encouraged to break off relations with them, with the questionable assurance that Castilian financial groups were ready and able to handle the financial needs of the crown. Thus, on the wave of financial nationalism, Philip II decreed the

[63] Ruiz Martín (1965). [64] Craeybeckx (1947), 96. [65] Craeybeckx (1967), 369.

suspension of payments on 1 September 1575. This time, however, his debts were not recognized in full. The legitimacy of many *asientos* was questioned with regard to specific clauses in the contracts or the rate of interest charged, and the *contadores* of the *Hacienda* were required to examine all contracts. While this investigation was taking place, the Spanish bankers in whom the king had placed his trust showed that they were totally unsuited to dealing with the sophisticated matters of capital transfers on the various European markets. On 5 December 1577, the king accepted a *medio general*, an agreement with his creditors which promised the Genoese *asientistas* a residual credit of 4.8 million ducats, one-third of which would be paid on the sale of *vassallos y jurisdicciones eclesiasticas* by granting them favourable conditions for such sales and the other two-thirds in *juros* at 3 per cent. The Genoese *asientistas* were allowed to pay their creditors in *moneda del decreto*, that is, not in cash but with bonds from the public debt at a low interest rate. Faced with these investment opportunities, the Genoese pledged new loans to the crown. This settlement exemplifies relations between the world of public and private finance. The subsequent *quiebra* of 29 November 1596 was regulated by the *medio general* of 14 February 1598 which recognized the total amount of the *asientos* contracted to a value of 14 million ducats: this refund was made two-thirds in *juros* at 5 per cent and the other third in *juros* at 7.14 per cent (of which half was on revenue from Milan and Naples).[66] At the end of the reign of Philip II in 1598 with a revenue of 10 million ducats, the total debt of the crown rose to 68 million.[67]

Three distinct phases may be discerned in the reign of Philip III. The first covers the period until 1609, when a truce was made with the government of the United Provinces; the second covers the period of the Twelve Years' Truce until the outbreak of the Thirty Years' War in 1618; and the third witnessed the opening of a new war front which would rule out any attempt at economic and financial recovery. Between 1598 and 1609 war in the Netherlands cost 37.5 million ducats, plus another 4.5 million in interest, excessive sums which were an immense burden for an economy which in the 1590s had entered into a phase of structural decline, indicated and analysed by many texts of the *arbitristas* (Chapter 6.2) and other sections of Spanish public opinion.[68] The reasons for the 1607 *quiebra* are not at all clear. Certainly monetary changes were a main cause, that is, the fact that the markets began to be flooded by *vellón* currency, a kind of copper with low intrinsic value. Both in Spain and in her imperial provinces there were two parallel monetary circuits: the first based on silver was intended for international transactions and the second tied to *vellón* regulated exchange on the internal market. In this situation, successive decrees on 6 November and 9

[66] Ruiz Martín (1968), 164–7. [67] Ulloa (1986), 830. [68] Elliott (1977), 43.

November 1607 imposed a new suspension of payments followed by a *medio general* on 14 May 1608, by which a short-term debt of 12 million ducats was converted into *juros* at 5 per cent. On this occasion, a council of the *medio general* was established, an organization strictly controlled by the Genoese which had at its disposal a fund of 6.5 million ducats to purchase *juros* at low prices and sell them again at higher prices.[69]

This type of speculation was eventually overtaken by events, as an organizational crisis broke at the end of the second decade of the seventeenth century, which forced the crown in 1621 to reduce the rate of interest generally on *juros* and *censos* to 5 per cent. With the new reign of Philip IV, Spain and a large part of her possessions were involved in the Thirty Years' War which opened up a bottomless pit in Spain's finances. The decree for the suspension of payments on 31 January 1627 marked an important turning-point in the development of Spain's finances, with a decisively reduced role for the Genoese, at least in strictly financial terms. The *medio general* of 17 September of the same year gave them a credit of 6.6 million ducats paid in *juros* at 5 per cent. Thus it was that the Castilian urban patricians avenged themselves. Yet there was no profound or salutary change in the crown's financial policy. The revenue sent by Castile outside Spain amounted to 72.6 million silver ducats between 1632–7; between 1635 and 1645 the Netherlands received at least 30 million ducats from Castile (Figure 31).[70]

The Spanish urban elites might have been less pleased at the humiliation of the Genoese had they realized their place was to be taken by a new group of *hombres de negocios* of Portuguese origin who between 1626 and 1650 contracted with the crown *asientos* to a total value of 81 million ducats, 40 per cent of which was spent on the Netherlands.[71] The terms imposed by the new financiers were no improvement from the point of view of the crown: indeed, after 1639 they required a clause in their contracts which suspended activities if the Treasury did not duly carry out their refunds.[72] The Portuguese bankers were no more successful than the Genoese in improving the position of Castile's finances. The increasing gap between revenue and expenditure continued to be a permanent problem in the financial system. In 1647, a decisive year for Spanish authority because of the outbreak of revolts in Naples and Sicily, estimated expenditure was four times higher than total revenues, while the revenues for the four subsequent years were already assigned to the *hombres de negocios*.[73] In these circumstances, a further bankruptcy was inevitable on 1 October 1647, followed by the *medio general* of 18 July 1648. Far from imposing a sense of moderation and

[69] Ruiz Martín (1970), 45–6.
[70] Ruiz Martín (1990), 105–6.
[71] Boyajian (1983), appx c.
[72] Domínguez Ortiz (1960), 57.
[73] Ibid. 68.

control of the financial machinery, high levels of debt continued to be incurred. In the three years 1648–51, new loans of nearly 30 million ducats were contracted.[74] No wonder, then, that it was necessary to resort to a new suspension decree on 31 July 1652, with a *medio general* on 18 August 1654. Nor was this the last in the reign of Philip IV, since he had to resort to the same measure again on 14 August 1662.

Slowly, however, a new attitude towards the management of Spanish public finance began to show itself, and this was first revealed in the 1662 crisis. The government resorted to the suspension of payments irrespective of the cash situation of the Treasury. Often these operations sought to reorganize the complicated system of Spanish public finance on a more rational basis. In this sense, the suspensions of 1665, 1692, 1693, 1695 and 1696 were not completely negative operations, but demonstrated the commitment to a reformed and less chaotic system. While it became less and less profitable for private finance to be committed in large loans to the crown, there was greater harmony among the various competing financial groups throughout Carlos II's reign. The system inherited in the eighteenth century was thus very different in significant respects from that which had preceded it between *c.*1516 and 1665. The Habsburg system had had its own intrinsic perversity, but for a very long time it had enabled Spain to control a vast but disunited empire and had influenced the destinies and fortunes of powerful economic elites.

[74] Ibid. 69.

CHAPTER 8

The Emergence and Consolidation of the 'Tax State'. I. The Sixteenth Century

Winfried Schulze

The early modern period is crucial for the development of modern structures of political organization and their legitimation: this seems to be a truism after so much research emphasis on national history, and rather less on comparative research. In nearly all political units the power of the centre was enhanced, marginalizing the regions and localities. Although there were specific differences within each 'national' development, there were also a great number of similarities in the processes of historical change. Indeed, by viewing historical change as a series of processes which do not fit a tidy model of periodization we can study parallel historical phenomena which interrelated in the process of change. Such an approach facilitates comparative research, even if the separate 'national' cases retain their own chronological distinctiveness.

The creation of 'national' states in the later Middle Ages and early modern period clearly drew upon trends going back far into the Middle Ages and even to the history of feudal organization. There were significant disparities between the pace of change in western Europe (principally Burgundy, France and England) as compared to central, east–central and southern Europe, where the central organization of state power developed more slowly. Whereas the pace of centralization must be seen as a long-term consequence of divergent feudal systems, the growth of fiscal power must be seen as a process of less divergent change. Indeed, we might speak of a 'first European world system' in the sense of an interlinked system of monetary interchange which was not totally uniform but meant that states tended to experience comparable problems at about the same period in time. Though there may be different rates of development for modern financial institutions in Europe—as Webber and Wildavsky observed—similarities outweighed the differences.[1] There was also a comparable economic

[1] Webber and Wildavsky (1986), 229. The author wishes to take the opportunity to thank the members of the Team for their helpful discussions but especially Richard Bonney not only for his

background and fiscal requirement. When the English king wanted to recruit German mercenaries in the mid-sixteenth century he had to pay roughly the same money to the soldiers as his German or French competitors. He could obtain this money from a Europe-wide money market dominated by German, Genoese, Florentine and Lyonnais bankers. If he did not need to borrow money, the ruler still had to extract the necessary money from a comparable economic system, though there were differences between purely agrarian-based economies and those which benefited from urban economic activity or from the European flow of commodities such as the Baltic trade taxed by the king of Denmark by means of the Sound tolls. Even if a kingdom wanted to avoid international commitments, its money went abroad if it had a balance of payments deficit. It could not avoid some degree of participation in European trade: Gresham's law was a contemporary formulation of this principle.[2]

When at the end of the sixteenth century Zacharias Geizkofler, the Imperial treasurer, and also a man with wide experience in helping to manage the Fugger enterprises, wrote a preparatory memorandum for the Imperial diet, he looked at other countries for guidance on methods of taxation which did not harm the economy but guaranteed huge sums of money: Venice and France were taken as the models. Trying to explain the lamentable state of the currency in the Holy Roman Empire, his insights into the workings of the European money and currency system may be considered comparable to the views of Sir Thomas Gresham. For Geizkofler, there was no doubt that the Empire gave away too much of its good money for foreign commodities and armies in Hungary. This clearly weakened its balance of payments, although this was a technical term not yet known to him.[3] Observations of this kind were close to the discourse on what we call today the 'price revolution' and may be observed in the work of Jean Bodin published in 1568 in refutation of that by Malestroit (Chapter 6.1). Europe was conceived of as an entity much earlier in financial and economic treatises than in other types of political theory.

8.1 *The Conceptual Debate on the Growth of the Fiscal State in the Sixteenth Century*

Historical research on the process of state making in the sixteenth century has tended to concentrate on the question of sovereignty, its theoretical foundation

difficult task in leading and encouraging the Team but also for valuable help with data and bibliographical support.

[2] De Roover (1949). [3] Schulze (1978).

and the extent to which it was capable of realization in different European countries: to what extent were the ideas developed by Jean Bodin put into practice? Another approach, exemplified by the volume edited by Charles Tilly on the formation of nation states in western Europe,[4] was more functional, taking into consideration in its various articles the stimulus of military forces and tax collection. For our purpose it seems adequate to return to a concept of periodization developed by Gerhard Oestreich. He tried to establish three phases of state formation: firstly, a prototype of a dualistic political system in the fourteenth and fifteenth centuries; then the first move towards the early modern state, which he called the 'finance state'; thirdly, there was a further development of the early modern state in the later seventeenth century, which he called the 'military, administrative and bureaucratic state'.[5] Although Oestreich's periodization drew upon his observation of the development of the German states in the late medieval and early modern period, his term 'finance state' remains applicable to the situation in western Europe in the later sixteenth century. It tries to depict the changing functions of the state in the sixteenth century and is more precise than the concept of 'dynastic state' which has found some acceptance elsewhere.[6]

We may conveniently combine the concept of the 'finance state' with the older ideas of Schmoller and Schumpeter.[7] Schmoller distinguished between a financial organization based on natural goods and the modern economic system based on money.[8] Following these lines, Schumpeter made an important observation on the significant step from the medieval 'domain state' to the modern form of 'tax state', the first phase of which may be seen as identical with Oestreich's 'finance state'. Schumpeter considered the concept of the 'tax state' to be a pleonasm,[9] but though the concept may be somewhat anachronistic for the sixteenth century, Petersen has used it to help explain the development of Danish state finance in the period (Chapter 4.6).[10] In a country such as France, the budget contained an insignificant and declining proportion of domain revenues (3.5 per cent of the total in 1523); but, as late as 1630, states such as Sweden and Denmark still derived respectively some 44.8 per cent and 36.9 per cent of their total revenues from the domain.[11] An apparently 'modern' German state such as

[4] Tilly (1975).

[5] Oestreich (1969), 279. Cf. Oestreich (1982).

[6] The most recent example is Bonney (1991*b*), though he discussed the term 'finance state' ibid. 352; the term 'dynastic state' was used earlier by Gerhard (1981), 88.

[7] The concept has been described by Krüger (1983). Cf. Buchholz (1990).

[8] Schmoller (1909). Schmoller's is perhaps the first comparative approach to European state finance.

[9] Schumpeter (1954*b*). [10] Petersen (1975). [11] Krüger (1988).

Prussia could still obtain nearly half of its revenues from domain income as late as 1778–9 (Chapter 13.3).[12] Notwithstanding the continuing importance of the domain, the concept of the 'tax state' underlines the crucial aspect of state building in the sixteenth century: the 'fiscal state' sought to develop itself simultaneously on several fronts (in the realms of ideas, action and institutional structure).[13]

At the end of the fifteenth century it might have seemed an open question whether the political structure would be controlled by a 'national' or territorial ruler or whether it would be decentralized under the control of great nobles or regional structures. The sixteenth century witnessed the triumph of the 'national' or territorial ruler: noble landowners had to compete with the central state for the limited surplus of money produced in peasant-based economies. This was a decisive stage in overcoming traditional power structures and inaugurating the modern tax state. Marc Bloch observed that the French provincial indendants of the seventeenth century were expected 'to protect rural communities, ripe material for taxation, from intemperate exploitation by their landlords'. We may interpret this trend towards protection of the peasantry by the state as a 'struggle between taxes and rents'.[14] This perspective has the advantage of linking the tensions between princes and their estates, between peasants and their landlords and between peasants and princes, various aspects of which may be seen at work in the frequent rebellions against taxation.

8.2 *Prerequisites of European State Formation in the Sixteenth Century*

Historians of the sixteenth century tend to agree that the period saw a decisive strengthening of political power in the hands of the ruler, who had finally emerged from a competing group of noble families in the late medieval period. The rules of succession were fixed, in France by the establishment of the *lois fondamentales*, in Germany by the Golden Bull in 1356, in England after the ending of the Wars of the Roses. Such rules could not guarantee a smooth process of transition in every case but the succession became more orderly: the succession of James VI of Scotland as James I of England in 1603 was clearly much smoother than the change of dynasty in 1485 or earlier in the fifteenth century. In Germany most territorial rulers established ordinances for the succession which aimed at establishing a secure and wealthy state by prohibiting partition and the alienation

[12] Mann (1937), 45.

[13] Cf. Bonney (1995) for the importance of 16th-cent. developments for a number of European countries.

[14] Jones (1988*b*), 132. For a later period: Root (1987).

of territory. The growing costs of government were a strong argument in favour of this tendency, and indeed there was an increasing regulation of government during the period.[15] Strong governments capable of action were what was needed: the idea of universal monarchy waned in importance in the course of the century.

Part of the process was a growing territorial cohesion in the state, which was not personal and corporate—*Personenverbandsstaat*, as the German medievalist Theodor Mayer once put it—but now had a much more clearly defined territory without interspersed patches belonging to another prince. With the French recapture of Calais in 1558, a long tradition of English territories within the realm of the king of France came to an end: in the fifteenth and sixteenth centuries the French national state found its definitive hexagonal form when several provinces were reintegrated in the realm.[16] Even so, there remained enclaves such as Orange until the end of the seventeenth century and the Comtat Venaissin at Avignon until the end of the *ancien régime*.

This process of territorial integration—Chaunu called it 'la superposition de l'État au Royaume'—which may be clearly observed in the Holy Roman Empire,[17] must be regarded as the essential precondition for regular taxation. The viable state was increasingly the state which had the capacity to levy taxation within a well-defined territory, to push to one side traditional exemptions (whether secular or ecclesiastical in origin) and to establish a degree of equity among taxpaying 'subjects'. In many western European countries (though not in the east), this process involved the suppression of noble autonomy. In England and Germany (though not France) noble rebellions came to an end in the sixteenth century (the last examples in the Empire were the *Sickingenfehde* of 1522 and the *Grumbachfehde* of 1567; Denmark had its Counts' rebellion in 1533, while England had its Northern Rising in 1569). In contrast, in central and eastern Europe the nobility retained its capacity for rebellion: this was true of Poland and Bohemia as well as in Hungary and Transdanubia (Siebenbürgen). Traditional noble service was in general converted into monetary payments to the ruler. Whereas the nobleman of the fifteenth century believed that his duty was to serve 'with his blood' and thus that he should be exempt from taxation, this attitude was challenged in the course of the sixteenth century. In Denmark the *rostjeneste* were brought under control; even the German Imperial knights, a difficult group of minor nobles immediately subordinate to the Emperor, had to accept his growing tax demands under the title of *subsidia charitativa*.[18]

[15] Kunisch (1982) cites the example of several European dynasties.

[16] Rowen (1980). [17] Cf. Sutter Fichtner (1990). [18] Press (1980).

The suppression of noble autonomy and rebellion resulted in the integration of noble lords within the customary law of the land (*Landrecht*) and the acceptance of a judicial system directed by the ruler; but it did not mean the end of the traditional bargaining for consensus in the different countries. Almost everywhere in western and central Europe, the late Middle Ages had seen the development of parliamentary assemblies, which had focused their attention on central issues of policy: the revenues of the ruler, and perhaps his 'budget' in a more modern sense; the development of legislation; and the rights of the ruler in these and other areas.[19] There were considerable differences between the various estates in terms of their success. The English Parliament continued to gain authority in the sixteenth century while adhering to its traditional policy that the king had 'to live of his own': the costs of government normally had to be found from the revenues of the royal domain or the grant of customs revenue. Some historians have argued that the English king was weak in comparison with his Continental colleagues in that he failed to obtain a regular income from Parliament (Chapter 5.9). The contrast was clear with France, where the *taille* was made permanent in 1439 and had become a regular source of income already before the sixteenth century.[20] The continuing distinction between the *pays d'états* and the *pays d'élections* (Chapter 13.5) and the sporadic meetings of the Estates General did not create any insurmountable problem for the French king, though a seventeenth-century French tract on taxation still regarded the *tailles* as 'quasi volontaires en France'.[21] The Spanish kingdoms retained their traditional assemblies but after 1522 these did not seek to enter into sustained opposition to Charles V or his son Philip II. The *Cortes* of Castile saw their emergency grants, the *servicios*, converted into regular subsidies. In 1541, the French King Francis I reminded the Venetian ambassador that Maximilian I once said that he was king of kings because no man did his bidding, while the Spanish king was a king of men because his subjects sometimes obeyed and sometimes disobeyed his commands and the French king was a king of beasts because his subjects always obeyed his commands.[22]

In the Holy Roman Empire, the Emperor had to struggle with the difficult machinery of the Imperial diets if he wished to levy extraordinary taxes against Ottoman aggression in Hungary (which was not a part of the Empire, but was linked to the Habsburg dynasty in a loose union), and often found that the Protestants linked any support to satisfaction of their religious demands. In the territorial states, most princes succeeded in requiring their estates to consent to a

[19] Griffiths (1968). [20] Cf. Collins (1988), 36 ff.

[21] Bercé in Genet and Le Mené (1987), 163.

[22] Alberi (1541) cited by Koenigsberger and Mosse (1968), 230.

semi-regular form of taxation on behalf of the Empire. After a meeting of the Imperial diet the territorial princes used the Emperor's own tax requirements (made manifest in the Imperial recess) as a justification for being granted taxes in their own right. By the end of the sixteenth century, the experience of a dozen or so Imperial diets had scaled down the traditional aversion to taxation, which had been characteristic of earlier noble behaviour. Territorial princes now had a better chance of obtaining the necessary money for their own growing armies, fortifications and diplomatic service or—more dangerous still—for writing off their excessive debts. The sixteenth century tended to regard taxation as increasingly necessary and also increasingly feasible in terms of the state's capacity for revenue extraction.

Growing control over ecclesiastical wealth was another basic precondition of the fiscal system of most European states in the sixteenth century (Chapter 15.2). It was not just Protestant rulers who profited from secularizing the church and for a while balanced their budgets as a result; Catholic rulers also did so. The growing control over ecclesiastical wealth helped facilitate the development of a more equitable distribution of the fiscal burden among the ruler's subjects. Ecclesiastical immunities lost their relevance and were encroached upon by the rulers. In Sweden nearly all estates belonging to the church were taken over by the crown as 'a virtually new financial basis of the state was created'.[23] In Castile, the *tercias reales* and the *cruzada* were made permanent taxes. In France, church wealth was also in effect taxed after the Contract of Poissy of 1561. The king succeeded in obtaining an annual grant *(don gratuit)* for six years, though the amount was smaller for the subsequent ten years.[24]

All discussion of the increase in taxation in sixteenth-century Europe must take into account the fact that it was a 'long century' of demographic and economic growth; there was a clear 'expansion of economic activity'.[25] The nominal increase in revenues discussed below has to be counterbalanced by the growing population and the increased amount of bullion and money in circulation.[26] A growing population was observed everywhere in Europe even though recurrent waves of the plague continued to check the upward demographic trend. The European population may have grown from 69 million in 1500 to about 89 million in 1600, albeit in divergent rhythms in different parts of Europe. However, it was perhaps not until around the middle of the sixteenth century that the number of European inhabitants in *c.*1300 was surpassed. The silver production of the central European mines and the import of gold and silver

[23] Cf. Lindkvist in Genet and Le Mené (1987), 61.

[24] Shennan (1969), 13–60.

[25] Spooner in Wernham (1971), 42.

[26] Spooner (1972).

bullion from America via Spain were essential to the various national tax systems:[27] the importation of 181 tonnes of gold and 16,000 tonnes of silver between 1500 and 1650 resulted in an increase in the money supply which eased the growing tax pressure.[28] Increased production for the market and growing monetary exchange were related preconditions for higher taxation.

8.3 *The Rise in Taxation and the Growth of the 'Public Sector' in the Sixteenth Century*

The cost of armies was a traditional reason for the growth of expenditure and hence taxation.[29] Yet while this became a central reason for increased taxation in the seventeenth century (Chapter 9.1), for the sixteenth century it has to be regarded as an argument only partially valid, since few states had standing armies at this date.[30] One should not forget other elements of the public sector were increasing at the same time as armies. The Bavarian government had 162 individuals on its pay list at Munich in 1508; 384 by 1552, 485 by 1556 and 866 by 1571. The number of councillors grew from 16 in 1511 to 45 in 1597. The decisive phase of growth took place in the second half of the century,[31] when there was a bureaucratic reorganization under the influence of Roman law. In effect a new culture of the written word came into place and, in this respect, the establishment of a central archive in Spain in 1549 might be seen as a decisive symbol for the rest of Europe. For France, it has been estimated that in 1515 about 7,000–8,000 office-holders worked for the king, whereas by 1665 this administrative corps numbered about 80,000.[32] A growing public sector, rather than simply the growth of army personnel during the so-called 'military revolution', better fits the broad spectrum of duties which was taken over by the early modern state.[33]

A more centralized jurisdiction carried with it considerable costs in its own right. Nearly all European countries developed a more centralized jurisdiction, with a codification of penal and civil law that made access to these central courts possible for nearly all subjects.[34] The sixteenth century may be seen in retrospect as a period of growing state interference in society. On the Continent, the reception of Roman law resulted in a growing number of trained jurists and

27 Elliott (1970), esp. ch. 3.

28 Van Cauwenberghe (1989).

29 Cf. the concluding remarks of Goldsmith (1987), 249.

30 Cf. Parker (1988), *passim*.

31 Cf. Lanzinner (1980), 22.

32 Cf. Greengrass (1991), 14. Though the figures are inflated by including clerks: Mousnier (1970*a*), 17–20.

33 Figures for military personnel are usually taken from Parker (1979), 96, but cf. the more detailed table in Greengrass (1991), 5.

34 Cf. Ranieri (1985), which also gives information about other central European courts.

newly established courts and chanceries. In England, the new courts of equity (Star Chamber and Court of Requests) developed at the same time. Newly established universities and quasi-universities, especially in the Holy Roman Empire, prepared the personnel for the growing state machinery but they also resulted in considerable costs. Princes tried to govern by statute law and by ordinances, which can be seen as a reaction to the growing expectations of different levels of society. The society of orders split up into competing interest groups seeking regulation by the state. These regulations could concentrate on domestic affairs (as on the Continent) but they might also concern matters of foreign trade and the currency, too, as in England and in the United Provinces.

The result of these growing costs of running a state in the European context was a general trend towards increased taxation. In his *Politicorum sive civilis doctrinae libri sex* (1589), Justus Lipsius followed Jean Bodin in comparing the money needed by the state with human muscles (*pecunia nervus rerum*): just as a man needed his muscles to walk, so the state could not do without its 'muscles', the sinews of finance. Writers all over Europe reformulated this remark and made it one of Europe's most famous political maxims.[35] Princes rapidly appreciated the advantages of a well-organized treasury. In 1611, Duke Maximilian I of Bavaria commented that 'reputation and *grandezza* did not mean spending money'. 'A prince who is not wealthy at times of adversity has neither authority nor reputation; if he loses these, the management of public affairs will collapse.'[36] The statistical evidence for the sixteenth century is rather patchy, but we can see evidence for the rise in taxation in specific localities such as at Montpellier, where—as elsewhere in the French Midi—the *taille* was *réelle*.[37] France, England and Spain all seem to have experienced an increase in revenue in real terms, even taking into account the population growth and inflation of the sixteenth century.[38] The Ottoman threat to the south-eastern borders of the Empire necessitated a substantial increase in the grant of Imperial taxes in the second half of the sixteenth century, increasing sixfold compared to the first half of the century, from a total of 4.3 million florins for the period 1521–56 to 23.3 million for the period 1557–1607. The Habsburg territories, including Bohemia and Moravia, carried a fiscal burden that was much heavier than the northern parts of the Empire; yet even the city of Augsburg saw an increase from 12,889 florins in 1498

[35] Cf. Stolleis (1983), 66. [36] Chroust (1903), 51 (15 Jan. 1611).

[37] Le Roy Ladurie (1966), ii, 1026.

[38] Miskimin (1977), 160, presents a graph of nominal figures, where the rate of growth is charted according to the percentage of the 'regional maximum during the time span for which statistics were available'. But cf. Hendricks (1976), who shows that the *Cortes* of Castile controlled more taxes than ever before during the reign of Charles V, and that it succeeded in restricting the rate of increase of taxes under its control.

to 71,346 florins in 1618. Data from elsewhere in Europe suggest a similar pattern of increase. Annual average revenues in England rose from £52,000 in the years 1485–90 to £382,000 in the years 1598–1600. Revenues in Castile increased from 1.5 million ducats in 1515 to 13 million by the end of Philip II's reign in 1598. In France, revenues paid to the Treasury increased from about 3.46 million *livres* around 1500 to 20.3 million in 1608. The revenues of the kingdom of Naples increased from 438,845 ducats in 1507–8 to almost 2.5 million in 1595. The revenues of Venice rose from 1.15 million ducats in 1500 to 2.45 million by 1600. Rome saw an increase from 118,000 ducats at the beginning of the century to 408,000 by the end, while the rest of the Papal States experienced a greater increase (from 236,000 ducats to 687,700 ducats).[39]

8.4 *Types of Fiscal System in Sixteenth-Century Europe*

In the sixteenth century Europe continued to have a variety of revenue systems.[40] There was not usually an overall annual budget; instead, different sources of revenues were dedicated to different sorts of expenditure (Chapter 13.2). As a general rule, the costs of peacetime government were laid upon the income of a prince from his domain, from customs and from regalian rights. Only in times of an external threat to the country might the prince ask his estates 'to grant him advice and help' in terms of cash. Whereas the English fiscal system at the end of the fifteenth century was still based on a mixture of 'domain-type' income with casual parliamentary grants, Spain and France already were remarkably developed 'tax states' (Chapter 5.9). In the German territorial states, in northern and central–eastern Europe, the fiscal state was still relatively underdeveloped: it was in these areas that the end of the sixteenth century and the beginning of the seventeenth century marks a decisive turning-point.

Krüger has shown, for example, that Hesse was a well-organized 'domain state' with a relatively efficient method of collecting at the *Ämter* the surplus produced from forest lands, salt production and trade. But this well-organized 'domain state' reached the limits of its fiscal capacity when Hesse tried to take part in wars. The debts of the country reached a million florins in the 1550s, that is, about ten times the income of the central Treasury. This crisis could only be

[39] Figures in Cipolla (1976), 45–6; Wilson and Parker (1977), 49–50, 213; Hartung (1898); Hendricks (1976), 271; Schulze (1978); Bonney (1991*b*), 352; Galasso in de Maddalena and Kellenbenz (1984), 45–88; Mieck (1982), 206; Miskimin (1989), 159–60. The two sets of figures for France from Bonney and Mieck demonstrate the fact that French royal revenues at least quintupled in our century. Cf. the general remarks by Richard Bonney on the methodology of a financial history of 16th- and 17th-cent. France in Genet and Le Mené (1987), 193–201.

[40] Cf. the overview in Koenigsberger and Mosse (1968), 226–31.

overcome by embarking upon a transition towards the 'tax state', requiring more and more money to be granted by the estates. Repartition taxes on personal wealth were established, and it was something of a triumph that the noble subjects of the prince were taxed together with non-nobles as a single cohesive group of equitably taxed subjects. This was a significant move towards a modern system of taxation. The other achievement was to establish a tax on wine and beer which was usually granted for a number of years and thus provided the prince with a secure income. Excises would prove particularly profitable as a source of revenue in the future.[41]

Much creative skill can be observed in the fiscal innovations of the sixteenth century, the central purpose of which was to seek out the most profitable forms of taxation, those which could guarantee the largest sums of money quickly and safely to the treasury. Three main ways of acquiring revenue were at hand. The first was revenue from direct taxes paid by the king's subjects: this could be of various types, such as taxation of the individual and his wealth (as with the 'common penny' in Germany), hearth taxes, taxes on landed and urban property, taxes on certain specific types of wealth, and taxes on livestock (Chapter 13.5). Secondly, there were indirect taxes on foodstuffs, on wine, beer and salt (Chapter 13.6). This form of taxation was later called the 'excise'. Technically, such taxes had to be granted in the same way as direct taxes but they tended to remain in force once granted. The third possibility was to borrow money. This became increasingly necessary as the sixteenth century advanced, since the fiscal systems of most states were unable to guarantee large sums just when money was urgently needed for a campaign or for other purposes. The deficit could only be bridged by short- and long-term borrowing (Chapter 14).[42] Large burdens of debt were a characteristic phenomenon of the fiscal systems of the sixteenth century, the model of which seem to have been the *Monti* of the Papacy.[43] The frequent recourse to borrowing has led to the hypothesis that state finance played a crucial role in the creation of capitalism.[44] Since the state's own credit resources were limited, different categories of moneylenders had to be asked for money. A first possibility was to ask for loans from private individuals. In Germany, there was a large range of moneylenders, from rich peasants and artisans up to the higher ranks of court officials. Ecclesiastical institutions lent money, as did cities and merchants or groups of merchants. Government bonds were usually guaranteed

[41] Cf. Krüger (1980), 291 ff.

[42] Cf. the relevant section in Bonney (1991*b*), 357–8; Webber and Wildavsky (1986), 251–2.

[43] Cf. Partner in Greengrass (1991), 42, and the general outline by Bauer (1928). For the important role of Jewish communities in the system of Papal finances: Stow (1982).

[44] See e.g. the German historian of the Fugger dynasty, Strieder (1932). Bauer asserted that without the system of Papal finance there could have been no emergence of capitalism: Bauer (1928), 475.

by local sources of income, whether from domains, from customs or other regalian rights. In France, the king developed a consolidated debt in the form of *rentes sur l'hôtel de ville*. These were interest-bearing obligations originally secured by the revenues of the municipality of Paris. Whereas these *rentes* did not exceed a million *livres* during the reign of Francis I, his successor Henri II sold about 6.8 million and by 1574 more than 25.9 million of *rentes* had been offered to the public. By the end of the century, the total sum of debts reached the enormous figure of 297 million *livres*, about fifteen times the annual revenue of the crown, which was insufficient to cover the costs of debt service. Under such circumstances it is no surprise that France developed an alternative strategy for coping with this financial problem. The systematic sale of offices began to form a second system of public debt. Judicial and financial offices were sold to wealthy competitors who could regard their annual salaries as a form of interest on the capital paid into the royal coffers.

When in 1581 Nicolas Froumenteau dedicated to Henri III his tract *Le secret des finances de France*, he wanted to 'discover the legitimate and necessary measures to rid the king of his debts, to discharge his subjects from taxes levied during the previous thirty-one years, and to recover all the money taken from His Majesty'. What Froumenteau attempted for France, Georg Obrecht, Jacob Bornitz and Christoph Besold tried to do within the Holy Roman Empire. These jurists emphasized that in the case of necessity the prince could do whatever was needed to rescue the state from invasion: *necessitas legem non habet*. Yet all taxation had to be justified by the *salus publica*, the public good. There had to be a just reason for extraordinary taxation; without this, the prince could and should be opposed. Jean Bodin had argued that extraordinary taxation should be the last and not the first resort of the prince (Chapter 6.1), and had justified his interpretation by the wording of the last will and testament of Louis XI that *tailles* and *aides* should not be levied on his subjects except for reasons of urgent necessity and evident utility as well as just cause, otherwise his successor would not be considered a king but a tyrant. But a generation after Bodin the German jurist Jacob Bornitz complained that extraordinary taxes had become commonplace.[45] How best to eliminate the royal debts or discharge his subjects from excessive taxes were crucial areas of discussion within the ruler's *arcana imperii*.[46]

Even if tax collection at the local level still remained a duty of the village community,[47] the obvious problems posed by the related duties of tax collection and the transmission of money from the periphery to the centre led to the establishment of a new group of officials who specialized in such matters. This

[45] Bornitz (1612), 61. [46] Froumenteau (1581). [47] Cf. Villain (1952), 22.

process of specialization is evident in France at a relatively early date. In 1523, the office of *trésorier de l'épargne* was established: this new official was responsible for all the revenues of the crown, including those from domains and from taxation; at first he was to be assisted by two *intendants des finances* and a *trésorier*, but in 1547 two *contrôleurs généraux* were also appointed. This was an important early step towards revenue unification, which demonstrated the relative homogeneity of the realm. In 1542, Francis I created sixteen *généralités*, administrative units in which a *receveur général* collected all the king's direct taxes. In 1577, the process was consolidated by the establishment of a *bureau des finances* in each *généralité*.[48] Through the acquisition of such offices, merchant and bourgeois families could enter royal service and become financial experts, with a strong tendency for the office to be seen as part of the family's property rights: office, indeed, was regarded as an 'irremovable status (*dignité*) with a public function' attached to it.[49] Financial administration and the judicial offices within the regional *Parlements* were open to recruits from the bourgeoisie at least during the sixteenth century.[50] In the Holy Roman Empire, the Exchequer was established in 1566 as a permanent office, whereas previously taxes had been collected by specially commissioned treasurers.

8.5 *Rebellions against Taxation*

One of the common features of European history is that modernizing processes were accompanied by strong resistance based on arguments of traditional law. Feudalism was in its deepest sense a system of mutual obligation. From the point of view of the lords, the taxation of their peasants at the same time as increased financial obligations on themselves was deeply unsettling. It threatened to undermine the traditional lord–peasant relationship by which the lord protected his peasants, who in return paid rents and provided labour services. It is true that there was a basic obligation on all subjects to save the country from an invading enemy, but this was not seen as a justification for regular taxation. Thus resistance to taxation in the sixteenth century could be legitimized with arguments concerned with the defence of the traditional order. Resistance was not

[48] These observations by Gaston Zeller are cited in Lloyd (1983), 65, who has much information about 16th-cent. French financial policy and administration.

[49] So runs the definition by Loyseau (1610): 'dignité ordinaire avec fonction publique'; cf. Mousnier (1971), 7. Lloyd in Loyseau, ed. Lloyd (1994), xxiii, translates this as 'dignity, with aptitude for public power'.

[50] For the complicated history of the French financial system in the 16th cent.: Mieck (1982); Wolfe (1972).

restricted just to the political classes within a *dominium politicum et regale*[51] but was also a traditional form of opposition used by peasants.

The tension between rents and taxes created certain structural conditions in which rebellions might take place.[52] In virtually all European states the peasants comprised an overwhelming proportion of the population and their production formed the core of the national economy. Their taxes and dues financed a large proportion of the noble estates and the national budget. During the sixteenth century (although this phenomenon was not restricted to this century alone) all European states were, to varying degrees, in a transitional phase between a subsistence and a market economy. This accounts for the fact that competition for taxation paid in money was fierce. During this century all European states experienced a degree of rivalry between autonomous feudal lords and centralized or centralizing monarchies. Both competed for control of the peasants. The process of 'state building' advanced very unevenly and in none of the European states was the peasant–landlord relationship as such a decisive factor. In all cases, the national monarchies emerged, to a greater or lesser extent, as the centre of power as a result of the state's increased fiscal capacity. Thus, a triangular relationship developed between peasants, feudal lords and central state authorities. In view of the growth of monetary exchange and generally favourable agrarian market conditions caused by the rise in population levels, feudal lords were eager to make the best possible use of obligatory dues and services. They opposed central taxation because it lessened the capacity of their peasants to pay rents and dues. The peasants were interested in securing as far as possible their individual and collective claims to land, their rights of inheritance and their rights to use or sell their products under favourable conditions. Only in this way could they achieve their exploitation of land for profit and gain a share in the market surplus which would enable them to pay their taxes. The central monarchies (or in the Empire, the territorial states) had an interest in fostering a prosperous population which was able to pay taxes. This enabled the rulers to assert themselves abroad and to stabilize their regimes at home.

The chronological sequence of peasant revolts in western Europe makes it clear that in the case of France and England the revolts came in relatively clearly defined cycles.[53] In France, the period from 1548 (the uprising of the *Pitauds* against the *gabelle* in Guyenne) to 1675 (the *papier timbré* uprising in Brittany) witnessed a cycle of what may be regarded as classic peasant revolts. The revolt of 1548 itself was the archetype, a rising against taxation epitomized by the rebels' slogan 'Long live the King, but without the *gabelle*'. The year 1675 may well not

[51] Koenigsberger (1986), 1–25.

[52] The author here follows his general remarks in Blickle, Rublack and Schulze (1984), 61–98.

[53] A good survey is offered by Kamen (1984), 258–91.

have been the definitive end of this type of revolt, but Le Roy Ladurie argues that between 1675 and 1685 the absolutist system was consolidated: taxation, in real terms, decreased; the confessional conflict was forcibly resolved with the revocation of the Edict of Nantes; and the intendants were able more effectively to defend the interests of the peasants. In England a comparable cycle can be observed extending from the revolts in Cornwall of 1497 to the agrarian revolts between 1628 and 1632. There were three distinct types of revolt: rebellions against taxation (which were characteristic of the early sixteenth century), revolts against the Reformation (chiefly a consequence of the dissolution of the monasteries in 1536) and anti-seigneurial revolts, such as occurred in 1549, 1607 and 1628–32. These revolts were obviously reactions to the three fundamental processes of modernization—the extension of fiscal policy, the Reformation and what we today regard as the early 'agrarian revolution'.

No comparable phenomena can be found in central, southern and eastern Europe. The great wave of peasant wars in this area in the late fifteenth and early sixteenth centuries were not the end of a cycle. At the end of the sixteenth and beginning of the seventeenth century a new wave of revolts occurred in the upper German and Habsburg regions; indeed, it may be argued that we find an almost continuous series of resistance movements of considerable variety which can be classified only in terms of the different territories in which they occurred. The same is true of east–central and south-eastern Europe, where revolts against the feudal system predominated, although there were also some revolts against taxation. Even the Ottoman empire saw tax rebellions between 1590 and 1607.[54] Viktor Buganov has referred to a 'relative delay' in Russia, where peasant uprisings did not reach their peak until the seventeenth and eighteenth centuries. This can be explained by the 'delayed' capitalist development in Russia, and the late emergence of absolutism there.[55] Josef Petran argues that peasant risings in Poland and Bohemia did not reach their climax until the second half of the eighteenth century.[56]

The different chronology of the revolts suggests that these movements should be seen in the context of the process of European state formation. This process involved the development of a centralized administration, a comprehensive taxation system, a predominant if not an exclusive religious denomination within the state, and clearly defined relations of power between parliaments and princes. This new stage in state organization was associated with strong resistance from the estates and with peasant revolts. In this broader perspective, the revolts were an important indicator of the extent, duration and success of the

[54] Faroqi (1991). [55] Buganov (1977), 119. [56] Petran (1969), 107–40.

process of modernization, and peasant resistance also helped to determine the direction of this development. Revolts against the process of state modernization had far greater scope than anti-seigneurial revolts. Resistance to fiscal policy or to reform 'from above' naturally extended further than the specific problems of individual landlords. Feudal disputes did not become really serious unless there was a generalized assault on the position of the peasantry, which rarely happened except perhaps in the case of the English enclosure movement or the Bohemian compulsory labour policy. Generally, however, anti-seigneurial movements were organized on a local or manorial or (at most) regional level, while the scope of the anti-state or anti-fiscal revolts was much broader.

8.6 *Conclusion: The Success of Taxation in the Sixteenth Century*

There can be no doubt that the sixteenth century witnessed the success of 'modern' taxation. If we compare the state of things at the dawn of the sixteenth century with the early seventeenth century, the achievements become quite obvious: *pecunia nervus rerum* had become the norm in states. Braudel argued that the state was 'increasingly emerging as the great collector and redistributor of revenue'; even if no more than 1 ducat per head was collected in Europe *c.*1600, this money was collected from the surplus production of a largely agrarian economy with uneven regional patterns of monetary circulation.[57] What had been strongly opposed at the beginning of the century (in Hungary, in the revolt of the *Comuneros*, and in the German Peasants' War) was accepted as necessary and inevitable by the end of the century. This was a revolution in political organization and perceptions. Within three generations, a total *renversement des mentalités* had taken place, even if there remain doubts as to whether the full impact of this revolution had occurred in the sixteenth century.[58] Leviathan now stood alongside the remaining seigneurial obligations as a second extractor of surplus peasant wealth.

This success of taxation must also have appeared surprising to governments. Royal councillors tended to think in terms of the likely discontent and even rebellion which their new fiscal measures might provoke. Whenever a tax measure was debated in a political context there was less argument about its economic feasibility than the potential reaction of the ruler's subjects. Comments on the avoidance of unrest, rebellion or sedition in the European political literature of the late sixteenth century are commonplace. Indeed, one cannot avoid the impression that contemporary discussions of taxation remained

[57] Cf. Braudel in Earle (1974), 26–8; Braudel (1973), i, 449; ibid. i, 451: 'the "fast-flowing blood" of the circulation of metal currencies . . .'

[58] Cf. Bonney (1991*b*), 352.

traditional,[59] perhaps even that they were now 'completely anachronistic'.[60] The king or prince was still held to have to 'live of his own'; his treasury must be strictly managed; the income from the domain was to be increased. A new tax remained an extraordinary event, which had to be justified by a legitimate reason or the lack of other financial resources. Subjects had to be asked for their consent before the tax was imposed and with the end of the emergency its levy had to cease. There was little by way of a general authorization for kings to levy taxes. Indeed, the reverse was held to be true: just as in the Middle Ages, taxes were seen as a significant encroachment on the private property of the citizen and lawful only under very strict conditions (Chapter 1.4).

Most of these comments were written by jurists who were well aware of the legal problems of encroachment on individual rights. Their cautious comments on taxation and attempts to rein in a voracious state were founded on the central argument of *necessitas*, which remained the only just reason for a tax.[61] *Necessitas* changed its nature from a real and controllable danger (for example the incursion of an enemy) to a general argument which could be defined by the prince himself. Referring to Livy, Georg Obrecht stated in 1597: 'It is most just because these taxes are a necessity and a duty without which the state is destined to perish utterly.'[62] What had been once understood by Jean Bodin as a fundamental threat to the security of the country was interpreted quite differently, as a relative phenomenon which included the duties of government as defined by itself. Few comments by European princes on their principles of taxation survive. Charles Emmanuel I of Savoy told Henri IV that the distinction between Savoy and Piedmont in terms of their fiscal capacity was that in the former he obtained what he could, whereas in the latter he levied what he required ('Je tire de Savoie ce que je peux et de Piemont ce que je veux').[63] When, in 1632, the Bavarian Elector Maximilian I—a prince whose attitude to fiscal matters was relatively 'modern'—recalled the remarkable growth of taxation during his reign, especially in those regions occupied by enemy armies, he wondered that this had been possible at all. Thirty years earlier, no one would have imagined that such sums could have been collected, and only the use of force had made it possible. This remark might be taken as a *post facto* legitimation of the 'modern' tax policy of European rulers from the mid-sixteenth century.[64] Among the lower levels of society, peasants naturally wanted to restrict their

[59] Stolleis (1983), 123–4; Schulz (1982), 28–9. These works deal with both the rich German literature and also the relevant European tracts.

[60] Schlögl (1988), 208.

[61] For the concept of *necessitas*: Pichler (1983), esp. 165–6.

[62] Schulz (1982), 65. [63] Cf. Stumpo (1979), 4. [64] Schlögl (1988), 21.

burden to the traditional, acceptable level. They did not accept the new scheme of things which made taxation a perpetual and ordinary burden, as in the Empire where peasants were burdened with an increasing number of *Römermonate* ('Roman months'). When, in 1598, a Swabian peasant community was confronted with a new set of about eighty 'Roman months' to pay within four years, the peasants wanted to return to their 'good old German months' (that is, to twelve annual payments instead of twenty). The official who tried to explain the system to the peasants had his doubts whether they were able to understand it.[65] One might conclude that they were indeed able to understand the new fiscal system, but that they refused to do so because they opposed the increased levy on principle.

There was a degree of solidarity between feudal lords and their subjects against the voracious centralized state. Such coalitions between nobles and peasants against the fiscal burden are evident in Bavaria and in France. Central taxation became an increasing danger for landlords who were dependent on their seigneurial income, as may be seen from the example of about fifty peasant estates under different landlords in the Bavarian *Rentamt* of Burghausen between the mid-sixteenth and the mid-seventeenth century.[66] There was a growing gap between the stagnation of rents paid in kind and the slow growth of rents paid in money on the one hand and the rapid increase in taxes on the other. The landlord was the loser in the course of this century, while the state emerged as the victor. Here again taxation has to be seen in relation to the interests of landlords and peasants.

By the end of the sixteenth century, more money was being collected on a more regular basis than ever before in the form of taxation. Taxation had been established as the only mechanism for running the state and paying for a bureaucracy and an army. Fiscal theorists of the seventeenth and eighteenth centuries depicted a circular model of taxation: money was taken away from the ruler's subjects only to return to society via charitable action.[67] In reality, the proceeds from taxation in the sixteenth century disappeared in expenditure on the bureaucracy and the armed forces, since the share of expenditure for education or the infrastructure was trivial in most states. Taxation thus only redistributed wealth among those strata of society which participated prominently in the business and financial affairs of the state: lawyers, soldiers, manufacturers of military goods, monopolists and financiers. Gerald Aylmer has called this the 'court–country' model: 'If all the material advantages of office-holding are included, as well as taxes in the narrower sense, then the "court–country"

[65] Schulze (1980). [66] Cf. graph in Schlögl (1988), 265. [67] Schulz (1982).

fiscal hypothesis may seem to fit the facts more closely than any other, at least for sixteenth- and seventeenth-century Europe and perhaps for parts of the Third World today.'[68]

[68] Aylmer in Burke (1972), 169.

CHAPTER 9

The Emergence and Consolidation of the 'Tax State'. II. The Seventeenth Century

Marjolein 't Hart

If we accept that 'centralized, productive revenue–expenditure systems began to emerge' in the early modern period,[1] it may be argued that it was in the seventeenth century that a significant increase in the scale of warfare accelerated this process. Military innovations and recurrent wars posed new challenges. Inflation resulting from the inflow of Spanish-American silver had raised the overall costs of government. As a result, the competition for resources was intensified between central states, provincial governments, cities and landlords. This intensity increased, in turn, the likelihood of war. Moreover, in much of Europe an economic recession altered the underlying conditions of the race for cash: private and public funds were restricted by the capacity of the population at large to pay, affected as they were by subsistence crises and recurrent outbreaks of plague. This was particularly true in the Mediterranean area, though less so in the north and west of Europe.[2]

The state developed its coercive potential in certain specific ways. Firstly, the financial burden of war was intensified and state expenditures rose dramatically. Secondly, the process of transformation of 'domain states' to 'tax states' was consolidated, a trend which established the finances of the state on a more permanent footing. Thirdly, a stable long-term public debt became imperative for the more belligerent states. And fourthly, the increased impact of the state on society posed a redefinition of property rights and access to the 'state-making' process, which increased the probability of domestic conflicts and turmoil. These trends were not exclusive to this age: they had begun in the late Middle Ages and were to continue throughout the last phase of *ancien régime* Europe. Yet they took on a definite shape in the course of the seventeenth century.

[1] Webber and Wildavsky (1986), 229. [2] De Vries (1976).

9.1 *Wars and New Centres of Power*

The multi-polar European state system led to an increase in militarization, for reasons both of attack and defence. Military innovations were invariably expensive and the number of military and naval personnel continued to grow.[3] More and more money was needed for these developments. Military expenses weighed heavily upon state budgets. For France, the increase was dramatic in the 1630s, following its entry into the Thirty Years' War. Expressed in real terms, there was a five- to eightfold rise from the early seventeenth century to the 1690s. Spain, which had already experienced an enormous increase in its military burden in the sixteenth century—probably unequalled by any other state—was confronted with a new peak in the 1650s.[4] Between the 1590s and the 1670s the English budget increased sixteen times in money terms, and more than this if we take into account the last decades of the seventeenth century.[5] In Denmark, comparing 1602 and 1700, state expenses rose twelvefold, with a significant rise after a standing army was created in 1637. And in the Dutch Republic, military costs as a result of the Eighty Years' War against Spain reached a peak during the 1630s and 1640s; there were equally high levels of expenditure during the Anglo-Dutch Wars and again during the Nine Years' War in the 1690s.[6]

The funds allocated for war increased in proportion to other expenses. Almost 90 per cent of the budget of the Dutch Republic was spent on war. This figure was even higher for the Empire: nearly 98 per cent of the tax income was spent on warfare, and similar tendencies are also apparent in some of the German principalities. Costs increased rapidly in Brandenburg–Prussia after the 1640s.[7] Expenses rose far less in states which did not participate in the competition for military power. The Swiss Confederation, for example, did not establish a permanent army, since it was only marginally engaged in warfare after 1650.[8] Yet such policy was possible only for the happy few, as the majority of states were caught in the spiralling rise of military costs.

The budget increased above all at the centre. Invariably, the 'core' regions of states became those most heavily taxed (for example, the province of Holland in the Dutch Republic, Castile in Spain, the *pays d'élections* in France, the kingdom in Denmark, and the English counties in the union of England, Scotland and Ireland).[9] Peripheral provinces paid relatively less. States that managed to

[3] Roberts (1956), *passim*; Parker (1988), 61–4; Kennedy (1989), 73.

[4] Bonney in Bonney (1995); Gelabert in Bonney (1995).

[5] Braddick (1991), 2; O'Brien (1988), 2.

[6] 't Hart (1993), 60–1; Petersen (1983), 43.

[7] Krüger in Witt (1987); Braun in Tilly (1975), 268, 311.

[8] Körner in Bonney (1995).

[9] Thomas and Meyer (1984), 467; Limm (1984), 61; Elliott (1984), 163; Kennedy (1989), 43, 53.

centralize and concentrate their resources were in an advantageous position, with England as the outstanding example in the later seventeenth century (Chapter 11.1).[10]

Yet the financial needs of monarchies could also strengthen the position of assemblies of estates, the strongest rivals to autocratic princes. Frequently, increased fiscal power was 'bought' at the expense of allowing domestic property-holders to gain access to new state power in meetings of representative institutions.[11] What was more, recurrently the meso-level of government (that is, government at the provincial and county level) had to be revived, because the centre had no choice but to rely upon the province's fiscal authority in the continuous pressure of military expenses. Examples of extreme meso-level states were the Dutch Republic (a union of seven provinces), the Swiss Confederation (a confederation of urban and peasant republics), and the Holy Roman Empire. In fact, even 'absolutist' France had to rely on the estates' administrators in certain of the *pays d'états*, while Spain may more properly be regarded as a union of separate states, such as Aragon, Catalonia, Valencia and Portugal, which were autonomous in fiscal terms.[12]

The administrative structures of the main cities, local towns, landlords and churches were overshadowed by territorial ones. Their budgets rose less as compared with the upper strata of government, while their autonomous resources were sapped by central state demands. Whatever their traditional privileges, they were increasingly under attack from modern taxation by the centre.[13] The enhanced coercive capacities of the state which accompanied increased warfare accounted for this development. Above all, the Thirty Years' War seems to have strengthened the grip of sovereigns. Absolutism was established in Sweden in the 1680s and in Denmark in the 1660s, while the personifications of this type of rule were the *roi soleil* in France and the soldier-king in Prussia.[14]

9.2 *The Transition to the Modern 'Tax State'*

In 'domain states', significant domain resources allowed princes to operate quite independently from the demands of society (Chapter 5.7).[15] In the 'tax state', the

[10] Brewer (1989), 3. [11] Tilly (1990), 99.

[12] Elliott (1992), *passim*; Heper (1985), 98; Kennedy (1989), 52–3.

[13] Rosenberg (1958), 33; Tilly (1986), 160; for regions with a strong local resistance: Blockmans (1989), 751; Prak (1991), 75.

[14] Petersen (1983), 46; Tilly (1990), 68; Duffy (1980), 4; Rosenberg (1958), 12; Press (1988), 266.

[15] Braun in Tilly (1975), 251.

larger part of public funds was to come from taxes paid in money. Even though the distinction between peacetime and wartime expedients (ordinary versus extraordinary) remained, ordinary taxation ultimately provided the main sources of revenue. Loans came to be guaranteed upon regular excises, customs and land taxes imposed upon the whole territory and, in some cases, granted by representative assemblies.[16]

This transition to the modern 'tax state' was furthered by the demands of war. The installation of a standing army or navy often triggered the shift towards permanent taxes. The income from royal domains could not meet the needs of a belligerent state as prices continued to rise, while war finance through extraordinary means such as exactions or 'contributions' levied upon conquered lands proved only sufficient as long as wars were victorious. For example, Sweden managed to construct a fiscal system upon contributions payable by the enemy, but military defeats might threaten to undermine the whole financial structure.[17] Innovations in fiscal systems were frequently drawn from the example of a competitor state, especially one which had been successful in securing a degree of equilibrium in the balance between income and expenditure. Not even the wealthiest states of the early modern period, such as France or Spain, succeeded in escaping from the problem that spending grew faster than receipts. The Dutch Republic, England, Denmark and Prussia certainly seemed more successful than others in developing methods for managing their rising expenditure. However, 'success' and 'failure' in public finance must be measured in terms of very narrow differences—all states experienced similar difficulties.[18]

Sales of crown lands, adopted as a convenient solution to pay military commanders, accelerated the process towards the establishment of a tax state. The monarchy in England, for example, had avoided taxation by selling crown property in the late sixteenth century, but by the seventeenth century (with the exception of the period of Charles I's personal rule) found itself utterly dependent upon Parliament for supply.[19] In Sweden too, as revenues were seldom sufficient, the income of the crown was sold or pawned to raise lump sums in cash.[20] The development in the state budgets of Denmark showed the transition clearly. Despite the fact that revenue from the domain did at first increase in absolute terms, by 1662 the proportion from this category was reduced to 10 per cent, whereas it had oscillated between 37 and 67 per cent in the first decades of the seventeenth century. The largest category of new revenue was the land tax,

[16] Bonney in Bonney (1995); Krüger in Witt (1987), 49.

[17] Limm (1984), 60.

[18] Bonney (1991*b*), 529; Webber (1986), 237; Elliott (1984), 71; 't Hart (1991), *passim*.

[19] Stone (1972), 60–6.

[20] Limm (1984), 60.

which had been necessitated by the drastic sale of crown lands during the Swedish wars in the 1650s. Furthermore, taxes formerly paid in kind were replaced by money taxes after 1660 as part of a new fiscal structure which was forged as Danish absolutism came into being.[21]

Wars might act as a kind of shock therapy for states and formerly impermanent sporadic taxes were made regular and permanent when a standing army was created. The Turkish War of 1593–1606 helped to establish something akin to a 'modern' system of taxation in the Holy Roman Empire. The Thirty Years' War forced several belligerents to break out of former fiscal constraints, as previously unthinkable tax burdens were imposed without reference to tradition (Chapter 8.6). Even agrarian societies proved to be more productive than was thought possible.[22] In Brandenburg–Prussia, earlier taxes were made permanent in the 1660s and were substantially increased, as were a group of excises and sale levies called the *Akzise*.[23] In England, a centralized system of customs, excises and land taxes had become the mainstay of state finances by 1688.[24] The French monarchy tried to reduce the noble exemption from the *taille*, the most important direct tax, at regular intervals. New land registers were constructed in areas of land tax and a 5 per cent sales tax (the *sol pour livre*) was introduced in 1640 in an attempt to make the fiscal burden more equitable: the tax had to be withdrawn because of resistance in 1643. A further new tax, the *capitation* (payable by heads of households), was introduced in 1695, while the farms of indirect taxes were consolidated in 1681 in an attempt to increase administrative efficiency.[25] In Denmark, the monarchy introduced new taxes on land (*hartkornskatter*) in 1662, doing away with the most important tax exemption of the nobility.[26] In the Dutch Republic, the Council of State imposed new taxes in the 'generality' lands gained after 1648, following the more advanced system pertaining in Holland.[27]

This evolution towards a 'tax state' did not occur everywhere at exactly the same moment. In Sweden, the earlier domain structures were reinforced in the 1680s. The Swiss Confederation had no overwhelming fiscal requirement necessitated by increased military expenditure and experienced no significant shift towards permanent taxation. Instead, a large part of the budget relied upon the economic activities of the republics.[28] Furthermore, even in modernizing tax states, traditional exemptions remained, such as the undertaxing of the nobility

[21] Petersen (1983), 34–8. [22] Zagorin (1982), i, 127; Elliott (1984), 64, 70.
[23] Rosenberg (1958), 34–40, 49; Braun in Tilly (1975), 269. [24] Brewer (1989), 95.
[25] Bonney in Bonney (1995); Bonney (1979), 12, 24. [26] Petersen (1983), 47.
[27] Kappelhof (1986), 79. [28] Körner in Bonney (1995).

and partial exemptions for whole cities. Nevertheless, in much of Europe the incidence of taxation rose, and as a result the 'tax state' was strengthened while the 'domain state' withered away (Chapter 13.3 discusses the exceptions, especially Brandenburg–Prussia).[29]

9.3 *The Novelty of Permanent State Indebtedness*

In the sixteenth century, few states contracted long-term debts, though certain of the city-states, and Spain, were the earliest and most notable exceptions. Yet by the end of the seventeenth century, almost all states were permanently in debt. Even the public debt of the city-state of Venice, so carefully managed up to 1600, rocketed in the seventeenth century to about 8 million ducats in 1641 and to over 50 million in 1714.[30] In the 'domain state', loans had been employed to bridge short-term financial difficulties. Often, parts of the domains had been pledged, and the obligations were paid back as soon as possible. In the 'tax state', loans were established as a part of the state's budget and guaranteed by regular taxation. Borrowing terms were improved by consolidating the short-term floating debt, which was issued at various interest rates, into long-term, fixed-rate obligations. The charges upon the debt were funded by permanent tax resources.[31]

War was again the force of propulsion. Military requirements tended to be financed by credit, since tax revenue could not be mobilized sufficiently quickly for the needs of armies and navies. Above all, highly commercialized and monetized states derived important advantages, as a symbiosis of state and capital became necessary. The permanency of the public debt paved the way for increased influence of the bourgeoisie, as cities and their financial elites assumed the function of providing loan capital for the state.[32]

The supply of money and credit was not only a 'transmission belt' for economic development, but also for success in wars. It was remarkable that the Dutch Republic not only escaped the worst effects of the economic crises of the seventeenth century, but was also able to manage a stable, long-term public debt. The Dutch could borrow more cheaply than any other government—excluding perhaps certain city-states—on bonds that were bought on a voluntary basis. The public retained great confidence in Dutch government certificates which were held by a large group of domestic investors. The public debt of the Republic's most creditworthy component, the province of Holland, increased

[29] O'Brien (1988), 16; Dent (1973), 232.

[30] Lane (1973), 402, 416; Petersen (1983), 45.

[31] Tracy (1985), 3.

[32] Tilly (1990), 89; Ardant in Tilly (1975), 189.

from 5 million guilders in the first decade of the seventeenth century to more than 190 million guilders in the 1690s. Yet rates of interest were reduced from 8.5 per cent to 3.75 per cent in the same period.[33] This process was facilitated by Amsterdam's role as the centre of the international bullion market; its municipal bank attracted capital from all over Europe.

In most cases, high interest rates pointed to weaknesses in public debt systems. Charges upon government obligations were raised in France in the 1640s and early 1650s. The French state in effect went bankrupt in 1648.[34] Spain, likewise, did not manage to reorganize its debt charges according to annual ordinary revenues. Traditionally, the treasure from the Americas had ensured the payment of interest on the debt. However, these resources failed to arrive in the 1630s and 1640s on the same scale as in the sixteenth century; as a result, bankruptcies were proclaimed with a degree of regularity in 1607, 1627, 1647, 1652 and 1662 (Chapter 7.4).[35] Denmark, too, was forced to declare a suspension of its payments in 1660, although the official rate of interest was relatively low, at only 6 per cent.[36] At this period, Charles II of England still had to pay interest rates of 10 per cent, while Louis XIV might even pay 15 per cent. In contrast, the elasticity of the Dutch domestic market for government obligations was revealed by the fact that the Union's government could obtain funds at a mere 4 per cent, despite the outbreak of another war in the 1660s.[37]

Because of burdensome interest rates, the need to increase taxation to fund them, and the pressing danger of state bankruptcies, all states aimed at reducing the total amount of debt. Few were successful. Until the 1650s, Sweden avoided the establishment of a huge public debt by selling crown revenues; however, in the subsequent decades indebtedness burdened this state too.[38] The Dutch could maintain their debt within certain limits after the 1650s, but only temporarily. Soon afterwards, wars overtook all good intentions. The policy of the Swiss Confederation was more successful, however. After 1650 the debt was amortized, a policy which could be sustained since the Swiss eschewed participation in military conflicts. What was more, by buying state obligations from other states, the Swiss even managed to obtain revenue from loan interest for themselves as other European states became heavily indebted.[39]

A typical phase of transition towards permanent indebtedness was the employment of intermediaries. A provincial or urban government provided loans to the state, the debt being administered by the mediators themselves.

[33] Dormans (1991), 65, 81; 't Hart (1993), 177–9.

[34] Dent (1973), 239; Bonney (1981*a*), 204–6, 320.

[35] Thompson (1976), 96–7.

[36] Petersen (1983), 47.

[37] Parker (1974), 574.

[38] Limm (1984), 60.

[39] Körner in Bonney (1995).

Principal cities, church and guild corporations, trade companies (for example, the East India Company) and provincial estates (for example, Holland within the Dutch Republic) furnished in this way enormous sums to central governments. As their fiscal apparatus was under close local scrutiny, thus guaranteeing the payments on the debt charges, interest rates could be significantly lower than those attached to direct loans of the central government. Indeed, investors were easier to find because of public confidence in the lower levels of government, such as the cities and provinces. The financial system of the Holy Roman Empire relied almost exclusively on the financial power of the cities: without their prefinancing of taxes in wartime, the wars of the Empire would have been impossible to finance. As a result, the German cities were heavily indebted after the Thirty Years' War.[40] The French crown raised long-term loans by selling annuities guaranteed by the municipality of Paris, as did the English in the 1660s through the city of London. In England, the main innovation was the selling of long-term government bonds through the national Bank which was established in 1694, a development which has been termed a 'financial revolution in the state'.[41]

Another way to borrow money was through the state's officials themselves. Civil servants and local authorities were approached, or even forced, to contribute to a government loan by alienating their capital. In the case of France, 'loans upon loans' were at times required from the tax-farmers.[42] Whereas using cities, provinces and banks as intermediaries seems to have enhanced the stability of the state, the internal arrangements with public officials constituted a parasitic growth which was inherently unstable. The total amount of debt became difficult to estimate, while the interest on those loans had to be provided from tax revenues which were often collected by the officials themselves. Consequently, the latter tended to enforce rigorously the levy of taxes paid by the population at large in order to safeguard interest payments on their own loans.

9.4 *'State Making' and Domestic Contention*

The demands of war provoked an intensive fiscalism almost everywhere. A strong reformism was inherent in this process, because fiscalism extended taxation to regions and social groups which had hitherto been shielded by customary privileges.[43] Yet precisely because of these reformist tendencies of central taxation, the seventeenth century typically witnessed a number of

[40] Gerteis in Genet and Le Mené (1987), 155.

[41] Parker (1974), 574–9; Dent (1973), 50; Braun in Tilly (1975), 288. Cf. Dickson (1967).

[42] Bonney (1979), 20–2.

[43] Elliott (1984), 141.

anti-monarchical rebellions. Fiscal innovation inevitably impinged upon traditional exemptions and was viewed as highly 'arbitrary' by the local populace. Yet 'arbitrary' taxation was not the only motive for revolt. The fiscal burden attained intolerable levels particularly where the demands of the state were exacerbated by adverse local circumstances. Resources could be drained by local taxes or feudal rights, or by armies of passage, occupation and siege. Acute subsistence crises might further erode the tax base, as in the years 1647–53 in France and 1650–1 in Spain. The economic situation inevitably had a direct effect on the tax yield, and in the seventeenth century there were frequent economic crises. A significant financial crisis occurred after 1619 as a result of a decline in mine production and bullion imports. Widespread debasement of the coinage, above all in the German territories, was the result (Chapter 13.4). Moreover, agrarian societies, especially in the less monetized regions, often found it difficult to make regular tax payments in money. A very successful harvest caused a fall in prices, which had the effect of reducing the incomes of peasant proprietors; yet a poor harvest with rocketing prices produced extreme distress for the non-grain producing agrarian communities.[44]

Apart from localized and religious causes, many rebellions of the seventeenth century were incited by the fiscal measures of the central state. In the Swiss Confederation, they provoked a general peasant uprising in 1652–3 which was crushed by the combined armed forces of the cities.[45] In Germany, anti-fiscalism was more often a cause of revolt in the countryside than the towns, although taxation was repeatedly an additional grievance in town disorders.[46] Tax disputes provoked challenges to the authority of the king of Spain, first by the Dutch revolt, then by rebellions in the Basque countries, Catalonia, Portugal, Palermo and Naples. There was widespread fiscal resistance among the clergy and the Basque provinces in the 1630s to the attempt of the Castilian government to impose a salt tax to replace the *millones* (excises upon articles of popular consumption), and in the event the proposed new tax was withdrawn. The Catalan uprising lasted from 1640 until 1652. Portugal also rebelled in 1640, in part because its autonomy had been undermined by the central Castilian state when a 5 per cent levy was imposed on all property. An independent Portuguese monarchy was established, although this was not acknowledged by Spain until 1668. Palermo rebelled after a poor harvest against the heavy excises on grain in 1647. The Neapolitan revolt began in the same year. The immediate cause was the imposition of another exaction, an excise on fruit, which was a staple diet for

[44] Ardant in Tilly (1975), 178–9; Bonney (1979), 17; Tilly (1986), 156–8; Kindleberger (1991), 149; de Vries (1976), 16.

[45] Bonney (1991*b*), 412; Körner in Bonney (1995).

[46] Gerteis in Genet and Le Mené (1987), 158.

the very poor. Control was soon restored, although the fruit tax was withdrawn.[47]

In the Dutch Republic itself, a province-based particularism overcame the centralist tendencies of the *Stadhouder* (the provincial governor, who might also be captain-general of the army) and the Council of State in a prolonged debate over sums to be spent by the Union. In 1650, the provincial government of Holland reduced the central state's budget from 20 million guilders on average to a mere 5 million. The size of the companies of soldiers and the number of warships with sailors were drastically reduced. The budget had to be restored with the coming of the Anglo-Dutch wars, but the *Stadhouder* was not reinstated until 1672.

In England, a long civil war increased the power of Parliament at the expense of the Stuart dynasty. The principle of parliamentary control over royal finances was reaffirmed and emphasized. Opposition had united during recurrent crises over the voting of tonnage and poundage in the 1620s. The attempt to introduce Ship Money in 1635, a tax hitherto imposed upon maritime counties but now extended to the whole kingdom, provoked outrage because it was seen as providing the state with fiscal powers independent of parliamentary consent. There was widespread tax resistance in England in 1640, coinciding with the outbreak of war with Scotland. Even after the Stuarts were restored in 1660, the monarch was made utterly dependent for his finances upon Parliament.[48]

Even the powerful French monarchy was shaken by recurrent revolts against taxation. The government's increased tax demands were accentuated by the economic recession after 1620. The *Croquants* in Quercy rebelled as royal agents came to replace the provincial tax collectors in 1624. The towns of Guyenne rose in 1635 as a new tax was imposed on wine sales in taverns. The multiple insurrections in Saintonge, Angoumois, Poitou, Périgord and other regions were due to the near-doubling of the *taille* and other fiscal demands placed upon these provinces. Hatred of taxation also inspired the revolt of the *Nu-pieds* in Normandy in 1639. Rebellion started as a protest against the crown's project to extend the *gabelle*, the salt tax, to previously exempt areas of the province, in addition to other fiscal grievances in this heavily taxed region. Peasant riots against the salt tax had been frequent.[49] Grievances arising from the government's policies to overcome the fiscal crisis gave the Fronde (1648–52) its momentum. The power of the royal government to levy taxes was contested. Protests against extortionate practices of the tax-farmers were voiced, and several tax-farmers were imprisoned. The city of Paris was irritated by royal exactions too, as the

[47] Zagorin (1982), i, 126, 247–9; Gelabert in Bonney (1995); Elliott (1984), 139.

[48] Zagorin (1982), ii, 141–5; Popofsky (1990), 45; Stone (1972), 94, 122; Roberts (1977), 74–5.

[49] Bonney (1991*b*), 392; Zagorin (1982), i, 215–20; ii, 11; Tilly (1986), 132–6.

monarchy tried to manipulate the interest payable on government bonds (*rentes*). Thereafter, resistance to taxation remained a dominant motive for rebellion in France. Another significant tax revolt, the 'stamped paper' (*papier timbré*) rebellion in Brittany, occurred in 1675.[50]

After seeking an explanation of the common causal factors in six significant rebellions in the seventeenth century, Roger Merriman concluded: 'In the first place, we find that the most immediate, though not always the most fundamental, cause of every one of them was finance; in every case it was arbitrary taxation in one form or another, and the complaints that it evoked, that brought matters to a head.'[51] The lack of sustained participation by local oligarchies in the revolt was crucial for the outcome of these rebellions. The oligarchies did not sustain their protest and refused to throw in their lot with the lower classes because they sought concessions for themselves. For example, the *gabelle* in France was advantageous to the elite, since much of the revenue from this tax was used for interest payments to the holders of annuities (*rentes*), which were owned largely by landlords and other property owners.[52] Discontent was likely to spread to ruling elites if their voice was not heard on a regular basis. As the French Estates General was not convened after 1615, the main forum for criticism was the sovereign courts (the *Parlements*) and the provincial estates. As a result, provincial autonomy was the focus for the fiercest power struggles between the state and the local elites. The traditional quotas for regional contributions to taxes were rarely adjusted, since such readjustment was likely to cause bitter discontent among the privileged.[53] This benign neglect of the issue of readjustment burdened the state with an inefficient fiscal system throughout the *ancien régime*.

The interests of major landholders were also affected by taxation. Property rights were redefined through the registration of title deeds, which in certain circumstances resulted in increased support for the state. Furthermore, specific elites were allowed to participate in the expanding functions of the state. In Languedoc, Louis XIV was particularly successful in linking the provincial elite to the crown, by allowing them authority in the regulation of troops passing through the province, allotting Mercantilist enterprises and canals to the province, and by suppressing the competing economic power of the Huguenots.[54] In eighteenth-century England, the effectiveness of the state continued to depend

50 Bonney (1981*b*), 830; Zagorin (1982), ii, 193, 210; Dent (1973), 28.

51 Merriman (1937), 15–16.

52 Hocquet in Genet and Le Mené (1987), 218.

53 Bonney (1992*a*), 162; Bonney (1992*b*), 112; Bonney in Bonney (1995).

54 Beik (1985), 281–7.

on the co-operation of county and village elites with the central government.[55] The form of administration which resulted was often a highly complex system with private and public elements mixed. Tax exemptions for the nobility might still survive: in Denmark, despite the imposition of a new general tax upon land, exemptions for their manors were granted to landowners in 1682 as a reward for their tax-collecting activities.

The complexity of the apparatus was increased through numerous semi-private arrangements. Contractors and officers necessarily thought in terms of their short-term security and profit, loyalty to their 'enterprises', not to the state.[56] The system of tax-farming was widespread. In return for a fixed annual rent, tax-farmers were responsible for the levy of the tax (Chapter 13.2). Any additional profits were theirs. In France, three farms (the *gabelle*, the *aides* and the *cinq grosses fermes*) provided 80 per cent of royal income from indirect taxes in the first half of the seventeenth century, and a significant, although fluctuating, proportion of total revenues until the end of the *ancien régime* (Chapter 13.6).[57] The prevalence of competing private interests within the state was most obvious with the sale of offices and titles. The purchase of an office or a title constituted a quick road to social respectability for the wealthy and upwardly mobile mercantile families. France was most notorious in this respect, although the sale of offices was practised to a lesser extent in almost all states. Revenues from the sale of offices for the French monarchy reached 55 per cent of ordinary revenue for one quinquennium (1630–4) in the first half of the seventeenth century. The capital value held in offices was estimated at 419 million *livres* in the 1660s.[58] A second great wave of sales of offices occurred during the period of Louis XIV's later wars, while reliance on semi-private contractors continued to the French Revolution and beyond. The consolidation of oligarchy was an alternative route for those states which did not experience a strengthening of central power in this period. The Dutch Republic and the Swiss Confederation were the most obvious examples of this process. A certain number of families secured access to the new bureaucratic structures and managed to expropriate part of the revenues for their own purposes. By excluding competing families, the number of ruling bourgeois families was restricted and power came to be concentrated in the hands of an oligarchy. This could in itself serve as a reason for the emergence of protest movements among those groups who were excluded from power, as is evident in the uprising of urban corporations in Basle in 1691.[59]

55 Braddick (1991), 3; Brooks (1974), 300.

56 Thompson (1976), 274–5.

57 Hocquet (1987), 46; Bonney (1979), 11.

58 Bonney (1978), 450 n. 2; Bonney (1981*a*), 313; Bonney (1992*b*), 108–9; Dent (1973), 233.

59 Körner in Bonney (1995); see also Prak (1989), 165.

9.5 *Conclusion*

Whereas the social impact of a 'domain state' had been small, the 'tax state' brought in its wake significant social and economic changes. Separate, atomized, households were obliged to meet their tax demands, which implied that they had to produce for the market, or sell their labour for a wage, in order to obtain the necessary cash for this purpose. Taxation assumed the existence of markets for the exchange of goods, while public borrowing assumed the existence of a capital market. The intrusive fiscal state combined a form of social disciplining that dated from the later Middle Ages along with the drafting of new property registers and the imposition of direct taxes, all of which served to focus the discontent of protest movements. The emergence and consolidation of the 'tax state' was both the cause and effect of much of the turmoil in the early modern states.[60]

Questions as to the 'legal' status of taxation were intensified as a result of the increasing fiscal burden, while economic recession affected the discussion in a negative way. Gradually, taxes were accepted as being indispensable for public peace. In this process, the states with more urbanized regions were at an advantage, since cash was more readily available in towns and the tax base was less restricted as compared to rural communities. Credit facilities were also concentrated in urban centres. The violent protests of the peasantry must be placed in the perspective of the problems associated with the imposition of taxes paid in money, whereas urban-based revolts often disputed the actual control of the funds collected.

However, most barriers to taxation were removed in the course of the seventeenth century. Central governments were strengthened,[61] with close relations between the central authority, local elites who supported the spread of central power, the military and those families who provided loans for the ever-growing public debt. The creation of a standing army left the state much stronger than it had ever been. War and resource extraction was a cyclical phenomenon, with the growth of a fiscal–military state as a consequence. By the eighteenth century, the majority of states were relatively compact areas of territory in which the central government exercised a degree of control over the economy, politics and society that would not have been thought possible in the later Middle Ages.

[60] Krüger in Witt (1987), 62.

[61] In particular after 1660: Bonney (1991*b*), 188.

CHAPTER 10

The Eighteenth Century. I. The Finances of the Austrian Monarchy and the Italian States

Carlo Capra

The emergence of the Austrian monarchy as a great power is one of the central features of European history in the decades around 1700. After the Turks were routed under the walls of Vienna in 1683, the whole of Hungary and Transylvania was subjected to Habsburg rule, and the frontier with the Ottoman empire was pushed further south with the conquest of Belgrade and the Banat in 1718. Meanwhile, the conclusion of the War of the Spanish Succession in 1713–14 had left Austria in possession of modern Belgium, the duchies of Milan and Mantua and the kingdoms of Naples and Sardinia, the last to be exchanged for Sicily in 1720. In less than forty years, the Habsburg territories had more than doubled in extent, while their overall population had grown from some 7 to over 18 million inhabitants. This meteoric rise was due to a combination of circumstances—the decline of the Ottoman empire, the fruitful alliance with the Maritime Powers in the struggle against Louis XIV's France, the military genius of Prince Eugene of Savoy—all of which helped to hide from contemporary eyes the real weaknesses underlying this imposing structure: the lack of geographic continuity and of any cultural and political homogeneity between such distant lands as Sicily, the Austrian Netherlands and Serbia; the economic backwardness of the core lands of the monarchy; and the persistent power of the estates which effectively limited the monarch's authority in most areas. All this has led one historian to speak of a 'baroque trompe-l'oeil';[1] and it goes far to explain why, with a much larger size and a population only slightly inferior to that of France, the Habsburg government could count on barely a fifth of France's financial resources around 1720.[2]

[1] Gherardi (1980), 81. [2] Ardant in Tilly (1975), 200.

10.1 *The Financial Structure in the Austrian Lands to 1740*

During this period of almost continuous warfare—the army was on a war footing in thirty-six out of forty-six years between 1695 and 1740—Austrian finances were naturally subjected to a severe strain. Nearly all the available revenue came at this time from two sources: the so-called *camerale* and the *contributionale*. Cameral revenue was collected *jure regio* (hence the name of *regalia* given to such incomes) and consisted of the yield from domain, mines, customs duties and excises. By the time of the death of Leopold I (1705), the Austrian monarchy had long ceased to be a 'domain state' after the fashion of Prussia or Denmark. Most crown lands had by then been given away, sold or pawned in exchange for ready cash.[3] By far the most important single item was the princely monopoly of the extraction and sale of salt, often called 'the most precious cameral jewel',[4] followed by the mining of silver, copper and other metals and by internal and external tolls. Of the many collecting agencies operating in the various territories of the monarchy, only a few produced a significant net revenue after administrative expenses and local assignments had been deducted. What remained, anyway, was sent to the *Hofkammer* in Vienna, the central financial organ for the whole monarchy excluding the Belgian and Italian provinces, and was used to cover civil expenses, such as the entertainment of the court, officers' salaries, pensions and gifts granted by the Emperor, and so on.

Military costs, on the other hand, were met in principle—though in emergencies part of the cameral revenue might be used for this purpose—by an entirely different form of imposition, the 'contribution'. This continued to be regarded as extraordinary revenue down to the middle of the eighteenth century and had to be voted by the estates of each land, who met every year in the Austro-Bohemian lands, and at longer intervals in the Hungarian provinces; the estates then proceeded to apportion and to collect their shares through their own agencies. In principle the contribution consisted of a land tax, though in Bohemia indirect taxes were also levied; the nobility were mostly exempt or were taxed at lower rates than the peasants. 'Contributional' revenue was transferred to the army through a special office, the *Hofkriegs-zahlamt*, and not through the *Hofkammer*.[5]

In spite of the built-in rigidities of the system and the inefficiency of the fiscal and administrative machinery, a considerable effort was made during the War of the Spanish Succession to raise the huge sums required by an army which in some years approached 140,000 men. According to Ingrao, after 1708 'the

[3] Bérenger (1975), 300–2; Mensi (1890), 300. [4] Mensi (1890), 10.

[5] For a clear description of the system: Bérenger (1975), 297–334.

Hofkammer could expect to raise between 16 and 17 million florins from the *Erblande* during most years, as opposed to less than 9 million at the end of Leopold's reign'.[6] This was the result, however, not so much of an increase in 'ordinary' taxation as of the adoption of a wide range of extraordinary measures, such as property and poll taxes, subsidies from the clergy, sales of offices, of crown possessions (the port of Finale was sold to the Republic of Genoa for 2.4 million florins in 1713) and even of crown jewels. Expenditure, moreover, varied in these years from 20 to 28 million, so as to make inevitable a massive recourse to credit, in spite of considerable financial help from Austria's allies.[7] Gundakar Thomas von Stahremberg, the able and hard-working president of the *Hofkammer* from 1703 to 1715, clearly understood that substantial improvement could only come from far-reaching structural changes, and at one time he proposed to replace the contribution with a 'universal excise' to be collected by royal order and through royal agents;[8] but he lacked the breathing-space and the support needed to effect such revolutionary plans. His greatest achievement was the creation in 1705 of the Vienna City Bank, which after surmounting an initial crisis became a viable credit institution and was able in time to shoulder most of the debts incurred by the state. He showed his concern, moreover, about the glaring injustices in the assessments for the contribution by persuading Emperor Charles VI (1711–40) to order new cadastral surveys to be carried out in Bohemia, Silesia and Lombardy.[9]

In spite of all this, Austrian finances offered throughout this period 'the spectacle of a state tottering in truly breakneck fashion on the brink of a precipice'.[10] This was partly due to the fact that the separation of cameral and 'contributional' revenues and the multiplicity of paying agencies—Stahremberg remarked once that 'there were almost as many paymasters as there were officers'[11]—made it impossible for the government to have a clear picture of the situation and to draw up a comprehensive budget. A considerable advance in this direction was represented by the creation in 1715 of a new state bank, the *Universalbancalität*, which though not fulfilling the high hopes that Charles VI had placed on it, led to a centralization of accounting; the next year the *Hofkammer* and the *Bancalität* were both placed under a so-called 'Finance Conference', which became the supreme advisory body in these matters. Under this new arrangement, an eleven-year forecast was submitted to the Emperor in 1721. Civil and military requirements for the period 1721–31 were estimated respectively at 69.5 and 88 million florins, to which 46.7 million were added for the servicing and repayment of debts belonging to various categories; the total

6 Ingrao (1979), 26.
7 Mensi (1890); Holl (1976), *passim*.
8 Holl (1976), 144–6.
9 Ibid. 238–72, 323–4.
10 Ibid. 437.
11 Ibid. 342.

amount needed thus exceeded 204 million, whereas the overall revenue expected was about 178 million. Including the additional burden resulting from the loans required to fill this gap, the total deficit ran to about 40 million florins.[12] This forecast did not include revenue from the Italian and Belgian provinces, which was spent on the maintenance of Imperial troops in those territories; the view held by some contemporary observers that Italian possessions were 'les Indes de la Cour de Vienne', as a Savoyard diplomat put it,[13] does not seem to be borne out by the facts, unless payments to the Emperor's secret funds and for pensions granted to his Spanish followers are taken into account. In the 1720s, the revenue from the Austro-Bohemian and Hungarian lands seems in fact to have averaged some 20 million florins, of which about half came from 'contributional' taxes and half from cameral taxes.[14]

The sorry state of Austrian finances was partially responsible for the military disasters of the 1730s, when Naples and Sicily were lost to the Bourbons, two Lombard provinces had to be ceded to the king of Sardinia and when even the Turks were able to recover some of their lost territory (the Peace of Passarowitz, 1739). The extraordinary costs of these unsuccessful wars were met, once again, by stopgap measures and by borrowing. The total public debt, which stood at 70 million florins in the 1720s, had climbed to 100 million by 1740, over half of which (54 million) was borne by the Vienna City Bank.[15] 'Contributional' and cameral revenues, in contrast, had barely risen to just under 11 and to 9.9 million respectively, including in the last figure 4.3 million transferred to the Vienna City Bank. The revenue from the monarchy's central lands in 1740 totalled about 22 million, which represents an increase of less than 3 million from the level of 1723 and barely 1.6 million from that of 1717.[16] Charles VI's best ministers, meanwhile, had either died, like Prince Eugene, or grown old and lethargic, while the particularism of the estates found powerful support in the Austrian, Bohemian and Hungarian Chanceries, manned by noblemen from the same families which dominated local life. It is no wonder that Maria Theresa, who succeeded Charles VI in October 1740, was to claim that she had found herself, faced with the aggression launched first by Frederick II, then by the Nymphenburg alliance, 'without money, without credit, without an army ... and finally also without counsel'.[17]

[12] Mensi (1890), 553–4.
[13] Marquis Ignazio del Borgo, quoted by Quazza (1965), 30.
[14] Dickson (1987), ii, 380.
[15] Mensi (1890), 705.
[16] Dickson (1987), ii, 380.
[17] Kallbrunner (1952), 29.

10.2 *The Situation in the Italian Lands before 1740*

The structure of public finance in the Italian states of the late seventeenth century was in part a legacy of the communal period, in part the result of a Renaissance 'state-building' drive which is now seen by historians, no longer obsessed by Italy's failure to develop into a national state, as parallel to, and indeed a forerunner of, similar processes in north-western Europe. One common feature of the financial policies adopted in the fifteenth and sixteenth centuries was the effort to spread a rapidly increasing fiscal burden more widely and in particular to tax landed wealth on a regular basis, though the notion that such levies were to be considered extraordinary rather than ordinary taxes died hard. At the same time public debt expanded at an unprecedented rate and new methods were devised to attract or coerce prospective lenders and to guarantee payment of the interests due to them: these methods ranged from entrusting creditors themselves with the collection of taxes and the management of state funds—as notably in Genoa and Naples—to disguising loans behind the sale of offices which were in fact sinecures, as in the Papal States. The economic decline that set in early in the seventeenth century and the weakening of Spain, the dominant power, put an end to this creative period. The financial systems existing *c.*1700 all reflected, in different ways, a complex balance in which privileged bodies—the nobility, the clergy, the towns—had reasserted their claims as rightful partners of the sovereign power, unless they held this power themselves, as was the case with the Venetian or Genoese patriciates. Cardinal Giambattista de Luca expressed this notion with a striking image when he compared the relationship between prince and state (meaning in fact its 'natural rulers') to that between husband and wife: state revenue was thus the equivalent of a dowry, of which the husband had the use and the administration, but not the full property.[18]

This political and financial stalemate was broken by the European wars of the first half of the eighteenth century, which brought about far-reaching changes in the political map of Italy. Spanish predominance came to an abrupt end in 1706–7, when Milan, Mantua and Naples were conquered by Austrian armies. Piedmont–Savoy, until then an insignificant principality straddling the Alps, acquired a new international weight thanks to the political skill and the military activities of Victor Amadeus II and Charles Emmanuel III; the acquisition of Sicily, exchanged in 1720 for Sardinia, gave them royal status, while their shifting alliances, now with Austria, now with France and Spain, enabled them to annex

[18] De Luca (1680), 13–14. Cf. Capra (1990), 141–6, for a fuller treatment and for bibliographical references.

piece by piece a substantial part of Lombard territory, extending as far as the Ticino river. Finally, the revival of Bourbon power in the 1730s, combined with the extinction of two old princely houses, the Farnese of Parma and the Medici of Florence, led to the advent of new foreign dynasties: Charles of Bourbon, son of Philip V of Spain, became king of Naples in 1734; the grand duchy of Tuscany was transferred in 1737 to Francis Stephen of Lorraine, later to be elected Emperor as the husband of Maria Theresa; while Parma and Piacenza were assigned to another Bourbon *infante* after a short spell under Austria. When the Peace of Aix-la-Chapelle (1748) stabilized the political situation of the peninsula for half a century, only the Papal States and the oligarchic republics (Venice and Genoa) preserved their old forms of government.

South of the Alps, too, the prolonged warfare of the first half of the century meant a sharp increase in the financial needs of the states involved, if not as belligerent powers then as victims of military invasion or of extortionate payments imposed on them by the Imperial Treasury—as was the case with Tuscany and the small principalities in the Po Valley.[19] Increased fiscal pressure was on the whole exercised through traditional channels, though attempts at reform were not lacking in Naples, both under Austria and under Charles of Bourbon, in Milan or in Florence. Piedmont–Savoy was unique, however, in experiencing a radical overhaul of its administrative and financial structures at this stage, and therefore deserves separate treatment.

According to one recent biographer, Geoffrey Symcox, 'Victor Amadeus' reforms ... endowed the Savoyard state with one of the most efficient administrations in Europe, far ahead of the cumbersome structures of the French and Spanish monarchies, or the outmoded institutions of other Italian states'.[20] In fact, as Enrico Stumpo has shown in his important work on finance and the modern state in seventeenth-century Piedmont, the building up of the Piedmontese administrative and financial apparatus was a slower and more gradual business than has usually been thought, and was inextricably tied up with the growth of the army and of military expenses.[21] Even under the personal rule of Victor Amadeus II (1686–1731), there is no doubt that the primary consideration was the raising of money to sustain the deadly struggle waged by this prince to free himself from French tutelage. The 31 per cent increase in ordinary revenue achieved from 1688 to 1700 was partly the result of the introduction of new levies, such as the stamp tax, but to a greater extent it was due to the tightening control of the provinces by the central organs of government. In the brief spell of peace enjoyed by Piedmont between the War of the League of Augsburg and the War

[19] On this aspect: Pugliese (1924). [20] Symcox (1983), 197. [21] Stumpo (1979), *passim*.

of the Spanish Succession, the provincial *direttori* or *referendari* were transformed into fully fledged intendants on the French model and sent into areas which had so far been immune from central interference. In the same years the great land survey was started which was eventually to lead to the *Editto di perequazione* of 1731, essentially a redistribution of the land tax (called *tasso* in Piedmont, *taille* in Savoy) among the communities on the basis of the capital value assigned to their territories. The link between these two initiatives is demonstrated by the fact that the work of measuring and evaluating land piece by piece was entrusted not to the communities themselves, as in the past, but to skilled surveyors appointed by the government and directed by the intendants. Indirect taxes too—the most important of them being the salt *gabelle*—were collected in more efficient and less expensive ways.

A complete restructuring of financial administration was achieved in 1717, when a new officer called *Controllore delle finanze* was appointed with the task of auditing accounts and preparing the yearly budget together with the already existing *Generale delle finanze*, and when the departments underlying an enlarged Council of Finance were regrouped into four *aziende*, one of which was made responsible for all collections and payments, thus replacing all the earlier agencies. Successful steps were taken by Victor Amadeus and his son, Charles Emmanuel III (1731–73), to reduce the burden of public debt, both by paying back short-term loans and cutting down interest on the long-term debt. Since the government's creditors belonged mostly to the privileged classes, this meant easing their stranglehold on the state's finances and reducing their influence over monarchical policy. In this respect, as in others, Victor Amadeus II anticipated the policies of Enlightened monarchs though he himself was far from being a paragon of Enlightenment.[22]

10.3 *The Reign of Maria Theresa to c.1756*

The story of how Maria Theresa, a young and inexperienced female placed at the head of an unwieldy conglomeration of territories at the most critical moment, succeeded in cutting her losses to a minimum and in preserving for Austria the status of a great power has often been told and need not be repeated here. The military costs of the War of the Austrian Succession have been estimated by Dickson to total 185.8 million florins.[23] Most of this expenditure was met by direct taxes on the central lands, whose burden became proportionately heavier

[22] More details on Victor Amadeus II's reforms in Einaudi (1908); Quazza (1957); Symcox (1983); Ricuperati (1990).

[23] Dickson (1987), ii, 119.

as a result of the loss of Silesia, and, secondarily, by subsidies from the Allies, while borrowing was kept down to a comparatively modest scale. This, however, led to near exhaustion towards the end of the war and raised serious doubts as to Austria's ability to repel another attack from Prussia, an event which seemed far from unlikely.

Already in the early war years Maria Theresa had shown her willingness to depart from old ways and institutions, for example by creating a new Court and State Chancery and by abolishing the Finance Conference. In the mid-1740s, she found a man after her heart in Friedrich Wilhelm Haugwitz, a Silesian refugee who had seen Frederick II's administration at work in his native country. Haugwitz's objective was to enable the central lands to maintain a peacetime military establishment of 108,000 troops, not counting the regiments in Italy and the Austrian Netherlands. This would require a contribution of 16.6 million florins, including 2.6 million for debt service, or nearly double the amount that the estates had paid in the last war years. Haugwitz thought this possible on two conditions: that the burden should be more evenly distributed, according to the principle of 'God-pleasing equality', and that the collection and management of taxes should be taken out of the corrupt and inefficient hands of the estates.

This project was carried out in 1748–9 in the teeth of powerful opposition, thanks to the unwavering support of the Empress. The estates were persuaded to vote for, or obliged to accept, contributions at the new higher level for a period of ten years. Financial and administrative responsibilities were entrusted to new territorial institutions called *Representationen und Kammern*, while at the centre a *Directorium in publicis et cameralibus* took over the tasks formerly filled by the *Hofkammer* and by the Austrian and Bohemian Chanceries. At the same time, a revision of existing *cadastres* was undertaken throughout the Austrian and Bohemian provinces. Seigneurial reports were to be verified by royal officers—this was the main purpose of the introduction of 'circle' administrations, or *Kreisämter*, in 1753—and though 'dominical' land was taxed at a lower rate than peasant settlements, tax evasion was made more difficult than before.[24]

The financial effects of this revolution in government were immediately apparent. 'Contributional' revenue jumped from 9.2 million florins in 1747–8 to 16.6 millions in 1749, and total revenue largely exceeded 30 million in the 1750s, an increase of nearly 50 per cent above the level of 1740.[25] State debts, other than

[24] 'Dominical' land was essentially land belonging to nobles or churchmen, as against 'rustical' land, which belonged to peasants and townsmen: Kain and Baigent (1992), 181, 191 [Ed.]. Haugwitz's reforms are discussed by, among others, Beer (1894); Walter (1958); Szabo (1979); Dickson (1987), i, 222–32, 264–72; ii, 7–23.

[25] Dickson (1987), ii, 399 (for the contribution), 380 (for total revenue).

those of the Vienna City Bank, were placed on a sounder basis in the same years by the skilful management of Francis Stephen, in whom Maria Theresa placed complete trust in such matters. The total debt fell from 124 to about 114 million florins in the period 1749–56.[26]

The arrangements of 1748–9 did not concern Hungary (though here, too, there was some increase of the military contribution in the 1750s), the Austrian Netherlands or Italy. Austrian Lombardy, however, offers a striking parallel to events in the central lands in the reforms projected and partly carried out by Gianluca Pallavicini, 'a kind of Italian Haugwitz' as Dickson has called him.[27] First as plenipotentiary and overseer of the Italian army, then as 'Minister of the Finances in Italy' (1749) and finally as Governor (1750–3), he unified financial administration, formerly divided into two magistracies, concentrated the collection of indirect taxes into a general farm on the French model and used the extra revenue and loans thus obtained to endow a public bank, aptly named *Monte di Santa Teresa*, which undertook the servicing and eventual repayment of state debts. But his greatest achievement is undoubtedly the resumption of the *censimento*, or cadastral survey, started under Charles VI in 1718 and which had been interrupted in 1733 as a consequence of the Franco-Piedmontese invasion. The second *Giunta Regia*, headed by the Tuscan Pompeo Neri, completed the laborious task of measuring and evaluating each parcel of land on the basis of its yearly produce, after deduction of the expenses for cultivation. Under the new system that came into force in 1760, all that was needed to apportion the land tax was to calculate it as a percentage of this capital value; this was a significant departure from the old practice of allotting a share of the total burden to each community or body of taxpayers, who were then left more or less free to distribute it among their members. Other direct taxes were maintained alongside the land tax, the most important being a poll tax to be paid by each adult man living in the countryside. But this was now fixed at a uniform and moderate level, so that its incidence was nearly halved on average. Two further aspects of the Lombard *censimento*, which became a model for similar surveys in Italy and elsewhere, deserve mention. First, fiscal reform was linked with administrative reform: communal affairs were henceforth to be run by administrators elected by all landowners, irrespective of birth or social condition, while strict obedience to the rules was enforced by new officials appointed by the government and called *cancellieri del censo*. Secondly, since the capital value of each property was assessed on the basis of what it produced at the time of the survey, every subsequent increase of productivity was practically tax free; this is thought by most students

[26] Ibid. ii, 29. [27] Ibid. ii, 23.

to have given a boost to agricultural improvement in late eighteenth-century Lombardy.[28]

There is some logic in dealing with developments in Tuscany here, since the grand duke of Tuscany, as has been said, was the same Francis Stephen who played an important role in the management of Austrian finances. The new authorities set up by Francis Stephen in 1737, the Regency Council and the Council of Finance, were superimposed on, rather than substituted for, the old tangle of magistracies and jurisdictions going back to the republican past or the early Medici period. In a sense, this was reflected in the arrangement adopted by Francis Stephen's powerful minister, Emmanuel de Richecourt, with regard to indirect taxes: their complicated and heterogeneous structure was not changed, but their collection was entrusted in 1740 to a company of French financiers, or *fermiers généraux*, who paid a fixed yearly sum for the contract. This led on the one hand to an increased revenue for the grand duke, who succeeded in extracting nearly 6.8 million *écus* from his Tuscan subjects in the period 1740–65;[29] on the other hand, it led to a sustained struggle against waste, privilege and fraud. The same effects were to be achieved in Lombardy by the *Ferma generale* created by Pallavicini in 1751. In time, a new structure emerged in the administration which broke almost completely with the traditional dominance of the Florentine patriciate. 'Towards 1759', it has been said, 'the institutional system set up by the Lorrainers included a head, the president of finances (who was none other than Richecourt himself), an administrative agency, the Secretariat, an auditing organ, the *Depositeria*, a jurisdictional court, the Grand ducal Chamber, and a fiscal apparatus, the *Ferma generale*.'[30] Nothing was done in Tuscany, on the other hand, to repay the huge state debt—though the rate of interest was reduced to 3 per cent—or to reform the outdated and faulty methods of assessing and collecting the land tax, until Peter Leopold succeeded Francis Stephen in 1765.

10.4 *The Impact of Cameralist Ideas and the Reforms of Kaunitz and Joseph II*

Before we proceed, brief mention at least must be made of the considerable change in concepts of public finance brought about by the Enlightenment in Austria and Italy in the third quarter of the eighteenth century. The Imperial

[28] On all this: Capra in Sella and Capra (1984), 310–28, 343–50; also Zaninelli (1963); Klang (1977); Cova (1982); Mozzarelli (1982).

[29] Waquet (1990), 563.

[30] Ibid. 567. On Tuscan finances under the Regency, see also Büchi (1915), 93–125; Dal Pane (1965), 43–72; Diaz (1987), 59–73.

Cameralist tradition that went back to Becher, Hörnigk and Schröder (whose *Furstliche Schatz- und Rentkammer* was instrumental in shaping Haugwitz's views: Chapter 6.4) was obsessed by the problem of increasing state revenues; economic expansion, to be achieved on a broadly autarchic basis, was regarded essentially as a means of increasing the taxable capacity of society. The concern for fiscal justice and for the well-being of subjects was more pronounced in such Italian works as the *Trattato de' tributi* by the Neapolitan Carlo Antonio Broggia (1743) or *Della pubblica felicità* by Lodovico Muratori (1749), whose thought was influential in the rise of Josephinism and who recommended that the prince 'be contented with the wool of his sheep, without stripping them of their skin'.[31] The real change, however, came with the spread of Physiocratic and utilitarian ideas, which decisively removed public finance from the sphere of politics into that of economics. It was no longer the prince's conscience or his wish for aggrandizement that must dictate fiscal policies, but the knowledge of 'natural laws' governing the production and exchange of goods. Economic development and the well-being of society became a goal in itself, and the state's financial needs took second place. In Austria these views found in Joseph von Sonnenfels their most articulate and influential spokesman (Chapter 6.4). After 1763, he taught Cameral science at the University of Vienna and his *Principles of Police* (1765–8) was used as a textbook in Austrian universities down to the middle of the nineteenth century and thus had a formative influence on several generations of Austrian state servants. 'The collection of revenue', wrote Sonnenfels, 'is in the sequence of things subordinated to the common well-being, because it is only a means to an end: all financial operations which upset this order and turn revenue into an end are harmful.'[32] The same note was sounded by a host of Italian writers, such as Pietro Verri and Cesare Beccaria in Milan or the so-called 'Physiocratic party' in Tuscany. One of the clearest expressions of the idea is to be found in Giuseppe Palmieri's *Riflessioni sulla pubblica felicità relativamente al regno di Napoli* (1790):

> The part concerning finances ... is so dependent on public economy, that it cannot have true principles or exact rules except those dictated and prescribed by the economic science; for if the public revenue is part of the income and wealth of the nation, it obviously follows that the principles governing the part must be analogous to those governing the whole.[33]

The 'spiritual kinship' (*Geistesverwandschaft*)[34] between Sonnenfels and the chief exponent of the Enlightenment in the Austrian government, Chancellor

[31] Muratori, ed. Falco and Forti (1964), ii, 1508.
[32] Sonnenfels (1971), ii, 209.
[33] Palmieri (1790), 3–4.
[34] Osterloh (1970), 37.

Wenzel Anton von Kaunitz-Rittberg, has often been noted. Commenting on Haugwitz's narrow fiscalism, Kaunitz wrote in 1757:

> It does not require much reflection or any profound insight to invent all kinds of ways and means of squeezing money out of our subjects. He who wishes to do so in a manner both reasonable and beneficial to the monarch and the state, however, must first, or at least at the same time, devote an equal measure of zeal to increasing the subjects' wealth so that they might bear this additional burden.[35]

As the Seven Years' War drew on, it became more and more obvious that the Austrian monarchy's administrative and financial machinery was unable to sustain the effort required. This induced Kaunitz to press for changes in government, which were carried out in 1760–1: the *Directorium in publicis et cameralibus* was abolished; financial matters were once more transferred to the *Hofkammer*, while political responsibility rested with a new joint Bohemian and Austrian Chancery, and auditing with a newly created chamber of accounts (*Hofrechenkammer*). Co-ordination among these and the other *Hofstellen*, or central organs of government, was to be ensured by a Council of State where the dominant influence was that of Kaunitz himself. This arrangement was to last until 1782, when Joseph II decided once more to unite financial and administrative responsibilities in a departmentalized central body called the *Vereinigte Hofstellen*.[36] On the other hand, growing dissatisfaction with the various fiscal expedients adopted to meet the huge costs of the war induced Kaunitz to support the plans put forward by his protégé Ludwig von Zinzendorf, whose central idea, largely based on the English model, was the mobilization of public credit through the creation of a new state bank and the issue of bearer-bonds to be circulated like paper money. Zinzendorf's plans, which met with powerful opposition from Hatzfeld, the president of the new enlarged *Hofkammer*, were to find only partial realization in the issue of the so-called *Banco-Zettel* later in Maria Theresa's reign. Meanwhile, an unexpected way had been found to lighten the overwhelming burden of public debt, which had soared to 284 million florins at the end of the Seven Years' War. Joseph II, who became Emperor in 1765 on the death of Francis Stephen, decided to place at the disposal of the state the immense wealth he had inherited from his father, amounting to some 32 million florins. A repayment fund was built up from this legacy, which enabled the government to present creditors with the alternative of either receiving back their capital or having the rate of interest reduced to a uniform 4 per cent. The operation was a complete success, since most creditors accepted the second option and the yearly drain on

[35] Quoted by Szabo (1979), 124.

[36] See the studies cited in n. 24 above, esp. Szabo (1979); Dickson (1987), i, 233–56.

the Treasury was thus reduced by some 3 million florins.[37] Kaunitz's and Zinzendorf's idea of free trade and economic development as the basis of sound public finance, however, gradually won acceptance in government circles, so that by the mid-1770s it became possible to abolish all internal customs duties and to start dismantling the guild system and the traditional controls on the buying and selling of cereals. This fostered the expansion of trade and consumption, which in turn helped raise the cameral revenue; better management, the maintenance in peacetime of the taxes introduced during the Seven Years' War and a more systematic recourse to tax-farming all worked in the same direction.

The growth in the yield of indirect taxation was thus mainly responsible for the 42.6 per cent rise in overall revenue between 1763 and 1778, as shown in Figure 33.[38] The share of indirect taxation, including the income from mines and coinage, rose from 26.8 per cent in 1749 to 44.4 per cent in 1778, though the trend was temporarily reversed in 1769–72. Direct taxation, in contrast, was responsible for three-fifths of the total amount in 1749, but for little more than two-fifths in 1778. Revenue from domains never exceeded 5 per cent, except in 1770, while the growth of 'other' incomes in the 1770s is explained by the inclusion in this item of Belgian and Italian subsidies. The constant surplus of revenue over expenditure after 1767, which appears from the comparison of Figures 33 and 34,[39] however, does not take account of the incidence of extraordinary expenditure, which in the years of the war scare about the first Polish partition alone (1769 to mid-1773) totalled over 18 million florins[40] and soared to new heights during the War of the Bavarian Succession (1778–9). A breakdown of expenditure, on the other hand, confirms the traditional pattern of military expenditure swallowing up about half the total, with debt servicing (interest plus repayment) taking second place at between a quarter and a third of the total (Figure 34).

For Joseph II's reign three separate statistical series exist, which do not agree with each another and present a difficult problem of interpretation.[41] Czoernig's 'official' series, which is given here in Figure 35,[42] does not allow for easy comparisons with data from Maria Theresa's reign. The striking growth in overall revenue is chiefly due to the inclusion of income from the Italian lands and the Austrian Netherlands, which totalled about 13 million florins in the mid-1780s.[43] Deflated against rising prices, however, the increase in revenue is much less significant: 'If ordinary state revenue under Joseph II nominally rose by

[37] Dickson (1987), ii, 52–7; Beales (1987), 161–4.
[38] Dickson (1987), ii, 380; ESFDB \austria\ausb006 based on \ausd003.
[39] Dickson (1987), ii, 385–6; ESFDB \austria\ausb007 based on \ausd004.
[40] Dickson (1987), ii, 105.
[41] Otruba (1985), 211–15; Czoernig (1864).
[42] Otruba (1985), 243; ESFDB \austria\ausb016 based on \ausd005 and \ausd006.
[43] Dickson (1987), ii, 113.

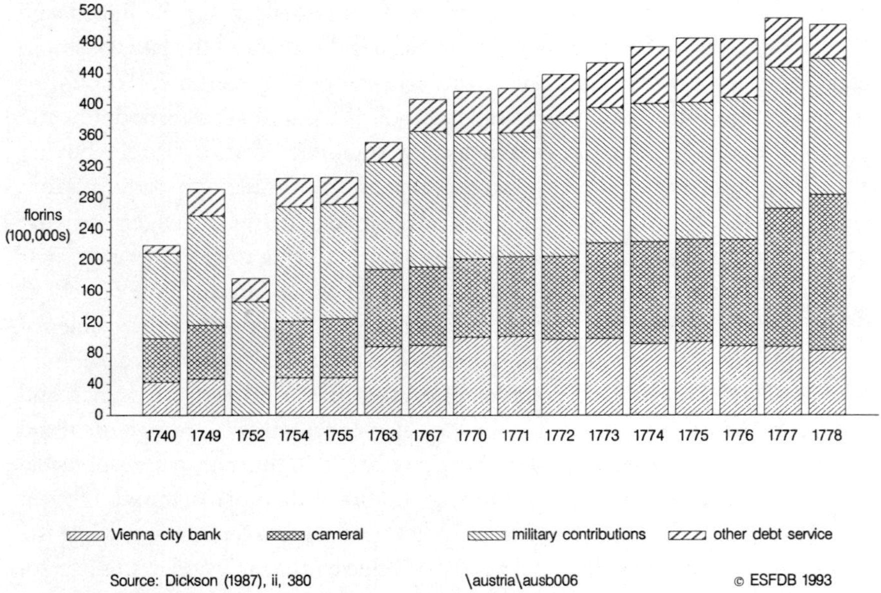

FIG. 33. Categories of ordinary net revenue of the Austrian monarchy, 1740–1778 (in florins)

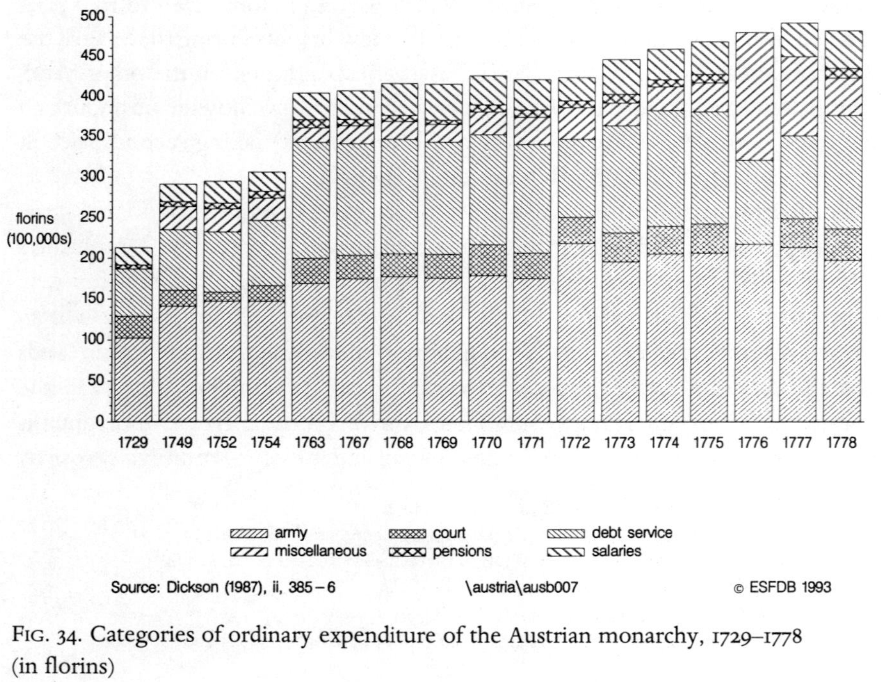

FIG. 34. Categories of ordinary expenditure of the Austrian monarchy, 1729–1778 (in florins)

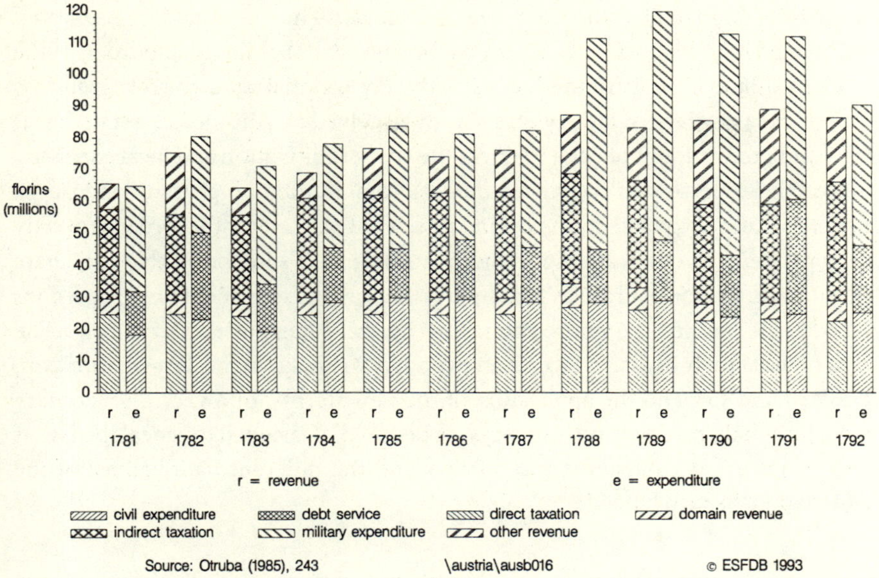

FIG. 35. Categories of net revenue and expenditure of the Austrian monarchy, 1781–1792 (in florins)

14.8 per cent, compared with a rate of inflation of 9.5 per cent, this means a real growth of only 5.3 per cent'.[44] On the expenditure side, the effects of the unpopular Turkish war of 1788–90 are clearly visible in Figure 35, as is, on the revenue side, the further fall of the share of direct taxation from an average of 35 per cent in 1781–6 to an average of 28.2 per cent in 1788–92.

It was partly to counter this tendency towards a relative decline of the contribution in the composition of revenue that Joseph II launched his great project for a land tax and agrarian reform, which, had it succeeded, would have undermined feudal relations in the Habsburg monarchy more than a half century in advance of the actual changes in the nineteenth century. A start was made in 1783 when the order went out to carry out a new cadastral survey in the Austro-Bohemian lands and in Hungary, in order to remedy the notorious shortcomings of Maria Theresa's land register and to introduce complete uniformity in taxation. There was vehement opposition to this project not only among the nobility, but in the ranks of the higher bureaucracy as well. All political and technical difficulties were overcome, however, as a result of the iron determination of the Emperor and the support given to him by some enthusiastic reformers and by the peasants, who took an active part in the heavy work of

[44] Otruba (1985), 219.

measuring land and estimating average yields. The new land register was completed in four years (1784–8): it was then decided that the total burden of the land tax should be redistributed on a strictly proportional basis; the relatively low rate of 12.22 per cent of gross yields was thus arrived at. Another 20 per cent was the estimated amount needed to cover the cost of cultivation and local expenses. Since the Emperor was convinced that the total burden on peasant land ought never to exceed 50 per cent of gross income, what was left for the lord was exactly 17.77 per cent. Even more important, it was Joseph II's intention that this share should in future be paid in cash and not in the form of services. These provisions were made law for the entire monarchy by the Patent of February 1789. The outcry was such as to induce the sovereign to make some last-minute concessions and suspend the application of the new norms for a year. By February 1790, Joseph II was dead and his successor Leopold II hastened to repeal the law as part of his effort to appease the nobility and the different nationalities of the Austrian Habsburg lands.[45]

10.5 *The Financial Position in the Italian Lands on the Eve of the Revolution*

In Italy, too, land registers remained one of the favourite means of redistributing the fiscal burden. The example of Piedmont and Lombardy was followed with various success by other states of the peninsula. In the republic of Venice local *estimi*, or *cadastres*, were revised according to uniform principles as early as 1740. In the kingdom of Naples the so-called *catasti onciari* (thus named after the *oncia*, the money of account in which rateable values were expressed) were drawn up for most communities in the central decades of the century, but the lack of precise measurements and the maintenance of feudal privileges largely frustrated the hopes of reformers. The main result was the partial abolition of the tax immunity for church lands, on the basis of a Concordat negotiated with the Papacy in 1741. The surveys carried out in the Papal States and in the duchy of Modena in the 1780s and 1790s were technically much more advanced, but they did not come into force until the beginning of the nineteenth century. Elsewhere the attempt failed, either because of the resistance of the privileged classes, as in Sicily or at Bologna (whose territory belonged to the Pope but was administered separately from the other provinces) or as a consequence of divergent views among state officials, as in the case of Tuscany to which we will return.[46]

[45] The most detailed account is Rozdolski (1961); but there is a good summary in Wangermann (1973), 92–4.

[46] For an informed survey and for bibliographical references: Zangheri (1979).

Indirect taxes included, in most places, state monopolies of salt, tobacco and saltpetre, excises on various items of consumption, such as wine, meat, flour and hides, duties on imports, exports and transfers from one province to another and tolls at city gates. Only part of the revenue from these levies went to the state; many of them were collected by the towns, by feudal lords, by collective bodies or by individual families who at some time in the past had purchased, or been granted, such rights. To bring order and rationality into the chaotic system of indirect taxation meant in the first place to reassert state control over these alienated revenues, called *arrendamenti* in Naples, *regalie* in Milan. In the kingdom of Naples a *Giunta delle ricompre* was created by Charles of Bourbon in 1751; but the right of the state to redeem alienated incomes had to be established before hostile tribunals and, even when this was done, the *Giunta* preferred in most cases to agree with the *arrendatari* on the payment of a lump sum and leave them in possession of their incomes. In 1783, alienated revenue still amounted to 3.2 million ducats, compared to ordinary state revenue of just under 4.9 million.[47] In Lombardy, by contrast, the Austrian government made good the decision taken in 1766 to buy back all the *regalie*, irrespective of the clauses under which they had been sold. The actual work of redemption took about twenty years and cost over 30 million lire. The benefit for the Treasury was evident, since these duties often yielded annually as much as 10 or 15 per cent of the amount spent on their repurchase.[48]

Another precondition of reform was the change from tax-farming to direct state administration. General farms, such as those established by the duke of Savoy as early as 1698, by the grand duke of Tuscany in 1741, by Gianluca Pallavicini for Milan in 1751, had the advantage of ensuring a higher revenue for the state while cutting through the intricate web of traditional privileges and exemptions. Once this was done, reforming governments were able to take over the collection of taxes and restructure them to the advantage of the national economy. This was the case notably in Milan and Florence, where contracts with general farmers were rescinded in 1768 and 1770 respectively. It then became possible to abolish a number of unpopular duties and above all to eliminate internal custom barriers: this unification of the home market was achieved after long preparation in Tuscany in 1781 and in Lombardy in 1787.[49] Less sweeping, but similar in intent, were the reforms carried out in the Papal States in 1786 and in the republic of Venice in 1794.[50] The system of controls and duties concerning

[47] Bianchini (1834–5), iii, 175. For general information and bibliography on the kingdom of Naples: Rao (1983).

[48] Capra in Sella and Capra (1984), 451–5.

[49] Ibid. 455–7; Becagli (1983).

[50] Caracciolo in Caravale and Caracciolo (1978), 503–4; Scarabello in Cozzi, Knapton and Scarabello (1992), 606.

the buying and selling of cereals and other victuals formed a special case. Peter Leopold was the first sovereign in Europe to abolish completely all restrictions on the import and export of corn, according to Physiocratic doctrines which found enthusiastic support in the upper reaches of the Tuscan bureaucracy in the 1760s and 1770s.[51]

Public debt weighed heavily on the finances of most Italian states, the main exception being Piedmont. The efforts of governments to consolidate floating debts, to reimburse creditors and to reduce the burden of debt servicing were helped by the general trend towards lower rates of interest, which by the second half of the century were everywhere at or near 3 per cent. The solutions adopted ranged from partial bankruptcies, as in Venice, to the creation of new public *Monti* where the old bonds could be transferred at lower rates. In Tuscany alone, however, there was a determined attempt to eliminate the debt completely; this followed a suggestion from Francesco Maria Gianni, Peter Leopold's closest counsellor in the 1780s, intended to counter the influence of the Physiocratic party, which advocated an *impôt unique* based on a new cadastral survey. Gianni observed that the existing inequities in the distribution of the land tax could be remedied simply by suppressing the tax itself. Since the yearly revenue from it was roughly equivalent to the amount of interest paid to state creditors, he hit upon the idea of extinguishing both at the same stroke. According to his project, creditors were to give up the bonds they held in exchange for the cancellation of the direct taxes they paid; those who owned no bonds, or had insufficient, were encouraged to buy them at reduced rates from church organizations, charities and other bodies, to which the bulk of them belonged. Gianni's bold plan was put into effect and, by 1790, when Peter Leopold had to leave Florence to take up his brother's inheritance in Vienna, two-thirds of the Tuscan debt had already been cancelled in this way.[52] Of course, this programme could only succeed if no direct taxation was established in any other form and if no new debts were contracted for in the grand duchy. Neither of these two conditions could be met by Peter Leopold's successors in the difficult circumstances of the 1790s.

Gianni's plan for the cancellation of state debt can be regarded as a notable exception to the eighteenth-century tendency towards an increase in state expenditure and state intervention. Tuscany, in fact, was one of the few European states where the fiscal burden decreased in absolute terms during this period of rising prices, from almost 11 million lire in 1758 to about 9 million in 1789.[53] In this respect, the Lombard experience under Maria Theresa and Joseph II was very different: here the total state revenue grew from 14 million lire in 1761

[51] Mirri (1972, 1980).

[52] Büchi (1915), 347–8; Dal Pane (1965), 139–47; Diaz (1966), 224–38.

[53] Dal Pane (1965), 64–5; *Governo della Toscana* (1791), 54–5.

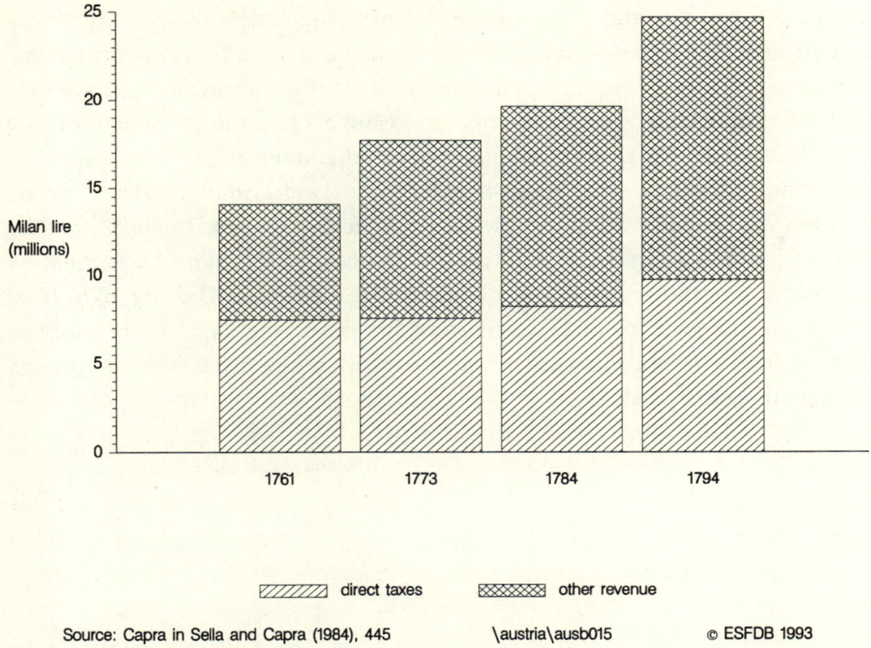

FIG. 36. Revenue of the state of Milan, 1761–1794 (in Milan *lire*)

to 24.7 million lire in 1794. As can be seen from Figure 36,[54] this rise was essentially due to the rapid rise in the income from indirect taxation, which represented 46.9 per cent of total revenue in 1761, but 60.5 per cent of total revenue in 1794. It should be emphasized, however, that this increase derived essentially from the reforms already mentioned (the redemption of alienated taxes and the substitution of direct administration for tax-farming) and from the natural expansion of trade and consumption, and did not therefore represent a heavier burden for individual taxpayers.

Around 1790 the average per capita burden was almost 20 lire in Milan, about 9 lire in Tuscany. Among other states, only Piedmont compared in this respect with Lombardy, whereas the corresponding rates were 9 lire for the republic of Venice, and 4 lire each for the Papal States and the kingdom of Naples.[55] These figures, however, only refer to state revenue: the significance of this becomes clear when it is noted that for each ducat that went into the state coffers, Neapolitan subjects paid 3 ducats to feudal lords, to the church, to local

[54] Capra in Sella and Capra (1984), 445; ESFDB \austria\ausb015 based on \ausd009.

[55] All figures are expressed in lire of Milan. The exchange rate with the Austrian florin was approximately 1 florin = 3.5 lire.

communities and to the *arrendatari*: in Milan at the end of the century, these groups took about 90 per cent of all the money extracted from the tax-paying population.[56] An analysis of expenditure in the various Italian states cannot be undertaken here, not only for reasons of space but because the data in many cases are not available. There is no doubt, however, that military expenses took up a much larger share of state budgets in Piedmont and Lombardy than, say, in Tuscany or in the Papal States, which had practically no army. But it is true that heavier taxation also meant, in Piedmont and Lombardy, more investment in administrative improvement, in public works, education and the like. It is perhaps no coincidence that Austrian Lombardy and the kingdom of Sardinia were destined to take the lead in industrialization and economic progress in nineteenth-century Italy.

[56] Bianchini (1834–5), iii, 170; Capra in Sella and Capra (1984), 448.

CHAPTER 11

The Eighteenth Century. II. The Struggle for Great Power Status and the End of the Old Fiscal Regime

Richard Bonney

Mercantilist and Cameralist ideas had made a lasting impression on European rulers by the eighteenth century. 'A financial system', wrote Frederick the Great in his memoirs, 'handed over by father to son and constantly improved, can change a government's position. From being originally poor it can make a government so rich that it can throw its grain into the scales of the balance between the great European powers.'[1] Rulers recognized that there was an intimate connection between economic growth, the prosperity of the inhabitants of their lands, and the growth in their fiscal and military power. Joseph II claimed that he was 'no more attached to the military than to finance'; had he been able to reduce the size of his army and make his subjects labourers he would have done so; but his responsibility was to 'combine the necessary security with the country's welfare'. On another occasion, he denounced rulers preoccupied with 'insignificant conquests' and 'futile advantages' while they diminished the true capital of the state and weakened its resources for years into the future.[2] Similar concerns were expressed by rulers of quite small states. Thus of the Landgrave Frederick II of Hesse it was said that he ruled his land well, loved his subjects and was loved by them; but also that his 'strongest passion' was the military, which was 'rooted in his love of money and profit'—though Hesse was exceptional because it had cornered the market in the German 'soldier trade'.[3]

Yet if rulers were better advised than ever before, and knew in principle what they wanted to do in terms of the management of their states, it does not follow that they necessarily made wise decisions. Prussian models were followed, in certain respects, by Austria and even Hesse; but the Prussian *régie*, itself modelled

[1] Hubatsch (1975), 147. The author is grateful to Professors François Crouzet, William Doyle and Patrick O'Brien, and Dr Hamish Scott for commenting on the draft of this chapter.

[2] Beales (1991), 16.

[3] Ingrao (1987), 87, 129.

on the French *ferme générale*, proved in the longer term to be faulty and some of the experimentation had to be abandoned even in Prussia itself.[4] The extent to which Physiocratic and Cameralist advisers were really able to evaluate the potential fiscal yield of states remains open to question. Here the most telling evidence comes from the abortive negotiations for the transfer of Bavaria to Joseph II in exchange for the Austrian Netherlands. It is true that this was always a difficult project to bring to fruition because of the risk of war with Prussia that it entailed, and the covert opposition of France. But in 1784–5, shortly before the death of Frederick II of Prussia, there was a real chance of bringing about a coup of profound territorial advantage, which would have brought significant administrative change in its wake, as Joseph himself recognized.[5] But Kaunitz, Joseph II's principal adviser, proved himself to be incapable of realizing the monarchy's true interests. Five of the six questions with which Joseph II concerned himself about the transfer related to finance, and the answer on each was negative. The Emperor would lose 400,000 men in terms of taxable population as a result of the transfer, and the Bavarian army was a mere 4,000 men; above all, there would be a loss of 4 million *talers* in revenue when a loss of only a million could be sustained. The Austrian advisers assumed that the revenues of the Austrian Netherlands were greater than those of the electorate, and that the gap would grow if the River Scheldt was reopened and Belgian commerce revived as a result. In fact, they did not perform satisfactorily the tasks of elementary addition, since according to their own figures the Bavarian revenues should have reached 6.25 million *talers*, much closer to the figure for the Austrian Netherlands than the assumed figure for the annual revenue of Bavaria of 4 million. The actual figures showed that Bavarian revenues were higher than those of the Austrian Netherlands (8 million as against 7.6 million), while under a more competent administration than that of Elector Karl Theodor they might have increased by perhaps a third. The potential revenue to be gained from Bavaria was perhaps not as great as from the Austrian Netherlands, which was also a source of loans, but, by 1787, Joseph II was openly regretting that an exchange had not taken place because the Habsburg 'core' lands would have been consolidated.[6]

A narrow preoccupation with fiscal issues, as against broader strategic and economic concerns, could thus be self-defeating. As a general rule, rulers in the eighteenth century could have expected their revenues to grow, particularly indirect taxes, as a consequence of economic development and, above all,

[4] For Prussia: Henderson (1963), 64–5, 164–5; a more positive verdict in Johnson (1975), 270–1, 278. For Hesse: Ingrao (1967), 90–1, 202.

[5] Bernard (1965), 160; Beales (1991), 17.

[6] Bernard (1965), 53, 153, 158–60, 172–3, 188, 205, 207, 217; Blanning (1983), 67, 69.

population growth. In both his *Anti-Machiavel* of 1739 and his *Testament* of 1768, Frederick the Great proclaimed the maxim that 'the real strength of a state consists in the number of its subjects'. He contrasted the vast emptiness of Russian Siberia unfavourably with small, but densely populated Holland, both from the point of view of revenues and military strength. Substantial sums were spent by the Prussian state in trying to entice immigrants, and by the 1780s some quarter of a million out of a population total of 4.75 million, or one in twenty of the population, were immigrants.[7] Other states, notably Austria and Russia, imitated the Prussian example with programmes of colonization, and it was not until the 1770s that the first real doubts were expressed as to the wisdom of encouraging immigration because of the inherent tendency of the population to rise. The image of a populous and prosperous Dutch Republic was displaced by Malthus in 1798 with that of a populous but impoverished China; but already in 1767 Sir James Steuart warned of a population which grew past subsistence, to be halted only by starvation, while Necker warned in 1775 of 'many privations' resulting from excessive population growth.[8] Such ideas were new and a minority opinion until the end of the century. Whether or not we accept the argument that between 1320 and 1720 there was little or no sustained growth in the size of the European population[9] (an argument which belies the evidence of England and Sweden to take two clear examples), after 1720 there was a real growth in population virtually everywhere. The population of the Austrian lands increased from 12.7 to 20.7 million between 1740 and 1787.[10] The population of France, which had been 19 or 20 million in 1715, rose to 29 million by 1789 and then remained stable at around 30 million in the Napoleonic period.[11] The notoriously small British population showed the most rapid rate of increase of all, rising by 46 per cent between the Glorious Revolution and the end of the War of American Independence, and reaching 10 or 12 million by 1815, 15 or 17 million if the population of Ireland is included.[12] Governments became much more concerned to count their populations than ever before; the age of the 'protocensus' (and not merely for fiscal purposes) had arrived, although a true census in the modern

[7] Hubatsch (1975), 110; slightly higher figures in Riley (1985), 76.

[8] Steuart, ed. Skinner (1966), i, 85: '... it is miserable and abusive procreation which starves so many.' Riley (1985), 137–8. In fact, the Dutch population would have declined sharply without immigration: van Zanden (1993), 24.

[9] Le Roy Ladurie (1981), 10–13.

[10] Dickson (1987), i, 36.

[11] Dupâquier (1988), ii, 60–5 and iii, 67–70, 123.

[12] Hall (1992), 1 and refs; ibid. 23 n. 2, quoting a report to Parliament which was higher than the estimate in Wrigley and Schofield (1981), 534; Wrigley in Stone (1994), 78–81.

sense was a nineteenth-century development.[13] Population pressure on food resources also became a serious political concern and the issue of grain 'liberalization', that is to say, the removal of traditional restrictions in the 'police' or administration of the grain trade became a significant factor in politics by mid-century,[14] as also the establishment of grain stores or magazines for times of war or scarcity.[15] The legitimate price of grain was a potentially critical issue, since it posed the question of government intervention in the market: this came to the fore most dramatically in the period of the 'maximum price' (*le maximum*) during the French Revolution.[16]

The state's revenue base might have proved sufficient for its needs with increased prosperity and a growth in population. Yet this failed to happen because of the rigidity of the fiscal systems of most European states; the structure of privilege and exemptions; the doubtful legitimacy of increased taxation; and the increased competition between states for great power status. Though crude 'population–army' ratios are of limited value (we need also to consider fluctuations in army size, variations in the numbers of foreigners serving in national armies, and so on),[17] it is clear that some states were much more heavily militarized than others[18] and that this might have a significant effect on their capacity for economic development and on the fiscal burden of their inhabitants. By 1786, Prussia was the thirteenth largest state in Europe in terms of its population, but the fourth (or perhaps the third) in terms of the size of its army.[19] However, even Frederick the Great had begun to recognize in his later years that the size of this military establishment was a drain on the economy and that it was more valuable for a state to have taxpayers and producers of goods than soldiers.[20] Hesse had an army size that was even larger in relation to its population than had Prussia. Since the British needed to recruit Hessian mercenaries, this had the effect of subsidizing the Hessian taxpayer, whose per capita fiscal burden was half that of his Prussian counterpart. Indeed, the Hessian per capita fiscal burden was one of the lowest in the Holy Roman Empire and actually fell during the eighteenth century.[21] The organizational capacity of states was therefore critical to their success or otherwise, and to the prosperity of their inhabitants. The reforms in Piedmont–Savoy made that state much more

[13] Dupâquier (1988), ii, 27–43; Perrot (1977), 8–21; Perrot and Woolf (1984), 19, 165; Dickson (1987), i, 25–7.

[14] Kaplan (1976); Miller (1992); Liebel-Weckowicz (1974), 70–1.

[15] For Prussia: Speier (1936), 309; Hubatsch (1975), 60–1; Johnson (1975), 162–3.

[16] Margairaz in *État, finances et économie* (1991), 399–427; Crouzet (1993), 260–4.

[17] Brewer (1989), 42.

[18] Jones (1988*a*), 29, 318–19.

[19] Hubatsch (1975), 137; Blanning in Scott (1990), 270.

[20] Craig (1955), 22.

[21] Ingrao (1987), 127, 132.

formidable than its size and population alone might have seemed to warrant (Chapter 10.2).[22]

11.1 *The Fiscal Outcome of Louis XIV's Later Wars*

By the end of the seventeenth century, as has already been seen (Chapter 6.3), the age of 'political arithmetic' had arrived. Commentators sought to advise their rulers on the relative virtues of one financial system against another and to compare the relative size of state revenues and debts. 'Happy are those kingdoms which abound in statesmen so qualified', wrote Charles Davenant shortly after the Peace of Ryswick (1697). He concluded that the French debt was much higher than had been imagined (he placed the debts of England at £17.5 million, those of Holland at £25 million and those of France at £100 million).[23] Davenant's figures are open to criticism but are important in that they remind us that the growth of the public debt was the supreme test of modernity in a state: debt management had already been of critical importance to belligerent states before 1698; it became one of the central issues in the long wars of the eighteenth century (Chapter 14).[24] The other concern of states was how to balance the outflow of expenditure on goods, services and payments to finance foreign warfare against the inflow of the same items. Without a balance of payments surplus, there would be a devastating effect on the exchange rate: 'if we have not effects to pay our army, the foreigners will have our silver to be sure, for the exchange is governed by the balance of trade'.[25] The states of Continental Europe had the advantage that their foreign wars were usually fairly close to hand. In the case of Austria, Prussia and Russia, they could supply their armies directly;[26] France and the United Provinces did not always practise direct supply, but much of the demand generated by the army resulted in spending taking place partially or wholly at home.[27] Even so, a net outflow of bullion from France was the norm during a foreign war in the eighteenth century, since France was not invaded between 1710 and 1792 and her armies operated in Germany, northern Italy, the Low Countries and north America.[28] After the Glorious Revolution, England's capacity to discharge war remittances depended almost entirely on the net earnings of foreign trade, an enormously risky policy since in the seventeenth century her trade usually fell in periods of war; moreover, foreign trade was

22 Symcox (1983), 118–33, 190–225.
23 Davenant, ed. Whitworth (1967), i, 250.
24 Dickson and Sperling in Bromley (1971), 286–94, 297–8, 300–2, 308–13.
25 Jones (1988*a*), 161.
26 Ibid. 35.
27 Ibid. 42–3.
28 Riley (1986), 84–5.

subject to losses to privateers, and it required a convoy system which might militate against the competing demands of the navy.[29]

The eighteenth century began and ended in the same manner, with European warfare which had as its basis the future of economic, as well as political, power, on a world scale. This was the essence of the struggle between England (or Britain after the Act of Union with Scotland in 1707) and France between 1689 and 1815, which has been called a 'second Hundred Years' War'.[30] France was viewed in England after the Glorious Revolution, and still more after the Hanoverian succession, as the realm's 'natural and necessary enemy'.[31] Yet the conflict was, of course, not between two states but five, with Austria usually on the British side and Spain in the French camp: with the possible exception only of Spain, the United Provinces was the first European state to succeed in mobilizing simultaneously a powerful army and navy;[32] and it remained the most powerful state in terms of its world economic position at least until 1740, notwithstanding the fact that the Treaty of Utrecht was a significant political defeat for the Netherlands and marked an important first step in Britain's supplanting of the Dutch as the dominant commercial power.[33] The Nine Years' War (1689–97; it was a Ten Years' War for France, beginning in late 1688) had witnessed the most systematic economic warfare ever attempted. England and the Dutch Republic, acting in a unique union in the lifetime of William III, were able to put pressure on their allies, Spain and Austria, to join the blockade of France. Such unity in economic warfare was not to be seen again until Napoleon's Continental Blockade, which was very different in nature.

The War of the Spanish Succession, in contrast, though necessary from the Dutch point of view for economic reasons, had seen only a partial ban on trade with France and the Southern Netherlands and no ban at all on commerce with Spain and Spanish America. Revived Dutch trade hegemony in the Southern Netherlands after 1706 had proved unpopular in Britain and significantly contributed to the growth of Anglo-Dutch tension in the later stages of the war. When the Dutch foolishly rebuffed the French peace overtures in 1709–10, it was left to the Tory government in Britain to reap the economic advantages of a separate

29 Jones (1988*a*), 41, 50, 60, 64–5, 166–8; Fayle (1923).

30 A term first used by Meyer and Bromley in Bédarida, Crouzet and Johnson (1979), 155–190, the best account of the naval aspects of the conflict. Also Meyer and Bromley in Bédarida, Crouzet and Johnson (1980), 139–72. Wallerstein (1980), 245, also used the term, but to describe the period 1689 to 1763 (*sic*). Wallerstein (1980), 256, noted the years of Anglo-French peace between 1713 and 1739. Cf. Crouzet (1985), 71, 316; Crouzet (1990), 78, 339.

31 O'Brien (1991), 14; Black (1985).

32 't Hart (1993).

33 Israel (1989), 375, 399.

peace with Louis XIV.[34] The exploitation of the possibilities of the *asiento* contract—the right of privileged access to the Spanish colonial possessions—never proved easy for Britain, however, and war between Britain and Spain resulted in 1739–48. The commercial treaty between the two countries in 1750 revoked the *asiento*.[35] Yet it was not a diplomatic victory in 1713 which secured British commercial primacy in the eighteenth century. Instead this primacy arose from the outcome of the last two wars of Louis XIV. During the War of the League of Augsburg, English trade almost collapsed, and the mechanism of payments was kept going only by coin clipping; even this could not prevent a serious fall in the exchange rate in 1695–6.[36] It was England's good fortune that, because of the impending crisis over the Spanish succession, France sued for peace at a time when it would have been very difficult to have continued the war. In contrast, the War of the Spanish Succession saw a strong British export-led growth, in part resulting from the demand for cloth in the swollen armed forces of northern Europe (Russia was an important market, although by regulation the Austrian and Swedish armies were clothed by domestic output) and the temporary eclipse of commercial rivals during the war as a result of direct military action or the imposition of high excises. The Great Northern War disrupted the Baltic grain trade and thus opened new markets for British grain exports.

Above all, the War of the Spanish Succession gave Britain a secure place in the two markets which really mattered because of their growth in the eighteenth century, and where Britain's future had been under threat in 1700: Portugal and Spain. Furthermore, Britain gained access to their colonial markets. Sales to Portugal and Spain, and their colonial empires, contributed on average half, and sometimes as much as two-thirds, of the total growth in British exports in the first four decades of the eighteenth century.[37] The exploitation of Britain's 'oldest alliance' with Portugal was critical to this success. In the seventeenth century, Portugal under the regime of the count of Ericeira (d. 1690), 'the Portuguese Colbert',[38] had tried to pursue Mercantilist policies aimed at excluding other countries from their colonial commerce. This protectionist policy was eroded by the growth of the Luso-Atlantic economy, and the rise in Brazilian gold exports in particular.[39] Favourable Anglo-Portuguese trading relations had been secured by Cromwell in 1654; but the Methuen Treaty of 1703 effectively gave England the status of most favoured trading partner and ensured that Brazilian gold would reach Britain via Portugal.[40] The Methuen Treaty provided a new source of

[34] Ibid. 342–3, 361, 364, 372, 374.
[35] Walker (1979), 210.
[36] Jones (1988*a*), 236.
[37] Ibid. 312–17.
[38] Hanson (1981), 161.
[39] Ibid. 187; Arruda in Tracy (1991), 385–9; Morineau (1985), 135–7; Sideri (1970), 65.
[40] Magalhães Godinho in Bromley (1971), 535; Jones (1988*a*), 194; Morineau (1985), 165–73.

bullion to ensure that British monetary circulation kept pace with her expanding production and trade (Figure 37).[41] Adam Smith was thus correct when he concluded that 'almost all our gold ... comes from Portugal'.[42]

The primacy of this world economic competition meant that the test of the military capacity of a belligerent power was not merely its ability to mount a significant field army but a navy as well. This was one of the distinctions between a first- and a second-rate power, and one recognized by contemporaries.[43] Uniquely, England had adopted the 'double forward commitment' of both army and navy from 1689, while France had been forced to abandon its main fleet operations in 1693 and 1704. As late as the Seven Years' War, France did not fund simultaneously a land army and a navy as large as Britain's.[44] For Britain, there could be no simple choice between a land or a sea war: 'The security of Europe is essential to the security of the British Empire. We cannot separate them', declared Lord Auckland in Parliament in 1799.[45] The cost of two types of simultaneous warfare, often within a world theatre of operations, had enormous implications for the growth of state finance. A second factor in the growth of military expenditure, and thus in the need to generate more revenue if high levels of indebtedness were to be avoided, was the increase in the size of armies. Despite much discussion by historians of a 'military revolution' before 1660, the size of individual field armies had rarely exceeded 25,000 to 30,000 men. In contrast, during the period of Louis XIV's last two wars, 50,000 to 100,000 men for field armies became the norm,[46] with even higher figures on the French side. The size of the French army had increased significantly by the last decades of the reign of Louis XIV: 158,000 men were under arms in 1689, but the figure had reached 273,000 by 1691 and peaked at almost 400,000 by 1693.[47] This figure of 400,000 remained the maximum army size in all theatres of war permitted by the resources of the French monarchy during the *ancien régime*, and in reality there was a marked decline in the size of French armies between 1710 and 1792, which were usually of the size of 150,000–200,000 men.[48]

This growth in the size of armies had obvious consequences for expenditure: Malet, one of the chief clerks of the finance minister, demonstrated that

[41] ESFDB \rjb\porboo1 based on \pordoo1; Morineau (1985), 167–8, 170.

[42] Sideri (1970), 22, 49, 51.

[43] Meyer (1991), 23.

[44] Jones (1988*a*), 28; Riley (1986), 80–1; Innes in Stone (1994), 108; Baugh in Stone (1994), 195–7.

[45] Mackesy in Dickinson (1989), 148.

[46] Lind (1987), 222 and his dataset ESFDB \armies\armdoo1. The author is grateful to Dr Gunner Lind (Copenhagen) for his helpful comments in the preparation of this chapter.

[47] Martin in Sonnino (1990), 120, 122–3. Napoleon later estimated that the army size under Louis XIV peaked at 546,000 in 1692: Woolf (1991), 159; but this could only be so if the militia was also included. Militia figures are excluded from the calculations here.

[48] Lynn (1980), 579, 581.

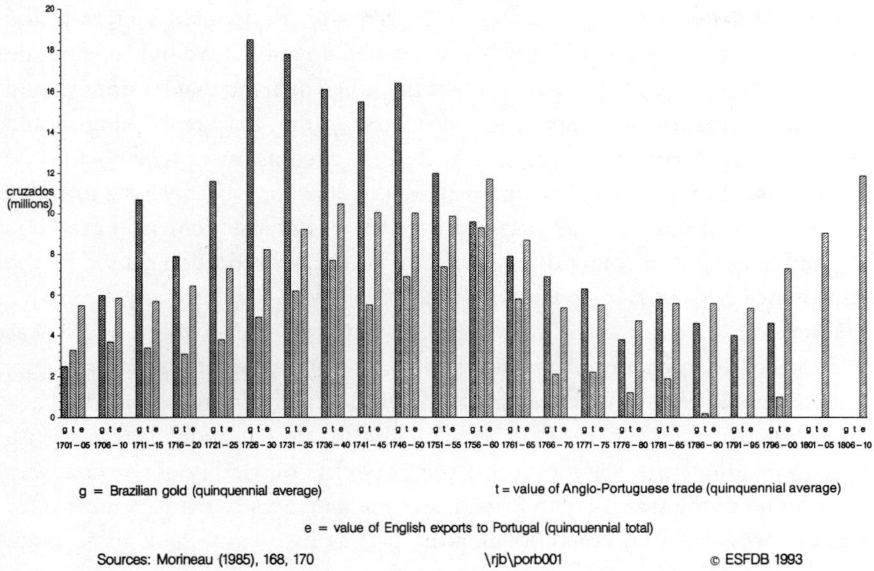

FIG. 37. Anglo-Portuguese trade and arrivals of Brazilian gold, 1701–1810 (expressed in *cruzados*)

expenditure by 1708–14 averaged 218 million *livres*, whereas in the Dutch war of 1672–8 it had averaged only 99 million.[49] The subsistence crisis of 1693 diminished the tax revenue of the state and it was only the relative success of a new tax modelled on Austrian Habsburg precedents, the *capitation* of 1695, which kept the war going.[50] The threat to the French frontiers meant that funds could no longer be spared for a great fleet after 1693. The vacuum was filled by privateers, who operated at first against English and Dutch vessels;[51] by 1709, French trade had spread illicitly (but with the earlier encouragement of the French minister of finance, Chamillart)[52] to the Spanish empire in South America, despite the alliance between Louis XIV and Philip V. Substantial bullion imports of 30 million *livres* in 1709 helped keep the French war effort going.[53] The failure of the

[49] Bonney (1991*a*), 190; Bonney and Bonney (1993), 23.

[50] Bonney (1992*a*), 162, 164.

[51] Symcox in Sonnino (1990), 137.

[52] Kamen (1969), 155. For the earlier arguments of French merchants that the Dutch and English were profiting from Spanish inability to defend its empire: A[rchives] N[ationales] G^7 183, nos. 239, 241, 260, 16 Sept., 23 Sept., 17 Oct. 1703; G^7 185 no. 120, 21 June 1705 and undated minute of Chamillart; Boislisle (1874–9), ii, 252.

[53] The rumour of 30 million was at first doubted: AN G^7 188, no. 371–3, 9 Apr. 1709. Both Malet and Desmaretz accepted the figure of 30 million: Malet (1789), 116; Desmaretz (1789), 13; Boislisle (1874–9), iii, 675. Kamen (1969), 192, gives annual figures (1701–13) in *reales de vellón*. At his conversion rate, this suggests only 16.25 million for 1709.

Gertruydenberg peace negotiations in March 1710 precipitated a crisis in the financing of the war: by mid-July, there seemed no alternative but to continue the war, unless Louis XIV were to accept the Allied demand that Philip V should no longer remain king of Spain and, if necessary, that the French king should make war on his grandson to expel him. In these circumstances, a new army had to be found, but there had been no real preparations for it because the tortuous negotiations of the previous year had raised hopes of a settlement on the one outstanding point of contention. Nor, after the social dislocation caused by the subsistence crisis of 1709–10 known as the *grand hiver*, was there any disposable tax revenue to pay for the new army. A new tax, the *dixième*, which was influenced by Dutch precedents, was rushed through in the late summer of 1710, after a drastic review of expenditure.[54] The French ministers seem to have considered the success of the new tax influential in bringing about a greater sense of realism among the Allies; in reality the Tory election victory of 1710 cut away the ground of the war party in Britain, and the Dutch were left to scramble for what concessions they could obtain after 'perfidious Albion' made its separate peace.

The weakness of the French currency, particularly in relation to the Spanish *doblón* or *pistole*, had played a critical role in undermining the French war effort against the Allies between 1689 and 1714. This was not assisted by the French government's more or less consistent policy of regular debasement during the two wars, while the Spanish government held to its policy of monetary stabilization after 1686. The exchange rate, which became a significant issue during the War of the Spanish Succession because of the French government's need to pay for its troops in the peninsula, thus moved more or less consistently in favour of Spain; French goods in Spain were much less attractively priced than Dutch or English contraband.[55] Thus although considerable amounts of bullion were imported into the French kingdom via Nantes, Saint-Malo, La Rochelle and Bayonne, it was equally true that, despite all the efforts of the government, substantial sums were exported illegally to Geneva via Lyon.[56] An acute problem of inadequate monetary circulation within the kingdom resulted.[57] Various expedients were adopted to try to overcome this difficulty, most notoriously the introduction of *billets de monnaie*[58] and subsequently the stipulation that such

[54] Bonney (1991*a*), 196–7; Bonney and Bonney (1993), 74–81; Bonney (1993*a*).

[55] Kamen (1969), 168–70; AN G^7 140, 25 May 1704; G^7 116, 27 Jan. 1705; G^7 117, 22 Sept., 3 Oct. 1708; G^7 118, 27 May 1710.

[56] On monetary networks: AN G^7 142 nos. 58, 76, 16 Feb. and 12 Apr. 1707.

[57] Thus Guyenne: AN G^7 140, 9 Oct. and 27 Oct. 1703; Boislisle (1874–9), ii, 154; G^7 141, no. 383, 22 May 1706; G^7 144, no. 20, 27 Jan. 1711; Boislisle (1874–9), iii, 348.

[58] On opposition to the *billets*: AN G^7 142, nos. 81, 86, 90, 30 Apr., 8 May and 21 May 1707.

paper should be used to pay for a quarter of the cost of all transactions.[59] After 1708, Desmaretz withdrew much of this paper from circulation and removed the stipulation on its use; but deficit finance remained the order of the day so that by the death of Louis XIV in 1715 the interest-bearing public debt was in the region of 1,739 million *livres* although this was not clearly visible from the way in which Desmaretz presented the figures.[60]

In the event, France had escaped lightly from the settlements of 1713–14, but was in no financial position to pursue an adventurous foreign policy. The serious fiscal pressure of the last years of the War of the Spanish Succession was bitterly resented by the privileged classes, who made it clear that their consent to the *dixième* had been for the duration of the war only: the Regent conceded its withdrawal in 1717. Then in 1718–20, Law's System attempted to expand the credit market, to reduce the public debt and to substitute paper for specie as the main medium of exchange. The excessive expansion of the scheme, rather than the resistance of vested interest groups, brought about the final collapse of the System on 17 July 1720. Confidence in financial innovation and paper money was damaged for the years to come,[61] while, far from reducing the public debt, Law had in fact succeeded in increasing it by some 700 million *livres* and (contrary to his intentions) in exacerbating the economic depression as well. Even after the arbitrary reduction of paper debts by the *visa*, the debt was still some 1,700 million and there is little doubt that it took the rest of the decade before France began to escape from the impact of the collapse of the System. The revaluation of the *livre tournois* in 1726, and its relative stability until 1785, provided much needed confidence in the currency, which had previously been the sacrificial victim of an aggressive French foreign policy. French revenues in peacetime expanded from 207 million *livres* in 1727 to some 344 million in 1768. This amounted to a modest increase in real terms by 1768, depending on the way in which inflation is calculated. Crucially, the peacetime burden of taxation seems to have declined in real terms from one era of peace to the next.[62] Military operations were on a relatively small scale before the outbreak of the Seven Years' War in 1756: the

[59] AN G^7 142, nos. 155, 158, 161, 5 Nov. and 26 Nov. 1707.

[60] Bonney (1992*a*), 171 n. 87; Desmaretz (1789), 54; Boislisle (1874–9), iii, 681. For criticism of Desmaretz's presentation of the debts: Steuart, ed. Skinner (1966), ii, 608; Bonney and Bonney (1993), 73; figures revised upwards from data supplied by Joël Félix.

[61] It may be said to have been restored somewhat with the establishment of the *Caisse d'escompte* in 1776: Marion (1914), 348; Crouzet (1993), 35–42.

[62] Mathias and O'Brien (1976), 604–5, concluded that there was no real increase, and their adjusted figure for 1768 is 178 million. Riley (1987), 232–3, recalculates the figure as either 234 or 249 million, depending on whether the Labrousse or the Posthumus series is utilized. On the figures as a proportion of gross output (a slight decline in peacetime): ibid. 236. The per capita fiscal burden remained more or less constant at 8.2 *livres* (1733) and 8.9 *livres* (1768): loc. cit.

financial demands of the War of the Polish Succession (1733–8) were contained successfully, while even the War of the Austrian Succession (1740–8) failed to produce a financial calamity for France.[63]

In contrast to France, and though Philip V kept his throne, Spain was made to pay heavily for the peace settlements of 1713–14, at least in terms of territorial concessions, but its financial position was considerably more favourable. Firstly, and conversely to what might have been expected, the revenues enjoyed by Philip V actually rose during the War of Succession: total income rose from 120.3 million *reales de vellón* in 1703–4 to 229.4 million by 1713, at the height of the war against Catalonia, chiefly due to ruthless exploitation of extraordinary sources of revenue such as those from the church, confiscations of the property of rebels and additional taxes.[64] A second, and later, aspect of financial recovery was the long-term effect of the abolition of the privileges of Aragon and Valencia in 1707, and of Catalonia in 1714. This permitted by 1718 the extension of effective direct taxation into the outlying regions which had always defeated the Habsburgs; by this date they were contributing about a tenth of all government income.[65] Thus whereas the estimates for May 1687 had suggested that revenue was 84 million *reales de vellón*, while expenses were in the region of 122.9 million, the position for 1717–18 was much healthier: expenses were 237.9 million, it is true, but income was 236.4 million.[66] Thereafter, the rate of revenue increase fell back and the 300 million barrier was not permanently breached until the War of Jenkins's Ear (1739–48) and then only to meet the growth of expenditure.[67]

The victor powers of the 1713–14 settlement experienced contrasting fortunes with regard to the growth of their public revenue and the stability of their finances. The Austrian Habsburgs were worst placed among the three victor powers, since under Leopold I both taxation and credit facilities had been largely controlled by the estates in the various constituent territories. The attempt to mobilize an army of 129,000 men in 1703 was an immense strain on resources.[68] Military expenditure had averaged over 20 million florins per annum during the War of the Spanish Succession, at least after 1704.[69] Under Charles VI, though new revenue policies were adopted, disposable revenue failed to grow in real

63 Morineau (1980), 303, 307; Riley (1987), 237.

64 Kamen (1969), 215.

65 Ibid. 224.

66 Ibid. 215, 228; Kamen (1980), 367.

67 Kamen (1969), 223, 230: the data underlying these two graphs has never been published or released by the author. Ozanam in Otazu (1978*a*), 51, 54; a lower evalutation is given by Artola (1982), 312.

68 Bérenger (1975), 276; Bérenger (1984), 221, 230.

69 Dickson and Sperling in Bromley (1971), 306.

terms; the state debt rose from 52.1 million florins in 1718 to 99 million by 1739, leaving aside separate debts of the governments in Brussels and Milan.[70] The Austrian Habsburgs inevitably became heavily dependent upon foreign subsidies in war, primarily from Britain until the diplomatic revolution of 1756.[71] Even so, Maria Theresa's *damnosa heritas* in 1740 (she described herself as 'without money, credit, and an army')[72] paved the way for military defeat in the War of the Austrian Succession and made necessary the reforms introduced by Haugwitz in 1747–9 (Chapter 10.3).

The second victor power of 1713–14, the United Provinces, was in better shape, but was bitterly disappointed by the settlement and clearly financially exhausted after three protracted and costly wars with France between 1672 and 1713.[73] The well-documented Dutch case demonstrates that only once before 1660 (in 1643) had the total size of the army exceeded 60,000 men. In the period of the Dutch war (1672–9), very high army sizes were recorded in the years 1673–5 (between 88,000 and 93,000 men); but not until 1695 did the army exceed 100,000 men. Between 1702 and 1713, in contrast, the size of the Dutch army *always* exceeded this figure (Figure 38);[74] the annual military estimates reached 24.4 million guilders in 1703, 27.7 million in 1708 and 29 million by 1712;[75] and it is not surprising that by the end of the War of the Spanish Succession the Republic's finances were seriously overstretched.[76] In 1713, it was calculated that the war had cost the Republic something approaching 128 million guilders, while the interest on the public debt of Holland alone had almost doubled between the Peace of Nijmwegen and the Peace of Utrecht.[77] Moreover, population growth was lower than elsewhere and a real increase in revenues was difficult to obtain. In terms of current prices, tax revenue increased by only about 25 per cent between 1725 and 1790 in Holland, compared to about 35 per cent in Britain and France; but unlike the two monarchies, in Holland tax revenues declined in real terms, that is, when they are recalculated at constant prices.[78] Worse still, as Isaac de Pinto came to argue in 1771, the main elements that had ensured Dutch primacy in world trade had begun to crumble by the 1760s.[79]

Britain was the unquestioned victor in 1713, although the national debt had

[70] Dickson (1987), ii, 6. [71] Ibid. ii, 158–72. [72] Ibid. ii, 3.

[73] Veenendaal in Hofmann and Norberg (1994), 127–9.

[74] Zwitzer (1991), 175–6; Vaupell (1898). The author is grateful to Professor Maarten Prak (Utrecht) and Dr Gunner Lind for these references. ESFDB \armies\netboo1 based on \netmoo1.

[75] Dickson and Sperling in Bromley (1971), 295.

[76] Aalbers (1977), 82.

[77] Schama in Winter (1975), 103.

[78] Aalbers (1977), 84–93; Fritschy (1990), 60–1; cf. Mathias and O'Brien (1976).

[79] Israel (1989), 379, 401, 377–98, *passim*, but the matter remains contentious.

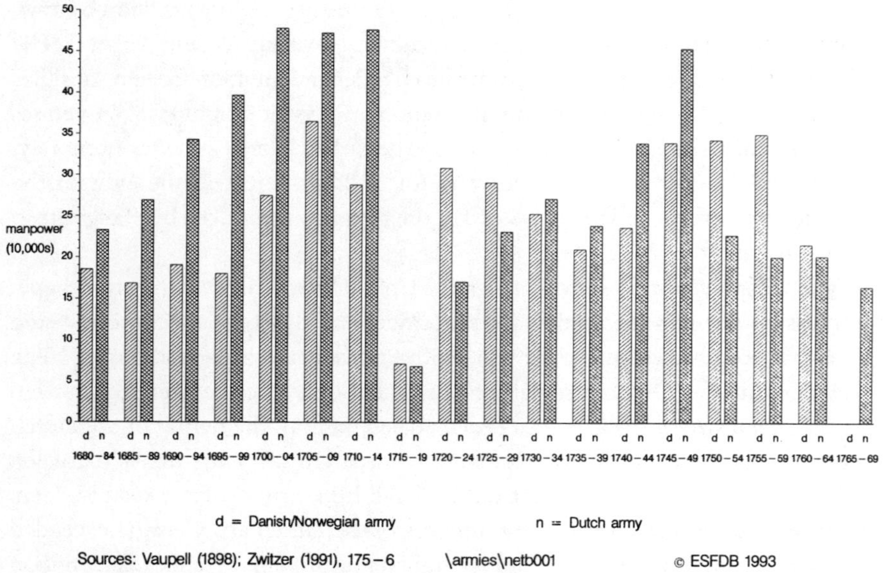

FIG. 38. Total manpower of the Danish–Norwegian and Dutch armies, 1680–1769 (manpower in tens of thousands)

more than doubled since 1697 (£36.2 million in 1713 as against £16.7 million in 1697), while average expenditure during the war had also been much higher than in the 1690s (£7 million instead of £5.5 million). The total number of men under arms—that is, in both navy and army—had risen from an average of over 116,000 in the Nine Years' War to an average of over 135,000 men in the War of the Spanish Succession. By the time of the financial crash of 1720 (the South Sea Bubble was in part at least a response to the apparent initial success of Law's System),[80] public indebtedness amounted to more than £50 million, but declined thereafter during the peaceful years of the 1720s and 1730s.[81] Even so, the debt more than doubled between 1713 and the end of the War of the Austrian Succession (1739–48) to £76 million, and it almost doubled again by the end of the Seven Years' War (1756–63), from £74 million to £132.6 million. In none of the wars after 1714 did the unfunded portion of the national debt exceed 20 per cent, however, and in most cases it was under 10 per cent: there had been a decisive shift towards long-term indebtedness (it was not until 1712 that funded exceeded unfunded liabilities).[82] Average annual expenditure during the War of the Austrian Succession was only marginally higher than during the last war against Louis XIV (£8.78 million as against £7.06 million), largely due to the fact that the

[80] Neal (1990), 62–80, 89–117. [81] Brewer (1989), 114. [82] Ibid. 119.

wartime army was smaller. However, expenditure more than doubled during the Seven Years' War, reaching an annual average of £18 million; the growth in the size of the army, to higher than 90,000 men, was a contributory factor.[83] By 1760, military expenditure was equivalent to a higher proportion of national income even than during the War of the Spanish Succession (an estimated 15.5 per cent in 1760 as against 14.5 per cent in 1710).[84] Apart from the size of the military establishment in wartime, there was also a heavy burden to discharge in foreign subsidies: £7 million during the War of the Spanish Succession alone, £24.5 million between 1702 and 1763.[85] If British subsidies were important to Austria, and later Prussia, British mercenary troop contracts were the lifeblood of Hesse–Cassel: between 1702 and 1763, 25 million *talers* or the equivalent of half of all government expenditure had arrived in the form of payment for mercenaries. 'These troops are our Peru', exclaimed Landgrave William VIII in 1745; 'in losing them we would forfeit all our resources.'[86] The British strategy was already clear during the War of the Austrian Succession: it was to tie down French power in warfare in Continental Europe by subsidizing the enemies of France; to blockade the French ports, so as to restrict the activities of its navy; and to use British seapower to make colonial gains and obtain the leading position in the carrying trade, subject only to the size of the merchant marine. At first, the policy was not entirely successful: the Spanish empire proved more difficult to dismember in 1739 than had been expected; only in the Seven Years' War was the policy brought to fruition, for this was the clearest example of a war in the eighteenth century during which British overseas trade grew with a consequential rise in customs revenue: this was partly thanks to military expenditure overseas.[87]

11.2 *The Fiscal Outcome of the Great War of the North and the Rise of 'Enlightened Despotism'*

The great struggle between Sweden and Russia for supremacy in the eastern Baltic had ended in 1721 with a decisive victory for Russia. Yet prior to 1697 the odds had still seemed to favour the continuance of Swedish hegemony in the eastern Baltic. Under Charles XI's allotment or *indelningsverket* system, Sweden had acquired a defensive standing army which could be financed in peacetime by the appropriation of specific revenues for its upkeep; this allowed the troops to live off the land without damaging the rural economy. Charles XI had reduced

[83] Ibid. 30. Note that the figures in O'Brien (1991), 34, differ because they are presented as centred 5-year averages rather than for the periods of the various wars.

[84] O'Brien (1991), 35.

[85] Brewer (1989), 32, gives slightly higher figures than Dickson (1987), ii, 158–60.

[86] Ingrao (1987), 127.

[87] Brewer (1989), 99, 175.

the national debt from 44 million *dalers* to 11 million and had put away nearly 2 million in his vaults to meet an emergency. When his son was attacked in 1700, the system bequeathed by Charles XI worked faultlessly and was resoundingly vindicated with the victory at Narva.[88] Thereafter, Charles XII had to return to the traditional policy of making 'war pay for war' in 1701–9; after defeat at Poltava in 1709 this was scarcely possible, though aggressive financial measures were adopted to keep the war effort going.[89] The death of the king in 1718 inaugurated the 'age of liberty' the following year, since Frederick of Hesse won the succession struggle for his wife only at the expense of sacrificing absolutism. Military adventures were thus at an end, not least for financial reasons: expenditure in 1718 was around twelve times the ordinary revenue (34.7 million silver *dalers* in expenses as against an ordinary revenue of less than half the 6.89 million laid down in 1696).[90] Worse than the purely budgetary consequences of war, the economy had been damaged by depopulation resulting from conscription for overseas service. Sweden ceased to be a great power, but the Swedish model had demonstrated earlier that a relatively small state in terms of population could become a significant military power, and attain regional hegemony, by efficient utilization of its resources, and by a high level of mobilization of its population for the war effort.

Of the victor powers in 1719–21, Denmark had the largest army in terms of the size of its population (Figure 38) and unlike Prussia had a significant navy as well.[91] Denmark had been influenced by the Swedish model but, unlike its rival, an absolutist regime with a high level of militarization remained the norm in the eighteenth century. Frederick IV hired out 12,000 men to the Dutch and English governments during the War of the Spanish Succession in return for a promise of naval support in any emergency.[92] Danish expenditure rose from 4.5 million *rigsdalers* in 1710 to 5.8 million by 1720; the cost of the army fell slightly in the period, but the costs of the navy and administration rose substantially. Uniquely among the Baltic states during the Great Northern War, Denmark had a healthy budgetary surplus in these years: total revenue rose from 5.3 million *rigsdalers* in 1710 to 6.9 million in 1720. Military subsidies from abroad played a significant part in creating this surplus: miscellaneous revenues were the largest component of the revenue budget (2.7 million in 1710 and 3 million in 1720).[93] Even so, the public

[88] Roberts (1967), 250; Åberg in Roberts (1973), 268, 286; Upton in Miller (1990), 118.

[89] Hatton in Bromley (1971), 672, 674–5.

[90] Roberts (1986), 18 n. 9.

[91] Lind (1987), 222, 241–2; Vaupell (1898).

[92] Stoye in Bromley (1971), 774.

[93] Jespersen (1989), 280, 282 and ESFDB \poul\dand010 and \dand014. The author is grateful to Dr Bjørn Poulsen for supplying this material.

debt had grown during the war, the coinage had been debased, and banknotes were issued for the first time in 1713. After 1721, army costs fell back below 2 million a year and (depending on which source is accepted)[94] did not exceed this sum before 1762. Despite fluctuations in the Baltic trade, Sound dues remained important to the Danish crown in the eighteenth century (Chapter 13.3).

Before the Russian victory at Poltava in 1709, the conflict with Sweden had been close-run: 96 per cent of Russian expenditure went on the war effort in 1705, the most critical year for the Russians.[95] By 1710, the proportion had fallen somewhat, to 80 per cent.[96] The fact that in 1710 only four-fifths of Russian expenditure was covered by taxation in a country with next to nothing in credit structures demonstrates the scale of the crisis: the deficit had to be met from debasement of the currency, a significant source of revenue between 1701 and 1709 (yielding some 4.4 million roubles)[97] and, later, from additional taxes.[98] Only at the end of the reign, in the accounts of 1725, was the total expenditure on the war needs (that is to say, army and navy) reduced to 6.54 million roubles or 64.5 per cent of total expenditure, a sum still nearly 2 million roubles higher than the total revenue of 8.5 million.[99] The military disaster at Narva in 1700 had taught Peter the Great to value the Swedish model in terms of both fiscal and military administration; through the German Heinrich Fick he learnt of Charles XI's achievements and received detailed information on the Swedish structure of government.[100] After the Russian naval victory at Hängo in 1714, Peter I introduced a modified Swedish system of administration into Russia, particularly the colleges, six of which were exclusively fiscal agencies or included revenue collection among their tasks.[101] Similarly, the Table of Ranks of 1722 drew upon the experience of both Sweden and Prussia, and confirmed the primacy of a military career for the nobility and the role of the head of the army in decision-making.[102] The most obvious consequence of the twenty-year war with Sweden was a permanently enlarged military establishment: even the fiscal crisis did not

94 We have accepted Vaupell's figures here. Nathanson (1836) has figures for other parts of the budget, but is not perhaps as reliable; he shows very high army costs in 1743 and 1744, exceeding 2 million, as also for 1759–61. Generally, Nathanson's military costs are higher than Vaupell's: ESFDB \poul\dand006. The author is grateful to Dr Bjørn Poulsen for supplying this material.

95 Anderson in Bromley (1971), 723.

96 LeDonne (1991), 276.

97 Anderson (1978), 95.

98 Klyuchevsky (1965), 73.

99 Dukes (1982), 91.

100 Peterson (1979), 162, 178, 411–13. Peterson, 412, concludes, 'the Swedish influence was especially strong when it came to the new fiscal administration ... Special interest seems to have been aroused by the so-called military *indelningsverket*, or military allotment system ...'

101 Anderson in Bromley (1971), 726; LeDonne (1991), 74, 240.

102 Dukes (1982), 79–82, who comments, 82: '... it was Prussia, Sweden and Denmark which had been of greatest influence, and probably in that order.' LeDonne (1991), 23, 50.

lead to a disbandment in 1724; instead, unpaid leave was granted to the officer corps.[103] Ambition fed on success, but the precondition for Russian territorial ambitions to the west was the collapse of Polish power. Fiscal reforms had been recognized as urgently needed in Poland, but were not carried out in the period after 1717 when the country fell under Russian tutelage. The 'Silent *Sejm*' of that year fixed state revenue at 10 million *zlotys* a year, a sum too small for military needs if Russia was to be confronted; the army size in any case was limited to 24,000 men.[104] A former great power, at least until the losses at the truce of 1667 were confirmed at the peace of 1686, was reduced to being a potential prey to partitioning powers. The state and the army were both weak in Poland because the nobility did not want to pay taxes. It was not until 1788 that Poland decided to create an army of 100,000 men, or 1 per cent of the population; and the partitioning powers made their final moves against Poland in 1793 precisely because the *Sejm* of 1788–92 had attempted to modernize the state and the army.[105]

'Enlightened despotism' cannot be interpreted narrowly in fiscal and economic terms, since it contained a conceptual element that was directly related to the spread of the ideas of the Enlightenment, and to the influence of Cameralism (Chapter 6.4).[106] However, there can be little doubt that at least in the case of the two largest German states—first Prussia, and later Austria—it amounted to an attempt to catch up with political, fiscal and economic developments in other European states such as Britain and the Netherlands. Britain and France would remain great powers which the others could not match. The question at issue was primacy among the second tier of states, and the competition for an alliance with the two great powers. Frederick II boasted that states such as Prussia and Austria were superior to a third category which could not finance an independent foreign policy without subsidies from abroad.[107] By this reckoning, most of the other German states would fall into the third category: there, enlightened despotism did not take quite the same form as in Austria and Prussia,[108] or was

[103] LeDonne (1991), 46.

[104] Gierowski and Kaminsky in Bromley (1971), 713–14; Filipczak-Kocur in Bonney (1995).

[105] Kochanowicz in Chirot (1989), 115.

[106] Beales (1991), 4–5; Scott (1990), 346; Raeff (1975, 1983).

[107] Roberts (1986), 19 n. 10; in class three he listed Sardinia, Denmark, Portugal, Poland and Sweden. Similar categorization of states in the lectures of Professor Koch at Strasbourg: Meyer (1991), 23–4. For the misplaced confidence of Frederick II, see the events of 1793–4 in Prussia described below.

[108] Blanning (1974), 139, in the context of Mainz; Liebel (1965), in the context of Baden; Vann (1984), 184, 186, 224–5, 275–9, in the context of Württemberg; Ingrao (1987), 6–7, 213, in the context of Hesse; Ingrao in Scott (1990), 227, for the smaller German states in general; cf. Morazé (1948).

not made manifest at all. At first, the rivalry between Austria and Prussia was obscured because of military co-operation during the War of the Spanish Succession (this won for Elector Frederick III the title of king in Prussia in 1701)[109] and the fact that Frederick William I (1713–40) usually pursued a pro-Austrian policy. Though historians rightly concentrate on the importance of the earlier achievements of the 'Great Elector', Frederick William, in establishing permanent taxation and the General War Commissariat,[110] it is often forgotten that Prussia, like Russia, had at first followed the Swedish pattern of military and fiscal administration; some improvements were made, but in the later eighteenth century the canton system in Prussia showed similar deficiencies to those of the Swedish system in the same period.[111] The maintenance of a standing army of 190,000 troops by the reign of Frederick II was a significant burden on the Prussian economy. The Austrian army was larger by a third, but Prussia raised twice as many troops in proportion to the number of inhabitants. Frederick William I had established the fundamental structure, the General Directory in 1722–3[112] (but he failed to introduce the Swedish and Russian *krigskollegium*, which did not appear in Prussia until 1787);[113] the canton system for the levying of troops was introduced in 1733.[114] He had also—like Charles XI after 1679—avoided war and built up a state treasure (*Staatsschatz*) of 10 million *Reichstaler* in gold coin by the time of his death in 1740. This and the powerful army, which was regarded in Europe as excessively large for a state with a population the size of Prussia's,[115] made possible Frederick II's seizure of Silesia in 1740, which decisively altered the course of European history in the eighteenth century.[116] After the occupation of Silesia, a reformed fiscal system was introduced there: taxation 'on a Prussian footing' was heavier than before but more equitable, though the balance of economic advantage lay with Prussia not Silesia.[117] Two-thirds of Frederick's war reserve was consumed in the two years of the First Silesian War; by 1745, the Treasury had been replenished to 6 million *Reichstaler*, although the Second Silesian War cost 12 million. By 1752, Silesia was yielding 28 per cent of Prussian revenues, and later it alone of the Prussian provinces paid its taxes

[109] Koch in Miller (1990), 154.

[110] Ibid. 146.

[111] Oestreich (1982), 235–6, 238–9. For the later Swedish problems: Roberts (1986), 22–3. For Prussian problems: Craig (1955), 22–3.

[112] Dorwart (1953), 167, 199–211.

[113] Peterson (1979), 399–402; Craig (1955), 29.

[114] Büsch (1962), 19; Sheehan (1989), 62, 64; Johnson (1975), 6–7, 26. It was introduced in 1743 into Prussian Silesia: Baumgart in Greengrass (1991), 168; but not into the former Polish territories acquired later: Speier (1936), 313.

[115] Hubatsch (1975), 128.

[116] Scott in Scott (1990), 23; Sheehan (1989), 21; Meyer (1991), 55–6, 86–7.

[117] Baumgart in Greengrass (1991), 165, 173; Johnson (1975), 148–9.

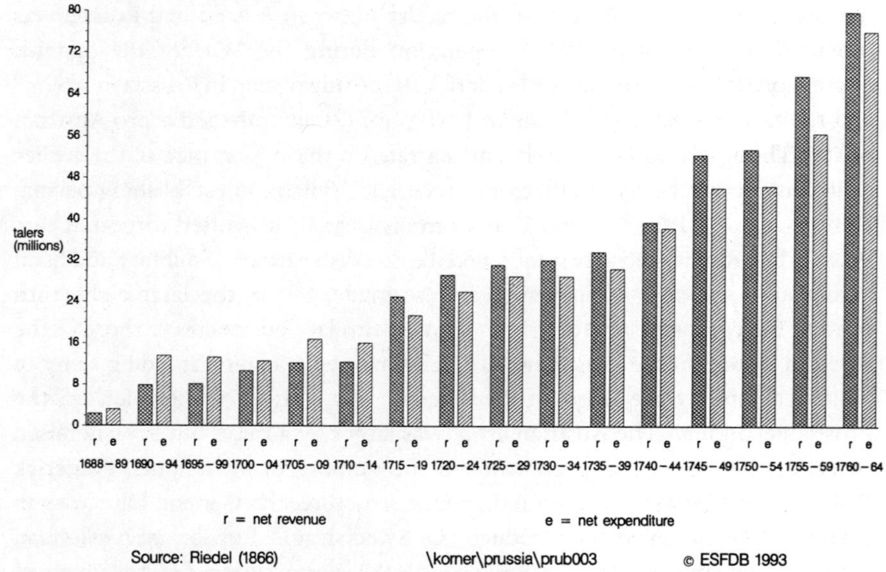

FIG. 39. Total revenue and total expenditure of Prussia, 1688–1764 (in *talers*)

regularly during the Seven Years' War.[118] War reparations and surpluses enabled the Prussian Treasury reserve to be rebuilt, this time to 20 million *Reichstaler*, by 1756 (Figure 39).[119]

Maria Theresa's response to the loss of Silesia was to make the issue of its restoration a life-and-death struggle: hence the two unsuccessful wars in the 1740s. Haugwitz's reform plans of 1749, which were intended to be a turning-point in the financial and military fortunes of the Habsburg monarchy, were influenced not only by Cameralist views (Chapter 6.4) but also by his experience as President of the Royal Bureau in what remained of Austrian Silesia after 1743, where he was well informed about the way in which Prussian reforms had been implemented across the border. He argued that the Prussian administration in Silesia had nearly doubled the yield in taxation, while the real fiscal burden had fallen because of greater fiscal efficiency.[120] The *Directorium* was an Austrian

[118] Johnson (1975), 144 n. 20, based on Frederick's *Political Testament* of 1752: 3.4 million *talers* from Silesia, 8.75 million from the other provinces combined. Henderson (1963), 65.

[119] ESFDB \korner\prussia\prub003 after \prum003; Riedel (1866). The author is indebted to Professor Körner for his interpretation of these tables. Note that cameral income is missing for the earlier period in Riedel's tables. Cf. Schremmer's comment on the limitation of Prussian accounting methods: Schremmer in Mathias and Pollard (1989), 414; Koser (1891), 551; Hubatsch (1975), 137–8.

[120] Dickson (1987), ii, 8–9; Scott in Scott (1990), 152–3.

version of the Prussian General Directory,[121] while the overriding aim was to create a standing army in peacetime of 108,000 men,[122] paid for by an increase in the contributions levied on the hereditary lands. This system failed lamentably in the great trial of strength, the Seven Years' War. The war cost Prussia 140 million *Reichstaler*. Although Russian troops (in alliance with Austria) occupied East Prussia for most of the war, Prussia in turn occupied Saxony, Mecklenburg and Swedish Pomerania: this yielded 53 million *Reichstaler*. The British subsidy of £670,000 per annum paid in gold yielded 27.5 million *Reichstaler* in all. Previous savings, increased taxation, a severe debasement of the coinage of occupied states (and, towards the end of the war, of Prussia's), the brutal exploitation of Saxony, and the failure to pay wages of officials helped boost revenue and cut costs. In 1763, Frederick II was able to emerge from the war with a considerable reserve (*Dispositionsfond*) of 14.4 million *Reichstaler*.[123]

There was a marked contrast on the opposing side. The Russian troops in East Prussia were unpaid at the time of Catherine II's accession in Russia. Expenditure in 1762 stood at 16 million roubles, of which 73.7 per cent was consumed by the military. The following year, expenditure was even higher, at 17.2 million.[124] Though revenue rose rapidly with the return to peace, it did not do so fast enough to remove the deficit, which stood at some 2.7 million in 1763, leaving aside arrears in the collection of taxes.[125] Paper currency had been considered by Peter III in May 1762, but his legislation was not confirmed by Catherine on her accession. The Austrian lands were in an even worse financial position by the end of the war. After a struggle for power between Haugwitz and Kaunitz in 1761, Haugwitz's *Directorium* lost most of its military and financial functions, with the exception of the 'contribution'. The decision-making process of the central government had to be altered to meet the challenge posed by the war. Whereas troop levels had reached 138,000 in 1704, the year of Blenheim, and a new peak of 162,000 in the Turkish war and its aftermath (1716–20), the early years of the Seven Years' War had seen numbers in excess of 200,000. Only in 1762–3 did a reduction occur to around 180,000 men.[126] Whereas total military costs during the War of the Austrian Succession had never exceeded 26.5 million florins a year, and the figures for 1744–6 were considerably higher than for the other years, the Seven Years' War had seen estimated military costs verging on 40 million

[121] Baumgart in Greengrass (1991), 166; Scott in Scott (1990), 152, 154.

[122] Dickson (1987), ii, 117–18.

[123] Koser (1903), 446; Henderson (1963), 39–40; Hubatsch (1975), 139–40.

[124] Madariaga (1981), 482; LeDonne (1991), 277; somewhat lower figures in Kahan (1985), 337.

[125] Kahan (1985), 341; cf. Madariaga (1981), 482.

[126] Dickson (1987), ii, 114–15.

florins a year, and consistently above 32 million.[127] Such an outlay in war expenditure required a substantially increased fiscal burden, although the Austrian government did not have recourse to the Prussian expedient of debasement. Instead, there was an increasing reliance on paper by 1761–3, when the paper credit rose to 18 million florins, equivalent to the sum required to finance at least half the costs of an entire campaign; interest on the loans was deferred, although the contribution and new war taxes were increasingly clogged by loan interest charges.[128] France had replaced Britain as the provider of the essential war subsidies, and had been a reasonably efficient ally, paying 7.5 million *livres* a year in 1760–2; but the initially very high figure in the convention of 1757 (12 million florins a year) could not be, and was not, honoured. By 1763, however, the Austrian government was disillusioned with subsidies as a means of financing any subsequent war, and was looking instead to the increase in national wealth, to the tax increases which might result, and to the growth of public credit.[129]

11.3 *The Outcome of the Seven Years' War and the New Colonial Struggle*

In terms of Anglo-Bourbon rivalry, the Seven Years' War had been a struggle for economic and commercial supremacy, which had been won convincingly by Britain. No state which aspired to the status of a global power could afford to let matters rest there. Accordingly, France took the initiative in considering in a comparative way the revenue basis for a future conflict, with emphasis on the reforming experience of certain Italian states (Chapter 10.5). An earlier French investigation of exchange rates ordered by Bertin provided a reasonable basis of equivalence of the other currencies to the *livre tournois*[130] and it is possible to extend the comparison over a longer timescale (Figure 40).[131] In terms of fiscal resources alone (that is, excluding credit), France still dominated in 1763, with an annual revenue of 321 million livres. Next came England with 224 million.[132] No evaluation was placed on Spanish revenues by the Spanish finance minister, who supervised the report for the French government, but these may be estimated at

[127] Ibid. ii, 119, 124.

[128] Ibid. ii, 132, 134–8.

[129] Ibid. ii, 173–84.

[130] Hartmann (1979), 22.

[131] ESFDB \rjb\malg049 based on \malm047 and numerous sources cited there. The conversion from £ sterling takes no account of the agio on the money, but is clearly close to the contemporary calculation for the conversion: the figure for English revenues in 1763 in dataset \malm047 is 222.8 million *livres*.

[132] These figures are documented in Bonney (1994), 74–5.

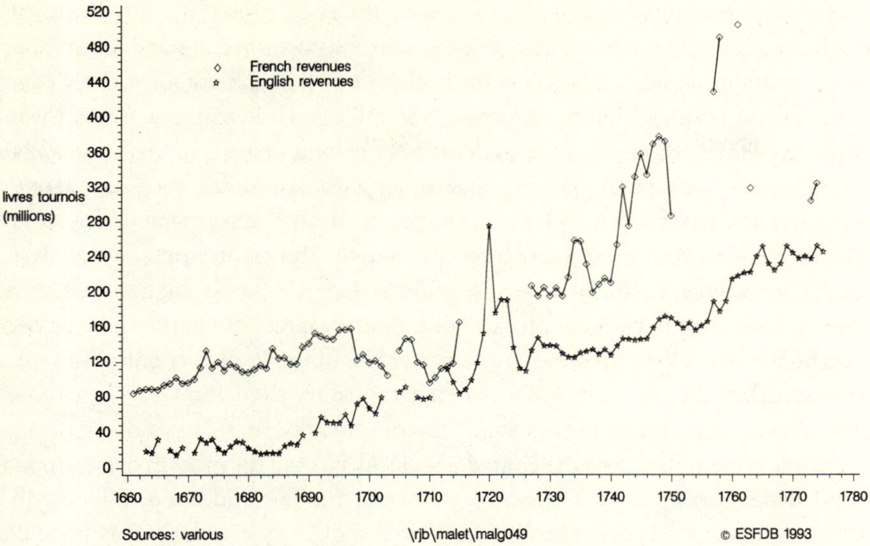

FIG. 40. Total revenues of the French and English monarchies, 1660–1775 (expressed in *livres tournois*)

131.8 million.[133] Thus, according to the evidence of the French enquiry, the United Provinces came third, with a revenue of 120 million, but this represented the total fiscal burden (that is, 'le revenu total des Etats Généraux et des villes'); disposable state revenue may have been as low as 85 million. The Austrian Habsburgs were close behind with 92 million excluding Lombardy and the Austrian Netherlands. The rising state was Prussia, whose revenues were not evaluated by the French enquiry, but which are thought to have been the equivalent of 49 million *livres*.[134] Prussian revenues were increasing so rapidly, however, that they may be estimated at nearly 90 million *livres* at the death of Frederick II in 1786,[135] while Dutch revenues had remained virtually static.

[133] The figure of 501.2 million *reales de vellón* cited by Pieper (1988), 88, converted by the multiplier used by Bonney (1994*a*), 74–5, n. 62. Pieper's work, which is fundamental for the period 1753–88, is discussed by Gelabert in Bonney (1995). Meyer (1983), 140, based on figures in Merino (1981), gives higher figures (140 million *livres* in 1752): but since Merino's figures in *reales de vellón* concern the reign of Carlos IV, neither the source nor the exchange rate is clear.

[134] Hartmann (1979), 222.

[135] Rousselot de Surgy (1784–7), iii, 417, records the figure of 46.1 million *écus* (or *Reichstaler*) equivalent to 166 million *livres*. This seems too high. Koser (1903), 119, records the figure of 21.73 million *Reichstaler* in 1784 (say 81.5 million *livres*), and ibid. 121, the figure of 23.8 million *Reichstaler* in 1786 (say 89.25 million *livres*). There is an error in Koser's addition, corrected by Henderson (1963), 66 n. iii. Koser's estimate is higher than the figures in Riedel (1866), table 14. Riedel and Henderson call the income *Taler*; Koser calls it *Reichstaler*.

Of the other European states covered by the enquiry in 1763, only Portugal, with a revenue of perhaps 50 million *livres*, was in a position comparable to that of Prussia, but its finances were more encumbered with fixed outgoings.[136] Sweden and Finland with 23 million, Naples with 27 million, and Denmark and Norway with 24 million were some considerable way behind Prussia, as were the Papal States (with perhaps 13 million) and other German states such as Saxony, Hanover and Bavaria. Though their reports attested to the permanent increase in taxes, relatively few of the French representatives abroad attempted an analysis of the per capita fiscal burden because of the lack of reliable population data.[137] A clear relationship between high rates of monetary circulation and sophisticated and highly developed fiscal systems emerged from the French enquiry. In some states, such as the Papal States and Sweden, monetary circulation was depicted as so low as to be almost non-existent. In contrast, the high levels of monetary circulation in England and the United Provinces assisted the growth of enormous funded debts (estimated respectively at 2,964 million and 2,100 million). Increased government debts in turn facilitated monetary circulation, as Isaac de Pinto recognized in 1771 (Chapter 6.5). Even some of the smaller Italian principalities such as Tuscany had significant public debts.[138] This tendency to accumulate debt, an inevitable consequence of the reliance upon loans because of the impossibility to finance wars by new taxes, became a general phenomenon in Europe and resulted in what has been called 'a pandemic of bankruptcy across Europe during the Revolutionary and Napoleonic wars', the origins of which are to be found in high debt–revenue ratios in the years following 1750.[139]

In accounting for this increase in the debt–revenue ratio, primacy must be accorded to the obstacles faced by European governments in establishing reformed tax structures, in eliminating privileges, and in taxing new forms of wealth. In France, such attempts failed dismally in the face of arguments that the government could not legitimately tax its population in an arbitrary fashion. It was clear by 1763 that radical reform was necessary in France because of the profound impact of the Seven Years' War on the royal finances.[140] Physiocratic influence over the French government reached its greatest extent at precisely the moment that the implementation of the *cadastre* was abandoned, that is to say with the resignation of Bertin as controller-general of finance in 1763. Bertin had drafted the reform measures for the liberalization of the grain trade, measures

136 Unpubd report of A. M. Hespanha to the Lisbon Team meeting and accompanying graphs.

137 Full references for these figures and detailed discussion of the enquiry in Bonney (1994); the conversion of the Swedish figure is a matter of debate.

138 Ibid.

139 Riley (1980), 114–18, 214; Ellis in Aerts and Crouzet (1990), 7.

140 Morineau (1980), 308; Riley (1986), xvi, 144–5, 159–61, 183–4; Riley (1987), 237.

which his successor L'Averdy implemented in full.[141] Grain liberalization was originally intended to be introduced simultaneously with the national *cadastre*, and it could be interpreted as a surrogate for, or prelude to, fundamental fiscal reform.[142] Moreover, the policy of grain liberalization received a measure of support (which the *cadastre* had not gained) in the *Parlements*.[143] Success in the area of economic reform might have helped to clear the way for later fiscal and institutional reforms. But the failure of grain liberalization—which began with the subsistence crisis of 1765 and was evident with the reversal of policy under Terray—foreclosed the possibility of any consequential fiscal reform as against a reform of the structural organization of the royal finances.[144] Terray's proposed territorial tax (*impôt territorial*) was stillborn;[145] but his partial debt repudiation, and conversion of *tontines* into life annuities, left a lasting legacy of bitterness, particularly among the holders of *tontines*.[146] When he came to office in 1774 after the fall of Terray, and under a new king who was committed in turn to reverse Terray's policies, Turgot, the controller-general closest to the Physiocrats,[147] was unable to introduce far-reaching reforms since by this date the ideas of the reform movement were largely discredited.[148] Yet if fiscal reform on the whole failed, colonial trade rebounded after the end of the Seven Years' War: whereas in the periods 1730–40 and 1740–54 French colonial trade had showed significant growth (respectively of 119 and 71 per cent), this sector had not recorded the largest rise (the Levant trade in the first period and the northern trade had showed larger percentage increases). But in the period 1765–76, French colonial trade grew faster than any other part of French trade, with a rate of increase of 76.7 per cent, at a time when trade with Spain declined by 6 per cent. The colonial trade was now nearly three times the size of any other sector of trade in terms of its value.[149]

For the British colonies, trade with the Spanish settlements was imperative,

[141] Kaplan (1976), i, 90–6, 136–7, 142. For Physiocratic influence over the drafting of the measures: ibid. i, 146–9.

[142] Ibid. i, 158–9.

[143] Ibid. i, 180; ii, 448; Antoine (1989), 799.

[144] Bosher (1970) and Bruguière (1990), 285–309, 493–7, both view the financial problems of the monarchy largely in terms of structural organization. Colbert's reform of indirect taxes in 1681, which endured for the rest of the *ancien régime*, demonstrated that it was possible to bring about a significant structural reform without altering the nature of the taxes themselves or their effect on the tax base.

[145] Marion (1910), 103, 362; Antoine (1989), 946–7.

[146] Weir (1989), 97, 121–4.

[147] Louis XVI had objected to his nomination precisely for this reason: 'Il est bien systématique, et il est en liaison avec les Encyclopédistes.' Faure (1961), 40. Turgot's ministry lasted only from August 1774 to May 1776.

[148] Kaplan (1976), ii, 661–2; Faure (1961).

[149] Butel in Tracy (1990), 163.

since this furnished their main supply of ready money. It was regarded as desirable to capture the enemy's colonial possessions, not only in order to retain them as markets and sources of supply, but because they, in turn, were a source of financial strength to the enemy, be it France or Spain.[150] The general balance of bullion exports to imports was favourable to Europe throughout the eighteenth century: the main outflows of bullion from Europe resulted from the trade with the Far East, but overall these were more than matched by the imports from America (Figure 1).[151] But Britain did better than other European powers, with the possible exception of the Dutch, whose trade in the Far East—at least until the Fourth Anglo-Dutch War in the 1780s—also prospered from the British defeat of the French.[152] The production of gold in Brazil peaked in 1726–30, and declined significantly after the 1750s, as did the flow of gold to Britain (Figure 37). Moreover, the economic dependence of Portugal upon Britain was resisted by the marquis of Pombal, minister during the reign of José I (1750–77), who adopted policies comparable to those of Enlightened despots elsewhere. Pombal was forced out of office after the death of the king, and some of his policies were reversed; but in general, Portugal prospered from its neutrality in the Anglo-French wars of 1778–83 and 1793–1802 and during this period its economic dependence on Britain was reduced.[153]

The new vigour of Spain[154] and France in their policy towards their colonies would have been less serious for Britain had it not experienced a crisis between 1763 and 1783 in its relations with its first empire in America, which resulted in the loss of the thirteen colonies. The crisis was provoked by the British attempt to make these self-governing colonies 'governable'. From 1763 to 1778, the British (or imperial) Parliament claimed the right to impose direct taxation on the American colonies in the form of the stamp tax. It ceased to do so in practice after 1778, simply because of the scale of rebellion there.[155] William Knox commented at the end of the American Revolution: 'it was better to have no colonies at all, than not to have them subservient to the maritime strength and commercial interest of Great Britain.'[156] The avowed purpose of the controversial Townshend duties, imposed in 1767, was to regulate trade rather than to raise revenue; but in the event of failure to enforce the duties it was thought 'absurd ever to

[150] Fayle (1923), 283, 285, 287; Arruda in Tracy (1991), 383.

[151] Barrett in Tracy (1990), 242–3, 253–4. There might well not be a national balance overall for a particular country such as Britain at a given moment.

[152] Neal in Tracy (1990), 221, 223; Prakash (1994).

[153] Maxwell in Scott (1990), 106, 112, 114; Sideri (1970), 98, 104–5, 110–11.

[154] Kuethe and Inglis (1985), 118, 122, who emphasize the reforming endeavours of Carlos III and Esquilache.

[155] D. K. Fieldhouse, paper at ESF plenary meeting at Lisbon (1992).

[156] Barrow (1967), 256–7.

think of preventing smuggling or collecting any revenue whether old or new'.[157] Previous taxation such as customs duties had been essentially a by-product of measures devised for other purposes, and in any case the proportion of duties paid by the Continental American colonies as against the West Indies had declined to infinitesimal levels;[158] but the need after 1763 for a permanent military establishment in the American colonies at a likely cost of some £224,000 per annum (civil administration had cost a mere £50,000) meant that new tax revenue had to be found in the colonies to meet the bill.[159]

With the outbreak of the American war in 1775, the British government was faced with unprecedented difficulties in feeding, clothing, arming and equipping large forces some 3,000 miles from their main sources of supply. On this occasion, in contrast to earlier wars, the British force of some 60,000 men (it rose to 92,000 men at the peak in 1780–1)[160] was denied local sources of supply by a 'refusal of all the colonies to supply the King's Troops with the Articles necessary for their support'.[161] Of critical importance was the British perception of the revolution: a long campaign was not expected, and every year was thought likely to be the last campaign; a false expectation of victory also meant that trade restrictions were not enforced vigorously enough.[162] With the entry of France into the war in 1778, and Spain the following year, the British navy was seriously overextended. The hostility of neutral powers, which brought the United Provinces into the war in 1780, further hampered the British blockade policy.[163] Once a large army had been provisioned in America and the West Indies for seven years, it became clear that the contracting methods used to supply it had been inefficient and expensive. There was also insufficient sea transportation to maintain a constant supply of men and provisions: had the war continued into 1783, the British army in America might well have been starved into submission.[164] This was the first (and only) war between 1689 and 1815 in which Britain fought both Spain and France without another 'war or object to draw off their attention and resources. We unfortunately have an additional war upon our hands which drains our finances, and employs a very considerable part of our navy and army ...'[165] George III consoled himself in September 1780 that the French and Spanish finances were in a poor state; 'this war like the last will prove one of credit'.[166] Despite Lord North's notorious 'parsimony of public treasure',[167] and largely because of rocketing naval costs,[168] the War of American Independence saw record annual

[157] Thomas (1975), 36.
[158] Barrow (1967), 75.
[159] Thomas (1975), 35, 38; Baugh in Stone (1994), 203–4.
[160] Baker (1971), 4.
[161] Ibid. 1.
[162] Mackesy (1964), 101.
[163] Ibid. 377, 378.
[164] Syrett (1970), 245–6.
[165] Ibid. 314.
[166] Ibid. 384; Harris (1979), 216.
[167] Mackesy (1964), 22.
[168] Ibid. 6; Bromley in Bédarida, Crouzet and Johnson (1979), 186, and Bromley in Bédarida, Crouzet and Johnson (1980), 169.

expenditure (at £20.3 million per annum on average) and significant tax increases: the land tax never fell below 3 shillings in the pound after 1775, and was at 4 shillings in the pound for most of the war; but excise was now much more important, yielding almost £6.5 million in revenue by the end of the war. Even so, the gap between expenditure and revenue was on average £8 million a year. It is therefore hardly surprising that the public debt nearly doubled from £127.3 million at the outset of the war to £242.9 million by 1783, since more than 80 per cent of the extra income to fund the war had come from loan revenue.[169] Expenditure incurred during the war had cost the country approximately £124 million, a sum greater by about a quarter than the entire national income for 1780. Taxation in real terms had risen by nearly a third during the war.[170]

Vergennes, the French foreign minister, knew that the maintenance of credit for the duration of the war was vital: 'it is truly a war of hard cash (*une guerre d'écus*), and there is reason to fear that if we drag it out we will not be the last to be exhausted.'[171] He believed that France would recover 'the public consideration that the misfortunes of the last war and perhaps other causes have greatly weakened'.[172] Turgot, the controller-general at the accession of Louis XVI, had opposed the war because for him it was internal reform within France that mattered. He thought that the whole colonial system was doomed by the American example; that the French colonies were not worth fighting for; that England, not France, would collect the profits of a new economic system which might follow upon the peace; and that 'the first cannon shot would bankrupt Your Majesty's government'.[173] Vergennes had the better of the argument and in the event Turgot's prophecies of doom were not fulfilled. Independence was conceded to the American colonies, though the other British colonies were successfully defended against the Bourbons. Britain herself emerged relatively unscathed from the last great war of the *ancien régime*, though having suffered a significant loss of 'reputation'. There was thus no return to the *status quo ante* 1763. Though some have argued that the American colonies had been of little economic benefit to the imperial power at the time of their independence, the

[169] O'Brien (1988), 4 (only 19 per cent of the extra revenue to finance the war came from taxation, the lowest figure for any of the wars between 1689 and 1815); Brewer (1989), 30, 95, 99, 114 (but at ibid. 38, annual expenditure of nearly £30 million is reported); Mackesy (1964), 370, 460, 464.

[170] O'Brien in Dickinson (1989), 171.

[171] Mackesy (1964), 386; Harris (1979), 209.

[172] Bromley in Bédarida, Crouzet and Johnson (1979), 185, and Bromley in Bédarida, Crouzet and Johnson (1980), 168; cf. Louis XVI's argument that the war was 'not with any idea of territorial aggression on our part, aiming solely to ruin their commerce and sap their strength . . . ': Hardman (1993), 92, 94.

[173] Harris (1979), 216; Dull (1975), 32–47, is fundamental on the Turgot–Vergennes debate.

reality is otherwise (America received 37 per cent of British exports in 1772–3, compared with only 10 per cent in 1700–1).[174] It is true that the colonists were in no position to close off British trade, particularly via the West Indies (and the French grand design of seizing the market from Britain failed miserably);[175] moreover, their finances were in desperate straits and in 1780 the paper money issued by Congress throughout the war was effectively repudiated, a significant precursor to events in Europe during the Revolutionary and Napoleonic wars.[176] It was not until Alexander Hamilton's report on public credit in 1790 that the situation was fully stabilized, although of course there was scarcely any comparison between the $80 million or so owed by Hamilton's government and the approximately $1,275 million owed by Pitt's government in Britain.[177] Above all, any French colonial advance at the expense of Britain had been decisively checked. Clive's victory at Plassey in 1757 had turned India into a 'real' colony yielding £7.5 million in net revenue by 1766–9. The French attempt to reverse the outcome of the Seven Years' War in India was defeated in 1781–2.[178]

During his first ministry (1776–81), Necker failed to implement more than an organizational change in the method of raising direct taxes; the nature of the taxes themselves was unaffected.[179] Influenced by the British example, and by the ideas of Isaac de Pinto on the need to create public confidence through the publication of accounts,[180] Necker financed French participation in the War of American Independence—which cost at least a billion *livres* over eight years[181] —essentially on the basis of loan income, rather than by raising taxes: he borrowed 530 million *livres* during his first ministry; some of the costs of debt service had been met from economies, but this left a heavy legacy of debt, and above all a high cost of amortization, by 1788 (Figure 41).[182] Towards the end of his ministry, it had become clear that this policy on its own could no longer work

174 The argument of Thomas and McCloskey in Floud and McCloskey (1981), 97, is refuted *inter alia* by Bromley in Bédarida, Crouzet and Johnson (1979), 189, and Bromley in Bédarida, Crouzet and Johnson (1980), 172; O'Brien and Engerman in Solow (1991), 185–6.

175 Mackesy (1964), 37; Crouzet (1985), 300; Crouzet (1990), 319–20; Richardson in Solow (1991), 249–50, 261 n. 73, 263.

176 Harris (1979), 210–11; Riley (1980), 185–7.

177 Swanson and Trout (1990), 631; Weir (1989), 98.

178 Parker in Tracy (1991), 184; Mackesy (1964), 494; though there were wild hopes of much greater profits from India: Lawson (1993), 107–8. Cf. Bayly in Stone (1994), 339–41; more generally, Marshall (1993).

179 Harris (1979), 91; Harris, ibid. 68, depicts Necker's first ministry as the 'culmination' of the reform movement after 1763.

180 Brewer (1989), 131.

181 Morineau (1980), 312; Harris (1979), 118–19 (less than a billion for the seven years of war to 1782: ibid. 247).

182 Harris (1979), 117, 120–1, 135–6; ESFDB \rjb\frb002 based on \frd008; AN AD IX 517.

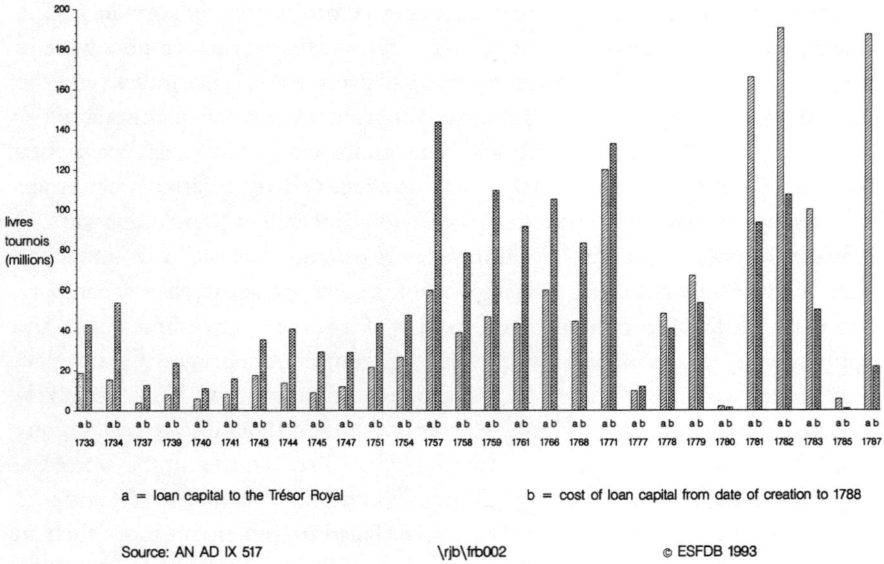

FIG. 41. Life rents and *tontines* in France, 1733–1788 (in *livres tournois*)

and that taxes would have to be raised. An erroneous report received in Britain was that Necker was forced out of office in 1781 because he opposed further war expenditure: 'the best men consider M. Neck[e]r's retreat as a fatal stab to the credit of France and to the independence of America.' The hope of a French financial collapse was widely held in Britain,[183] but even Vergennes believed this likely by 1781. In reality, although Necker was involved in an abortive peace initiative, there is no evidence that he opposed an extension of taxes once the capacity for further savings and all possible forms of loan income had been exhausted. His resignation was occasioned by the king's refusal to accept his demand to be admitted to the *conseil d'en haut*, which in turn had been occasioned by the rise in naval costs.[184]

Mirabeau subsequently denounced Necker's recourse to very expensive life rents (*rentes viagères*),[185] though whether the average annual interest rate of 6 per cent was excessive compared to that paid by his predecessors, or in view of prevailing market conditions, has been questioned.[186] A report produced by the

[183] Mackesy (1964), 384.

[184] Dull (1975), 227, 279–80, 297–8, 345–50; Harris (1979), 225: Hardman (1993), 62, 66.

[185] Harris (1979), 117, 132–4; but cf. Hardman (1993), 60, who talks of '10 per cent (proportionately less if more than one life was being insured)'.

[186] White (1989), 559. Though whether the French government fully realized the growing financial sophistication of the market is another issue (Chapter 6.8).

French government in 1782 estimated the comparative cost to Britain and France of the war and its effect on the public debt in the two countries. Using an exchange rate of 23.17 *livres* to the £ sterling, the French government calculated that the British armed forces in the seven years after 1776 had cost 2,834 million *livres*; subtracting ordinary peacetime expenditure, war costs were reduced to 2,270.5 million. During the same period, the French armed forces had cost 1,732.5 million *livres*; again, subtracting the ordinary peacetime expenditure, war costs were reduced to 928.9 million. The cost of the British war effort was therefore over double that of the French, who had not been fighting a land as well as a sea war. The effect on the public debt showed a similar pattern. The British debt, including Exchequer notes, notes issued by the armed forces, and arrears, stood at 5,532 million *livres* bearing an annual interest charge of 220 million (the figures for the consolidated debt alone were respectively 4,538 million and 170 million). In contrast, the French debt (including the loans for 1782) was 3,315.1 million, bearing an annual interest charge of 165.4 million.[187] This comparison remained valid until the outbreak of the French Revolution. The French debt was smaller than the British in terms of value, and considerably so in terms of its ratio to gross national product (56 per cent as against 182 per cent) and to income per capita. However, debt becomes significant when it cannot easily be serviced. When expressed as a proportion of the debt, debt charges in France were much more significant than in Britain (7.5 per cent as against 3.8 per cent), while the proportion of debt service costs to tax revenues was also higher (62 per cent to 56 per cent). France maintained a consistently lower burden of debt interest on its tax revenues, but gained no benefit from its policy, since Britain paid for its national debt by raising taxes, whereas France was forced to contain its debt by partial defaults such as in 1770. One consequence of this tradition of partial default before 1774 was that the rate of interest was higher in France than Britain: the market lacked confidence in the French crown as a borrower. 'Default risk' thus added a persistent premium to the cost of the French debt in comparison to the British debt.[188] Until Pitt became Chancellor of the Exchequer in 1783, Britain did not redeem a significant proportion of its debt via the Sinking Fund, but at least 30 per cent of the cost of French debt service was for amortization.[189]

[187] Harris (1976), 247–50.

[188] Velde and Weir (1992), 5, 18–19, 30, 35–7; Bordo and White (1991), 309; Bordo and White in Bordo and Capie (1994), 250; Schwarz in Bordo and Capie (1994), 379, questions the argument of Bordo and White that the British government had greater 'credibility as a borrower' than did the French because of 'its long record of fiscal probity'. However, the research of Velde and Weir appears conclusive on this point.

[189] Weir (1989), 97–103; Brewer (1989), 123–4.

After 1783, there was a change in British policy: Pitt transformed navy bills and other short-term debt into perpetual and irredeemable debt and also used new tax revenue both to pay interest on the debt and also to repay some of its principal. In this task, he was assisted by an increase in revenue from about £12 million per annum in 1782–4 to over £16 million per annum in 1790–2.[190] The revised Sinking Fund of 1786 envisaged redemption of the debt within thirty-five years and therefore assumed a more harmonious relationship between Britain and France as manifested in the Anglo-French trade treaty of that year. The peace of 1783 led to a fundamental reappraisal of British policy objectives with regard to colonial trade. Adam Smith had intended Book 4 of *The Wealth of Nations* ('On systems of political oeconomy') to persuade British statesmen to reform the empire politically and commercially. His influence on the British government has been greatly exaggerated, but an apparent *entente* with France was manifested in the Anglo-French commercial treaty of 1786: most goods from each country were subject to moderate, reciprocal duties, and in effect each country had most favoured status in the other's trade.[191] French colonial trade had suffered during the War of American Independence, but the return to peace after 1783 marked its apogee before the Revolution. By 1784–8, the average annual value of French trade had almost quintupled since 1716–20, from 215 million *livres* to 1,062 million (expressed in current prices).[192] This growth was part of a general revival of the Atlantic economy which had been in recession since the 1760s. The years 1783–92 also saw the British economy rebound after the economic depression during the War of American Independence, with an annual average rate of growth of exports of 6.9 per cent, much higher than for subsequent periods before 1815. There is no doubt that there was a sharp rise in British exports to France following the Eden Treaty of 1786.[193] On the other hand, many examples of British tariff reductions in the years 1783–93 seem to have been prompted by the Exchequer's interest in the reduction of smuggling and increased customs revenue. The British government's aim to flood the Continental market with cheap manufactured goods remained unchanged, and there was a stubbornly 'Mercantilist' stance until the repeal of the Corn Laws in 1846.[194]

[190] O'Brien in Dickinson (1989), 174–6.

[191] Crowley (1990), 339–41, 353, 360.

[192] Butel in Tracy (1990), 153–4, 162; Riley (1986), 106–11, esp. the construction of a curve in constant values: this puts French exports in 1780 at 154.9 million, deflated by an index based on 1721–45 (ibid. 110).

[193] Crouzet in Dickinson (1989), 190–1; O'Brien (1989), 369; Crouzet (1985), 43–4, 91–2, 171–3, 187; Crouzet (1990), 36–7, 107–8, 217–19, 236–7; O'Brien and Engerman in Solow (1991), 183. Somewhat different calculations: Thomas and McCloskey in Floud and McCloskey (1981), 88–9.

[194] O'Brien (1988), 25–6; O'Brien and Pigman (1992), 92–3.

11.4 *The French Revolution: The Epoch of Paper Inflation*

In an extreme reaction to the policies of the previous years, Louis XVI had made a conscious choice at his accession in 1774 not to repudiate the public debt, and this remained his position throughout the reign.[195] Yet without periodic repudiations, of one type or another, the state could not survive because of the persistent, and growing, deficit which arose from 'a political system that completely separated the privilege of spending from the obligation to pay taxes and at the same time left the public enough political power to resist taxation'.[196] The escalation in peacetime borrowing was the inevitable consequence of Louis XVI's policy: between April 1783 and November 1787, the sum of 570.4 million *livres* was raised in net borrowing. Debt servicing costs in peacetime more than doubled from 28 per cent of total expenditure in 1751 to 49.3 per cent in 1788.[197] Calonne's ministry (1783–7) is usually taken to be the turning-point in the fiscal origins of the French Revolution. It marked the peak of peacetime borrowing (a sum of 335 million in net loan revenue was raised), while the minister's critique of the fiscal structure and his proposals for reform were the most far-reaching under the *ancien régime*.[198] The failure of his plans was a severe shock to the political system. Brienne's more limited plans were also blocked, and the Estates General was summoned as a last resort, when the crisis in the Treasury had become insoluble because of the difficulty in finding new loans. The Estates General was promised that it would consent to taxation and control the budget, including the king's personal expenditure.[199] The first decision of the newly sovereign National Assembly in June 1789 was to declare that it had 'voted unanimously to agree provisionally on behalf of the Nation that taxes and contributions, although illegally established and collected, should continue to be levied in the same manner as hitherto'.[200]

Though intended as a measure to ensure that the king and his ministers would not be able to govern if the assembly ceased to meet, the decision was disastrous

[195] Root (1994), 211, 228–31, discusses the reasons for the king's attitude.

[196] Velde and Weir (1992), 36. The authors provide details of new loans (1747–88): ibid. 20. They describe the earlier types of default policies: ibid. 8–10. Cf. Crouzet (1993), 61–2, 77–83, 127–32.

[197] Velde and Weir (1992), 20 (table 2); Crouzet (1993), 61, 78 (citing different estimates of Taylor and White).

[198] Marion (1914), 350–99, 386–401; Bruguière (1991), 342; Vovelle (1984), 75–7; Hardman (1993), 103–7, 235–6; Bonney in Bonney (1995); Doyle (1989), 68, calls it 'the most radical and comprehensive plan of reform in the monarchy's history'.

[199] Aftalion in Aerts and Crouzet (1990), 24; Aftalion (1990), 30; Hardman (1993), 142; Doyle (1989), 78–85, esp. 85: 'the bankruptcy of the monarchy was . . . not only financial, but political and intellectual, too.'

[200] Aftalion (1990), 51; cf. Doyle (1989), 105.

since it provoked massive tax resistance to the new Revolutionary government.[201] No new (and therefore *ipso facto* 'legitimate') tax system could be put rapidly in place; and successive Revolutionary governments lacked the means, and perhaps the will, to resort to massive coercion since this would end the taxpayers' honeymoon which was for many the main political advantage of the Revolution.[202] Necker was clear that a new emergency tax was needed to overcome the triple problem of the decline of existing taxes ('dépérissement des impôts existants'), the delays in introducing new ones, and the risks of structural reform ('hasards inséparables d'un systême complet d'innovation'). Delay had caused in the provinces 'un contentement très-favorable à la révolution'; yet the people had confused fiscal reform with tax remission ('la libération des impôts qui lui étoient onéreux, & la diminution de tous ...').[203] Instead, the National Assembly voted away the hated indirect taxes without waiting to find a suitable replacement, thus depriving the new state of the most lucrative of the revenues of the *ancien régime* and ensuring that the balance would shift from indirect to direct taxes in a totally unplanned way.[204] Morever, it suspended and then abolished the clerical tithe,[205] which, however hated, was again potentially a useful source of additional revenue to the new state if the clergy was in any case to be expropriated (as happened by the secularization of church properties, which were renamed *biens nationaux*).[206] Necker was particularly critical of the decision of the National Assembly to introduce paper money in December 1789—the notorious *assignats*, which were anticipations on the sales of this church property, initially to the value of 400 million *livres*. Although the decision had been taken in principle, the actual issue of the new paper money (*numéraire fictif*) was deferred until April 1790.[207] A new triple system of direct taxes was introduced (the *contribution foncière*, the *contribution mobilière et personnelle* and the *patente*). The new land tax contained a number of serious deficiencies (for example, in the absence of a national land register it continued to be levied on the

201 Marion (1916); Marion (1919), 67–89; Rose (1969).

202 Aftalion (1990), 101; Crouzet (1993), 120–3.

203 Necker (1791), 130.

204 Marion (1919), 249–57; Bonney (1992*a*), 175; Doyle (1989), 131; Aftalion (1990), 93.

205 Aftalion (1990), 54, 75.

206 Doyle (1989), 134; Aftalion (1990), 65–7; Crouzet (1993), 99–103.

207 Necker (1791), 131–4, who opposed the scheme in part because of his preference for a revised *Caisse d'escompte*; Marion (1919), 100–21; Harris (1930), 41; Harris (1986), 724–7, 730–1, 759–60; Aftalion (1990), 66; Doyle (1989), 133–4; Bruguière (1991), 371–83. These were notes bearing interest at 3 per cent at the time of their first issue in 1790: Crouzet (1993), 111–12, 572, whose study of the *assignat* experiment is now the definitive interpretation. For Crouzet's criticism of 'le caractère fallacieux du gage territorial': ibid. 209.

basis of taxpayers' declarations, while its repartition was based on *ancien régime* precedents) but above all it was introduced far too late and on the basis of far too optimistic assumptions about the likely yield. Throughout 1790 and 1791 the monarchy's monthly expenditure was consistently in excess of its income.[208] The 1791 levy for the land tax had yielded only 34 million *livres* of an estimated 300 million by December 1792; yet the state's expenses in 1791 were running at 822.7 million a year, while only 249 million had been collected in taxes (as against 587 million predicted).[209]

Brissot and his followers succeeded in inciting the deputies in the National Assembly to declare war on Austria (April 1792), whereupon war became for the French Revolutionary government a 'financial operation against the coalition of the princes'.[210] War was necessary for the Revolution's creditworthiness in a political sense (to deprive the *émigrés* of any base for a counter-revolution) and in a literal sense (to give the *assignats* international convertibility): Brissot told the Jacobin Club on 31 December 1791 that 'not to start a war is to seek to destroy the credit of our *assignats*'.[211] The exchange rate might be restored; in the circumstances of a successful peace the *assignats* might flood the rest of Europe, thus giving it a vested interest in the success of the Revolution.[212] On the opposing side, France was deemed to be 'without disciplined armies, without experienced generals, without money . . .' and thus powerless to resist the coalition forces.[213] The introduction of the *assignats* took place notwithstanding the bitter experience of Law's System and in full knowledge of the disastrous consequences of paper currency in the United States, Denmark and Sweden and, though the full effects were not apparent until later, Russia and Spain (Chapter 13.4).[214] Though taxation provided the French Revolutionary government with 13 per cent of all revenues between 1790 and 1795, the paper *assignats* were deliberately expanded both to cover the deficit and to remedy the shortfall in revenue. They provided 7,000 million *livres* in revenue (at stable *assignat* values of 1790), equivalent to

[208] Aftalion (1990), 72 (graph based on Braesch's figures); for the *foncière*: Marion (1919), 179–94; for the *mobilière* and *patente*: ibid. 194–224.

[209] Marion (1919), 332–4; Aftalion (1990), 93, 103. Different recent calculations of the deficit: Bordo and White in Bordo and Capie (1994), 250–1; Crouzet (1993), 123, 213–17, 571, summarizes the differences between the figures of Bordo and White (from an earlier working paper) and those of Harris (1930).

[210] Aftalion (1990), 106.

[211] Blanning (1986), 105; Dorigny in *État, finances et économie* (1991), 348–9.

[212] Blanning (1986), 105–6; Kohn (1967), 55; Crouzet (1993), 207.

[213] Blanning (1986), 114–15.

[214] Aftalion (1990), 81, citing Boislandry, a merchant from Versailles, on the disasters in America, Denmark, Sweden and Russia.

fourteen years of normal revenue.[215] After January 1793, the issue of new *assignats* became the crucial measure for financing the war.[216] But the economic cost was enormous. The paper in circulation was not matched by any new economic resource. Much of the early confidence in the *assignats* originated in their land security, that is to say, that the paper money would be redeemed through the sales of *biens nationaux*: but the actual sales of church lands and possessions belonging to the *émigrés* did not amount to much more than 900 million in *assignats* at stable values.[217] The *assignats* were disbursed first in Paris and spread out into the *départements* at an unequal rate, and there were great local variations in their value between one *département* and another.[218] Though introduced for different reasons, the system of maximum prices introduced in 1793 (that is, prices which were fixed at rates below market prices) helped at first to sustain the value of the *assignats*, at least until the inability to convert the paper into bread purchases became apparent at times of subsistence crisis. Because of its policy of supplying bread to the capital, and requisitioning bread and other supplies for an army of 750,000 men in the summer of 1794,[219] the government itself escaped much of the depreciation of the *assignats*.[220] By 1795, the government was planning to collect revenues with *assignats* accepted at their market rates (*au cours*); but by the time the scheme came to fruition, the *assignats*—reduced in early 1796 to less than 1 per cent of their nominal value—were too depreciated to be continued. The attempt to find a replacement paper money (by the issue of so-called *promesses de mandats territoriaux*) was also rapidly undermined.[221] Inflation became the real form of taxation resulting from the excessive issue of *assignats*; and this form of taxation was even more regressive than the

[215] Marion (1921) is a detailed account; Harris (1930), 52–3; Bruguière (1991), 371–83; Crouzet (1993), 562, accepts Harris's calculations and comments that compared to Brienne's budget for 1788 (with 472 million in fiscal revenues), 'L'État révolutionnaire se serait donc assuré des ressources trois fois supérieures à celles que l'Ancien Régime obtenait'.

[216] Crouzet (1993), 213, 572–5; cf. Aubin (1991). Ramel later commented that the Convention 'abandonna presque la partie des rentrées [fiscales], soit par principe de conduite, soit à cause de leur insuffisance': quoted in Crouzet (1993), 300.

[217] The nominal figure was 2,100 million: Harris (1930), 85. The law of 18 March 1796 noted 'la disproportion entre la quantité en émission et la valeur du gage': quoted in Crouzet (1993), 412.

[218] Caron (1909); Aubin (1991), 760; White (1991); Crouzet (1993), 433, 576–8.

[219] Graph of the (theoretical?) size of the French army, 1789–99, in Delmas (1992), 242; Crouzet (1993), 268, 273, 367. Crouzet deflates the figures on paper for the size of the army: ibid. 304.

[220] Harris (1930), 159. For war financing during the Revolution: Brown (1990); Pinaud (1991).

[221] Harris (1930), 187–8, 200. Graph of the depreciation of the *assignats* (after Caron): Hincker (1989), 134; Aftalion (1990), 96; Crouzet (1993), 581. Crouzet gives details of the fiasco of the *promesses de mandats*, which were discredited even more rapidly than the *assignats*: ibid. 411–20.

hated taxes of the *ancien régime* (low denominations of *assignats* were only printed from May 1791).[222]

The gulf between revenue and expenditure became a yawning chasm after the declaration of war in April 1792. The accounts of September 1793 dealt with a twenty-six-month period from 1 July 1791, of which sixteen months had seen hostilities. Expenditure had risen to 2,652 million *livres* in this period of which 2,322 million had been on the war (including 714 million for subsistence for the army, 490 million for its pay and 324 million for its uniforms). Only 226 million of the war costs had been paid in cash.[223] Yet 5,600 million (or 82 per cent) of the 6,800 million in revenues which had financed the war effort arose from the creation of *assignats*; tax revenues and the income from national lands were much lower, amounting respectively to 368 million and 130 million.[224] On 15 December 1792, the institutions of the former Austrian Netherlands were laid aside and arrangements were enacted for the exploitation of the local resources to feed the French armies; the *assignats* were to be introduced into occupied territories.[225] As the war turned into a national crisis, the Convention was forced in August 1793 to decree the *levée en masse*. At a stroke, the effective *ancien régime* limit on the size of the French army (200,000 men in 1789) was cast aside: by September 1794, the army was nominally at the level of 1.17 million men, although only about 750,000 were fully equipped and trained for battle, and desertion was soon a significant problem.[226]

At home, the costs of the army could be paid for by a command economy with the regime of the 'maximum price' (May 1793–December 1794), which opened up the prospect of 'inexhaustible treasures' to the Convention: 'since the *maximum*', it was said, 'the depreciation of the *assignat* is onerous to the government only in the acquisition of imports.'[227] The costs of the army abroad were another matter. An army with 400,000 men actually present cost 354 million *livres* in year V (141 million in pay; 158 million in provisioning; and 55 million in additional expenses, including 34 million for transportation costs excluding the transport of

[222] Aftalion (1990), 98, 185; Crouzet (1993), 217–21, 406, for the 400 printing presses needed to print the *assignats*. On the cost of inflation, Crouzet comments that 'il s'agissait d'un impôt en nature' but whose incidence was 'très arbitraire et inégale': ibid. 319.

[223] Belhoste in *État, finances et économie* (1991), 322–3; Bordo and White in Bordo and Capie (1994), 250–1, provide other figures for these years.

[224] Belhoste in *État, finances et économie*, 323–4.

[225] Doyle (1989), 199; Marion (1921), 19–22, 193–9.

[226] Lynn (1980), 579; Doyle (1989), 204–5; Woolf (1991), 17; Delmas (1992), 242.

[227] Harris (1930), 45, quoting Mallet du Pan. The two detailed studies are Margairaz in *État, finances et économie* (1991), 399–427, and Crouzet (1993), 255–79. 'Tenez pour certain', wrote Mallet du Pan, 'que le principe fondamental du comité [de salut public] est de nourrir la capital et les armées': quoted in Crouzet (1993), 273. To some extent, the 'maximum price' assisted the value of the *assignat*: ibid. 310.

provisions).[228] In the occupied territories, the initial welcome for the French occupation soon turned sour with the enforced circulation of the *assignats* and requisitions without payment. The terrible winter of 1794–5 saw the occupied territories stripped bare. By March 1796, local claims (which were almost certainly excessive) were made in the area between the Rhine and the Maas that foodstuffs and goods to the value of 257.5 million *livres* (valued in hard currency) had been seized or lost; 54.7 million of this total sum had been paid for in *assignats*, while a further 49.2 million was regarded as a loss attributable to the fall in the value of the *assignats*.[229] A precise calculation of the exactions on occupied countries and 'sister republics' is an impossibility, given the accounting methods adopted even within France;[230] but a conservative estimate is that at least 360 million francs were levied between 1792 and 1799, a sum which represented perhaps a quarter of the Directory's revenues by years VI and VII.[231] Pitt the Younger once boasted that he could predict the financial collapse of Revolutionary France. 'But who', Wilberforce is alleged to have replied, 'was Attila's Chancellor of the Exchequer?'[232]

As the *assignats* and *mandats* declined in value, the official accounts of year III (September 1794–September 1795) had to convert the paper into its value at the time of redemption. Total expenditure then stood at 457 million *livres* in terms of hard currency, of which 252 million had been paid directly in cash; 213 million of the cash payments had been directly committed to the war effort.[233] The available cash resources in this accounting period amounted to a mere 271 million. Of this sum, 51 million arose from taxation including part of the proceeds of the forced loan of 1793 (the full yield of which may be valued at 228 million in *assignats*)[234] and sums levied on the annexed departments formerly of the Austrian Netherlands. In contrast, 122 million arose from contributions on the *pays conquis* (including 105 million from Holland and 12 million from Italy) and 55 million from secret cash purchases by means of *assignats* (7,400 million in *assignats* and 450 in *mandats* were necessary to produce this cash sum!).[235] A budget for year V (1796–7) suggested that receipts were at only 422 million (mostly made up of taxes), while expenditure stood at 842 million: the scarcity of precious metals made it difficult to expand the revenues from taxation, while the

[228] Belhoste in *État, finances et économie* (1991), 320–1.

[229] Kohn (1967), 57; Blanning (1974), 327; Diefendorf (1980), 57 n. 11.

[230] Harris (1930), 45.

[231] Woolf (1991), 17, citing Godechot's estimate; Crouzet (1993), 331 (for the pricing of requisitions in Belgium), 437–45, 497–502 (for the balance of gains abroad).

[232] Mackesy (1964), 35–6.

[233] Belhoste in *État, finances et économie* (1991), 325.

[234] Mascard in *État, finances et économie* (1991), 374.

[235] Belhoste in *État, finances et économie* (1991), 327–8, 331–3.

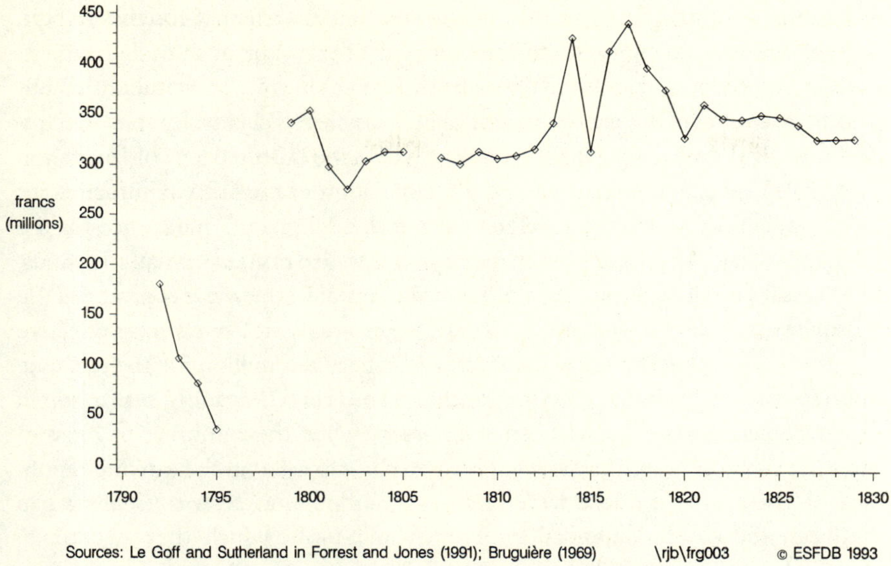

FIG. 42. Revenue from direct taxes in France, 1792–1829 (in francs)

size of the army inevitably fell to some 400,000 men by the end of 1795 simply because the state lacked the resources to finance a larger force.[236] The return to monetization was a slow and painful process, with *promesses de mandats* and other fiduciary devices in circulation failing to assist the republic in the transitional period.[237] During the *assignat* period, there was also a massive decline in the exchange value of the French currency, explicable in terms of the exportation of capital, purchases of wheat abroad, and restrictions on the exportation of gold.[238] Loss of confidence, and the destruction of the French export trade during the war were also crucial factors. But the expansion of paper had been so rapid that the return to a metallic standard was bound to be extremely difficult, though the easier access to bullion imports resulting from the Franco-Spanish alliance of 1795–6 and the export of gold from Britain (resulting from its heavy military expenditure abroad and purchases of grain) probably helped.[239]

By 1797, the effectiveness of tax collection within the French republic had been somewhat enhanced and revenue stabilized in nominal terms (Figure 42), while there can be little doubt that low agricultural prices increased the real fiscal

[236] Harris (1930), 232; Crouzet (1993), 366.

[237] Harris (1930), 226, 231–4; Crouzet (1993), 377, notes in the localities primitive exchange on the basis of grain values.

[238] Harris (1930), 258; Crouzet (1993), 285–99.

[239] Bruguière (1991), 432, 502; Crouzet (1993), 445–51.

burden of the land tax.[240] In the *banqueroute des deux tiers* (September 1797), Ramel, the finance minister, cut the cost of debt servicing at a stroke from 250 million (itself a greatly reduced figure from the debt in 1790) to 80 million.[241] But the army contractors were the government's privileged clients. By short-circuiting Treasury control, the Directory placed half of the expected levy of 320 million *livres* from specified departments at the disposition of the army contractors, of which a half (or 80 million in specie) was to be designated in advance for the companies' use. The remainder of the payment was to be made in national lands, a proposal described as placing a pistol at the throat of the army contractors ('le pistolet sur la gorge aux fournisseurs'). This was a relatively cost-effective method of meeting the army contractors' costs of 160 million for the last nine months of 1798.[242] By the end of 1798, the various revolts against French rule in the occupied territories had been suppressed, while the resources of most of western and southern Europe were ready to be exploited in the satellite republics.[243] The costs they bore were significant, although there was usually a gap between the sums demanded by French and those which they eventually received. The Treaty of The Hague (May 1795) imposed by Sieyès and Reubell on the Dutch required an indemnity of 100 million guilders for their liberation from the yoke of the 'tyrant of Orange', and the normal penalties of requisitions and the free circulation of *assignats*. This succeeded in crippling the finances of the fledgling Batavian Republic.[244] A new 8 per cent tax on income was proposed in November 1797 and enforced from April 1798.[245] The deficit on ordinary revenue stood at 44 million guilders by 1800, total expenditure having risen in that year to 78 million. Betwen 1795 and 1804 it was estimated that the Dutch paid over 229 million guilders to the French or rather more than one year's gross annual income of the republic. The Dutch were paying per capita more taxes than any other nation in Europe. In 1803, it was calculated that citizens of France paid 15.2 francs in taxes, while those of the Batavian Republic paid the equivalent of 64.3 francs.[246]

[240] Le Goff and Sutherland in Forrest and Jones (1991), 71; Bruguière (1969), 13; ESFDB \rjb\frg003 based on \frd009; Crouzet (1993), 459–62.

[241] Marion (1925), 55–70; Aftalion (1990), 178; Crouzet (1993), 466–71. Crouzet quotes (453) Ramel's hopes for a balanced budget.

[242] Brown (1990), 72–3.

[243] Blanning (1986), 196.

[244] Schama in Winter (1975), 111; Schama (1977*a*), 207, 238; the guilder was equivalent to 42 *sous* 6 *deniers*, but due to various remissions, the annual payment was in the region of 15.3 million francs: Marion (1925), 22 n. 1.

[245] Schama (1977*a*), 293–5, 305; Schama in Winter (1975), 111 (for the treaty and obligatory reception of the *assignat*), 112 (for French army costs), 115–16.

[246] Schama in Winter (1975), 117–18; Schama (1977*a*), 385, 446; somewhat different figures in Crouzet (1993), 500.

11.5 *Napoleon: The Return to Monetary Orthodoxy and the Financial Exploitation of Continental Europe*

The fruits of this exploitation of dependent territories were harvested not by the Republic but by the First Empire. Napoleon has been termed a man of the *ancien régime* in that he rejected the entire Revolutionary experience of paper money in favour of a strict monetarism.[247] He completed the Revolutionary governments' work in limiting the size of the national debt; and once he had taken over other states, too, such as Holland in 1810, he followed the same policy there.[248] In many respects, he rejected the banking experiments under the Directory,[249] since the Bank of France (founded in January 1800, but with rules of operation specified by a law of 14 April 1803) had essentially limited functions. It held a monopoly of issuing banknotes, but these were limited to a value of 500 *livres* each, and were convertible only in Paris. The circulation of such notes never exceeded 112 million *livres* under the Empire, and therefore could not play a significant role in the mechanism of state payments. The Bank's deposits scarcely exceeded those of the *Caisse d'escompte* on the eve of the Revolution. Napoleon confronted the 'paper pound' with monetarist rectitude: the so-called *franc de germinal* of 1803 had the same value as the *livre tournois* of 1785.[250] The Emperor did not wish to enter into large-scale borrowing, but fiscal discipline was also imposed by the absence of government creditworthiness: Ramel's debt repudiation in 1797 in the aftermath of the *assignat* fiasco had undermined public confidence to such an extent that even if loans had been forthcoming they would have been prohibitively expensive.[251]

If he was a man of the *ancien régime* in his distrust of paper money, Napoleon also detested financiers, whom he called scourges and lepers ('le fléau, la lèpre de la nation'). Not that he could dispense with their services: from 1806 the receivers-general were in effect back in business as the government functionaries for the levy of direct taxes.[252] Indirect taxes, too, in the form of the *douanes* and *droits réunis* made a significant comeback under the First Empire,[253] though they

[247] Gabillard (1953), 549; Woolf (1991), 138; Crouzet (1993), 399, notes Bonaparte's comment in January 1796 that 'Il faut en venir à l'argent'.

[248] Marion (1925), 334–41; Ellis (1991), 39; Pinaud (1991), 424.

[249] Jacoud (1991); Bergeron (1978*a*), 87–119.

[250] Marion (1925), 246–50; Braesch (1936*a*); Gabillard (1953), 550; Jacoud (1991), 134; Ellis (1991), 37–8; Plessis in *État, finances et économie* (1991), 257–8; Hincker (1989), 201–6; Bruguière (1991), 432–4. The fundamental accounts are Thuillier (1983), 63–152, and Crouzet (1993), 530–39.

[251] Velde and Weir (1992), 17–18; Bordo and White (1991), 314–15; Bordo and White in Bordo and Capie (1994), 266–8; Crouzet (1993), 567–8.

[252] Gabillard (1953), 552; Bergeron (1978*a*), 147–66; Théret (1991), 154. They had been in place since 1802, but without the title of *fonctionnaires banquiers*. For Mollien's reforms: Marion (1925), 290–3.

[253] Marion (1925), 297–307; Gabillard (1953), 557; Hincker (1989), 197–200; Bruguière (1991), 425–6.

were not administered as a single revenue farm (Chapter 13.5). Thus if Napoleon did not entirely recreate the fiscal system, he certainly strengthened it and confirmed a process of centralization based on Paris.[254] He was also a Mercantilist in his viewpoint: the purpose of the Continental Blockade was financial, in the words of Mollien, his Treasury minister (1806–15), 'to strike a monetary wound against England that was deeper than any which France received'.[255] Mollien considered that Napoleon's blockade 'had shaken the principal support of England's power . . .'. The Emperor, he thought, had sought to ruin 'her credit, whose measure he wrongly sought in the capricious course of the exchange, and to exhaust the source of the subsidies which she could have given to the new coalition'.[256] Thus Napoleon eagerly studied the exchange quotations, and deviations in the Hamburg[257] or Danzig rates were seen as proof that specie was being drained from the Bank of England, not as the result of Continental Europe importing Manchester cottons or Jamaica sugar.[258] The purpose of the Continental Blockade was thus in a sense defensive, to keep British products out of Europe.[259] The Continental System in a general sense had a more positive purpose: the set of military, diplomatic and dynastic alliances, fiscal and administrative reforms and the systematic exploitation of resources in the satellite states sought to make the Empire self-financing and economically prosperous.[260]

It was essential that the Empire should be self-reliant because of the spiralling costs of war: 5,100 million francs were spent between 1806 and 1814, with 817 million in the record year, 1813, after the disaster in Russia.[261] Napoleon presided over an extraordinary growth of expenditure, which (if the figures are to be believed) virtually doubled in nominal values between 1801 and 1813, from 549.6 million to 975.5 million, attaining a billion francs in 1811 and 1812 (Figure 43).[262] On the revenue side, the most important single source of income arose from military success, which provided indemnity and other extraordinary levies paid into the

[254] Bruguière (1991), 179–84, esp. 179: 'c'est la fiscalité qui nous a conduits à cette tyrannie administrative.'

[255] Gabillard (1953), 553: 'Faire à l'Angleterre une plaie d'argent plus profonde que celle que recevait la France.' Cf. Connelly (1965), 47, who calls Napoleon both a Mercantilist and a bullionist.

[256] Mollien quoted by Silberling (1924), 423. On Mollien: Bruguière (1991), 446–9. Cf. also Root (1994), 220, quoting Bonaparte in Russia in 1812.

[257] On Napoleon and Hamburg: Bruguière (1991), 137–51.

[258] Silberling (1924), 423.

[259] Gabillard (1953), 553.

[260] Ellis (1981), 108–9, makes the distinction.

[261] Tulard (1980), 490; graph of military costs in Delmas (1992), 314.

[262] ESFDB \rjb\frg001 based on \frd002 and \frd005; Tapiès (1845), 191; cf. Chabert (1949), 292–3; Flora (1983), 378–9. On expenditure and the financial difficulties at the end of the First Empire: Marion (1925), 322–8, 365–71. Bordo and White in Forrest and Capie (1994), 251, provide even higher figures for total expenditure but a similar figure (816 million) for military costs in 1813.

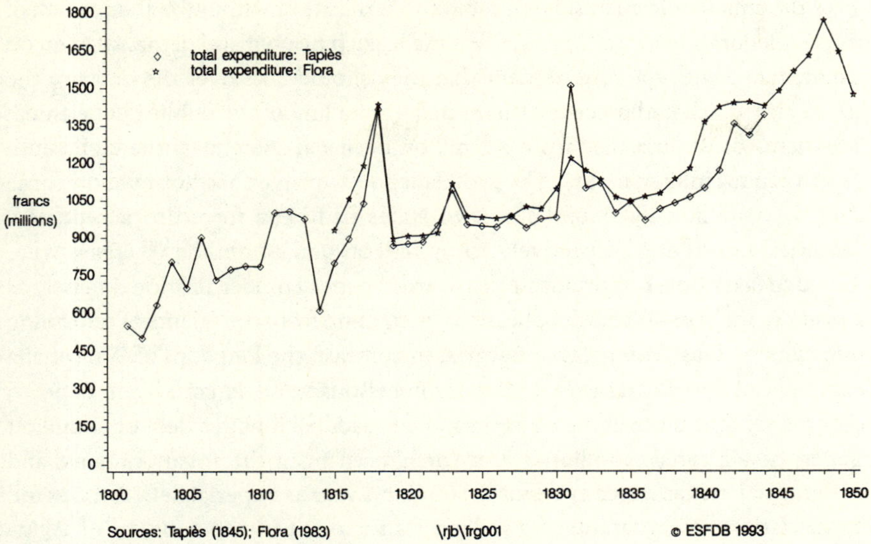

FIG. 43. Total French expenditure, 1801–1850 (in francs)

Emperor's *domaine extraordinaire*.[263] Napoleon crushed the combined Russian and Austrian forces at Austerlitz in December 1805 and by the Treaty of Pressburg imposed contributions of 40 million florins on the Empire in lieu of a direct levy on the cities. Not all the contributions and indemnities were paid by the defeated or occupied powers. Portugal was supposed to pay 100 million francs in 1807, but remained basically pro-British and paid only 7 million.[264] Despite many uncertainties due to Napoleon's retrospective balancing of the budget,[265] it seems that the campaigns of 1806 and 1807 yielded revenues which covered one-third of France's budgeted expenditure, in addition to the maintenance of the army abroad.[266]

Fiscal reforms were introduced into the occupied states and the semi-autonomous kingdoms, many of them based on French models (these included the separation of public revenues from domain or crown revenues; the destruction of feudal privileges, and the compilation of land registers; unification, rationalization and simplification of the administration of revenues and expenditure). These reforms laid the basis for modern systems of public finance.[267] Napoleon

263 Marion (1925), 350–4; Gabillard (1953), 558; Dufraisse (1984), 33; Tulard (1980); Bruguière (1991), 414–16.

264 Woolf (1991), 172; Hall (1992), 106, 113, 167–8; Sherwig (1965), 140, 191, 198–9.

265 Gabillard (1953), 556; Hincker (1989), 206: 'pas de budget mais une cour des comptes.'

266 Woolf (1991), 172.

267 Ibid. 104–5.

gave the smaller German states a rapid modernization within the framework of the Confederation of the Rhine.[268] He made such heavy fiscal demands even on client states, with the requirement that they should take over the debts of the territories which had preceded them, that a spiralling of the public debt ensued. The debts of Bavaria rose from 20 million florins at the end of the eighteenth century to 105 million in 1818. Those of Baden rose from 65,000 florins at the same date to 31 million by 1818. These two states had been forced to accept new liabilities amounting respectively to 93 million and 15 million.[269] They were forced to take some important steps towards financial modernization precisely as a result of the size of their debt burdens, benefiting from the talents of reforming ministers such as Montgelas in Bavaria. In contrast, the kingdom of Westphalia experienced a fiscal disaster under Jérôme Bonaparte. It could not hope to become solvent, since at the outset Napoleon saddled it with a debt of 34 million francs; he allocated 7 million a year for himself from the royal domains, and designated lands and incomes worth 5 million a year as imperial fiefs. A thousand beneficiaries were guaranteed 7 million francs, or nearly 20 per cent of Westphalia's public revenues. The domestic debt thus rose from 47 million in 1808 to 220 million by 1813; revenues, it was thought, could not rise above 34 million while war contributions would cost 31 million, leaving aside the maintenance of an army of 25,000 men at a cost of a further 11.5 million. Though the rate of land tax was increased from 5 per cent to 20 per cent by 1812, domestic revenues actually fell, so that the annual deficit rose from 8 million in 1808 to 31 million by 1813.[270]

The kingdom of Italy under the viceroyalty of Eugène de Beauharnais was the most successful of the satellite kingdoms, yet even here revenues only increased by 50 per cent between 1805 and 1811, while the deficit rose from 1 to 5 million lire.[271] Eugène's finance minister, Giuseppe Prina, set the capitation rate at 176 Milanese lire or 134 francs, and this was not increased during the reign, though new indirect taxes were added in 1809.[272] The kingdom benefited from the cession of Venetia, although one-fifth of its revenues, as well as national properties to the value of 30 million francs, were attached to new fiefs; a further annual income of 1.2 million francs was set aside for distribution to generals, officers and soldiers nominated by Napoleon.[273] In the kingdom of Naples under Joseph Bonaparte, feudalism was formally abolished in August 1806 and

268 Von Aretin in Aerts and Crouzet (1990), 50; Brandt in Witt (1987), 82–3.

269 Ullmann in Witt (1987), 65–7; Sheehan (1989), 248–9, 253, 262–3, 267.

270 Connelly (1965), 207–9; Woolf (1991), 173, 183.

271 Woolf (1991), 105.

272 Connelly (1965), 45–6.

273 Woolf (1991), 182.

Roederer introduced a single land and industrial tax on French principles to replace twenty-three pre-existing taxes. Joachim Murat reaped the benefit of the reforms. There was a deficit in 1808, but the following year the budget was almost balanced, and there was an increasing surplus in 1810 and 1811, while the debt had been more than halved; only in 1812–15 did military expenses produce new deficits. Revenues rose from 48 to 72 million lire between 1808 and 1811, but army and navy costs consumed 71 per cent of expenditure in 1813 (57 million lire out of a total of 80.4 million). Roederer calculated that the fiscal burden in Naples was 12 francs per inhabitant, as compared to 27 or 30 francs per inhabitant in France in 1808; but in a predominantly rural and poor economy this was probably a substantial burden, and one which increased under Joachim Murat.[274]

The experiences of Holland and Spain under the Empire were more disastrous than elsewhere. It is true that in 1806 Gogel, the Dutch finance minister, managed to impose a reformed fiscal system which owed more to his earlier abortive reform in 1801 than to French experience.[275] Before this reform, the gap between income and expenditure for 1804 was estimated at 38.2 million florins, and expenditure for 1805 seemed set to rise.[276] Gogel's reform secured a revenue increase of some 16 million florins, but gross annual income remained more or less static between 1806 and 1809 at around 52 million florins (say 113 million francs); the net figure was above 50 million only in 1809.[277] The admitted deficit fluctuated at between 18 and 28 million florins; but the figure rises to 135 million or so on average if the rise in the public debt is included in annual expenditure. The inability of Louis Bonaparte to achieve financial reform—in May 1809 he dismissed Gogel, judging that his sternness was affecting public morale—was a precipitating factor in Napoleon's annexation of the kingdom in 1810.[278]

In Spain, the Bourbon debt of 7,200 million *reales de vellón* (say 1,920 million francs)[279] was taken over by the regime of Joseph Bonaparte, and ostensibly redeemed against 'national properties' (that is to say, confiscated monastic and rebel holdings, valued at 9,700 million). The Bourbon paper money (*vales reales*)

[274] Rambaud (1911), 309–68, esp. 38; Connelly (1965), 80, 116–17; Davis (1988), 165–6; Woolf (1991), 104, 173.

[275] Woolf (1991), 104.

[276] Schama (1977*a*), 497.

[277] The figures in Connelly (1965), 143–4, are modified by Schama (1977*a*), 514, 697 n. 121; see also Schama in Winter (1975), 136 n. 85.

[278] Connelly (1965), 142–51.

[279] Ibid. 241 n. 4 accepts an exchange rate of 1 franc to 3.75 *reales*; Artola (1982), 459, has a debt of 7,099 million, presumably at a slightly earlier date.

was directly exchangeable for property, but was to be replaced with 'mortgage notes' (*cédulas hipotecarias*) which would be turned in for property and then burned. The scheme, which had some of the features of the discredited *assignats*, was poorly administered, and other types of paper money were in circulation, since Joseph's fiat only extended over part of the country. The result was that there was a rapid depreciation of the paper, which by November 1809 was worth only 25 per cent of its face value. Since some 100 million *reales de vellón* a year in revenue had been sacrificed by abolishing royal monopolies and gambling houses and the previous tariff policy, the new domestic debt rose steadily and reached 327 million *reales de vellón* by June 1813 (87 million francs). Once the debt to France by that date is included (620 million *reales de vellón* or 165.3 million francs), a more realistic picture of indebtedness begins to emerge, although the inflation of the Bourbon debt remains obscure due to the inadequacy of the debt redemption policy. The total cumulative cost of the French army in Spain rose from 532 million *reales de vellón* in 1808 (142 million francs) to 3,242 million by June 1813 (865 million francs over five years). An exaggerated estimate is that five years of war in Spain cost Napoleon a billion francs in specie and an additional 3 billion in loans and paper.[280]

11.6 *Reform in the Ancien Régime Monarchies and Resistance to French Expansionism (to c.1815)*

'Soon Amsterdam will be your counting house', Cambon had told the Convention.[281] The occupation of the Austrian Netherlands and Holland would cure France's financial deficit and destroy the confidence which was the basis of British credit. It is not always sufficiently acknowledged how close successive Revolutionary governments came to achieving their objectives. The French invasion of Holland in 1794 had temporarily deprived foreign powers such as Russia of their main money markets,[282] while in general the Coalition forces ranged against France (with the exception of Britain) comprised powers which were less advanced both economically and in terms of financial structure.[283] Napoleon dealt even more devastating blows than the Republic. The four most significant *ancien régime* monarchies on the Continent were either forced to sue for peace, or were defeated by Napoleon between 1800 and 1806: Russia sued for peace and seemed almost to turn pro-French in 1800;[284] Austria, Prussia, Russia

280 Connelly (1965), 241–4, 344. The figures in the table (ibid. 241) are open to question.

281 Mackesy in Dickinson (1989), 148.

282 Riley (1980), 118, 290; Anan'ich and Lebedev in Aerts and Crouzet (1990), 38; Buist (1974), 154–5.

283 Bergeron in Aerts and Crouzet (1990), 16.

284 Schroeder (1987), 282–3.

and Spain were defeated or occupied, respectively in 1805, 1806, 1807 and 1808 (and Austria was defeated again in 1809). In each state the period of war had an immense fiscal significance. The implications of the changes that resulted need to be reviewed together because they had certain features in common.[285]

The central objective of each of these four states was to emerge at least no weaker from the period of Revolutionary and Napoleonic expansionism; in the minds of their rulers and political leaders, it was clearly desirable for each state to exploit the opportunities presented by the European conflict to emerge stronger than its rivals. The balance of gains and losses in comparison with Prussia and Russia was carefully considered, for example, by Austria in the period of the Second Coalition.[286] Many of the most prominent thinkers of the Enlightenment were highly critical of the contemporary practice of international relations, which after the example of the Prussian seizure of Silesia in 1740 was marked by an occupation and partition mentality.[287] Analysis of the devastating effects of the Seven Years' War[288] often neglects the fact that Prussia's finances were on a sounder footing than any of the other Continental belligerents. Indeed, there was a paradoxical long-term benefit which accrued from having started the conflict in 1740: Prussia was at war for a shorter period of time than any of the other main European powers between 1740 and 1786.[289] Moreover, this breathing-space was used to good effect in Frederick the Great's *rétablissement*, or period of post-war reform. By 1786, Frederick had a reserve fund of 51.3 million *Reichstaler* in his *Staatsschatz* and its associated funds,[290] equivalent to perhaps 192 million *livres*. The French government never had an operating surplus, let alone a comparable reserve fund in this period. The apparent Prussian 'ascendancy' in the period between 1763 and 1793 coincided with the partial eclipse of France in a financial as well as a political sense.[291] For Austria and Russia, whose finances after 1763 were more encumbered than Prussia's, financial considerations alone dictated that a prior division of the territorial spoils of war was a pre-requisite for mobilization.

The peace of 1763 had revealed to Maria Theresa that the attempt to wrest Silesia back from Prussia was a 'chimera'.[292] Joseph II, co-ruler with Maria Theresa from 1765 in a scarcely workable political arrangement, tried to introduce a version of the Prussian canton system into the Austrian lands. The

[285] Holzmair (1949) makes comparisons but does not discuss Spain.

[286] Schroeder (1987), 253–4.

[287] Scott in Scott (1990), 25–6.

[288] Ibid. 17.

[289] Blanning in Scott (1990), 281.

[290] Koser (1903), 474; Hubatsch (1975), 147.

[291] Cf. Blanning (1986), 208.

[292] Beales (1987), 110.

policy was not without its inconsistencies, since Joseph was convinced that Frederick the Great's 'purely military government so [enervates] his provinces that he cannot extract further resources from them when war comes'.[293] Nevertheless, it was not Joseph but Maria Theresa who opposed the full implementation of the canton system, though much was achieved by 1771.[294] By the end of her reign, the military reforms, combined with the rise in population, had made it possible to raise forces in wartime so large that the cost—65 million florins in 1779 alone—was excessive.[295] The War of the Bavarian Succession in 1778–9 was an indirect attempt to make Frederick pay for the seizure of Silesia in 1740. The Austrian monarchy mobilized 195,000 men in 1778, and sought to increase the figure to 308,000 the following year;[296] the war petered out inconclusively, but the financial cost was significant. The monarchy, in Joseph II's words, was 'effectively without allies' and thus had 'to find its resources within itself and rely on them alone'. As Kaunitz had predicted, a huge army did not guarantee results against Prussia,[297] but it did guarantee a huge expense. For an expenditure of 100 million florins, and the dashing of financial reforms painstakingly introduced since 1763, the gains were pitifully small: the acquisition of the Innviertel, a small territory of 1,000 square miles, with a population of 120,000 persons yielding a revenue of about half a million florins a year.[298] The three-year conflict with the Ottoman Turks (1788–90) was much more damaging (Figure 35). Joseph II had recognized that such a war was of questionable economic and financial benefit: 'even if it is successful, the money and the number of men it costs, especially through sickness, make it always very damaging, without taking into account all the provinces which are devastated, and the depopulation and infertility of those which can be conquered'.[299] The army, with some 315,000 troops mobilized, incurred 207.7 million florins in expenditure. Though revenues rose from 65.8 million florins in 1781 to 87.5 million by 1788, the rate of increase was insufficient. Paper issues (*Banco-Zettel* or *Bankozettel*) had reached 28 million florins by 1790 to cover the deficit, and the national debt by this date stood at 400 million.[300] The failure of Joseph II's plans for fiscal reform thus assumed momentous significance. Despite his pronouncement that 'as regards the financial articles of faith, I have become an atheist',[301] his single tax on land at its inception bore close resemblances to the Physiocratic *impôt unique*. The tax and

[293] Ibid. 189.

[294] Ibid. 227; cf. 184, 222, 344–6.

[295] Dickson (1987), ii, 150, 154.

[296] Following Dickson (1987), ii, 149, rather than Beales (1987), 404, 414.

[297] Beales (1987), 186.

[298] Ibid. 403–4, 414, 422.

[299] Ibid. 276.

[300] Dickson (1987), ii, 115, 155–6; Blanning (1978), 56, 86; Macartney (1968), 179.

[301] Blanning (1978), 53–4.

agrarian regulation was promulgated in February 1789, and henceforth any peasant holding 'rustical' lands which were not part of the lord's domain would pay 12.22 per cent of his income as taxation, with 17.77 per cent as a permanent commutation payment to the nobility; 70 per cent would be retained for the support of his family. The tax reform was impracticable in war time and Joseph II arbitrarily changed the nature of the tax from a levy on the net to one on the gross product of agriculture. This led to the prospect of a real increase in the fiscal burden of the peasantry, while at the same time reducing aristocratic incomes; the reform thus contributed towards revolt in Hungary and general disaffection elsewhere.[302] Joseph's intention to divert a greater proportion of Hungarian tax revenue towards Austria was well known (in Joseph's words, Hungary would thus become 'another Peru discovered').[303] Faced with simultaneous upheavals in the Austrian Netherlands and Hungary, Leopold II withdrew these reforming measures immediately on his accession in 1790; though this did nothing to assist the financial crisis of the monarchy, Leopold did effect some reduction in extraordinary military expenditure (from 41.8 million florins in 1790 to 16.4 million in 1792) but the public debt had risen somewhat by 1792 (to 417 million).

Hostility to the war against France was rife in the Austrian Habsburg lands, but support was gained by the suggestion that the war would be short and that taxes would not have to be raised; this promise was broken in 1794.[304] In only one year between 1781 and 1818 did Austrian revenue exceed current expenditure.[305] The accounts for 1793 showed a deficit of 10 million florins (about £1 million).[306] Conforming to a precedent established in 1702, the Austrian authorities attempted to use their credit to raise a loan in the British money market. By December 1794, Pitt recognized that a loan guarantee to the Austrians of £6 million was probably necessary in return for a force of 200,000 men in the field. By January 1795, this loan guarantee had been reduced to £4 million or 40 million florins, later raised to £4.6 million, despite fears of an impending Austrian bankruptcy and reservations about the likely inaction of its army. Fox regarded the loan guarantee as akin to a subsidy, and events proved him right.[307] By the end of the War of the First Coalition, Austria's foreign indebtedness was about 116 million florins, or a fifth of the total state debt.[308]

302 Liebel-Weckowicz (1974), 78, 80; Scott in Scott (1990), 185–6.
303 Beales (1987), 100.
304 Wangermann (1969), 121, 123, 147–9.
305 Riley (1980), 107; Mitchell (1981), 733, 742–3.
306 Helleiner (1965), 3, 11.
307 Ibid. 2, 28, 33–4, 49–50, 54, 56, 106.
308 Macartney (1968), 179 n. 1.

The withdrawal of Prussia from the war in 1795 left Austria to bear the brunt of the fighting, and by 1796 a total of 46.8 million florins in paper money was all that kept the finances going; the following year the convertibility of banknotes into specie was suspended.[309] As military defeat sapped the Habsburgs' financial strength, fiscal weakness made a successful war effort increasingly difficult.[310] Though the British were suspicious of Austrian objectives, and preferred alliances with Russia and Prussia, British loans to Austria amounted to 31.3 million florins between 1800 and 1808.[311] Such sums were insufficient to stave off bankruptcy resulting from the costs of two mobilizations and defeats in 1805 and 1809. The Austrian financial crisis in 1805 was exacerbated by the fact that the British had to suspend payments in case the money was simply syphoned off into the enemy Treasury; even so, in all probability the £1 million Austria had received in British subsidies found its way to France in war indemnity.[312] By 1806, nearly 450 million florins of *Bankozettel* were in circulation, and the discount rate was 175.[313] Austria was subsequently defeated again at Wagram in July 1809, by which time Britain had remitted £1.19 million in specie to finance the Habsburg war effort.[314] These two Austrian defeats led to indemnities of 350 million francs in total, much of which was spent on the occupation; but some 120 million francs entered the French Treasury.[315] In December 1809, the government was forced to call in all the silver held by its subjects (except in Hungary) in order to pay the second French indemnity. The *Bankozettel* in circulation had increased to 846 million by this date, while their discount rate was 469, recalling the notorious fate of the French *assignats*.

Shortly before the reform measure of February 1811, the total circulation of *Bankozettel* had reached 1,060 millions at a discount rate of over 800.[316] By the reform, all *Bankozettel* and all small coins were called in and exchanged for new paper issues, called redemption bonds (*Einlösungsscheine*), at the rate of one new for five old, of the same face value. Since all taxation was to be paid in the new currency, as were government pensions and salaries, taxes and salaries were thus multiplied by five. But the rate of interest on loans was cut by half; the issue of paper money was never to exceed the figure of 212 million, and that sum was to be amortized gradually. The scheme had to be implemented by decree in

[309] Ibid. 179; Riley (1980), 204; Blanning (1986), 176.
[310] Sheehan (1989), 282–3.
[311] Schremmer in Mathias and Pollard (1989), 416–17 and n. 11; Schroeder (1987), 283, 287 n. 96.
[312] Helleiner (1965), 144–5; Sherwig (1969), 170.
[313] Macartney (1968), 183.
[314] Sherwig (1969), 212–13; Hall (1992), 176.
[315] Woolf (1991), 172; Gabillard (1953), 559.
[316] Macartney (1968), 183, 195; Holzmair (1949), 129.

Hungary after September 1812, since consent could not be obtained from the diet.[317] It failed in its purpose in the Austrian lands, for when serious rearmament began again in April 1813, the government was forced to issue another 45 million in paper (this time called *Anticipationsscheine*) and there were seven secret issues thereafter, which resulted in a discount rate of 408 by April 1815. The amount of paper in circulation, old and new, was now 635 million.[318] British subsidies were therefore much needed, but relatively little could be offered since the coalition had been established before Austria entered the war and Britain's resources were exhausted: £1 million was the extent of the commitment in 1813, although half a million in supplies were also provided. The following year the subsidy was slightly smaller because of the ending of hostilities.[319] The decision to limit the army size to a nominal 400,000 men (200,000 to 230,000 in practice) and to keep the military budget to 45–50 million florins (the official limit was first 40 million, later raised to 44 million) was only possible after 1815 because Austria enjoyed nearly thirty-five years of peace (apart from military intervention in Italy in 1820–1). These savings, together with a rise in ordinary revenue from 50.7 million florins in 1814 to almost 94 million in 1817, which was largely the result of the return of the territories lost in 1809, might have offered some prospect of balancing the budget. The problem was that annual deficits were still incurred, and the state debt rose from 739 million in 1816 to 905 million in 1823, while the interest charge trebled from 12 to 36 million in the intervening period. Even the British government's renunciation of all but £2.5 million of the £23.5 million debt owed to it in 1823 could make but a small impression on this debt mountain.[320]

Prussian budgetary data remain elusive or misleading.[321] The surviving accounts suggest that revenue regularly exceeded expenditure, even in time of war (Figure 44).[322] However, everything we know from other sources suggests that the reverse was true after 1786, and that the surplus left by Frederick the Great was eroded because Frederick William II refused to limit his foreign policy commitments. By the end of 1793, it was certain that Prussia could not long continue in the war without subsidies. Of £13 million left by Frederick the Great in 1786, less than £3 million remained—or so Grenville, the British foreign secretary, was informed—while Prussian revenue was regularly falling short of

317 Macartney (1968), 196–7; Hanák (1991), 91.

318 Macartney (1968), 194–8.

319 Sherwig (1969), 310, 323; Hall (1992), 200, 205.

320 Macartney (1968), 203–6; Helleiner (1965), 147–79; Sherwig (1969), 343.

321 Schremmer in Mathias and Pollard (1989), 414–15.

322 Riedel (1866); ESFDB \korner\prussia\prub004 after \prud004.

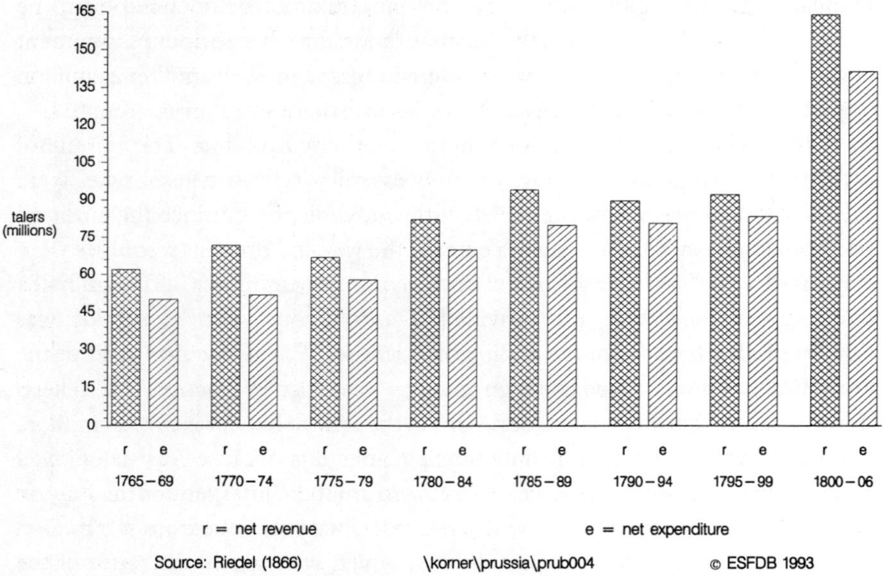

FIG. 44. Total revenue and total expenditure of Prussia, 1765–1806 (in *talers*)

expenditure.[323] Prussia let it be known that a force of 100,000 men in the field required 22 million *talers* (or £3.5 million) from her allies: so much for Frederick the Great's boast that states of the second rank needed no foreign subsidies in time of war.[324] By 1794, the Prussian public debt was 38.1 million *talers*, which helps explain the withdrawal from the war the following year.[325] A state which in appearance had been one of the most effective of the *ancien régime* monarchies on the Continent had in fact suffered from internal political divisions and structural weaknesses which necessitated a neutral stance against France after 1795 and suggested the inevitability of defeat when a direct military confrontation came in 1806.[326] Prussia was defeated at Jena in October 1806 before its request for a renewal of the 1794 subsidy treaty could be agreed by Britain. Though it was rumoured that the equivalent of £2 million in specie had been removed from the Prussian Treasury before Berlin had been captured, the British considered Prussian resources 'not only weakened and exhausted but ... scarcely ... to exist'.[327] The price of defeat was heavy: its territorial extent was more than halved (from 335,000 to 158,000 square kilometres) and as a result almost half its population was lost to other states (the population fell from 10.7 million to 4.9

323 Sherwig (1969), 35. 324 Helleiner (1965), 1.
325 Schremmer in Mathias and Pollard (1989), 415.
326 Schroeder (1987), 267–8, 274, 286; Sheehan (1989), 224–5, 233–4.
327 Sherwig (1969), 179.

million).[328] Defeat was little short of a fiscal catastrophe with momentous political consequences, bringing the state to the verge of extinction as a significant power.[329] As late as about 1812, total revenues were only 17.2 million *talers* as against 29.7 million in about 1800.[330] The debt in 1807 stood at 53.7 million *talers*, to which was added a huge war indemnity imposed by Napoleon: 515 million francs was to be levied, of which 220 million francs were to be paid to the war Treasury and a similar amount spent on the occupation forces; the indemnities amounted to more than the total annual income of the truncated Prussian state.[331] Not surprisingly, the debt grew rapidly, reaching 100 million *talers* in 1810, 112 million in 1811 and 206 million in 1815.[332] By the spring of 1810, the Altenstein–Dohna government had still not succeeded in paying off the French indemnity in full and was recommending the cession of the province of Silesia: Hardenberg on his return to office that year promised Frederick William III to find the means of paying off the indemnity in full.[333] In reality, the Prussian government sought every means at its disposal to elude payment of the French indemnity, which was moderated to 198.7 million francs (56.3 million *talers*), of which 154.5 million remained unpaid on 12 July 1807. It was expected that 15 million of this would be paid in cash, 45 million by ceding royal domains, and 90 million in commercial credits. Though reduced by various expedients to 108.4 million in November 1807, the debt still stood at 44.4 million in March 1813.[334] Even so, reform of the Prussian fiscal economy became a dire necessity, and began after the Peace of Tilsit in 1807, though the process of reform was still incomplete in 1820: in Hardenberg's words, a state which did not embrace Revolutionary principles 'must either face their forcible imposition or its own extinction'.[335] The short-term objective was the levy of an extraordinary direct tax on personal incomes in 1808; the longer-term aim was a more equitable distribution of the land tax, including the abolition of exemptions, and the levelling of tax distinctions between town and countryside. Stein was the initiator of these ideas and the cause was then taken up by Hardenberg. Stein's ideas were certain to alienate the nobility, and did so, whereupon in 1811

[328] Schremmer in Mathias and Pollard (1989), 417.

[329] Sheehan (1989), 291; Simon (1971), 232, comments that 'a direct chain of cause and effect ... linked the constitutional crisis of 1811 to Napoleon's financial pressure'.

[330] Schremmer in Mathias and Pollard (1989), 416.

[331] Ibid. 415; Woolf (1991), 172; Dufraisse (1984), 33; Gabillard (1953), 559; Sheehan (1989), 255; Simon (1971), 14.

[332] Sheehan (1989), 305; 287.6 million in 1815 according to Schremmer in Mathias and Pollard (1989), 454.

[333] Simon (1971), 49; Sheehan (1989), 305.

[334] Lesage (1924), 12, 29, 79, 93, 116, 182, 251, 258–9, 290–1, 298, 307. Lesage, 299, states that there was a fixed exchange rate for the purposes of the indemnity of 85 *talers* to 300 francs.

[335] Schremmer in Mathias and Pollard (1989), 421; Sheehan (1989), 252.

Hardenberg had to beat a retreat on far-reaching reform by the removal of exemptions.[336]

Russian revenues rose steadily between 1763 and 1796, but the costs of collection increased in absolute terms and as a percentage of the revenue obtained. When Catherine II assumed power in 1762, the field army fighting against Prussia had not been paid for eight months and payments totalling 17 million roubles had not been honoured.[337] There was no certainty at all in the accounting process (one estimate placed the revenue in 1764 at 9.3 million roubles, but another in 1769 at 19.9 million).[338] A more probable figure for 1764 is a gross revenue of 21.9 million reduced by collection costs of 4.2 million to a net revenue of 17.7 million (a collection overhead of 19.2 per cent). By the end of Catherine's reign in 1796, gross revenues had jumped to 73.1 million, reduced by collection costs of 17.7 million to a net revenue of 55.4 million roubles (a collection overhead of 24.2 per cent).[339] If the fiscal organization of all states was 'expenditure-driven' (Chapter 12), this was particularly true of Russia, where revenue increases followed upon the growth of expenditure after a significant time-lag (Figure 45).[340] Expenses rose from 21.6 million roubles in 1764 to 78.2 million by 1796. The deficit had to be covered by the emission of paper money, the *assignat* roubles.[341] An *assignat* bank and paper money had been established at the end of 1768 to help finance the First Russo-Turkish War (1768–74); by 1786 some 45 million *assignat* roubles were in circulation, when the ceiling on issues was raised to 100 million in order to finance the Second Russo-Turkish War (1787–92); and by the end of Catherine's reign in 1796 some 156.7 million had been printed. The result was the collapse in the value both of the *assignat* and the exchange value of the currency, for example against the Dutch guilder (which was of crucial importance because of the importance of Russian borrowing on the Amsterdam money market).[342] The Russian finances were in the worst state of all the potential coalition partners: by 1796 the national debt had reached 215 million roubles, and with annual income and expenditure respectively at 55.4 and 78.2 million roubles, the debt was set to rise rather than fall.[343]

336 Simon (1971), II, 54–5, 57–60, 83–7. On Hardenberg, see also Klein (1965), 21–34; Nolte (1990), 32–9, 49–50, 93–105.

337 Duran (1970), 485; Madariaga (1981), 470.

338 LeDonne (1984), 245.

339 Kahan (1985), 341; Madariaga (1981), 481, somewhat exaggerates the collection overhead.

340 Kahan (1985); Khromov (1950); ESFDB \russia\rusb002 based on \rusm002. The figures before 1796 provided by Kahan are those for net revenue. Khromov's figures include extraordinary revenues and borrowing.

341 Kahan (1985), 341, 346; LeDonne (1984), 259–60.

342 De Bloch (1899), i, 71; Khromov (1950), 121–2; Riley (1980), 154–7; LeDonne (1984), 260; LeDonne (1991), 280.

343 Saul (1970), 22; Blanning (1986), 188.

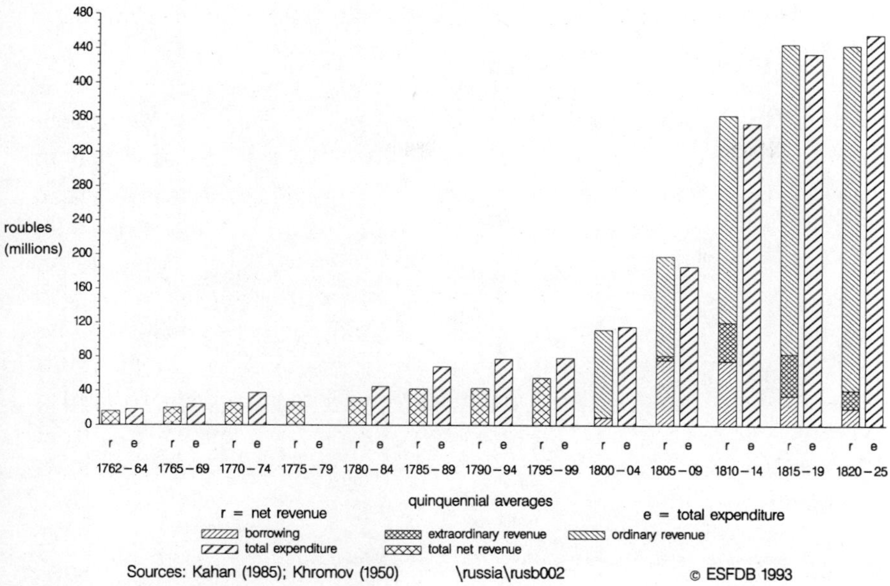

FIG. 45. Categories of Russian expenditure and revenue, including borrowing, 1762–1825 (in roubles)

Russia was hostile to the French Revolution, but until 1797 her war against Jacobinism was restricted to military intervention in Poland, despite Austrian and Prussian demands for military assistance. Even the prospect of a favourable loan from Britain in 1795 (£1 million for a force of 55,000 men) failed to stir Russia from neutrality.[344] The preferred ally of Britain had to operate furthest from the main theatre of war at a time when its finances were in the worst state of three main potential allies. The period of peace with France under Paul I halted the spiralling deficit, but in the first decade of Alexander I's reign financial affairs went out of control. In 1803, revenues stood at 95.5 or 101.6 million *assignat* roubles, but expenses were at 109.4 million. By 1805 revenues remained more or less stable (at 100 or 107.2 million) but expenditure had reached 125.5 million. The disastrous war against Napoleon which ended with the Treaty of Tilsit saw expenditure in 1809 rise to 278.5 million against 127.5 or 133.8 million in revenue. The Russian government had asked Britain for £6 million to continue the war, but the negative response had been motivated by fear that the Russians would renegue on the debt; the British in any case considered that the war was being fought to preserve Russian territory and interests and should therefore be financed without assistance. Finally, in November 1807, in line with undertakings

[344] Helleiner (1965), 80.

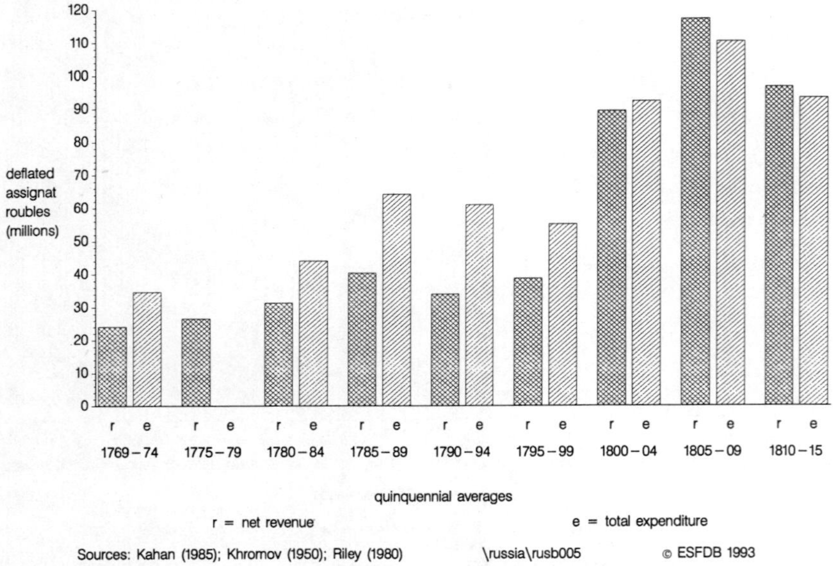

FIG. 46. Russian deflated expenditure and revenue, including borrowing, 1769–1815 (expressed in deflated *assignat* roubles)

made at Tilsit, Russia declared war on Britain. Moreover, seeing an opportunity for compensation for the Treaty of Tilsit, Alexander I sought to annexe Finland, thus incurring a further round of costs.[345] As before, the new military commitments were financed by further issues of *assignat* roubles, indeed for record amounts in 1808–10 (respectively for 95 million, 55.8 million and 46.2 million), taking the total amount in circulation to 477.4 in 1808, 533.2 million in 1809 and 579.4 million in 1810. By 1810, the *assignat* rouble had hit an all-time low of one-quarter of its nominal value in silver (25.4).[346] The new financial adviser to the government, Michael Speransky, argued that the absolute priority was to reduce the quantity of *assignats* in circulation, to stop further issues of paper money, to reduce expenditure and to float a domestic loan equivalent to the French *Caisse d'amortissement*. Speransky's plan was accepted in a decree of February 1810: the *assignats* were recognized as a state debt for which full redemption was promised, and further increases in their emission were forbidden. Subsequently, a limit of 577 millions in circulation was announced, but it could not be maintained. The extraordinary financial burdens of the wars of 1812–15, comparable in importance to the culmination of the struggle with

[345] Lower figures from de Bloch (1899), i, 113, as compared with Khromov (1950), 440–1, 446–7; Raeff (1969), 83–4; LeDonne (1991), 281–3; Sherwig (1969), 179–82; Hall (1992), 137, 163–4.

[346] Riley (1980), 156; de Bloch (1899), i, 110–11; Raeff (1969), 84 n. 1.

Charles XII in 1709, prevented the adoption of such a financial solution.[347] Subsidies of £4 million a year were demanded from Britain for a resumption of hostilities, but this was more than Britain could pay given that the Spanish peninsula was its priority. Moreover, in so far as Britain wished to make payments at all, paper issues were proposed rather than specie; British subsidies were relatively small in comparison with the financial need, in part because the Russian will to resist Napoleon was doubted until the extremely costly French victory at Borodino.[348] The gap between revenue and expenditure continued to widen due to the inflexibility of the Russian tax base and loan revenue and other expedients were needed to retrieve the situation (Figure 46).[349] By 1815, 825.8 million in *assignat* roubles were in circulation and their value had depreciated somewhat since 1810 (from 25.4 to 23.8). The debt continued to grow even with the return to peace, and reached 1,300 million by 1825.

The move towards a fairer distribution of taxation largely failed in *ancien régime* Spain, which explains the fiscal limits on the revenue system and the country's vulnerability to the Napoleonic takeover in 1808.[350] The key idea under Carlos III was the 'single tax' (*única contribución*), originally conceived before the spread of Physiocratic ideas in Spain. A reform commission was set up to demonstrate the benefits of revenue amalgamation in contrast with the diversified system which prevailed in the eighteenth century. This reported in positive terms in April 1756.[351] Nothing was done at first, but the idea was revived in 1760. The Spanish government tried to shift the burden away from indirect taxes, but in the event failed (due to aristocratic and popular opposition to Esquilache, which culminated in the riots of 1766).[352] A further attempted reform in 1770 proved abortive. The recourse to paper currency, and subsequently the disentailing of the church during the Revolutionary wars, were the inevitable consequences of the inability to reform the fiscal structure earlier in the eighteenth century. Before 1768, the *rentas provinciales* had never exceeded 90 million *reales de vellón* in a single year. Nevertheless, improved fiscal efficiency after 1779, with the removal of farming of the *rentas provinciales* and the recourse to direct

[347] Raeff (1969), 95–7, 101–2, 104–5.

[348] Sherwig (1969), 282, 289–90, 294–5, 301–4; Hall (1992), 198–200.

[349] Kahan (1985); Khromov (1950); Riley (1980), 156; ESFDB \russia\rusb005 based on \russia\rusm004.

[350] Noel in Scott (1990), 123, 131, 134, 142; Barbier and Klein (1981).

[351] *Mémoires*, ed. Moreau de Beaumont (1768), i, 493–4. These figures have been compared with those of the *Junta*, dated 30 April 1756: Matilla Tascón (1947), 92–3. On Ensenada's reforming efforts in general: Lynch (1989), 164–75.

[352] Herr (1989), 8–10; Noel in Scott (1990), 134.

administration, led to a rise from 102.6 million *reales de vellón* in 1779 to 158 million by 1793 (Figure 47).[353]

'America is the soul of our greatness': the central role of the colonies to the Spanish monarchy was restated in the aftermath of the Peace of 1763 (following the disastrous defeat of Spain the previous year, when the British captured Havana).[354] The growth of Spanish naval and military strength in response to the need to exclude the British interlopers was dependent on an increase in royal revenue. The Spanish empire was regarded as a source to be exploited as well as defended,[355] and there is no doubt that imperial revenue grew in the course of the eighteenth century; income from the Lima Treasury recovered after 1750, though it was not until 1780 that it reached the peak years of the seventeenth century.[356] Though Spain gained Minorca and Florida from its war against Britain (1779–83), its finances plunged into a chronic deficit which could be bridged only by the emission of a form of paper money, the *vales reales*. During the war, Spain had issued *vales reales* to the extent of 452 million *reales de vellón*, and the paper had depreciated by 13 per cent by the end of the war (at one point, it had depreciated by 22 per cent below face value). Confidence in the paper currency was restored only with the return to peace in 1783, and the government was able to issue a further 99 million by 1789, to help pay for a canal-building programme.[357]

Within two years of the French declaration of war in 1793, the collective will of Godoy's government to resist France had collapsed in the face of conspiracy at home and a spiralling deficit. New loan income had been quickly exhausted in the war as had the capacity for sustained expansion of the ordinary revenues (Chapter 13.3). Excluding the colonies, expenses had risen to 709 million *reales* in 1793, and rose still further to 946 million in 1794, and 1,029 million by 1795. The total deficit for the four years 1793–6 was estimated at 1,269 million *reales* of which about three-quarters (964 million) was covered by paper issues (*vales reales*).[358] The Spanish navy was too weak to maintain neutrality between the two great maritime powers; Carlos IV opted for alliance with France and war with Britain, respectively in August and October 1796. The effectiveness of the

353 Artola (1982), 306, 343, 349; ESFDB \rjb\spain\spg003 based on \spd005.

354 Noel in Scott (1990), 121, 123–4; Lynch (1958), 14–15; Walker (1979), 222.

355 Lynch (1958), 15–16, 18, 116–18.

356 TePaske and Klein (1981), 122–3; Lynch (1958), 121–2; Brading in Bethell (1984), 409.

357 Riley (1980), 167–8; Herr in Otazu (1978*a*), 124; Herr (1989), 79, 768–9; Artola (1982), 369–87; Harris (1979), 211.

358 Barbier and Klein (1981), 321; Herr (1989), 80–3. Note the difference between Barbier and Klein's figures and those of Cuenca Esteban (1981), which are 20 per cent lower for ordinary income in the years 1788–92: Herr (1989), 79 n. 3. Herr in Otazu (1978*a*), 124; Artola (1982), 404–5, 417.

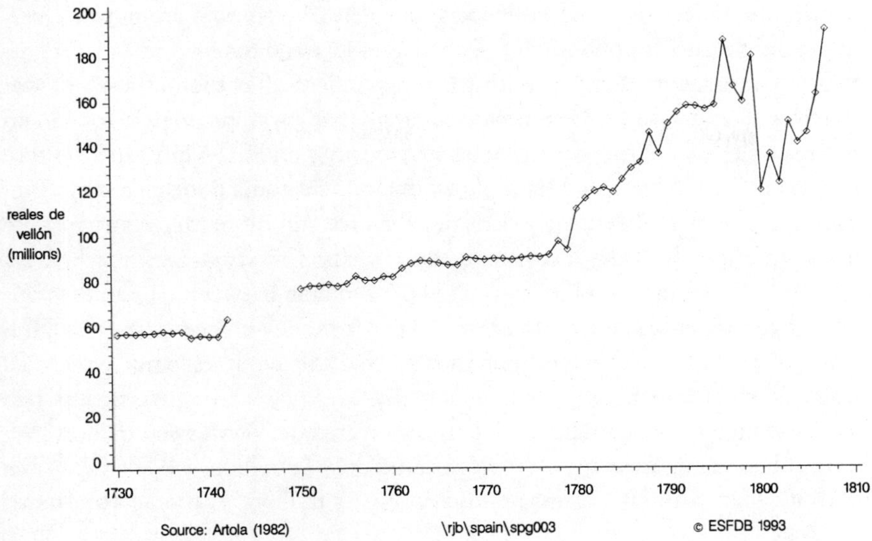

FIG. 47. The value of the *rentas provinciales* in Castile, 1730–1807 (in *reales de vellón*)

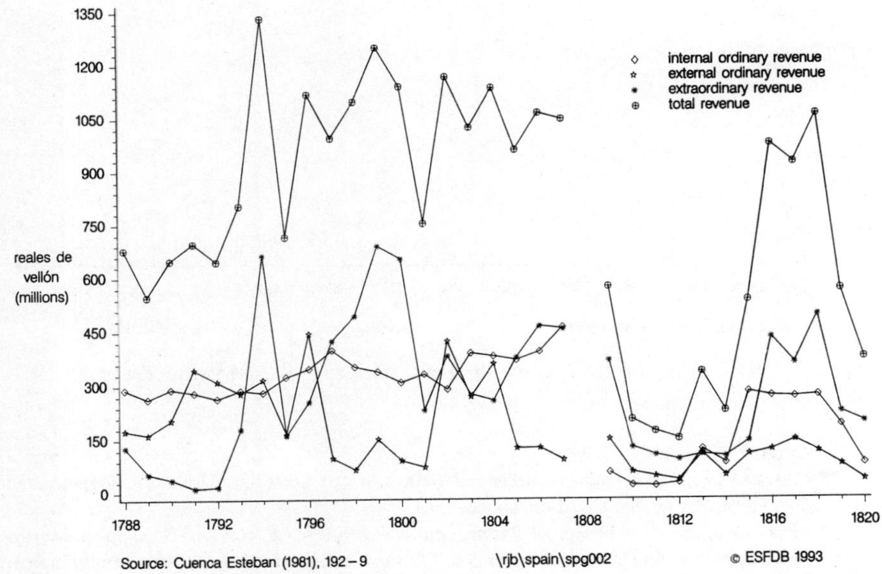

FIG. 48. Net revenue of the Spanish General Treasury, 1788–1820 (in *reales de vellón*)

British blockade[359] resulted in financial disaster. The sources are not in agreement, but the income of both the General Treasury and the Madrid Treasury, its largest constitutent element, both show a problem after the outbreak of war (Figures 48 and 49).[360] One estimate suggests that royal income, which in 1793 had been 584 million *reales de vellón*, fell in 1797 to 487 million, while expenses rose to 1,423 million, leaving a deficit of 945 million. Customs duties, an important source of revenue, inevitably fell, as did a source still more important, income from America: the latter had averaged 123 million in 1793–5 and reached 232 million in 1796, only to fall to an average of 17 million between 1797 and 1801.[361] The government was forced to accept its paper money at face value, though it was discounted by 15 to 20 per cent: thus in 1797, it paid out 1,080 million in *vales reales* to meet expenses of 900 million. By May 1798, the government had outstanding bills of 26 million, while the predicted deficit was 800 million.[362]

A public gift to assist the war effort raised only 23 million, while a repayable patriotic loan without interest produced only 1.5 million. At the end of August

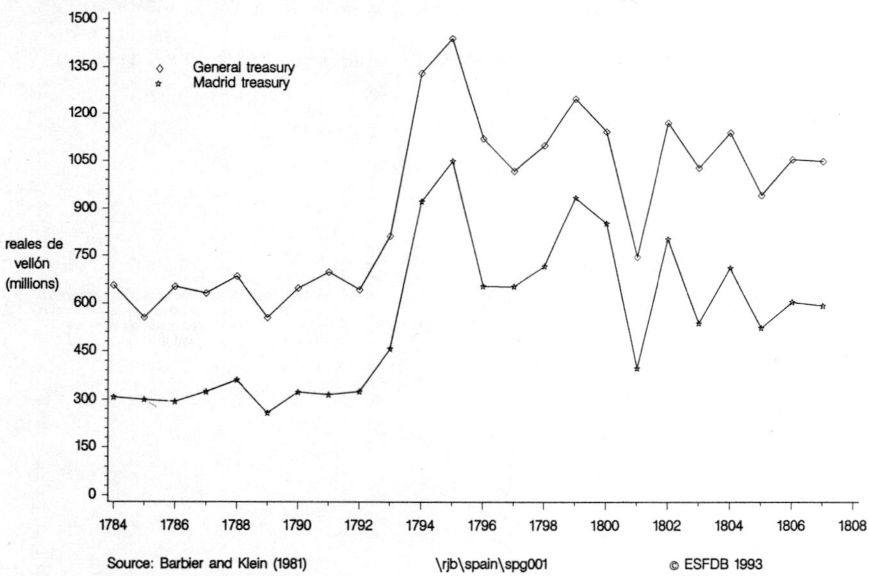

FIG. 49. Total income of the Spanish General Treasury and the Madrid Treasury, 1784–1807 (in *reales de vellón*)

[359] Brading in Bethell (1984), 434–5.

[360] Cuenca Esteban (1981), 191–9; Barbier and Klein (1981), 318, 338; ESFDB \rjb\spain\spg002 based on \spd004; \rjb\spain\spg001 based on \spd001.

[361] Herr (1989), 84. The figures of Barbier and Klein (1981), 338, remain more optimistic for revenues and (ibid. 326) for American revenues. The same is true of the figures of Cuenca Esteban (1981), 192–9.

[362] Herr (1989), 85, 87, 770.

1798, Soler reported on the need for 'extraordinary measures to produce massive funds'. The proposal, enacted in four royal decrees in September, was to attack directly the wealth of the church; the *vales reales* could be used in payment for the ecclesiastical properties, while the paper would be gradually withdrawn from circulation. The cost of servicing the royal debt was reduced by a quarter, but the success of Soler's plan depended on the product of the sales being placed in an amortization fund, which in turn relied on a balanced budget which was scarcely possible during the war against Britain. Almost immediately a new loan was floated and, in April 1799, *vales reales* of almost 800 million were issued; the value of the *vales reales* fell to between 30 and 45 per cent below par in the first half of 1799, and ranged between 62 and 72 per cent by August 1800. Only in 1802, with the peace between France, Spain and Britain did the *vales reales* recover to a discount of 10–20 per cent. In August 1800, in an attempt to boost confidence, all *vales reales* issued since 1780 were recognized as a legitimate debt of the monarchy, and a separate consolidation fund was established: according to figures given to Napoleon in 1808, this eventually redeemed some 300 million of the 2,193 million *vales reales* in circulation. The government failed singularly to take advantage of the sale of ecclesiastical properties, a mere 340 million in total coming from the process of disentail; the remaining 1,653 million constituted a new debt.[363] The renewal of war between France and Britain in May 1803 overturned the attempted policy of debt redemption. Carlos IV was forced by Napoleon to pay a 'neutrality subsidy' of 6 million francs (24 million *reales de vellón*) in October 1803, retroactive to the outbreak of the war. Since there was no available source of income, the consolidation fund had to meet the bill; but it proved unable to do so and in September 1805 Carlos IV had to sign a contract with the house of Hope and Co. of Amsterdam for 10 million florins (80 million *reales de vellón*) at 5.5 per cent interest. In 1808, the debt to the French stood at 31.6 million *reales de vellón*, with an additional 318 million to Dutch bankers.[364]

Britain's response to the Spanish 'neutrality subsidy' was to capture three or four Spanish frigates on their way from Mexico to Spain, laden with silver; Spain in turn declared war on Britain in December 1804.[365] Royal income from the Indies collapsed from an average of 193 million for 1802–4 to 28 million for 1805–7, while average income from the customs was halved, from 187 to 85 million.[366] According to figures given to Napoleon, expenditure was at 637 million in 1807, as against income of 505 million, leaving a deficit of 132 million. New taxes were

363 Ibid. 88–9, 93–6, 100–2, 112–14 (esp. 114 n. 56), 117–18, 151.

364 Ibid. 141, 145–7; Buist (1974), 298–304; Riley (1980), 170–4.

365 Hall (1992), 112.

366 Herr (1989), 138, based on Cuenca Esteban (1981). The figures in Barbier and Klein (1981), 338, again differ.

desperately unpopular and failed to produce much income to bridge the deficit.[367] One factor precipitating the Bonapartist takeover in Spain in 1808 was Napoleon's fear of the fiscal collapse of his ally: Spain, he believed, had vast wealth which its incompetent rulers were unable to tap, and the reports he received only served to bear out his contention.[368] What he failed to recognize was that the war had fatally cut Spain's relations with its American colonies. Here the contrast with Portugal is clear. The successful Franco-Spanish offensive against Portugal in 1807–8 chased the government out of the kingdom, forcing them to withdraw to Brazil, where their hold on the colony was consolidated, and resistance to Spanish rule in America could be organized.[369] In contrast, the Spanish colonies were seething with discontent with the imperial government; the colonists were split on whether to recognize Fernando VII, Joseph Bonaparte or to declare independence: within the framework of a 'loyalist' revolt emerged the idea of 'the liberty of a nation'.[370] These discontents and splits, combined with the enforced isolation from the imperial government because of the British blockade, ensured the loss of much of the Spanish empire in 1808–10 and altered the entire course of its financial history. By the time of Fernando VII's restoration the die was cast. The rebels in Spanish America had made permanent the almost complete cessation of bullion remittances imposed by the British blockade in 1804.[371] External revenues (customs duties and remittances from the colonies) declined from about a quarter of all government revenues prior to the war of 1793 to less than 10 per cent after 1815. The silver remittances disappeared entirely. The estimated economic loss to Spain was between 2.3 and 5.6 per cent of national income, with between 1 and 1.3 per cent resulting from the loss of silver remittances alone.[372] The restored Fernando VII (1814–20) was committed to the recovery of the American empire, with only minimal concessions to local autonomy. The result was political and financial bankruptcy. Only American silver could stave off bankruptcy, yet only a solvent state could reconquer America.[373] In reality, Spanish America was irretrievably lost.

[367] Herr (1989), 140–2. These figures differ both from Barbier and Klein (1981) and Cuenca Esteban (1981). Artola (1982), 458, has total income in 1807 at 570.2 million (*integro*) and 475.9 million (*líquido*).

[368] Herr (1989), 155, 713.

[369] Ibid. 154; Lynch (1958), 275–6; Mansuy-Diniz Silva in Bethell (1984), 508; Maxwell (1993), 223, comments that this event removed Lisbon as an intermediary in the Luso-Atlantic economic system and led to 'direct access between Europe and the ports of Brazil'.

[370] Lynch (1958), 266–9, 274; Carr (1975), 102; Brading in Bethell (1984), 438–9.

[371] Morineau (1985), 437. At ibid. 438, he ends his quinquennial averages in 1804 as also (ibid. 435–6) his annual figures.

[372] Prados de la Escosura in Aerts and Crouzet (1990), 80–3.

[373] Carr (1975), 122–3, 143–6.

11.7 *The Cost of Achieving British Economic and Financial Hegemony*

It was France which had declared war on Britain and the Dutch Republic in February 1793. Though Britain went to war in 1793 over the balance of power in Continental Europe and not for imperial gain ('the [French] islands in the West Indies are not worth to us one year of that invaluable tranquillity of which we are now enjoying' had been Grenville's view in 1791),[374] once embarked upon the war, the British aims expanded to the acquisition of the French overseas empire 'with the view of enlarging our national wealth and security' and becoming 'the paramount commercial and naval power of the world'.[375] Henry Dundas asserted in 1801, that '... the present strength and pre-eminence of this country' resulted from 'the extent of its resources arising from its commerce and its naval power which are inseparably connected'. However, it was vital that Britain's 'industry and commercial enterprise' should not 'outrun the extension of its foreign markets'.[376] Indeed, the French colonial trade collapsed early in the war, following the slave revolt of 1791 at San Domingo (the base of three-quarters of the trade).[377] Much of the French West Indies were occupied within the first eighteen months of the war, but complete control (the elimination of enemy garrisons of any sort and the establishment of seventeen separate garrisons) did not come until 1810. The British sea blockade established in 1793 destroyed the French merchant marine, and French industrial output collapsed until 1796 with the closure of Continental markets. Almost at a stroke, therefore, the economic power of Britain's principal rival was seriously undermined and a decisive step taken towards British world economic hegemony.[378] As Ricardo maintained (Chapter 6.7), the cost of the war had to some extent been paid for by a real growth in the British economy, and this in large measure tilted the balance in the struggle in Britain's favour. Yet war brought economic losses as well as gains. Between 1792 and the Peace of Amiens in 1802, British exports grew on average by 5.9 per cent, more slowly in the early years of the war than in the period 1798–1802. Woollens, and above all cottons (which grew on average by 5.6 a year between 1790 and 1811), played a decisive role in the export success. Thus part of

[374] Blanning (1986), 158.

[375] Duffy in Dickinson (1989), 130; Mackesy in Dickinson (1989), 150.

[376] Mackesy in Dickinson (1989), 150; O'Brien (1991), 21; O'Brien and Engerman in Solow (1991), 177.

[377] Crouzet (1985), 282; Crouzet (1990), 297; Doyle (1989), 412–13; Villiers in Solow (1991), 225; Tarrade in *État, finances et économie* (1991), 562; Butel in *État, finances et économie* (1991), 568.

[378] Crouzet (1985), 282, 296, 301; Crouzet (1990), 297, 313, 320–1.

the £21.2 million of British government subsidies to allies between 1793 and 1801 was recycled in the form of expenditure on British goods.[379]

Napoleon's Continental Blockade, enacted by the Berlin decree of November 1806, was an attempt to reverse these gains by a measure of economic autarchy: British goods were simply to be closed out of those European markets under Napoleon's control. The policy was relatively successful. British growth rates slowed down significantly: exports increased by 3.1 per cent annually between 1802 and 1814 as against 5.9 per cent in the period 1792–1802. Even the spectacular growth of cotton exports (17.2 per cent per annum between 1792 and 1802: cotton achieved the position of 24 per cent of manufactured exports by value in 1800, 42 per cent by 1815) slowed down to an average annual increase of 8.4 per cent between 1802 and 1814.[380] Britain was forced to take decisive countermeasures, firstly to defend its imperial interests and guarantee its transatlantic trade. Until 1807, neutrals had been allowed a substantial share in the transatlantic carrying trade. American shipping had filled the vacuum left after 1792 by the elimination of the traditional rival in the colonial trade, France. The value of American exports rose from $20 million in 1792 to $108 million in 1807, its record level in the period; in the same period, its merchant marine replaced the French as the second largest after Britain. A crisis in the British imperial economy resulted, to which the response was the adoption of the Orders in Council of November 1807, which prohibited Americans from trading with enemy countries, except via British ports.[381] The Orders in Council were not repealed until June 1812, but four days earlier Madison had proclaimed a state of war with Britain. The war of 1812–14 was a not insignificant diversion of British resources at the time of the culmination of the struggle with Napoleon; but the outcome of the economic rivalry with America between 1807 and 1815 was that the American merchant marine was chased from the seas and ceased to be a significant threat to British hegemony. British control of Canada was preserved and America became a virtual British economic satellite.[382] Relations with the traditionally friendly Denmark also reached a nadir as a result of the prospect of Orders in Council against neutral trade; the Danes declared war in September, but the British had already decided (by a pre-emptive strike against Copenhagen) on the elimination of a rival navy which might fall into Napoleon's hands.[383]

[379] Crouzet (1985), 173; Crouzet in Dickinson (1989), 191, 200; Crouzet (1990), 219; O'Brien (1989), 369.

[380] Crouzet (1985), 179; Crouzet (1987), xii, xv, xix; Crouzet in Dickinson (1989), 191; O'Brien (1989), 370–1; O'Brien and Engerman in Solow (1991), 184.

[381] Crouzet (1985), 302; Crouzet (1990), 321–2; Crouzet in Dickinson (1989), 192.

[382] Crouzet (1985), 313, 318; Crouzet (1990), 335, 340; Hall (1992), 197–8.

[383] Hall (1992), 161–2.

A second British response to the Continental Blockade was a more vigorous attempt to close off, and preferably seize, the specie remittances of both Spain and Portugal from their colonial possessions.[384] The French Revolutionaries had argued that the Spanish empire was in a state of terminal decline and ready for liberation (they talked of 'l'imbécillité du joug espagnol'),[385] but due to the primacy of British seapower they had been in no position to lend the settlers a helping hand. British needs for bullion imports to facilitate the payment of foreign subsidies placed a new urgency on 'intercourse with Spanish America'.[386] In 1806, Popham temporarily captured Buenos Aires and sent home £1.1 million in prize money;[387] but subsequent military activities against Buenos Aires were unsuccessful and it is doubtful whether the financial and commercial advantages could have offset the cost of operations.[388] The change of dynasty in Spain and the rebellion against French rule in 1808 enabled Britain to penetrate the Spanish American market much more effectively than before, though the Spanish Junta was unwilling to throw open the colonial market.[389] To these benefits were added a significant gain which accrued from the French attack on Portugal in 1807: the British transferred the Portuguese court to safety at Rio de Janeiro and in 1810 a treaty of commerce and alliance opened up the Brazilian market (and, through Brazil, the trade of Angola) to British goods, free of restrictions. By 1812, English exports to Brazil were exceeding the value of those to Portugal. The treaty was a classic example of a British pre-emptive strike in economic terms: privileged access to cheap raw materials was gained; new markets were opened up to British goods; and retaliation by foreigners was forestalled. Moreover, the Portuguese government was powerless to prevent the reversal of much of its policy since the time of Pombal: from 1807 until John VI returned from Brazil in 1821, mainland Portugal was governed by a regency council, the most influential member of which was the British General W. Carr Beresford. Portugal could scarcely have paid a higher price for British support, and in 1825 was forced to concede Brazilian independence.[390] Britain retained its empire but clearly benefited from the enforced decolonization of two of its former rivals.

At the outset of the war in 1793, Pitt, the British prime minister, was said to have commented that 'he had two millions [in pounds sterling] ready, and that he

[384] Gabillard (1953), 554; Lynch (1989), 369–70.

[385] Dorigny in *État, finances et économie* (1991), 350.

[386] Sherwig (1965), 200. [387] Hall (1992), 144. [388] Ibid. 148.

[389] Sherwig (1969), 201; Crouzet (1985), 175; Crouzet (1990), 221–2; Crouzet in Dickinson (1989), 192.

[390] Magalhães Godinho (1955), 276–80; Crouzet (1958, 1987), 314–17; Sideri (1970), 120–9; Hall (1992), 168; Miller in Solow (1991), 132.

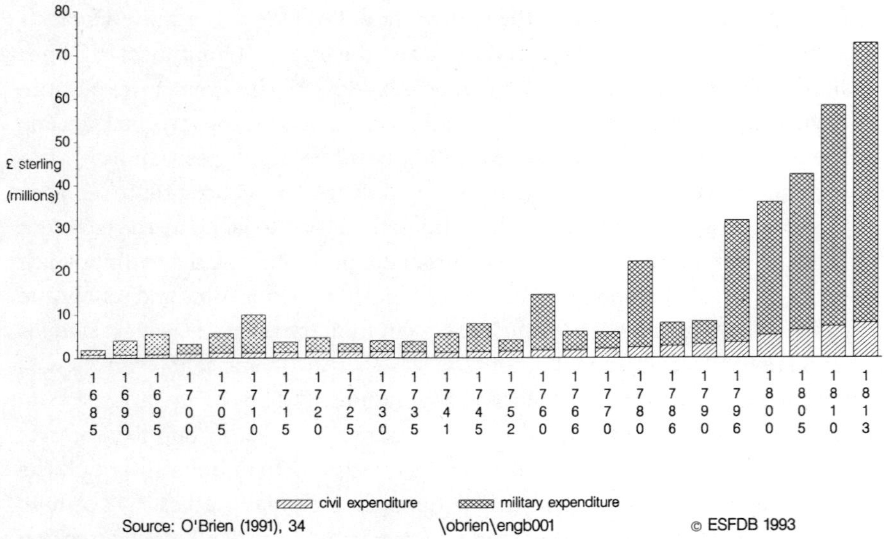

FIG. 50. Categories of expenditure of the British government, 1685–1813 (expressed as five-year centred moving averages in £ sterling)

trusted the surplus of the permanent revenue would be £600,000 a year . . .'[391] Such sums were wholly unrealistic for the scale of the conflict which followed. Annual expenditure in Britain rose six times during the period of war as against its pre-war level and the total bill between 1793 and 1815 was in the region of £1,039 million at current prices. Expenditure on warfare predominated throughout the eighteenth century (Figure 50).[392] The cost of war had averaged £5.2 million a year in the War of the Spanish Succession, £9.5 million a year during the Seven Years' War and £9.9 million a year during the War of American Independence; in the final wars with France, the figure commenced at an average of £22 million in 1793–7 and peaked at £84 million in 1815. In real terms, average annual expenditure rose from £13.2 million a year in 1798–1801 to £28.3 million a year during the last years of the war.[393] Expenditure had clearly risen in real terms when allowing for inflation (Figure 51).[394] It had also risen as a proportion of national income during the last period of warfare, from about 6 per cent in 1792 to perhaps a quarter by the peak years of 1808–15, and was higher than in all previous conflicts.[395] One evident consequence of this enormous jump in expenditure was an equally significant rise in the face value of the national debt from £290 million

[391] Blanning (1986), 155.

[392] O'Brien (1991), 34; ESFDB \obrien\engb001 based on \engd011.

[393] O'Brien in Dickinson (1989), 177.

[394] O'Brien (1991), 34; ESFDB \obrien\engb002 based on \engd011.

[395] O'Brien in Dickinson (1989), 177; O'Brien (1989), 341–2; O'Brien (1991), 35; Crouzet (1987), lxii.

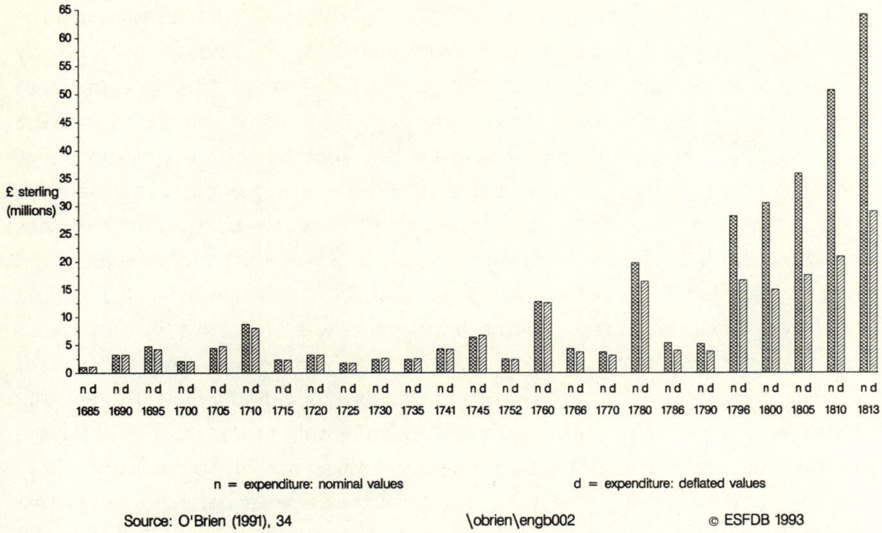

FIG. 51. Military expenditure of the British government, 1685–1813 (expressed as five-year centred moving averages in £ sterling, nominal and deflated figures)

in 1788–92 to £862 million by 1815. Inflation marked the war years, and the sums lent to the state, valued in prices of 1788–92, actually declined from an annual average of £18 million in the first stages of the war (1793–7) to £11 million in the middle period (1798–1812), but rose again to above £18 million in the expensive last phase (1813–16). Throughout the war, the real rate of interest declined, although the nominal capital of the public debt trebled. Though the point remains open to discussion, it seems that investment in the British economy was restrained but not entirely 'crowded out' by the government's heavy demands for loans, since the share of national income invested remained roughly constant for most of the war.[396]

The increased borrowing of the British government resulted in interest payments to creditors totalling some £236 million between 1793 and 1815. These sums could not have been discharged, nor the credit of the government sustained during the war, without a substantial increase in taxation: some 60 per cent of the extra taxes collected from the public between 1793 and 1815 were transferred as interest payments or as monies to redeem the debt. The percentage (though not the amount in money terms) was roughly the same as the 63 per cent of extra taxation falling upon the incomes and consumption patterns of the rich during the war years, although this would suggest a degree of financial planning which was entirely absent: Pitt and his successors 'simply concocted policies as they

[396] O'Brien (1989), 345–7, 355; Crouzet (1987), liii–liv.

went along, from budget to budget'.[397] Most of the extra tax revenue between 1793 and 1815 (some 55 per cent) arose from increasing the rates of taxes already available to the government before the outbreak of war; 36 per cent came from some twenty-one new taxes. Among the latter, the most important was the income or property tax of 1799, which was proposed by Pitt in November 1797 and enacted in January 1798: this yielded £1.86 million in 1798 and £6.05 million in 1799.[398] The combined effects of increased revenue demands, continued reliance on indirect taxes, and price inflation was that Britain—which already before the war was the second most heavily taxed nation in Europe after the United Provinces—became at some point during the war the most heavily taxed European state. Between 1803 and 1812, the British paid three times more taxes than the French on a per capita basis in terms of wheat equivalent. By 1818, the British public revenue was the equivalent of 1,184 million francs, the French 732 million. The repudiation of the public debt in France, and Napoleon's unwillingness and inability to borrow, tended to increase the disparity between the relative debt burden: the per capita public debt burden in Britain in 1818 was the equivalent of 1,210 francs, while in France it was a mere 80 francs.[399]

Bullion and currency reserves stood at £7 million in 1793 and peaked at £9 million in April 1794.[400] Between 1793 and 1815, £65.8 million was paid by Britain in subsidies to allies, almost half of which (£30.7 million) was spent in the last five years of the war; the total subsidy payments amounted to about 10 per cent of the revenue collected during the period of war. The total amount of 'offshore expenditure', excluding the cost of British armed forces, was £163 million between 1793 and 1815, again with a peak after 1812 (Figure 52). In real terms, the figures for the later years were substantially reduced because of the significant inflation of prices.[401] Before 1808, foreign subsidy payments were relatively modest, except in 1795 (Figure 53),[402] and did not amount to more than 1 or 2 per cent of national product. Grenville had objected to more than £2 million a year on the grounds that the 'German Princes think England a pretty good milch cow';[403] Pitt thought that it would have been more satisfactory for the king of Prussia to have acted 'on his own bottom, and from his own resources'.[404] In

397 O'Brien (1988), 13, compared to O'Brien (1989), 349; O'Brien in Dickinson (1989), 177.

398 Seligman (1914), 62, 65, 115; O'Brien (1988), 22; O'Brien in Dickinson (1989), 182–3.

399 Mathias and O'Brien (1976); Crouzet (1987), lxii; Crouzet in Dickinson (1989), 208; Wrigley in Stone (1994), 74–5.

400 Sherwig (1969), 86; Gayer, Rostow and Schwartz (1953), i, 49.

401 Anderson (1974), 618; ESFDB \rjb\engb001 based on \engd001; Crouzet (1987), lxxi–lxxiii, esp. the explanatory note at lxxi n. 3; Sherwig (1969), 345; Silberling (1924), 227. In Fig. 52, Anderson's nominal figures are deflated by the price index in Crouzet (1987), lxx.

402 Sherwig (1969), 365–8; ESFDB \rjb\engb002 based on \engd002.

403 Sherwig (1969), 37.

404 Ibid. 43. Figures for the payment: ibid. 52, 365.

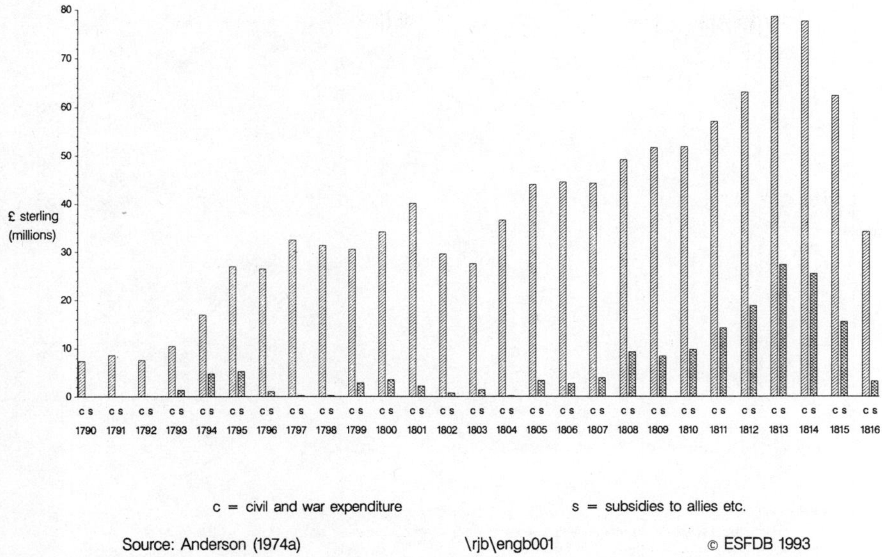

Fig. 52. Great Britain: civil and war expenditure and subsidies to allies, 1790–1816 (in £ sterling)

defence of the subsidy policy, which was criticized by Fox as likely to lead to 'the whole expense' of the war falling on Britain, Grenville argued that Britain had at all times considered it 'cheaper and more politic to pay foreign troops, than to take our own youth from the plough, and the loom, and thereby not merely put a stop to all domestic industry, but also drain the island of its population, and diminish our national strength'. British superiority over France in naval power, commerce and wealth was 'manifest' but 'in point of population, and of the means of raising armies, Britain must yield to her rival . . .'[405] The Austrian loan guarantee was only one of several factors which strained British financial resources to breaking-point in 1797: between January and March bullion and currency reserves fell from £3.3 to £2.2 million, the low point for the period. It is true that, despite the attempts of the Revolutionary government in France to curtail the transfer of specie abroad, both *émigrés* and bankers who remained in France took active measures through placing investments in London to avoid devaluation of their deposits during the *assignat* period.[406] The reserves of the Bank of England were significantly improved by such foreign investments during the conflict with France, but the main growth was after 1801.[407] In 1796–7, the

[405] Ibid. 44. [406] Antonetti in *État, finances et économie* (1991), 261–72.
[407] Neal (1990), 206–14.

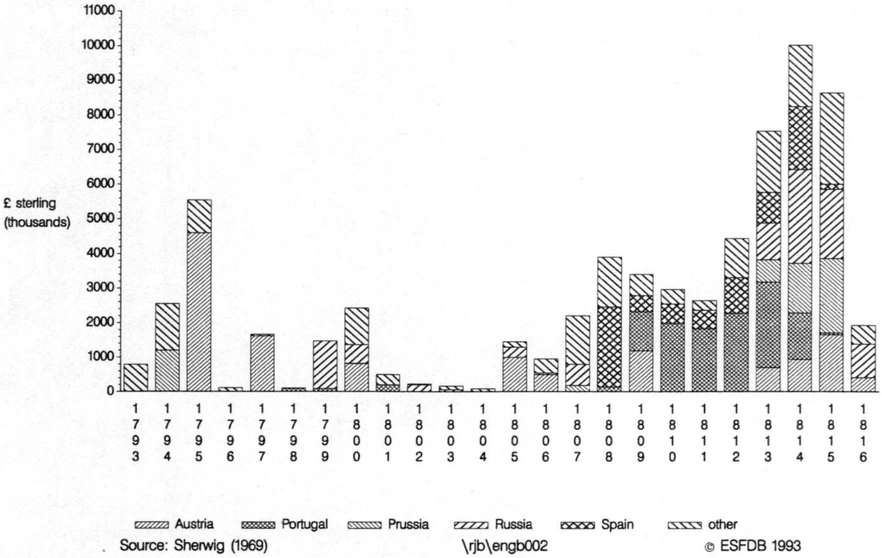

FIG. 53. Subsidy payments by the British government to its allies, 1793–1816 (in £ sterling)

return to a metallic standard in France had operated against the interests of the Bank of England, though on what scale is impossible to determine.[408] Pitt's opponents seized on the foreign subsidies as the chief cause for the bank crisis of 1797: Britain had remitted at least £13 million for the military effort, either in specie or bills of exchange, and had made subsidy payments of £10 million.[409] However, £4 million had been spent in the year preceding the bank crisis just in the purchase of grain from abroad,[410] so that the balance of payments crisis was not merely caused by war expenses and subsidies to the allies. Pitt's decision was not that subsidies to allies should be stopped, but that a far higher proportion of public expenditure than hitherto had to be financed from taxes. The exchange rate and the balance of payments remained a central preoccupation; bullion and currency reserves were also a consideration,[411] but it was assumed, probably correctly, that the position of the reserves would automatically improve if the exchange rate and the balance of payments position were maintained.

[408] Silberling (1924), 232 n. 3; Crouzet (1993), 445–51.

[409] Sherwig (1969), 87.

[410] Silberling (1924), 227 (i.e. £2 million plus £2.5 in his table, which is the figure in excess of £2 million); Sherwig (1969), 88.

[411] Helleiner (1965), 62, 87.

The Suspension Act of February 1797 ended payments in cash from the Bank of England.[412] This restriction on the convertibility of Bank of England notes into gold bullion or coin began the period of the so-called 'paper pound', which lasted until 1821. One effect was to lock foreign investments in Britain because, had they been transmitted abroad through bills of exchange, they would have lost value because of the fall in the London exchange rate.[413] The money supply expanded, and there was a risk of inducing a 'hyperinflation' in Britain comparable to the French experience. This never happened, despite the fear of bullionist critics of the government and a fierce attack on the policy of successive ministries in 1809–10 led by David Ricardo. Britain could not have funded Wellington's and the Allied armies in Europe if the country's limited gold reserves had been redeployed to ensure full convertibility.[414] At first, Napoleon's Continental Blockade had a disruptive effect on Britain's capacity to make foreign subsidy payments. The balance of payments position in 1808 was critical at a time when there was once more a need to enter into subsidy arrangements; the Spaniards were told that it was impossible 'to find a sufficiency of silver to meet the many demands at the moment upon our resources' and payment had to be made in Treasury bills.[415] Once the crisis of 1808–9 was overcome, the British government was once more able to resume payments abroad on subsidies and its armed forces: the average annual payment of £16.1 million between 1808 and 1815 was equivalent to 5.3 per cent of the national product in 1811, while the effort in 1813 was truly remarkable—£27.4 million was paid out in that year, equivalent to at least 8 per cent of the national product.[416]

This national effort resulted in a peace settlement very much in Britain's interest, securing an economic hegemony which was to last for much of the nineteenth century. It is true that Britain's alliance at Waterloo resulted in Prussia's being accorded Rhineland territories, 'a mistake which was to prove fatal' for British interests, but this was in the longer term.[417] Palmerston was clear that Britain had 'neither the power nor the might to prevent independent states' from joining the Prussian-led customs union of 1834, the *Zollverein*, even though this might become a threat to British exports.[418] The union was founded partly as

412 Gayer, Rostow and Schwartz (1953), i, 49; Silberling (1924), 398–9, 402–3; Neal (1990), 192 n. 31, 217; O'Brien in Dickinson (1989), 180; O'Brien (1989), 351.

413 Neal (1990), 215, 217.

414 Silberling (1924), 420–39; Gayer, Rostow and Schwartz (1953), i, 107; O'Brien in Dickinson (1989), 181, 185–6; O'Brien (1989), 373. This point was contested somewhat by Crouzet (1987), 560–1, on the grounds of the counter-productive inflationary effect of the paper pound.

415 Sherwig (1969), 214; Crouzet (1987), lxxii–lxiii, 540; Neal (1990), 204–5; Hall (1992), 174.

416 Anderson (1974), 618; Crouzet (1987), lxxiii.

417 Crouzet (1985), 239; Crouzet (1990), 284.

418 O'Brien and Pigman (1992), 95.

a reaction to the discriminatory British Corn Laws, and economic rivalry between the new German customs union and Britain was inherent from the start.[419] In general, bilateral trade agreements entered into by Britain after the Congress of Vienna simply removed discriminatory tariffs against British merchandise or discriminatory port duties on British ships. This Mercantilist protectionism was reciprocated. Some states, such as Spain and Portugal, knew only too well the consequences of an 'open door' policy and rejected any new treaty. Restoration France flirted for a few months with free trade in 1814, but once its disastrous consequences were clear it reverted to a protectionist stance until 1860, though tariffs were consistently lower than in Britain from 1820 until about 1880.[420] The continuation of Mercantilist policies abroad after 1815 was matched by *laissez-faire* at home. Lord Liverpool's government adopted a regressive fiscal policy, which (after the repeal of the income tax in 1816) relied on indirect taxes to pay interest charges on the public debt and the costs of the enlarged peacetime military and naval establishment (which in 1820–5 cost over two and a half times the amount paid in 1788–92). As a final example of financial conservatism, the 'paper pound' was abandoned in 1821 with the return to the gold standard. Even the abandonment of any pretence of debt redemption in 1828 might be depicted as a conservative act, in the sense that the Sinking Fund had been an innovation. Above all, there was no reversal of the growth of state expenditure in the new conditions of peace, so that taxes stood at nearly three times their pre-war levels in 1816. Those holding shares in the public debt did much better on the whole out of the peace than did ordinary taxpayers.[421]

11.8 *Conclusion*

Kersaint had assured the Convention in 1793 that 'the credit of England rests on fictitious wealth'; Napoleon, too, was convinced of the 'gnawing worm' (*ver rongeur*) of the British public debt, which might lead to the overthrow of its economy. On the British side, even before the outbreak of war Lord Grenville had written that 'the bubble of French finance must . . . inevitably burst'.[422] The assumption that war would be of limited duration because of the financial problems of states proved to be a delusion during the Revolutionary and Napoleonic period. The British were slow to adapt to the new conditions of warfare since, with the exception of the loss of the thirteen American colonies, they had been astonishingly successful in fighting the limited warfare of the *ancien régime*, which resulted not in the overthrow of states but in quantitative

[419] Kiesewetter (1991), 277–8, 298. [420] Nye (1991), 27, fig. 1, table 1.

[421] O'Brien (1989), 374, 379; Crouzet (1987), lxxxvi–lxxxvii.

[422] Mackesy in Dickinson (1989), 148, 158; Crouzet (1985), 241; Crouzet (1990), 285.

issues of wealth and power.[423] The British constitutional principle was that since 'all modern wars are a contention of purse' the war minister should therefore be the minister of finance;[424] even so, before 1807–8, British strategy was preoccupied with commerce and the colonies, not with operations in Continental Europe. Necker had understood the same constitutional principle at a time when France enjoyed its best opportunity for making colonial gains at the expense of Britain, but in 1781 he failed to persuade Louis XVI of the need for the finance minister to become chief minister.

'The French revolutionaries', it has been said, 'waged total war of an unprecedented intensity and on an unprecedented scale.'[425] Napoleon continued their work, 'setting new standards of rapacity wherever he went'.[426] Other states, including eventually even Britain, were forced into emulation of some of the techniques of mass mobilization and resource extraction simply in order to survive. It was estimated that Britain had some 615,000 men available for the nation's defence; a more conservative figure of 500,000 men would have amounted to 3 or 4 per cent of the population directly involved in military service on land (excluding another 110,000 men or so at sea). To have matched Britain's proportion, France would have had to have levied somewhere around a million men, as against a force of front-line troops in 1805 of some 310,000 men from a population of 29.6 million.[427] Over half Napoleon's Russian invasion force of 500,000 or 600,000 men came from outside France, while the total contribution of soldiers from beyond the frontiers amounted to perhaps a million men. The maximum number under arms under Napoleon was 2.8 million in theory, but in reality there were 1.1 million men mobilized in 1813, not all of whom were Frenchmen.[428] There thus remained a significant difference in the size of the British and French armed forces, arising largely from the overwhelming superiority of France in terms of overall population. To bridge the gap, a coalition had to be built and subsidized by Britain. Napoleon's last campaign in 1815 cost Britain nearly £7 million in subsidies for a war lasting a hundred days. The calculation was clear, however. It was cheaper to spend £11 2*s*. a year recruiting a soldier abroad than mobilizing and maintaining a British soldier in Europe at a cost of between £60 and £70.[429] Subsidies could therefore be depicted as an economy,

423 Mackesy (1964), 4–7.

424 Aspinall and Smith (1959), 124–5; Mackesy (1964), 21; Mackesy in Dickinson (1989), 149.

425 Blanning (1986), 211.

426 Ibid. 128.

427 Hall (1992), 6–7, with the population figure corrected from Dupâquier (1988), and Postel-Vinay (1989), 1024 (stable territorial boundaries); Colley in Stone (1994), 167.

428 Woolf (1991), 159, 172; Ellis (1991), 62; much lower figures for contingents to the Imperial army in Emsley (1993), 142, 146.

429 Sherwig (1969), 337–41.

and the impecuniousness of the Continental powers saved Britain enormously greater war costs in defeating Napoleon.

The experience of the Revolutionary and Napoleonic periods suggests that an even more radical reshaping of the boundaries of Europe could have occurred, and been rendered permanent, in which perhaps two 'superstates', Britain and France, could have emerged with vastly superior resources than they had under the *ancien régime*: this would have resulted if the Peace of Amiens of 1802 had become a permanent settlement. The survival of the pre-existing states of the *ancien régime* therefore depended on their capacity to mobilize fully their resources in time of war. Austria in 1805, and Prussia the following year, were found wanting and were swept aside by Napoleon. In terms of fiscal exploitation, too, the Revolutionary and Napoleonic periods were of immense significance. One of the great successes of Napoleonic administration abroad (if not at home) was the rationalization of public finance and an increase in public revenues; but the benefits were almost entirely lost with the spiralling increase in the costs of war.[430] The almost uninterrupted period of warfare between 1793 and 1815 greatly accelerated the long process of the creation of the modern fiscal state in Europe.

It is tempting to conclude that Britain finally won the conflict against France in 1815, and permanently eliminated the Napoleonic threat to its hegemony, because of a preceding 'financial revolution' that made it adapt earlier than other states to meet the costs of war on a global scale. It might even be argued that the experience of total war confirmed an economic lead in the Industrial Revolution because of the 'catalytic influence of military impulses on economic growth', that is military requirements as 'the principal determinant of the structure of production'.[431] In the course of European history there have been many technical innovations which might amount to a 'financial revolution'; to single out the English version of 'Dutch finance' as the sole factor in success is clearly an oversimplification, though the English public debt alone avoided the excesses of 'hyperinflation' in the 1790s and thereafter. To succeed, credit structures have to adapt constantly in order to command confidence among successive generations of investors. The English public debt had to be consolidated first into permanent, non-redeemable, stock; later, a prospect of redemption had to be offered; and in the period of the Revolutionary and Napoleonic wars, both tax increases on an unprecedented scale and the abandonment of a metallic standard for the conversion of currency were needed in order to bolster the financial system in an era of total war. A sensible British strategy still had to be adopted in order to guarantee success. And, perhaps crucially, economic growth had to be

[430] Woolf (1991), 104–5, 172–3. [431] Sen (1984), 93.

maintained to generate a taxable increase in the gross domestic product. None of this could be guaranteed or was even foreseeable. The peaceful consumption of cotton was more important than military requirements as the source of foreign earnings and there is an argument, which has not been entirely laid to rest,[432] that 'peaceful' investment in British economic growth was 'crowded out' by the financing of war—in other words, that the British economy might have done better had first the Convention, and then Napoleon, not been confronted in an almost permanent war between 1793 and 1815. The change in the balance of power caused by French expansion was such that isolation was never a serious political option. There would have been a longer-term economic cost in the potential closure of European markets to British goods. The converse position to the 'crowding-out' hypothesis is that the prosecution of war raised overall levels of demand and absorbed manpower and resources which might otherwise have been unemployed or underutilized. Taxes and loans for the military effort arose from increases in national income which might not have materialized but for the rise in government expenditure as a result of the war. Britain needed its population rise of between 3.7 and 4.3 million persons between 1791 and 1811; without it, the economic cost of the war effort would have been much more difficult to sustain. Britain also needed its colonial seizures and windfalls in terms of increased colonial penetration after the events of 1807–10, though here there is also a counterargument which suggests that no more than 15 per cent of investment in the Industrial Revolution arose from British overseas trade with the 'periphery', that is, Latin America, the Caribbean, Africa and Asia.[433] If this last argument is true, were the benefits of the British 'blue water' policy worth the costs? Again, as with the Continental war, the answer is likely to be found in the counterproposition that economic losses might have resulted from other states penetrating colonial markets in advance of Britain and closing them off to British exports: for example, in 1808 the British Cabinet thought that 'the interval may be short between the seizure by France of the Spanish government at home, and the occuption by the same power of its colonies abroad . . .'[434] What might have happened to Britain's share of world trade had she been forced to sue for peace with Napoleon, who sought to turn his military ascendancy in Continental Europe to economic advantage? It is likely on balance that there was some net reduction in investment at home attributable to a 'crowding-out' effect in wartime, but the economic benefits accruing from the elimination of the threat posed by the most powerful state of the *ancien régime* in Continental Europe

432 Williamson in Aerts and Crouzet (1990), 31–2, restates his thesis. But cf. Neal (1990), 221–2; O'Brien (1989), 354, 356; Crouzet (1987), lii–lvii.

433 O'Brien (1982), 7; cf. Klein in Tracy (1990), 303 n. 46.

434 Hall (1992), 91; cf. ibid. 77.

clearly outweighed such losses: the total value of French exports in 1788 was not achieved again until about 1826. Without a vigorous debt repudiation policy, France could no longer afford her status as a great European power in 1789.[435] The Revolutionary upheaval and the wars of 1792–1815 brought about the loss of her relative position as a powerful threat to British economic superiority.[436]

[435] Crouzet (1993), 70–83, 127–32, 561; Bordo and White in Bordo and Capie (1994), 249–51; Root (1994), 228–31.

[436] Ellis (1981), 267, 285–6; Ellis in Aerts and Crouzet (1990), 11; Ellis (1991), 98–9, 106; Dufraisse (1984), 23–5, 30; Hincker (1989), 45–6, 149, 183.

PART III

Structures

CHAPTER 12

Expenditure

Martin Körner

Anyone wishing to express an opinion on the finances of the early modern state should reflect on the obligations of that state. Its first task, according to Fernand Braudel, was 'to secure obedience, to gain for itself the monopoly of the use of force in a given society, neutralizing all the possible challenges inside it and replacing them with what Max Weber called "legitimate violence"'. Its second task was to control and organize economic life, the circulation of goods, and to establish the material and legal infrastructure to facilitate the proper workings of production and exchange. The third and final task of the state was to play a part in cultural and spiritual life, by keeping watch over, and channelling, ideas and intellectual movements.[1] Yet when writing of the obligations and budget of the state, Braudel described the latter as an intrusive Leviathan which sought to procure the ever-increasing financial resources required to achieve the objectives it set itself. He pointed out one constant feature—that expenditure generally outran revenues, with the result that borrowing was always necessary.[2]

12.1 *Problems of Perspective and Method*

Most previous studies of the finances of early modern states have concentrated largely on revenues, and especially on those raised through taxes and loan income.[3] Despite a balanced title focusing on both the raising and the disbursement of revenue, the proceedings of the 1984 conference on *Prélèvement et redistribution* organized by the CNRS at Fontevraud consisted almost exclusively

[1] Braudel (1981–4), ii, 515. The author and the Editor thank Dr J. A. Bergin (Manchester) for preparing this translation.

[2] Ibid. ii, 519–20.

[3] Ziegler (1981); Schulz (1986); contributions of Corbier, Depeyrot and Hocquet in Genet (1990).

of studies on revenues, with very little discussion of expenditure apart from the central issue of how much states spent on warfare.[4] Systematic, comparative research on state expenditure in relation to its volume, its structures, its growth and its fluctuations has yet to be done.[5] However, in preparing this chapter, the author was able to rely on a number of excellent monographs, both old and new, whose proto-statistical material has proved very interesting and valuable.[6]

Clearly, Fernand Braudel, along with numerous other historians, focused somewhat too narrowly on the monarchical variant of the early modern state, that is, the monarchies which grew and established themselves securely from the fifteenth century onwards. Without wishing to deny the European monarchical states their dominant role in the creation of a form of early modern state which distorted or shattered 'preceding structures and institutions—provincial estates, free cities, *seigneuries*, smaller states'[7]—it should be recognized that many of these small-scale states survived and resisted the encroachments of monarchies until after the end of the *ancien régime*. This in turn prompts the comment that such alternative forms of state possessed a real dynamism and a capacity to modernize which also enabled structures that may appear archaic to survive. Cities in particular established a modern and efficient administration of local and territorial public finances long before Europe's monarchies, which subsequently benefited from this product of merchant and urban culture. It was on this model that most rulers depended in order to develop the financial administration of their duchies and kingdoms.[8]

The analysis of state expenditure needs to be conducted on several levels. At the first level, we find local expenditure which does not figure in the accounts of any higher financial administration because it was autonomous and even sovereign. Examples of this are the numerous urban republics and free cities such as Geneva, Zurich, Nuremberg and Hamburg. The same would also apply to the various small lordships, ecclesiastical or lay, of which there were many in the Holy Roman Empire. The existence of the Empire on a higher level did not deprive its members of their status as states. Equally, we should not overlook those cities which did not enjoy sovereignty but were part of larger territories

[4] Genet and Le Mené (1987).

[5] With one main exception for the Middle Ages and the early modern period but this study concerns cities and urban republics: Körner (1981), 93–9; Körner (1989).

[6] For these works see the notes to ESFDB \korner\swid006.

[7] Braudel (1981–4), ii, 515.

[8] e.g. the dukes of Burgundy created their first *Chambres des Comptes* in the 14th cent. at Dijon and Lille: Richard (1978), 183. For the Empire in general: Orth in Schulz (1986), 74–86; Möhring in Schulz (1986), 87–99; Henning (1985), 64, 120–2. See also Boyer-Xambeu, Deleplace and Gillard (1986). The Swiss towns extended their financial administration at the pace of their territorial consolidation: Körner in Bonney (1995).

and subordinated to a prince, such as French cities to the king of France, or to a patrician class, such as Bergamo to Venice after 1427 or Lausanne to Berne after 1536.

The pace of chronological development also poses a problem: the state in 1600 was not that of 1400, any more than that of 1800. Even with regard to apparently immobile structures, history, as we have known for a long time, is a matter of movement and change.[9] The history of Berne from the thirteenth to the sixteenth century illustrates this point: formerly a subordinate city, it achieved effective emancipation, became a sovereign republic and even came to dominate an extensive territory containing other towns and rural communities. The city of Berne thus dominated bourgeois, peasants and even noble lords.[10] Certain duchies failed to preserve their rank as states and, as was the case with Brittany and Burgundy, were incorporated into the kingdom of France during the last quarter of the fifteenth century.[11] In addition, the Spanish Netherlands and Lombardy tend to be regarded from the sixteenth century onwards as states, because of their territorial separation from Castile, the centre of the Spanish empire (Chapter 7.1).[12] In discussing the expenditure of early modern states, we should therefore bear in mind the different models or the different possibilities of state evolution: free city, ecclesiastical or lay lordship, province, county, duchy, kingdom, confederation, empire. Even then, we should distinguish between the Holy Roman Empire with its somewhat federal, and notably electoral, structure on the one hand, and the Spanish empire with its highly centralized administration built around a personal union and a hereditary monarchy, on the other. Indeed, in order to underscore the differences, we should also remember the confederations of towns and provinces like Switzerland from the late medieval period onwards, and of the United Provinces after the war of independence in the sixteenth century.[13]

It is in the light of these divergent aspects, whether they be institutional, political, social or geographical, that similarities and differences in expenditure, as well as the changing volume of expenditure, take on a greater significance. Even so, this attempt at comparison is subject to considerable margins of error as a result of the enormous variety of methods used by states to calculate their expenditure. We find gross and net figures, which may include or exclude local administrative costs and expenses. Added to this are the obstacles faced by historians in the form of the archival records of previous financial

9 A striking demonstration of this was provided by Braudel (1973).

10 Feller (1946–60).

11 Richard (1978), 180–205; Kerhervé (1987).

12 Durand (1969), 146–62, 185–92.

13 Ibid. 178–208; Peyer (1978); Blockmans (1989).

administrations—whether the accounts were kept carefully or negligently; a survival of documentation that may be either complete or dispersed; and so on. As a result, absolute and comparative figures quoted in this chapter never account for all expenditure, but amount only to a reasonably plausible approximation. Finally, the different approaches, methods and scholarly techniques which are evident in published studies on public finance have forced us to make unavoidable and painful choices. The interpretation of statistical data needs to be based on significant differences rather than on the insignificant specifics of each case study. In order to make quantitative comparisons of the volume of expenditure, the sums given in territorial units of account or real money have been converted into metric tonnes of silver.[14]

12.2 *Theorists and Theories of Expenditure*

The problem of expenditure appears to have been less important in the works of the best-known and most-quoted early modern thinkers on the state than in those of their later medieval predecessors (Chapters 1 and 6). From the sixteenth century onwards, they seem to have been obsessed with one idea, that of finding yet more new ways of increasing the ruler's revenues. Those who dared to criticize the use to which revenues were put, or who suggested limitations on revenues, can be counted on one hand. By claiming that the king of England sometimes demanded more money than he needed, Sir William Petty (1623–87) was one of the first to reflect on the question of the primacy of expenditure over revenue (Chapter 6.3). About a century later, the Cameralist Johann Heinrich Gottlob von Justi (1720–71) stated that the extraction of revenues should not outstrip the financial needs of a state in its endeavours for the common well-being of a country in general, and of its inhabitants in particular.

It was the spokesmen for the Cameralist school who, from the 1720s onwards, asserted the need for budgets for both public revenues and expenditure. From their perspective, it was clear that the volume of receipts determined that of expenditure, and that state debt was tolerable only in extreme cases and in order to cover extraordinary expenditure.[15] Yet from the sixteenth century onwards, it was held that the private economy could be given stimuli in the form of state expenditure, particularly by the grant of loans to worthwhile entrepreneurs. This idea, already aired by Georg Obrecht (1547–1612), was taken up later by Wilhelm

[14] Braudel and Spooner (1967); Guéry (1978); Körner (1984).

[15] Spokesmen for the Cameralist school included Julius Bernhard von Rohr (1688–1742), Simon Peter Gasser (1676–1745), Jakob Friedrich von Bielfeld (1717–77), Johann Friedrich Pfeiffer (1718–87), J. H. G. von Justi: Dittrich (1974), 77–8.

von Schröder (1640–88), Theodor Ludwig Lau (1670–1740), Johann Georg Leib (1670–1727), Justi and Joseph von Sonnenfels (1732–1817), who, in addition, insisted on the links between state expenditure and general employment levels.[16] Starting from this assumption, these Cameralists, and others such as Christoph Besold (1577–1638), Kaspar Klock (1583–1655), Maximilian Faust (active *c.*1641), Johann Joachim Becher (1635–82) and Justus Christoph Dithmar (1678–1737), formulated a vision of the state as an entrepreneur. The establishment of public banks, manufactures and state monopolies in sectors where certain private enterprises had failed or had abused their monopoly position, would enable a government to deal with economic crises by intervening over interest rates, prices and employment on the one hand, and to derive welcome profits from them which would complement taxes, tariffs and other receipts on the other.[17]

As far as the practice of expenditure was concerned, we should note two functional types which became established over time. The first type involved the intervention of a class of great financiers who were often war suppliers, and who were connected to state finances through credit and cash advances destined to cover items of expenditure in anticipation of actual revenues. The state leased certain kinds of revenue to them, and also entrusted a considerable share of expenditure to them. It was a decentralized approach, and one which was controlled by 'financial technicians'. 'Pillars of the monarchy', they acted as the indispensable intermediaries between the monarchy and the privileged wealthy classes who refused to pay taxes, but who were not averse to investing their money in activities which underpinned the royal finances.[18] This method of managing public expenditure placed the state at the mercy of a powerful and unscrupulous group of men. In addition it facilitated corruption and fraud. Introduced in the thirteenth and fourteenth centuries in some of the Italian city-states, it was gradually improved, but in general it proved highly expensive for the financial administration of states. It was to be found especially in the Latin world, most notably France and the Spanish monarchy.[19] To some extent, it was also to be found in the financial administration of certain cities. Until the early eighteenth century, tax-farming was still the norm in Geneva before direct state administration took over.[20]

The second type of financial administration was less spectacular. It was borrowed from urban finances and also dated from the Middle Ages. Its central

[16] Ibid. 66–7, 103–4.

[17] Ibid. 44–5, 83–4, 103–4.

[18] Goubert's preface in Bayard (1988).

[19] Bayard (1988), above all the conclusion, 451–5. See also the conclusion of Calabria (1991), 130–2.

[20] Hiler (1982–3), 24.

principle was the centralized supervision of the administration of public finances—of both revenues and expenditure—by one or more chambers of accounts,[21] which throughout the year were mainly engaged in checking the accounts which the administrators in the various departments at the centre or the periphery were obliged to submit. Throughout the municipalities, rural communities and parishes of a particular state, *baillis* or governors elected for a given period of two, four or five years, relied on sworn representatives, selected or proposed by community assemblies for election to their governing council. This method of professionalizing public administration promoted civic consciousness and the mutual supervision of administrators and subjects, and it largely avoided substantial fraud and financial abuses. It was widely established north of the Alps, in those states where Cameralism was practised—for example in Bavaria and Prussia, though the most striking instance was that of the Swiss republics.[22] The fact that this system cost less, that it was more 'transparent', and that it bore a greater resemblance to the running of a business, leads one to conclude that it was more 'modern', in that it was more akin to the financial administration of twentieth-century states.

These points made, the questions which need to be asked about public expenditure will enable us to deal with three main issues: firstly, the volume of expenditure in relation to variable factors and the importance of individual states, and changes in the level of expenditure through the centuries; secondly, the structure and fluctuations of expenditure in relation to the functions and needs of the state; and thirdly, the growth and the evolution of the expenditure of early modern states seen primarily as distributors or redistributors of wealth.

12.3 *The Volume of Expenditure*

Clear divergences of scale between the different states[23] were already evident in the fourteenth and fifteenth centuries. Expenditure by most cities, such as Basle, Berne, Frankfurt, Schwäbisch Hall, Lucerne, Munich and Vienna, fluctuated in the fifteenth century between 0.2 and 1 tonne of silver. Among lordships, counties, duchies and bishoprics, expenditure by Brandenburg, Saxony, Bohemia, the Welfs, Ansbach in Bavaria and the bishopric of Cologne scarcely

[21] These were known as *Rechenkammer*, staffed by *Rechenherren*.

[22] Barudio (1981), 222–30; Hinze (1988). For Lucerne: Körner (1981), 17–43. For Zurich: Frey (1910), 8–57; Sigg (1971). For Basle: Vettori (1984), 42–176. For Schaffhausen: Schmuki (1986), 37–168.

[23] The expenses of central and regional powers must not be aggregated. Instead, we must seek to ascertain the expenditure possibility of the state, whether it was a significant central, regional or local power. If centralization had taken place, or a federal structure had come into being, some degree of aggregation may be accepted.

exceeded 1 tonne of silver. Württemberg spent around 2 tonnes, Bavaria, the Palatinate and Tyrol about 3 tonnes. At least one city north of the Alps achieved the same financial capacity: Nuremberg's spending rose from 1.5 to 2.7 tonnes. In 1438, Austria spent the equivalent of 4.5 tonnes of silver, almost as much as the 5 tonnes which the Holy Roman Empire had at its disposal only by the end of the fifteenth century. In the fourteenth century, the kingdom of Navarre had already overtaken this figure with expenditure of 5.9 tonnes in 1390, which had risen slowly from 1.2 tonnes after 1360, before falling back again to 3.6 tonnes at the turn of the next century.

Above this threshold, we find the middle-ranking powers whose ambitions were well known in the fifteenth century. Brittany spent 7 tonnes, Burgundy 12, the Burgundian Netherlands 8 to 15, the Papacy 10 tonnes of silver. But their financial resources were no match for those of their contemporary great powers. Until about 1470, they could still just about match Venice's expenditure of 6 to 12 tonnes, but after 1490, the mercantile republic definitively joined the ranks of the great public spenders with a figure of 37 tonnes, which far exceeded the expenditure of Lombardy and Naples with 22 tonnes apiece. Among the great spending states we also find England with figures between 17 and 44 tonnes, Castile with figures between 12 and 76 and, of course, France with figures between 42 and 91 tonnes.

A simple arithmetical exercise enables us to plot the evolution of Europe's powers at the end of the fifteenth century. By adding the expenditure of their ducal lands to that of the Netherlands, the dukes of Burgundy, with 20 to 27 tonnes of silver, had almost the financial resources of a great power at their disposal. The Habsburgs, whose *Hausmachtpolitik* saw them bring together Austria, the Tyrol, Bohemia, as well as Franche-Comté (part of the old duchy of Burgundy), the Netherlands and Hungary, reached a potential expenditure figure of at least 35 tonnes, which placed them among the great powers. If we add to that the expenditure of Lombardy, the Habsburgs were in possession of nearly 60 tonnes, unless of course the French monarchy prevented such an accumulation. Moreover, acquisition of the kingdom of Naples provided the king of Castile with the means to spend more than his French counterpart.

In general, the average volume of expenditure by each group of states rose during the sixteenth century. That of most of the cities varied between 0.3 and 2.5 tonnes of silver. Hamburg, one of Germany's future metropolitan cities, reached the upper limit. Milan's budget totalled 5.9 tonnes at the end of the century. Nuremberg's expenditure, which fluctuated between 2.3 and 8.1 tonnes, was always on a par with that of a middling German duchy. Indeed, the expenditure of Hesse rose during the first half of the century from under 1 to 6.6 tonnes, but fell back later to 2.8 tonnes. Württemberg's budget increased dramatically from 3.1 to 10.4 tonnes. Austria and the Tyrol together totalled 6.6 tonnes. If we add together the expenditure of the Swiss republics, the Confederation, with 5 to 7 tonnes, disposed of financial resources comparable to those of an Imperial duchy. Switzerland's neighbour, Piedmont, spent an average of 9 tonnes between 1559 and 1580. Towards the end of the sixteenth century, new middling powers revealed their financial capacity, among them Poland, with 20 tonnes of silver. Venice's expenditure rose from 46 to 66 tonnes. In 1550, the budget of Naples was, at 42 tonnes, twice what it had been at the end of the fifteenth century; it would rise still further to exceed 100 tonnes. French expenditure grew more than any other state except Spain, reaching a maximum figure of 444 tonnes during the 1580s. But during the same decade, Spain broke all sixteenth-century records with expenditure of over 500 tonnes, to which should be added the expenditure of Naples just cited.

The seventeenth century appears as an extension of these sixteenth-century developments in state expenditure. Firstly, we have confirmation of the provincialization, or the moderation—depending on one's perspective—of most urban expenditure, which no longer grew, but settled at figures between 0.2 and 2.9 tonnes of silver. The expenditure of metropolitan cities grew rather feebly: Nuremberg spent between 6.4 and 12.5 tonnes, Hamburg between 7.1 and 13.8, Milan between 5.9 and 11.6 tonnes. However, they still constantly exceeded the modest expenditure of a small territorial state like the bishopric of Bamberg, with its 2.2 to 5 tonnes, and also that of the duchy of Württemberg, whose budget fluctuated around 10 tonnes. With between 20 and 30 tonnes, Sicily and Genoa reached the position attained a century before by Piedmont and Poland, while the latter now managed, as did Bavaria, to spend more than 40 tonnes. Among the middling powers, we note the rapid growth of Denmark's expenditure, moving from 6 to 113 tonnes, and that of Prussia, whose budget rose from 56 tonnes during the 1680s to 156 tonnes twenty years later.

The expenditure of the Dutch Republic during the seventeenth century was even more considerable. The young Republic's spending in 1641 amounted to around 264 tonnes of silver, evidence of the powerful financial capacity, particularly of the towns, of this 'newcomer' among early modern states.[24] If we settle, perhaps a trifle arbitrarily, on a boundary between middling and great powers at 250 tonnes, then the United Provinces just about find a place among the great powers. Austria, encompassing the hereditary Habsburg lands, definitively maintained its position in the same group by raising its expenditure from 68 tonnes during the 1650s to 288 tonnes by the end of the century. But the three dominant great powers again pulled away from the other states. During the early decades

[24] 't Hart (1989).

of the century, the combined expenditure of Castile and Naples oscillated between 500 and 600 tonnes, that of England rose to 926 tonnes, while that of France exceeded 1,600 tonnes at the end of the seventeenth century.

In the eighteenth century, both continuity and discontinuity are evident in the evolution of different states' expenditure. If towns with modest resources—for example, Hanover, Überlingen and Lucerne—continued to be those whose expenditure averaged at around 1 tonne of silver, that of other cities expanded quite markedly. Munich's budget reached 3 tonnes, but other cities exceeded 5 tonnes. The expenditure of Basle stood at 5.3 tonnes, that of Frankfurt between 4.3 and 8.2, that of Ulm at about 6 tonnes, that of Zurich at about 8 tonnes, and that of Berne at 14 tonnes. Expenditure fell during the century at Nuremberg from 11.3 to 5.7 tonnes, and at Milan from 7 to under 4 tonnes. With such expenditure levels, several of these cities on their own possessed financial resources equivalent to those, for example, of the duchy of Württemberg. Moreover, the combined total of the budgets of the Swiss urban republics provided the Confederation with resources of about 40 tonnes, which placed it on the same level as other regional European powers.[25] Sicily and Genoa, for example, each spent 27 tonnes, Switzerland's neighbour Piedmont 45 tonnes, and Bavaria between 41 and 73 tonnes. Around 1720, Lombardy's budget ranged between 49 and 66 tonnes—in other words, about six times the combined expenditure of Milan and the nine provincial administrations.

After the end of the War of the Spanish Succession, Piedmont and Sicily were similarly placed, albeit only for a few years, with expenditure of at least 69 tonnes of silver. Venice's budget for 1783 was equivalent to 118 tonnes. The newer northern powers continued the rise begun in the previous century. Denmark's expenditure rose from 86 tonnes at the beginning of the century to 360 tonnes in 1801. That of Prussia grew in stages from 112 to 485 tonnes, and ranked alongside the United Provinces, with 439 tonnes in 1795. The Austrian Habsburgs, whose spending fell during the first decades of the century from 495 to 345 tonnes, took off again after the War of the Spanish Succession thanks to the acquisition of Lombardy and Naples which, after the exchange of Sicily for Sardinia in 1720, brought additional spending of at least 100 or 150 tonnes. France succeeded in retaining its dominant position as a great power into the second half of the century. Average expenditure during the 1780s reached 3,000 tonnes, and climbed to 3,660 tonnes during the wars after 1800. But after 1790, France was overtaken by Britain, whose budget provided for an expenditure equivalent to 8,500 tonnes.

[25] The Swiss Confederation may be considered a prototype of a federation of states with a significant degree of administrative and financial decentralization.

12.4 *The Pattern of Expenditure during the Fourteenth and Fifteenth Centuries*

In order to conduct a comparative analysis of expenditure, it is essential to divide it into clearly defined and meaningful categories—expenditure on the court, civil administration, public buildings and other such work, internal and external security, debt servicing, financial and social transfers, productive investments, as well as miscellaneous items which cannot be assigned to one of these categories. Despite their modest number, the 256 examples summarized in the accompanying charts enable us to form a clear idea of developments.

In the fourteenth and fifteenth centuries, princely states devoted between about 10 and 40 per cent of their spending to the court (Figure 54).[26] In general, the relative cost of the court was high because spending to internal and external security was low. This impression is strengthened if one adds to the outgoings on the court those arising from civil administration. The fact that the latter accounted for between 50 to 71 per cent of the budget of Burgundy and the Netherlands in the fifteenth century suggests that civil administration was especially developed in these lands. If it is permissible to form a judgement based on expenditure figures alone, civil administration there claimed a share of the budget which was twice or three times that of England, France, Castile, Navarre or Württemberg. It is from this perspective that we should also judge the distribution of expenditure in the Empire, whose principal duty internally was to handle conflicts between its members, and externally to ensure the security of the Empire as a whole. The 17 per cent of total expenditure spent on its administration towards the end of the fifteenth century corresponded to the modest costs of the Imperial diet and court, both of which were still rudimentary governmental institutions, while the 83 per cent spent on war testifies to the importance and steep cost of armed conflicts.

A surprising feature is the apparently complete absence of resources devoted to servicing the debt before the end of the fifteenth century. We should not conclude from this, however, that monarchical states had not become indebted before then. Clear proof to the contrary is available.[27] This analysis of public finance leads rather to the conclusion that the volume of outgoings on interest payments and redemptions had not yet reached the scale of later developments (Chapter 8.4). Moreover, in order to cover their planned expenditure, rulers still had fiscal options that awaited more effective exploitation. Castile, which spent

[26] ESFDB \korner\swib003 based on \swid006, which contains a detailed list of sources too long to repeat here. Note that in this and the following charts there is some missing data, or data that does not equal 100 per cent due to rounding.

[27] This point was demonstrated magisterially in a paper read to the Team at Arc–et–Senans in 1991 by the late Derek Knights but which remains unpublished.

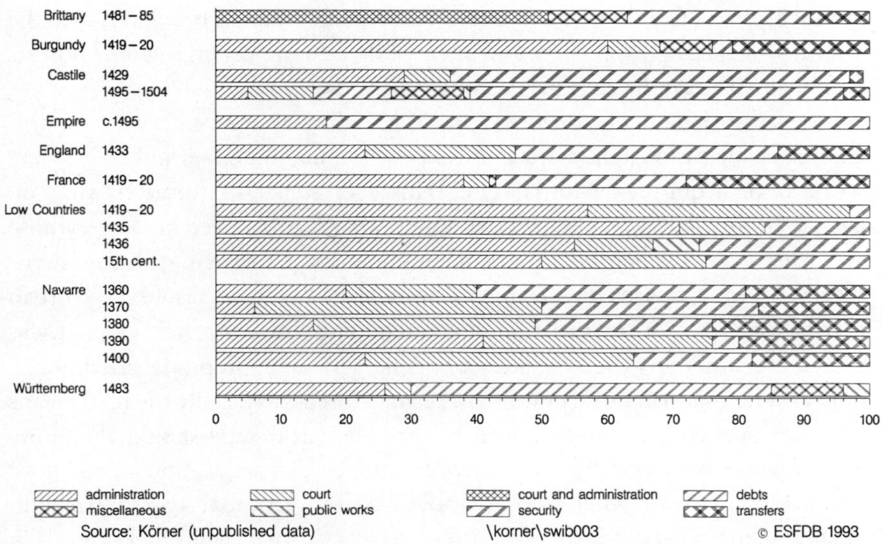

FIG. 54. Categories of expenditure of the Holy Roman Empire, European principalities and kingdoms, *c.*1360–1504

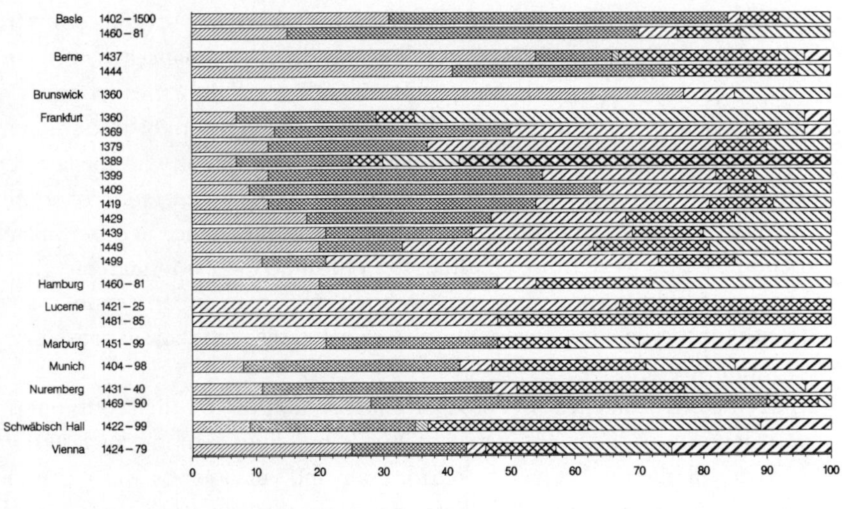

FIG. 55. Categories of expenditure of European republics and towns, *c.*1360–1500

12 per cent of its budget in 1500 on debt servicing, and Württemberg, which spent as much as 55 per cent in 1483 on interest payments, were early adherents to the option which the great powers and some of the less important regional powers would adopt from the sixteenth century onwards.

One surprising (and erroneous) conclusion which might be drawn from this analysis, is that monarchies apparently spent nothing on either public building works or on acquiring territorial rights. However, such an extreme view has no basis in historical reality. On the contrary, rulers generally lived in castles whose construction had usually been partly financed by domain revenues and by labour services from subjects, or which had been placed at their disposal by urban communities. As for the question of the acquisition of territorial rights, it was settled by combining the hereditary principle with an appropriate matrimonial policy. When succession disputes arose, armed force was usually the final means of action. Spending on external security by monarchical states should, therefore, be at least partly regarded as an investment for the acquisition of rights of domination, at least when war was followed by territorial aggrandizement. Finally, spending in the form of transfers, which attained their highest levels in England, France, Burgundy and Navarre, where they ranged between 14 and 28 per cent, consisted mainly of gifts and subsidies for the upkeep by the rulers of a political and military clientele.

In cities where institutional and political organization was influenced by republican practices, the structure of expenditure differed on several counts from those of monarchical states (Figure 55).[28] Firstly, in urban finances there were no direct outgoings on a prestigious court. Spending on the cities' councils and political leaders was included in the costs of public administration, which proportionately cost no more than in the monarchies. But as with the latter, the relatively low (at 8 per cent) or relatively high (at 50 per cent) ratio of administrative costs to the overall budget in cities was a consequence of other forms of expenditure that were more sensitive to cyclical accidents. In general, government and administration were relatively cheap for an urban republic in the fifteenth century in comparison to monarchical states with their expensive court and administration.

The majority of cities devoted at most a quarter of their outgoings to investments in, or the maintenance of, public buildings. Among the latter were the town hall, the market hall, stores for grain and salt reserves, mills, churches, bridges, but also the town's fortifications. From this perspective, part of these expenses should be considered alongside those required for external security even if, from the vantage point of economic analysis, public building works are

[28] Sources as for Figure 54; ESFDB \korner\swiboo4 based on \swidoo6.

all of a kind. With a few exceptions where the differences are not significant, the proportion of expenses devoted to war was smaller than that devoted to building work. War expenditure was always lower compared to administrative and building expenses. As relative proportions, both the average (15 per cent against 29 per cent) and the median (14 per cent against 26 and 27 per cent) of security expenditure were in any event lower than in monarchical states, the Empire excluded. Were cities less aggressive than princes? Cities with their eyes on either an acquisition or on territorial aggrandizement had less frequent opportunities than princes of invoking a right of succession. Among the items which resulted in 52 per cent of Lucerne's budget being spent on public building and the redemption of rights of sovereignty for the years 1481 to 1485, we find the cost of buying out the city's ancient subordination to the abbey of Murbach, as well as acquisitions of sovereignty from a number of both neighbouring and distant *bailliages*.

It also emerges as certain that in order to pay for their security needs, the cities contracted debts. The cities of the Empire were permanently threatened with the prospect of subjection to territorial states.[29] During the fifteenth century, they were prepared, or even obliged, to assign at least 12 per cent (but most of the time between 25 and 50 per cent, or even over 60 per cent) of their budgets to debt servicing. For certain cities, this financial effort enabled them to sustain not only their autonomy as free cities of the Empire, but also their position as sovereign republics exercising sway over territorial states which would henceforth bear their name, as in the case of Venice, Genoa, Berne, Lucerne or Hamburg, to mention typical examples drawn from three different parts of Europe. At the end of the fifteenth century, one of them, Lucerne, even succeeded in eliminating its public debt for good.

For cities which failed to shake off their subjection to a territorial state,[30] the structure of expenditure contained a category not to be found in sovereign republics, that of the transfer of contributions payable to their ruler. The cases of Marburg, Munich and Vienna show that these transfers could amount to between 15 and 30 per cent of their expenditure. This also meant that subject cities of monarchical states not only paid for protection by their ruler, but also for the upkeep of his court! But even Imperial cities had to transfer contributions to the administration of the Empire, to which Nuremberg contributed 4 per cent and Schwäbisch Hall 11 per cent respectively of their outgoings. The urban republics of Switzerland had already freed themselves from this type of transfer. In fifteenth-century Berne, this budgetary item already involved gifts and subsidies to institutions within the city.

[29] Isenmann (1988), 174–9.

[30] These were known as *Landstadt* or *Munizipalstadt*.

12.5 *The Structure of Expenditure in the Sixteenth Century*

In the towns, the structure of expenditure changed only slightly during the sixteenth century (Figure 56).[31] Several median values were close to those of the previous century: 16 and 17 per cent against 20 per cent for administration, 19 per cent against 18 per cent for building, and 30 per cent against 30 and 34 per cent for debt servicing. However, they spent less on their security, and the median value for this category was now only 5 per cent, compared to 14 per cent in the previous century. This was clearly the result of territorial peace in Switzerland after 1531 and in Germany after 1555. It would be interesting to have comparable studies of urban finances in France and the Netherlands in order to measure the true extent of this difference.

As to transfer expenditure, all German cities continued to contribute between 3 and 41 per cent of their annual budget to the princely or Imperial administration. In contrast, the Swiss republics systematically allocated between 10 and 38 per cent of their expenditure on financial investments abroad, the interest on which brought them welcome annual revenue. They also invested in proto-industrial activities and even in service abroad via military enterpreneurs, in order to stimulate business in times of economic recession.[32] Other cities like Schwäbisch Hall and Überlingen engaged with some success in a similar financial policy. In contrast with the Swiss city republics, money was spent on basic foodstuffs; the gross return on the sales of such products eventually appeared in the cities' revenue receipts either the same year, or one or two years afterwards. Other cities in Europe had participated, as had the Swiss republics, in a policy of collective food-provisioning since the fourteenth century and had established grain, salt and wine administrations, each with their own accounts. Only the net gain from this subsequently figured in the accounts of the central state. On the expenditure side, we find only traces of the initial investment, made as an advance of working capital. Finally, when, during the Reformation, the Swiss republics incorporated church property into their assets, they contributed from then on to the working of their reformed territorial churches, as in the case of Zurich, which spent 12 per cent of its budget in this way.[33]

In the monarchical states, however, the structure of expenditure in the sixteenth century clearly changed from that of the previous century, although this view is based on limited statistical evidence—the Holy Roman Empire, Castile, Naples, the principality of Hesse and the duchy of Württemberg—though these states are typical representatives of the different forms of

[31] Sources as for Figure 54; ESFDB \korner\swib006 based on \swid006.

[32] Körner (1980), 430–40.

[33] The reformed territorial churches are known as *Landeskirche* or *Église nationale*.

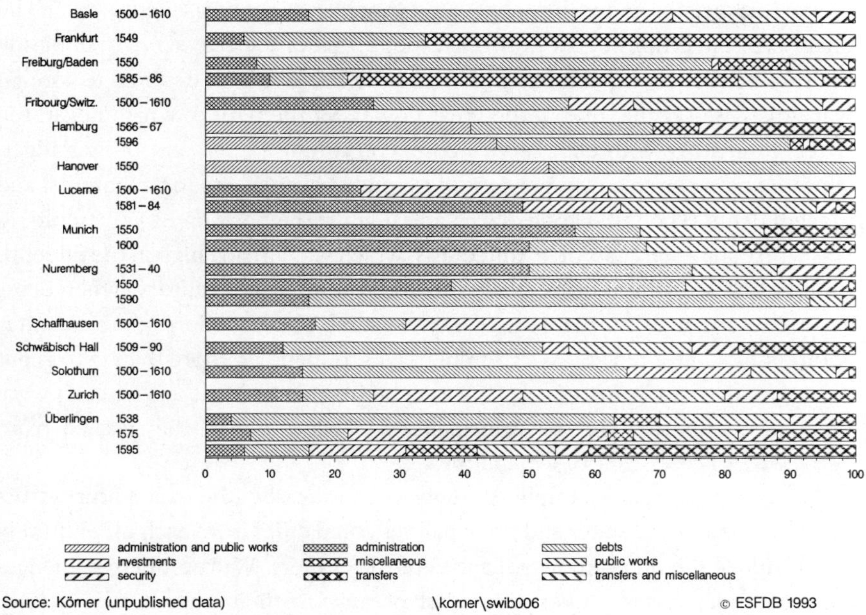

FIG. 56. Categories of expenditure of European republics and towns, 1500–1610

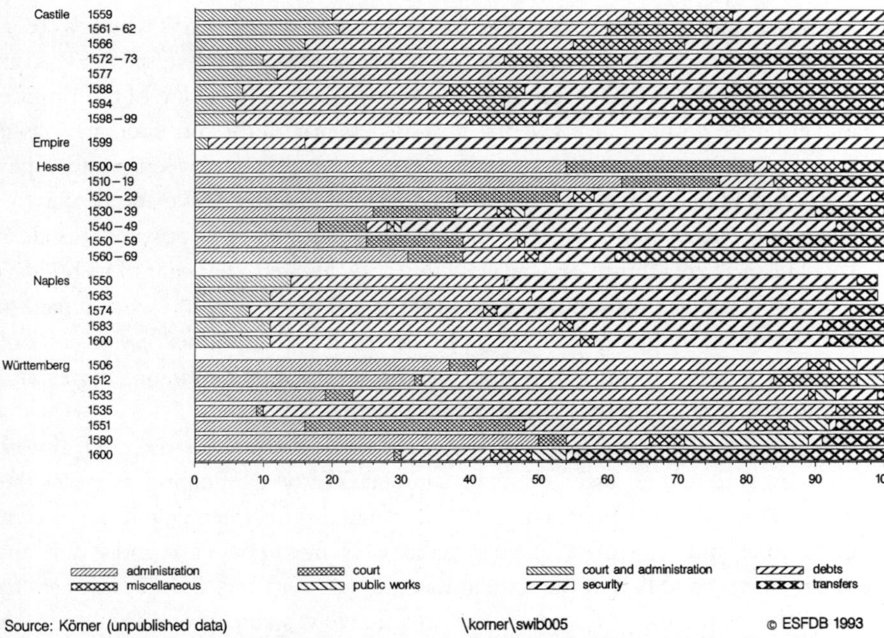

FIG. 57. Categories of expenditure of the Holy Roman Empire, European principalities and kingdoms, 1500–1600

monarchical states and principalities in the sixteenth century (Figure 57).[34] The finances of the Empire show only one change, that of the debt service, alongside the tiny item covering administration and the massive sum devoted to foreign war. Likewise Castile, one of the great powers of the period, which began the sixteenth century with debt service costs consuming 12 per cent of its budget, allocated between 30 and 45 per cent of expenditure after 1559 to pay interest and redeem debts. The same applied to Naples, while the position of Württemberg was worse still. The costs of indebtedness, which was already high in the fifteenth century, grew further during the first half of the sixteenth century, when debts accounted for over 80 per cent of expenditure. The situation improved after about 1550, while after 1580 Württemberg was to spend no more than 12 to 13 per cent of total expenditure on servicing its debt. In contrast, debt service costs were much less important in the principality of Hesse, where they varied from between 2 to 9 per cent of expenditure.

These two German examples show how considerably the expenditure structures of monarchical states and principalities could differ from each other, purely as a result of the differing personalities of their rulers. Württemberg's finances suffered under certain dukes whose behaviour cost their lands dearly, as with Duke Ulrich who was placed under Imperial ban in 1519 and expelled from his duchy. Its reconquest by the duke in person and by Philip of Hesse in 1534 was mainly financed by loans repayable by the restored duchy, loans which were in effect a mortgage on its finances for several decades. In contrast, the landgraves of Hesse adapted more successfully to the turbulent political life of the Empire and emerged without heavy debts. This success was all the more remarkable in that during Germany's religious wars, Hesse had to spend between 35 and 63 per cent of its budget on the requirements of armed security. If we add to this the sums transferred to the Imperial administration and to other powers, it is clear that Hesse's expenditure on war was constantly above 50 per cent of its budget. Württemberg was in a similar situation at the end of the century, when it paid 45 per cent of its outgoings to the Empire. In the long run, the excessive costs of building modern fortifications undermined several middle-ranking states and nudged the great powers towards bankruptcy.[35]

The hegemonic ambitions of the great powers involved them in almost constant war, and necessitated financial policies in which floating debt was the norm. The military expenses of Castile fluctuated at between 14 and 29 per cent of the total, and those of its Italian province of Naples between 34 and 51 per cent during the second half of the sixteenth century. Over time, Castile managed to keep the two types of expenditure in relatively stable proportion to each

[34] Sources as for Figure 54; ESFDB \korner\swiboo5 based on \swidoo6.

[35] See above, n. 11. Margolin (1977), 713–19.

other—with that on war fluctuating around 20 per cent, and debt servicing at around 40 per cent. In the kingdom of Naples, however, military costs fell from a high of 51 per cent in 1574 to only 27 per cent in 1627, while debt service costs rose from 31 to 56 per cent during the same period. In tandem with this trend, both states progressively increased the share of expenditure devoted to gifts, subsidies and pensions to an increasingly numerous political clientele. In Castile, this budgetary item generally stood around 20 per cent, while in Naples it rose noticeably, yet remained below 10 per cent during the sixteenth century; it later continued to rise to a maximum of 12 per cent. The payment of subsidies was a policy openly followed, and one which provoked competition with other enemy powers, such as France. As a consequence, the recipients of subsidies learned to play this game with a degree of virtuosity: the Swiss republics reformed their public finances in part thanks to such subsidies.

In addition, the relative share allocated to civil expenditure, whether on the upkeep of a princely court or the general costs of central administration, tended to fall in both Castile and Hesse during the sixteenth century. In the case of the Spanish monarchy, this was a result of the huge inflation of the total volume of expenditure mainly following the transfers, in the form of subsidies and payments, from Spain to the Netherlands. In Hesse the fall is illusory, for during each decade of apparent reduction, we find an exceptionally high percentage in another category of expenditure—security during the 1540s because of the Schmalkaldic Wars, and transfers during the 1550s because of payments made to the Empire and dynastic arrangements with the house of Nassau. In Naples and Württemberg, the proportion of expenditure on the court and civil administration seems to have been relatively stable (the high costs of the Württemberg court for 1551 should be seen in terms of the expenses of Duke Christoph's accession).

12.6 *The Structure of Expenditure in the Seventeenth and Eighteenth Centuries*

The apparent reduction of expenditure on the court and general administration in seventeenth-century Austria and Denmark should be interpreted with some caution (Figure 58).[36] Like other powers before them, these two states increased the overall level of their expenditure, and expenditure on war in particular. The same can be said of the bishopric of Bamberg in the second half of the century. In other states such as Piedmont and Sicily, there were only modest increases in expenditure, while its structure remained relatively constant (Figure 59).[37] In

[36] Sources as for Figure 54; ESFDB \korner\swiboo7 based on \swidoo6.

[37] Sources as for Figure 54; ESFDB \korner\swiboo8 based on \swidoo6.

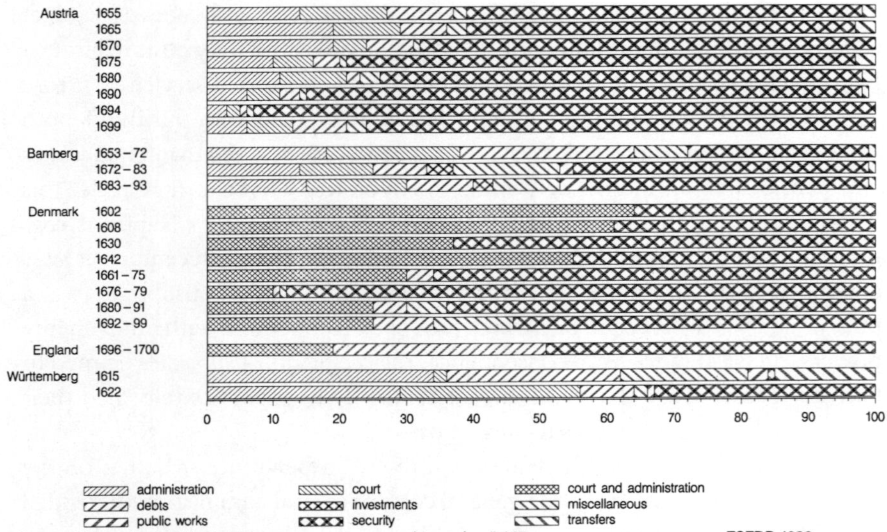

Source: Körner (unpublished data) \korner\swib007 © ESFDB 1993

FIG. 58. Categories of expenditure of north European principalities and kingdoms, 1602–1700

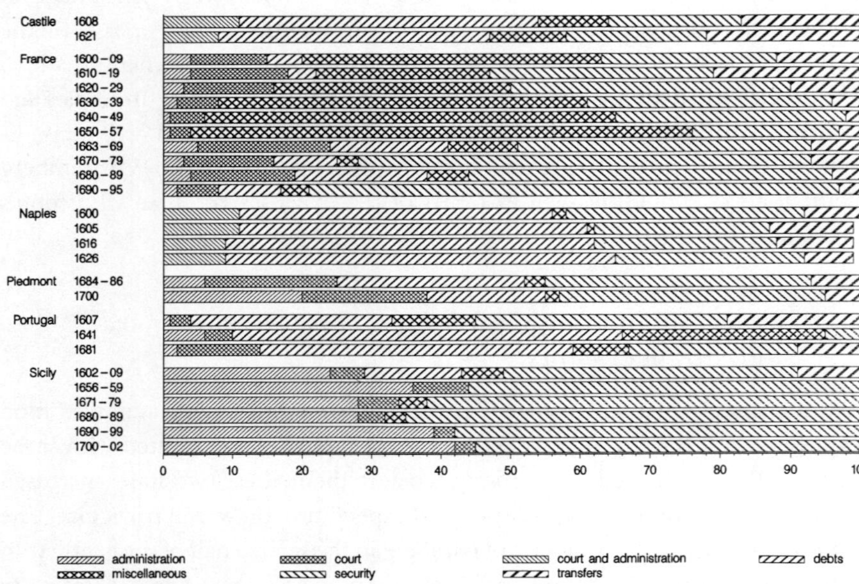

Source: Körner (unpublished data) \korner\swib008 © ESFDB 1993

FIG. 59. Categories of expenditure of south European principalities and kingdoms, 1600–1702

France, too, the proportion of military expenditure rose rapidly after the 1660s, with a resulting decline in expenditure on the court, administration and other services or items of consumption. Only in Naples did the decline in military spending which had commenced in the sixteenth century continue into the 1620s, when it amounted to only 27 per cent of the total. But as a general rule, the monarchical states devoted almost half of their budgets to military activity, with median figures at 44 and 45 per cent. Contrary to what might have been expected, the highest figures were not reached during the Thirty Years' War but during the last decades of the century, when Sicily spent 65 per cent of its total expenditure, France 76 per cent, Denmark 88 per cent and Austria 93 per cent, on war.

On the other hand, the monarchies seem to have redirected their policies on subsidies and pensions. Before the 1620s, the highest figures were around 20 per cent of total expenditure, but this proportion fell to under 10 per cent by the end of the century. As for the costs of debt servicing, it seems that it was the states of the Spanish monarchy, as well as England, which had to make the greatest sacrifices. Naples devoted fully half of its expenditure to it, Castile about 40 per cent, and England 30 per cent. The other states for which there are figures available managed to reduce such expenditure to below 20 per cent or to keep it under 10 per cent. This holds good even for Austria and Denmark, whose military spending grew enormously during the century. France, which seemed to have kept the costs of debt servicing under control during the early decades of the seventeenth century (largely because such costs were hidden),[38] also saw them rise under Louis XIV to just under 20 per cent of the total.

Among the republics, the structure of the finances of the Dutch Republic in the seventeenth century resembles that of the Holy Roman Empire during previous centuries, with military expenditure in excess of 80 per cent, low outgoings on central administration and, like other rising powers, debt servicing costs that were still inconsiderable (Figure 60).[39] Despite numerous institutional differences, the analogy with the Empire is clear as far as the central finances are concerned. The main objective and activities of the United Provinces were directed towards maintaining the mutual independence of their members. The density of administrative institutions was greater, and administration was far more developed at provincial and urban levels. This was also a continuing trend among most of the urban republics and other cities during the seventeenth century, while the relative proportion of expenditure devoted to administration and public works was always higher among the urban republics generally than

[38] Bonney (1981*a*), 298, 308–10; Bonney (1992*b*), 104–5, 110–11.

[39] Sources as for Figure 54; ESFDB \korner\swib009 based on \swid006.

the European monarchies. It took a long time for the monarchies to follow the lead of the cities in this respect.[40]

As for external security, Hamburg alone spent at least half of its expenditure budget on this item. The other German cities and the Swiss urban republics succeeded in keeping the proportion down to 20 per cent or even lower. Indeed, where this item of expenditure exceeded 10 per cent in a single decade, this was because of an extraordinary effort to improve fortifications or to modernize military equipment. However, cities which had had to transfer considerable sums to their rulers or to the Empire during the sixteenth century, had to bear an equivalent, or even an increased, burden during the seventeenth. Transfers of this kind from Munich varied between 7 and 23 per cent of total expenditure; at Nuremberg the proportion was between 8 and 39 per cent; at Schwäbisch Hall the figure was 31 per cent; at Überlingen, it oscillated wildly between 7 and 68 per cent, while at Milan it also varied between 31 and 58 per cent. Even when a proportion of this spending was devoted to local social and religious institutions—between perhaps 1 per cent and 5 per cent of the total, as in the Catholic republic of Lucerne—the greater part of the sums transferred left the city for the coffers of the central administration. The Swiss republics continued to be the exception in this regard, transferring between 11 and 20 per cent of their budget to their territorial churches, while also retaining their traditional policy of financial investments.

This policy was pursued at the same time as the service of the public debt, which could vary between 17 and 56 per cent of total expenditure and continued to represent a heavy burden for the exchequers of certain urban republics in the early decades of the seventeenth century. However, by the end of the century, this element had disappeared entirely from the Swiss republics' finances, even though other cities continued to spend between 11 and 65 per cent of total expenditure on servicing their debts. In general, the median value of the proportion of expenditure devoted to debt servicing was, at 22 per cent, lower than during the previous century, when it had stood at 30 per cent.

Eighteenth-century developments brought about no significant new changes to the structure of the finances of towns and urban republics (Figure 61).[41] On the contrary, the structures established previously were consolidated, and some of their typical features were accentuated. In Milan, for example, we may note an overload in the form of sums transferred directly to central government because the city had accepted responsibility for the costs of their garrison, which regularly accounted for between 72 and 88 per cent of total expenditure. Similar transfers by German cities were less onerous, amounting to 25 per cent at most.

40 Hildebrandt (1977).

41 Sources as for Figure 54; ESFDB \korner\swib010 based on \swid006.

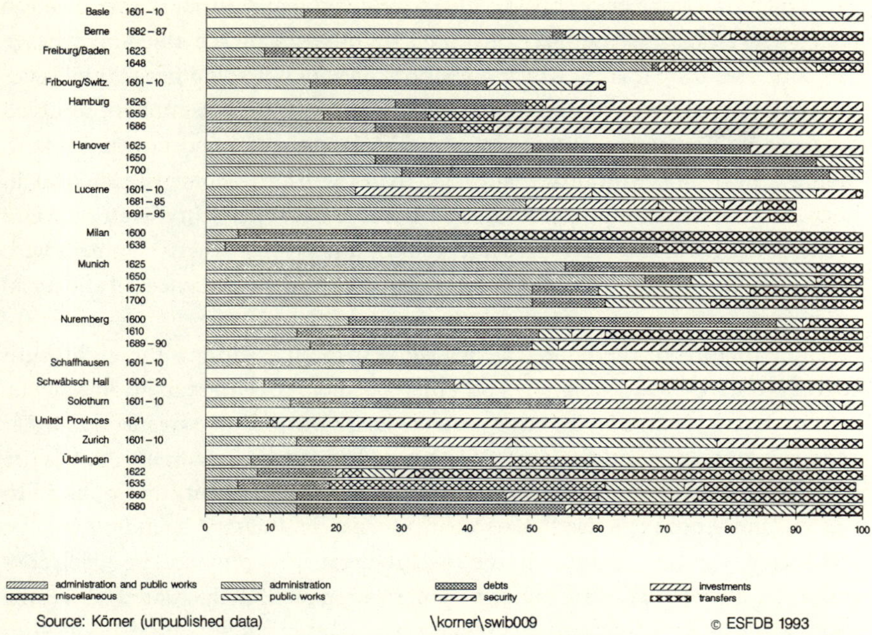

FIG. 60. Categories of expenditure of European republics and towns, 1600–1700

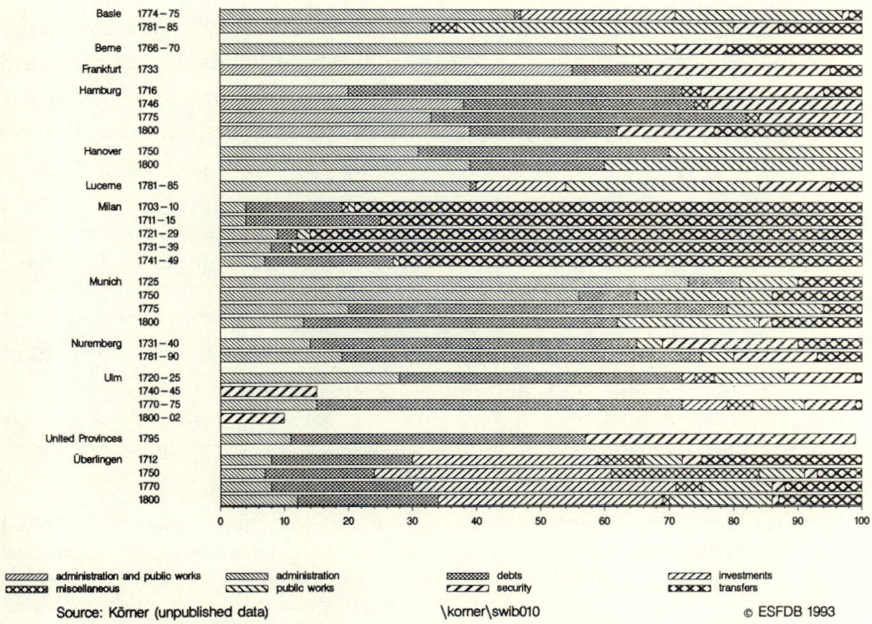

FIG. 61. Categories of expenditure of European republics and towns, 1703–1802

But then they spent a greater part of their outgoings, generally between 10 and 20 per cent, on security. The share devoted to debt servicing remained on average the same as during the seventeenth century, although it could be slightly lower or slightly higher from city to city. For their part, the Swiss republics preserved their special position: spending on security was minimal and devoted less to military protection from external threat than to ensuring internal peace, as in Lucerne, where the outgoings for this purpose rose to 11 per cent towards the end of the century. Finally, we should note the continuity of the Swiss republics with regard to the absence of debt servicing and the importance of financial investments.

The structure of the United Provinces' expenditure during the eighteenth century differed hardly at all from that of the great monarchical powers. Administrative costs continued to remain relatively low (Figures 62 and 63).[42] Spending on war claimed 42 per cent—the median for the monarchies was 54 per cent—and the cost of debt servicing amounted to 46 per cent, that is, close to French and English levels.[43] The relative cost of military spending by the monarchies can be illustrated in the case of Great Britain where, between 1685 and 1813, the share of private investment in relation to GNP fluctuated between 4 and 8.8 per cent, while that of military expenditure alone varied between a minimum of 2 per cent in peacetime and 17.6 per cent in wartime.[44] Lucerne's total expenditure amounted to nearly 3 per cent of GNP at the end of the sixteenth century, but was less than 2 per cent at the end of the eighteenth century.[45] In proportionate terms, the difference between the tiny republic and the powerful English monarchy in peacetime, and even in wartime, was not enormous. The differences lay in the scale of activities and in the number of years of warfare.

12.7 *Conclusion: The Evolution of Expenditure in the Long Term*

The growth of expenditure in the different types of European state was not a uniform phenomenon. If we calculate at random the annual rate of growth of forty states over a minimum period of 30 years and a maximum of 380 years among cities, urban republics and republics which were at one time or another

[42] Sources as for Figure 54; ESFDB \korner\swib011 and \swib012 based on \swid006.

[43] Calculations based on figures in 't Hart (1991), 41, and Schremmer in Mathias and Pollard (1989), 320, 326. Patrick O'Brien argues that the cost of debt service, that is interest and reimbursement of capital, should be considered an aspect of war expenditure since in England loans served the unique purpose of financing war expenditure. According to his figures, the proportions for Britain rise to 60 per cent in peacetime and 87 per cent in time of war (1688–1815): O'Brien (1991).

[44] O'Brien (1991), 35. [45] Körner (1981), 376.

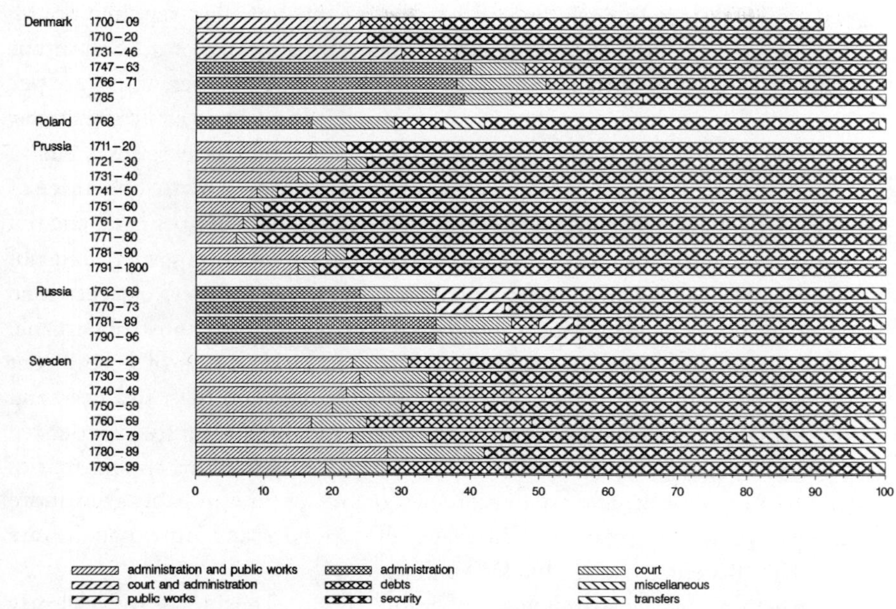

Source: Körner (unpublished data) \korner\swib011 © ESFDB 1993

FIG. 62. Categories of expenditure of duchies, kingdoms and empires of the Baltic region, 1700–1800

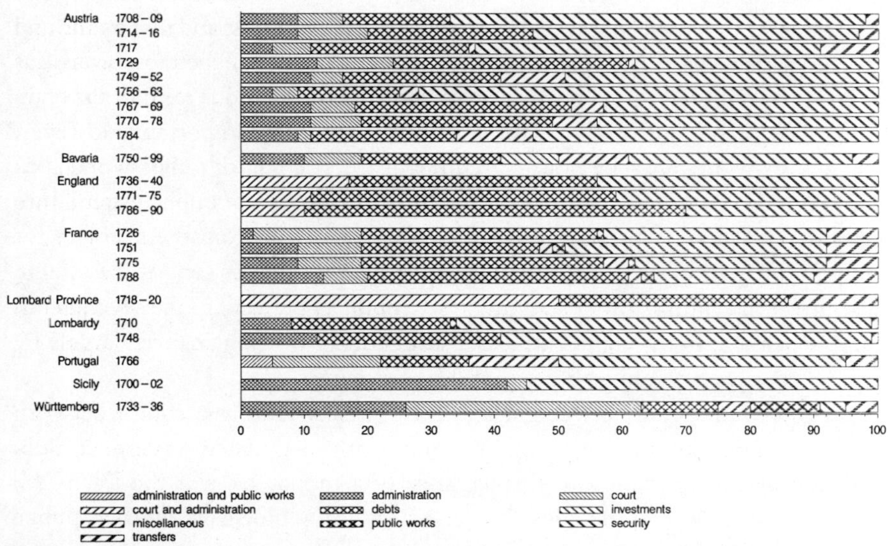

Source: Körner (unpublished data) \korner\swib012 © ESFDB 1993

FIG. 63. Categories of expenditure of non-Baltic duchies, kingdoms and empires, 1700–1799

great powers—that is, including such states as the Venetian republic or the United Provinces—we obtain negative or zero annual rates of growth in ten instances, positive growth of under 1 per cent in twenty-two cases, and over 1 per cent in thirteen, with two cases of maximum growth of 2 per cent.[46] A similar exercise covering thirty-two rates of growth in monarchical states yields a noticeably different result—only two examples of negative growth, only three of growth less than 1 per cent, twenty-three with growth of over 1 per cent, and ten above 2 per cent. With the exception of the high expenditure growth rates of Navarre in the fourteenth century and of the bishopric of Bamberg between 1600 and 1680—both calculated for a relatively short period—the most remarkable growth rates were those of Denmark with an annual increase of 2.7 per cent between 1600 and 1700, England with 3 per cent between 1690 and 1770, and Russia with 4.3 per cent between 1762 and 1796. French expenditure experienced its greatest relative expansion between 1590 and 1690 with an annual rate of growth of 2.2 per cent. The expenditure of monarchies thus probably grew more strongly over the long term than did that of the republics, and more than the rate of growth of Venice or the Dutch Republic.

A structural analysis spanning just over four centuries enables us to see clearly where the money went. It was neither the court nor the administrative machine of rulers which, in the long term, weighed most heavily in the scales of monarchical expenditure. On the contrary, while it is true that in the fourteenth and fifteenth centuries these items of spending were still of some importance, it is no less clear that their share fell during subsequent centuries, and that by the end of the *ancien régime* it had reached a very modest level. For all their importance as historic monuments, public works were in no sense a serious item of expenditure, though the construction of fortifications might still be important. However, such costs were generally not entered under the heading of public works, but rather under that of external security. The great scourge of public expenditure was the growing proportion devoted to war, as is clear from the averages for those monarchical states for which we have figures—40 per cent of the total in the fifteenth century, 27 per cent in the sixteenth, 46 per cent in the seventeenth and 54 per cent in the eighteenth. As a consequence of wars financed largely by credit, there was the huge burden of debt servicing.[47]

In the competition between states, cities usually had little choice between three options—submission, armed resistance or a negotiated settlement. Submission and integration into the territory of a monarchy was the lot of the majority of cities, and the consequence was a heavy mortgage on their public expenditure in the form of transfer payments as the price to be paid for the peace

[46] Rates of growth calculated on units measured in metric tonnes of fine silver.

[47] For France: Morineau (1980), 318; for England: O'Brien (1991).

and protection guaranteed by the ruler. For many of the cities this meant higher expenditure on fortifications, war and repairs. Other cities, such as Genoa and Venice during the Middle Ages, or those of the United Provinces in the late sixteenth century, opted for resistance at any cost or even aspired to be first-rank powers, which carried its own high price. The Swiss republics probably found the most economically efficient solution to the problem, that of political compromise, at the beginning of the sixteenth century, but this came only after they had tried the military option during the fifteenth century and had paid the usual price for it in the form of burdensome debt servicing costs. Once they had opted for a peaceful instead of an aggressive strategy, the expenditure of the Swiss republics generally remained below the volume of revenue. Deficits became the exception, profits the rule.

To demonstrate this point, it suffices to compare the chart of the spending of a Swiss urban republic, that of Lucerne (Figure 64),[48] which can serve as an example for the others, with that of a great monarchical power, France. From 1435 to 1795, Lucerne's expenditure always experienced fluctuations of a small or medium range, which was entirely normal. Peaks in the graph reflect wars which were more frequent in the fifteenth and early decades of the sixteenth centuries than later.[49] The temporary but noticeable increase in the years 1693–1702 is evidence of the extraordinary effort to rearm at the time of the War of the League of Augsburg. But all of these wars were very short-lived episodes without disastrous consequences for the equilibrium of Lucerne's budget. In the 1760s, a more significant rise in spending was caused by the establishment of a permanent, specialized police force intended especially to strengthen internal security. This shows clearly how far the budgetary position of the republic depended on the savings achieved by the principle of an armed militia and the absence of a permanent army.

It was under Francis I and his successors that the expenditure of the French monarchy began to increase significantly.[50] But the hegemonic policies of the seventeenth and eighteenth centuries produced an expenditure explosion, the first peak beginning with the Thirty Years' War and direct French intervention during the 1630s and 1640s (Figure 65).[51] After a brief cessation of war with the advent of Colbert, expenditure rose again with the Dutch War and that of the League of Augsburg, reaching a second peak with the War of the Spanish

[48] Körner (1981); ESFDB \korner\swib002 based on \swid005.

[49] These were: the battle of Saint-Jacques-sur-La-Birse in 1444, the Burgundian wars of 1474–6, the Swabian war against Emperor Maximilian in 1498–9, the Italian wars in 1513–15, the First War of Religion of 1528, the Second War of Religion in 1531, the Peasants' War of 1653, the First Villmergen War of 1655, and the Second Villmergen War or the Toggenbourg War of 1712.

[50] Guéry (1978), 227–8.

[51] ESFDB \rjb\malet\malg048 based on \malm046 and the sources cited there.

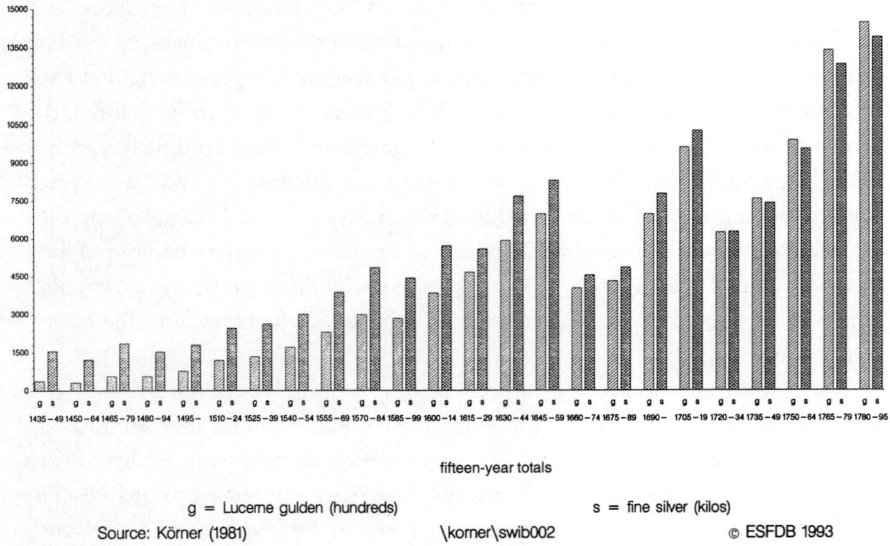

FIG. 64. Expenditure of the city and state of Lucerne, 1435–1795 (expressed in Lucerne *gulden* and in kilos of fine silver)

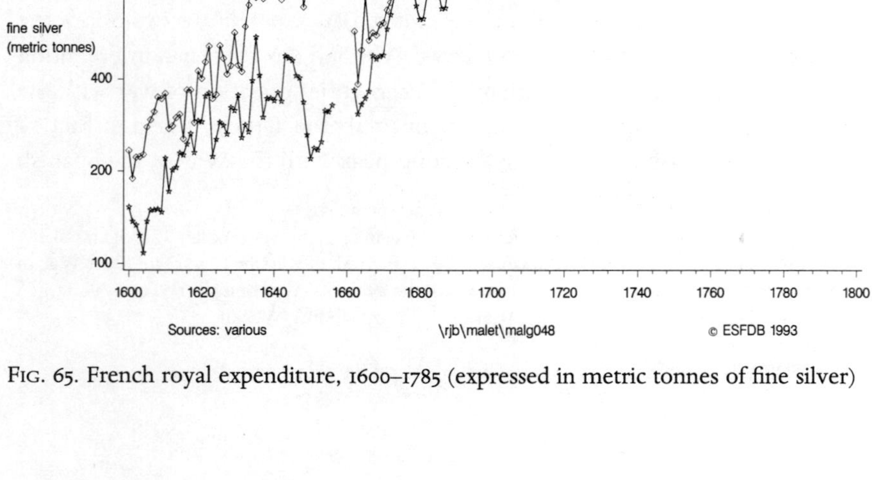

FIG. 65. French royal expenditure, 1600–1785 (expressed in metric tonnes of fine silver)

Succession, and a third with the Seven Years' War. The difference between each of these surges in total French expenditure lay, however, in the fact that each lasted several years and that the costs of war weighed far more heavily in the overall structure of the budget. Above all, the gulf between ordinary and total expenditure had grown considerably (Figure 66).[52]

But there are also similarities between the graph of the expenditure of the French monarchy and that of the tiny republic of Lucerne. The 'long' sixteenth century was the period of greatest growth in expenditure. The dynamism of the finances of both urban republics and kingdoms was 'the measurable sign of the emergence and establishment of the early modern state'.[53] Growing budgetary spending does indeed appear to reflect faithfully the increased means of intervention which states had at their disposal. In the monarchical states, this was expressed above all in war and the costs of debt servicing, while the increase in the number of royal servants trailed after these two dominant items.[54] At the other end of the spectrum, as in the Swiss republics, the state grew along more rational lines, with a collective, aristocratic and oligarchical leadership at the top which still managed to integrate the population at the communal level. Among such states, expenditure on war was virtually negligible.

We should also note divergences in expenditure growth and cycles between sovereign cities and cities forming part of a kingdom or an Empire. On the one hand, the outgoings of Nuremberg, one of the richest cities of the Holy Roman Empire, appear to have risen strongly during the sixteenth century, while in the eighteenth century they appear to have stagnated in nominal value and to have fallen in real terms. While sovereign cities such as Lucerne were faced with the growing financial demands of being a territorial state, an Imperial city could limit its normal expenditure to local needs. On the other hand, the fluctuations in the charts of Nuremberg's expenditure (Figures 67 and 68)[55] are a forceful reminder of the contributions imposed on Imperial cities for prolonged and costly wars. These were most noticeable during the wars of Maximilian I from 1498 to 1513, the wars of the Reformation period, especially the Schmalkaldic War of 1546–7, during at least three phases of the Thirty Years' War, during the War of the League of Augsburg followed by that of the Spanish Succession, and finally—and particularly severely—during the Seven Years' War.[56]

The strong surges and fluctuations in the expenditure of Baltic monarchical

[52] ESFDB \rjb\malet\malg050 based on \malm046 and the sources cited there.

[53] Braudel cited by Guéry (1978), 321.

[54] A divergent view is expressed by Guéry (1978), 231.

[55] Sander (1902), 698, 750, 780–1, 804–7; ESFDB \korner\nurb001 based on \nurd001; ESFDB \korner\nurb002 based on \nurd002.

[56] Sander (1902).

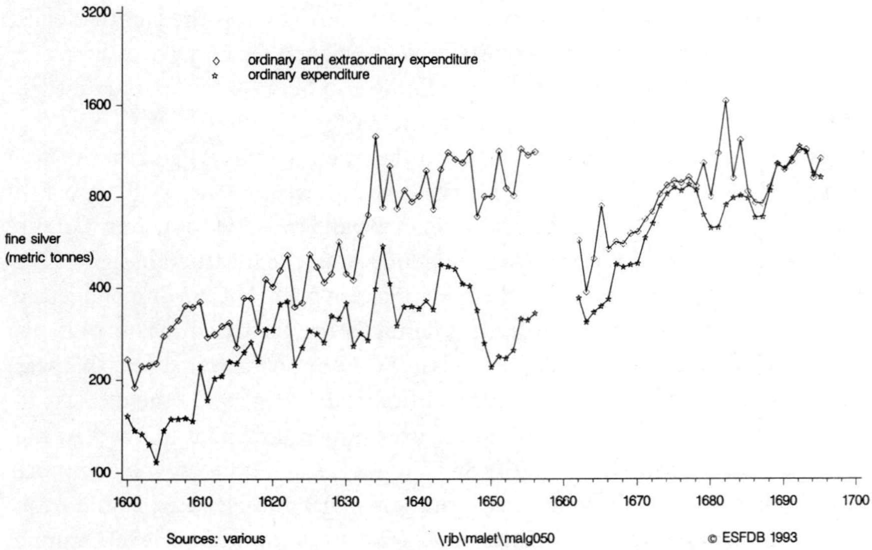

FIG. 66. French royal expenditure in the seventeenth century (expressed in metric tonnes of fine silver)

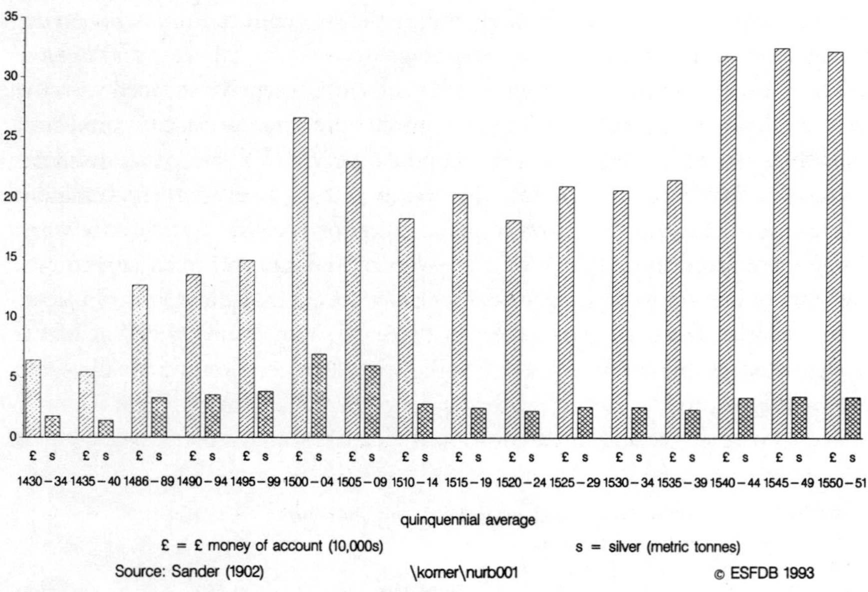

FIG. 67. Expenditure of the city of Nuremberg, 1430–1551 (expressed in £ of money of account and in metric tonnes of silver)

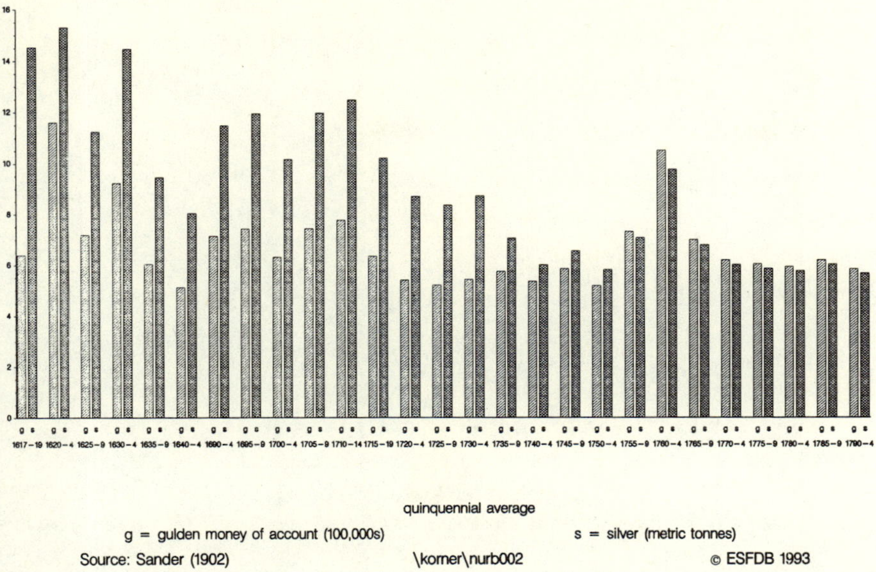

FIG. 68. Expenditure of the city of Nuremberg, 1617–1794 (expressed in *gulden* of money of account and in metric tonnes of silver)

states in the eighteenth century also reflect the dominance of military spending and the cost of debts contracted as a result (Figure 69).[57] The rise in Sweden's expenditure during the 1740s was a consequence of a costly war with Russia in 1741. This level of spending was subsequently maintained because of the costs arising from the Seven Years' War. Above all, it was a new war against Russia in 1788–90 which led to a peak in expenditure.[58] The curve showing Prussian expenditure in Figure 69 reflects Prussia's wars, especially the Silesian War, which included the Seven Years' War, and the constant advance of militarization, as well as the administrative integration into the kingdom during the 1780s of newly acquired territories. The sustained rise in the curve is powerful evidence of the rise of Prussia during the eighteenth century.[59] The same applies to the rise to great power status of Russia under Catherine the Great: the curve of Russian expenditure reflects its military efforts against the Turkish empire in 1768–74 and 1787–92, as well as the creation after 1783 of a Black Sea fleet linked to Russian expansion into the Crimea.[60] Lastly, Denmark, after it had made a huge financial

[57] Åmark (1961); Riedel (1866); Nathanson (1836); Kahan (1985), 345; ESFDB \korner\eurg001 based on \eurd001.

[58] Åmark (1961). [59] Riedel (1866). [60] Kahan (1985).

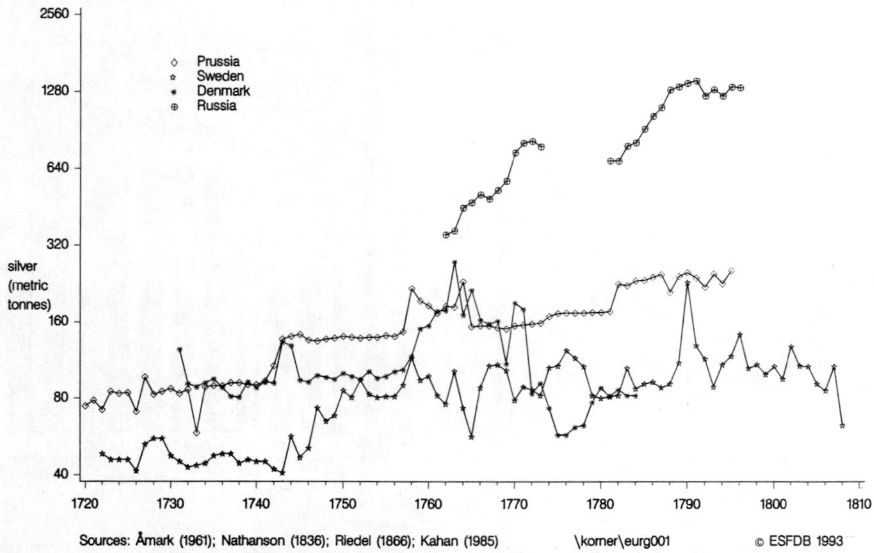

FIG. 69. Total expenditure of Prussia, Sweden, Denmark and Russia, 1720–1808 (expressed in metric tonnes of silver)

effort during the Seven Years' War as a consequence of its maritime union with Sweden, subsequently opted for neutrality if not for military self-restraint, the effect of which was immediately felt by a massive reduction in its expenditure after 1770.[61]

[61] Barudio (1981). Data supplied by Dr Bjørn Poulsen: ESFDB dataset \poul\dand006.

CHAPTER 13

Revenues

Richard Bonney

Where a programme of research covers such a vast area of study, it is necessary to begin by setting its parameters. It is impossible to study the evolution of the revenue systems of every European state, let alone the evolution of the main types of revenue in each one. Our more modest objective is to describe the evolution of certain types of revenue which we may take to be reasonably representative of their kind within western Europe, and to attempt to discern the relationship between these types of revenue and political and economic developments. In other words, certain types of political, economic and social development were necessary for particular forms of revenue to be adopted by states. As has been seen earlier (Chapter 6.5), at least by the eighteenth century, theoreticians were clear that some types of revenue were better adapted to particular governmental and economic systems. Part of our purpose is to determine whether (for example) Montesquieu's views on the relationship between state structure and revenue systems were true and to debate the nature of a 'fiscal constitution'. In so doing, we must necessarily leave aside the case of the Papacy because of its universalist claims. The revenues of the Avignon Pope John XXII (1316–34), which averaged 228,000 Florentine florins a year, were less than those of the government of Florence itself, and substantially less than those of the kings of France, Naples or England. Unlike those rulers, however, the Pope drew his revenues from all parts of Europe. Papal finance is an important case study in state development; but, except in terms of the income drawn from the Papal States themselves (which constituted under half the total receipts until the sixteenth century), the case of the Papacy is wholly exceptional. The Papacy gave a lead to secular rulers in a number of fiscal devices, however, notably the sale of offices, and it also provided a serious threat by drawing bullion from their kingdoms.[1]

Before we can proceed to an analysis of the evolution of revenue systems over time, some categorization of public revenue and taxation is required. This is extraordinarily difficult. How can one compare like with unlike even within the same period? In Russia, during the period of the Mongol Yoke (1240–1480), perhaps a dozen taxes were collected as tribute to the conquerors, in addition to levies commanded by the princes and their retinues. There was little or no native currency, and no native silver mines; but substantial amounts of foreign currency in circulation were transported to the Mongol conquerors. The fiscal system was dominated by the 'feeding system' (*kormlenie*), whereby favoured servants of the ruling princes were dispatched on rotation from the capital to the provinces in effect as governors. Much of their revenue was collected in kind, making a calculation of the medieval tax burden impossible.[2] Contrast the situation in England in the thirteenth century, where an elaborate classification of royal revenues may be undertaken, and sophisticated calculations as to the purchasing power of those revenues in real terms may be hazarded.[3] A further contrast between the situation in England in the 1290s and in the 1790s[4] demonstrates again the complexity of any classification of a revenue system. The mutation of the system within the same country was very considerable over the period under review in this book. When the evolution of other states is taken into consideration, the problem becomes multi-dimensional. In general, it may be agreed that as the structure of the economy changes, so too does the nature of the tax base, and with it those items subject to taxation. The economic objectives of tax policy vary with stages of economic development, as do the criteria by which an efficient tax structure is judged. The changes, however, result from institutional decisions and are not an inherently economic matter, although it is true that, as a more highly developed, monetized, economy develops, then a much wider range of tax bases becomes available.[5] The capacity of a ruler and his officials to evaluate wealth affects what kinds of property can be taxed and where. Before the general European trend towards land surveys and cadastral maps in the

[1] Partner in Bonney (1995); Delumeau (1957–9, 1961); Spufford (1989), 157–8, 183; Lunt (1934), i, 57–136; Prodi (1987), 57, 208 n. 85. In the case of France, 53.4 per cent of coinage output was drained off by the Papacy between 1404 and 1408: Miskimin (1984), 79. The author thanks Professor Patrick O'Brien for commenting on a draft of this chapter.

[2] Hellie in Bonney (1995).

[3] Ormrod (1995).

[4] O'Brien (1988). O'Brien and Hunt (1993) and O'Brien and Hunt in Bonney (1995) deal with the evolution between 1485 and 1815.

[5] Musgrave (1969), 125–36, is fundamental; Tilly (1990), 88, offers a visual representation.

eighteenth century, for example, an equitable distribution of the land tax was an impossibility.[6]

Compounding our difficulty in perceiving the structural evolution of fiscal systems is the relatively scant guidance we find from contemporaries. It is questionable whether they had any notion of fiscal systems in their entirety before the early modern period, and few early modern theoreticians apart from Sonnenfels (Chapter 6.4) and Mirabeau (Chapter 6.5) wrote systematic analytical treatises. In the English language, Smith and Ricardo for all their insights (Chapter 6.7) were not primarily interested in the subject, and it was not until J. R. McCulloch's *A Treatise on the Principles and Practical Influence of Taxation and the Funding System* (1845) that there appeared a 'publication, of any authority at least, that exclusively deal[t] with the subject of taxation'.[7] Thereafter, the philosophy of modern taxation as a subject in its own right really begins.[8] Apart from the inherent complexity of revenue systems, which rendered analysis difficult for contemporaries as it does for us today, it is not difficult to see why contemporary theoreticians tended to eschew global analysis of the subject. They were obsessed by their own form of systems theory, according to which there was one preponderant or guiding system for an economy. Though such deductive reasoning was denounced by Condillac in his *Traité des systèmes* (1749), and Steuart called such systems 'mere conceits', we find such guiding principles underlying the Physiocratic concept that (in Locke's words) taxes 'for the most part terminate upon Land', as also in Smith's discussion of 'agricultural systems', the 'mercantile system' and his advocacy of the 'simple system of natural liberty'.[9] It is not surprising, therefore, that contemporaries were more concerned with guiding principles in a tax system than with global analysis. It has already been seen that to some extent von Justi anticipated Adam Smith's 'four canons' of taxation (Chapter 6.7). Other theorists before Smith sought to identify the principles underlying tax efficiency. For Ernst Ludwig Carl (1682–1743), writing in 1722–3, the most important points were the ease with which taxes were paid by the people to the government; that the money should pass immediately from those who owed the taxes to those to whom they were due (thus, he was hostile to intermediaries such as tax-farmers); that taxes should be 'proportional', by which Carl meant that they should be levied in accordance with the ability to pay;[10] and that taxes should not damage or destroy the wealth

[6] Levi (1981), 455–6; Kain and Baigent (1992), 336–41. The English land tax remained the exception to the European trend: ibid. 340.

[7] McCulloch, ed. O'Brien (1975), xv (a quotation from *The Times*, 27 Sept. 1845).

[8] Smith is the only earlier writer discussed in Groves (1974).

[9] Hutchison (1988), 325, 338, 358.

[10] True proportionality in tax is taken by modern economists to mean that the rich pay the same as the poor, as distinct from progression (where the rich pay a larger proportion than others) and

of the state by their disproportionality, multiplicity or uncertainty.[11] In his *Meditations on Political Economy* (1771), Pietro Verri (1728–97) laid down five principles for taxation: taxes should not fall immediately on the poor; they should be imposed in a manner which minimized the cost of collection; tax legislation should be clear, precise, inviolable and impartial; taxes should never raise transport costs; and finally taxes should never penalize the growth of industry.[12] A final example of pre-Smithian fiscal theory, and one which certainly influenced Smith himself, is provided by Lord Henry Home Kames's *Sketches on the History of Man* (1769), which contained a long discussion of tax issues. Kames enunciated six 'rules to be observed in taxing'. When the opportunity for tax evasion existed, he contended that taxes should be moderate so as not 'first to tempt and then to punish' for yielding to temptation. Taxes which were expensive to levy should be avoided. Arbitrary taxes were 'disgustful to all', since the amount paid was determined by the 'vague and conjectured opinion of others'. Kames advocated a degree of progression, arguing that the poor should be relieved of any significant tax burden in order to remedy the 'inequity of riches'. Taxes that sapped the strength of the nation should be avoided since they contradicted the very nature of government 'which is to protect and not oppress'. Finally, taxes should not be levied with the requirement of an oath from the taxpayer, on grounds of both morality and effectiveness ('the imprudent multiplication of oaths [for tax enforcement] has not only spread corruption . . . but by annihilating the authority of the oath over conscience, has rendered it ineffectual').[13]

Despite the importance of some of the ideas advanced by contemporary theorists, we are perhaps better guided by modern fiscal theory developed in the context of developing countries. This is a relevant comparison because of the endemic fiscal deficits of developing countries. It becomes evident that, in the absence of social upheaval, significant changes in tax administration come about only over a relatively long period of time: when tax revenue falls significantly, it is inappropriate to speak of a decline in the efficiency of the administration of taxation since the cause is usually economic, or a result of the interaction of economic policy with fiscal policy.[14] Several characteristics of tax systems in developing countries are similar to those of medieval and early modern European states. Firstly, there are usually a significant number of taxes. As a fiscal

regression (where the poor pay a larger proportion than the rich): Adams (1993), 76. Carl used the term 'proportional' in the same sense as Francis Hutcheson in 1755, that 'a just proportion to the wealth of the people should be observed in whatever is raised from them': Hutchison (1988), 197.

[11] Hutchison (1988), 162.
[12] Ibid. 305–6.
[13] Adams (1993), 286–7.
[14] Tanzi (1991), 116, 133.

principle, the 'proliferation of taxes not only complicates their administration, [but] confuses tax payers and facilitates or even invites tax evasion ...'[15] Secondly, there is a relationship between the tax burden, the rate of saving and the balance of payments. If the tax system creates distortions and thus decreases the ability of a country to earn foreign exchange, quite low levels of taxes may prevent capital formation;[16] the criticisms of contemporary theorists such as Ustáriz of Spanish fiscal practice in the eighteenth century illustrate the principle (Chapter 6.2). In developing countries, increases in real revenue are likely to occur when the delays in the collection of taxes are short, and the tax systems are elastic, but these are primarily characteristics of industrialized countries. A drastic fall in real revenue may result from the combination of an inelastic tax system, a long delay in the collection process and high inflation.[17] The development of the tax base that can be used by governments in developing countries to raise the desired level of revenue depends on a number of factors such as the level of per capita income (often taken as a proxy for economic development); the degree of urbanization; the literacy rate; the degree of monetization of the economy; the ratio of exports and imports to the gross domestic product (GDP); the share of mining or agriculture in GDP; the size of the country and so on. In addition, there are a number of qualitative factors which are of importance but which are difficult to quantify, such as the quality of tax administration; the resources which the country allocates to this function; the honesty of the taxpayers; the degree of corruption among tax collectors which in turn may be influenced by the level of their wages; the size of the penalities for non-compliance by the taxpayers and for corruption by the tax administrators; the income distribution of the country; the importance of the subsistence sector; the attitude of the citizens towards the country, which may be influenced by the efficiency with which tax revenues are spent; the form of government; and so on. Because of the complexity of the problem, there are no simple criteria for tax structure development. The only feasible approach is to develop 'model tax structures' applicable to groups of countries with more or less similar characteristics with regard to available tax bases and levels of per capita income.[18]

The difficulties of the fiscal historian of medieval and early modern Europe are compounded by the intractability and incompleteness of the surviving statistical

[15] Ibid. 17, 159. Proliferation 'renders very difficult the use of an active fiscal policy because if the government wants to raise more revenues ... it must change the nominal rates of many taxes'. 'Small, nuisance taxes obfuscate the tax system ... Low yielding taxes often demand as much administrative effort as much more productive ones.'

[16] Ibid. 25.

[17] Ibid. 104.

[18] Ibid. 117–18; Musgrave (1969), 166.

evidence. Where this survives from certain European states, even in the eighteenth century the normal separation between 'revenues' and 'expenditure' is sometimes unclear.[19] In part, this arises from the practice of assigning expenses directly against specific revenues, but there are other accounting reasons peculiar to specific states. Another difficulty arises from contemporary accounting practice, which usually distinguished between ordinary and extraordinary revenues: in the case of the Austrian Habsburg lands after 1682, extraordinary taxes meant the 'Turk taxes' (*Türcken-Steuer*) for the defence of Vienna and reconquest of Hungary (Figure 70).[20] Apart from the observable phenomenon, noted by Giovanni Botero in 1589, that over time extraordinary taxes tended to become ordinary,[21] comparison between states is hindered by this distinction since one state's definition of what was 'extraordinary' differed from that of another. Even so, the conceptual framework of administrators remained intensely traditional: even Necker's celebrated accounts of 1781 (the first to be published in France) presented only ordinary expenditure and ordinary revenues in the form of single-entry book-keeping. Indeed, Necker was critical of the English failure to

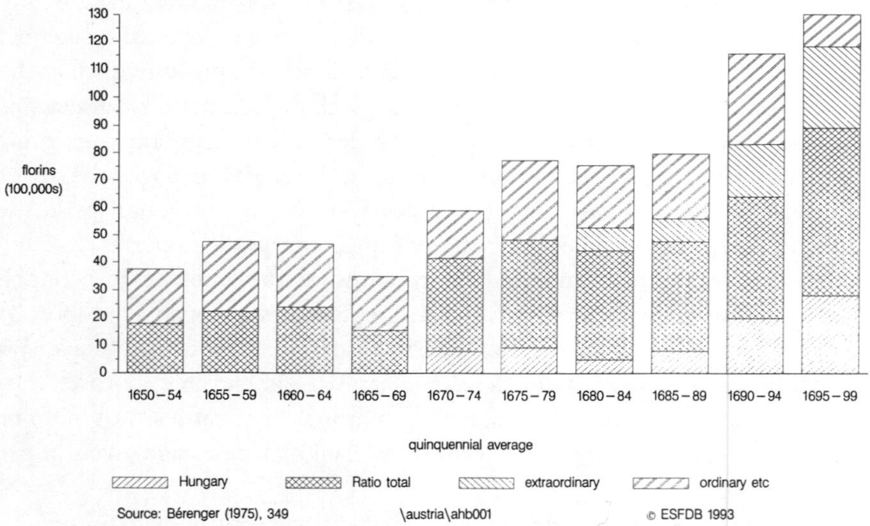

FIG. 70. Categories of ordinary and extraordinary revenues from the Austrian Habsburg hereditary lands, 1650–1699 (in florins)

[19] Johansen (1985), 313 n.1.

[20] Bérenger (1975), 335–7, 349; ESFDB \austria\ahb001 based on \adhd002; note that between 1664 and 1674 extraordinary taxes were paid in kind and are not evaluated in the table upon which this dataset draws.

[21] Bonney (1991*b*), 353, after Botero, ed. Waley (1956), 135.

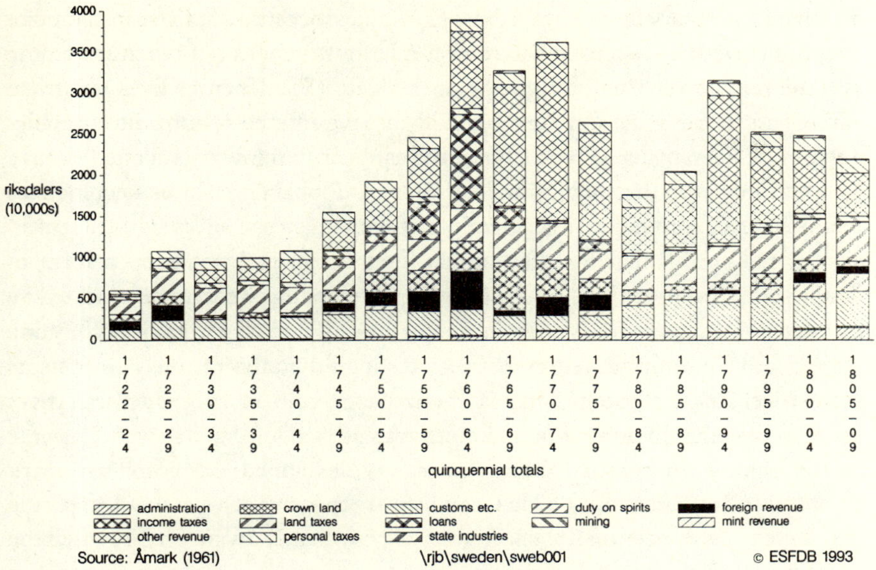

FIG. 71. Categories of revenues of the Swedish state, 1722–1809 (in *riksdalers*)

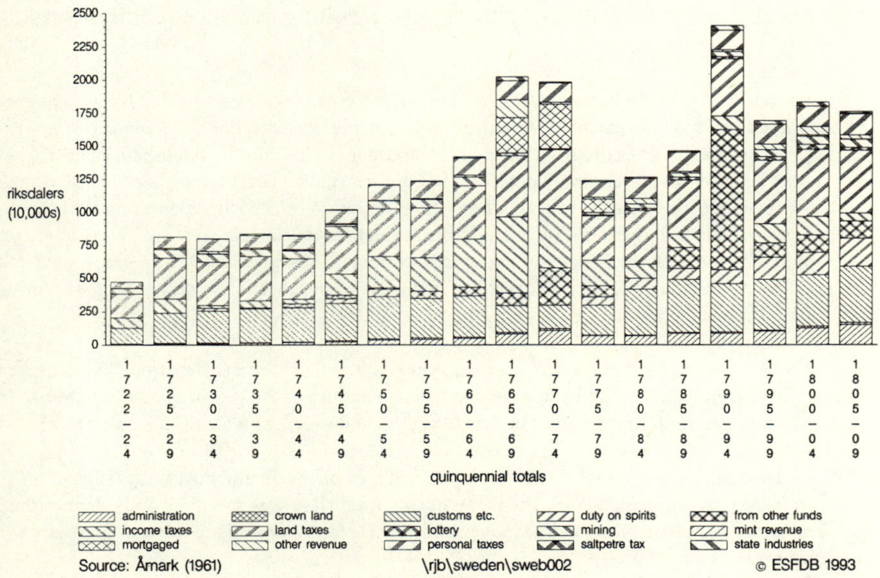

FIG. 72. Categories of domestic revenues of the Swedish state, 1722–1809 (in *riksdalers*)

distinguish ordinary from extraordinary revenues; because of this, it was impossible, in his view, to ascertain the correct relationship between revenue income and the regular or 'fixed' outgoings of the state ('les dépenses fixes').[22] Much earlier, under Sully, Simon Stevin is said to have offered to introduce double-entry book-keeping into France, but the great finance minister is alleged to have refused to take up the suggestion.[23] In France, double-entry book-keeping was not introduced into the various accounts of state finance at all levels until 1808.[24] This is not to say that for the various funds there had not been a form of double-entry book-keeping in place earlier: witness the weekly accounts of the proceeds of the new *dixième* tax in France in 1711.[25] Such forms of accounting were relatively sophisticated in that they distinguished the various components in the mechanism of receipts and payment (paper, coin, assignment)[26] but there was no possibility of presenting accounts at a national level in this way. It is only in the eighteenth century that some states developed the combination of technical and administrative advances necessary to arrive at a state budget for the first time: in the case of Russia, it was in 1781, nearly twenty years after the accession of Catherine II.[27]

Russian practice had been heavily influenced by Swedish models. In Sweden, double-entry book-keeping was introduced by the Dutchman Abraham Cabeljau or Cabiliau in 1623; by the 1630s there existed a personnel budget, an appropriations budget and the 'general disposition'.[28] Even with the relatively sophisticated accounting techniques prevailing in Sweden, and an almost unbroken run of statistics from 1722 to 1809 (Figure 71), the resulting evidence requires careful

[22] Necker (1791), 145; Harris (1979), 122, 224–5; contrast Vergennes's objection that Necker sought to base his conduct 'on the example of England, which publishes its accounts . . .': Hardman (1993), 66. Necker agreed that extraordinary expenditure accounts should not be published, since it was imprudent to provide the enemy with too much information: Harris (1986), 230. Harris notes Necker's terminological change in 1789, after which he referred to fixed expenses and revenues (previously he had used the term 'ordinary' expenses and revenues): ibid. 412.

[23] Buisseret (1968), 85; the Paris brothers, who were great tax-farmers under the regency, are said to have attempted double-entry book-keeping at the *ferme générale* but the experiment was 'sans lendemain': Perrot (1992), 21.

[24] Théret (1991), 172.

[25] AN G^7 1140, 16 May 1711, 'caisse du dix^e, Bordereau de la recette et depense'. This has the income from the tax on the left-hand page and the expenditure of the proceeds on the right-hand page. There is a sum of the difference between receipts and expenses which is the amount which 'Reste en caisse'.

[26] For income, it was specificied whether 'en argent'; 'en billets de monnoye'; 'en assignations'; or 'en rescriptions'. For expenditure the name of the beneficiary was specified, and whether the payment was 'en argent'; 'billets de monnoye'; 'billets' or 'rescriptions' of the *receveurs généraux*; or 'assignations sur les pays d'états'.

[27] Duran (1970), 485, 493.

[28] Buisseret (1968), 85; Peterson (1979), 191–3.

interpretation.[29] Loan income, both from home and abroad, was included as revenue in terms of providing the state with an increased capacity to spend. Loan income nevertheless must be regarded as a deferred tax: loans have to be repaid, and in the long term only a growing economy permits borrowing to repay borrowing. In some states in the Middle Ages, loans (whether voluntary or forced, and whether repayable or not) were akin to direct taxes: forced loans (*preste* or *prestanze*) and voluntary loans were used more frequently at Siena, for instance, than direct taxes before 1355.[30] Forced loans and unrepaid loans should be regarded as a form of wealth tax. In contrast, 'genuine' loans had to be voluntary and repaid, whatever the contemporary accounting practice. Foreign income and subsidies were also an important source of revenue for states such as Sweden in the eighteenth century, but these figures need to be removed from the calculations if the purpose is to study purely domestic revenues (Figure 72). Finally, contemporary accounting practice included as income other items such as the carry-over of revenue from previous years and the projected deficit against expenditure, which we would not consider as part of the annual revenue.[31] For these reasons, and bearing in mind that accounting practice in other states was often less advanced than in Sweden, comparison between one fiscal system and another is rendered extremely hazardous.

13.1 *Fiscal Constitutions: Coercion, Consent and Administration*

It is important to recognize that all states have held a 'revenue position', an independent standpoint in fiscal terms. Implicitly or explicitly states have asked similar questions of any new tax measure. Was the proposed tax economical, or would it cost too much to collect? Was it within the powers of the government to levy, and of the administration to assess and collect, or was it too complicated to be workable? Would the tax be specially open to evasion? Would the imposition of the tax tend to damage the economic activity which was the source of the revenue, for example a particular trade? Finally, would it create political difficulties and unrest?[32] In the context of the discussion which follows, the term 'fiscal

[29] ESFDB \rjb\sweden\sweb001 based on \swem001. All the Swedish data from the period after 1719 is drawn from Åmark (1961), 400–14, who publishes an almost complete run of statistics for the period, or from Jörberg (1972), i, 78–85; ii, 127–44. Further interpretation of the data is required, in the manner suggested for Denmark by Professor H.-C. Johansen at the seminar on Danish state finance held at Odense on 1 Oct. 1993.

[30] Bowsky (1970), 166, 189, 223–4.

[31] Sources as Figure 71; ESFDB \rjb\sweden\sweb002 based on \swem002. These last two items are included under 'other revenue' in the chart. The categorization follows Åmark, who summarizes the presentation in the accounts.

[32] Stamp (1921), 92–3.

constitution' is consciously adopted in a sense broader than that given by its originators and discussed earlier in the introduction to this book. All states had some form of fiscal constitution, and it was the interrelationship between this and economic development which defined the revenue capacity of the state. We start with the assumption that in all societies taxation has been regarded as potentially objectionable, particularly if levied in an innovative, oppressive or arbitrary manner. The nature of the relationship between those in power who determined both the amount and the type of taxation, and those excluded from central decision-making but who had to pay the taxes decided by others, is therefore crucial. We may assume that there have always been gradations in this relationship, but that its nature is unchanged throughout history: there is inevitable tension between rulers and taxpayers, even if the members of the governing class are themselves taxpayers or profit from the handling of tax receipts. All fiscal policy is politicized and involves a greater or lesser degree of political conflict. The degree of this tension depends on the nature of the fiscal constitution. In some medieval Italian city-states, tax measures were used as a weapon of oppression by one party against another. Fiscal policy became subject to factional politics. Even that great reforming measure at Florence, the *catasto* of 1427, was intended primarily as a more precise instrument to be used for party political purposes: the 'people' were said to be in favour of the reform (*laudat populus catastum*).[33]

Where there was a degree of representation in the state, the standing of the representatives of the taxpayers within their own communities and *vis-à-vis* the government became crucial, as did the extent of their control over the fiscal process. The vicissitudes of the *Cortes* of Castile and its standing committee in the period between the death of Philip II and Philip IV demonstrated the fluctuations in the balance of power that could occur even over a relatively short period of sixty-seven years (1598–1665).[34] Fiscal resistance and rebellion might serve to undermine, or enhance, the status of the representatives who attempted to modify government fiscal policies through mediation. Even in England in the late sixteenth century, though there were regular meetings of Parliament and no outright rebellion against taxation, the memory of tax revolt in the early Tudor period was significant in limiting the fiscal options considered by the government.[35] On the other hand, even when Charles I sought to govern without Parliament during the so-called 'eleven years' tyranny' (1629–40), resistance to

[33] 'Le catasto n'est pas une simple réforme de la fiscalité; il a aussi servi de machine de guerre aux factions politiques désireuses d'abattre leurs adversaires': Herlihy and Klapisch-Zuber (1978), 34.

[34] Thompson (1982, 1984); Fortea Pérez (1991); Thompson in Hoffman and Norberg (1994).

[35] Bush (1991). On Elizabethan parliamentary policy towards finance: Hartley (1992), 38–58.

the hated Ship Money was ineffective and royal revenues, at least during the second half of the decade of personal rule, were sufficiently buoyant that without the failure of two disastrous military campaigns against the Scots there would have been no fiscal necessity to summon Parliament.[36] By the eighteenth century, it has been argued, 'representative institutions, not absolute monarchy, proved superior in revenue extraction. Where representative bodies held the ultimate authority, as in the Netherlands or eighteenth-century England, they facilitated taxing.'[37] On the other hand, when a national assembly with fiscal powers emerged in France after 1789, popular pressure prevented the imposition of heavier taxes. The inflation caused by the emission of paper money, at least at first, was a less unpopular decision (Chapter 11.4), and French taxpayers remained chronically 'undertaxed'.

Where there was no representation and hence no mediation by representatives, fiscal resistance and rebellion assumed even greater significance, moulding the government's fiscal policies. Policy was shaped directly, in that resistance and revolt sometimes forced governments to abandon attempts to tax in certain specific ways simply because the opposition was too great: the 5 per cent sales tax (known variously as the *sol pour livre*, the *pancarte* and the *subvention générale*) had to be abandoned twice in France, in 1602 and 1643, because of resistance.[38] Policy was sometimes shaped indirectly, in that fear of a repetition of such resistance led to the abandonment of some types of fiscal solution before implementation was attempted. Certain avenues for tax reform were thus closed off to governments because of previous events or resistance in a country's fiscal history. Instead of innovation and reform, fiscal conservatism tended to result. What may seem to historians a relatively primitive fiscal system in one country is explicable by the operation of such rules within a particular fiscal constitution in which the evolution of power relations over time was crucial. The taxation of noble and clerical wealth was possible in some states, such as Prussian Silesia after 1740, but impossible to implement (though not unthinkable) in other states such as France at the same date. Thus, the revenues enjoyed by the French monarchy from clerical taxation fell between 1561 and 1788, both in real terms and as a proportion of the total expenditure of the crown, from some 15 to less than 1 per cent.[39]

That such a policy was impossible to implement, even if not unthinkable, poses two subsidiary questions: what was the nature of tax compliance within a particular European state, and how effective was its revenue-raising system?

[36] Sharpe (1992), 105–30, is the most detailed discussion.

[37] Hoffman and Norberg in Hoffman and Norberg (1994), 306; cf. ibid. 310.

[38] Bonney (1992*b*), 124–5.

[39] Michaud (1991), 9, 543.

In conceptual terms, tax-operating costs combine two elements, compliance costs and administrative or 'overhead' costs. Tax compliance theory suggests that different tax systems have variable costs related to the extent of tax evasion: how heavy does the penalty have to be before a tax will be paid voluntarily? In general, both administrative and compliance costs grow with the complexity of the tax. If they become too high, this generates tax evasion and an anti-tax mentality. Two of Smith's 'four canons' of taxation (the last two, concerning convenience and economy) were a contemporary statement of compliance cost theory (Chapter 6.7), and even the first canon on equity has relevance to the issue, since the costs of complying with tax laws might fall inequitably on different taxpayers. Arguably, Smith's second canon on certainty was also relevant, since administrative and compliance costs have their own timescale (the commencement costs of a tax need to be distinguished from the temporary costs which follow whilst a growth in understanding the tax takes place, both on the part of administrators and those taxed, and from the regular costs for continuing the tax).[40] Tax evasion was endemic in all medieval and early modern states. One of the great weaknesses of all early modern systems of direct taxation was the unwillingness of states to instigate an 'inquisition' into the wealth of their citizens. As late as 1845, McCulloch castigated income taxes because 'They require a constant interference with, and inquiry into the affairs of individuals, so that, independent of their inequality, they keep up a perpetual feeling of irritation'.[41] Voluntary declarations of wealth were always preferred to the systematic recourse to family papers and notarial acts. Sir William Petty was almost unique in asking the question 'where is the evil of so exact knowledge?' (Chapter 6.3). The Scottish nobles thought otherwise in 1556, rejecting a new tax assessment on the grounds that 'they meant not to put their goods in inventory, as if they were to make their last wills and testaments'.[42] That supposedly most 'absolute' of rulers, Louis XIV, when forced to order the levy of the *dixième* in the great crisis of his reign (1710), was unable to secure accurate declarations of wealth from taxpayers. Contemporaries considered that under the first *dixième* (1710–17) wealth was underassessed by more than half. Since the penalty for underassessment was a quadruple payment of tax, the penalty (and the government's reluctance and inability to enforce it) was seen as a sign of weakness. It was therefore insufficient to prevent significant tax evasion.[43]

All taxation requires the threat of coercion to ensure its implementation and a

[40] Sandford (1980), 155–7; Sandford, Godwin and Hardwick (1989), 16–17, 24–6.

[41] McCulloch, ed. O'Brien (1975), xxxiv, 133–4.

[42] Goodare (1989), 23.

[43] Petty, ed. Hull (1899), i, 53–4; Bonney (1993*a*); Marion (1910), 273 (declaration of 14 Oct. 1710, article 11).

belief among potential taxpayers that the threat can be implemented successfully by the governing power. The question at issue is not the implicit threat, but the explicit action. In seventeenth-century France, for example, coercion had to be introduced during the Thirty Years' War to ensure that popular protest at increased direct taxes was overcome and that payments to the central government essential for the war effort were received on time. The population did not appreciate the need for the war and the resulting increased taxes imposed arbitrarily by the central government. Coercion was implemented by brigades of troops.[44] Gradually, in the more settled decade of the 1660s, such coercion was abandoned in most provinces, although there were some notable exceptions such as Dauphiné[45] and Guyenne,[46] where the war system continued longer. Reforming ministers such as Colbert criticized the comparatively higher collection costs in provinces where coercion remained the norm. During the War of the Spanish Succession, the same opposition to paying greatly increased taxes revived, and coercion returned with a vengeance in a number of provinces and was not abandoned until after the death of Louis XIV. In the later eighteenth century coercion was used once more, since it was found to be cheaper than judicial sanctions against the parish community.[47]

The French example demonstrates that overt coercion was an important aspect of revenue raising. Indeed, at times it was crucial in ensuring the flow of revenues. Some states, such as Habsburg-reconquered Transylvania in the eighteenth century, depended entirely on it.[48] Coercion cannot be ignored in the historical development of the state. Arguably, it was the essential element in the political evolution leading to a 'higher' form of state development or towards a more authoritarian form of government.[49] The transition from the 'tax of violence', that is to say, the uncontrolled looting by troops, to a formal contributions system played a crucial role in enhancing political stability and the viability of the tax system. The presence of the army in a province, treating it as a

44 Bonney (1978), ch. 10.

45 AN G^7 239, no. 12, 'Projet d'ordonnance pour la levée des tailles en Dauphiné', *c.*24 Apr. 1679; G^7 240, no. 60, 'Mémoires des principaux abus qui se sont introduits dans le recouvrement des deniers des tailles de la province de Dauphiné', *c.*7 July 1683; G^7 240, no. 180, ruling of Le Bret, 18 Nov. 1684.

46 Ruling of Le Goux de La Berchère in the *généralité* of Montauban: AN G^7 391, no. 50, 4 Nov. 1685. On the difficulties of suddenly reducing the reliance on coercion: G^7 391, no. 244, 14 Aug. 1686, and no. 256, the intendant's printed ordinance, *c.*4 Sept. 1686.

47 Marion (1910), 14–15.

48 AN K 879 no. 80/9: 'C'est un gouvernement purement militaire; le souverain peut y etablir tels impôts qu'il juge convenable ... '

49 Downing (1992) discusses the rise of what he calls 'military-bureaucratic absolutism'; cf. Levi (1981), 458: 'The predatory theory of rule suggests that a ruler will always seek to maximize his wealth and power.'

conquered land, was seen by French finance ministers as late as the 1650s as the reason why the revenue system could not produce the tax income expected from it, and the problem was not much better even a decade later.[50] Sporadic military contributions raised by foreign armies of occupation might be extremely significant to the local taxpayers, for they were often higher than the taxes normally levied by the government if the army was in a position of strength.[51] Border areas tended to pay relatively low regular taxes in peacetime.[52] The total cost of the Allied contributions levied on Artois in 1708 was 2 million *livres tournois*, of which a quarter was to be paid within one month; in contrast, the French crown had earlier in the year required a normal tax levy from Artois of only 400,000 *livres*, of which the first payment was not due until some five months after the enemy invasion![53] Military contributions were more burdensome for the peasants of Artois, but they were an impermanent revenue paid to a foreign occupying power, in this case the United Provinces. Only rarely do we find the statistical evidence of revenues gained by one state from the occupation of another's territory (for example, the French occupation of Savoy during the War of the Spanish Succession),[54] or clear evidence of the value of contributions in offsetting a state's own military costs and making 'war pay for war': calculations on surviving French accounts and estimates suggest that the value of contributions might vary between 18 and 43 per cent of the total cost of the army, but that forage requisitions might surpass contributions in value.[55] Contributions might also be levied during civil wars, and again in such cases there is evidence that they were higher than preceding levels of peacetime taxation. There was occasionally some regard to the sensibilities of the local taxpayers, as in the north Midlands during the English Civil War, when rival sides collected contributions on consecutive days with no apparent attempt to hinder each other.[56] In most cases, overt coercion in the form of military contributions did not alter the nature of the revenues collected. The method of tax collection took on an arbitrary, or military, aspect; but its nature was unchanged unless payment was discounted against the cost of billeting of troops or unless it was paid in kind. In this

[50] Redlich (1959); Bonney (1978), 260–3, 280–3; Bonney (1981*a*), 248–9; Lynn (1993), 293.

[51] Lynn (1993), 298 n. 28, notes that the Spaniards set the level of contributions in 1689 to half the value of taxes paid in the French provinces concerned in 1687. Clearly, their army was in a weak position.

[52] Potter (1993), 235, 241, suggests for Picardy that border areas might pay relatively low taxes even in wartime.

[53] AN E 1946, fos. 136, 184, 7 July and 14 Sept. 1708.

[54] AN G^7 249 no. 242, 'Estat des sommes imposées en Savoye depuis et compris le 15 nouembre 1703 jour de l'occupation du pays par les troupes du Roy jusqu'en 1711 inclusivement . . . '

[55] Lynn (1993), 303–6, is the best discussion; he argues that contributions might represent on average 25 per cent of the costs of land warfare.

[56] Bennett (1986), 8.

discussion, we should not confuse the enforced levy of taxation by military means with the distinction made by certain states—such as in the Austrian Habsburg lands after 1749—between military contributions[57] and 'cameral' or civil contributions.[58] This distinction, which drew upon the Prussian model,[59] was intended to earmark specific revenues to specific expenditure needs.

Even without coercion, it is clear that all forms of revenue raising require administration, and to some degree leadership. There is a striking contrast between the effectiveness of the French fiscal system, particularly in the levy of direct taxes, before and after fiscal powers were accorded to the provincial intendants in 1642. Their role in preventing the self-defeating competition between direct and indirect taxes was recognized by successive finance ministers, and it is significant that their recall from most of the *pays d'élections* during the years of the Fronde (1648–52) was a temporary aberration by a weak government capitulating to political opposition. In normal times (1642–8, 1653–1790), the services of the intendants could not be dispensed with, and they remained the linchpin in the administration of direct taxes in France until the Revolution.[60] The French example illustrates the development of a new form of administration for the supervision of direct taxes because the previous system, based on a multiplicity of venal office-holders, had been tested and found wanting during the Thirty Years' War. Tax collectors' compliance is an important aspect of the fiscal efficiency of all states, and as significant a factor as tax compliance.[61]

An administrative infrastructure had to be constructed at an early date if revenues were to be exploited effectively. The development of English customs revenue administration in the Middle Ages was a particularly precocious example of this for the levy of one form of indirect taxation. A new hierarchy of officials came into being, associated with the assessment and the collection of the various duties and the control of possible fraud. London, the port with the greatest activity in overseas trade, had by far the most impressive collection of officials engaged in what had become, by the late fifteenth century, a more professional business. By 1490, there were forty-two customs officials attached to the port. None of the other English ports sustained such a large complement, but probably Bristol, with two collectors, one controller, one searcher, four 'waiters'

[57] Dickson (1987), ii, 398–400; ESFDB dataset \austria\ausb004, reprod. in chart form in Bonney (forthcoming), fig. 9.

[58] Dickson (1987), ii, 398–400 and ESFDB dataset \austria\ausb005, reprod. in chart form in Bonney (forthcoming), fig. 10.

[59] Dorwart (1953).

[60] Bonney (1978) provides an analysis of the early period of the intendants' administration. The author is working on a study of the intendants of Louis XIV.

[61] Musgrave (1969), 128.

employed to guard shipments which had been valued and numerous clerks attached to these offices, had the next biggest customs organization. The importance of the leading or 'head' ports grew and even became institutionalized as a result of financial legislation passed by Parliament. The result of this government selection of a small number of head ports for regulating the export trade of medieval England was that a comprehensive range of documentary evidence was drawn up within the port which, where it survives, gives a record of the movement of shipping through these ports, together with the value of the shipments, the names of merchants who used the ports for their trade and the type and quality of their exports, a record which is largely unrivalled in other European states.[62] The records also enable estimates to be made of the royal income from indirect taxation on cloth and wool exports, and on other items such as wax, hides and 'general merchandise'. England is thus a particularly well-documented example for the purposes of studying the long-term evolution of a revenue system (Chapter 13.7).

13.2 *Revenue Collection, Revenue Unification and the Assignment of Revenues*

John Law's attempt to unify the system of direct and indirect taxes in France in 1719[63] and the Physiocratic idea of a single tax on net agricultural income (Chapter 6.5) were two different eighteenth-century ideas of revenue unification, the first a unification of the whole tax system, the other a single tax to replace a multiplicity of levies. Adam Smith extolled the 'uniform system of taxation . . .' in Britain, which left 'the interior commerce of the country, the inland and coasting trade, almost entirely free ... This freedom of interior commerce, the effect of the uniformity of the system of taxation' was considered by Smith 'one of the principal causes of the prosperity of Great Britain . . .'[64] In contrast, 'in France, the different revenue laws which take place in the different provinces, require a multitude of officers to surround, not only the frontiers of the kingdom, but those of almost each particular province . . .' But such 'various and complicated revenue laws were not peculiar to France'. Drawing upon the French enquiry of 1763, Smith commented that the duchy of Milan was divided into six provinces, each of which had a different system of taxation, while the smaller territories of the duke of Parma certainly had three.[65] Reform might be easier to introduce in

[62] Bonney (1992*c*), and the datasets in the ESFDB therein cited.

[63] Bonney (1992*a*), 172.

[64] Smith, ed. Campbell, Skinner and Todd (1976), ii, 900.

[65] Ibid. ii, 901–2. For Milan: *Mémoires*, ed. Moreau de Beaumont (1768), 264; AN K 880 no. 10. The price of salt, for example, was different in Parma, Piacenza and Guastalla: ibid. 367; AN K 880 no. 8. Smith states that there were 'three or four' systems in the territories of the duke of Parma.

smaller states such as Piedmont and Savoy, but clearly small states had many of the same problems as large ones in terms of organization.

Such ideas on revenue unification in the seventeenth and eighteenth centuries were relatively recent. In monarchical states apart from England earlier attempts at revenue unification had met with failure. The Knights Templar managed the royal finances in France for almost a century after 1200 'as one account in their keeping'; but this early and incomplete development in revenue unification came to a sorry end in 1307–14: the prosecution of the Templars seemed to demonstrate the risks for the king's revenue when it was farmed to any single organization or individual, out of overall royal control, apart from the dangers run by his servants resulting from a sudden change of royal policy.[66] In the Middle Ages, the guiding principle of revenue raising in many states seems to have stressed the advantages of fragmented revenue collection. An efficient tax-farmer needed specialized knowledge of commodities and their markets, which suggested a small scale of operations. In November 1297, for example, the commune of Siena announced the sale or farming of thirty-eight separate *gabelles*—the Italian term *gabella* was almost certainly of Arabic origin (*qabala*)—on such items as gaming tables; on animals slaughtered in the city and its boroughs; on the rental of those squares in the city in which fish were sold; and even on the prisons.[67]

Fragmented revenue collection meant a larger number of people to invest in, and thus potentially to profit from, revenue collection; the specific revenues to be collected could be adjudicated at the best price; and, perhaps above all, the risks resulting from insolvency among the revenue collectors were reduced, since each unit of collection would have had its own sureties. In Russia in the later eighteenth century, leases for the collection of liquor revenues were always fragmented, to encourage a broader-based participation, including merchants, nobles and even peasants.[68] There were also two fundamental administrative difficulties which pointed in the direction of fragmented revenue collection: rates of tax varied considerably from one area to another, for example between city and countryside; there were also different, and frequently very complex, rates of collection for the different leases, so that to amalgamate them risked introducing confusion. Where a 'great *gabelle*' or '*gabelle* of the eight *gabelles*' existed, as at Siena, the component parts of the tax were not revealed and it must have been

[66] Lot and Fawtier (1957–62), ii, 188. The *Trésor du Temple* was transferred by ordinance on 19 Jan. 1314: Favier (1963), 104, 204. On the general background: Barber (1978), 40–1, 246.

[67] Bowsky (1970), 122–3; though the process of tax-farming seems to have been developed first by the ancient Greeks: Adams (1993), 66–7.

[68] LeDonne (1976), 190.

difficult for the city government to have evaluated its separate elements.[69] Likewise, two ubiquitous taxes at Siena and other Italian city-states, the *gabelle* on contracts and the *gabelle* of the gates, posed immense administrative complexities in themselves, since there were many kinds of notarial transactions and hundreds of separate items passing through the gates of the city. A more unified approach was adopted with the taxation of the dependent countryside (*contado*) of the Italian city-state: witness the establishment of the *contado gabelle* in Siena in 1291 in place of a number of *gabelles* formerly collected there, and in principle distributed proportionately to the ability of each community to bear its share of the cost.[70]

From an early date, states were faced with the choice between direct administration and the leasing or sale of revenues for a limited duration. The pawning or alienation of revenues were more extreme versions of the sale of revenues, usually under more onerous conditions for the state and implying a degree of permanency. The pawning or sale of crown lands is an obvious example of the alienation of a domainal possession which carried with it the loss of an annual revenue. Ordinary taxes were also sold, even as late as the seventeenth century: this was true in France before 1634 (where the sales of rights to collect additional increases of the *taille* were known as the *droits aliénés*), and in the kingdom of Naples before the revolt of 1647.[71] In Italian city republics, direct taxes were on the whole directly administered, while the *gabelles* were leased. Whereas, for example, in seventeenth-century France direct administration was chiefly reserved for direct taxes and leasing for indirect taxes (though even here, as will be seen, there were exceptions), this was less true in medieval Italy: the shift from *dazi* to *gabelles* cannot be explained entirely as a shift from direct to indirect taxes, because some *gabelles* were direct taxes.[72]

No single factor determined the decision whether to lease, or to collect revenue directly, although by the mid-eighteenth century there was a strong tendency away from farming and towards direct administration (*régie*), both in theory (most notably in the writings of Montesquieu: Chapter 6.5) and practice (Chapter 10.5).[73] The decision instead depended on a number of interrelated issues such as the financial position of the state concerned (whether there was a

[69] Bowsky (1970), 145–6. [70] Ibid. 226, 230.

[71] For France: Bonney (1981*a*), 165–6; Collins (1988), 135–43. For Naples: Villari (1993), 75, 102–3, 195–6.

[72] Herlihy (1964), 393; Bowsky (1970), 100. La Roncière distinguished artificially between *gabelles* in general and 'true gabelles' or indirect taxes: La Roncière (1968), 146.

[73] Dickson (1987), ii, 51–2. Though Zinzendorf considered that farming might give a higher yield: ibid. ii, 51 n. 54; cf. Bonney (1994), 68, 71–2. Copland and Godley in Butcher and Dick (1993), 45–68, provide an overview of revenue farming in the early modern period.

pressing crisis or not), the number of potential or actual state servants as against potential or actual lessees; and more intangible issues such as the extent of tax compliance within the state and the nature of its fiscal constitution. In the early Italian city-states, leasing (*appalto*) appeared to offer a secure, predictable revenue on the proceeds of which fixed expenditure could be assigned. At Genoa until 1326 the municipal government had to decide each year whether to farm its *gabelles* or collect them directly. However, in 1340 it passed a law ordering the farming of all direct taxes. The *gabelles* multiplied in number and became the mainstay of the state's revenues: by 1457, fifty-five were listed, but this excluded those on foodstuffs.[74] Virtually all the indirect taxes were eventually removed from the control of the municipal government and became the possession of the banking house, the *Casa di San Giorgio*, and were used by it to underwrite the repayment of interest on the state debt (*luoghi delle Compere di San Giorgio*). With the rapid growth of the state debt between 1454 and 1464 (from 8 million to 11 million *lira*), it became imperative for *San Giorgio* to be able to ascertain in advance the size of its revenues so that it could determine whether or not the same rate of interest could be paid. Thus renting of the *gabelles* for a fixed period became desirable, and from 1472 five-year leases became the norm.[75] At Florence, the development of the public debt (*Monte*) similarly may have encouraged a trend towards the projection of future revenues, but there the policy of relying increasingly on officials for the collection of *gabelles* was adopted—not least when it proved difficult in the 1350s to find revenue farmers in a period of declining consumption after the Black Death.[76]

The change in Florentine practice may also have been a reaction against the revenue farmers' demands for remissions of rent and the discounting of leases. There seem to have been different practices with regard to relief given to revenue farmers, even at an early date. Florence granted such relief only rarely, but the government of Siena was much more generous in this respect.[77] Remissions of rent payable by revenue farmers undermined the very concept of the revenue farm, which was that the farmers estimated in advance the profitability of their activities and were held to what they had promised whether the year was good or bad.[78] In practice, the longer the lease the greater the chance of

[74] Heers (1961), 125; cf. ibid. 597.

[75] Ibid. 130–1; cf. Bowsky (1970), 120 n. 28 at 121.

[76] Herlihy (1964), 400–1. La Roncière (1968), 182–5, stresses that it was the 1350s which witnessed the increased reliance on communal officials.

[77] La Roncière (1968), 179; Bowsky (1970), 134, 285.

[78] This principle was well stated by Chancellor Séguier during the Fronde: Bonney (1979), 17. For evidence of remissions during the 1630s and 1640s: ibid. 18–19.

a change of circumstances, particularly a sudden, unpredictable, fall in consumption or the interruption of commerce as a result of war. Later leases, such as those of the French revenue farmers towards the end of the seventeenth century, distinguished between rents payable in wartime and peacetime; but this did not altogether remove the problems and the demand for remissions, since the rent reduction in time of war was never regarded as sufficiently substantial to meet the revenue farmers' losses. The fixed condition of the lease tended to screen the actual value of the taxes at a given moment and the extent to which they fluctuated according to economic circumstances. When rent payments were made promptly, when the farmers were ready to provide additional credit, and when their prospective successors were prepared to place a much higher valuation on the revenue of the farm, it is reasonable to assume, for example, that the English customs revenues were buoyant. It is also reasonable to assume that this buoyancy was the result of a trade revival after the conclusion of war.[79] Alternatively, in a period of sudden commercial depression such as the 1620s, the English customs revenues could become 'over-rented' and the crown might have to accept a reduction of the lease.[80] The crux of the problem is to determine where economic influence ended and the efficiency or otherwise of the revenue-raising machinery began.

A further difficulty is that rulers did not see the revenue-raising machinery of their states in purely objective terms with a view to obtaining maximum efficiency. On the contrary, they tended to confuse revenue structures and credit structures: indeed, in some states the revenue structure became the main structure of public credit in the absence of alternative banking mechanisms which were sufficiently developed: in England, the early Stuarts came to rely increasingly upon the revenue farmers to provide them with short-term loans, that is to say advances of current rent, and later on with longer-term loans, anticipating the rents two or three years in advance.[81] There were two contradictory tendencies at work: the consolidation of leases enabled a government to extract more by way of borrowing or anticipation of the rents of the farm. This was the fundamental purpose underlying John Law's attempt to consolidate the direct and indirect revenues in France in 1719 and Philip V's consolidation of the leases of the *rentas provinciales* after the War of the Spanish Succession.[82] Fragmentation of leases resulted from disputes between partners, or a bankruptcy. In some cases, such as France in the early seventeenth century, it was explicitly stated that the partners refused to participate in a general lease because of the size of the liability.[83]

[79] Chandaman (1975), 24. [80] Ashton (1960), 95. [81] Ashton (1956, 1960), 97, 99.
[82] Bonney (1992*a*), 172; Artola (1982), 301; Mounier (1919), 68; Ustáriz, trans. Kippax (1751), i, 267.
[83] Bonney (1979).

Direct administration might seem a less costly alternative to revenue farming. This could take a number of different forms. One sort of reform was to vest fiscal management in administrative boards or government departments. Thus in England, the customs were taken over as a government department in 1671, under Sir George Downing's chairmanship, and this precedent was followed with regard to the excise in 1683. The salaried personnel of these two departments grew substantially in the eighteenth century.[84] This was also the Swedish model, a modified version of which was later introduced into Russia.[85] In Sweden, at least until the reign of Gustavus III, the Paymaster General's Office (*Kungliga Statskontoret*) was the centre of both tax collection and expenditure, and also the preliminary institution for budget preparation. Money, however, was handled by the Treasury (*Kungliga Räntekammaren*), in collaboration with the Bank of Sweden and the local provincial revenue offices (*lanträntererna*). The aim of the reformers in Russia was to establish the College of Revenue as the chief collecting agency of the government, but the reform of June 1731 proved short-lived. The establishment of the Expedition of State Revenues (February 1775) was a further step in the same direction; but it was not until after 1811 that the Finance Ministry emerged clearly in Russia as virtually the only tax-collecting agency as well as the Treasury, though even this did not preclude revenue farming in the localities.[86]

An alternative approach was to collect taxes through officials who were paid a fee, and who later purchased their offices. In France by 1665 there were about 46,000 office-holders, whose offices were worth 419.6 million *livres* at current prices. There were 8,468 judicial office-holders and 4,968 financial office-holders.[87] The sale of offices was at times a vital revenue of the French monarchy in the seventeenth century, particularly in the 1630s and 1690s, and the market for offices remained buoyant in the eighteenth century.[88] But its consequences for financial administration were no less important. In the central government, the *intendants des finances*, who were subordinate only to the finance minister, owned their offices and acted with considerable independence. In the provinces, the older forms of direct taxes such as the *taille* (but not the *capitation* of 1695, or the new taxes of the eighteenth century, the *dixième* or the *vingtième*) were apportioned by office-holders (the *élus*) under the supervision of the provincial intendants after 1642. The collection of taxes was undertaken by non-venal collectors who received fees (*taxations*), but the sums collected were held by

[84] Roseveare (1973), 40; Brewer (1989), 101–14.

[85] Peterson (1979).

[86] LeDonne (1984), 246–7 and (1991), 240–1.

[87] Mousnier (1970*a*), 20; Véron de Forbonnais (1758), i, 329.

[88] Mousnier (1971); Doyle (1984).

receivers for each administrative subdivision or *élection* (*receveurs particuliers*) and then for each *généralité* (*receveurs généraux des finances*). Multiple funds resulted: there were some 418 offices of receiver towards the end of the *ancien régime*.[89] At first, such a system of multiple funds was regarded as more secure than a general fund. A *Caisse commune des recettes générales* was established in June 1716 with Geoffroy d'Assy as *caissier général*. John Law saw this reform as insufficient, and argued that the multiplicity of funds meant that the ruler's money failed to circulate ('les amas particuliers d'argent . . . mettent une obstruction léthargique dans les affaires').[90] The time-lag between the collection of revenues and the actual payment to the treasury was a crucial weakness of the fiscal system of almost all European states. Receivers were able to make use of the cash balances in their accounts for their private purposes, which were detrimental to the interests of the central government. Indeed, this was the principle underlying the establishment of 'financiers', who recirculated the crown's own money; the reason that they participated in financial affairs was precisely the constant use of cash in hand which their accounts commanded.[91] In France, it was not until Mollien introduced the *Caisse de service* in 1806 that the central government gained full possession of its own resources.[92]

The establishment of a single Treasury has been seen as a fundamental test of modernization, both for the purposes of revenue unification and budgetary control. The concentration of budget making in a single office (the Expedition) in Russia was the essential first step towards establishing a national budget in 1781.[93] Necker's reforms in France in 1780 (though reversed in 1781) are similarly seen as heralding the changes of the French Revolution, whereby the collection of revenue was eventually placed in a single treasury and the agents of revenue collection transformed into quasi civil servants. But under the Empire and Restoration some of the changes were reversed: in particular, surety payments demanded of receivers were required once more after 1800, thus returning them to a status akin to the office-holder of the *ancien régime*.[94] In England, too, there was a move towards creating a powerful Treasury in 1667–8, under the influence of Sir George Downing, who urged that there should be a deliberate attempt to exceed the Dutch in creditworthiness by placing all revenues under its control. But this was not enough, as was evidenced in Burke's speech on 'economical

[89] Bosher (1970), 79. [90] Bonney (1992*a*), 172.

[91] Bosher (1970); Thomas in Hoyle (1992), 75, for a specific example (Wentworth as receiver of recusant revenues in England in 1637). Cf. Tanzi (1991), 160–1: 'When such delays are possible, the tax system cannot be efficient, regardless of how well designed it may be in theory.'

[92] Marion (1925), 290–3.

[93] LeDonne (1991), 283, 289.

[94] Bosher (1970); Théret (1991), 151–2, 172.

reform' in February 1780. In his view, the Treasury required an unfettered superintendence of public income and expenditure instead of being obstructed by 'subordinate treasuries'—the independent empires of the departmental paymasters—and by an anachronistic Exchequer (which was not abolished until 1834).[95] These moves towards Treasury unification were relatively late, and for the most part multiple treasuries and fragmented accounting remained the order of the day. This was the norm in countries such as Prussia, Austria and Spain towards the end of the *ancien régime* and is one reason why it is so difficult to re-establish a proper 'budget' for those states.

A further complication arises from the process whereby specific revenues were assigned to meet expenditure, so that these revenues did not pass into the central Treasury and accounting process. This process of assignment requires careful definition. It was common practice in Mughal India, where the revenues thus assigned (*jagirs*) were held for periods as long as three or four years as a payment for service.[96] One recent estimate is that about 82 per cent of the revenue collected by the Mughal emperors in about 1595 never went to the central treasuries, but was instead appropriated by 1,671 members of the ruling class in order to enable them to maintain a fixed quota of troops. The office-holders in turn spent about two-thirds of their salaries in maintaining their contingents in what was essentially a circular and unproductive process, revenue being used to pay for troops who ensured that the revenue was collected. Revenues from the land financed a town-centred ruling class.[97] This process seems more akin to an alienation or pawning of revenues than an assignment or *assignation*, which more typically represents a payment discharged on the yield of a specific revenue within a given accounting period. Such assignments to crown officials in lieu of wages (*beställningar*) were a feature of Swedish accounting practice from the reign of Gustavus Vasa.[98] Under Gustavus Adolphus, both temporary and more permanent alienations of revenues increased greatly. Temporary assignments (*förläningar*) amounted to some 5 per cent of ordinary revenues in Sweden in 1632, while more permanent alienations had risen to nearly 7 per cent.[99] The two most significant changes in Sweden in the second half of the seventeenth century were the full-scale resumption of alienated lands and revenues in 1680 (*reduktionen*) and Charles XI's introduction of the 'allotment' system (*indelningsverket*) to finance a military reserve (Chapter 11.2). The royal domains which had been restored through the first process were sub-

[95] Roseveare (1973), 22–9, 63, 65.

[96] Habib (1963), 257–61. For Mughal finance generally: Richards (1993).

[97] Moosvi (1987), 221, 272, 299; Pearson in Tracy (1991), 54–5.

[98] Krüger (1988), 143. [99] Roberts (1953–8), 74.

sequently 'allotted' or permanently assigned to pay for royal officials and military personnel. This process became fossilized with the adoption of the new Form of Government in 1720, which stated that the budget for 1696 should not be exceeded.[100] The process of temporarily assigning revenues to meet specific payments also, of course, continued, and Swedish practice here was once again followed in Russia.[101] The *Kriegskammer* or *Kriegskommissariat* in Brandenburg–Prussia controlled all assignments for army needs from the 1680s until the establishment of the General Directory in 1722–3.[102] A more permanent form of assignment was the alienation of revenues to pay interest on the public debt, which was a feature of Spanish and Portuguese finance in the seventeenth and eighteenth centuries, and a cause of the financial problems of those states.[103]

As a result of changes introduced by Colbert, French accounting practice after 1660 distinguished between gross revenue (the *montant des impositions et baux*), assignments and net revenue (the *partie du Trésor royal*). Within this definition, assignments were made essentially on current revenues, which were thus distinguished from disposable revenue.[104] The importance of Colbert's accounting change was that for the first time in France it was possible to calculate reasonably precisely the total amount of assignments and thus the fiscal burden for the country as a whole with regard to direct taxes. Even so, a calculation of the total fiscal burden on the provinces remained problematic because of the administration of indirect taxes as separate revenue farms, whose borders did not necessarily coincide with those of the provinces.[105] Short-term assignments of revenues should be distinguished from the more permanent alienation of taxes, such as occurred in France in the 1620s with the creation of the so-called *droits aliénés*, a policy which was then reversed in 1634, when these alienated taxes were revoked. Clearly individuals bought alienated taxes for the profit they yielded. In the kingdom of Naples in 1642–3, Bartolomeo d'Aquino bought direct taxes on hearths and on feudal successions with a nominal value of 2.9 million ducats for 1.6 million ducats or a premium of 59 per cent; other direct taxes on hearths having a nominal value of 2.16 million ducats were sold by d'Aquino to the leading feudal lords of the kingdom for 1.1 million, that is an average premium of 49 per cent.[106] The different aspects of assignment and alienation discussed above

[100] Peterson (1979), 180, 193–5. [101] Ibid. 204–7.

[102] Carsten (1954), 199, 224, 259–63; Dorwart (1953), 136–7, 151–2, 203–4.

[103] For the problem of financing the *juros* under Philip V: Kamen (1969), 224–8.

[104] Bonney (1991*a*), 204; Bonney and Bonney (1993), 41.

[105] Bonney (1992*a*), 169–70; Bonney (1992*b*), 116, 118; Collins (1988), 109–10, distinguishes between 'regular' and 'irregular' assignments.

[106] Villari (1993), 102–3, 195–6.

demonstrate the truth that the disposition of revenues is an important aspect of the efficiency of the fiscal system, and one that is no less important than the level of revenues analysed in this chapter and elsewhere in this book.[107]

13.3 *Lands, Enterprise and Colonies: Types of Early Modern Domain State*

Perceptive commentators in the eighteenth century recognized that a state's revenue system was the product of a long evolutionary process and that without a historical perspective it was impossible to understand how the system had come into place. Thus the French intendant of finance, Moreau de Beaumont, argued in the eighteenth century that the French kingdom had originally been a domain state, with the royal revenues derived from proprietary wealth in income from land and forests; from casual seigneurial revenues, including confiscations; and from specific seigneurial rights within each domain.[108] These resources were inadequate when a kingdom developed an aggressive foreign policy. They were too small, too sporadic and incapable of expansion: real wealth in the economy had to be taxed more effectively. At a higher level of economic and political organization (what we might call, after Schumpeter, the 'tax state'), Moreau de Beaumont postulated that revenues tended to have common characteristics, since only certain sorts of wealth were susceptible to taxation. He thought that in the main these were landed property; income from various sources (thinking of France, he called these *rentes*); items of consumption ('les fruits et les consommations'); and finally commerce and industry.[109] Moreau de Beaumont's analysis was an early attempt to describe within a monarchical state the transition from a 'domain state' to a 'tax state', a change which occurred in different monarchies at different periods and defies simplistic analysis: France was still a 'domain state' at the beginning of the Hundred Years' War whereas England was not (Chapter 5.7). Indeed, the period of the so-called 'domain state' may scarcely have existed at all in England, which helps explain the relatively small attention devoted to it in Anglo-American historiography.

In France, there seemed no prospect of reviving the 'domain state' in the sixteenth century. Though inalienable according to the fundamental laws of the kingdom, the domain had been sold cheaply or leased out on long leases so that much of the estimated revenue of between 3 million and 4.5 million *livres* from

[107] Brennan and Buchanan (1980), 135.

[108] *Mémoires*, ed. Moreau de Beaumont (1769), ii, p. vii.

[109] Ibid. ii, p. xiii. Moreau de Beaumont's fourth volume contains a detailed analysis of legislation concerning the royal domain in France.

this source had been lost to the crown. Sully devoted part of his considerable energies in an ultimately futile attempt to reverse this process under Henri IV: he signed leases for a capital value approaching 40 million, but this would have yielded only some 1.3 million in additional annual revenue. Colbert's achievement in reviving domain revenue (excluding domainal rights) was greater than Sully's in nominal terms, as well as more enduring (Figure 73).[110] Domain revenue (excluding domainal rights) continued to grow in the eighteenth century, and played a crucial role in the period of transition from the *ancien régime* to the new fiscal system of the Revolution.[111] It was of critical importance that the royal domains (or in other states, ducal domains) should not be alienated to provide for the maintenance of the princely family: only once this policy was reversed, for example in Württemberg in the 1730s, could domain income increase from 32.4 per cent to 46.1 per cent of total revenues.[112] Such high proportions of domain income were by no means unusual even in the eighteenth century. Around 1704, 52 per cent of the landgrave's income in Hesse arose from domain receipts.[113] Adam Smith declared boldly in 1776 that no 'civilized state' derived 'the greater part of its publick revenue from the rent of lands which are the property of the state'. He contended that crown lands were invariably neglected in comparison with the revenue yield of the same lands when placed under private ownership; and he added that 'the rent of all the lands in the country, managed as they probably would be if they all belonged to one proprietor, would scarce perhaps amount to the ordinary revenue' which rulers levied 'upon the people even in peaceable times'.[114]

Smith's contention underlined the characteristic of the domain, which was that its administration lay at the intersection between estate management and the profitability of land on the one hand and public finance and the solvency of the state on the other. A recent collaborative study of the administration of the English crown lands between 1558 and 1640 concludes that their progressive

110 Malet (1789); ESFDB \rjb\frmalet\malb029 based on dataset \malm044. Note that the domain revenue is so small that it only shows on Fig. 73 after 1670. Note also that in this chart the practice adopted in Bonney (1981*a*), 305 n., is used of counting revenue from the *parties casuelles* as ordinary revenue. For the period 1611–56, Malet failed to include this item in his total for ordinary revenue: Bonney and Bonney (1993), tables 12 and 19, pp. 149 and 172 nn. For the history of domain revenue in general: Clamageran (1867–76), ii, 198, 221, 244, 246, 253; Bonney (1981*a*), 33, 62–3, 81, 111, 130–1, 133. The calculation is based on a capitalization at *denier* 30.

111 Braesch (1934), 41; but there were serious infringements of forest rights at the outset of the Revolution: Marion (1919), 327–31; Massaloux (1989).

112 Vann (1984), 67, 107, 112–16, 228–9.

113 Krüger in Witt (1987), 59, who comments 'domain and tax state were almost in equilibrium'. For the earlier period, cf. Krüger (1980); for the later period, cf. Ingrao (1987), 38–9, 105–7, 190–2.

114 Smith, ed. Campbell, Skinner and Todd (1976), ii, 823–4.

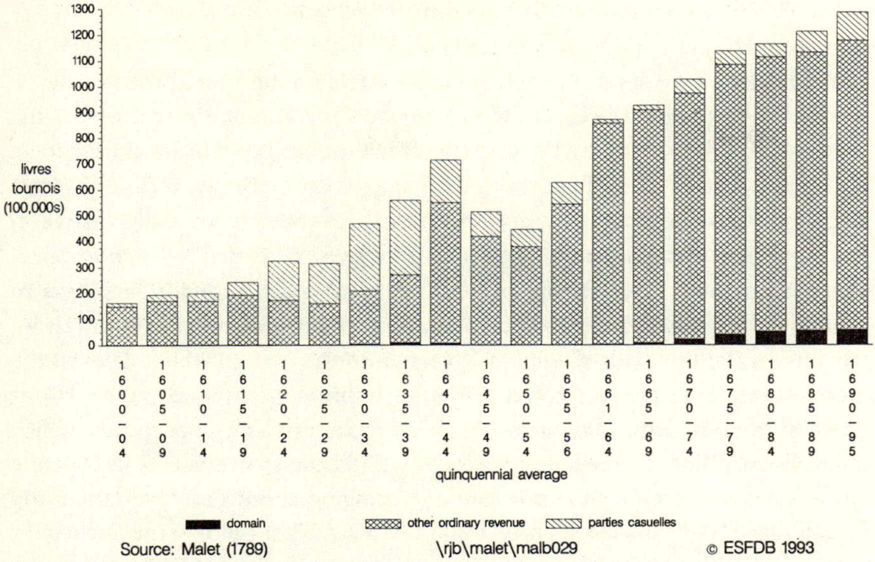

FIG. 73. Categories of ordinary revenue in France, 1600–1695 (in *livres tournois*)

decline 'was a decisive factor in the emergence of the modern state',[115] a comment which might be taken as representative of views on the decline of the 'domain state' expressed elsewhere in this volume. There are two important caveats, however. The first, which has already been remarked upon, is that royal or princely income from the domain did not decline uniformly throughout Europe, and by this test of modernity Prussia, for example, was not a 'modern' state even in the eighteenth century. The second caveat is that the administration of the domain was a paradigm of the administration of the fiscal system in general; the problems encountered in running crown lands were in many respects similar to those which would be encountered under the so-called modern 'tax state'. The first difficulty was the dispersed nature of the royal lands, which was comparable to the multiple taxes of medieval and early modern states: in England, although the crown estates had a privileged legal position there was no uniform system of administration; there were several estates, not one, and 'there was a constant circulation of lands in and out of the crown's hands . . .'[116] Income from these estates was inflexible and inelastic, comparable to much of the tax revenue of the state. Though there was a rise in the nominal gross value of the crown lands in England between the 1550s and 1603, this was more than offset by the rapid rise in prices and bore little relation to the increase in land values.

[115] Hoyle in Hoyle (1992), 432. [116] Ibid. 9.

Crown lands were let out at far below their real value and consequently were sold at much higher rates than other lands.[117]

In England, the rules of customary tenure could not be altered and the crown was forced into a policy of sales which negated any attempt to restructure the estates along 'modern' lines; the lands became the equivalent of a war fund to be raided rather than a set of estates to be managed on their own terms, not least because sales were less costly in terms of lost revenue than the alternative of financing the costs of borrowing.[118] The state's vision tended to be short term, rather than the 'long horizon' needed for fiscal reform: unlike landlords in general, it was always forced into premature renewal of leases on disadvantageous terms; the lands were leased years into the future, which delayed the moment when the crown could act as an improving landlord; inevitably, it missed the optimum moment for introducing reforms, an opportunity which improving landlords were able to seize.[119] Could the crown act as an effective 'projector' or 'entrepreneur', for example bringing about disafforestation and land drainage? Key officials such as Sir Julius Caesar, Chancellor of the Exchequer in England under Elizabeth, and Sully, *surintendant des finances* in France under Henri IV, were sound managers of their own lands.[120] Expertise was not lacking, but such changes required a long-term perspective and investment; neither was forthcoming, and the most that the state achieved in England was to license an alteration in land use which others exploited at their own risk. Instead, the crown relied on a drive against 'concealments' of its income from lands, employing 'searchers' to discover losses of forest, lessees with defective titles, encroachments and so on. In England, there was an 'unprecedented search for documentary proofs of title' which 'presaged unending argument' and created great resentment among landowners which was reflected in the Grand Remonstrance of 1641.

Matters were made worse by the fact that the most notorious 'concealment hunters' in England, such as Sir Giles Mompesson, were corrupt:[121] but, as with an aggressive fiscalism, the sums raised were relatively trivial and wholly disproportionate to the political damage incurred by irresponsible entrepreneurs and officials. The administration of the royal estates thus posed the same issues of tax collectors' compliance, peculation and corruption which have already been

[117] Ibid. 12; Thomas in Hoyle (1992), 58–9, 86.

[118] Hoyle in Hoyle (1992), 3; Thomas in Hoyle (1992), 32–3.

[119] For the 'long horizon': Tanzi (1991), 188 ('The costs of the reforms are always immediate; the benefits are almost always spread over the future'). Hoyle in Hoyle (1992), 373, 421–3, 427.

[120] Thirsk in Hoyle (1992), 299; Aristide (1990).

[121] Thirsk in Hoyle (1992), 306, 327–8, 348–51; Thomas in Hoyle (1992), 69–70.

observed for fiscal systems in general. Moreover, if there was to be a 'shifting and shaking of men's estates' then there had to be adequate proof to back the crown's claims: surveys alone would permit fines according to the value of lands rather than the often outdated rental of lands. No general cartographical survey of the crown estates was undertaken, however, for reasons of expense and technical difficulty.[122] The inadequacy of surveyors compounded the ignorance of officials, although here, too, the 'domain state' anticipated the difficulties of the 'tax state' in introducing cadastral reform in the eighteenth century. Private landlords could afford surveyors, just as they could afford to invest in their property, because they had a longer persepective which came from settled ownership. Improvement of the crown lands was hard: sale was easier, either the permanent alienation of property, or the sale of assets such as timber, or the granting of new leases which might raise substantial sums at a given moment but then required the lapse of a generation before the asset could be exploited again.[123]

Adam Smith was probably correct in his contention that crown lands were invariably neglected in comparison with the revenue yield of the same lands if placed under private ownership, but we must beware of too narrow a definition of the 'domain state'. This might be defined somewhat arbitrarily as a state in which the income from the domain was regularly equivalent to half or more of the total revenue. A further refinement of such states might distinguish between 'primitive', 'less primitive', 'entrepreneurial' and 'colonial' types. By a 'primitive' domain state, we mean those where the ruler was obliged to consume the produce of his estates *in situ*: there were no sales for the market, or to a central collection point which could manage the sale of goods and thus secure the transfer from payment in kind to cash. The disadvantage of this 'primitive' system was that the ruler was trapped into a peripatetic lifestyle if he wished to benefit from his revenues in kind; moreover, the system was inflexible and inappropriate in time of war. This was the problem faced by the dukes of Schleswig around 1490.[124] It is clear that domain states of a 'less primitive' kind, where there was a central and local administration which ensured the collection, storing and consumption of goods in kind, were better placed. Denmark in the sixteenth century illustrated this type of state finance. There, income from the domains increased threefold in nominal terms between 1533 and 1574; since prices rose substantially in the intervening period, the real rise in domain income was even greater. Consolidation of the domains was also important as a contributory factor in leading to a rise in real revenue in Denmark.

122 Barber in Buisseret (1992), 79–82, discusses what was done on the royal estates.

123 Hoyle in Hoyle (1992), 211–17, 261–2; Thirsk in Hoyle (1992), 320; Bonney (1994), 78–9.

124 Poulsen (1990), 63.

Small fiefs in Denmark yielded a fifth of the income from the domains in 1533, but their share had decreased to almost a seventh in 1574.[125] An expanding domain helped as well: 115 of the 215 small fiefs at the beginning of the reign of Christian III had been confiscated from the bishops, while former monastic estates in 1574 yielded about a fifth of all the income from the domains. By this date, the lands formerly held by bishops were no longer separately accounted for, but had been integrated into the large and small fiefs. No doubt Denmark could have continued as a relatively stable domain state had not Christian IV ventured on an aggressive foreign policy. Swedish war indemnities after the War of Kalmar in 1611–13 helped repay his costs, but the Danish intervention in the Thirty Years' War in the years 1625–9 was disastrous. Extraordinary taxes rose to more than a fifth of the net revenues. Although the figures as recorded in the ordinary accounts appear to suggest a surplus of revenue over expenditure (Figure 74),[126] when loan income is eliminated from the figures, it may be seen that war expenditure in the seventeenth century could no longer be financed by a state relying on relatively inelastic sources of domain revenue (Chapter 4.6 and Figure 75). In 1630, the domain represented almost 37 per cent of Danish net revenues.[127]

Yet the comparison with Sweden suggests another possible transition, from a 'less primitive' type to an 'entrepreneurial' domain state. In the sixteenth century, the collection and utilization of significant payments of taxes in kind rather than in money safeguarded the crown against sudden price fluctuations or shortage of goods. The crown lands were concentrated in the provinces to the north of Stockholm (Uppland, Västmanland, Värmland, Dalarna, Dalsland, Norrland) and in Finland, whereas the nobility dominated in the southern provinces (Södermanland, Närke, Öster- and Västergötland, Småland). The royal domains (*gårdslän*) were administered by non-noble bailiffs who sent on the surplus to the central government. Possessions scattered about larger areas were combined in the county hundreds, where the hundred bailiffs collected the taxes and fines, paying them over to the central government. In 1524, Gustavus Vasa had ordered them to 'record all the incomes of the crown in their area—both in money and in kind—as well as the number of free peasants and of peasants of the crown living in each fief'. The peasants held by the clergy before the Reformation had been transformed into crown peasants, while those of the nobility

[125] Krüger (1988), 135.

[126] Krüger (1970), 212–17; ESFDB \krug\danb003 based on \dand001 and \dand002. The author acknowledges generous assistance from Professor Krüger in the preparation of Figure 74. At the seminar on Danish state finance at Odense on 1 Oct. 1993, it was pointed out that the evidence used by Professor Krüger was the equivalent of ordinary accounts elsewhere in Europe.

[127] Sources as for Figure 74; ESFDB \krug\danb004 based on \krug\danm001; Krüger (1988), 130; the figures in Krüger (1970) have been reworked to exclude loans, debt servicing and surplus revenue.

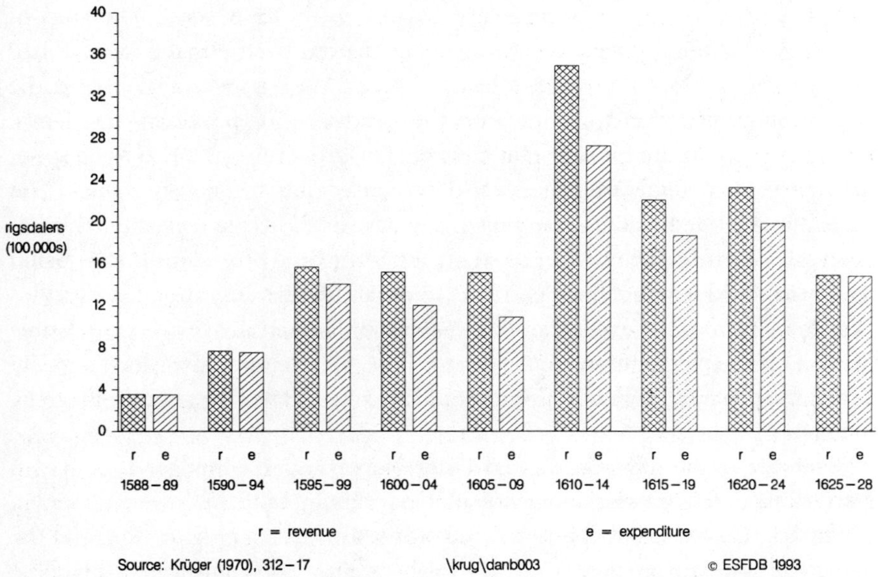

FIG. 74. Revenue and expenditure of the Danish *rentmeisters*, 1588–1628 (in *rigsdalers*)

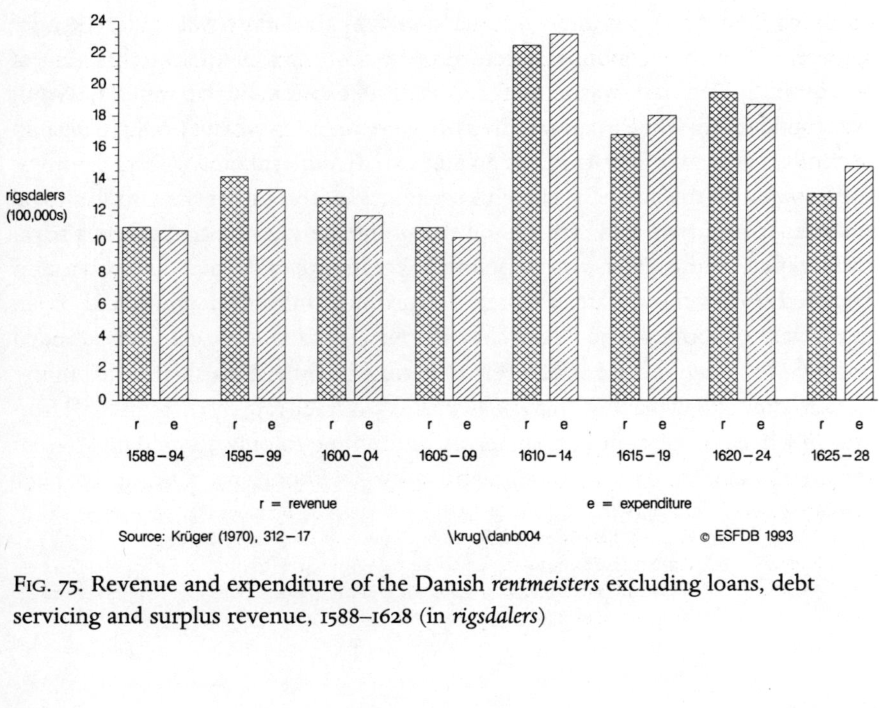

FIG. 75. Revenue and expenditure of the Danish *rentmeisters* excluding loans, debt servicing and surplus revenue, 1588–1628 (in *rigsdalers*)

were to be registered.[128] Comprehensive manorial rolls (*jordeböcker*) were subsequently compiled, listing every farm and its tax burden. The sum of the crown's ordinary annual income, as evidenced by the manorial roll, had to be indicated and the officials had to submit their annual accounts to the central administration together with the *jordebok*, thus providing the centre with the prerequisite for stringent control. The gross revenues had to be specified as paid in kind; they were also converted into monetary values. Net revenues after deductions (*avkortning*) were also listed, as were expenses such as deliveries to the court or other royal offices, wages and provisions for the bailiff and his subordinates, and assignments to royal officials. Any monetary surplus was to be paid to the exchequer (*räntekammare*), though this proved impossible with regard to payments in kind. After 1530, the government established regional warehouses where payments in kind could be collected and the goods sold on the market.[129]

Superior accounting practice and a more sophisticated administration may in part explain the greater longevity of the domain state in Sweden than in Denmark. Gustavus Adolphus ordered a Swedish land survey in 1628, and the resulting *Geometriska Jordeböckerna* was certainly a sophisticated mapping achievement for the period; whether it had a clear fiscal purpose is doubtful, however, since tax rates remained unchanged after surveying and mapping had taken place. In contrast, Frederick III's *matrikel* in Denmark, a fiscal reform first undertaken in 1662 and then revised in 1663–4, was not based on surveying and mapping, and it was not until 1668 that a systematic survey was undertaken.[130] Differences in the economic structure of Sweden and Denmark were also of importance. Denmark was famous for its cattle exports, but no mineral wealth was found there, while iron and silver ore were found in Norway only in 1624. In contrast, silver was discovered at Sala in Sweden in 1510, and profits from the exploitation of this industry came to assume a central importance to the royal finances. The crown laid claim to all the profits derived from silver as a royal prerogative. Some silver was mined in royal monopolies, but the crown also imposed duties on private production. Income from silver amounted to an equivalent of about 10,000 *Reichstaler* before 1530, but in a record year exceeded 200,000 *Reichstaler* in 1536. The average annual income from this source in the decade after 1538 was almost 140,000 *Reichstaler*, but fell rapidly thereafter.[131] Iron was much less important in fiscal terms, amounting to only about 9 per cent of income in kind in 1530,[132] though this grew in importance during the later

[128] Krüger (1988), 142; Lindkvist in Genet and Le Mené (1987), 61.

[129] Krüger (1988), 143.

[130] Kain and Baigent (1992), 53–6, 66, 77–8.

[131] Krüger (1988), 146.

[132] Ibid. 147.

sixteenth and seventeenth century because of the needs of the armaments industry.[133] The other important mining activity in Sweden was that in copper. Once copper prices increased on the European market after about 1570, this became a potentially profitable enterprise, the more so once Sweden came temporarily in the seventeenth century to enjoy a virtual monopoly on the European market. The Swedish crown twice established a royal monopoly in copper (in 1580–9 and 1619–28).[134] At other times, the crown imposed duties on copper, and thus participated in the profits of the copper business. The policy ran into deep trouble with the decline in the value of copper in the late 1620s.[135] Oxenstierna concluded that the best policy for the crown was to follow neither management by a company nor royal control of the industry—the first was a monopoly, the second subjected crown revenues to the chances of a speculative market—but a free trade, which would yield a revenue in the form of export duties. Even in the crisis of 1629–31, Gustavus Adolphus drew more revenue from the mines of Falun than from any other national source (in 1623, income from this source had amounted to the equivalent of more than 291,000 *Reichstaler*, or more than 23 per cent of net revenue)[136] and only the temporary cession of the Prussian tolls proved a more important source of war finance.[137]

More advanced, or 'entrepreneurial' states might thus escape some of the inherent limitations of primitive domain states. The trained manpower of a state might be used in an entrepreneurial way—the Swiss Cantons had set the example with the export of their mercenary troops in the fifteenth and sixteenth centuries; they had also exacted a high price for an alliance with other European powers. The inability of Henri IV to pay his Swiss mercenaries in the 1590s had been a crucial factor delaying his reconquest of the kingdom from the Catholic League.[138] Other states, including Denmark, Hesse, Württemberg (for a relatively short period before the Seven Years' War)[139] and ultimately Russia (in the last stages of the Napoleonic wars: Chapter 13.6), followed the Swiss example. The net effect of marketing the export of mercenaries was to reduce the taxes required from the internal resources of the state and thus the fiscal burden on the ruler's subjects. The levy of a toll on foreign merchandise, though an indirect tax, had a similar effect in circumstances where the productive wealth of the ruler's subjects remained unaffected. Such levies might be heavily dependent on a temporary military ascendancy: the 'Prussian licences' were enjoyed by Sweden

[133] Roberts (1953–8), ii, 104.

[134] Krüger (1988), 148; Roberts (1953–8), ii, 92 states that the company projected in 1615 was not actually established.

[135] Roberts (1953–8), ii, 99.

[136] Krüger (1988), 130–1.

[137] Roberts (1953–8), ii, 103–4.

[138] Körner (1980), 110–16; Bonney (1981*a*), 35–8.

[139] Vann (1984), 265.

only in the aftermath of a successful campaign in Prussia by Gustavus Adolphus; once Swedish military power declined after the king's death, the cession was revoked by Poland.[140] Other external tolls were of much longer duration, and survived military crises. Denmark succeeded in levying dues on the Baltic commerce passing through the Sound from about 1426 until 1857: Adam Smith pronounced it 'the most important transit-duty in the world'.[141] The toll registers have been studied by economic historians interested in the history of international commerce, but not in a systematic way by financial historians.[142] The Sound toll was originally set at between 1 and 3 *rosenobels*—a gold coin worth 4 *Reichstaler*—per ship. The toll rate was raised drastically during the War of the North, in 1567, when an additional duty of 1 *Reichstaler* for every *last* (2 tons) of merchandise, and half a *Reichstaler* for every 2 tons of ballast, was imposed on cargo. A linkage was thus established between the volume of trade and the toll revenue which was independent of the size of the ships. Toll revenues jumped from about 45,000 *Reichstaler* in 1566, to over 132,000 *Reichstaler* the following year, of which 92,000 *Reichstaler* came from the new levy on cargo. This success was not repeated again until the end of the sixteenth century, but in 1630, for example, the equivalent of nearly 183,000 *Reichstaler* or 29 per cent of net Danish revenues were derived from this source.[143] A provocative toll policy—that is, a rapid increase in rates—was adopted by Christian IV in 1613–14 and after 1638: on the second occasion, Danish revenues from this source doubled (and in one spectacular year, 1639, trebled) without any corresponding increase in the traffic through the Sound. The Swedes and the Dutch responded by separate armed intervention—the Swedes with their land army in 1643, the Dutch with their navy in 1645: the rate of toll was lowered as a result.[144] Toll income retained its importance into the eighteenth century, notwithstanding the fluctuations of the Baltic trade (Figure 76).[145]

A comparable toll, though one less effectively enforced, was the Spanish tax on exports from Seville (the *almojarifazgo*)[146] and another tax, the *avería*, which helped to finance armed escorts for the fleets and was levied on outbound and homebound cargoes (Figure 77).[147] Juridically part of Castile, the Spanish empire

140 Roberts (1953–8), ii, 80–5.

141 Smith, ed. Campbell, Skinner and Todd (1976), ii, 894.

142 Jeannin (1964); Israel (1989), 20, 51, 93, 118, 144, 214–16, 301, 366.

143 Krüger (1988), 130–1, 138.

144 Israel (1989), 94–5, 146–9, esp. table 5.9 (ibid. 147), which compares the number of ships passing through the Sound with the yield from dues, 1627–31 and 1636–42.

145 ESFDB \poul\dang003 based on \poul\danm001, and ultimately Nathanson (1836). Data kindly supplied by Dr Bjørn Poulsen.

146 Chaunu (1977), vi pt. i, 52–7, 434–53, 470, 472–4; Phillips in Tracy (1990), 82.

147 Chaunu (1977), vi pt. i, 46–51, 414–20, 466–74; ESFDB \rjb\spain\spb004 based on \spm001; Phillips in Tracy (1990), 83.

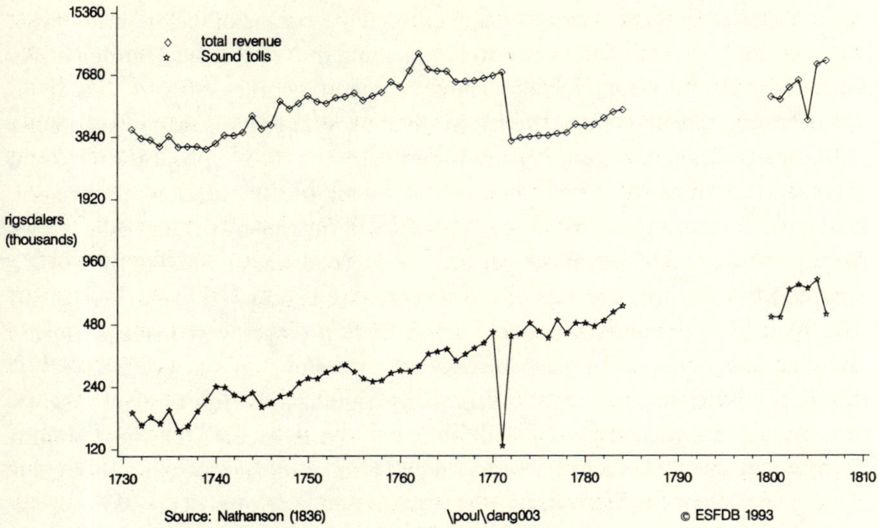

FIG. 76. Revenue from the Sound toll set against total revenues of the Danish monarchy, 1731–1806 (in *rigsdalers*)

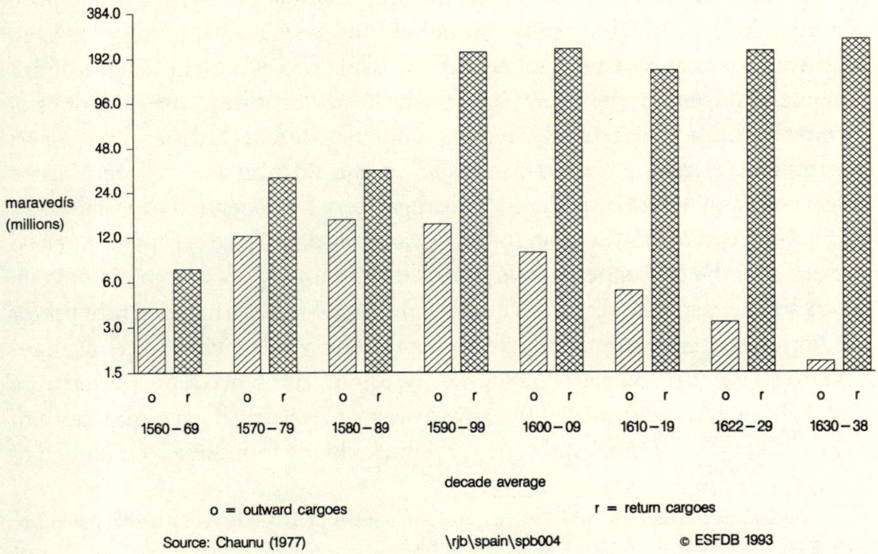

FIG. 77. The *avería* levied on outward and return cargoes between Castile and the Indies, 1560–1638 (in *maravedís*)

may be regarded as in one sense a domain state: the proportion of American bullion exports and tax revenue which entered the coffers of the Spanish crown was a net saving to the domestic tax revenues and thus to the fiscal burden of the king's subjects in mainland Spain. The seventeenth-century crisis in New Spain has been much debated, and the fall in silver remittances to Castile had a clear political significance. Revenues from mining production as a proportion of total royal income in Mexico fluctuated in the course of the seventeenth century, falling to as low as 12 per cent of the total in the decade 1680–9. But at other times the figure was much higher—30 per cent of the total was attained in the decade 1620–9, while in three decades of the seventeenth century (1610–19, 1650–9 and 1690–9) the figure reached 25 per cent of the total. Attempts were made in Mexico and Peru to levy new taxes, to increase old ones and to eliminate corruption; but this was insufficient to increase royal income significantly. It was silver production which maintained the overall stability in the income of the Mexican Treasury in the seventeenth century, while after 1720 there was a spectacular growth in revenues. In contrast, Peru witnessed a severe depression in the second half of the seventeenth century from which there was no real recovery until 1780 (Figure 78). By 1800, total revenues from Peru were only one-sixth of those of Mexico, whereas between 1580 and 1660 Peru had sent Castile twice as much bullion as had Mexico. Castile, however, did not benefit as greatly as might have been expected from the recovery of revenues in eighteenth-century Mexico, since after the decade 1611–20 the proportion of public revenue shipped abroad had declined consistently throughout the seventeenth century.[148] Even so, the importance of American income to Castile was clear. The decline of this revenue at the end of the *ancien régime*, which is evident from the categories of income of both the General Treasury and the Madrid Treasury, its largest constitutent element, proved a disaster to the Spanish position in Europe (Figures 79 and 80; Chapter 13.6).[149] Portugal, too, had operated its empire as a form of entrepreneurial domain state from an early date, since except for a period in the 1460s, the Portuguese crown claimed a monopoly on all imports of gold, slaves and pepper. The accounts of 1506 and 1518–19 suggest that gold receipts for the Portuguese crown remained steady at 120,000 *cruzados*, while spice revenues rose from 135,000 to 300,000 *cruzados*. The two items combined represented more than half the total revenues of the crown (valued respectively at a minimum of 500,500 and 772,500 *cruzados*).[150] Such revenues, chiefly from Brazil, continued to

[148] TePaske and Klein (1981), 122; (1982), i, 284–421; ESFDB \tepaske\tepg001 based on \tepm001. Data kindly supplied by Professors TePaske and Klein.

[149] Cuenca Esteban (1981), 192–9; ESFDB \rjb\spain\spb003 based on \spd004; Barbier and Klein (1981), 338; ESFDB \spb002 based on \spd003.

[150] Magalhães Godinho (1969), 830; Phillips in Tracy (1990), 50.

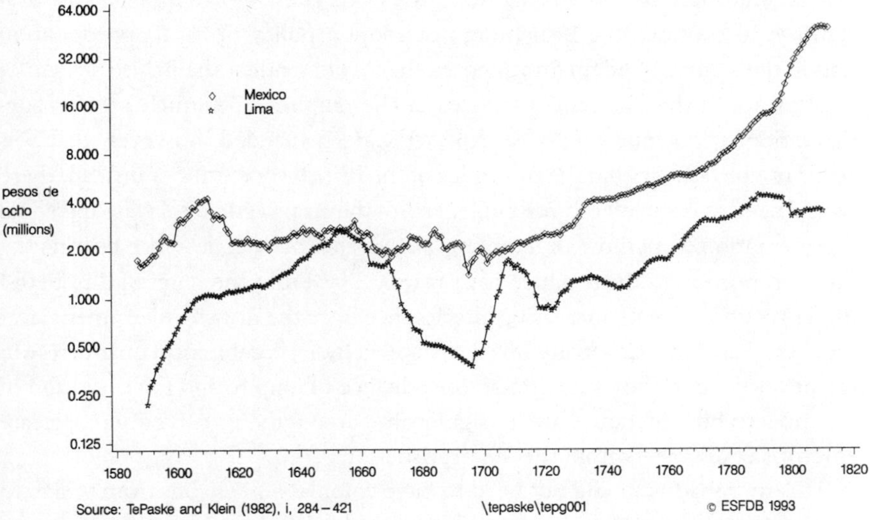

FIG. 78. Eleven-year moving averages of total revenues of the Mexico and Lima Treasuries, 1587–1812 (in *pesos de ocho*)

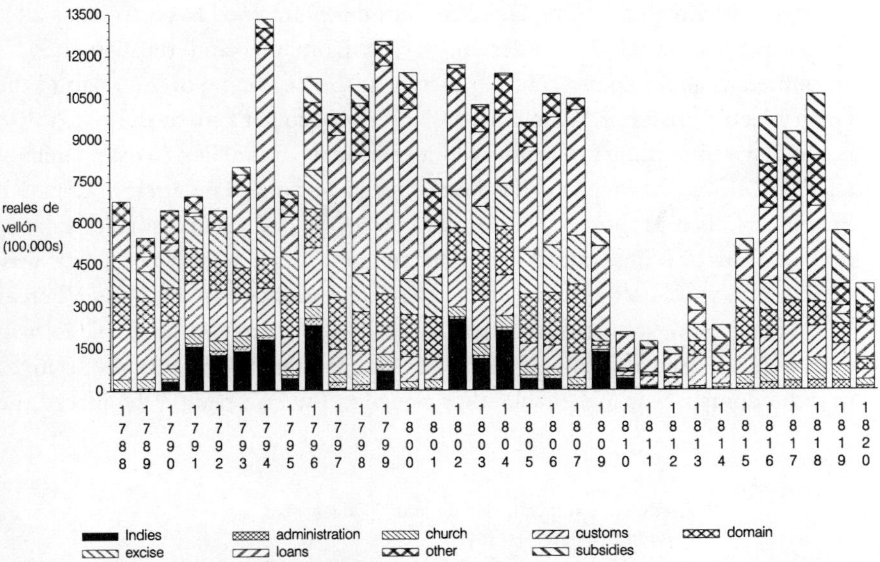

FIG. 79. Categories of income of the Spanish General Treasury, 1788–1820 (in *reales de vellón*)

play an important part in the income of the Portuguese crown in the eighteenth century. In contrast, the British did not adopt a policy of fiscal appropriation within their empire. Adam Smith noted that 'by extending the British system of taxation to all the different provinces of the empire ... a much greater augmentation of revenue might be expected'. He concluded, however, that this could not be done within the principles of the British constitution. Instead, there would need to be in effect a States General of the empire, that is, 'a fair and equal representation of all those different provinces, that of each province bearing the same proportion to the produce of its taxes ...'[151] From the reign of Elizabeth I until 1858 (though with increasing interference from the British government after 1763), the East India Company was the 'state' in India, combining a unique role in the development of overseas trade, the advance of empire and the evolution of the modern bureaucratic state. In significant parts of the British empire, private enterprise prevailed within the 'enterprise' state.[152]

An 'enterprise' state did not need to have colonial possessions from which to extract revenue in order to limit its subjects' tax burden: it needed only to acquire new territory, or to exploit its domains more effectively and encourage economic development. In this respect, the classic example is Brandenburg–Prussia. Domainal income was important at the origins of the state and throughout its history, beginning with the careful accounting required of the commanderies of the Teutonic Knights.[153] The Hohenzollern dukes retained large domains after the secularization of the Order in 1525.[154] Domainal and regalian income amounted to about 60 per cent of revenue at the beginning of the reign of the Great Elector Frederick William (1640) and about 50 per cent at the end (1688), the total revenue rising in the intervening period from 1 million to over 3 million *taler*.[155] During the reign of the first 'king in Prussia', Frederick I, Christian Frederick Luben proposed that the domain be divided up and smaller estates, mills and inns be rented out on leases that might become heritable property: this, he thought, would act as an incentive to more intensive exploitation. Whereas Wartenberg and Wittgenstein tried to adapt the plan, the regional domain chambers opposed and sabotaged it.[156] In 1713, Frederick William I pronounced that the domain was inalienable, thus rejecting Luben's plan;[157] he placed the

151 Smith, ed. Campbell, Skinner and Todd (1976), ii, 933.
152 Lawson (1993), 116–25, 164.
153 Burleigh (1984), 57; ibid. 58–62, for details of domain income.
154 Carsten (1954), 151.
155 Ibid. 266.
156 Koch (1978), 73–4.
157 Ibid. 85; Braun in Tilly (1975), 274 n. 35, 277.

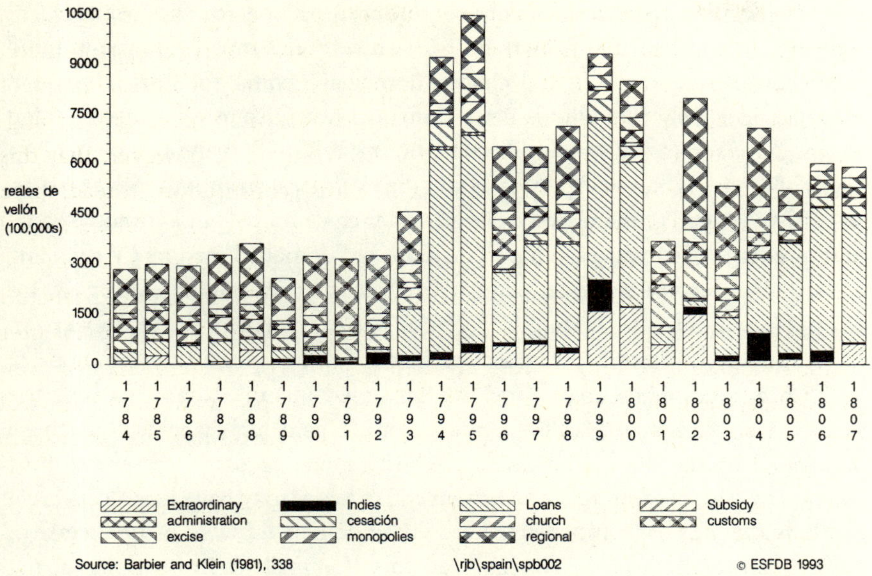

FIG. 80. Categories of income of the Madrid Treasury, 1784–1807 (in *reales de vellón*)

General Directory of 1722–3 in charge of domain commissions which would examine ways in which the domain might be improved or leased out more profitably.[158] There was a small rise in the relative importance of domain income during his reign: revenue from this source rose from 1.6 million *taler* in 1713 to 3.4 million in 1740 (an increase from 40 to 46 per cent of net revenue).[159] Frederick the Great acquired new territory, and with it new domains: domain revenue represented nearly 23 per cent of revenues from Silesia in 1743.[160] In contrast, the acquisition of West Prussia cost 6.7 million *Reichstaler* in investment costs in the years 1774–86, at least 0.46 million being spent in setting up new royal domains and purchasing estates.[161]

Historians have concluded from the evidence of these high administrative costs that the great period of domainal development had reached its peak before the reign of Frederick the Great, despite the acquisition of three new provinces.[162] Certainly, domain revenue fell from its peak of 46 per cent of net revenue at the beginning of the reign in 1740. By 1778–9, it yielded 9 million *taler* out of a total income of 22.8 million (or 39.5 per cent); at the end of the reign in

[158] Dorwart (1953), 209.

[159] Schremmer in Mathias and Pollard (1989), 415; Koch (1978), 93.

[160] Baumgart in Greengrass (1991), 165.

[161] Hubatsch (1975), 189. [162] Ibid. 174–5.

1786, the figures were respectively 8.5 and 23.8 million (or 35.7 per cent).[163] However, the spectacular growth in Prussian revenues must be borne in mind when considering the relative decline of domainal income: total net revenue in 1740 had been only 7.4 million. Thus, domainal revenues rose during the reign (from 3.4 million to say 8.5–9 million),[164] but more slowly than tax income. As a result of Frederick's policy, particularly in the *rétablissement* after the Seven Years' War, the Prussian domains were placed under civil control but administered by entrepreneurs.[165] It was possible to increase net domainal income by reducing costs, increasing the price of leases (there was a review of leases in 1768, for example), and by investigating surreptitious enlargement of noble domains in 1777. The application of Cameralist principles, and especially the methods of 'English agronomy',[166] may also have increased income somewhat, but the suspicion remains that leaseholders could have paid higher rents than those demanded by the domain chambers, which tended regularly to renew short leases. The leaseholders' fear of non-renewal of leases may have led to conservative bids and thus have impeded the growth of domainal revenue, the reverse of the English problem of the sixteenth century.[167] Finally, there was a growing belief that the canton system for the maintenance of the army—heralded as a great reform when it was introduced in 1733 (Chapter 11.2)—was an impediment to agrarian progress and economic development;[168] it was not formally revoked until June 1813, although it had in effect been abandoned five years earlier.[169]

Notwithstanding its decline in real terms, domainal income still represented 28 or 30 per cent of total net Prussian revenue respectively in 1800 and 1806:[170] the 'entrepreneurial' domain state might thus have appeared a relative success. There was debate in Prussia at the beginning of the nineteenth century as to whether taxation should be renounced altogether in favour of an enlarged domain. However, a calculation made in 1803–5 revealed that the government would have had to own almost 22 per cent of the productive land for this to become a possibility.[171] Any chance of this was dashed with Napoleon's crushing victory at Jena and the resulting loss of territory (Chapter 11.6). The French

[163] Henderson (1963), 66 n. 1; Koser (1903), 465.

[164] There seems to have been no growth in the period between 1778–9 and 1786. Schremmer in Mathias and Pollard (1989), 415, places domain income at 6–7 million in 1786. This is much lower than Koser's figure.

[165] Johnson (1975), 79–80.

[166] Ibid. 237–41.

[167] Hubatsch (1975), 173–6.

[168] Johnson (1975), 263–6.

[169] Koch (1978), 186.

[170] Schremmer in Mathias and Pollard (1989), 415–16.

[171] Ibid. 410.

government sought repayment of its war indemnity by means of a transfer of domain lands, but Frederick William IV sought to retain them ('le roi tient beaucoup à ses domaines'). Daru, the energetic French representative, doubted whether they could have been sold for 50 million francs given the difficulty in realizing capital after the war. The estimated income from the domains was only 10.3 million francs.[172] No cession of domain lands to France took place, but income from public property had fallen to 23.6 per cent of net income by 1821 (15.9 per cent if income from the salt monopoly is excluded).[173] Nevertheless, the tradition of owning substantial public property remained throughout the nineteenth century, when heavy industry and railways were added to the more traditional forms of domain and forests: direct and indirect taxes actually fell in the last quarter of the nineteenth century as an increasing proportion of revenue was drawn from state enterprises.[174] Though modern historical interpretations stress the inevitability of the transition from a 'domain state' to a 'tax state', the Prussian example might suggest that improved domain administration, and the incorporation of new types of enterprise into the ordinary revenues, might serve as one test of modernity in the process of state building.

13.4 *Monetization, Coinage Profits and Fiduciary Issues*

Taxes paid in kind were probably the earliest form of revenue in states with predominantly agrarian economies and were characteristic of the feudal mode of production. Adam Smith noted that the land tax could be levied in either money or kind. In China, where it was usually levied in kind, the ruler had always derived the greatest part of his revenue from a land tax, 'estimated so very moderately, that, in many provinces, it is said not to exceed a thirtieth part of the ordinary produce'.[175] Under the Ming dynasty (1368–1644), the land tax provided about three-quarters of all revenue or 27 million *peculs* of grain; tax rates remained substantially unaltered in the first decades of the Ch'ing or Manchu dynasty (1644–1911). The land tax was equivalent to about 10 per cent of agricultural output, although there were significant regional variations in the basic assessment in *peculs* of grain.[176] Smith denounced the payment of land tax in kind: 'a publick revenue, which was paid in kind, would suffer so much from the mismanagement of the collectors, that a very small part of what was levied upon the people would ever arrive at the Treasury of the prince'. He considered

172 Lesage (1924), 79–80, 85, 87, 95 n. 1.

173 Schremmer in Mathias and Pollard (1989), 435.

174 Ibid. 418–19.

175 Smith, ed. Campbell, Skinner and Todd (1976), ii, 838. Cf. ibid. ii, 683.

176 Huang (1974), 40, 46, 49, 164, 183, 308; Huang (1969), 89. For the continuing importance of the land tax under the Manchu dynasty: Chen (1914), 56, 66–9.

that the Chinese administrators and tax collectors would 'find their advantage' in continuing this system; certainly Smith was correct that there was a vast difference between the tax burden in China and the sovereign's revenue.[177] In Mughal India (1556–1707), the rate in kind paid by peasant cultivators was translated by means of complex tables into a cash equivalent for the benefit of the army commanders. In time, differences between the rates of different provinces, and within the same province, became marked and a range of rates was permitted within the province for different localities between maximium and minimum figures. Subsequently an investigation was held, rates were tabulated, and a range of rates was allowed depending on whether high value cash crops were cultivated or not. The system was thus divorced from the actual value of the harvest in a given year. The process of converting annual tax payments in kind into actual money required an increasing money supply in the late sixteenth and early seventeenth century. Silver currency output in the Mughal empire is estimated at just under 160 metric tonnes a year between 1605 and 1635, compared to 75.3 metric tonnes a year in France between 1631 and 1660.[178]

Even in Europe, some states made a relatively late transition from taxes paid in kind to monetary payments. The Swedish debt to Lübeck was repaid in kind in 1532, part payment of which was in butter.[179] In Muscovy, Peter the Great wanted to secure payment of taxes in silver, thus adopting German practice;[180] but there was never enough silver coin in circulation for this to be a practicable policy and military operations during the Seven Years' War, for example, were financed by the minting of copper coinage. Insufficient silver currency compelled the Russian government to commence printing money in 1768: the two *Assignat* banks founded that year began the virtually unrestricted printing of money which helped finance an expansionist foreign policy and especially the culmination of the protracted conflict with Napoleon (Chapter 11.6). Even so, the scarcity of money meant that payment in kind remained extensive. The three main categories of such payment—fiscal services, labour exacted in the form of *corvée* and the supply of housing and food, which were known collectively as contributions from the land (*zemskie povinnosti*)—remained a heavy burden on the peasantry, and the means by which the state administrative apparatus was paid for, until well into the nineteenth century.[181]

The French enquiry on comparative revenues in Europe, which was launched in 1763, revealed that the trend was firmly away from payment of taxes in kind

[177] Smith, ed. Campbell, Skinner and Todd (1976), ii, 839; Huang (1974), 268, 271.

[178] Habib (1963), 201–12; Moosvi (1987), 97–107, 361–2.

[179] Heckshер (1953), 213–14.

[180] Montesquieu, ed. Cohler, Miller and Stone (1989), 216.

[181] LeDonne (1991), 269–75.

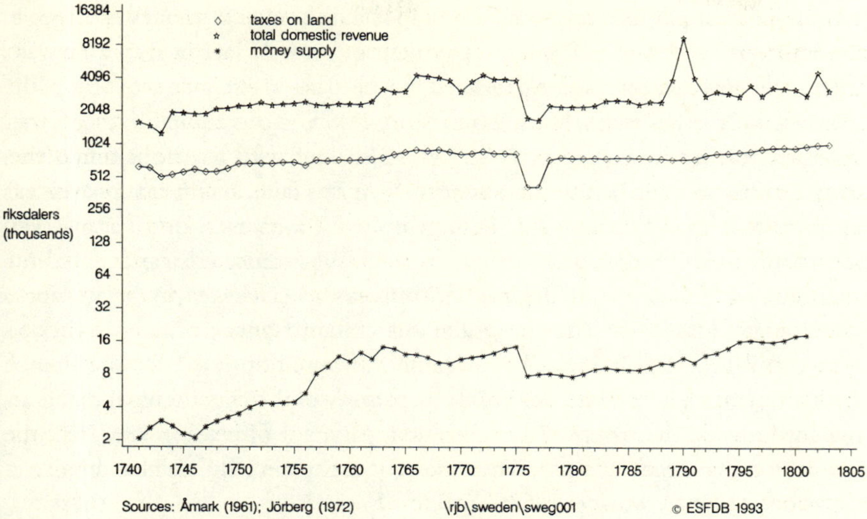

FIG. 81. Revenue from taxes on land and total domestic revenue in Sweden set against total money supply, 1741–1803 (in *riksdalers*)

elsewhere in Europe. The commutation to money payments was enacted in Denmark in October 1763,[182] although Sweden still practised mixed payment. The result was that at the time of the French enquiry the evaluation of Swedish revenues was considered difficult because of the survival of payments in kind.[183] This did not prevent the Swedish government from arriving at a purely monetary evaluation of revenue after 1719, however, and what becomes clear from the analysis of the figures (Figure 81) is the eclipse by the eighteenth century of domainal revenues, which never comprised a full 1 per cent of total revenue for a single decade between 1722 and 1809.[184] However, the land taxes amounted to a considerable proportion of domestic revenue, fluctuating between a low of 22 per cent in the 1790s and a high of 40 per cent in the 1730s;[185] these revenues were calculated, and largely paid, in units of natural produce such as grain. They were earmarked for the remuneration of crown servants, and the resulting system though it was relatively inflexible, nevertheless protected royal officials from the

[182] Hartmann (1979), 119; *Mémoires*, ed. Moreau de Beaumont (1768), 63, noted that the reform was 'à la grande satisfaction des peuples'.

[183] Hartmann (1979), 71, 73; *Mémoires*, ed. Moreau de Beaumont (1768), 27, 29.

[184] Åmark (1961), 400–14; Jörberg (1972), i, 80; ii, 131–2; ESFDB \rjb\sweden\sweg001 based on \swem002 and \swed003.

[185] Under our criteria here, domestic revenue excludes loan income, whether from abroad or at home and the carry-over of revenue from one accounting year to another. It also excludes the projected deficit against expenditure.

erosion of their pay as a result of fluctuations in the value of money.[186] Even in France there were late examples of payment in kind. As late as 1725, a new tax called the *cinquantième* was established, to be paid in kind directly from the proceeds of the harvest. Although in theory it was more equitable than other taxes, in practice it proved unworkable; it also met with ferocious opposition from clerical and aristocratic landowners.[187] At this date, such a tax in kind was an aberration and it was revoked within two years. Payment in kind was reserved for wartime extremities such as 1709–10, when subsistence crisis prevented the munitioning of the army on the frontier, and only special levies on the provinces could avert disaster.[188] The exception was certain frontier provinces such as Alsace and Franche-Comté. They became the munitions base for the French armies operating abroad because of the proximity of their predominantly agrarian economy to the troops. The substantial payment of taxes in kind, and the requisition of peasant labour and transportation, explain why the new direct tax, the *dixième* of 1710, was not established in Alsace.[189]

Such requisitions and payments in kind were unusual in western Europe in the early modern period. The thirteenth century had seen extensive monetization which had facilitated the transfer from payments in kind to monetary payments with a resulting increased reliance of states on tax income (Chapter 5.3).[190] In the early Middle Ages, levies on coinage and taxes for the 'confirmation' of money had counted as one of the earliest regalian rights.[191] These levies were transmuted into a more settled and regular right of seigniorage (*seigneuriage* or *moneyage*), more akin to a general tax than a regalian right.[192] We are not always accurately informed about this aspect of regular royal income: both Sir James Steuart and Adam Smith thought that the French king in the eighteenth century levied a seigniorage of about 8 per cent, a rate which would have been quite unrealistic, since, as David Hume pointed out, 'nobody would bring bullion to the mint'; the true figure, according to Necker, was about 3 per cent, but fluctuated in different periods, as did the profit from recoinage.[193] In his *De moneta* in the fourteenth century, Nicholas Oresme had argued that debasement was in effect a tax, and the reason why a ruler altered the coinage was simply the

[186] Åmark (1961), 884 (English summary). The author thanks Dr Paul Hart for translating some of the Swedish fiscal terminology.

[187] Bonney (1992*a*), 153–4.

[188] Ibid. 154 n. 18.

[189] Ibid. 154 n. 19.

[190] Cf. Spufford (1989), 246–7, 383.

[191] Bisson (1979).

[192] Morineau in Genet and Le Mené (1987), 120–1; Einaudi (1953), 240, 257–8; Boyer-Xambeu, Deleplace and Gillard (1986), 83; Ardant in Tilly (1975), 191.

[193] Smith, ed. Campbell, Skinner and Todd (1976), i, 62; Steuart, ed. Skinner (1966), ii, 431, 575; Bonney (1992*a*), 156 n. 21; Boyer-Xambeu, Deleplace and Gillard (1986), 82.

desire for profit or gain (Chapter 1.4).[194] By the eighteenth century, such monetary manipulations were condemned by contemporaries: Adam Smith went much further than Oresme, and called them 'a simple augmentation . . . an injustice of open violence; whereas an adulteration is an injustice of treacherous fraud'.[195] In some years, gains from coinage alteration formed an extremely significant proportion of royal income. The French debasement of 1298–9 brought in an income one and a half times that from all other sources combined; Philip VI's debasement in 1349 provided the equivalent of 67 per cent of total income, and yielded a sum a hundred times that of the contemporary debasement by Edward III; while in 1420 and 1421, debasements in France produced an income respectively four times and eleven times as much as all other sources of revenue combined, though the events of these two years were thoroughly exceptional.[196] John the Fearless nearly quintupled his 'normal' revenue from the two Burgundies by debasements in 1416–19,[197] but it was above all in Castile in the later Middle Ages that debasement ran riot, with a fall of about 95 per cent in the value of the *maravedí* over a period of about 130 years. There are no surviving records of Castilian mint outputs, which might question the prevailing notion of a monetary contraction in late medieval Europe:[198] but it is clear that any short-term gains from mint profits were eroded by the catastrophic decline in the real value of the crown's ordinary revenues. In real terms, the Castilian revenue in 1504 had increased by only 40 per cent since 1429.[199] Thereafter, the *maravedí* remained stable until the disastrous introduction in the seventeenth century of copper coinage (*vellón*), minted largely from Swedish copper sold at Amsterdam.[200]

Perhaps the most important role for mint profits was in the period when revenues from the royal domain were no longer sufficient, but when the system of taxation had not yet reached its fullest stage of development: thus, for example, the peaks of gold and silver coinages in France occurred during the fourteenth- and not the fifteenth-century debasements.[201] Yet the historical experience of the main European states does not bear out the contention that states debased their coinage before a tax system was fully in place: Frederick the

194 Spufford (1989), 295, 300, 306–8; Oresme, ed. Johnson (1956), 24, 36, 41.

195 Smith, ed. Campbell, Skinner and Todd (1976), ii, 932.

196 Spufford (1989), 302, 305, 308–10, 317; Day (1978, 1987*a*), 53; Day in Depeyrot, Hackens and Moucharte (1987); Miskimin (1984), 50 n. 48, suggests that Day's figures understate the French coinage output in the first years of the 15th cent. and overstate it for the later years.

197 Spufford (1989), 311–12.

198 Day (1987*a*), 53–4, 64–7, tabulates the main surviving series elsewhere. Cf. Day (1984).

199 Spufford (1989), 299, 314–15; Ladero Quesada (1970, 1973), 43–4; Ladero Quesada in Bonney (1995).

200 Spooner (1972), 60.

201 Einaudi (1953), 258; Miskimin (1984), 50.

Great was forced into a massive debasement towards the end of the Seven Years' War because his revenue system was inadequate for his needs in wartime.[202] The experience of the great German debasement of the years 1619–23 (the *Kipper- und Wipperzeit*), which was largely started by a number of smaller princes in an attempt to build up their revenues at the outset of the Thirty Years' War, demonstrated the disastrous consequences of competitive copper debasements. Adam Smith contrasted large states such as France or England, which could control their own currencies, with smaller ones such as Genoa and Hamburg, which could not.[203] But while Smith's observations had become generally true by the eighteenth century, except for the smaller states in the Holy Roman Empire, they were misleading for earlier periods. England was relatively unusual in the Middle Ages, because its island status allowed the crown to prevent the circulation of foreign coin.[204] This was not possible on the Continent: foreign coin still circulated freely in sixteenth-century France, for example. Regional mints drew their coin from different foreign sources, and it was only gradually in the course of the seventeenth century that most of this foreign money was recoined and issued as 'French' money.[205] Once this had occurred, a convinced bullionist such as Colbert was, almost for the first time, in a position to consider the relationship between the amount of revenue extracted in taxation and the amount of coin in circulation in the kingdom.[206] Even after this creation of a 'national' coinage, there remained a distinction between the 'real' money in circulation and the money of account, an abstract unit used to calculate the value of actual coins in circulation and to bind them into one system. In such a system, debasement could be effected by the process of 'crying up' the actual coins in circulation in relation to the money of account.[207] If more than one system of account was in operation simultaneously, then the political and economic cohesion of a large state might be placed in doubt.[208]

One English commentator in 1621 compared the hammers of the mint in a state to the human pulse: 'For as if these beat strongly, it argues health; but if faintly, weakness in the body natural.'[209] By this reckoning, although the mint outputs of England and France showed substantial increases over the long term (Figure 2), output was irregular with short-term peaks (often after coinage

[202] Henderson (1963), 40–1; Hubatsch (1975), 139–41.

[203] Smith, ed. Campbell, Skinner and Todd (1976), i, 479–80; Kindleberger (1991), 153.

[204] Mayhew in Challis (1992), 131–2.

[205] Richet (1961); Spooner (1972), 306, 316; Boyer-Xambeu, Deleplace and Gillard (1986), 110–12, 220–1.

[206] Hecksher (1953), 221–2; Bonney (1981*a*), 282 n. 2.

[207] Einaudi (1953), 248–9; Boyer-Xambeu, Deleplace and Gillard (1986), 102.

[208] Einaudi (1953), 244; Boyer-Xambeu, Deleplace and Gillard (1986), 39, 204.

[209] Challis in Challis (1992), 307.

alterations) followed by periods when mints lapsed into relative inactivity which might augur ill for the health of the body politic and above all the economy.[210] One feature which was evident of France throughout, and remained true for England at least in the Middle Ages,[211] was the proliferation of regional mints. As with regional taxation, regional mints have their distinctive histories, and the variations in the outputs of local mints are not explicable by any single factor: there were differences in local market conditions, in the entrepreneurial effort and skills of the local mint masters, and the opportunities created by the state varied from one local mint to another.[212] Some regional mints were much nearer the point of arrival of precious metals than others, which was of crucial importance since bullion flow was perhaps the single most important consideration determining mint output.[213] For all these reasons, plus the impact of technological change and the vicissitudes of royal power (after Parliament seized the mint in 1642, Charles I found that he was unable to achieve any significant rival mint output during the English Civil War),[214] the history of the mint output even of one country is extraordinarily complex. The principal concern from a revenue point of view must be the royal profit from minting, recoinage and debasement. Here the most important conclusion of the revised history of the English mint is that profitability to the crown was rarely a significant aspect of royal policy, either in the Middle Ages or in the early modern period. The introduction of a fixed seigniorage and mintage charge of 1 shilling in the pound (though this fluctuated from time to time) was of crucial importance, since it replaced a more dispersed and erratic source of income. Sound money remained the order of the day for most of the Middle Ages, and even Edward IV made his large profits from the mint by adjusting his seigniorage charges rather than debasing the coinage for fiscal purposes. For most of the early modern period, the fiscal return from the mint was low.[215] A similar situation prevailed in fourteenth-century Florence, despite two debasements caused by external pressures rather than fiscal reasons (a crisis in the gold–silver ratio in 1345–7 and the 'invasion' of Pisan currency in 1366–71): the state relied on its rights

[210] Ibid. 190, 192; Dyer and Gaspar in Challis (1992), 431.

[211] Mayhew in Challis (1992), 83, 149, for the 'withering of the provincial mints' in England. His chapter is entitled 'From regional to central minting, 1158–1464', but there remained some regional mints after this date and others were subsequently created.

[212] Challis in Challis (1992), 240–1; Sussman (1990), 155; Williams (1991) discusses a local example (in this case, Agen).

[213] The maps in Spooner (1972), 222–45, remain fundamental for France; Mayhew in Challis (1992), 130. Bullion inflow ceased to be of primary importance in England only after 1815: Dyer and Gaspar in Challis (1992), 484.

[214] Challis in Challis (1992), 281, 283.

[215] Mayhew in Challis (1992), 85, 89–90, 133–5, 138; Challis in Challis (1992), 216, 332.

of seigniorage, the tax on minting activity, for its profits.[216] Though recoinage was intended to be profitable or at least self-financing, disastrous mistakes could be made, as in the great English recoinage of 1696–8, urged on the government by John Locke, which led to coinage issues in silver of £6.8 million at a cost of some £2.7 million. For all its importance, Locke's monetary theory failed the crucial tests of being self-financing in its application or appropriate in its economic consequences.[217] In contrast, the period of systematic fiscal exploitation of the mint, Henry VIII's 'great debasement' of 1544–51, the full effects of which were not eliminated until after 1561, resulted in issues of debased coin worth £4.4 million at face value, the majority of which was in silver. Of every £100 which left the mint in silver, the crown took no less than £46 in profit excluding overheads.[218]

Though the techniques of manufacture were different, debasement was no different in kind from the printing of money. The first serious issue of paper money occurred in France in the first decade of the eighteenth century, precisely at a time when there was a rapid debasement of the coinage: *billets de monnaie* were issued after 1701 to those who brought their bullion or coin to the mints for reissue, and by 1708 total paper of various types to the face value of 343.7 million *livres* had been issued, of which the *billets de monnaie* constituted 72 million. Since this paper money was not fully convertible, there was a rapid depreciation in its exchange value, which had declined by some 60 or 70 per cent by 1707.[219] Some 600 million of the paper debt in 1715 was reduced to 250 million in *billets d'État*, and it was this paper which was rapidly inflated under the impact of Law's 'splendid, but visionary ideas' as Adam Smith termed them. Smith commented that 'the idea of . . . multiplying paper money to almost any extent, was the real foundation of what is called the Mississippi scheme, the most extravagant project both of banking and stock-jobbing that, perhaps, the world ever saw . . .'[220] Sir James Steuart explained the origins of the scheme:

> the debts of France were . . . above 2,000 millions. The coin, at this time, in France, was reckoned at about 1,200 millions . . . The Regent thought, that if he could draw either the whole, or even the greatest part of this 1,200 millions of coin into his bank, and replace the use of it to the kingdom, by as much paper, secured upon his word, then he should be able to pay off, with it, near one half of the debts of France . . .

At the time of the collapse of Law's System, however, there were '2,235 millions

[216] Cipolla (1982), 88; Cipolla (1990) is a detailed comparison between monetary policy in Milan and Florence.

[217] Challis in Challis (1992), 381–2, 386, 397; Locke, ed. Kelly (1991), 55–67, 110–21; Appelby (1976).

[218] Challis in Challis (1992), 228, 232–3, 239.

[219] Bonney and Bonney (1993), 70–1; Seligmann (1925).

[220] Smith, ed. Campbell, Skinner and Todd (1976), i, 317.

of discredited banknotes in circulation, and a small sum of coin to make them good ...' The inevitable consequence of 'the fatal bankruptcy in 1720' was a recoinage in 1726:

Upon that last general coinage, the same principles of enriching the King by the operation directed the conduct of the minister. The old specie was cried down, and proscribed in circulation: but it was thought, that as it was the King's coin, he had a liberty to set a price upon it, at a different rate from any other bullion of the same fineness: and that he had also a right to command the proprietors of it to bring it to the mint at his own price.[221]

Law's experiment was not repeated in France until the Convention began systematically to finance its war effort against the *ancien régime* monarchies by the issue of *assignats* (Chapter 11.4), which were correctly seen by Necker as paying for today's policies by tomorrow's inflation.[222] Napoleon rejected such expedients (Chapter 11.5): with the issue of the *franc de germinal* in 1803, previous monetary mutations were declared disastrous, the fiscal purpose of monetary change was rejected for the future, and the distinction between money of account and 'real' money in circulation was finally abandoned.[223]

Other countries followed Louis XIV's example in issuing a form of paper money, but for the most part on a more modest scale. Denmark had first introduced paper to supplement tax revenues during the Great Northern War, but these notes had been withdrawn by 1728. Issues recommenced in 1736, and expanded rapidly in the 1760s until the end of the War of American Independence. After ministerial changes in 1784, the issue of paper was reduced somewhat, but by 1789 banknotes had regained the level of 1783.[224] In Sweden, domestic tax revenues had expanded less rapidly than note supply and the value of the *riksdaler* in exchange transactions had fallen accordingly. The first great expansion occurred during the Seven Years' War, when the amount of notes rose from 13.8 million *riksdalers* in 1755 to 44 million in 1763; there was a reduction to 31.8 million by 1769. Current account deficits during the Russian war were met by foreign loans and further emissions of paper, especially *riksdaler riksgälds*, which were not convertible into silver: Sweden had passed from the silver standard reintroduced in 1775 to a paper standard by 1789–90.[225] Until the currency conversion of 1803, Sweden had two parallel standards: these comprised Riksbanknotes or *riksdaler banko* (which were convertible into silver), and National

221 Steuart, ed. Skinner (1966), ii, 538, 556, 583.

222 Harris (1986), 759–60; Necker (1791), 132: 'il en résulteroit un tel empressement de réaliser une pareille monnoie, que tous les objets d'échange s'éleveroient peut-être à un prix deux ou trois plus considérable que leur juste valeur.' Du Pont de Nemours had predicted the inflationary effect of the *assignats* in 1790: McLain (1977), 148; Hutchison (1988), 407 n. 11.

223 Braesch (1936*a*), 146–59, esp. ibid. 159; Thuillier (1983), 84–91.

224 Riley (1980), 136–41.

225 Jörberg (1972), i, 78–85; ii, 127–44; Riley (1980), 144–51.

Debt Office bonds or *riksdaler riksgälds* (which were not convertible into silver). However, it is clear that the land taxes, which were paid in kind, were much more significant than the issue of money either in the form of paper or silver coin. By the end of the eighteenth century, as has been seen, most of the main European states were financing their wars by borrowing, and in several cases by the emission of paper money. The French had given the lead in the creation of fiat money, and brought the system to its disastrous climax in the 1790s. Money creation thus came to be viewed as a revenue instrument, enlarging the state's sources of financing and thus the size of its deficit; indeed the deficit came to feed upon itself, leading to ever greater monetary expansion.[226] The French state came to enjoy a monopoly franchise in the creation of fiat money in the eighteenth century, once it had eliminated constraints on its behaviour imposed by the presence of competing monies. Other states followed suit when they found themselves in a comparable need (Chapter 11.6).[227]

13.5 *Direct Taxes*

Originally conceived in some states as a voluntary gift of subjects to their ruler (*don gratuit*, a term still used on the eve of the French Revolution for the taxation of sectional groups such as the clergy, in the context of privileged provinces[228] or in the case of cities which normally enjoyed exemption from direct taxes),[229] taxation in a modern sense is a manifestation of the government's power to coerce, to take money from individuals. Direct taxation may take the form of a tax on a person's property, or his various assets including income; a tax on the income from an asset is equivalent to a tax on its capital value.[230] Adam Smith doubted the capacity of states even in the eighteenth century to tax the interest earned on deposits as effectively as the rent of land. Whereas the quantity and value of the land held by an individual could be ascertained with great exactness, his capital stock was 'almost always a secret', and thus difficult to estimate, apart from being subject to variation. Smith concluded that in 'all countries a severe

[226] Cf. Tanzi (1991), 79, 102.

[227] Cf. Brennan and Buchanan (1980), 109–11; Ardant in Tilly (1975), 192. In the Austrian lands, Zinzendorf had warned in the late 1760s and early 1770s of the danger of creating an unredeemable paper money which would sink to a discount as had the French *billets d'État*. Zinzendorf's predictions proved correct in the two decades of inflation of paper money after 1787: Dickson (1987), ii, 72–3.

[228] For examples in the later 17th cent.: Bonney and Bonney (1993), 201–4, 297 (tables 26, 49); for Louis XVI's use of the term: Hardman (1993), 62.

[229] Descimon (1989), 72. For increasing taxation on the French towns in the 16th cent.: Chevalier in Genet and Le Mené (1987), 150–1; Knecht (1982), 123–4.

[230] Ardant (1965), i, 22–3, 32; Brennan and Buchanan (1980), 8, 84–5; Guéry (1984).

inquisition into the circumstances of private persons has been carefully avoided'. In the cantons of Unterwald and Zurich, self-assessment of wealth upon oath was the order of the day, while at Basle merchants provided a three-monthly statement of the tax due from their exchange transactions.[231] In contrast, the merchants of Hamburg would have considered such a declaration of their trading activities prejudicial, but they were prepared to pay a tax of 0.25 per cent on their wealth, which—since their assets consisted principally in stock—was equivalent to a tax upon stock.[232]

Most Italian city-states seem to have developed advanced and sophisticated fiscal systems at a relatively early date in the Middle Ages: the deep political rivalries within the Italian peninsula were sufficient to ensure that city-state competition became also a struggle for fiscal resources with a premium on the adoption of efficient revenue-raising devices.[233] The Florentine *catasto* of 1427 is merely the best known example of this, because it was to have great influence on the introduction of subsequent land registers, though it was a sophisticated attempt to include nearly all wealth within the tax net.[234] Elsewhere, other states developed a form of direct taxation at a relatively early date: the extent to which such taxes were levied on a regular basis inevitably relates to the social, and above all the political, development of each state.[235] What needs to be studied here is how direct taxes were conceived, in terms of the evaluation of wealth; the extent of the fiscal base encompassed by the tax; and the mechanism of the levy. In each of these areas there was increasing sophistication from the fifteenth to the eighteenth centuries, so that by the period of the Revolutionary wars direct taxes came to be regarded as an equitable, and (at least, in France) as the fairest form of contribution by taxpayers.

One of the earliest forms of direct taxes was the undifferentiated hearth or poll tax, which took no account of the ability to pay, except perhaps for the poverty-stricken. This was the type of tax imposed, for example, at Siena in 1323 (with the provision that those in the *contado* would pay double the rate in the city).[236] It was the celebrated third English poll tax of 1380–1 which precipitated the Peasants' Revolt of 1381: this was a tax of a shilling per head on all adults over

231 *Mémoires*, ed. Moreau de Beaumont (1768), 163, 166–7, 171; AN K 879 no. 107. For earlier *impôts sur la fortune* at Schaffhouse and Saint-Gall: Körner (1980), 93–4.

232 *Mémoires*, ed. Moreau de Beaumont (1768), 74; Hartmann (1979), 139; Pelus in Bulst and Genet (1988), 252.

233 The best overview is Herlihy (1964), repr. in Herlihy (1980). See also the comment of Burke in Hall (1986), 141.

234 AN K 881 no. 3, 'Mémoire sur le cadastre de Toscane et l'imposition qui en résulte'. Herlihy and Klapisch-Zuber (1978, 1985); Veseth (1990), 48–50.

235 This is one of the themes of the separate contributions to Bonney (1995).

236 Bowsky (1970), 69.

fifteen years, except for genuine beggars.[237] The first poll tax of 1377 had been lighter (but had been extended to adults over the age of fourteen); only the second poll tax of 1379 had been graduated according to the social and economic status of taxpayers (graduated poll taxes were also imposed at a later date, for example in 1641 and 1660). Undifferentiated taxes were also imposed on special groups, but in such cases there was sometimes a minimum property qualification. Thus, for example, in 1342 the Golden Penny (*gulden pfennig*) was levied on Jews in the Holy Roman Empire: it was a 1 florin tax to be paid by all Jews, including widows over the age of twelve who possessed 20 florins of property.[238] Similar arrangements are found for Jews in Poland in the late sixteenth and early seventeenth centuries (for example, a poll tax of 1 *zloty* or more per head).[239] In 1695, Charles Davenant called the poll tax 'odious', indeed 'so great a badge of slavery' that Turks 'impose it upon none but Christians'.[240] Montesquieu, as has been seen (Chapter 6.5), followed this line of reasoning in the eighteenth century. Adam Smith remarked that 'Taxes of so much a head upon the bondmen employed in cultivation, seem antiently to have been common all over Europe. There subsists at present a tax of this kind in the empire of Russia.'[241] In fact, the *capitation* or poll tax was introduced in Russia by Peter the Great in 1724–5 on the basis of a census of 5.4 million persons, with the rate set at 70 *kopeks* to produce a yield of 4 million roubles. The *capitation* rate was unchanged until 1794; it thus remained a tax incapable of sustaining a growing budgetary need, since it could be increased no faster than the rate of population growth unless there was to be a substantial increase in the levy, which would be unacceptable politically. As a proportion of total Russian revenue, it therefore tended to decline in the eighteenth century.[242] Smith postulated that

> capitation taxes are levied at little expence [*sic*]; and, where they are rigorously exacted, afford a very sure revenue to the state . . . It is in general, however, but a small part of the publick revenue, which, in a great empire, has ever been drawn from such taxes; and the greatest sum which they have ever afforded, might always have been found in some other way much more convenient to the people.

However, the Russian poll tax or *capitation* was not representative of *capitation* taxes in western Europe, where there was some attempt to proportion them

237 Dobson (1986), 117; Hilton (1973), 162. For the yield: ESFDB datset \orm\engd010. It was the enforcement of the levy by parliamentary commissioners which provoked the revolt: Harding in Hilton and Aston (1984), 169.

238 Isenmann in Bonney (1995).

239 Tollet, unpubd paper.

240 Davenant, ed. Whitworth (1771), i, 22.

241 Smith, ed. Campbell, Skinner and Todd (1976), ii, 857.

242 Klyuchevsky (1965), 116–18, 169–76; LeDonne (1984), 251–4; Kahan (1985), 328–34; LeDonne (1991), 259–60, 277–8.

according to social rank. Smith observed this with regard to the poll tax introduced in England on the accession of William III and Mary: 'In the assessment of a tax which was not very heavy, a considerable degree of inequality had been found less insupportable than any degree of uncertainty.' The French *capitation* of 1695, introduced by Pontchartrain, was modelled on the tax ordered by Emperor Leopold I in his hereditary lands in 1690 (it included the clergy in its provisions; the French version did not).[243] The French government originally intended making the tax a personal one, with scarcely any exemptions—this had been the intention also of the Austrian government.[244] But the French government changed its mind at the last moment before the introduction of the *capitation* in January 1695, so that it became a tax payable by heads of households, which conformed more to French social structure than to the original purpose of the tax.[245] The tax was revoked at the end of the War of the League of Augsburg but it was reintroduced in 1701. It became a permanent tax for the rest of the *ancien régime*, but one principally under the control of the intendants and independent of the *bureaux des finances*, the *élections* and the *Cours des Aides*; and its purpose changed radically. The levy was increased in 1701 by half as much again, and many intendants resorted to levying it as an accessory to the *taille*, while corporate groups were encouraged to make lump sum payment (*abonnement*).[246] Adam Smith stated that in England poll taxes had 'never produced the sum which had been expected from them' but that 'the more severe government of France assesses upon each generality a certain sum, which the intendant must find as he can.' That part of the *capitation* payable by the nobility was 'the least considerable. The largest [proportion] falls upon those subject to the taille, who are assessed to the capitation at so much a pound of what they pay to that other tax.'[247] The *capitation* was one of several French taxes which Smith thought should be abolished.

An alternative method for the collection of direct taxes, used, for example, by the commune of Siena as early as the years between 1168 and 1175, was to evaluate wealth as the basis for a levy: in the case of Siena this was known as the *alliramento*, or the making of the *lire*, which was carried out by assessors possessing a minimum of taxable wealth, who were selected from the body of citizens. Their task was to evaluate the real (*possessioni*) and movable (*mobile*) property of the head of each family: sometimes, though not always, differential

243 Bérenger (1975), 338.

244 B[ibliothèque] N[ationale], Paris, MS. fr. 8852, fo. 83^{v}, 31 Oct. 1694; Bérenger (1975), 338 n. 204.

245 Guéry (1986), 1048. Pontchartrain was quite specific about the change of plan in his letters: BN MS. fr. 8853, fos. 82, 240, 14 Jan. and 16 Feb. 1695.

246 Bossenga (1991), 27; Bonney and Bonney (1993), 75.

247 Cf. *Mémoires*, ed. Moreau de Beaumont (1769), ii, 421; Rousselot de Surgy (1784–7), i, 177.

rates might be applied to the two types of property.[248] None of this was easy: should there be a single evaluation of wealth, with the two forms of property separately listed? What was meant by value? Was it the estimated market price, the annual rental income or the return that could be expected annually from the sale of its produce? Rental income seems to have been the norm at Siena, as it was at Treviso.[249] The wealth of about 7,000 taxpayers was evaluated in the three separate Sienese levies of 1285, a not inconsiderable administrative feat in itself.[250] A second type of evaluation, the Tables of Possessions (*Tavola delle Possessioni*), was attempted at Siena between 1316 and 1320: this was a more complex measurement, description and evaluation of real property (and perhaps movables as well) within the city-state, which was to be established with the aim of creating a just and equitable fiscal system. The experiment was too complex and it was abandoned in 1324. The Florentines repeated it in 1346, but they, too, had to abandon their scheme nine years later.[251]

For the purposes of direct taxes, Florence relied instead on forced loans (*prestanze*), the assessments of which were controlled in the interests of powerful citizens who protected themselves, rewarded friends and punished enemies. As their significance increased (Figure 82), complaints about the unfairness of their distribution multiplied.[252] A rural assessment (*estimo*) had been implemented in 1422–4. The Florentine *catasto* of 1427, based on the Venetian regulations of 1411,[253] was introduced with the purpose of establishing individual responsibility for the payment of taxes; providing evidence of liquid wealth, such as cash and business investments, so that taxation was not based solely on landed property; and, above all, eliminating fiscal injustice. The law of 24 May 1427 required declarations of their wealth from Florentine citizens and subjects as well as from adult servants. The unit of assessment was the fiscal hearth or tax-paying household. For landed property, instead of the 'just estimate' provided by neighbours, the basis for calculating the land's taxable value was to be the rent or return it yielded (taken to be half the total harvest). Property owners were required to draw up an exact list of rents received from each piece of property over the preceding three years: the rent was assumed to represent 7 per cent of the capital value of the property. The assessment of movable property was carried out by surveyors who entered what they considered to be its fair market

[248] Bowsky (1970), 70–2, 75–6, 78–9.

[249] Herlihy (1958), 78 n. 25.

[250] Waley in Denley and Elam (1988), 177.

[251] Bowsky (1970), 87–90, 96–7, 110–12.

[252] Molho (1971), 62, 76–7; Conti (1984), 81–3; ESFDB \rjb\italy\flogo01 based on \flodo01.

[253] Molho (1971), 79; Herlihy and Klapisch-Zuber (1978), 56–8, (1985), 9. The etymology (from the Greek *kata-stikhos*) suggests that the Venetians borrowed the word, and perhaps the method of assessment, from Byzantine practice.

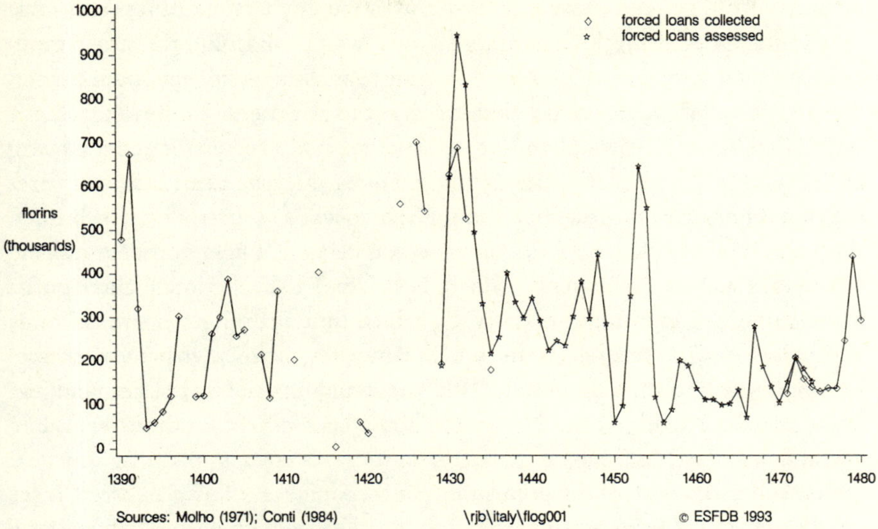

FIG. 82. Florentine forced loans, 1390–1480 (in florins)

value, with the proviso that in the case of disputes there had to be agreement between the owner and the officials. With the exception of shares in the public debt (*Monte*), liquid assets were more difficult to detect, but the surveyors could require the presentation of merchant account books, and compare the respective claims of debtors and creditors. In general, the difference between assets and liabilities constituted the taxable wealth (*soprabondante*) of the household, which was taxable at 0.5 per cent of the capitalization.[254] Despite the great sophistication of the Florentine *catasto*, it is worth remembering that the reform was of short duration: the quality of the information declined markedly in the two later *catasti* of 1430 and 1433. Fiscal pressure provoked further attempts to levy new funds 'by way of *catasto*' (*via catasti*) in 1442, 1451, 1458, 1469 and 1480; but in 1495 the system was permanently abandoned in favour of the *decima* or tithe.[255] This was in principle a 10 per cent property tax, which paid no attention to the size of the household. In practice, it was a tax of 10.5 per cent on households, and of 11.66 per cent on the yield of rent in the countryside; by the mid-eighteenth century it had risen to a tax of about 14 per cent on net revenue within the city, but less outside.[256]

The *catasto* was a product of a highly sophisticated urban political, social and

[254] Herlihy and Klapisch-Zuber (1985), 14–17 and (1978), 59–71; Molho (1971), 81; Herlihy (1972), 42–3 [repr. in Herlihy (1980)].

[255] Herlihy (1972), 45; Conti (1984), 320, 326.

[256] AN K 881 no. 3, 'Memoire sur le cadastre de Toscane et l'imposition qui en resulte', 31 May 1765.

administrative system. It was difficult to maintain this effort even in this environment; by definition, such techniques were impossible for larger monarchical states to emulate. No such experiment at fiscal equity was attempted in the French *bonnes villes*, which were reluctant to impose direct head taxes as a form of *taille*, and rarely adopted a consistent method of assessment over a long period of time.[257] Similarly, the Dutch towns in the seventeenth century preferred indirect taxes to direct ones; though there was a *capitation* tax, the burden on the smaller cities and the countryside was relatively light compared to the great cities such as Amsterdam, Leiden, Haarlem, Delft, Dordrecht and Gouda, at least until the eighteenth century, by which time tax on government bonds and other stocks levied by reducing the interest payment (the *100^e^ en 200^e^ penningen*) had become important.[258] In the kingdoms of Naples, England and France by the sixteenth century, the method of assessment for direct taxes had become fossilized and increasingly unrealistic as a means of taxing any real increase in the wealth of the population. In the kingdom of Naples, direct taxes nearly trebled between 1550 and 1638, but failed to keep up with inflation, since the levy was related to the number of hearths, which increased only modestly. Additional direct taxes became increasingly burdensome in the 1620s and 1640s, while the faults of the system were compounded by the fact that taxes were frequently collected by delegates of the state's creditors. Direct taxation represented 80 per cent of government income in 1550, but only 55 per cent by 1638.[259]

In England, the Tudor dynasty found the medieval tenths and fifteenths an insufficient basis for direct taxation, and established an intermittent lay subsidy (there were twelve subsidy acts in the forty-five-year reign of Elizabeth, for example),[260] which was intended to tax property and incomes more effectively. The form of this tax varied from 1513 until 1553, but in Mary's reign the rate was fixed at 4*s*. in the £ sterling for landed incomes, and 2*s*. 8*d*. in the pound for other property. These rates remained the same under Elizabeth: after 1563 the commissioners no longer had to make their returns under oath, while after 1566 individuals assessed themselves for tax purposes. The Privy Council suspected that wealthy men underassessed themselves at the expense of 'persons of the meaner sort'.[261] The result was that the subsidy was hopelessly out of date by the seventeenth century. (A similar situation prevailed with the quite separate assessment systems in Scotland by the end of the sixteenth century.)[262] Charles I

[257] Favier (1970), 40–60; Chevalier in Genet and Le Mené (1987), 145; Descimon (1989), 73–4.

[258] 't Hart (1989), 675–6; Fritschy (1990), 66–7.

[259] Calabria (1991), 58–66.

[260] Hartley (1992), 40. In 1589, the grant became a double subsidy (£280,000 over four years), and the last Parliament of the reign (1601) agreed to a contribution of four subsidies.

[261] Ibid. 52.

[262] Goodare (1989), 23–5, 46.

tried to innovate with the imposition of Ship Money during the 'eleven years' tyranny', but while his fiscal position was quite advantageous in time of peace, it was wholly inadequate in time of war without recourse to Parliament.[263] A permanent new form of taxation, the assessment, was not introduced until the Interregnum; this continued (with modifications) under the Restoration. A modified subsidy was introduced in 1671 and a hearth tax was added in 1660. All these various measures suffered from the disadvantage that there was no realistic valuation of property for tax purposes, and there were regional inequities. Charles Davenant had little difficulty in calculating that Ship Money had been more realistically assessed between the Home Counties and the rest of England than any subsequent direct tax prior to the land tax of 1692.[264]

A similar intractability of the system of direct taxes was evident in France. The *taille*, the chief direct tax in France, had been levied permanently on the *pays d'élections* since 1439. It had reached its apogee in real terms during the reign of Louis XI, and had not outstripped inflation again until the reign of Henri III.[265] Adam Smith commented on the *taille personnelle*: 'No man subject to such a tax, it is evident, can ever be certain, before he is assessed, of what he is to pay. He cannot even be certain after he is assessed ...'[266] Smith's viewpoint does not, perhaps, do sufficient justice to the government's attempts at reform and the real achievements brought about by reforming intendants in certain provinces. L'Averdy issued a declaration in 1768 which served to moderate some of the abuses in the apportionment of taxes,[267] while some of the experiments in a *taille tarifée*—at Limoges and Châlons,[268] but most notably the work of Bertier de Sauvigny in the *généralité* of Paris[269]—made a considerable advance in establishing a more equitable system (even if this was not always popular). Nevertheless, for the *pays d'élections* as a whole no advance was possible: the idea of a national *cadastre* was abandoned in 1763, almost at its inception. Necker's position on the *taille* was clear: it might not be possible to do without it, but there should be no further increases without registration in the *Parlements*, a measure enacted in February 1780.[270] In the long term, inflation would thus reduce the proportionate importance of the tax.[271]

263 Sharpe (1992), 105–30, 567–95.

264 Davenant, ed. Whitworth (1771), i, 38–9.

265 ESFDB \rjb\frd007 reprod. by Bonney in Bonney (1995); cf. Guéry (1985), 62.

266 Smith, ed. Campbell, Skinner and Todd (1976), ii, 855.

267 Marion (1910), 39–40, 159–64.

268 Ibid. 35–7, 153–6. The discussion of reform in *Mémoires*, ed. Moreau de Beaumont (1769), ii, 80–113, referred to the instructions of 1767 and the declaration of 1768, as well as to the intendants' work in the two *généralités*. Kain and Baigent (1992), 218–19.

269 Marion (1910), 43–4, 168–71; Touzery (1983); Kain and Baigent (1992), 220–1.

270 Harris (1979), 190; Necker (1791), 137; Marion (1910), 46, 174–8.

271 Bonney (1992*b*), 119, and ESFDB \rjb\elego06.

These comments apply only to the areas of *taille personnelle* within the *pays d'élections*. This was the greater part of France, but within some of the *pays d'états* the land tax (*taille réelle*) operated according to its own rules, which were specific to each province. Adam Smith noted that 'the real taille, as it is imposed only upon a part of the lands of the country, is necessarily an unequal, but it is not always an arbitrary tax, though it is so upon some occasions'; the land register of the *généralité* of Montauban, which was reformed by the intendant Claude Pellot in 1666, was deemed by 1727 to be 'altogether unequal'. It had to be remedied by additional assessments and remissions controlled by the provincial intendant.[272] Only in Dauphiné was a substantial reform undertaken on the initiative of the intendant Bouchu (called a *revision des feux*); but this task of reform, which was the most sophisticated in Louis XIV's France, proved to be of long duration and it was not completed by the time of the Regency and its abandonment in 1716.[273] The very term 'hearth' posed intractable problems of comparability between one province and another, given the differences in administrative practice for example between Burgundy and Brittany.[274] In Brittany, the number of hearths was of crucial importance, because there had never been a *cadastre*, and the number of taxable hearths (*feux roturiers*) had been reduced since the fifteenth century.[275]

Adam Smith equated the *vingtième* in France with the English land tax, which he took as the principal example of a fixed levy unrelated to fluctuations in rent. He was in no doubt about the superiority of the *vingtième* to the *taille*.[276] Originally introduced as a wartime measure in 1710, the tenth or *dixième* had been abolished in 1717, reintroduced in 1733 during the War of the Polish Succession, and again in 1741 at the outbreak of the War of the Austrian Succession. The regulations governing the administration of the tax remained unaltered; it was only in 1749, at the end of the war, that the *dixième* was revoked and a successor tax, the twentieth or *vingtième* replaced it in peacetime. This tax, too, was

[272] Smith, ed. Campbell, Skinner and Todd (1976), ii, 836, 854; *Mémoires*, ed. Moreau de Beaumont (1769), ii, 145; AN G^7 391, nos. 362, 367–437, 21 Nov. 1687 and *avis* of the intendant, 26 Nov. 1687.

[273] AN G^7 243, no. 409, 3 Sept. 1697 and above all nos. 434 and 435, instructions and decree of the council authorizing the 'revision generalle des feux de la province de Dauphiné', 27 Aug. 1697. On the revocation of the commission: AN G^7 251 nos. 7, 8, 21, 5 Sept., 8 Oct. 1716, 28 July 1718.

[274] AN G^7 190 no. 191, 6 Nov. 1710.

[275] Kerhervé (1987), ii, 549, 551, 578; (1992), II, 21. The original evaluation of 79,748 *feux contribuables* and 18,699 *feux exempts* was never realistic because of exemptions and the lower number of real hearths in the 15th cent.; subsequently there were *affranchissements des fouages* in 1577, 1638 and 1640 which were confirmed in 1710.

[276] Smith proposed the abolition of the *taille* and *capitation*, and an increase of the *vingtième*: Smith, ed. Campbell, Skinner and Todd (1976), ii, 904.

administered initially by regulations based on those of 1710; but Machault, the controller-general, tried to implement it as a significant fiscal reform. The attempt ended largely in failure in 1754. It was not until 1763 that a later controller-general, Bertin, tried to ensure that two *vingtièmes*—that is to say, the equivalent of the old *dixième*—should be levied and appropriate measures be taken to ensure a proper estimation of wealth (the idea of the land register or *cadastre*). The concerted resistance of the sovereign courts to this proposal forced the government to retreat, and in real terms the levy from the *vingtièmes* remained level or in decline until 1771. The Maupeou *coup d'état* encouraged Terray to attempt a revision of the method of assessment, such as Machault had envisaged in 1749: this would have formed the basis of a revised national tax, the *impôt territorial*.[277] Despite the work of verification by the controllers of the tax, the problem of realistic assessments remained: in the face of the resistance from the sovereign courts, only 4,902 parishes out of 22,508 within the *pays d'élections* had their rolls verified between 1772 and 1782; but this resulted in an increased levy of nearly a half in the parishes concerned.[278]

The English land tax of 1692, introduced to finance 'a vigorous war against France', was established without any surveying or mapping. The tax returns listed the owner and/or occupier of each property, its rack rent and the amount of tax paid; but they did not always give the name of the property, nor did they indicate its acreage or boundaries.[279] Originally equitable at the time of its establishment, the English land tax necessarily became 'unequal in process of time, according to the unequal degrees of improvement or neglect in the cultivation of different parts of the country'. The fixed nature of the tax had worked to the advantage of the taxpayer rather than the ruler, since rents had risen continually since the establishment of the tax in 1692 but the value of the money had remained constant.[280] Considered by foreign observers in the 1760s to be in general terms equivalent to a tax of one-fifth on land, but subject to the greatest regional and personal inequities,[281] the land tax was a heavy burden in wartime until the 1740s, as a result of agricultural depression. However, the failure to revise the national land values drawn up in 1692 meant that landowners' new-found prosperity after 1750 was not taxed. Improved husbandry was

277 Marion (1910), 103, 362–5.

278 Ibid. 107–8, 317.

279 Kain and Baigent (1992), 257–9, who comment: 'A mapped or surveyed cadaster would necessarily have been in the hands of professional surveyors under the control of central government and would have removed control of the tax from the local landowners and as such was unthinkable.'

280 Smith, ed. Campbell, Skinner and Todd (1976), ii, 828–30.

281 Hartmann (1979), 50–2.

not discouraged by the land tax; it may even have been encouraged, as some foreign observers such as Pagnini believed;[282] more correctly, perhaps, Smith thought that it neither encouraged nor discouraged improvement.[283] It may also have been the case that the costs of the English land tax were fundamentally borne not by the landlords but by farmers and their labourers, though this issue remains contentious.[284] Doubtless landlords sought compensation through increasing their rents, but it is unlikely that the full burden of direct taxes was shared by this means. A comparison of rent movements with fluctuations in the rate at which land tax was collected in England does not suggest that the fiscal burden was fully transferred from landlord to tenant, no doubt because of the length of leases, which ensured that changes in rent levels would lag behind alterations in the tax rate. By the 1790s, the land tax was no longer biting as it had done earlier in the century.

Adam Smith noted that the Physiocrats had recommended as 'the most equitable of all taxes' a tax upon the rent of land which 'rises and falls according to the improvement or neglect of cultivation'. He drew upon the French survey of 1763 to illustrate his argument, using as an example the Venetian tax of one-tenth of the value of arable leases, which he considered to be 'certainly more equal than the land tax of England' although expensive to administer. He considered the 'moderate abatement' of tax to those landlords who cultivated their own land a desirable encouragement to agricultural improvement, but in general a variable land tax on the Venetian model served rather as a discouragement.[285] Smith also noted the advantages of a register of leases, and was fully aware of the importance of the European movement for cadastral reform (Chapter 10.5): he talked of 'an equitable valuation in consequence of an accurate survey, like that which was lately made in the Milanese, and in the dominions of Austria, Prussia and Sardinia'.[286] The Bohemian *cadastre* was not particularly influential since it

[282] AN K 881 no. 3, 'Memoire sur le cadastre de Toscane et l'imposition qui en resulte' (31 May 1765): 'M. Pagnini . . . croit que le meilleur cadastre a sa connoissance est celui établi en Angletere en 1698, ce qu'on reconnoit encore par les effets merveilleux qu'il y a produit, surtout à l'avantage de l'agriculture . . . '

[283] Smith, ed. Campbell, Skinner and Todd (1976), ii, 839. Ricardo denied that any land tax could be an encouragement to agriculture: Ricardo, ed. Sraffa and Dobb (1951–5), i, 188.

[284] O'Brien (1988), 19; Brewer (1989), 203; Beckett and Turner (1990), 387. Ricardo had his own views on the shifting of the burden: Ricardo, ed. Sraffa and Dobb (1951–5), i, 186.

[285] Cf. *Mémoires*, ed. Moreau de Beaumont (1768), i, 240; AN K 880 no. 1. The proprietor paid 8 per cent of his revenue.

[286] Smith, ed. Campbell, Skinner and Todd (1976), ii, 934. For Austria: Vann in Buisseret (1992), 165–6; Kain and Baigent (1992), 191–2.

was the product of a gradual evolution over a century.[287] Prussia introduced a new *cadastre* in Silesia, which it occupied after 1740, and noble landholdings were taxed at 3 per cent higher than those on base tenure;[288] the revenue of the church was taxed more heavily than that of lay proprietors (at 50 per cent as against 38.33 per cent of net revenue) because the greater part was a burden upon the rent of land.[289] Referring to the French enquiry of 1763, Smith also noted the movement for cadastral reform in Savoy and Piedmont[290] and in the duchy of Milan, 'the most accurate [*cadastre*] that has yet been made'.[291] He concluded that for its effectiveness, cadastral reform depended on 'the continual and painful attention of government to all the variations of the state and produce of every different farm in the country'; such an attention, in his view, was 'so unsuitable to the nature of government, that [it] is not likely to be of long continuance, and which, if it is continued, will probably in the long-run occasion much more trouble and vexation than it can possibly bring relief to the contributors'.[292]

It should be noted that Smith's remarks contrast strongly with the tone of his source material, the French enquiry of 1763, particularly with regard to the perceived advantages of the cadastral survey in the realms of the king of Sardinia.[293] Smith could not have anticipated the success of the French *cadastre* introduced under Gaudin, and of the French influence on other European countries, where the new land registers were introduced together with the metric system and the Napoleonic Code.[294] Even in Napoleonic France, however, the implementation of the *cadastre parcellaire* was slow because of the time taken to carry out the surveys: 9,000 communes, comprising 12 million hectares, were surveyed between 1808 and 1814. The task was not completed until 1850, by which time it was recognized that fundamental revision was

[287] *Mémoires*, ed. Moreau de Beaumont (1768), 183; AN K 879 no. 70. For the Bohemian *cadastre* of 1747 and subsequent reforms: Dickson (1987), ii, 224ff.

[288] *Mémoires*, ed. Moreau de Beaumont (1768), 119; AN K 879 no. 81. Hartmann reprinted detailed classifications of types of cultivation and the distribution of taxes: Hartmann (1979), 203–13; Baumgart in Greengrass (1991), 165. Doubtless the Silesian *cadastre* was based on earlier Prussian experience in Cleves: Kain and Baigent (1992), 153–7.

[289] Cf. *Mémoires*, ed. Moreau de Beaumont (1768), 119; AN K 879 no. 81; Rousselot de Surgy (1784–7), iii, 409.

[290] Cf. Symcox (1983), 123–7, 202–6; Kain and Baigent (1992), 188–90, 213–17.

[291] Cf. Klang (1977); Kain and Baigent (1992), 181–5.

[292] Smith, ed. Campbell, Skinner and Todd (1976), ii, 836.

[293] Cf. *Mémoires*, ed. Moreau de Beaumont (1768), 312–15; AN K 880 no. 59.

[294] Marion (1925), 256–9, 307–12; Ardant (1971–2), ii, 197–209, and (1965), i, 227–9, 456–7; Pro Ruiz (unpubd) argued that 'the Napoleonic cadaster was to be the model on which all cadasters of Continental Europe would be worked out, making allowances for the autochthonous traditions of each region, inherited from the seventeenth century'; Kain and Baigent (1992), 233–4.

necessary.[295] Napoleon was a man of the *ancien régime*, and the *cadastre* was an *ancien régime* reform, yet even the Revolutionary governments, for all their loathing of indirect taxes, were remarkably conservative in their reforms of direct taxation. The Revolution proclaimed the principle that taxes should be 'apportioned equally among all citizens according to their capacity to pay'[296] and introduced a land tax, a (largely unworkable)[297] tax on movables and a commercial profits tax (Chapter 11.4). The most important of these was the *contribution foncière*, the new direct tax replacing the cluster of *ancien régime* taxes on land (*taille*, *vingtièmes* and so on), which accepted an important Physiocratic principle in that it was to be a tax on net revenue (the *foncière* was not to exceed one-sixth of net revenue).[298] Though the proportion of taxes on land to direct taxes as a whole may have fallen slightly (from about 80 per cent before 1789 to about 75 per cent after 1790),[299] this relatively trivial change was accompanied by a significant attempt to improve the equity of tax assessments through the abolition of privilege. On the other hand, until the whole country could be surveyed for the *cadastre*, continuing reliance was placed on the tax rolls of the *ancien régime*, which perpetuated glaring regional disparities.[300] The sums actually collected were much lower than the nominal levy for the land tax, which stood at 240 million francs in 1791 and 1792 (Figure 42).[301] Another aspect of continuity with the *ancien régime* was the continuing reliance of the Revolutionary direct tax system either on estimates of wealth or voluntary declarations: asking people voluntarily to declare their profits was like saying 'lie to me' (*mens-moi*), it had been argued in 1775.[302] Direct taxes are particularly susceptible to changes in the methods of collection and enforcement. Here, the most significant change was the revocation of the provincial intendants in 1790, who had played a crucial role under the *ancien régime*. With the exception of the forced loan of 1793, the Revolution failed to secure tax compliance from its subjects until effective collection and enforcement procedures were introduced in 1797, when these

[295] Herbin and Rebereau (1953), 23–9; ibid. 21, for the linkage in Napoleon's mind in 1807 between the Code and the *cadastre*; Kain and Baigent (1992), 228–9.

[296] Doyle (1989), 119; Bonney (1992*a*), 176, both quoting article 13 of the Declaration of the Rights of Man and the Citizen.

[297] Gross (1993), 108.

[298] Hincker (1989), 100, who summarizes the details of the fiscal changes of the Revolution. Cf. Du Pont de Nemours' criticism of the *dîme* and call in 1789 for a tax on net revenue: McLain (1977), 146–8.

[299] Le Goff and Sutherland in Forrest and Jones (1991), 83 n. 60.

[300] Sutherland (1989), 103.

[301] Mascard in *État, finances et économie* (1991), 374; Marion (1919), 193, commented that the levy was too high, as a result of the predominance of Physiocratic theories and an overestimate of net landed income (1,440 or 1,500 million).

[302] Gross (1993), 101.

responsibilities were conferred on new directorial tax commissioners who had the power to billet troops in cases of non-compliance. Napoleon built upon the system created by the Directory.[303] However, the land tax was unpopular with the landed classes, who were offended by the continuing discrepancies in fiscal burden according to location and its detrimental effect upon producers. Physiocratic arguments were stood on their head when, under Napoleon, the case for indirect taxes was presented: 'it may be true that all comes from the land and must return to the land' but it certainly was not 'true that all must fall as direct taxes upon the land'.[304]

The most lasting innovation of the eighteenth century was not the Revolutionary reform of direct taxes, or the Napoleonic *cadastre*, but income tax. As has been seen (Chapter 6.5), Boisguilbert, Vauban and Saint-Pierre had all wrestled with the idea of progressive direct taxation. The chevalier de Jaucourt in 1765 had argued that the principle of geometric progression could be applied to all forms of taxation, while Jean-Louis Graslin in 1767 introduced the expression 'progressive' in relation to taxation and argued that while the rich man might pay a quarter of his revenue in tax, the lower classes would pay one-fifth, one-eighth, one-twentieth and so on downwards, until the last class was reached of those who would pay nothing because all they had were physical necessities. Condorcet and Théodore Vernier both proposed progressive tax schemes in the 1790s, but it was not until the crisis of the war in 1792–3 that Robespierre tabled a new draft Declaration of the Rights of Man which asserted the principle of progression: 'Those citizens whose incomes do not exceed what is necessary to their subsistence shall be exempted from contributing to public expenditure; the others shall support it progressively, according to their fortune.'[305] A forced loan was levied in 1793, which was in effect a 'progressive income tax' and resulted in a levy of about 300 million francs on the basis of voluntary declarations. Nearly all the money was collected at a moment of great national crisis; but the effort was not repeated.[306] As Ramel observed, there was a considerable difference between a public loan imposed once only and a permanent progressive tax which should aim at equalizing fortunes gently ('par des voies douces'). Nevertheless, the forced loan with its notional ceiling of 4,500 *livres* in income after tax (thus the fifteenth tax band of 15,000 *livres* in taxable income required a payment of 10,500 *livres* in tax), together with other radical proposals, provided a fairly clear idea of

[303] Sutherland (1989), 346; Doyle (1989), 333–4, 384; Théret (1991); Hardman (1993), 178; Crouzet (1993), 454, 460–2.

[304] Marion (1925), 297–307; Collins (1989), 85.

[305] Gross (1993), 115.

[306] Sutherland (1989), 310, 325–6, gives the traditional figures; Mascard in *État, finances et économie* (1991), 374, 384, revises these upwards.

the sort of tax policy which would have been pursued after the war had the Jacobin experiment succeeded. After 1794, graduation in French tax structures was ruled out, tainted as it was by the stigma of Jacobinism.[307]

The influence of Jacobin rhetoric and action in 1793 was considerable outside France. The Dutch, who had earlier inspired Lord North's additions to the stock of English direct taxes during the War of American Independence,[308] were clearly influenced by it under the Batavian Republic, when the first tax on incomes was levied in 1797 at a rate of 8 per cent after a very close vote (58 to 54) in the National Assembly. In 1798 and 1800, income taxes with progressive rates were levied. However, even the dedicated reformer Isaac Gogel was unable significantly to alter the balance of taxation between heavy indirect excises on primary necessities and an intermittent income tax. Rather than continue with the income tax, with its possible resort to search, sequestration and imprisonment, Gogel preferred the continuation of the *verponding* of the *ancien régime*, a tax on all forms of property, which had the advantage of being open to legal certification and for which there were cadastral maps.[309] Under the Batavian Republic and successor regimes, this constituted about 20 or 25 per cent of total revenue as against 10 per cent under the old *verponding* of Holland. Gogel insisted on assessments being carried out by government-appointed officials without local interests and on rental averages over fifteen years, rather than relying on market prices which were depressed as a result of the recession in wartime.[310]

The English income tax of 1799 was no more a permanent solution to the problem of insufficient tax revenue than its Dutch counterpart, though this owed less to its deficiencies than to political opposition to its continuation after the end of the war. Critics argued that income tax was 'worthy only of the French Council of Five Hundred' and that its introduction would amount 'to neither more nor less than the introduction of a plan for equalizing fortunes'.[311] A precursor of the income tax was implemented in 1798 (the Aid and Contribution Act), which divided taxpayers into three categories; while the normal rate of tax was 10 per cent, rates were progressively reduced on all incomes below £200, until at £60 no tax at all was payable. Above £200, taxpayers were invited to make additional voluntary contributions, so as to ensure that they paid 10 per cent of

[307] Gross (1993), 115–17, 121–2; this loan, and later experiments, are discussed by Crouzet (1993), 247–8, 250, 479–82.

[308] Seligman (1914), 59.

[309] Kain and Baigent (1992), 27–32, for the situation before the reform of 1805; ibid. 32–9, for the reforms of 1805 and subsequently.

[310] Schama in Winter (1975), 123, 126, 136 n. 84; Schama (1977*a*), 292–4, 305, 385; Fritschy (1990), 70–1.

[311] Gross (1993), 122.

their income. The triple assessment of 1798, which used expenditure as a proxy for income, proved a failure: the yield proved disappointing, £2 million instead of the £4.5 million estimated by Pitt, a consequence (in Pitt's words) of 'the difficulties which the measure encountered from the shameful evasion, or rather the scandalous frauds by which its effects were counteracted'. Voluntary contributions amounted to £2 million instead of the estimated £1.5 million, however.[312] The Act of 1799 for Taxing Income imposed taxation on all aspects of an individual's income, divided into four sections or heads (income from landed property; personal property and from trades, professions, pensions, stipends, employments and vocations; income arising outside Britain; and income not falling under any of the other rules). Pitt had estimated the yield at £10 million, but it produced only just over £6 million.[313] In two important respects, it was a conservative measure: firstly, taxation was limited to a flat rate of 2 shillings in the pound, or 10 per cent of total income; moreover, the declarations of wealth were voluntary. Contemporary opinion conceded that the tax was just and equitable precisely because it was not progressive, but left 'those persons ... affected by it in precisely the same relative situation, one towards another, after its operation as they were previously to its imposition ...'[314] Addington's modifications to the tax in 1803 fundamentally changed the method of assessment, providing in effect for a series of taxes assessed under different categories or schedules. Schedule A dealt with the 'landlord's duty', levied on the annual rent of lands and tenements less deductions for repairs. Schedule B dealt with the 'tenant's duty', while Schedule C taxed all 'profits arising from annuities, dividends (that is, interest on moneys invested in government funds or securities) and shares of annuities', which were to be paid by the stockholders or their agents. Schedule D taxed the profits arising from all property not taxed in the previous schedules or chargeable under Schedule E (the latter comprising income from public office or employment). The principle of stoppage at source was introduced in 1803, which produced a yield from the tax (£5.35 million) that was almost the same as in 1801, yet the rate of tax had been halved. In 1806, the principle of stoppage at source was greatly extended, so that the Bank of England itself was to make the assessment under Schedule C; the rate of tax was increased from 6.25 per cent to 10 per cent, and the combined effect of these changes resulted in a doubling of the yield to £12.8 million, while in most years until the end of the war in 1815 the figure was higher than this (Figure 83).[315] Pitt had

[312] Seligman (1914), 66, 71.

[313] Ibid. 79, 87.

[314] Sabine (1966), 27–8; Hope-Jones (1939), 17; Shehab (1953), 48.

[315] Seligman (1914), 102, 105, 115; ESFDB \obrien\engb003 based on \engm010; yield of different schedules in Hope-Jones (1939), 77–8; the effectiveness of the schedules discussed ibid. 117–18.

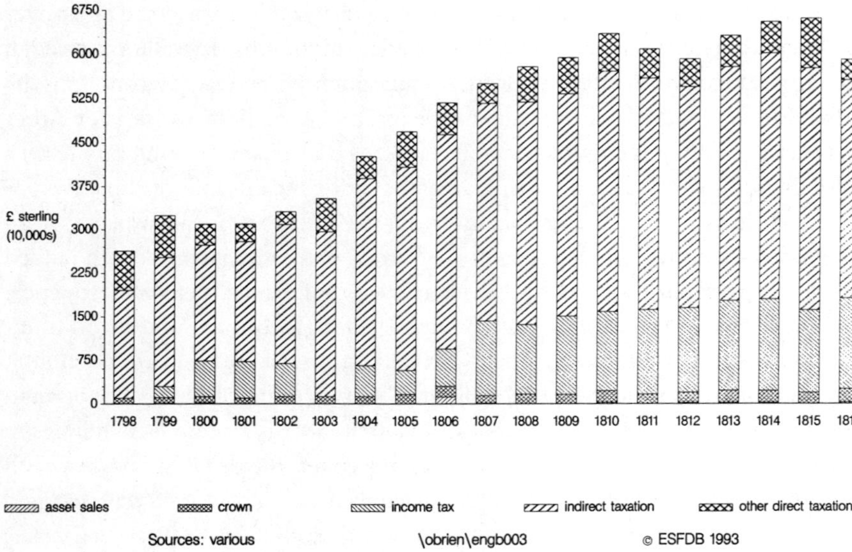

FIG. 83. Categories of revenue to the British government, 1798–1816 (in £ sterling)

assured Parliament that the Act sought to avoid 'improper disclosures of circumstances which were repugnant to the manners and customs of the nation', and after its repeal in 1802 and 1816, the papers held by the income tax commissioners were destroyed.[316] The City of London called the tax 'insupportable': 'the manner in which the tax is carried into execution (by means of an odious, arbitrary, and detestable inquisition into the most private concerns and circumstances of individuals)' was considered vexatious, unjust and oppressive, and repugnant to the principles of the British constitution.[317] Indeed, only the success of the armies of Revolutionary France and the probable collapse of public credit prompted the political classes in England to accept the Act as a temporary measure in 1799, subject to its immediate repeal after a peace treaty.[318]

13.6 *Indirect Taxes*

'The impossibility of taxing the people, in proportion to their revenue, by any capitation', according to Adam Smith, 'seems to have given occasion to the invention of taxes upon consumable commodities.' Historically, Smith's verdict may not be correct, though it is undoubtedly true that there was a

[316] Seligman (1914), 88, 113; O'Brien in Dickinson (1989), 184.

[317] Seligman (1914), 110; Hope-Jones (1939), 114–16.

[318] Hope-Jones (1939), 116; O'Brien (1988), 22.

European-wide move towards consumption taxes and excises in the eighteenth century as wealth became more diversified and the *capitation* or poll tax no longer an appropriate or sufficient instrument for fiscal purposes.[319] As Smith put it,

> the state not knowing how to tax, directly and proportionably [*sic*], the revenue of its subjects, endeavours to tax it indirectly by taxing their expence [*sic*], which, it is supposed, will in most cases be nearly in proportion to their revenue. Their expence is taxed by taxing the consumable commodities upon which it is laid out.[320]

Indirect taxes appealed to governments because of the apparently voluntary payment of taxation at the time the item was purchased. The ancient Greeks had thus seen indirect taxation as the badge of liberty, while direct taxes were chiefly levied against outsiders.[321] The incidence of taxation appeared to be hidden in the sale price of the product, which led the Swedish Chancellor Axel Oxenstierna to pronounce indirect taxes 'pleasing to God, hurtful to no man, and not provocative of rebellion'.[322] (In contrast, where indirect taxes were less clearly hidden, and the tax was levied on commodities such as bread, this maxim was proven wrong—this was the case with the revolt at Palermo in 1647, where the oppressive nature of the tax was evident in the form of a reduction in the weight of bread from 11¾ ounces to 10 ounces; a popular revolt ensued.) Sir Matthew Decker proposed in his *Essay on the Causes of the Decline of Foreign Trade* (1744) that indirect taxes should be paid annually, half-yearly or quarterly by the purchase of licences. (Decker wanted to cut indirect taxes, and to reduce and simplify customs duties in the hope both of stimulating trade and eliminating smuggling.)[323] Adam Smith pointed out that such a scheme would diminish 'one of the principal conveniencies [*sic*] of taxes upon goods of speedy consumption; the piece-meal payment'. In a system of indirect taxation where there was no monopoly right or coercion of payment, individuals paid their taxes as they consumed their goods, and when they could afford to do so.[324]

It has already been seen—in the context of revenue administration and unification—that in the medieval Italian city-states there was widespread recourse to the farming of taxes, particularly *gabelles*, and that while not all *gabelles* were indirect taxes most were. The majority of *gabelles* applied to and were collected in the city, rather than the countryside, as was recognized at Siena in 1334.[325] The greater proportionate reliance on indirect taxes in the cities was not

319 Seligman (1914), 11.

320 Smith, ed. Campbell, Skinner and Todd (1976), ii, 869.

321 Adams (1993), 52, 54.

322 Roberts in Aston (1965), 200.

323 Kennedy (1913), 114–15, 132–3; Brewer (1989), 216.

324 Smith, ed. Campbell, Skinner and Todd (1976), ii, 877–8.

325 Bowsky (1970), 118–19.

unique to the Italian republics: a similar situation prevailed at Ghent, for example, where regressive taxes on the 'popular' varieties of wine, on beer, the grain assize, and the tax on firewood had serious social consequences. There were 548 tax receivers and revenue farmers at Ghent between 1348 and 1455, the two types of official being drawn from the same social group (whose members were Flemings to a man). There was a distinct preference for tax-farming, particularly once the harvest had been collected and its success was known: direct administration or *régie* was practised only at the beginning of the fiscal year, when potential tax-farmers were likely to be cautious in their bidding because the state of the harvest was an unknown quantity.[326]

At the risk of oversimplification, indirect taxes may be divided into three main types of tax (it has already been seen that Adam Smith and David Ricardo distinguished them according to economic function: Chapter 6.7). The first is toll revenue, which might be levied on internal or external trade and defined by the state or the city. This might take the form of the multifarious gate *gabelles*, that is to say, differential rates of tax levied on the entry of goods into the city, practised by the Italian city republics at an early date—for example at Siena and Florence.[327] The administration of internal toll revenue in sixteenth-century Muscovy was certainly farmed out, on the whole to merchants in the towns.[328] The fluctuations in toll revenue in states with a high proportion of foreign trade in transit can reveal the relative importance of different trades and shifts of economic importance from one area to another.[329] Alternatively, tolls might be levied at a convenient transit point for shipping, such as the Danish Sound. Other states with a less convenient geographical position could nevertheless seek revenue from a comparable source: though not originally intended for this purpose, the great English revenue source in the later Middle Ages was the tax on wool exports, and later cloth exports and imports.[330] In the years after 1670, customs revenue did not grow as fast as excise receipts, but in constant prices had risen from an average of £0.2 million in the 1670s to £2.2 million in the 1770s. In current prices, they rose from £3.3 million in 1785 to £18.8 million in 1810. As a proportion of revenue, however, customs duties tended to fall, from about one-third of royal income in the period 1675–85 to less than a quarter a century later, though with a marked tendency to rise once more after 1790.[331] Adam

[326] Boone (1989), 113–18; Boone (1990), 213–18. The author is grateful to Professor Maarten Prak for drawing attention to these works and providing an English summary of the article cited above.

[327] Bowsky (1970), 158–9; La Roncière (1968), 152–5, 163–5.

[328] Bushkovitch (1978).

[329] Körner (1992).

[330] Prestwich (1982), 55; Bonney (1992*c*), 24.

[331] O'Brien (1988), 14; ibid. 9 (table 4), and 15 (table 6, col. 4); Brewer (1989), 96–9. Beckett and Turner (1990), 379–81, show a decline to 19.5 per cent in 1796–9, however.

Smith quoted 'the opinion of many people, that, by proper management, the duties of customs might ... without any loss to the public revenue, and with great advantage to foreign trade, be confined to a few articles only ...'[332] In reality, increased customs revenue was a consequence of a growth in English trade rather than a policy of increasing duties. Bilateral treaties presented a constraint on the possibility of raising more revenue in the form of duties on retained imports, while after 1722 exports were not only untaxed but in the case of some commodities enjoyed bounties or subsidies when sold abroad.[333]

It was a weakness of the Castilian financial system in the late Middle Ages that because the Mesta gained great privileges over transhumance grazing rights, the fiscal aspects of the *servicio y montazgo* were insufficiently exploited by the crown.[334] On the other hand, the important wool exports of Castile were taxed, by the *derecho nuevo* and the *derecho antiguo*: the second tax, unlike the first, was levied at differential rates according to the quality of the wool and was collected only on the south and east coasts; the north-coast wool exports were exempted since they already paid an ordinary export duty (*diezmo de la mar de Castilla*).[335] In the kingdom of Naples, with a predominantly pastoral economy, the control of transhumance grazing rights was systematically exploited by Alfonso V of Aragon and royal commissioners collected fees based on the number of animals.[336] Revenues from the Foggia Sheep Customhouse remained an important aspect of royal income in Naples particularly until 1611.[337] After 1553, the sheep census (*numerazione*) was replaced by a complex system of estimation called 'free bidding' (*professazione voluntaria*) in an attempt to extract more revenue. The result was an inflated rise in the number of sheep. A fixed tax arrangement (*transazione*) was substituted for the free bids in 1615, and for the next forty years this was renegotiated and increased at regular intervals: the graziers paid an agreed fixed sum plus an additional levy, but there were clearly abuses ('The powerful people declare fewer sheep than they really have and they make the poor pay more than is their due ...'). The 'free bidding' system was re-established in 1661 to encourage renewed pastoral investment, and this system continued until 1805 (Figure 84).[338] In general, the crucial point about the levies discussed above is that they reflected primarily the volume of internal or external trade, or the success of a primary pastoral activity depending on the nature of the

332 Smith, ed. Campbell, Skinner and Todd (1976), ii, 883.

333 O'Brien (1988), 23–4.

334 Ladero Quesada in Genet and Le Mené (1987), 41, 44; Ladero Quesada (1989), 42.

335 Israel (1980), 196, n. to table 2.

336 Ryder (1976), 359; *Mémoires*, ed. Moreau de Beaumont (1768), 428–9; AN K 881 no. 25.

337 Calabria (1991), 69–73.

338 ESFDB \rjb\italy\napgoo1 based on \napdoo1, based on Marino (1988), 277–83; ibid. 30–1, 34–5, 149–51, 283; Villari (1993), 145–6.

levy and the point at which it was made.[339] An administrative infrastructure was required, and in some cases (as with the Foggia Customhouse)[340] surveys and maps were needed to enforce the right to tax. Since the ruler could manipulate the rate of tax, the impersonal forces of the economy did not necessarily determine the revenue yield; but an economic depression would inevitably reduce revenue even if the rates of tax were temporarily lowered at the same time, while an accident such as the decimation of sheep in 1611–12 at Naples clearly had disastrous fiscal implications.

Levies on commercial transactions or on consumption were a second main type of indirect tax. These, too, were subject to demographic and economic fluctuations; but in general a rise in the price of goods and a growth in population would tend to yield more revenue to the state. The converse is also true: indirect taxes added substantially to the cost of living in a period of inflation and could thus be oppressive. For example, prices doubled at Florence between the 1350s and 1370s; but taxation by itself raised the price of oil by 13 per cent, the price of casked wine by 22 per cent, and the retail cost of wine by 66 per cent.[341] Over the long term, the increase in tax revenue arising from wine sales at Lucerne, for example (Figure 85),[342] was a consequence of economic growth and a rise in personal expenditure. Yet a rise in indirect taxes on sales may also reflect a greater capacity on the part of government to tax commodities which were in demand, and which may in turn have restricted that demand. The rise in the English malt and beer duties in wartime after 1702 is a case in point. Adam Smith contended that 'it has probably been the interest of this superior order of people . . . which has hitherto prevented a change of system that could not well fail both to increase the revenue and to relieve the people', but his proposed single tax on malt was not introduced until the Napoleonic wars, while the beer tax remained until 1830.[343] There was a general European trend, probably based on Dutch experience, to move towards a broad excise on goods (although, it has been observed, the Dutch had no general excise but multiple excises; nor is it certain that the term 'excise' was of Dutch origin).[344] The French 5 per cent sales tax of 1640–3, although abortive, was specifically modelled on the Dutch, though it is uncertain whether the earlier experiment in the reign of Henri IV had also been

339 Körner (1980), 100–1.

340 Marino in Buisseret (1992), 15–16.

341 La Roncière (1968), 186–7.

342 ESFDB \korner\swig003 based on \swid004; Körner (1981), 140–1 and unpubd data supplied by Professor Körner.

343 Smith, ed. Campbell, Skinner and Todd (1976), ii, 893. Cf. his refutation of Davenant at ibid. ii, 891. For Davenant's view that 'as the duty now lies, the whole people contribute towards it, as traders or consumers . . . ': Davenant, ed. Whitworth (1771), i, 223; Mathias (1959), 355–61.

344 't Hart (1991), 43–4.

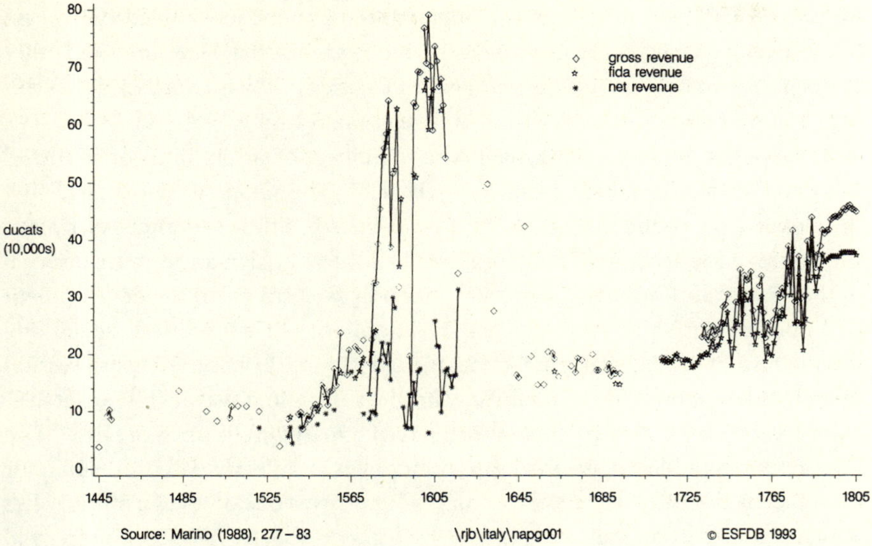

FIG. 84. Revenue from sheep in Foggia, 1445–1805 (in ducats)

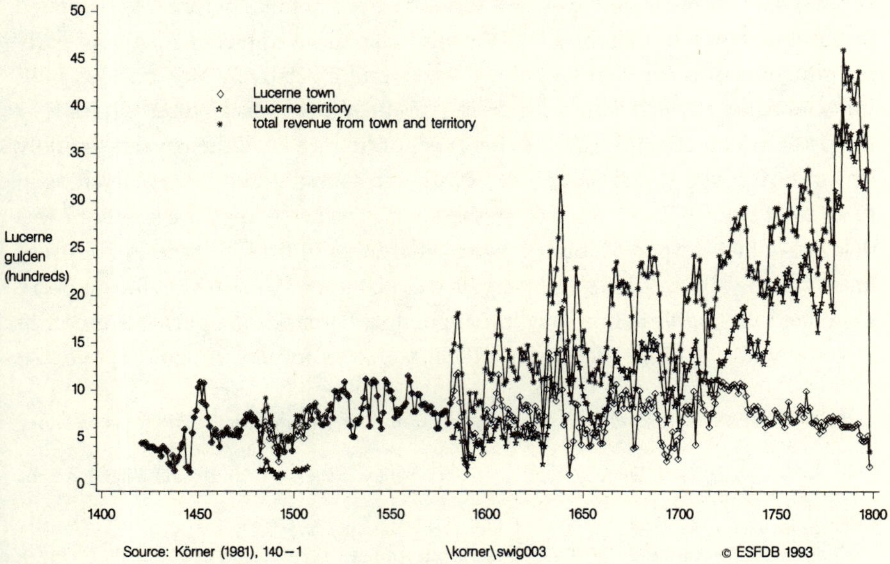

FIG. 85. Revenue to the state of Lucerne from taxes on wine sales, 1421–1798 (in Lucerne *gulden*)

influenced by this example.[345] In England, Parliament introduced excises on tobacco, wine, cider, beer, imported silks, furs, hats, leather, lace, linen and other items in 1643 to help finance its war against Charles I. It was contended that this was 'the most easy and equal way' of raising tax revenue.[346]

Monopolies formed a third main type of indirect taxation. In most countries salt was a monopoly item from an early date. The Chinese empire had first developed a salt monopoly under the T'ang dynasty in the years after 758; by 780, the salt revenue accounted for more than half the annual income at the disposal of the central authorities.[347] The salt monopoly was critical in the development of Venetian public finance and had a central role in its political, social and commercial life.[348] Similarly at Genoa, the salt monopoly became the possession of the banking house, the *Casa di San Giorgio*, in 1454 and was highly profitable, although care was taken to prevent excessive increases in the price of salt.[349] The Tuscan city republics developed salt monopolies at an early date—at Siena, for example, by the early thirteenth century, where it was one of several monopolies which included iron, grain, oil and fish.[350] Florence, too, had a state monopoly in salt. An individual or a community had to buy a given quantity of salt at a given price. The fiscal yield could be improved either by increasing the prescribed quantity of salt, or by raising the price, both of which were done in the fourteenth century.[351] By the first third of the fifteenth century it was yielding a revenue second only to the *gabelle* of the gates.[352]

Thus the salt monopoly was well tested in city republics before it was applied to the European monarchies.[353] We may take as examples a relatively early introduction of a royal monopoly (France) and a relatively late one (Russia). Introduced for the first time perhaps in 1331, the salt tax was an intermittent levy in northern France until 1366, when a royal ordinance gave the royal monopoly its juridical basis, which was to last (with substantial amendments, such as in 1680) until 1790.[354] The extension of the tax into other parts of the kingdom was delayed, which helped account for the differences in fiscal regime in the provinces which were to prove enduring: it was not until 1411 that the duc de Berry organized the *gabelle* definitively in Languedoc. Later on, the personal union of Brittany with the lands of Charles VIII in 1491 created new difficulties, because

345 Bonney (1981*a*), 14, 50, 183–5. Sully was silent on any Dutch origins for the idea in 1596: Bonney (1992*b*), 125 n. 74.

346 't Hart (1991), 44–5; Kennedy (1913), 54–5. For hostility to the word 'excise' in England: Adams (1993), 261.

347 Twitchett (1963), 51–2.

348 Hocquet in Bonney (1995).

349 Heers (1961), 136–40.

350 Herlihy (1958), 83.

351 La Roncière (1968), 158–61.

352 Molho (1971), 54.

353 The two syntheses on the salt monopoly are Hocquet (1985) and Adshead (1992).

354 Hocquet (1985), 283–5; *Mémoires*, ed. Moreau de Beaumont (1769), iii, 3–6.

the Bretons demanded permanent exemption from the tax. The attempts of Francis I and Henri II to create a unified tax regime for the *gabelle* failed as a result of the concerted opposition of that other privileged region, the provinces of the south-west, which had known only a light salt tax (called *quartage*) under their former English masters. The concessions made to them by Charles VII in 1445, in the last decade of the struggle to secure English expulsion, thus proved enduring. The territorial acquisitions of the seventeenth century did not lead to any gain from the point of view of an extension of the *gabelle*. Instead, Colbert's reforming ordinance of 1680 fossilized the status quo: France was divided into twelve *généralités* within the *pays de grandes gabelles*, with 253 *greniers*, some of which were *greniers de vente volontaire*, others *greniers d'impôt*; an area known as the *pays rédimés et provinces exemptes*; a number of provinces with *petites gabelles*, including Languedoc, where the tax was first levied in France, but which never experienced its (objectionable) full impact; and finally the *pays de salines et de quart-bouillon* (notably that part of Normandy which experienced the revolt of the Va-Nu-Pieds in 1639). The complexity of the divisions required a heavy administrative apparatus for enforcement of the farmers' rights, which in turn led to mapping.[355]

The fiscal burden represented by the *gabelle* varied enormously between these regions, but for all its incompetence and corruption, the French monarchy was aware of these variations in the level of so-called 'indirect' taxation and sought to compensate for them by increasing direct taxes in those provinces which were privileged:[356] but it may be doubted whether the crown was able to do so effectively.[357] Where the tax was most oppressive, within the *pays de grandes gabelles*, its description by historians as an 'indirect' tax requires modification. A true indirect tax is one which the consumer consents to pay because he is free to choose whether or not to purchase the item which is taxed; there is an element of social equality in the tax, because both rich and poor pay the tax according to their level of consumption. The *gabelle* in northern France fits neither of these definitions of an indirect tax. Since salt was an essential item of consumption, individuals could scarcely choose whether or not to purchase it; in any case, they were in many cases required to purchase a set amount. In 1638, the *cahier* of the estates of Normandy contained a protest against this policy.[358] The rise in the French monarchy's revenue from the salt taxes was a relatively late development

[355] Buisseret in Buisseret (1992), 99–100.

[356] Hocquet (1985), 351.

[357] Marion (1919), 207–10.

[358] Part of the province was within the *pays de grandes gabelles*, and the discrepancy between the rates of tax there and in the *pays de quart-bouillon* must have been striking ('demandons qu'aucun ne soit forcé de prendre en vos greniers plus de sel que ce dont il a besoin'): Hocquet (1985), 380–1; Porchnev (1963), 433.

(despite the attempts of Francis I and Henri II, the real exploitation of this revenue came in the seventeenth century). In 1681, the combined *gabelles* amounted to 18.2 million *livres*; by 1726 they amounted to 26.5 million; by 1762, 35.2 million; by 1774, 45.6 million; and by 1788, 58.5 million. However, as a proportion of the total indirect taxes within the royal general farms, the *gabelles* showed a tendency towards decline, as other revenues, such as the tobacco monopoly, were first incorporated into the farms (after 1730, in the case of tobacco) and then became more important: the proportion was 31.5 per cent of the total in 1681, 33.1 per cent in 1726, 28.4 per cent in 1762, 30 per cent in 1774 and 24 per cent in 1788.[359]

The salt monopoly in Russia was introduced by Peter the Great in 1705. It was temporarily suspended in the years 1728–30, but was reinstated in 1731; by the 1740s, if not earlier, the monopoly was conceived as having essentially a fiscal purpose, exploiting a natural resource in which Russia was particularly rich. Yet the price of salt failed to rise in line with inflation and the depreciation of the currency in the last third of the eighteenth century. This, combined with the high transportation costs given the huge distances of the Russian empire, meant that the salt revenue did not rise and operational profits were eventually converted into losses: a 2.2 million rouble profit in 1762 became a net loss of 1.2 million roubles by 1795. Where the monopoly succeeded was thus not in the area of revenue raising, but in the distribution of salt throughout the empire: a law code in 1781 required the regional salt stores to keep a two-year reserve so that salt would be available at all times in adequate amounts. Operational difficulties and the high costs incurred by the state nevertheless forced the abandonment of the salt monopoly and the return to a free trade in salt in 1811. Had Catherine the Great shown less 'motherly compassion' for her subjects and exploited the salt monopoly as ruthlessly as in Poland, or especially France, perhaps this would not have occurred.[360]

Other countries introduced monopolies in other areas. China attempted a liquor monopoly as early as 782, but there is no evidence that it became as significant a revenue as the salt monopoly.[361] In Russia, there was a royal monopoly of the sales of liquor after 1478, while the nobility gained a primary share (and, between 1716 and 1728 and again after 1754, a monopoly) in liquor production. Nobles who declared their intention to produce for the market were required to sign four-year contracts to deliver their liquor at a stated price. Early on, attempts were made to place the collection of revenue with various institutions of municipal government, but there was an increasing tendency towards

359 Calculations based on Bayard in Bluche (1990), 632; Matthews (1958), 88.

360 LeDonne (1975), 185 and n. 56.

361 Twitchett (1963), 59, 62.

revenue farming by the eighteenth century. With effect from 1767, the entire liquor revenue, except for Siberia and other borderlands, was farmed out, usually in small farms with a duration of four years. A severe problem was posed by rising sales of bootlegged liquor, which was encouraged by revenue farmers subcontracting their rights of collection: by the 1790s, this had become so serious that vigorous measures had to be taken against bootlegging, while the townsmen's near-monopoly over the sales of liquor was broken. Total revenues from liquor sales rose from 15.6 million roubles in 1793 to 22 million by 1798 as a result of these changes, while the net profit to the crown almost doubled from 8.7 million to 15 million. Except for the years 1817–27, this system of revenue farming on four-year contracts was retained until the introduction of the excise in 1863.[362]

New habits of consumption, such as the spread of smoking after the introduction of tobacco in the later sixteenth century, permitted the development of new sources of taxable revenue. In France and elsewhere a tobacco monopoly was developed in the seventeenth and eighteenth centuries. At first the growth in revenue from this source was slow, reaching only 4 million *livres* in 1717 and 7.5 million by 1730; but by 1788, royal revenue from the tobacco monopoly had reached the significant figure of 30.5 million. As a proportion of the revenue from indirect taxes, the tobacco monopoly had risen from about 8.6 per cent in 1730 to about 12.2 per cent in 1788. At its peak, it perhaps accounted for 7.3 per cent of total royal revenue.[363] Necker considered the tax upon tobacco the lightest and most imperceptible of all imposts, ranked with reason in the class of the most skilful fiscal inventions.[364] Adam Smith, too, thought it a proper subject of taxation, since along with sugar and rum it was a commodity which was not a necessity but which had become an item of 'almost universal consumption'.[365]

By the mid-eighteenth century, therefore, governments were faced with a much wider choice than ever before of items of consumption for the purposes of taxation. In particular, they could determine the extent to which new 'luxury' items could be taxed as against traditional basic commodities; the number of indirect taxes levied had to be settled (was it worth levying numerous very small taxes?); governments also had to decide the extent to which reliance was placed on indirect as against direct taxes. In the view of the commentators reporting to the French government in the years after 1763, Tuscany was a state which had

[362] LeDonne (1976).

[363] Matthews (1958), 118; *Mémoires*, ed. Moreau de Beaumont (1769), iv, 614–15; Price (1973), i, 361–75, esp. i, 374–5.

[364] Price (1973), ii, 789.

[365] Smith, ed. Campbell, Skinner and Todd (1976), ii, 936.

failed to limit the number of indirect taxes. Instead, numerous very small levies occasioned more vexation than they were worth.[366] Milanese indirect taxes were considered disastrous, since they simultaneously raised labour costs in the city while damaging the prosperity of agriculture.[367] Spain offered the clearest example of a state which had lost the necessary balance between indirect and direct taxes: 'lands pay practically nothing [in tax] in this kingdom', the marquis d'Ossun commented to L'Averdy in May 1765, 'and most of the taxes are carried by consumption.' This had succeeded in destroying Spain's internal commerce, while agriculture was not being improved in the manner of other European states.[368] Moreover, the nature of the indirect taxes compounded the problem. The *alcabala*, denounced by Ustáriz and Smith, for example, was exacted on all goods sold, whether movables or immovables, at a rate of tax between 8 and 14 per cent. The tax was levied on each transaction so that frequently the tax exceeded the intrinsic value of the goods sold, which encouraged fraud and collusion between taxpayers and the authorities.[369]

In the United Provinces, too, Smith was later to denounce the impact of high excise duties on labour costs (Chapter 6.7). Here, he drew on the earlier comments of the French enquiry, which had stated:

> Excise duties are generally too numerous and excessively heavy. Labour costs rise steeply as a result, and the collapse of manufacturing industries which cannot compete with foreign competition is a daily occurrence. Town dwellers not involved in maritime commerce are impoverished, and even merchants find it difficult to keep going. This same element of high wage costs ... affects ... herring fishing, whaling and even ship construction, which necessarily has an impact on commerce in general.[370]

This contrasted with the situation in the countryside, where farmers were generally prosperous because there was a ready market for their goods: farmers in a real sense paid their taxes with the money they earned from consumers (Chapter 15.6). There was thus a growing fiscal differentiation between town and countryside, and in the effect of taxation upon different economic activities. Nevertheless, although taxes upon necessities amounted to a quarter of indirect taxes in the United Provinces, the growing interest burden of the state was

[366] Bonney (1994), 70; AN K 880 no. 6, 14 June 1765. Waquet (1990) is the definitive account of the Tuscan tax structure; Capra in Bonney (1995) makes comparisons between the various Italian states in the eighteenth century. In Tuscany, there was no attempt to tax the profits from trade, manufacturing or banking.

[367] Bonney (1994), 70; AN K 880 no. 13.

[368] Bonney (1994), 70; AN K 881 no. 51, 20 May 1765.

[369] Bonney (1994), 71; the rate of tax had been reduced by the time that Smith denounced the *alcabala*.

[370] Bonney (1994), 69; *Mémoires*, ed. Moreau de Beaumont (1768), i, 202; AN K 879 no. 123. On the general theme, Wilson [1969], 114–27.

financed out of the rapid increase in revenues from taxes upon luxuries.[371] The precise importance of the taxation of wages in the Dutch Republic, and the impact of high wages on economic development, remains contentious, however. Moreover, external changes may have been more important than internal developments in determining the relative economic decline of the United Provinces in the later eighteenth century (Chapters 11.1 and 11.3).

The French Revolution, inspired by the criticisms of the *cahiers* of 1789 and the abuses of the revenue farmers, took its stand firmly against indirect taxes, so that in 1791 it was estimated that indirect taxes had fallen from 287.2 million to 133 million *livres*, while direct taxes had risen in proportion (from 171.2 million to 300 million).[372] Indirect taxes were restored first under the Directory in 1798. Napoleon confirmed the trend, because this provided him with a source of revenue which could be manipulated free from parliamentary control.[373] The fiscal purpose was clearly regressive. Indirect taxes, it was argued, by raising the price of commodities would encourage people to work harder to obtain both necessities and luxuries. Taxes were established on tobacco and drinks and were directly administered by a *régie* known as the *droits réunis* rather than as a tax farm. Taxes on foodstuffs were avoided, and it was argued that tobacco and drinks were not absolute necessities: only people who could afford to buy them did so; on the other hand, clearly they were commodities which were so widely used that the taxes would fall upon a great many people.[374] After the Peace of Amiens, customs duties were levied on imports and exports on the grounds that without them France would become a 'tributary' of Britain, but these required a substantial mechanism of enforcement against smuggling.[375] The result of these two changes was that the new indirect tax revenue became more closely related to political events and the fate of the economy: customs revenue fell during the British blockade after 1806, while income from the *droits réunis* dipped during the economic crisis of 1810–12. Yet by 1813 there was almost a balance between direct and indirect sources of revenue (the yield from direct taxes was 340.7 million francs in 1813, as against 315 million from indirect taxes). With the Restoration in 1814–15, the balance shifted once more towards direct taxes.[376] The Revol-

[371] Fritschy (1990), 69. At ibid. 67, she points out that 25 per cent of indirect taxes in the Netherlands (unlike Britain and France) arose from taxes on the milling of grain. The significant long-term economic consequences (especially for the preservation of the craft structure in industry) of the complex excise regime is stressed by van Zanden (1993), 137–8. 'The ossified structure of the craft industry' was not weakened until the abolition of the excise tax on milling in 1855: ibid. 148–9.

[372] Bonney (1992*a*), 175.

[373] Doyle (1989), 334; Sutherland (1989), 380; Hincker (1989), 197–200; Collins (1989), 85.

[374] Collins (1989), 85.

[375] Ibid. 86.

[376] Bruguière (1991), 425. His figure for indirect taxes (471 million) includes 156 million from the *enregistrement* and *domaines*, which should more correctly be viewed as domainal; this figure has

utionary attack on indirect taxes was echoed outside France (except, of course, in Britain). One of the features of the Revolution of 1820 in Spain was the spontaneous abolition of the *consumos*, indirect taxes levied on prime necessities. When the government tried to reimpose them, radicals warned that taxation was the yardstick by which the public judged their institutions.[377]

13.7 *Conclusion*

No survey of revenue systems can conclude without mention of the glaring discrepancies in many countries between the tax structures of the town and the countryside or the contrasts between the fiscal systems of the different regions within the same state. In part, a province defined itself by its fiscal structure and fiscal privileges, often defended by a representative institution. Even in that model state for 'modernity' in terms of its financial organization, the United Provinces, there was virtually no unified tax structure. Instead, the separate provinces had their own fiscal systems. There was a regional or quota distribution, but this was for costs; how the costs were met against taxes was largely the concern of each province, and the system proved very difficult to reform even in the period of the Batavian Revolution.[378] If one reads the pages of Rousselot de Surgy's *Encyclopédie méthodique*, edited shortly before the end of the *ancien régime*, one can hardly fail to be struck by the fact that his definition of a French province's privileges was largely fiscal in character.[379] The fiscal historian rarely possesses a full range of quantitative economic data sufficient to pass judgement on that elusive concept, regional 'taxable capacity'. Clearly there is 'taxable capacity' in a political sense: the money may be safely extracted without risk of rebellion. There may be 'taxable capacity' that is knowable in a demographic sense: it may be possible for certain regions to build relatively precise demographic evidence into the picture so as to arrive at something approaching a quantification of the 'real' fiscal burden on a per capita basis. It is most unlikely that for Europe as a whole we could arrive at anything as precise. What it may be possible to do is to convert into constant silver values this sort of statistical evidence, so that it may be possible to make comparisons on a per capita basis with other regions in roughly speaking the same period (say, the same half century). Much work needs to be done before we can arrive at this desirable

been excluded here. Bruguière (ibid. 520) claimed direct taxes as 57.6 per cent of the total of 590 million in 1815, as against indirect taxes at 22 per cent, and domainal income (*enregistrement, domaines* and *bois*) at 20 per cent.

[377] Carr (1975), 133.

[378] 't Hart (1993), 77–80; Schama in Winter (1975), 123, 126, 136 n. 84; Schama (1977*a*), 292–4, 305, 385; Fritschy (1990), 70–1; Veenendaal in Hoffman and Norberg (1994); Price (1994), 279.

[379] Rousselot de Surgy (1784–7); Bonney (forthcoming).

outcome. But is there any possibility of studying regional 'taxable capacity' in a broader, economic, sense? Here, it seems that the range of materials available to the historian is too sporadic and uneven from one country to another and from one region to another for any realistic comparison to be made. And the question posed may arise from a false premise: if regional fiscal divisions were in large measure a question of privilege then we should not expect any clear relationship between economic wealth and fiscal burden. Just as in the French peasant revolts it was often the privileged regions which protested first and loudest at the smallest infringement of their privileges, so we may deduce that in many, though not necessarily all, cases a light fiscal burden was not a recognition of inherent poverty but a sign of political caution: the province that was most troublesome was that which was least heavily taxed, starting with the frontier regions (provided that the transfer of sovereignty was permanent).[380]

As Sir William Petty and Adam Smith observed, the nature and timing of tax payments crucially affected the capacity of the population to pay. In a rural community, this meant that payments to the state depended in large measure upon the state of the harvest: peasant sales of produce were often made all at one time.[381] This was perhaps most obviously true of direct taxes in a year of subsistence crisis such as 1693 in France.[382] But in a local economy dependent on viticulture, tax returns depended not simply on the success of the grape harvest, but on the capacity of landowners to sell abroad: the interruption of the Bordeaux wine commerce because of the onset of war in 1689 thus had a serious effect on the tax yield.[383] This reality of the harvest, which was a constant for much direct taxation, was somewhat less significant for most indirect taxes, where payment was made piecemeal as the item of consumption was purchased. It is argued elsewhere in this volume that the real measure of the fiscal burden is its relationship to the success of the harvest in a given year (Chapter 15.5).

The comparison between the revenue systems of states over long time periods is complicated by significant frontier and population changes. Thus England has been chosen as the example for the evolution of a kingdom's revenue between *c.*1200 and *c.*1800 because of the advanced development of its administration; the early reliance on monetary payments rather than payments in kind; the kingdom's administrative uniformity; and the unique survival of relatively complete

[380] Where the transfer of sovereignty was impermanent, there was much to be said for extracting as much revenue as possible for the duration of the occupation. Even so, difficulties might be experienced. Cf. the Dutch experience in the 'generality' lands: 't Hart (1993), 94–100.

[381] Spufford (1989), 382.

[382] AN G^7 393, 13 Sept. 1693.

[383] AN G^7 134, 5 Mar. 1689, 26 Dec. 1690; AN G^7 135, 3 Feb. and 5 June 1691.

documentation in many areas of the fiscal system.[384] The long-term evolution of tax revenue may be viewed by recalculating the figures as index numbers which refer to a common base index (1451–75 = index 100), and inflation may be taken into account by using a deflator for prices devised by Phelps-Brown and Hopkins (Figure 86): the figures are presented as eleven-year moving averages.[385] It is also possible to discern the long-term evolution in the balance between direct and indirect taxes in the same state over roughly the same period between 1315 and 1815 (Figure 87).[386] For much of the Middle Ages indirect taxes had provided the lion's share of taxation, and given the sporadic nature of direct taxes it had sometimes provided 100 per cent. (The graph shows the proportion of total taxation, not total revenue: there were always other elements such as domainal income in the total revenue figures, but it is not always possible to calculate these items for the Middle Ages.) After 1530, however, indirect taxes did not exceed 50 per cent of total taxation until 1571 and then did so only five times during the rest of the sixteenth century. Under the early Stuarts, the position was reversed—indirect taxes provided less than 50 per cent of total taxation for only eight years in the period 1603–40. After the Commonwealth, when direct taxes were clearly dominant, indirect revenues resumed their former importance under the Restoration. They consistently provided more than 60 per cent of taxation under the Hanoverians, and between 1750 and 1799 this proportion rose to over 70 per cent of taxation. The English political classes anticipated the conclusions of J. R. McCulloch, who argued that indirect taxes, levied on both home-produced goods and imports, had the ability to produce revenue with the least disruption of economic growth. In contrast to property and income taxes, indirect taxes did not for the most part require investigation and were therefore politically more acceptable.[387]

However, it is argued elsewhere in this volume that indirect taxes did not necessarily assist economic growth, but could actually impede it, the fundamental criticism for example of the Spanish fiscal system in the seventeenth and eighteenth centuries (Chapter 15.6). This prompts consideration of the positive or detrimental economic consequences of fiscal policy and the 'shifting' which

384 The author acknowledges the generous collaboration of Dr Mark Ormrod for medieval England and Professor Patrick O'Brien for modern England. Their separate chapters appear in Bonney (1995). Subsequently to the preparation of the graphs shown here, O'Brien and Hunt (1993), 148–50, reworked the figures using their own deflator rather than that of Phelps Brown and Hopkins.

385 ESFDB \obrien\engg001 based on \engm002 and \engm003; unpubd data kindly supplied by Dr W. M. Ormrod and Professor P. K. O'Brien; index from Phelps Brown and Hopkins (1962).

386 ESFDB datset \obrien\engg002 based on \engc001; unpubd data kindly supplied by Dr W. M. Ormrod and Professor P. K. O'Brien.

387 McCulloch, ed. O'Brien (1975), xxxvi–xxxviii, 170–1.

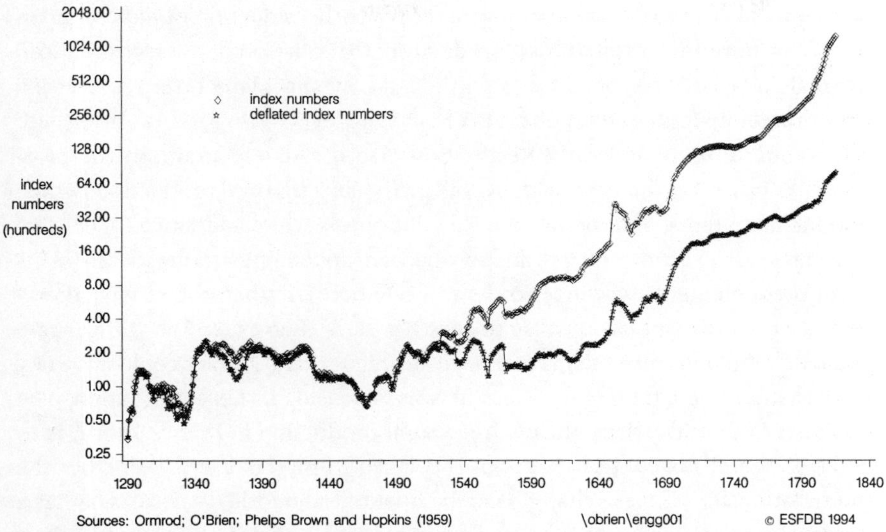

FIG. 86. Eleven-year moving averages of index numbers for total revenue from taxation in England, 1290–1815, set against deflated index numbers for this revenue

might occur in wartime away from productive capital investment. The 'crowding-out' thesis is a subject of some debate among English historians of the period of the Revolutionary and Napoleonic wars (Chapter 11.8). In France itself, the fiscal changes of the Revolutionary era, it is argued, did not tax property so

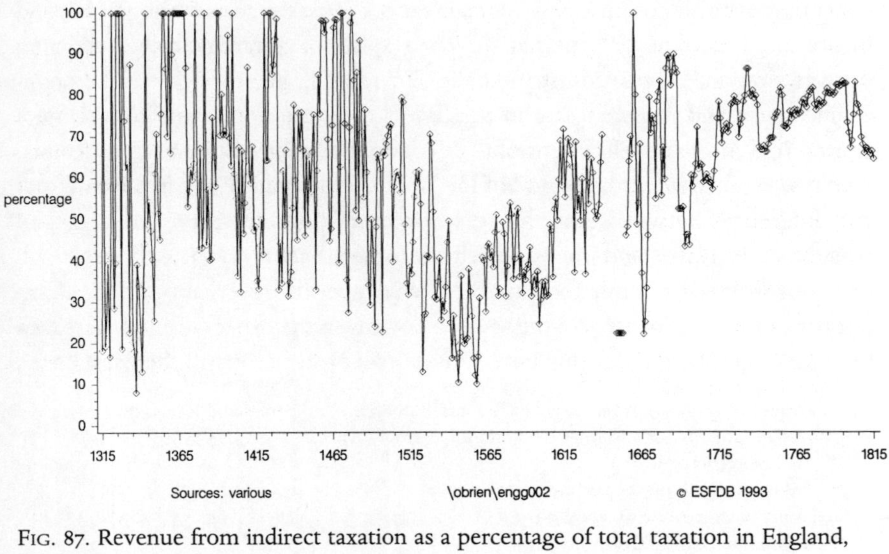

FIG. 87. Revenue from indirect taxation as a percentage of total taxation in England, 1315–1815

heavily as to act as a break on investment, while the reduction of indirect taxes acted as a stimulus to agricultural production; the inflation of the 1790s reduced the real value of levies of all types on the land; even so, land taxes represented about three-quarters of total direct taxes and the level of the land tax in the late Napoleonic Empire and early Restoration placed a severe strain on the peasantry.[388] Taxes formed part of an overall *prélèvement* on rural production, which also included rents, and (before the Revolution) the tithe and feudal dues. The total levy, or exaction, on production had an upper limit though each of its constituent elements was independent. If one part fell, then the others, after a period of adjustment, would rise to take the slack. Land taxed at a lower rate could be rented for more than land taxed at a higher rate. Nobles could not exact increased rents at a time when the state was increasing its tax contribution. The abolition of the tithe theoretically freed rural production in France after 1791 to make a greater tax contribution, but this failed to materialize.[389] Whether the interrelationship of these changes can be quantified (in other words, whether a 'multiplicand'[390] can be constructed for a particular period to take account of fiscal change as a positive factor in the economy) is to be doubted.

The sophistication of west European fiscal structures has been stressed in this chapter. It is tempting to contrast an arbitrary form of taxation in eastern Europe, and its correlation of economic stagnation, with a measured fiscal burden in western Europe, and its correlation of economic growth.[391] Such a contrast risks oversimplification even if we assign to fiscal change the positive role of motor within the economy as a whole. The economics of backwardness had causes other than arbitrary or unsophisticated taxation, causes such as demographic and institutional weakness,[392] perhaps even a spirit of autarchy rather than an outward-looking, expansionist mentality.[393] Yet if large cities generated economic wealth and progress, late in the day[394] the state, too, came to assume a central role in the development of the economy even in a state such as Russia. And it was precisely in the period of the late development of the fiscal state that the differences between east and west, or more properly between successful western-style states and those which remained backward (Russia, after all, overtook Poland), became most marked. Whatever the reservations of contemporaries about the capacity of the state to borrow in the expectation of increased revenues (and the relationship between the size of the debt and the fiscal base),

388 Postel-Vinay (1989), 1019, 1043; Le Goff and Sutherland in Forrest and Jones (1991), 69.

389 Le Goff and Sutherland in Forrest and Jones (1991), 69.

390 Anderson (1974*a*).

391 Ardant (1965), i, 188–95 and (1971–2), i, 303–11.

392 Gunst in Chirot (1989), 53–72, 81–3.

393 Kochanowicz in Chirot (1989), 105.

394 Bérenger and Tollet in Genet (1990), 58–9.

the emergence of 'mountains of debt' and high debt–revenue ratios was a feature of modernity in the west. At the very moment that this more adventurous fiscal policy was emerging, the Ottoman state became more conservative. Military fiefs (*timars*) were first converted into tax farms (*iltizam*); in the eighteenth century, these tax farms were then held on a lifetime basis (*malikane*), with a consequential depressing effect on potential revenue growth. As the absolutist states of western Europe sought more effective taxation geared to developing capitalist economies, the late Ottoman state became 'risk averse', in part because of a retarded capitalism.[395] The capacity of governments to borrow, and the interaction between the constraints on borrowing and the power to tax, became the real test of the fiscal powers of the 'modern' state by 1800–15. It is to the evolution of those techniques of public credit that we must now turn.

395 Berktay (1991), 252–3; cf. Adanir in Chirot (1989), 146–9.

CHAPTER 14

Public Credit

Martin Körner

The earlier chapters of this section dealing with the financial structures of the state revealed the fact that the inadequacy of states' fiscal foundations constantly compelled those in power to borrow money (Chapter 13), and that servicing the debt, which included both the payment of interest and the repayment by instalments of the money borrowed, constituted in most states one of the most significant, if not the most significant, items of expenditure (Chapter 12). The state which successfully repaid its debts and managed to produce an annual surplus—in short, the 'savings state'—was the exception. Where this happened, the problem was how to manage the profits—whether this should be by creating a cash reserve, by purely financial investments, or by other forms of profitable investment.

Public credit, whether it be that of princes or of cities, was tied to business, to financial and banking techniques. From at least the twelfth century, the services of bankers and financiers were indispensable in providing the capital required by the state or lordship when its normal receipts were insufficient to cover expenditure. The same group of people advised rulers over decisions regarding the investment of surplus funds, or the regional or international transfer of capital on behalf of princes and republics. From the late Middle Ages, merchant bankers held a wide range of positions in the financial administration of city-states as well as in those of princes and kings. We find them active as mint-masters, managers of silver mines, receivers of taxes and holders of state monopolies.[1] Princely finances attracted them and, in return for their services, they obtained economic advantages. If they were members of the prince's inner circle, they were well informed, especially concerning the prospects of war or peace, which in principle

[1] Unpubd paper read to the Team at Arc–et–Senans in 1991 by the late Derek Knights. Van der Wee (1991), 71–103. The author and the Editor thank Dr J. A. Bergin (Manchester) for preparing this translation.

enabled them to spread their commercial risks, and their general banking activities, more advantageously. They quickly learned that lending money to princes brought advantages, and enabled them to make a profit which was not only rapid but also substantial—unless, of course, they fell victim to overambitious speculation. But they could also lend to cities, which was safer, although lending to a single city was also less profitable.[2]

During the later Middle Ages, modern credit structures gradually emerged. These included the techniques required for the transfer of funds, international loans and double-entry book-keeping. The application of such techniques can be seen in the business relations of Tuscan bankers and the Roman Curia, and in their relations with the princes of western Europe. These ties were disrupted by the crises of the sixteenth century, when international banking fell apart and was subsequently transformed into national systems in the seventeenth century. Indeed, the eighteenth century witnessed the appearance of state banks which administered the public debt in what was increasingly a world economy. This development will be sketched, with examples relevant to the problem of public debt and credit, in what follows.

14.1 *The Later Middle Ages*

The majority of the bankers and financiers concerned with, and living off, the public debt may be classified in terms of the scope of their activities—whether this was local, regional, national or international. As early as the mid-twelfth to the mid-thirteenth century, the loans required for military undertakings in the Empire or for the crusades were effected by merchant bankers. Of course, Italians were active on both sides of the Alps; but a considerable proportion of the world of high finance involved in these transactions came from England, Flanders, Artois, Cologne and northern Germany, and these bankers were also active both north and south of the Alps. The Hardels, Bukerels, Rengers and Eswy-Adriens were prominent merchant bankers from London. William Cade and William Fitz Florence came from Saint-Omer, while Gerhard Unmaze and Fitz Thedmar, as well as Bernardus Teutonicus, the associate of the Ziani in Venice, were from Cologne.[3] Around 1200, the world of Bernardus Teutonicus was just as international as that of the Tuscan banking houses of Siena, Lucca, Piacenza and Florence which made a place for themselves in the financial affairs of the kings of England from the late thirteenth century onwards (Chapter 5.2).[4]

[2] Favier (1987), 365–82; Van der Wee (1991), 103–17; Lüthy (1959), i, *passim*.

[3] Fryde (1985), 41–8; Stromer in Dubois (1986), 62–71.

[4] Favier (1987), 58–67, somewhat exaggerates Italian preponderance.

One of these banks, that of the Scotti from Siena, lent money in 1249 at Limassol to Louis IX, then a prisoner, and he promised to repay them the following year at the fair of Provins. In 1253, the Scotti lent money in Siena at the request of Pope Innocent IV. Between 1271 and 1276, they were the favourite bankers of Gregory X in Rome. In 1282, they lent money to Edward I of England, and secured repayment in Paris in 1287. After them and their contemporaries, the Bonsignori and the Ricciardi, came the great trio, the Bardi, Peruzzi and Acciaiouli, who dominated international finance until about 1350. Finally, the second half of the fourteenth century saw the rise of the Frescobaldi, Gualterotti, Strozzi and especially the Medici bank, whose supremacy lasted until the end of the fifteenth century. The power of these houses was based on the connection between their commercial and banking activities. Engaged in mercantile business on a large scale and over long distances, they possessed branches and correspondents throughout virtually all Europe. The Tuscan houses bought huge quantities of wool in England. Instead of paying for the wool with money shipped from Italy, they did so with the taxes they collected for the Apostolic Chamber in England and northern Europe. They paid equivalent sums into the Papal treasury from funds they derived from the resale of finished goods in southern Europe. They were also engaged in public credit operations in England.

In order to reform his finances, in 1275 Edward I reorganized the customs system, ceding its financial management in the form of a lease to Tuscan merchant bankers. The latter made ever bigger advances, secured on import and export taxes, to the king, but the crown's needs were so vast that on his death in 1307 Edward left enormous debts. A wave of Italian bankruptcies followed in both England and Tuscany. This did not prevent other merchant bankers from returning during Edward III's reign, which was the apogee of the three great banking houses, especially of the Florentine Bardi and Peruzzi who embarked on ill-advised loans to the king in order to service his financial needs during the first phase of the Hundred Years' War. When it became clear in 1339 that Edward III lacked the means to repay his huge debts, his creditors went bankrupt: the Peruzzi in 1342, the Bardi in 1346; after that, Italian bankers ceased to participate in the English crown's credit operations. The Italians' downfall in England also resulted in serious difficulties for the finances of the Apostolic Chamber under Clement VI.

Towards the end of the thirteenth century, Tuscans were active, though to a lesser extent. The king of France borrowed large sums from the Guidi brothers, who represented the Florentine firm of Franzesi, in 1294–5. Subsequently, during the fourteenth century, the king scarcely ever used the Italians as sources of loans.[5] Yet they were very active in the Midi, in close cooperation with the Apostolic Chamber which was entrusted with managing Papal finances. The great banking houses which oversaw the collection and transfer of Papal revenues throughout Christendom to Avignon, the Popes' residence from 1308 to 1378, made current account advances or loans in response to instructions from the Papacy. With the Papacy's departure from Avignon, the Florentines' centre of activity shifted to Geneva. Moreover, the main banking firms no longer concentrated their efforts primarily in the field of royal finance and credit. Admittedly, in the fifteenth century the Medici lent large sums to Edward IV and Charles the Bold—which were not repaid—but these sums were an insignificant proportion of the total volume of their business.

It is probable that the ease with which they obtained small short-term advances from Italian merchant bankers whetted the appetites of kings and princes for loans to compensate for the difficulties they experienced in wartime because of the insufficiency of their ordinary tax revenues. In order to satisfy this demand, the great Italian firms, acting together, mobilized more substantial sums by floating loans as virtual banking syndicates. One of the best known examples was that of the Bonsignori who, through a group of Tuscan bankers, secured a loan of 200,000 *livres tournois* for Charles of Anjou to enable him to acquire the kingdom of Sicily. In their loans to English kings, in particular, the bankers mistakenly accepted both the monarchs' word and their ability to repay. Once faced with demands from a small number of their depositors for the return of their funds, the bankers were all too easily subject to liquidity shortages caused by the dubious value of their loans to kings.

From the fourteenth and especially the fifteenth centuries onwards, public credit was increasingly organized in national, regional or local frameworks. In England, the crown could henceforth rely on the rising class of English capitalists in the City of London, one of the first of whom was William de la Pole, who was later joined by rich princes of the church such as Henry Beaufort, bishop of Winchester.[6] In France, Jacques Coeur, the celebrated merchant banker from Bourges, succeeded in dominating the king's finances. By advancing money to the king and the nobility, he gradually became Charles VII's trusted man, and in turn supplier of the court, master of the mint, king's treasurer and head of the royal financial administration. In 1449, for example, he lent 200,000 florins to the king for the war in Normandy. He regularly represented the king in loan negotiations with third parties. In 1451, he was accused of lending to the king sums which, as treasurer to Charles VII, he had taken from the royal Treasury. Condemned by the great council of the realm, he fled to Rome.

[5] Dubois in *Banchi pubblici, banchi privati*, ii, 763–4.

[6] Ormrod in Bonney (1995).

Charles VII did not base his finances upon loans. Louis XI (1461–83), on the other hand, experienced liquidity problems at a time when fiscal pressure was high, and resorted to a variety of loans—forced loans through non-payment of officials' salaries; arbitrary confiscations of sums deposited with law courts; short-term loans from royal officials; loans secured by intermediaries from individuals; demands for money from towns (in the form of loans or gifts), especially from Lyon; and loans from the clergy. Louis XI also borrowed from Italians, from Giovanni Arnolfini, and later from the Lyon-based Medici and Pazzi banks, sometimes using the city of Lyon as his intermediary. But these loans were in no way systematic, and merely served to bridge gaps in the case of temporary liquidity problems. Interest and capital were generally repaid when cash arrived from the tax receipts of the following year.[7]

On the other hand, various French princes resorted more readily to borrowing, since their expenditure generally outstripped their resources. They included the counts of Champagne, the dukes of Burgundy and Brittany, and princes of the house of Valois. While occasionally using the services of Italian bankers, they relied more on the financial operators in the towns of which they were lords.[8] Admittedly Philip the Good had recourse to the Geneva fairs early in his reign, but in general the three successors of Philip the Bold mainly borrowed capital in the towns of the Netherlands.[9] A similar trend is observable in Spain where, from the late fourteenth century, the kings of both Castile and Aragon used primarily the credit of the towns and bourgeoisie to satisfy the borrowing needs of their respective treasuries.[10]

In Spain and elsewhere in Europe, the revival of towns was accompanied, from as early as the thirteenth century, by a considerable enrichment of urban society, thanks in part to the intensification of production, and to local and regional trade. In the urban localities of France, England, the Netherlands, Germany and Switzerland, merchants from towns like Asti, Chieri, Novara and Alexandria in Lombardy, and from Cahors in southern France played an important role in pawnbroking. Lombards and Cahorsins increasingly supplanted the Jews in this sphere by creating networks of pawnbroking banks. They were also present in Spain, though they were less numerous there. When approached for loans by municipal authorities or by princes, they imitated the merchant bankers by forming loan syndicates with a view to spreading the risk.[11] Their economic

[7] Dubois in *Banchi pubblici, banchi privati* (1990), ii, 764.

[8] Ibid.; Kerhervé (1987), ii, 615–36.

[9] Dubois in *Banchi pubblici, banchi privati* (1990), ii, 766.

[10] Ladero Quesada in Dubois (1986), 32–4.

[11] Amiet (1876–7); Nabholz (1944); Irsigler in Bestmann (1987), 122–62; Van der Wee (1991), 75–80.

success placed them at the top of the fiscal elite in many cities.[12] But gradually, the Lombards were in turn replaced by the financial networks developing among old local families. Occasionally, this transformation gave rise by the early fifteenth century to the first attempts to establish public exchange or pawnbroking banks.[13]

Side by side with the Italian merchant bankers who are well known because of their eminent position in the financial system of the Roman Curia and of the kings of western Europe, and overshadowed by them, there developed in Germany, the Netherlands and England a noble and bourgeois world of high finance the fortunes of which were based on either local domestic industry (*Verlagssystem*), long-distance trade in textile and metallurgical products, or the shrewd management of landed estates. This world of high finance exercised growing political influence, earned through its capacity to make loans, its control of the money markets, and its complete understanding of the management of urban finances. From the late fourteenth and fifteenth century, central Europe came to be dominated by the high finance of Nuremberg and Augsburg.[14]

Similarly, the birth of public banks (*casa*, *taula*, *Stadtwechsel*) is observable in Italy, Spain, the Netherlands and south Germany during the fourteenth and fifteenth centuries. One of the common features of these institutions, apart from the exchanging of currencies in circulation, was the management of public borrowing. Urban authorities increasingly resorted to the sale of life annuities, the most common form of long-term credit, in order to cover more frequent deficits in their annual accounts caused by the steep costs of security and the aids demanded of them by their rulers. Both the organization of such subscriptions and the payment of the annuities were made largely the responsibility of money-changers or public banks of the towns. Thanks to the relations between the public money-changers of the towns of a region, the towns attracted purchasers of life annuities from an expanding geographical area.[15]

If such new wealth sought profitable investments, the availability of such liquidity also sharpened the appetite of princes, especially if they were successful in extending their territorial domination over regions of high urban density. The dukes of Burgundy after Philip the Bold, for example, increasingly borrowed from the towns of the Netherlands. In 1422, the towns of Flanders and Brabant were obliged to redeem annuities previously sold, with their agreement and

[12] Sosson in Dubois (1986), 46–52.

[13] Stromer in Vannini Marx (1985), 229–54; Körner in Bestmann (1987), 245–68.

[14] Stromer (1970); Stromer in Dubois (1986), 62–71; Fryde in Bestmann (1987), 128–45; Fryde (1989), 1–12; Hucker in Bestmann (1987), 147–88; Irsigler in Bestmann (1987), 357–81.

[15] Stromer in Vannini Marx (1985), 229–54; Mueller (1987), 145–55; *Banchi pubblici, banchi privati* (1990); Van der Wee (1991), 90–4.

surety, by the counts of Holland, so as to avoid confiscations for late payment detrimental to the interests of their merchants. To be able to act in this way, as well as to cope with the growth of their fiscal obligations, cities like Ghent, Brussels, Leiden and others continued to increase their public debt after the fifteenth century.[16] Allowing for specific variations, a large number of cities of the Empire came to labour under a comparable burden of debt which was becoming more and more oppressive.[17]

The public and permanent nature of the debt also characterized a large number of independent and sovereign cities. It appeared in Venice by the late twelfth century.[18] Genoa and Florence are well-known examples, but the case of Swiss cities such as Zurich, Berne, Lucerne, Fribourg, Solothurn, Basle and Schaffhausen is generally unknown. If the striking growth of the public debt of the Italian cities enabled them to enjoy the role of great powers in Italy and the Mediterranean world in the fourteenth and fifteenth centuries, the analogous position of the Swiss cities enabled them to finance their attempts at emancipation both from their lords and from the Empire north of the Alps. Italian cities generally engaged in forced loans[19]—albeit with variations peculiar to each city—calculated pro rata on the immovable wealth of the bourgeoisie and at compound interest;[20] the bonds were negotiable at widely fluctuating rates, depending on economic and political circumstances.[21] In the humbler world of the Swiss cities, the usual practice was the familiar one of selling life annuities and issuing repayable loans for subscription by the bourgeoisie, allied cities and the neighbouring nobility. Part of the debt was subsequently repaid from the proceeds of an extraordinary direct tax levied on the wealth of the bourgeoisie and the rest of the population.[22]

Despite differences in name and the definition of what constitutes a loan, the various forms taken by public credit in a whole range of social and political contexts during the Middle Ages can be reduced to a few key elements. Money was advanced or lent for short periods from three to six months, or sometimes until a fixed date in the following year. The security for such short-term loans lay in the item pledged—jewels, lands, the output of mines or tax revenues. Interest was not involved, but rather the right to a repayment of capital: the amount was determined in advance. In the fourteenth and fifteenth centuries, for example, the kings of Denmark obtained additional funds almost wholly by pledging royal

16 Blockmans in Genet and Le Mené (1987), 77–90.

17 Isenmann (1988), 174–81.

18 Hocquet in Bonney (1995).

19 *Prestanza, compera.*

20 *Estimo*, and later, *catasto*. Hocquet in Bonney (1995).

21 Day (1987*a*); Mueller (1990), 39–64.

22 Körner (1981), 274–80; Rosen (1989), 148–74; Gilomen (1982).

fiefs (Chapter 4.6). Different forms of security were the norm in the realm of private credit. In addition, we find the pledging of revenues which, for example, the Emperor granted to a prince or a city for their profit, usually for a limited period, without any prior loan in the form of capital. This form of pledge (*Pfandschaft*) served to reward, usually for a limited period of time, services rendered to the Emperor by the holder of the pledge. If the grant and repayment of a loan were not made in the same place, letters of exchange were employed, particularly when the person repaying the sum was not the individual who took out the original loan.[23] Short-term lending offered the highest profit margins—12 per cent, 20, 25, 33.3 or 43.3 per cent and so on per annum, depending on circumstances, regions and economic trends, and the abundance or scarcity of money in circulation.

Long-term lending took essentially two forms: life annuities and loans (also called annuities in some places), the term for repayment being left to the discretion of the borrower. With life annuities,[24] the lender received no security, but in return he periodically (once a year, or else every four or six months) received an annuity which mostly represented between 7 and 10 per cent of the capital involved. This right died with him. Repayable loans were not usually defined in these terms,[25] but were mostly called 'purchases of money' or 'sales of dues' (*cens*).[26] The lender purchased the right to an annual payment stipulated in the contract, which would continue until the capital was repaid.[27] The security was generally a piece of immovable property, since the annuity was originally the right to share the fruits of land or immovables.[28] In public credit, the immovable property pledged by a prince or a king was usually a town with its goods and revenues. The same was true of towns which offered themselves as pledges, as well as for merchants and bourgeois whose merchandise a lender could impound in the event of non-payment. Interest rates varied, but usually fluctuated between 4 and 6 per cent. In order to avoid talk of interest, which was officially frowned on during the Middle Ages, it was common practice to refer to 'gifts'. In cases of uncertainty, the lender could demand the additional surety of an individual or a group.

The state had no right to interest on its deposits where public deposit and clearing banks were concerned, but drew its recompense in the form of the security and the services of the banks, which were viewed as a specialized section

[23] Considerations of space preclude a discussion of the mechanism of the *lettre de change*. Consult: De Roover (1953*a*); Munro in *Banchi pubblici, banchi privati* (1990), i, 47–80.

[24] *Lybding, Leibgeding, juros, rente.*

[25] *Préstamos* in Spain, *prestito* at Venice.

[26] *Geldkauf, Zinskauf.*

[27] *Hauptgut.*

[28] Schnapper (1957).

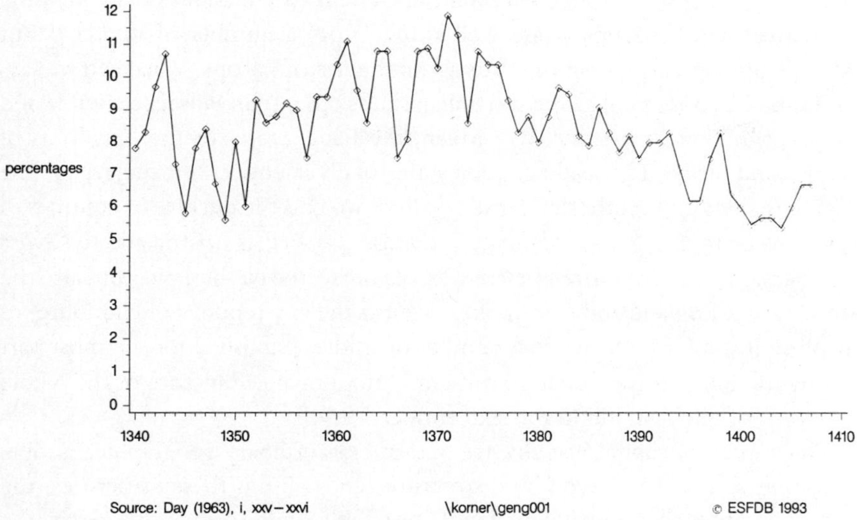

FIG. 88. Interest rates at Genoa of the consolidated debt, 1340–1407

of public administration. If, however, the state was a shareholder, it shared in a bank's profits. This was particularly so in Genoa, where the *compere*, the creditors of the commune of Genoa, were grouped in syndicates for the purpose of administering the domainal and tax revenues of the state—the various *gabelles*, the alum mine of Phocea and so on. Depending on profits and economic trends, interest rates reached 8 or 9 per cent, but they could be as low as just over 5 per cent (Figure 88).[29] It was also in the Italian cities that the consolidated debt was invented: this enabled the state, which was now no longer able to repay its ordinary debt, to transform it into a consolidated debt by issuing life annuities. On the other hand, a distant monarchy far from the Mediterranean such as Sweden did not have any kind of organized credit until the end of the fifteenth century.[30]

14.2 *The Sixteenth Century*

In view of the fact that there was a public debt in practically every kingdom, duchy and republic in the sixteenth century, it is scarcely surprising that there was an almost universal growth in the demand for capital (Chapter 8.4). The examples of the Empire under Charles V, of France, and of Spain under Philip II,

[29] Day (1963), i, xxv–xxvi; ESFDB \korner\gengoo1 based on \gendoo1; Favier (1987), 239–64.
[30] Svanidze in Vannini Marx (1985), 49–51.

with their financial centres, their financiers, and their techniques of borrowing, repayment and bankruptcy, are well known from a number of studies.[31] But what do these grand syntheses tell us about the rest of Europe? What can we say, for example, about public credit in Italian states other than Florence, Genoa and Venice, whether in the duchy of Milan, the Papal States or the kingdoms of Naples and Sicily? The leading studies are totally silent on the subject for the Alpine regions and southern Germany where we find the duchies or counties of Savoy, Württemberg, the Palatinate and Hesse, as well as Austria and the Swiss republics. In northern Europe, there was, of course, the Netherlands, but also the kingdoms of England and Denmark, as well as the city republic of Hamburg, to mention just a few. Thanks to a number of studies published for the most part during the 1980s, it is possible to present a more nuanced picture of the whole spectrum of public credit in the sixteenth century.[32]

The supply of capital was diverse and of extraordinary geographical scope, reflecting as it did the economic structures and, within these structures, the sectors and branches which were highly profitable. In the sixteenth century, the highest profits were made in Mediterranean and Atlantic maritime trade, and were concentrated in a number of port cities of the first rank; in the production (through the *Verlagssystem*) and commercialization of goods finished on the Continent, and especially in southern Germany and the Rhineland; and also by combining trade in goods and in money in the industrial and commercial centres. There were also the profits from land rents and the cattle trade, as in Schleswig, Holstein, the great plains and the Alps. Added to this was the wealth of the clergy and religious houses, the alienation or confiscation of which helped to repay parts of the public debt. Everywhere financial officials and administrators were pressed to make advances against the state's revenues. Areas enjoying peace, where states achieved budget surpluses thanks to the limitation of expenditure on war, were not insignificant either. Nor were those with a high concentration of military enterpreneurs who made their profits from the various associated functions of war. Finally, we should not forget those powers or towns which were themselves borrowers, but which also, in certain circumstances, provided allied states and rulers with urgently needed loans. This is not the place to discuss the impact of bullion imports from America on the supply of European capital (Introduction). Instead, we may note that the minting, circulation, transfer and dealings in gold and silver imports were highly profitable for the merchant-banking class (Chapter 7.3).

[31] Carande (1967); Braudel (1981–4), ii, 522–5; Boyer-Xambeu, Deleplace and Gillard (1986); Van der Wee (1991), 162–80.

[32] See particularly Kellenbenz (1986).

A similar role to that exercised by towns with fairs in the area of merchant trade and banking was carried out by financial centres in the search for 'public' credit. Sometimes the same venue performed all three roles (trade, banking, public finance), though this was neither the general rule, nor was it necessary. A financial market attracted capital through the advantages it offered, such as its range of investments, attractive interest rates, the reliability of borrowers, or the 'modernity' and transparency of its financial techniques. But because public borrowing was not solely based on commercial capital tied to exchange terms, sixteenth-century financial markets were all located in regions known for their intense economic activity. They needed a flourishing regional economy from which surplus capital could be syphoned off for investment. Ultimately, a financial market was distinguished by the abundance of capital on offer. Lack of space does not allow us to place each of the financial markets with public credit operations in its historical context. In addition to these purely economic or technical financial considerations, there were institutional and political limits on each sixteenth-century financial market. Thus, in Venice, the *Signoria* monopolized the sources of wealth for its own public credit operations, and the capital market serviced those needs to such an extent that no other power even dreamed of floating a loan on the closed financial market of the Rialto.[33] On the other hand, Genoese capital circulated freely in other markets and supplied public credit demands in Naples, Lyon, Antwerp, Madrid and Valladolid. In several markets, the dominance of Genoese bankers as state creditors became overwhelming—for the kings of France at Lyon, and for the kings of Spain at Antwerp, the *Bisenzone*, Milan and Naples.[34] In the kingdom of Naples, the Genoese held between 17 per cent and 24 per cent of the state bonds (*juros*).[35] Around 1617, they held about 30 per cent of the financial instruments underwriting the Venetian public debt.[36]

After the Italian wars, Francis I made Lyon his primary borrowing centre in France. Among the foreign merchant bankers there we find above all the Genoese, but also Florentines and Lucchese, as well as Germans and Swiss.[37] In 1558, the Swiss obliged Henri II's representatives to accept a term loan, and the duration of the contract was fixed at six years in accordance with the practice at Lucerne.[38] But Lyon was not the monarchy's sole borrowing centre. Through their ambassadors, every French king from Francis I to Henri IV also obtained loans in Switzerland, particularly from the Basle market between 1521 and 1591, with the largest borrowings coming after 1560. On the other hand, the kings of

[33] Favier (1987), 362.

[34] Carande (1967); Castillo Pintado (1963*b*).

[35] Calabria (1991), 115–17.

[36] Hocquet in Bonney (1995).

[37] Mauro (1966), 199–200.

[38] Körner (1980), 419–20; Doucet (1933), 6.

France raised nothing at Antwerp, which was the financial market both of the Empire and of western Europe under Charles V, and of Spain under Philip II. England, however, enjoyed access to the Antwerp market in order to raise short-term loans.

Although the main Italian banking houses had branches at Antwerp, the market was dominated by the Fuggers, whose base was in Augsburg. From the beginning of the century, the Fuggers added to their activities as merchant bankers and mining-contractors the functions of official bankers to the Papacy in Germany, Poland, Hungary and Austria, running the sale of indulgences, collecting Papal taxes, and organizing the transfer to Italy of the sums they raised. In 1519, Jakob Fugger headed the consortium of bankers which put together the capital which Duke Charles of Burgundy had promised the German electors to secure his election as Emperor Charles V. From that date, the great banking houses of southern Germany, led by the Fuggers and the Welsers, remained the Emperor's principal bankers, playing an increasingly dominant role in the Antwerp market. The Habsburgs also needed to mobilize large sums in Vienna for the struggle against the Turks, and appealed for money to the great banking houses, the nobility, and the leading officials of the Chamber of Accounts. The court and the provinces borrowed first and foremost from the Fuggers but, towards the end of the century, increasingly from Viennese and also Italian bankers.[39]

In northern Europe, Hamburg was important, but it was above all the Kiel money market (*Kieler Umschlag*), located in the duchy of Holstein, which in the sixteenth century played a central role in borrowing, in the payment of interest and annuities, and in liquidating the public debt of the kings of Denmark who were heavily in debt to the nobility of Schleswig and Holstein (Chapter 4.6). In southern Germany, cities such as Frankfurt-am-Main, Strasbourg, Augsburg, Nuremberg and others each acted as a financial market for regions of varying sizes.[40] Any 'republic' or state, ranging from the numerous urban communes to the principal duchies of the Empire, might find money to borrow in these capital markets which it is legitimate to describe as international, so extensive was their clientele. Basle is one of the best-studied cases. Located on the frontier between Switzerland and the Empire, it served as a genuinely international financial market, thanks to its bankers and its public bank. The bank floated loans for all Swiss towns of any importance, for the Confederation's peasant republics, for neighbouring counties such as Gruyère, Neuchâtel and Fürstenberg, as well as for cities such as Strasbourg and Frankfurt-am-Main. In addition, Savoy, Württemberg, the Palatinate, Hesse, Austria and France increased their public debt in

[39] Bérenger (1975), 430. [40] Kellenbenz (1986), 318–26.

the sixteenth century by loans floated in Basle. Basle, Freiburg-im-Breisgau, Strasbourg and Frankfurt kept each other informed of the liquidity levels of their respective markets, a practice which became increasingly common.[41]

Other more important markets such as Milan, Genoa, Florence, Naples, Barcelona, Seville, Lisbon, Paris and London might also be described here, as well as the small regional markets that were even more numerous. But these examples should suffice as evidence of a European landscape which was dotted with financial markets, whether municipal, regional, interregional or international, in the service of public credit, either through their merchant bankers or the range of their borrowers, or at times both. Of course, they were not all equally important, either in the volume of their business or in their general economic or specific financial roles. They evolved in response to structural conditions and various types of economic and political change.

During the sixteenth century, states and their banker-financiers refined the techniques developed in the later Middle Ages, and innovated with new institutions and forms of public credit. The simultaneous emergence of public banks in Alsace, Switzerland and Italy was a notable institutional development.[42] But this is not mentioned, even in the most recent research, which only refers to public deposit banks, clearing banks or pawnbroking in Palermo, Turin, Florence, Genoa, Messina, Venice or Milan in Italy, Barcelona, Valencia and Saragossa in Spain, banks which were either founded or were reactivated during the second half of the sixteenth or early seventeenth century.[43] Yet Strasbourg probably had a public exchange open for fixed hours during working days from the late fifteenth century, Basle had one after 1504, and Geneva from 1568 to 1581. In fact, to judge by their terms of operation, these were real banks which acted as centres of exchange for foreign currencies and for the circulation of local currency; they issued and honoured letters of exchange and promissory notes beyond the dates of the fairs; they accepted deposits and made loans against pledges or mortgages; they transferred sums from accounts held by their clients when given orders in writing; they floated loans at least for the political authorities on whom they depended; and they ensured the payment of interest and repayment of capital invested with them.[44]

With regard to the floating of loans, a distinction should be made between the ordinary and extraordinary procedures. In markets not subject to excessive pressure and where demand did not outstrip supply in scale or regularity, money could be borrowed in untroubled conditions and at reasonable rates of interest.

41 Körner (1980), 335, 340–2; Krüger (1980), 232–5.

42 *Banchi pubblici, banchi privati* (1990).

43 Kellenbenz (1986), 324; Van der Wee (1991), 131–3.

44 Lütge (1966), 233; Körner (1980), 331–86.

The Continental interior, embracing Germany, Alsace and Switzerland, was a vast region where, at the beginning of the century, money was relatively cheap, at 4 to 5 per cent for repayable bonds and 10 per cent for life annuities. On its western and southern extremities, as well as near the Mediterranean and Atlantic, capital flooded into markets where interest rates were significantly higher. Beyond Ticino (near Milan) and Geneva, Lyon's neighbour, interest rates on Swiss borrowing experienced pressure from the mid-century onwards. Although generally holding at around 5 per cent at Geneva, rates tended in exceptional instances to rise towards 7 and 8 per cent, and at times even to 10 per cent.[45] On the other hand, in the more expensive parts of Europe, interest rates were higher early in the century and tended to fall thereafter, as in the case of Charles V's short-term loans in Antwerp and the *juros* of Spain and Naples (Figure 89).[46]

The pledging as surety of domain revenues, towns, and villages was common, as can be seen in the borrowing of the kings of Denmark, France, Spain and Naples, the rulers of Hesse, Württemberg and Savoy, as well as the Italian cities and those north of the Alps. When the surety appeared too unreliable to the lenders, interest rates soared. Charles V's Genoese, German, Spanish and Flemish bankers were paid an average of 18 per cent for the *asientos* at Antwerp between 1520 and 1532, 21 per cent between 1533 and 1542, 38 per cent between 1543 and 1551, and 49 per cent between 1552 and 1556. Promises of repayment based on domains located in Castile or on the arrival of precious metals from America appeared too unreliable. Above all, it was the financial necessity and the haste, first of the Emperor, and then of Philip II, in seeking credit in order to pay for wars in Flanders and the Netherlands which drove up interest rates, and the Genoese bankers knew how to take full advantage of their dominant position.[47]

Henri II of France was in a comparable position, and paid up to 16 per cent for loans floated in Lyon during the 1550s. The outcome was that the French and Spanish treasuries declared themselves insolvent, the French in 1559 and 1598, the Spanish in 1557, 1560, 1575 and 1596. Many historians describe these financial crises as royal bankruptcies.[48] They are not wholly mistaken in doing so, because the mechanisms were those of commercial bankruptcy. But as neither monarchy entirely lost its credit, they were rather moratoria, each of which was followed by a deal with the creditors and a consolidation of the floating debt.[49] The French

[45] Körner (1980), 350–65; Krüger (1980), 232.

[46] Calabria (1991), 143–5; Ruiz Martín (1975), 739; Blockmans in Genet and Le Mené (1987), 86; ESFDB \korner\eurg002 based on \eurd002.

[47] Gelabert in Bonney (1995).

[48] Bonney (1981*a*); Braudel (1981–4), ii, 525: 'the bankruptcy of 1575'; Van der Wee (1991), 170–80.

[49] Steele (1986), 159–65; Steele in Dubois (1986), 76–87; Steele in *Banchi pubblici, banchi privati* (1990), i, 183–204.

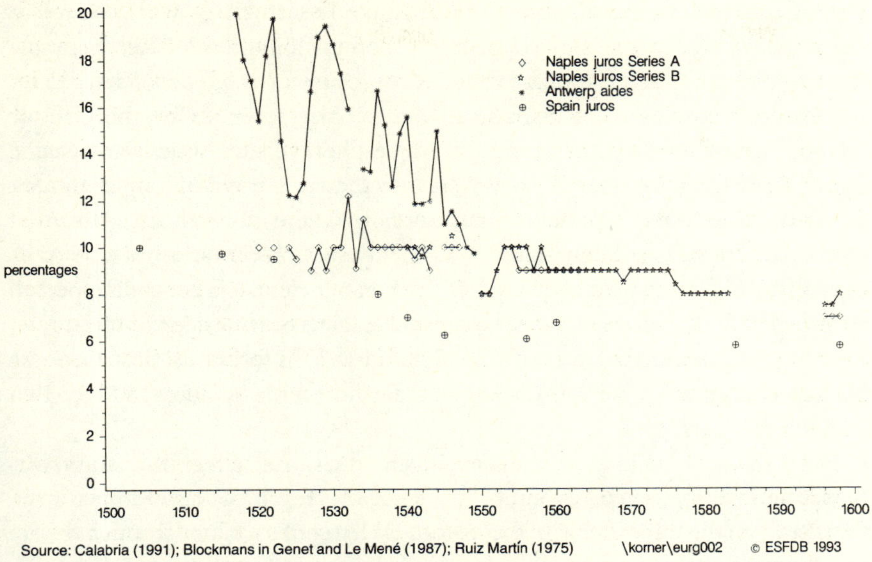

FIG. 89. Interest rates on the public debt of various states, 1504–1598

and Spanish monarchies survived these traumas, as did the strongest banks, but the remainder were obliged to sell their bonds at a loss; with each crash, a certain number of banks folded. But the kingdom's floating debt was rescheduled as a loan at lower interest rates, and with repayment terms spread out. In Spain the *asientos* were converted into *juros*, while in France the trend was to create more annuities (*rentes*).[50] State bankruptcy was very different. This was the fate of small territories unable to manage any longer, an experience illustrated by the county of Gruyère. The count was in debt after the 1540s, and in 1555 he could no longer pay interest or capital, nor obtain credit or sureties. The diet of the Confederation assembled as a chamber of justice, divided up Gruyère's lands between Berne and Fribourg, which undertook to honour the debts of the county. Count Michel was expelled from his lands.[51]

The rise of heritable annuities continued during the sixteenth century, and the monarchies strongly promoted them. In France, a proportion of the annuities after 1520 came in the form of salaries payable to those who had invested their capital in the sale of offices. Another set, that of the annuities on the Paris *hôtel de ville* which were assigned on the *aides*, the *gabelles* or Paris city taxes, began in 1522 at 8 per cent interest. Because of the king's growing demands for loans, annuities were introduced at Provins in 1553, at Moulins in 1559, at Rennes in 1569 and at

[50] On the different types of *juros*, see Steele in Dubois (1986), 76–87; Van der Wee (1991), 177–8.

[51] Körner (1980), 150–1, 405–6.

Marseille in 1571.[52] From the 1560s onwards, the French clergy were obliged to pay a subsidy in order to service the interest on the annuities.[53] Their heritable character meant that the annuities quickly constituted a large consolidated debt. In Castile, annuities were guaranteed on colonial revenues by the *Casa de Contratación* of Seville (Chapter 7.4). In Naples, heritable annuities also became important during the 1550s.[54] They were also the instrument of long-term debt which cities preferred, especially in those regions where more advanced forms of credit had not hitherto penetrated.[55] In the Swiss Confederation, where most urban republics managed to get rid of their public debt, life rents disappeared (Figure 90).[56] They were replaced by repayable loans bearing a low interest rate, which were either heritable or of limited duration.[57] As for the *asientos*, Genoese bankers continued to use them as part of their short-term advances to Philip II in subsequent years.[58]

In the field of banking and financial techniques, the sixteenth century witnessed innovation, even revolution, if we are to regard as revolutionary the passage from the transferable to the negotiable letter of exchange through the act of endorsement, a measure which developed at, and spread from, Antwerp by the end of the century.[59] Valuable bonds changed hands with greater ease and across geographical zones of increased size. Letters, bills and repayable bonds, deeds, annuity contracts and letters of mortgage were transferable and, therefore, were also used as methods of payment in fiscal and public credit transactions, all of which extended the range of financial markets in areas such as the Swiss Confederation and Naples.[60]

Another innovation—or perhaps a technical rationalization—was the floatation of state loans through subscriptions open to the public. This was a clear advance on the Italian *luoghi* which had existed since the Middle Ages, since it was independent of the tax revenues of the place where the loan was floated. It was one of the specialities of the Basle public bank.[61] At the request of a Swiss or a foreign state, the bank set the loan in motion, advising its clients in an approximately 150-kilometre radius of Basle, preparing the bonds, collecting the

[52] Mauro (1966), 229–34; Boyer-Xambeu, Deleplace and Gillard (1986), 88–90.

[53] Michaud (1991), 102–46.

[54] Toboso Sánchez (1987); Calabria (1991), 104–9.

[55] For e.g. northern Germany: North (1990), 212–23; North in *Banchi pubblici, banchi privati* (1990), ii, 809–26.

[56] Körner (1980), 302, and original data supplied by the author; ESFDB \korner\swig002 based on \swid003.

[57] Körner (1980), 227–330.

[58] Lapeyre (1953), 11–20; Castillo Pintado (1963*b*).

[59] Van der Wee (1967); Van der Wee (1991), 180–95.

[60] Körner (1980), 368–76; Calabria (1991), 104–29.

[61] *Stadtwechsel*.

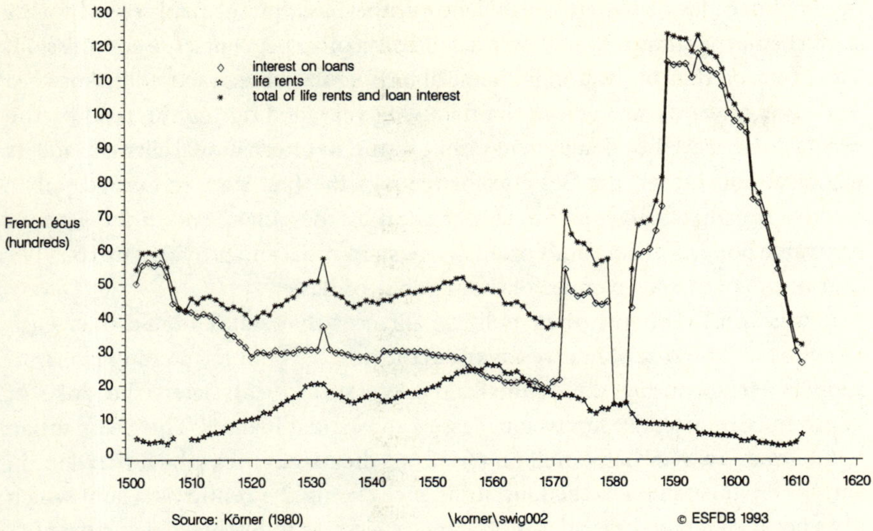

FIG. 90. The growth of interest on loans and life rents in Basle, 1501–1611 (expressed in French *écus*)

amounts subscribed and so on, until the total sum was delivered to the representatives of the borrower state. Clearly the issuing bank acted as the market for the payment of interest and, eventually, for the repayment of the loan. The first such loan in Basle was in 1506, and was followed by several similar ones. During

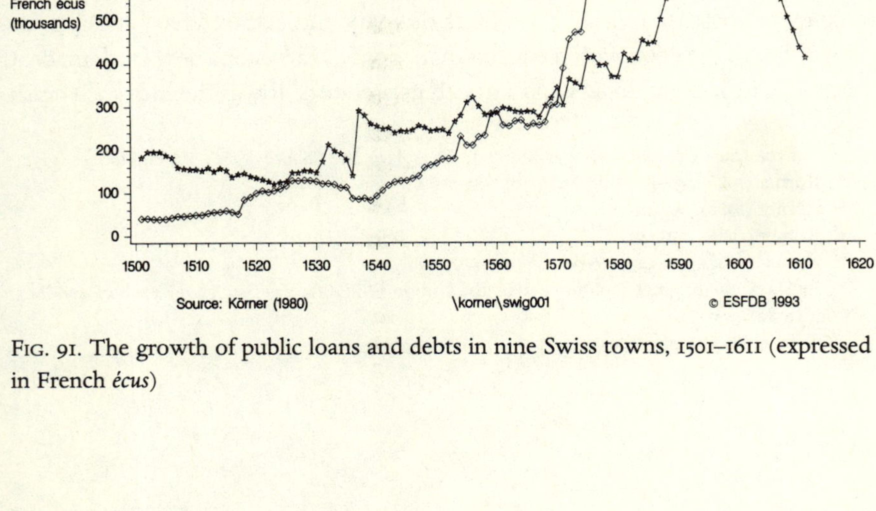

FIG. 91. The growth of public loans and debts in nine Swiss towns, 1501–1611 (expressed in French *écus*)

the final decades of the sixteenth century, the Basle public bank raised for its state-clients the sums required with a deduction of a 2 per cent issue commission. Variations on this innovation in financial techniques were practised in Antwerp from 1542 onwards, at Lyon in the following year, and during the 1550s by the *grand parti* there.[62] But thanks to its public status, its international clientele and its technical innovation, the Basle exchange was the first state-supported public bank to organize loans open to subscription by the public, and in the form of repayable bonds.[63] The bank's profits were substantial and provided up to 12 per cent of the ordinary revenues of the republic of Basle.[64]

It was consistent with their political alliances that states should offer each other loans. The king of France advanced the sum of about 100,000 *écus* in 1547 to support Hesse during the Schmalkaldic War. Ten years later, the duke of Württemberg acted as surety for Hesse's substantial loans.[65] The Swiss urban republics drew over half a million *écus* from their treasuries which they lent in various circumstances to the kings of France during the century—a sum which does not include the other debts of France's kings to individual Swiss citizens.[66] The Swiss states were also in a position to practice an unexpected form of public credit during the sixteenth century. Since they gradually succeeded in redressing their financial position once and for all (Figure 91), they were able to undertake *ad hoc* investments in public works and to finance promising economic enterprises, especially in textiles and the various lucrative aspects of mercenary warfare.[67]

14.3 *The Seventeenth Century*

Between 1598 and 1621, the Spanish monarchy avoided armed conflicts, but it failed to take advantage of peace in order to reduce its debt. Worse still, an incompetent administration and the corruption of the Council of Finance and of the *junta del desempeño* during the ministry of the duke of Lerma led, in November 1607, to a new liquidity crisis which forced Philip III to declare the crown insolvent.[68] Subsequently the crown continued to borrow money and to employ an increasing proportion of its ordinary and extraordinary receipts for the service of the debt, with the result that twenty years later a new crash made it necessary to seek an understanding with its creditors. It was the fifth such crash

[62] For the traditional view: Boyer-Xambeu, Deleplace and Gillard (1986), 87; cf. Doucet (1933).

[63] Körner (1980), 331–86; Körner (1990), 885–7.

[64] Körner (1980), 95, 382–6.

[65] Krüger (1980), 226, 233.

[66] Körner (1980), 133–225, 416–30.

[67] Ibid. 432, and original data supplied by the author; ESFDB \korner\swig001 based on \swid002; Körner (1989), 949–81.

[68] Gelabert in Bonney (1995).

since 1557, and three more would follow in 1647, 1652 and 1662, during the Thirty Years' War and the long Franco-Spanish conflict (1635–59).[69]

For its part, France began to repay part of its debts during Sully's ministry.[70] The reign of Henri IV and the early years of Marie de Médicis's regency were years of peace, but from 1613 onwards internal and foreign war disrupted budgetary expectations. In its efforts to follow its policy as the foremost power of western Europe, the French monarchy found a solution in state-organized credit which, by excluding banks, was based on relations with private financiers. Sully, Richelieu and Mazarin constantly complained of the difficulty of satisfying the state's creditors. Cash shortages and indebtedness were a constant feature of the crown's finances (Figure 92).[71] Serious shortages of funds became more and more frequent, and even ended with the cessation of all payments to creditors in 1648.[72] 'Arrangements' were negotiated with creditors, and expedients continued to be the unvarying norm.[73]

From 1544 to 1574, England floated short-term loans on the Antwerp market. After her accession to the throne, Elizabeth moved to repay them quickly, and Gresham, her financial adviser on foreign loans, fully succeeded in doing so. Under the Stuarts, however, the floating debt began to rise again. In the period of the civil war, and later the Protectorate of Oliver Cromwell (1653–8) and even under the restored monarchy of Charles II (1660–85), the public debt continued to grow. This was particularly true of the years 1665–7, with the financial demands of the Second Anglo-Dutch War. Repayable term-loan bonds were a great success, but the Treasury rapidly proved unable to honour its commitments with regard to interest and capital repayments. On 1 January 1672, the Treasury was obliged to suspend all payments, which as a result led to the bankruptcy of many of its creditors. As for the public debt, the answer lay in the conversion of term-bonds into heritable annuities bearing fixed interest, and it was these which formed the core of the English public debt thereafter.[74]

In the sixteenth century, the kings of Denmark also succeeded in rapidly reducing the public debt which had grown as a result of the wars in which they were involved. In Schleswig–Holstein as well as in the royal lands, the volume of the public debt was virtually insignificant by 1600. In the early seventeenth century, the Danish monarchy was even in a position to advance large sums to its

[69] Ibid.

[70] Körner (1980), 427–8.

[71] Bonney (1981*a*), 315–17; Spooner (1972); ESFDB \rjb\kingdebt\kdg002 based on \kdm001; Bonney (1992*b*), 113.

[72] Bayard (1988), 68–74.

[73] Ibid. 455.

[74] Van der Wee (1991), 246–9.

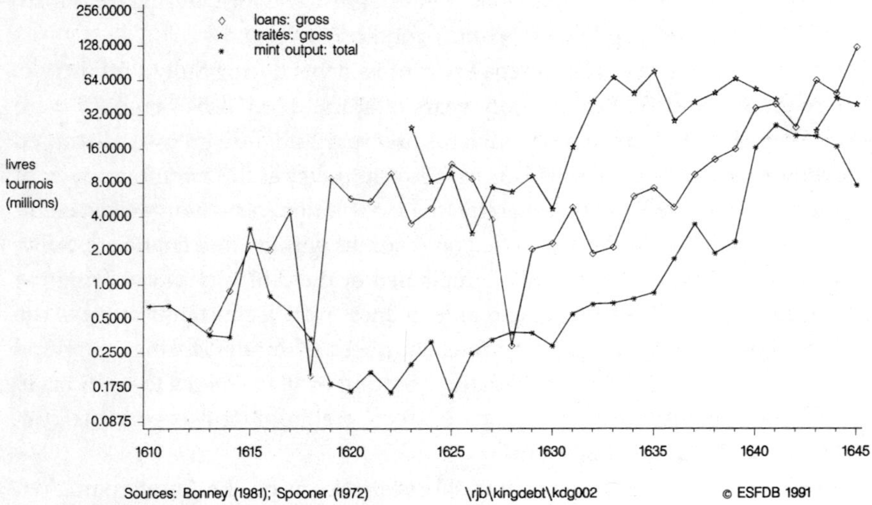

FIG. 92. Royal borrowing and *affaires extraordinaires* in France, 1610–1645, set against mint output (in *livres tournois*)

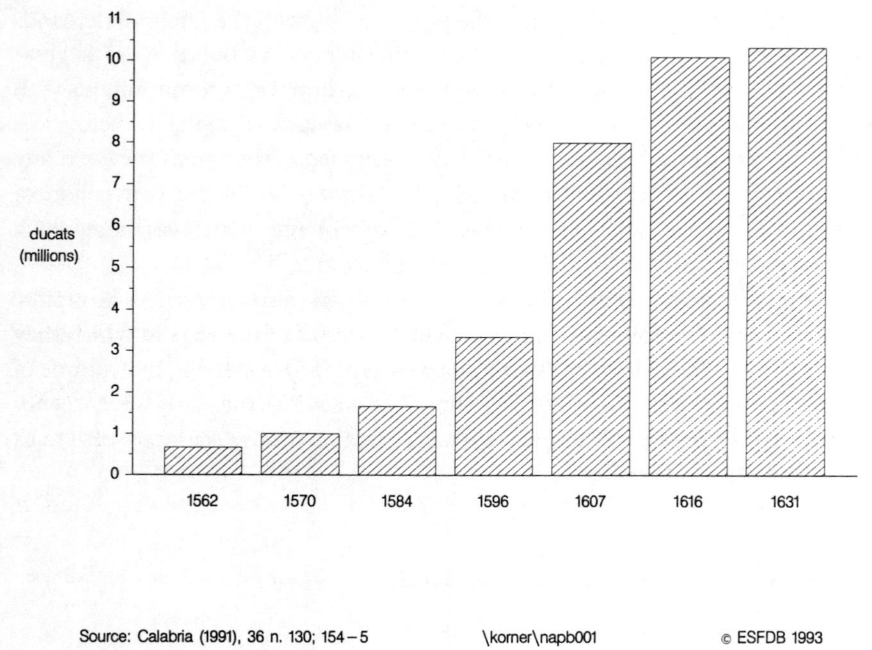

FIG. 93. The public debt of Naples, 1562–1631 (in *ducats*)

nobility and to other powers. The 1630s were a new turning-point. Expenditure during the Thirty Years' War and in the war of 1657–60 against Sweden resulted in a burden of debt which the kingdom's treasury was no longer able to service; nor could creditors be repaid their capital. Denmark suspended its payments in the autumn of 1660. To deal with the problem and finance the service of the debt, the crown mainly sold off domain lands (Chapter 4.6).

Debts were certainly contracted by rulers during the sixteenth century in the various states comprising the Holy Roman Empire. The dilemma of rulers can be seen in the examples of Württemberg and Saxony, where the gap between growing expenditure and relatively static revenues could only be bridged by public debt.[75] When Frederick William, the Great Elector, acceded to Brandenburg and Prussia in 1640, the country was heavily in debt because of the impact of military costs during the Thirty Years' War. Despite numerous reforms of the financial administration, he failed to reduce the debt, and between 1674 and 1688, the last years of his reign, he was still obliged to borrow.[76] The Austrian monarchy also sought credit between 1593 and 1606 in order to undertake the campaigns of the Thirteen Years' War. Both the court and the provinces were in debt. Between 1587 and 1611, Bohemia's debt tripled as a result of Habsburg borrowing. The situation at the end of the sixteenth century remained virtually unchanged by 1650. The Chamber of Accounts had to seek credit to bridge the deficit in the absence of money in the Treasury.[77] The second half of the century was no more tranquil for Austria than the first, and the Emperor was still obliged to borrow in order to supplement his revenues. Between 1612 and 1711, the state's debt, expressed in florins of account, doubled in size.[78]

The public debt of the kingdom of Naples also rose in the early decades of the seventeenth century, seriously affecting the finances of the city itself (Figure 93).[79] Venice's indebtedness to its state bank, the *Banco del Giro*, escalated with the opening of the Thirty Years' War, and never fell back to its pre-1620 levels (Figure 94).[80] As soon as it became a *de facto* independent state in the 1580s, the United Provinces set in motion its 'credit machine', which operated on three levels—at the level of the towns, the provinces and the Union. From the early seventeenth century, the national or Union debt grew continuously. The debts of the Generality in 1649 were divided as follows: 32 per cent for soldiers' wages, 6 per cent for military support costs, 26 per cent for fortifications, 13 per cent for foreign policy, 10 per cent for the admiralty, 2 per cent for sundry items, and 12

75 Klein (1974), 18–19.

76 Ibid. 41–5.

77 Bérenger (1975), 432–5.

78 Klein (1974), 24–6.

79 Calabria (1991), 36 n. 130, 154–5; ESFDB \korner\napb001 based on \napd001.

80 Tucci in Vannini Marx (1985), 182; ESFDB \korner\veng001 based on \vend001.

per cent for the consolidated debt.[81] Yet at the end of the Thirty Years' War, the debt of one of the provinces, Holland, which stood at approximately 130 to 140 million florins, was around ten times that of the Union.[82] In contrast, there is the opposing, if exceptional, case of regions which succeeded in remaining unaffected by international armed conflict for a long period of time. At the beginning of the seventeenth century, the Swiss republics took advantage of the first debt repayments agreed with debtor-states, of which France was one, as well as of subsidies, in order to reduce substantially their own debts (Figure 91). For the remainder of the century, borrowing was episodic and of no consequence. Even Geneva, the most indebted state in sixteenth-century Switzerland, managed finally to shed its public debt shortly after 1650.[83]

As far the institutional dimension of public credit is concerned, we should distinguish between states where private or public banks were the principal intermediary between capital and the state, and countries such as France, where public credit remained largely in the grip of a class of great financiers. *Traitants* and *fermiers* were active in proposing fiscal measures, the holders of tax farms, financial contracts and offices, and provided the monarchy with a ready supply of loans guaranteed against future tax revenue. They discreetly borrowed money from the upper classes of French society which they then lent to the crown.[84] While allowing for specific national differences, broadly similar types of financier were to be found in the lands of the Spanish monarchy, in the Austrian empire, the United Provinces and, to a lesser extent, England. They were often simultaneously merchant bankers, and they might hold a decisive position in the royal financial administration. But everywhere their role was that of raising, either at home or abroad, the sums which princes, kings and the Emperor desperately needed.[85]

In the Mediterranean lands, the merchant bankers of Genoa remained active, but others began to compete with them. Portuguese Jews entered the world of Spanish royal finance.[86] In the kingdom of Naples, Genoese supremacy, especially that of the Spínolas, declined, to the benefit of wealthy Neapolitan intermediaries such as the Aquinos and Marescas.[87] Yet the Genoese began to

[81] 't Hart (1993).

[82] 't Hart (1989), 678.

[83] Körner (1980), 431–4; Körner in Bonney (1995).

[84] Bayard (1988), 267, 290.

[85] For Spain: Gelabert in Bonney (1995). For Naples: Calabria (1991), 54–75, 104–29. For Austria: Klein (1974), 25; Bérenger (1975), 440–2. For England: Van der Wee (1991), 247.

[86] Boyajian (1983), 205, cited by Gelabert in Bonney (1995).

[87] Villari (1967).

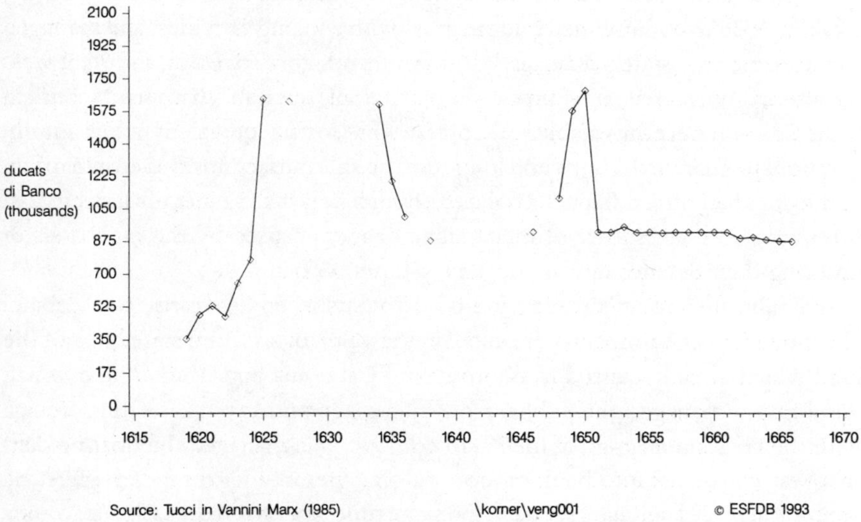

FIG. 94. The public debt of Venice at the *Banco di Rialto*, 1619–1666 (in ducats *di Banco*)

acquire shares in the Venetian public debt in 1617, and by 1673 they held nearly 30 per cent of it.[88] From 1685, they were active as lenders to the Viennese court, but their contribution to Austrian credit was slight compared to that of the financier Samuel Oppenheimer and his associates, who sometimes raised as much as 47 per cent of the short-term loans.[89] Moreover, powerful Dutch bankers like Louis de Geer, Elias Trip and Jean Deutz, dominated not merely the public credit of the United Provinces, but also raised the capital for several loans requested by Austria, Brandenburg and Sweden.[90]

The social range of those who invested or saved by means of government bonds also broadened considerably. Among them we find nobles and bourgeois, bishops and ecclesiastics, office-holders and state servants, merchants and artisans, male and female servants and, naturally, local bankers who took deposits in order to invest them at a profit either with financiers and significant bankers, or directly in a public investment institution.[91] Within towns, this function was increasingly entrusted to public banks. In the United Provinces, the state's credit was based on public confidence in the credit of the towns, which raised, through their own administrative services, most of the sums which they were required to place at the disposal of the Generality.[92] Confidence in public treasuries and

88 Hocquet in Bonney (1995). 89 Bérenger (1975), 437–9.

90 Ibid. 436; Van der Wee (1991), 263.

91 Bérenger (1975), 440–2; Bayard (1988), 454; Van der Wee (1991), 247; 't Hart (1993).

92 't Hart (1989), 678–80.

banks was also the norm in Switzerland. At Geneva, the *chambre des blés*, established in 1628, combined trade in grain with banking activities, and managed to reorganize the state's finances.[93] In seventeenth-century Basle, the *Stadtwechsel* also administered at a profit the capital of the salt chamber.[94] Zurich, Saint-Gall and Lucerne established a *Stadtwechsel*, or an equivalent public administration, to guarantee short- and long-term credit transactions.[95] German urban authorities had similar financial policies, though they were generally less successful, owing to the disorder of their public finances caused by the high costs of ensuring their defence during the Thirty Years' War.[96]

In Spain, the crown's suspension of payments in 1575 gave rise to a debate, albeit one without immediate results, on the value of a central state bank of the kind which already existed in the towns of Catalonia and Aragon, and which would have managed the public debt.[97] This step was taken instead at Venice with the creation, in 1587, of the *Banco del Giro*. This managed the floating debt that was converted into bank money and thus became legal tender, while the *Banco della Piazza di Rialto*, set up at the same time, was given the task of currency reform and remedying deficiencies in the manner in which payments were made.[98] The Bank of Amsterdam, established in 1609, performed functions similar to those of the *Banco di Rialto*, although it was a public institution guaranteed by the city. Officially, its functions were not those of the *Banco del Giro*, but in fact it lent capital to the city government and to the East India Company. The public banks of Middelburg (1616), Hamburg (1619), Delft (1621) and Rotterdam (1635) operated in a similar way.[99] The creation of a public bank on the Dutch model was discussed in Danzig during the 1630s, but the project came to nothing.[100]

The Bank of Stockholm, with its two departments, the *Wexelbank* and the *Länebank*, was a different case. Set up in 1656, it issued, from 1661 onwards, notes payable to the bearer, which were unnumbered and convertible into copper currency. These monetary instruments made it possible to finance state borrowing, but the bank was closed after a panic in 1663. In 1668, the Estates (*Riksdag*) founded the *Riksens Ständers Bank*, which did not issue notes, but which engaged in currency exchange and lending against security, as well as in raising large loans for the Swedish state.[101] In France, Colbert tried to solve the problem of the

93 Blanc (1941).

94 Hallauer (1904), 144–9.

95 Weisz (1944), 143–4; Sigg (1971), 34–6; Körner (1981), 306–9.

96 Mauersberg (1960), 427–8; Bühler (1977), 158–72; Gerteis (1986), 91; Roeck (1989), 568–78.

97 Hernandez-Esteve in *Banchi pubblici, banchi privati* (1990), ii, 963–1033.

98 Tucci in Vannini Marx (1985), 171–228.

99 't Hart (1991), 51; Van der Wee (1991), 196–216.

100 Bogucka in Vannini Marx (1985), 297–307.

101 Van der Wee (1991), 226–9.

floating debt, especially the increasing number of annuities payable by the state. He established the *caisse des emprunts* at Paris in 1674, with a view to exchange deposits progressively from private individuals for the existing annuities. Individuals would instead receive interest-yielding certificates convertible into currency after due notification. But the coffers of the *caisse* were often empty, with the result that settlements were constantly delayed. The *caisse* was abolished when Colbert died in 1683, and its deposits were converted into annuities.[102] Shortly afterwards, England made much more significant progress than its Continental rival. It was in 1688–9, with the arrival of limited monarchy, that the conditions were established for the creation of the Bank of England six years later, amidst a general atmosphere of confidence. This was the first genuine state bank, which integrated short-term public credit into a modern system of semi-public currency banking. As a result of its success, English bonds gradually gained recognition in foreign financial markets, especially at Amsterdam. In 1695, the Bank of Scotland, enjoying similar prerogatives, was founded.[103]

The early seventeenth century brought no innovations in the specific area of public credit. Familiar credit instruments were used—the sale of offices, short-term advances in anticipation of state revenues, *asientos*, various life annuities and an increasing volume of long-term bonds that were both transmissible and negotiable.[104] To make state borrowing more attractive, *tontines* and the 'million lottery' were tried in France. *Tontines*, named after their inventor, Lorenzo Tonti, a relatively obscure financial adviser to Mazarin, divided the investors in a loan into groups of equal size, and distributed the sums payable to dead investors among the survivors of each group, until the last one had died. In the lottery, investors whose names were drawn by lot received annuities a hundred times higher than the rate agreed in the contract.[105] The second half of the century saw the birth of the modern banknote not guaranteed by bullion deposits. Anticipated by the printed, non-interest bearing notes payable to the bearer issued by the Bank of Stockholm from 1661 to 1663, banknotes made their definitive appearance as promissory notes in the form of tallies and new orders of payment issued by the Bank of England.[106] It was only at the end of the century, and in England, that real innovation had occurred.

The interest rate levels observed in medium- and long-term public credit contracts varied between areas of cheap and of dear money. In the United

[102] Ibid. 232–3.

[103] Ibid. 249–50.

[104] A striking example, to judge from the portfolio of contracts he left at his death, is Louis de Geer of Amsterdam: 't Hart (1989), 679.

[105] Van der Wee (1991), 250–1.

[106] Ibid. 228, 252–3.

Provinces, rates fell during the century to 4 and 3 per cent.[107] In the Swiss Confederation, 5 per cent was the highest figure, with 3 per cent also in evidence.[108] Rates also fell in Venice to 5 and 4 per cent.[109] In Austria, we find rates of 5 per cent, but 6 per cent was more common.[110] England also had rates of 6 per cent.[111] At times of intense demand, short-term rates for loans in England and France rose to 10, 14 and 15 per cent, while in Poland they varied between 12 and 18 per cent.[112] It is thus not surprising that it was in the republics, and later in the first constitutional monarchy, that an atmosphere of order and confidence prevailed. They were the states which benefited from relatively low interest rates and which were able to export capital, with the consequence that during the seventeenth century, Amsterdam and London emerged alongside Genoa as the financial centres which dominated the market in government loans.[113]

14.4 *Conclusion: The Achievements of the Eighteenth Century*

As had previously been the case, the public debt evolved during the eighteenth century as a function of the incidence of war and its attendant costs. The problems were the same, whether it was a matter of financing a military campaign, raising capital for the fitting out of ships, or for obtaining subscriptions to government loans. As ordinary budgets were constantly inadequate, it was always necessary to resort to raising money by credit. After the Wars of the League of Augsburg and the Spanish Succession, there was a period of respite, during which governments tried successfully to reduce or to consolidate the burdens of debt which had inflated between 1689 and 1714.[114] Until the mid-century, Continental states such as Austria, Bavaria and Württemberg succeeded at least in preventing their debt from continuing to rise.[115] France reduced its debt by one-third between 1716 and 1771.[116] The grand duchy of Tuscany also repaid some of its debt.[117] As a result of interest-rate manipulations, the value of Venice's debt fell by two-thirds in 1715.[118] Denmark achieved a similar result

107 't Hart (1989), 679.
108 For example, at Lucerne: Körner (1981), 306–7.
109 Tucci in Vannini Marx (1985), 176–7.
110 Bérenger (1975), 431.
111 Van der Wee (1991), 249.
112 Day (1987*b*), 88; Van der Wee (1991), 250, for the *tontine*; Bogucka in Vannini Marx (1985), 307.
113 For the Swiss Confederation: Körner (1986), 225–37.
114 Bergeron (1978*b*), 120.
115 Mensi (1890), 478–517, 748; Schmelzle (1900), 222–37; Müller (1932).
116 Morineau (1978), 153.
117 Waquet (1990), 116.
118 Hocquet in Bonney (1995).

through redemptions between 1730 and 1754.[119] Under Frederick William I, Prussia even managed to put together a substantial treasury surplus between 1713 and 1740.[120] Thanks to draconian administrative reforms, Prussia met one of the long-standing demands of the Cameralists,[121] achieving the financial health which the Swiss republics had enjoyed since the late sixteenth century.[122]

Prussia sustained this movement in the second half of the century. It was only after 1794 that it was obliged to borrow money to fight its wars against Napoleon.[123] Bavaria, which had allowed its debt to rise during the 1740s, succeeded in reducing it in subsequent decades.[124] But despite numerous attempts at financial reform, borrowing by many important and less important powers—from Württemberg, Venice, Lombardy, Piedmont, Tuscany, Naples and the Papal States to Austria, France, Denmark, Sweden and England—reappeared on a large scale, thanks to successive military confrontations such as the Austro-Turkish war, the War of the Austrian Succession, the Seven Years' War, and the American War of Independence. This upsurge in loans was at its most intense during the years 1770 to 1795, with the Napoleonic wars to follow.[125]

The supply of capital was more international than ever before. Part of the money borrowed by states was always foreign in origin. Since the financial resources of Tyrol, the hereditary lands and of Further Austria (*Vorlande*) were inadequate, Austria raised loans in the German states of the Empire, the Austrian Netherlands, the United Provinces, England, the Swiss Confederation, Genoa and other Italian states.[126] In Italy, the grand duchy of Tuscany raised 10 per cent of its capital beyond its borders, half of it from the Genoese, the other half from creditors in the Papal States, Piedmont and the rest of Italy; non-Italian contributions were insignificant.[127] Denmark borrowed in the markets of Hamburg, The Hague, Amsterdam, Geneva and Genoa.[128] In 1784, its creditors were to be

[119] Unpubd paper delivered to the Team by Dr Bjørn Poulsen.

[120] Klein (1974), 48–54.

[121] The need for a financial reserve was argued by Johann Bornitz (1577–1638), Klaus Klock (1583–1655), M. Faust (active *c*.1641), Hans Conring (1605–81), Wilhelm von Schröder (1640–88), Theodor Ludwig Lau (1670–1740), J. H. G. von Justi (1717–71), Joseph von Sonnenfels (1733–1817): Dittrich (1974), 46–7, 62–3, 103–4.

[122] Körner (1980), 116–32; Körner in Bonney (1995).

[123] Klein (1974), 60–1.

[124] Schmelzle (1900), 237–49; Klein (1974), 70.

[125] Klein (1974), 6–7, 26, 75–8; Feldbaek (1982), 131, cited by Dr Bjørn Poulsen in an unpubd paper read to the Team; Bergeron (1978*b*), 121; Capra (1990).

[126] Mensi (1890), 300–422; Dickson (1987), ii, 272–339.

[127] Waquet (1990), 351.

[128] Unpubd paper read to the Team by Dr Bjørn Poulsen.

found in Holland, Brabant, Germany, Switzerland and Italy.[129] In 1794–6, Prussia raised one-third of its loans in the Netherlands.[130] Viewed from the perspective of the lenders, the case of the Swiss Confederation, admittedly a modest exporter of capital, reveals an impressive geographical range of investments. Between 1700 and 1750, both individuals and the Swiss states purchased English, Dutch, Austrian, German, Savoyard and French bonds; in the second half of the century they also bought the bonds of Denmark, Sweden, Ireland and America.[131]

The movement of capital invested by a wealthy and privileged public in the international markets for government loans was for the most part controlled by four financial centres, Amsterdam, Genoa, Frankfurt and Geneva, during the last quarter of the eighteenth century. The first three were both commercial and financial centres, while Geneva's role was almost exclusively confined to political finance. London and Paris were not active as brokers but rather as borrowers of capital. Most of the other banking centres played a regional or a municipal role.[132] The geography of their clienteles shows that Geneva turned to France, and Frankfurt to the German states. The Genoese historically followed a policy of distributing risk on a wide geographical and political scale. The Dutch, about half of whose capital was invested around 1780 in English bonds, later diversified their investments to northern and eastern Europe, to France and Spain.[133]

The eighteenth century witnessed, even in France, a relative decline of offices as a source of finance, and the return of the banking houses to a principal role in raising capital in national and international markets. Whether it be the French *Banque protestante* in association with the *international huguenote* centred in French-speaking Switzerland, Frankfurt, Hamburg, Amsterdam and London, or the network of Portuguese Jews active in Bordeaux, London and Hamburg, or again the spider's web of the *Banque catholique* dominated by Italians, the world of international finance was controlled by groups of banking houses connected to each other by the affinities peculiar to social, economic, professional and confessional minorities, which developed exceptional strength thanks to their cohesion, their internationalism, and their personal and family ties. From the middle of the century, Protestant banking eclipsed all its rivals because of the universal scale of its dispersion, the rapidity of its rise to riches and, in the last resort, by its exceptional ability to seize control of advanced sectors of economic and financial activity—slavery, the China trade, calico textile printing and public credit.[134]

129 Nathanson (1836), 229, cited in unpubd paper read to the Team by Dr Bjørn Poulsen.

130 Klein (1974), 61.

131 Veyrassat (1982), appx 2; Peyer (1968), 158–66.

132 Bergeron (1978*b*), 125.

133 Ibid. 129–30.

134 Ibid. 122, 131; Lüthy (1959–61), ii; Fisher (1971).

During the eighteenth century, governments set up central banks with powers to issue notes payable to the bearer, in order to control both monetary circulation and their public debt at home. Austria did so with the *Wiener Stadtbank* in 1703, Denmark with its *Kurantbanken* in 1736, Stockholm with the reforms of the *Riksens Ständers Bank* in 1762, Berlin with the *Königliche Giro- und Lehnbank* in 1765, Moscow and St Petersburg with the *Assignationsbank* in 1768, Paris with the *Caisse d'escompte* from 1776 to 1793, and Madrid with the *Banco de San Carlos* in 1782.[135] Others, like Bavaria with its *Schuldentilgungskasse* of 1728, restricted themselves to institutions for the redemption of their debt.[136] In Switzerland, where the state had long ceased to depend on loans, private banks had taken over the investment abroad of surplus public and private capital; it was these groups which, in 1744–6, pressed for the winding up of the *Basler Stadtwechsel*.[137] In Zurich, on the other hand, an initiative launched by private bankers led to the founding, in 1755, of a public bank, the *Banque Leu et Cie*, which was designed, through the issue of cash vouchers, to tap the enormous supply of capital with a view to investing it abroad via the international network of private bankers.[138]

The establishment of central banks empowered to issue notes was considered the ideal method for states which needed to raise money; but insufficient attention was paid to the fact that paper money in circulation should not exceed a certain volume if it was to retain its value and public confidence. In the system of the *Banque générale* and the *Compagnie d'Occident* set up in France in 1716 at the prompting of John Law and based on the English model (Chapter 6.6), the vast quantities of notes issued in a few years lost their value and flowed back towards the counters of the *Caisse générale*. As the bullion reserves of the *Caisse* were inadequate, the holders of notes panicked. Since the government withdrew the official rates for the notes in October 1720 and also refused to accept them in payment transactions, the collapse of the *Banque générale* was inevitable. Moreover, when the *Compagnie d'Occident* lost its privileges, the price of its shares, which had been subject to wild speculation, also collapsed, and the financial crisis reached its peak. The consequence was a profound suspicion in France of public credit institutions and of wealth in the form of movable effects.[139] At the same time England was subject to similar speculation and inflationary processes with the South Sea Company, though there were two differences. The Bank of England had enough reserves in order to advance, in agreement with the East India Company, the funds needed by the troubled South Sea Company, while

135 Schneider in *Banchi pubblici, banchi privati* (1990), i, 133–69.

136 Klein (1974), 67.

137 Hallauer (1904), 61–83.

138 Körner in *Banchi pubblici, banchi privati* (1990), ii, 889–90; Peyer (1968), 133–44.

139 Morineau (1978), 500–3.

Parliament fully guaranteed the Company's shares in order to protect shareholders. At no point was the credit of the Bank of England undermined.[140] Nevertheless, these two experiences of 'speculative bubbles' in France and England delayed progress before the 1760s in the powers of European central banks to issue convertible notes.[141] The *Kurantbank* of Copenhagen did not issue large quantities of banknotes until the end of the century.[142]

Another development influenced the range of instruments available for loans. In the absence of a genuine financial market in France, the traditional system preserved the many types of life annuity during the eighteenth century. Since the redemption of the public debt was effected only through the death of the *rentiers* or by a state 'bankruptcy', annuities became the object of clever speculation with a view to postponing their 'natural' redemption for as long as possible. The perpetual loan, redeemable at an unspecified term and issued at a lower interest rate than life annuities—and accordingly less expensive for the state in the long term—existed only in England. It was encouraged by the effectiveness of the London financial market, and it enjoyed the confidence of the public whose patriotism was stimulated by the political system. Parliament controlled the budget in England and guaranteed the loans which it voted after open, public debate. The redemption mechanism, the timescale of which was decided by the borrower-cum-government, made possible a more flexible budgetary policy. Elsewhere in Europe, a more characteristically 'early modern' method was followed, that of the term loan, usually limited to ten, twelve, or fifteen years. This trend reflected, on the one hand, the weakening credit of states which had too readily resorted to borrowing and, on the other, the increasing power of private banks *vis-à-vis* the authorities.[143]

However, turning to the case of the United Provinces, we find that the public credit of the Generality, the seven provinces, the admiralties of the five maritime provinces, the municipalities and the *waterschappen* (independent administrations in charge of the polders) enjoyed the confidence and support of the public. This was all the more evident in that, despite the expansion of the overall public debt of the country, the rate of interest remained a very low 2.5 to 3 per cent. Of course, the fact that repayment dates were fixed at the outset stimulated the administration to manage the debt reasonably, which both reassured the lender and boosted confidence.[144] The trend towards lower rates was also generally the rule for long-term public loans. In northern Europe, Denmark paid between 4 and 5 per cent on its debt.[145] In Tuscany, the loans made early in the

[140] Ibid. 503–5.

[141] Henning (1985), 277.

[142] Unpubd paper read to the Team by Dr Bjørn Poulsen.

[143] Bergeron (1978*b*), 122.

[144] Van der Wee (1991), 259–60.

[145] Nathanson (1836), 229, cited in an unpubd paper read to the Team by Dr Bjørn Poulsen.

century by the *Monti* cost 6, 5 and 4 per cent. After 1723, they cost only 4 per cent, after 1726 even as low as 3.5 per cent.[146] In central Europe, Austria usually paid between 5 and 6 per cent for its domestic loans during the first four decades of the century.[147] These rates fell during the 1760s and 1770s to 4 and 3 per cent (Figure 95).[148] In the Swiss republics, rates also dropped even more than during the previous century towards 4 and 3 per cent.[149] Funds for long-term loans seemed to have become cheaper in most of Europe, despite the sharp rise in the overall indebtedness of states. On the other hand, short-term advances in a different market remained subject to higher rates—for example, 20 per cent in Austria early in the century, 8 to 12 per cent subsequently.[150] The rate in the grand duchy of Tuscany was usually 12 per cent.[151]

Across the long time-span from the later Middle Ages to the late eighteenth century, interest rates on public credit clearly fell, both in short- and long-term lending. Yet for centuries states borrowed both short- and long-term money at both high and low rates of interest. The reason was always the same—the

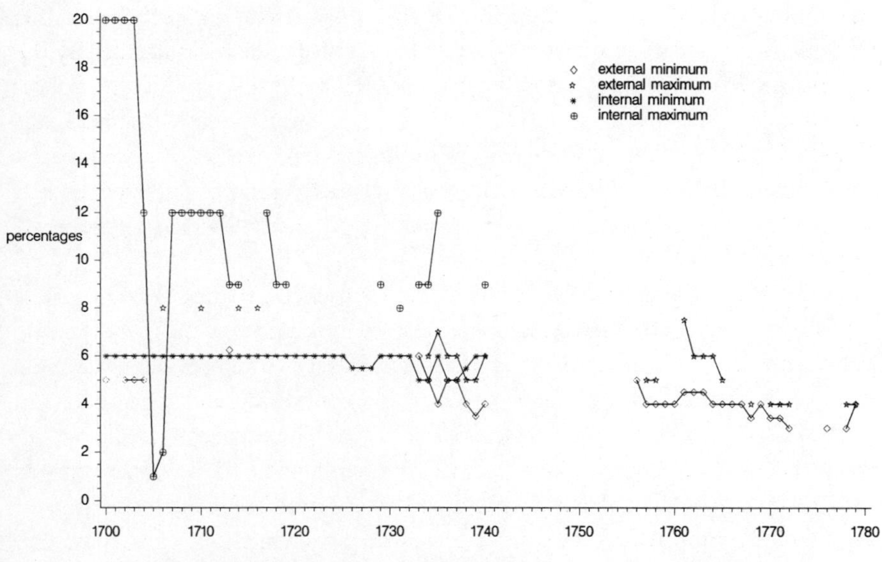

FIG. 95. Interest rates on Austrian loans, 1700–1780

146 Waquet (1990), 116. 147 Mensi (1890), 755.
148 Dickson (1987), ii, 402–18; ESFDB \korner\ausg001 based on \ausd001.
149 Peyer (1968), 130–44; Körner (1981), 307–8.
150 Mensi (1890), 755. 151 Waquet (1990), 101.

immediate need for money which they could not themselves produce until later. Most states generally abused the credit which merchant bankers and financiers, eager for profit and economic privileges of all kinds, granted them too readily. When public credit moved in the opposite direction, from the state towards individuals, as it did in the Swiss Confederation by the sixteenth century, it produced revenues for the state treasury. Most of the other states had to concentrate on tax increases in order to meet their current expenditure and to honour their financial commitments. The next chapter will, therefore, examine the fiscal burden.

CHAPTER 15

The Fiscal Burden

Juan Gelabert

*H*istorians who have studied the fiscal burden of a particular locality during a given period have usually been content to offer figures which represent the tax burden as accurately as possible by means of a wide variety of indexes. Rarely has much attention been paid to the underlying issues and the reasons why such figures differ so much from one place to another; why direct taxation predominated in some places while indirect taxes were the rule in others (Chapter 13); or why some systems were successful at raising money while others failed. Without completely disregarding quantitative data, the aim of this chapter is to address these issues, and to offer some suggestions towards an understanding as to why discussion of the fiscal burden ought not to be reduced simply to the calculation of a per capita fiscal burden, the lot of the 'average taxpayer', even within a particular country. There are various contributing factors which created the disparities in the tax burden on taxpayers in different countries. Leaving aside the question of the differential increase in state expenditure (Chapter 12), the aim is to focus on a geography of the tax burden in early modern Europe, something which Jean Bodin had already envisaged in the later sixteenth century.

This contribution will survey the various causes which contributed to creating and maintaining such differences. In the first place, it will be seen how differences in the extent of the royal domain at the end of the fifteenth and beginning of the sixteenth centuries meant that rulers had more or less need for recourse to the purses of their subjects. The maxim that the sovereign ought 'to live of his own' was generally accepted; the key question was what was understood to be 'his own'. Secondly, once it was considered necessary to demand an *auxilium* from his subjects, the choice of the mechanism to be used—a decision which was generally left in the hands of the representative assemblies—seems to have determined not only the type of taxes that were to be collected but also who should be the taxpayers. It seems obvious that where rulers were able to proceed without convening representative assemblies, indications of a greater tax burden are likely to be found. On the other hand, assemblies of estates tended to accentuate fiscal disparities, which constituted a defining element of the political constitution of the *ancien régime*. Thirdly, the religious convulsions of the sixteenth century were of decisive importance in the final outcome of the fiscal relationships between the rulers and their subjects. Wherever the Reformation, in any of its different forms, managed to prevail, the ruler's resources grew significantly, and the need to tap the subjects' wealth could, at least in theory, be reduced. No less important was the 'social discipline' which gradually asserted itself in the political relations between rulers and subjects. This point is particularly important in countries where the Catholic Reformation triumphed and the decrees of the Council of Trent were enforced. From the viewpoint of comparative fiscal history, developments such as the reinforcement of the immunity of the clergy and their properties must be emphasized. This drastically reduced the prospects of an equitable distribution of taxation among the various classes of society. No less significant were the influences (sometimes more than merely ideological) which were transmitted by the Catholic clergy to the taxpayers, who as a result questioned the justice of certain fiscal demands.

Thus, politics and religion appear to have had a profound influence on the design of European fiscal systems and, consequently, were contributing factors to the variety of fiscal systems as well as a means of accentuating inequalities in the tax burden. The capacity of each fiscal system to achieve its purpose of generating the maximum amount of revenue was to a considerable extent dependent on the development of the economy. Direct taxes proved to be suitable for periods of recession (for example, in seventeenth-century France), whereas exactly the opposite was true of indirect taxation (for example, in sixteenth-century Spain). Even if there was only relatively slow growth in population and consumption, indirect taxation might prove to be the appropriate mechanism (for example, in eighteenth-century England). However, fiscal systems were unable to adapt easily to changing economic cycles, even if they were of relatively long duration. The same political factors which had given rise to the fiscal systems also restricted their capacity for adaptation. As a result, the increased fiscal burden in the seventeenth century had significant consequences for the form of the economic crisis in certain countries, as well as for the subsequent development of the states themselves.

15.1 *Taxation and Politics*

In the *Testament Politique*, Cardinal de Richelieu asserted that there was a clear limit to the fiscal burden to be borne by the taxpayer; if this limit was exceeded such an action would make the prince unjust. He added that common sense ought to be able to determine this limit, bearing in mind the balance between the amount of the burden and the strength of those who had to bear it. Richelieu gave precedence to questions of justice, which were commonplace in the political culture of early modern Europe, over crude calculations and statistics. According to W. F. Church, this 'brief but crucial' passage of the *Testament* proposed 'to extend to the lower elements of the social hierarchy Richelieu's recommendations concerning the policies that were both just and necessary to its proper functioning'.[1] Another passage from the *Testament* merits inclusion in its entirety:

All political thinkers agree that if the common people were too comfortable, it would be impossible to hold them to the dictates of their duty. This maxim results from the people having less capacity for understanding than the other orders in the state which are much more cultivated and instructed; if they were not restrained by necessity, they would not easily remain within the conventions prescribed for them by reason and law. Reason does not permit them to be exempted from all burdens because, if they lost all evidence of their subjection, they would also forget their status (*condition*); if they were freed from paying tribute they would also believe themselves freed from obedience. They must be compared to mules which, being accustomed to burden, are more troublesome after a long rest than by work. But just as the mules' work should be moderate and their burden proportionate to their strength, so it is with regard to taxes on the common people. If they are not moderate, even though they might be useful to the public, they would still be unjust.[2]

Even the distinguished advocate of *raison d'état* could not avoid dealing with concepts such as moderation, proportion and justice when considering the sensitive issue of the fiscal burden. Richelieu was not alone. Towards the close of the sixteenth century, Justus Lipsius ranked torture (*supplicia*), censorship (*censura*) and taxes (*tributa*) as equally iniquitous.[3] In the political culture of the *ancien régime*, paying taxes was not only considered undesirable for the taxpayer but also weighed heavily upon the conscience of those rulers who asked for an *auxilium* from their subjects. Thus, in 1607, James I wrote to his council that 'the only disease and consumption which I can never apprehend as likeliest to endanger me, is this eating canker of want, which being removed, I could think myself as happy in all other respects as any other King or Monarch that ever was since the birth of Christ'.[4] And in 1635, the year of the outbreak of hostilities with France, Philip IV of Spain wrote to the president of the Council of Finance that 'if God

[1] Church (1972), 488. [2] Richelieu, ed. André (1947), 253–4.
[3] Oestreich (1982), 47. [4] Tanner (1930), 354.

were to put it right, I will not only excuse larger burdens but also most of those which exist today'.[5] Such statements from both sides should serve as a reminder to those who nowadays may consider the custom of paying taxes as a political practice firmly established in the relations between governors and governed during the early modern period. This was not the case: new tax levies were generally regarded as something verging on robbery. Although they had to be paid, the prevailing viewpoint was that taxes were an episodic matter requested in response to a specific need so that, once the need had been met, it no longer made sense for rulers to continue asking their subjects for money on a regular basis. A placard that appeared in the streets and squares of Avila in 1591 stated: 'And you, Philip [II], be happy with what is yours, and don't take away someone else's.'[6] Jean Bodin himself wavered considerably in granting to the sovereign power in the fiscal sphere comparable to that bestowed on them in other areas, though there was a degree of inconsistency in his viewpoint (Chapter 6.1).[7] The power of the English kings was no weaker than that of others because they had to resort to Parliament in search of *auxilium*, since it was not in the power of any ruler to 'levy taxes on the people at his pleasure any more than he has the power to take another's goods . . . '[8]

Underlying this predisposition against taxation was the widespread conviction that the prince ought 'to live of his own' (*vivre du sien* or *conformarse con lo suyo*). In general, 'his own' consisted of—although it was not always confined to this kind of patrimony (Chapter 13.3)—a landed royal domain whose returns, it was thought, ought to be sufficient to maintain the *état royal*. In most of the monarchies of western Europe, the fundamental laws or their equivalent took meticulous care to protect the integrity of this patrimony, attributing to it an inalienable character.[9] Princes were entrusted with the management of this patrimony, although the possibility of misuse had already made Sir John Fortescue write that it would be better supervised under Parliament's jurisdiction (Chapter 1.5).[10] Thus subjects had an understandable interest in the maintenance and, of course, in a possible expansion of the royal domain. If the returns generated in this manner did not suffice, the door remained open for the introduction of taxes. The Estates General pointed out to Charles VII that 'if the king gives away part of his domain, the equivalent has to be levied on the poor people' in the form of taxes. When, in 1555, Mary Tudor resorted to Parliament in request of financial help because of 'the great intolerable charges wherewith Her

[5] Gelabert (1990), 557.
[6] Kagan (1990), 165.
[7] Marongiu (1985), 371.
[8] Bodin, ed. Franklin (1992), 21.
[9] Kantorowicz (1965*a*), 145.
[10] Mosse (1950), 11.

Majesty hathe byn many waies burdened', the initial response from Parliament was that it was not proper to alleviate the Queen's necessity with 'parliamentary supply', but that the crown should enforce its claims against debtors, particularly those who had seized the church's revenues.[11] On the other hand, even the use that the prince made of the revenues from the domain had its limitations. Apart from the fitting upkeep of the royal household, the resources placed at the disposal of a king had to be allocated to the defence—in the broad sense of the word—of the kingdom. There were numerous images and symbols which spoke of a marital contract between the king and his kingdom, which served as his wife. As in any other marriage, a dowry—the royal domain—was conferred upon the husband so that he could meet the general needs of the state from his own revenues. Thus, the royal domain was a *dos pro oneribus*, an inalienable dowry. In the coronation ceremony of Henri II of France (1547), the conferral of the *anneu royal* symbolized precisely this marital contract—'le Roi espousa solennellement le Royaume'. And in his first speech to Parliament, James I declared: 'What God hath conjoined then let no man separate. I am the husband, and all the whole island is my lawful wife; I am the head, and it is my body; I am the shepherd, and it is my flock.'[12] In 1516, the Castilian *Cortes* found itself in the position of having to remind its new—and foreign—king that it considered him a 'mercenary' at the service of the kingdom.

Nevertheless, already at the beginning of the early modern period the days when kings could *vivre du sien* had become a thing of the past. However, the same could not be said of the ideological, political and constitutional framework which delimited the relations between kings and kingdoms. In seventeenth-century France, the extent to which 'l'ancienne conception demeurait vivace' has been demonstrated.[13] Richelieu in effect argued that the psychological aspect of taxation, what has been called the 'pression fiscale psychologique ou subjective',[14] was more important than the size of the fiscal burden and the ability of the taxpayers to bear it. To ensure effective collection, taxes should be fair (the moderation, proportion and justice to which Richelieu alluded), an issue which first of all required the taxpayers' consent (*Quod omnes tangit* . . .). In the race for political preponderance which accelerated in Europe in the sixteenth century, not all countries began at the same level of development in terms either of the extent of the domain or the willingness of subjects to consent to becoming

[11] Alsop (1982), 11.

[12] Kantorowicz (1965*b*), 388. The 'shepherd-king' image appears as early as 2000 BC in Egyptian and Babylonian texts: Todd Lowry (1987), 17.

[13] Meuvret (1971), 295.

[14] Bercé (1974), i, 71.

taxpayers (Chapters 8.4 and 8.5). When Jean Bodin suggested something like a fiscal geography of the Europe of his time, according to which northern countries were freer than those in the south, he surely had in mind inequalities like those which have just been mentioned.

In late medieval France, income from the royal domain may have represented a significant proportion of the king's ordinary revenues.[15] But the Hundred Years' War gave rise to the progressive introduction of a parallel extraordinary taxation, which soon surpassed in volume the revenues from the domain (Chapter 5.8). Besides, this was done under the pretext of the permanent state of need created by the war, without waiting for the subjects' consent; in short, 'the marriage between taxation and representative assemblies did not take place . . . in most of France'.[16] In 1523, the domain contributed only 10 per cent of the revenues, about 4 per cent in 1567 and 2.5 per cent on the eve of Sully's ministry.[17] Its partial recovery—40 million *livres* out of an estimated total value of 150[18] —showed the king and his minister in a good light, an enviable accomplishment achieved by none of his successors until Colbert (Chapter 13.3). The indisputable anti-fiscal nature of most of the popular movements which arose in seventeenth-century France must have been a consequence not only of the unbearable nature of the burden but also of the dubious legality of the constitutional mechanisms through which the sovereigns claimed *auxilium*. From the beginning of the sixteenth century, France was clearly the paradigm of a 'tax state'; yet such precocity carried with it a heavy political price.

On the other side of the Channel, England was showing symptoms of a relative 'backwardness'. Bodin's fiscal geography was beginning to make sense. Even though F. C. Dietz's old calculations have been the object of severe criticism, it can still be asserted that 'the basic components of the permanent royal revenues at the end of Henry VII's reign appear still to have been land revenues and customs, but with land revenues now providing the larger sum'.[19] While customs revenues increased by about one-quarter between 1485 and 1509, land revenues rose by about two-fifths. The restoration of the royal domain and the growth of customs revenues brought about a proportionate decline in parliamentary taxation. From 1487 to 1496, Henry VII collected approximately £310,000 in this manner, that is, an average annual sum of £30,000. From 1496 until Henry VIII's accession to the throne, he resorted to parliamentary taxation on only one occasion—in 1504—so that the average annual sum of parliamentary

[15] Rey (1965), 99.

[16] Major (1980), 15, 58, for differences between the *pays d'états* and *pays d'élections*. On the quantitative aspect: Collins (1988), 232.

[17] Wolfe (1972), 355. [18] Bonney (1981*a*), 55. [19] Wolffe (1964), 251.

taxation for the whole of his reign was reduced to some £13,500 per annum.[20] The crown lands yielded some £40,000 by 1502, so that Henry VII deserved praise from English taxpayers similar to that given to Henri IV of France by French taxpayers at the beginning of the seventeenth century. Denmark was not left behind: 'His Danish Majesty received some 75 per cent of his net revenue from crown lands in 1500', certainly 'an anomaly in the European context' (Chapter 4.5).[21]

Further south, the kings of Castile could lay claim to a royal domain comparable in size to that of the neighbouring French monarchy. The *Cortes* of Castile regularly granted *servicios* requested by the king in addition to his ordinary revenues. The most important of those ordinary revenues was the *alcabala* (a sales tax), although in her will and testament of 1504 even Isabella expressed doubts about its status as part of the regalian rights (*regalia*). In practice, although it was attacked by lawyers and loathed by taxpayers, the *alcabala* was collected regularly, which allows us to regard Castilian revenues as divided into ordinary and extraordinary taxes. Between 1482 and 1504, parliamentary taxation (or extraordinary revenue) accounted for approximately a quarter of the overall revenue,[22] with a tendency for it to fall in relation to ordinary revenue. Thus, in the early years of Charles V's reign (1516–20) the *alcabala* and the *servicios*, the two most important items of revenue, amounted to 83.6 per cent and 16.4 per cent respectively of total revenue.[23]

In Holland in the years 1521–30, revenue from the royal domain amounted to about 13 per cent of total revenue (2.5 million *livres* out of 15 million).[24] In the provinces of the Low Countries as a whole it amounted to almost one-third (30.6 per cent) in 1534, falling thereafter to just over a quarter (27.6 per cent) in 1545. The remainder was made up of subsidies, that is to say, taxation in the strict sense of the word.[25] This was precisely the kind of development which taxpayers were trying to avoid. They undoubtedly shared the opinion of Stein, the Prussian minister of excise, customs, manufacture and commerce at the beginning of the nineteenth century:

> The income from the domains is the economic foundation of the sovereign kingdom and therefore of independent internal and external state building, because the crown's domain is the foundation of the material independence of kings against the dominion of the strong corporations of the estates. Hence, domains exist and will continue to exist as long as there are kingdoms, inasmuch as the two are not only historically but also organically linked conceptions.

[20] Schofield (1988), 231.
[21] Petersen and Jespersen (1987), 479.
[22] Ladero Quesada (1976), 315.
[23] Hendricks (1976), 222.
[24] Tracy (1985), 30.
[25] Baelde in Cohn (1971), 213–14.

Taxpayers would have been likely to dismiss out of hand Adam Smith's opinion that the preservation of the domain cost society at large more than it yielded.[26]

15.2 *Taxation and the Reformation*

At the beginning of the sixteenth century the fiscal systems of southern Europe continued to offer a clear contrast with those of the north. The French Estates General had been swept aside as a representative assembly with any control over taxation. In the contrasting case of Castile, the role of the *Cortes* as intermediary between king and kingdom was perhaps its most characteristic feature. But new developments tended to widen the gap between northern and southern Europe during the first half of the sixteenth century. One of the most distinctive features of the Reformation was the secularization of church property, its incorporation into the domain of the reformed princes, or the sale of church lands. This process of secularization was spurred on in some instances by pressing financial needs. The most significant case was that of Denmark. The so-called 'Count's War' which resulted in Christian III's accession to the throne,[27] gave rise to a summons of the diet in 1536, at which there was general approval for secularizing church property in order to keep down the cost of the recent war from the point of view of the taxpayers ('bishops' properties should come under the crown and for their protection, so that the people will not be so frequently taxed'). It has been calculated that in this way revenues from the domain trebled between 1533 and 1574 (Chapter 13.3). The Swedish experience was comparable. In 1521, the church owned one-fifth of the land in the kingdom (21 per cent) and the crown 5.5 per cent. The debts incurred by Gustavus Vasa in his war against Christian II acted as a powerful stimulant for the first steps towards confiscation in 1522–3. In the *riksdag* which was summoned to meet at Västeras in 1527, Gustavus Vasa proposed and obtained approval for the secularization of church property. When he took his coronation oath the following year there was no longer any mention of the defence of the church's properties and rights.[28]

The impact of the Reformation on the German principalities was a gradual, and not a uniform, process, but in general terms, 'recent research strongly suggests that princes gained far more than used to be thought' from the secularization of church property.[29] The profits served a multitude of purposes

[26] Braun in Tilly (1975), 295–6. [27] Kirby (1990), 62. [28] Krüger (1988).

[29] Cohn in Kouri and Scott (1987), 168. Foreign subsidies allowed Frederick of Hesse by the late 18th cent. not only to avoid convoking the estates, but to reduce substantially the per capita burden on his subjects (from 3 to 2.2 *talers* as against 3.8 in Bavaria, 5.3 in Cologne and 6.2 in Zweibrücken): Ingrao (1987), 127.

which varied according to the religious devotion of the princes, their earlier level of indebtedness, the power of the nobility within the estates, and so on. However, there is little doubt that regardless of the precise mechanisms for distributing church lands, princes could extend their patronage system, neutralize the political and legal powers of the church, and provide their subjects with funds for schools, universities and hospitals. In 1533, Philip of Hesse declared that the construction of the University of Marburg and grants for its students, the building of hospitals, and dowries for noblewomen, were ways in which he had managed to improve the lot of his subjects without having had to increase taxes. A Protestant critic of Henry VIII's use of secularized church properties cited as a counter-model 'the godly Christian Germans [who] divided not such goods and lands among the princes, but . . . put them into the use of the commonwealth and unto the provision for the poor according to the doctrine of the Scripture'.

The dissolution of the monasteries in England roughly doubled the crown's ordinary income.[30] Between *c.*1540 and *c.*1552, £3.5 million had been disbursed in war-related expenses. Direct taxation provided about 35 per cent of this sum and almost the same amount (32 per cent) was raised from the sale of church properties previously secularized and by the debasement of the coinage. With a little imagination one could draw the conclusion that the use by Henry VIII of the secularized church properties along with the debasement of the coinage spared the English taxpayers from a doubling of the fiscal burden. Alternatively, if he had not chosen either of these expedients, Henry VIII might have had to eschew an active role in European affairs.

It has been suggested that one of Henry VIII's sources of inspiration for the Anglican Reformation was the French model provided by Francis I in his relationship with the Gallican church. From a fiscal point of view, the Concordat of Bologna (1516) marked the beginning of the systematic breakdown of fiscal immunity for the clergy. In theory, every Concordat signified an agreement between equals. The Pope, *de jure*, reserved for himself the right of consent on the question of whether members of the Gallican church were to pay taxes to the French monarchy. In reality, Papal authority in this area was so weakened that it may be considered virtually to have disappeared.[31] Francis I requested one, two, three and even four 'tenths' annually from the French clergy (each worth approximately 100,000 *écus*), but it is difficult to ascertain how much of the revenues of the French crown came from taxation of the clergy before 1561. In that year, in order to remedy the disastrous financial situation bequeathed by Henri II, assemblies of the third estate and the nobility suggested to the

[30] Davies (1977), 95.

[31] Wolfe (1972), 100.

Chancellor Michel de l'Hôpital the alienation of a part of the church's properties. On 21 October 1561, the so-called Contract of Poissy was signed, which specified that the French clergy were to contribute on a regular basis fixed annual sums to the crown. It has been calculated that the collective contribution of the church to the Valois Treasury between the signing of the Contract and the death of Henri III (1589) amounted to between 15 per cent and 20 per cent of the crown's total revenues.[32] In the case of France, the Reformation was not neeeded to achieve financial results similar to the consequences of secularization, for example, in the German principalities. However, it is also true that in France such large contributions were not repeated between the end of the sixteenth century and the Revolution.

Under the 'Catholic Monarchs', decisive steps were taken in Castile to break down the fiscal immunity of the clergy. During the sixteenth century, the church contributed through the *subsidio* or *décima* ('tenth'); the crown also withheld the best part of the so-called *Bula de la Cruzada* (the 'Crusade Bull'). The Popes had granted the Castilian crown two-ninths of all the tithes (the royal *tercias*) and, in 1567, Philip II obtained another new contribution, the so-called *excusado*. Furthermore, in 1523, Pope Adrian VI, Charles V's former tutor, had entailed on the crown the administration of the *Maestrazgos*, the extensive lands and properties of the Military Orders. These items amounted to about 15 per cent of the crown's total revenues at mid-century (1555–9),[33] that is to say, a similar proportion to that of clerical taxation in France after 1561. Estimates based on other sources[34] would suggest that one-third of total revenue for the period 1530–1630 came from ecclesiastical sources, a figure which seems exaggerated. Nevertheless, the difference between France and Castile lay in the fact that, whereas the French kings could take for granted the church's annual contribution (although in certain years, such as 1640, there were difficulties in dealing with the Assembly of the Clergy), both the *Bula de la Cruzada* and the *subsidio*, and later the *excusado*, were 'grants' which depended on Papal agreement. Thus, they were subject under Charles V, Philip II and their successors to periodic crises in the relations between crown and Papacy. As far as the ecclesiastical contribution to ordinary revenues was concerned, the kings of Castile thus relied solely upon the profits from the farming-out of the *Maestrazgos*; and even these profits did not go directly to the Council of Finance but rather to the Council of the (Military) Orders, as legally speaking the revenue remained a *fiscus ecclesiasticus*.

[32] Michaud (1991), 146. [33] Ulloa (1986), 129. [34] Hermann (1989), 392.

15.3 *The Social Implications of Taxation*

Another significant aspect which ought to be taken into consideration before undertaking a purely quantitative study of the fiscal burden, is whether taxation was direct or indirect (Chapters 13.5 and 13.6). A preference for forms of indirect taxation which had been characteristic of medieval cities was one of the hallmarks of the so-called 'new monarchies'. It has been observed, for example, that in the cities of the Low Countries indirect taxes amounted to at least 63 per cent of total tax revenue at Ypres, rising to 88 per cent at Lille, 93 per cent at Dinant and 98 per cent at Ninove.[35] It is not coincidental that in France the *aides* were collected at a national level before the *tailles*. Neither is it a coincidence that whereas the *alcabala*, an indirect tax, finally succeeded in establishing itself as a *regalia* in Castile, the *servicio*, a direct tax, was in Castile a parliamentary grant from medieval times to the end of the *Cortes* in 1665.

Contemporaries were fully aware of the regressive character of indirect taxation, but the repudiation of direct taxes made much sense in a society based precisely on privilege and legal inequality. Even in England, where fiscal privilege already seemed out of place in the fifteenth century, it did not mean that those who had the most paid the most. In any case, at the height of the sixteenth century, direct taxation—with Parliament's consent—did not give *de jure* recognition to the *de facto* exemption gained by some sections of the population, thus laying the foundations for those who had more to contribute more. Fifteenths and tenths and 'subsidies' conformed to these characteristics. Fifteenths and tenths were fixed in 1334 and modified only slightly thereafter. The tax was subsequently distributed throughout the country in such a way that every village, town or city knew in advance how much they had to pay. It was left to the discretion of each community of taxpayers to determine how this amount was to be shared out amongst its members. With the basis for the distribution of the taxes laid down in the distant past, it was inevitable that over time certain parts of the country found themselves overburdened while there was under-assessment for other areas. In order to eliminate these inequalities, 'subsidies' came into existence in the Tudor period. In theory, the 'subsidy' was a progressive form of direct taxation, since individuals were assessed for taxation according to the net value of their annual income and movable capital, which included outstanding debts owed to them. The rich were subject to the tax, since there was a lower limit below which the subsidy did not apply. In 1524–5, approximately 10 per cent of the rural population of Norfolk escaped taxation for this reason; in Exeter and Leicester the proportion rose to one-third, while it was as

[35] Blockmans in Genet and Le Mené (1987), 78.

high as 47 per cent in Coventry.[36] Changes were made to this lower limit in each particular subsidy, with the result that in any one area from time to time those paying the tax might range from 23 per cent to 75 per cent of the total population. In general, the subsidy was fairer than the fifteenths and tenths. In mid-sixteenth-century England, the crown seriously believed that this form of taxation was borne fundamentally by the rich, and in its origins the subsidy was a first-rate fiscal device, both from the administrative point of view and in relation to contemporary ideas about fiscal justice. Most of the tax revenue approved by Parliament reached the royal coffers, and thus the subsidy adhered to the fourth maxim—economy in its collection—which Adam Smith required of taxes in general (Chapter 6.7). Its only drawback was the fraudulent assessment of wealth. Collusion between local magnates and tax collectors had worked so well throughout the reign of Elizabeth I that in 1601 she required henceforth the assessment of taxes 'in some farr better proportion than heretofore hathe bene done'. It has been estimated with reasonable accuracy that whereas during Henry VIII's reign the fortunes of the peers had, on average, been valued at between £800 and £900, in 1580 they were assessed at £300. By the close of the sixteenth century, the subsidy was undergoing a dangerous perversion: the undervaluing of assets was liberating the very rich and penalizing those who were less well-off. In the final years of Elizabeth I's reign, Parliament was obliged to grant 'double subsidies' in order to compensate for the shortfall in tax returns.

In other countries, such as France and Castile, different political sacrifices and social concessions had to be made when direct taxation was introduced. In 1856, Tocqueville commented on the establishment of the *taille* as a permanent direct tax in fifteenth-century France that 'the aristocracy were cowardly enough to let burdens be imposed upon the third estate provided that they themselves remained exempt', which fatally undermined the capacity of the French monarchy to undertake reform during the *ancien régime*. Much nearer the event, Commynes had remarked that Charles VII thereby assumed a serious responsibility for himself and his successors and inflicted an injury upon his kingdom from which it would long suffer (Chapter 1.5).[37] Current historiography does not refute the argument that most of the fiscal burden in France was shouldered by the non-noble population, the *roturiers*, the least powerful both in political and economic terms. The *taille*, which amounted to approximately two-thirds of tax revenues under Charles VII, reached as much as 83 per cent under Louis XI; it was

[36] Schofield (1988), 233.

[37] Tocqueville, ed. Mayer (1967), 180. Commynes's *Mémoires* are frequently quoted by Bodin when dealing with the royal domain and taxes; his influence is evident in statements such as that the Papal States were 'the best governed in the whole world, for they do not pay tailles nor other taxes' (!) or that the ideal state meant the absence of taxation: Bouwsma (1990), 193–7.

reduced under the following two monarchs, with indirect taxes making up the difference. Under Francis I, despite having been doubled in value, it became relatively less important amounting to rather less than 40 per cent of total revenue at the end of the reign in 1547. At the beginning of the seventeenth century, the *taille* stood at about 54.8 per cent of total revenue in 1600–4 (for the *pays d'élections* alone), 58.8 in 1607 and 57.5 per cent in 1614.[38]

In Castile, inclusion on the tax rolls (*padrones*) for the payment of direct taxes (*servicios*) was the unmistakable mark of a *pechero*—literally a taxpayer, usually a peasant or artisan. In 1516–20, direct and indirect taxes represented respectively 16 and 84 per cent of total tax revenue; by 1551–5, the proportion had changed dramatically, with the *servicios* amounting to almost 31 per cent.[39] The new strategem which was proposed to Charles V in 1536 by the *Cortes* of Castile, and accepted by him without any hesitation, consisted in freezing the annual amount of sales tax by means of a general *encabezamiento* (similar to the French *abonnement*) applicable to the whole of the kingdom in exchange for a substantial increase in the *servicios*. The result, in terms of the displacement of the fiscal burden, was apparent even to contemporaries. Representatives of the cities who sat in the *Cortes* looked favourably upon the fact that the *alcabala*—which was levied on all kinds of commercial transactions—would remain stable (initially for a period of ten years) and that the losses for the royal Treasury were to be replenished by increased direct taxes payable by the *pecheros*.[40] The relief that this must have provided to urban economies already enjoying economic expansion is difficult to quantify but easy to imagine.

However, it was not only in Castile or France where urban economies succeeded in shaking off a good part of the fiscal pressure by diverting it to the rural surroundings. In general, it can be said that wherever the co-operation of urban representatives in the assemblies of the estates was necessary in order to approve the taxes, they did not miss the opportunity of favouring their fellow citizens. In Holland, both the *ordinaris* and the *extraordinaris bede* granted by the provincial states usually went hand in hand with the corresponding *gratien*, that is, discounts on the quantity initially granted which could amount to as much as one-third. It is hardly necessary to add that the larger cities (Dordrecht, Delft, Gouda, Leiden, Amsterdam, Haarlem), those with the greatest political and economic weight, were particularly favoured by the discounts.[41] Between 1524 and 1545 these six cities shared out between 66 per cent and 80 per cent of the total *gratien* derived from the *ordinaris bede*; from 1523 to 1552 the figure varied between 77 and 100 per cent with regard to the *extraordinaris*. In Flanders between 1476 and

[38] Collins (1988), 234; Bercé (1974), i, 67; Bonney (1981*b*), appx 2.
[39] Hendricks (1976), 222. [40] Carande (1943–67), i, ch. 12. [41] Tracy (1985), 53–5.

1477, a scheme was designed for the distribution of the fiscal burden according to which the urban population (36 per cent) would have to pay just over half (54 per cent) of the contributions, which in principle seemed quite fair. However, the larger cities obstructed the approval of these subsidies by demanding specific discounts, so that the justice of the distribution system was diluted to a considerable extent.[42] In the kingdom of Naples, people living in the capital were exempt from the *focatico*, 'the core of the fiscal system', a tax on property 'movable and not' which in 1550 provided 80 per cent of total tax revenue.[43] When it became necessary to increase the tax demands of the state, the municipalities preferred to resort to indirect taxes in order to collect the extra amounts. In 1638, although direct taxes had trebled, they constituted only 55 per cent of total revenues, while indirect taxes had multiplied fifteenfold since 1550.

15.4 *Tapping the Wealth of the Privileged*

If there were obvious inequities in the situation of urban and rural taxpayers, there were other types of inequity which require explanation in order to qualify any definition of the 'average or typical taxpayer'. These disparities were inherent in a society that was generally based on juridical inequality with respect to taxes. The case of the immunity of the nobility has already been discussed. However, the privileged situation of the church and the clergy was even more scandalous. German historians of the 1980s coined the term 'confessionalization' to refer to the 'problems of the specific mediations of religion and social formations in early modern (or "Old European") societies in general'. According to one of its most outstanding exponents, confessionalization 'drove forward the modern secularization of political life'. With regard to the territories of the Holy Roman Empire and to their princes—'often equipped with but modest means of power'—it has been said that 'deliberate confessionalization became a welcome instrument for the intensification of authority and for building up the state'. Moreover,

> not only did confessionalization present an opportunity to domesticate the church and eliminate it as a rival for power, but the confessional churches also incorporated all subjects into a system of pastoral and moral influence and control. The churches thus promoted the formation of a uniform body of princely subjects.

In conclusion, Gerhard Oestreich argued that 'confessionalization was a prep-

[42] Blockmans in Genet and Le Mené (1987), 79; Craeybeckx (1947), 91.

[43] Calabria (1991), 58.

aration for the social discipline of absolutism'[44] and the term 'confessional absolutism' is now frequently used.[45]

In the countries where a 'Catholic confessionalization' had the best opportunity for development (Spain, Italy and Portugal), no comparable process may be observed. Instead, immediately after the Council of Trent, the Catholic church not only managed to bring about the consolidation of ecclesiastical jurisdiction but, by so doing, erected a permanent barrier in the *respublica christiana* separating the clergy from their fellow-citizens.[46] Two specific episodes, both of which are, moreover, related to the position of the clergy within the community of taxpayers, will serve to illustrate the significance of this desired separation. In the final sessions of the Council of Trent, the Catholic church attempted to establish itself as a society parallel to lay society at large; by resurrecting its medieval role as the principal guide of the *respublica christiana*, it aimed to set the course for lay society and for the relations between society and princes. Hence the emphasis placed on the defence of ecclesiastical immunity—including fiscal immunity—and the motivation for hindering the deployment of fiscal power by Catholic rulers. The Council was not content with merely reforming the church; it also aimed to achieve a *reformatio principum*. Several drafts were made of the document that was given this name in 1562 and 1563.[47] The French ambassador in Venice, du Boistaillé, perceived it as a disaster for the crown. Other French observers referred to it as the seed of disobedience and rebellion, and as a clear example of Papal intervention in the sphere of domestic policy. The Chancery of Ferdinand I warned that the document would have extremely grave consequences, making the financial position of kings untenable. It is not difficult to imagine its original tenor. Moderated in the course of four successive drafts, it advised Catholic princes on respect for ecclesiastical rights, liberties and immunities (excommunication was now restricted to royal servants); it mentioned the canonical provisions that the Council had decided to renew and requested that they be respected. The ecclesiastical hierarchy perceived that the state-building process was leading to a reduction in the power that the church had enjoyed in better times. The church viewed the Council of Trent as an opportunity for restoration. But from a political, princely point of view, attitudes and texts such as those described did little to help attain a 'uniform body of princely subjects', the 'secularization of political life' or 'building up the state', the objectives of rulers following a policy of 'deliberate confessionalization'.

After this first campaign, the Catholic church took the offensive once again in

[44] Oestreich (1982); Schilling (1988), 266; a good synthesis is Po-Chia Hsia (1989).

[45] Bireley in Evans and Thomas (1991), 232–40 [Ed.].

[46] Prodi (1957), 233.

[47] Prosdocimi (1939), *passim*; Alberigo (1979), 172–3.

1578 by reissuing the bull *In Coena Domini*. The purpose of this bull, which had been published every Maundy Thursday from the fourteenth century, was to make public a list of persons and groups who had been excommunicated. In 1511, during Julius II's pontificate, it included heretics as well as usurpers of church property, pirates, bandits and so on. The fifth chapter of the bull, in its 1568 text, read as follows: 'Also we excommunicate and anathematize all those who impose new tolls or rents in their lands or increase them except in cases permitted to them by law or by special licence of the Apostolic See, as also we excommunicate and anathematize those who exact the prohibited impositions or increases.'[48] In effect, the text subordinated the fiscal sovereignty of Catholic rulers to the supreme authority of the Pope. Although the text was modified under Gregory XIII so that only non-sovereign powers were considered to be affected, the Tridentine Papacy once again took very seriously its role as shepherd of the entire Catholic flock—a role which all other indications suggested the princes were determined to prevent it from exercising, at least on fiscal matters. The Republic of Venice prohibited the publication of the bull in its territory. In Tuscany, Cosimo de' Medici allowed it to be made public, but the lower ranks of the clergy took it as a pretext for not paying taxes.[49] In 1578, Philip II—who had commenced his second debt rescheduling two years earlier and badly needed *nova pedagia seu gabellas*—was extremely offended by the attitude of the Pope, who had to explain that he had not intended to diminish in any way the king's authority in fiscal matters.[50]

Thus whilst princes who had introduced the Reformation increased their fiscal power with the secularization of church property and had reduced, at least in theory, the fiscal pressure upon their subjects, Catholic rulers had to tolerate the maintenance, or even strengthening, of the principles of ecclesiastical immunity. The result was a reduction in the number of subjects and property liable to taxation, which aggravated the fiscal burden on the rest. It has been shown that in sixteenth-century Lombardy properties with ecclesiastical immunity (*sub clypeo immunitatis ecclesiasticae*) were initially set aside when making the assessments of the *mensuale* (a tax on lands, houses and commercial profits). Consequently, the areas where church property was most abundant (Cremona, Novara, Pavia and Como) were those in which the burden was the heaviest for the lay taxpayers. In order to eliminate these inequalities, new assessments had to be made in which financial officials proceeded as if ecclesiastical wealth did not exist![51] Lay properties which were incorporated by donation or inheritance into the holdings of the

[48] Prodi (1989), 15.
[49] Bizzochi (1989), 363.
[50] Caracciolo (1983), 37.
[51] Coppola (1989), 314.

church were immediately removed from taxation, while, on the contrary, fiscal exemption remained when the ownership of ecclesiastical properties was transferred. When the civil authorities declared that properties should be transferred with their fiscal burden (*bona transeant cum onere suo*), the clergy used canon law in their defence, the bull *In Coena Domini* and similar authorities, which seem to have been effective arguments at least until the eighteenth century. Even then, the method of the Concordat (that is an agreement between the ruler and Pope as sovereign powers) was seen as the only means to neutralize (at least partially) ecclesiastical fiscal privilege.

Even in the case of the Catholic monarchy *par excellence*, that of Spain, the exact nature of the ecclesiastical *auxilium* enjoyed by the ruler, which has been estimated by some historians at 30 or even 36 per cent of the gross income, is worth careful examination.[52] So, too, is the comparison with other Catholic kingdoms such as France or with those countries in which secularization of church property occurred. In short, the church in Spain mainly acted as a point of transmission between the taxpayers and the crown, yielding up to the ruler a proportion of those funds the king's agents should have collected from the people direct and which should have been paid directly into his coffers.[53] By means of this mechanism, the *tercias* (two-ninths of the tithes) and the revenues from the Military Orders reached the royal Treasury. During the reign of Philip II, the remaining fiscal concessions granted by the Pope, with which the clergy were supposedly burdened, started to be sarcastically called 'The Three Graces'. One of them, the *excusado*, also consisted of a portion of the tithes; the *cruzada* was an ecclesiastical tax only in the sense that it depended upon Papal authorization and was theoretically earmarked for religious purposes (that is, the crusade against the Turks), since those who paid it were, in fact, ordinary taxpayers. Thus, in the last analysis, the *subsidio* was the only tax paid by the clergy, and its collection encountered a great deal of opposition in the first half of the sixteenth century, as the clergy kept up a firm defence of their fiscal immunity even though the Pope briefly changed his position on the matter. In 1532, the Castilian clergy temporarily went on strike against the tax: 'no Mass was said, neither the dead buried, nor the church bells rang', reads a contemporary account. Most of the so-called ecclesiastical contributions were, in fact, simple transfers; they were part of the fiscal contribution made by lay taxpayers, although it was the church that handed them over to the royal Treasury. A recent study of the weight of ecclesiastical contributions in the total ordinary and extraordinary taxes of Castile (which takes into account neither the revenues from the masterships of the Military Orders nor the *tercias*—proof of the

[52] Reinhard (1989), 472. [53] Artola (1982), 61.

confusion that reigns in this matter) estimates that they represented 16.4 per cent of tax revenues in 1561–5, 18.9 per cent in 1575–9 and 17.3 per cent in 1590–4, with a maximum of 26 per cent and a minimum of 12 per cent over the period as a whole.[54] The *subsidio*, the only tax that actually came out of the ecclesiastical purse, represented 6.1 per cent of the tax revenues that Philip II received from all his subjects between 1563 and 1598. Something similar to the French alienation of the *temporel*[55] also took place in Castile on a few occasions but, in comparison with the amounts involved in these operations in France, those of Castile were a mere drop in the ocean.[56] Ecclesiastical property, as well as the fiscal immunity of the clergy, remained practically untouched until shortly before the end of the *ancien régime* when Soler began the sale of church lands (Chapter 11.6).

There was only one Catholic territory which took measures that were similar in quality—although perhaps not in quantity—to those taken in the Reformation countries: Austria. The Turkish threat that weighed heavily on its inhabitants for almost three centuries brought about extremely unusual developments. Religion, politics—parliamentary consent to taxation—and war were united there in such a unique way in the sixteenth century that the saying 'Fiscus est Respublica' truly made sense. In 1452, the Turkish threat had already led Pope Nicholas V to grant to Emperor Frederick III the authority to demand taxes and subsidies from the clergy in case of need without consulting the bishops.[57] After the battle of Mohács (1526) in which the Turks defeated the Hungarian army and killed the last Jagellion king, Ferdinand I, brother-in-law of the late king, appropriated church properties and made use of them 'at his pleasure and as a consequence of necessity'. The Turkish threat also made it necessary to summon the estates frequently: here, the nobility, in exchange for their consent to taxes, managed to win concessions regarding the practice of Reformed worship from a Catholic ruler. Later, in 1541–2, the General Diet of Prague established the principle that the fiscal privileges of the clergy and nobility might be annulled, a principle which was largely unparalleled in early modern Europe. With some later modifications, the *cadastre* (*Steuerkataster*) elaborated at that time served as the basis for the tax system until the mid-eighteenth century, by which time the political, financial and economic development of the Austrian Habsburg lands had been considerable since the sixteenth century (Chapter 10). Haugwitz commented in the mid-eighteenth century that 'the privileges of the Estates are always to be regarded by a Christian sovereign as high and sacred', although in

[54] Bilbao (1990), 59. [55] Wolfe (1972), 126.
[56] Nader (1990), 100. [57] Pickl (1989), 123.

situations of pressing need the 'God-given principle of equality prevailed'.[58] Lord Stormont's description of the Austrian fiscal system in 1765 emphasized how the *auxilium* that the crown claimed from the estates was apportioned 'according to a fixed equitable proportion without any privilege, or exemption being allow'd . . . and the Clergy paying through their full Share'. He also pointed out that 'in Austria the Clergy are likewise subject to the ordinary Civil Jurisdiction *in Temporalibus, et active et passive*'. Such anomalies led him to place the following reflections in writing:

It seems something extraordinary, that in a Country where Zeal for the Roman Catholick Religion has run so high, and where the Interests of the State have been so often sacrificed to that Zeal, the power of the Clergy should have been brought, and kept within such narrow Bounds. Whatever may have been the Cause of this (for I Have not been able to meet with any Thing satisfactory under that Head, tho' Writers agree that Things have been upon this Footing for at least three hundred years) it is now a fixed, generally received, and uncontroverted principle.[59]

In general it was not until the spread of the Enlightenment that most Catholic states took the first steps towards the progressive elimination of privilege. When these measures were taken, it could be seen that not only was the fiscal pressure distributed more fairly, but also, as a consequence, the burden could be lightened without any appreciable impact on the income of rulers.[60] Until these radical changes took place, accompanied obviously by a new political and social climate, it proved to be practically impossible to broaden the social tax base and thus achieve greater fiscal justice. As Montesquieu had observed, 'the nature of taxes is relative to the government' ('la nature des tributs est relative au gouvernement').[61]

15.5 *The Fiscal Burden in the Sixteenth Century*

Richelieu pointed out the relationship between the fiscal burden and fiscal capacity. There is a need for precision on the amount of tax revenue which finally reached the Treasury (Chapter 13.2), which may have been very different from the fiscal burden carried by taxpayers. In this respect, the experiences of Austria and Castile were diametrically opposed. The net revenue of the *Haussteuer* in Austria (1671–1705) constituted 99 per cent of the sums agreed by the estates,[62] but usually the collection process for the *servicio de millones* in Castile supplied the Treasury with only one-third of the sums granted by the *Cortes*. Differences like

[58] Dickson (1987), ii, 185. [59] Ibid. i, 393. [60] Capra (1980), 7.

[61] Montesquieu, ed. Cohler, Miller and Stone (1989), 222; Braun in Tilly (1975), 247.

[62] Bérenger (1975), 326.

this bring to the fore not only the question of fraud to the detriment of the royal Treasury, but also the possible 'redistributive' character of a fiscal system, according to which financial loss for the Treasury may be beneficial to its administrators.

Fiscal capacity is much more difficult to assess. Some historians have taken an indirect approach, perhaps similar to the attempt to relate the fiscal burden to economic trends; it was argued that fiscal capacity might be reflected in the evolution of prices, or in a combination of prices and demographic trends.[63] However, there are serious doubts as to whether a general price index, let alone an index based on agricultural prices alone—as in the example cited previously—reflects anything but variations in the success or otherwise of harvests.[64] With due respect to the compilers of such indexes, other possible indicators will be evaluated here, such as the evolution of the volume of coinage (France), or the formation of monetary stock (Castile), in an attempt to deal with the issue in the broadest sense. Both contemporaries and historians have tried to estimate the fiscal burden of the 'typical peasant'[65] or the 'typical taxpayer'. In such cases, the search for a method of analysing the evolution of the fiscal burden is usually sacrificed in order to obtain results for a given moment in time.

The most reliable figures for Castile in the first half of the sixteenth century come from the evidence of the *alcabalas* and *servicios*, which represent considerably more than half the total tax revenue. Between 1516–20 and 1551–5 both sources of income increased by 140 per cent, while prices rose by 170 per cent between the same dates. The rise in wages (145 per cent) was less than that of prices, but slightly more than the increase in tax revenue.[66] The accumulated monetary stock (also counting the outflow of specie) grew by 272 per cent in the same period.[67] In short, against whichever index the evolution of the fiscal burden is measured, these were golden years for the taxpayer, in comparison with what was to come. Nevertheless, the relative immunity gained from oppressive taxation was not enjoyed to the same degree by all social groups. In 1516–20, indirect taxation (*alcabalas*) contributed 83.6 per cent of the total of *alcabalas* plus *servicios* and 69.2 per cent in 1551–5. Since the *servicios* were paid by the non-privileged, the humblest groups in both the towns and the countryside were hit hardest. It could be argued that, in terms of the per capita fiscal burden, indirect taxation was more oppressive since it was a more significant tax and was

[63] Calabria (1991), 57. [64] Morineau (1985), 32–3.

[65] Collins (1988), 166. The search for the 'Français moyen' has been called a 'fiction statistique inéluctable': Morineau (1988), 93.

[66] Hendricks (1976), 223. [67] Pieper (1985), table vi.

also more prevalent in cities than rural areas. Yet, though the urban population of Castile was still growing, it had not reached 10 per cent of the total population by 1550. In reality, indirect taxes were not more burdensome than direct ones because of the administrative procedures adopted. Each district was responsible for payment of the sum fixed for the levy of *alcabalas* and *tercias* (two-ninths of the tithe). The administrators farmed out the *tercias* of the district to the highest bidder and this amount was deducted from the total; then, the part of the *alcabala* payable by retailers coming from outside the administrative boundaries was also farmed out; what remained was finally shared out amongst the mass of taxpayers.[68] Taxpayers were assessed regardless of whether they lived in cities or rural areas; when there were no sales on which taxes could be collected, the remainder of the tax was shared out according to individual wealth, so that instead of remaining an indirect tax it was transmuted into a direct tax. This administrative procedure governed the two most important tax revenues in Castile during the first half of the sixteenth century, and is explicable only within the framework of the political relations between the king and the kingdom represented by the *Cortes*.

Since 1494 the fiscal administration had accepted the principle that the cities that were heads of a fiscal district should collect the *alcabalas* and *tercias*; part of the agreement was a moratorium on tax increases. More and more cities joined the system (*encabezamiento*) until in 1536 it embraced the whole of Castile. The loss of income for the Treasury was evident, especially at a time of rapid economic growth. Taking the years 1526–30 as index 100, *alcabalas* and *tercias* increased from index 96.9 in 1516–20 to only index 110.8 in 1551–5. The *servicios* rose somewhat higher, from index 63.6 in 1516–20 to index 165.6 in 1551–5. In 1556, when Philip II began to assume his responsibilities in the government of Castile, both he and his team of financial advisers were clear on at least two points: that the fiscal system had become profoundly unjust and that its administration had been incapable, for political reasons, of maximizing tax revenue or at least indexing the crown's share to the dramatic increase in wealth which had occurred in the kingdom during the last half century. Such dynamic sectors as trade with America contributed very little to the Treasury. In order to stimulate trade and the colonization of the New World, no specific tax was placed on the movement of goods until the *almojarifazgo* of the Indies was introduced in 1543. In the following year, this tax contributed a relatively modest 6 per cent to the total revenues. From 1544 to 1566, the year in which there was a spectacular rise in the rate at which the tax was levied, the ratio between the total tonnage and the

[68] Fortea Pérez (1992), 162.

collection of the *almojarifazgo* was 0.598—as opposed to 1.191 for the period 1573–96 and 0.986 for the years 1616–47.[69]

This situation did not change substantially until 1575. Thus, the Castilian fiscal system can scarcely be seen as aggressive in the light of the wealth that was being generated during the first three-quarters of the century. There are indications that in such vast and economically important areas as Andalusia, the overall fiscal pressure may actually have been less in the 1560s and early 1570s than in the 1520s. What can be said about the situation of the 'typical peasant'? In 1575, Philip II charged a team of inspectors with the task of making a survey of the villages of Castile by means of a questionnaire comprising 57 items; in 1578, the operation was repeated but this time with 45 questions. The answers from some 600 villages still exist. They have been examined by historians with a view to finding answers to questions similar to those which are being considered here.[70] In 1575, the total of the major taxes (*alcabala* and *servicios*) which the 'typical peasant' household had to pay came close to 8 per cent of their annual income as estimated by the surveyor. In 1590, the *servicio de millones* was introduced, which raised the rate to almost 10 per cent.[71] That is to say, by the end of the sixteenth century the 'typical Castilian peasant' was paying the Treasury the equivalent of another tithe. Whether this was a heavy or a light burden cannot be estimated except in relation to the size of the annual harvest. Adam Smith cautioned, in his second canon on taxation, that taxes should be 'certain and not arbitrary'. On most occasions, the 'typical peasant' knew beforehand the amount payable, that is, the real fiscal burden. The uncertainty lay in the variations of his annual income. Historians are frequently surprised that the per capita fiscal burden is not inevitably excessive during periods of acute fiscal pressure. The taxable male population of Russia, for example, carried an increasing fiscal burden in the sense of heavier taxes: but when calculated as a share of the per capita income, the 'real' fiscal burden fluctuated between 12 and 15 per cent.[72] Therefore, it was harvest fluctuations ('l'inégalité des récoltes')[73] which eased or increased the fiscal burden, and not the actions of the state on its own. Indeed, such fluctuations constituted one of the essential characteristics of the peasant economies of the

[69] Author's calculations based on Chaunu (1977), vi pt. i, 334–6, and Ulloa (1986), ch. 7.

[70] Salomon (1964), 234; Gentil da Silva (1967), 50.

[71] The precise figures are 7.73 per cent in 1575 and 9.79 per cent in 1590.

[72] Kahan (1985), 345. Morineau (1988), 92–4, arrives at the following estimates for France for the percentage of taxes on the country's wealth: 18 per cent (1450); 10 per cent (1525); 16 per cent (1607); 31 per cent (1683); 38 to 40 per cent (1789), considering the gross wheat production. If total agricultural production was twice that contained in the base calculation, then the percentages would be halved. A second approach—in monetary terms per caput—at the same dates yields the following figures: 4, 6, 34, 118, 340–60 *sols*. A third approach—expressed in the number of working days of an 'average worker'—yields the following figures: 1.33, 2.8, 3.4, 7.8, 17–18.

[73] Vilar (1974), 42.

ancien régime. There was more predictability about the tax collector than the climate.[74]

It is not easy to make similar calculations in the urban areas. Nevertheless, some trends seem apparent in Castile by about 1575. Until then, town dwellers, who were also subject to the payment of *alcabalas* and *servicios*, dealt with these in a different manner from the rural population. The burden of the *servicio* in the urban areas does not seem to have been intolerable. As has already been pointed out, it was a tax which marked the distinction between the privileged and the non-privileged. Obviously, a significant proportion of the urban population was non-privileged or commoner (*pechero*), but there were also very high concentrations of privileged inhabitants in comparison to the average for the kingdom.[75] This made inequities in terms of class and their fiscal consequences particularly significant. Local authorities tried whenever possible to reduce the amount of the taxes (they had to vote for them in the *Cortes*, even though they themselves were not taxed) and to prevent an adequate knowledge of the numbers of commoners subject to taxation by circumventing a revision of the roll of taxpayers. In 1528, when crown officials attempted to draw up such a roll in Burgos, they were forced to desist because, as they reported to the *Cortes*: 'if it be wanted to do it now, it would be a great scandal and riot, and . . . they did notify and admonish us not to meddle in doing any sort of taxpayers' roll.' In Avila they resorted to the levy of *sisas* (excise taxes) paid on consumer goods or with the council's own funds; only in the most extreme cases was there a repartition of taxes. The crux of the matter was to maintain the nature of the *servicios* as a form of parliamentary taxation. This allowed the cities' representatives in the *Cortes* to bargain for other concessions in return for their consent to the levy of taxes and the preservation of the prevailing legal-political order (which perpetuated fiscal inequity). At the same time, the towns attempted to keep the commoners' contribution from becoming so oppressive that it might become a justification for social discontent.

As for the *alcabala*, nobody could avoid paying it. It has been seen that the *encabezamiento* was collected by first deducting the *tercias*, then the amount paid by retailers from outside the city; and finally the remainder of the tax was shared out within the city itself. It can be asserted that prior to the great increase in 1575, most of this third part, that which was shared out within the city, was collected on sales of consumer goods (soap, wine, fish and so on). Other kinds of transactions more closely related to commercial and industrial activities seem to have been less affected. But after 1575 it was very difficult to continue such a

[74] Collins (1988), 90.

[75] Moliné-Bertrand (1973), 13 (for the clergy); Moliné-Bertrand (1974), 68 (40 per cent of the nobility lived in urban centres).

discriminatory tax policy without endangering the provisioning of the cities, since the *alcabala* was collected from those who sold goods.[76] In the city of Avila, the contribution of the 'typical *pechero*' to the *alcabala* in the first fifty years of the century ranged between a minimum of 557 *maravedís* (in 1536) and a maximum of 761 *maravedís* (in 1534), while it increased to values between 1,413 *maravedís* (in 1597) and 1,954 *maravedís* (in 1577) in the second half of the century. The values for the *servicio* ranged from 75 *maravedís* in 1503, to 79 (1519), 170 (1549), 192 (1594) and reached 1,182 *maravedís* in 1610. These figures express both the nominal increase in taxes (in the case of the *alcabala* from 1575 onwards, with respect to the *servicio* from 1539) and the decrease in the taxable population after its peak in the quinquennium 1570–4.[77] For one reason or another, and perhaps earlier in the cities than in the countryside, the weight of taxation began to be felt in Castile from 1575 onwards. And there was to be a further demographic setback before the end of the century.

The French monarchy managed to triple its revenues from 10 to 30 million *livres* between the beginning of the reign of Francis I and the final years of Henri IV. Both the rate of taxation and the amount of tax revenue went up sharply during the sixteenth century. With hardly any significant changes in the structure of the fiscal system (that is, the ratio between direct and indirect taxes), direct taxes 'rose a bit more than general prices until the 1550s, but they did not keep pace with the rampant inflation of the 1550–85 period'.[78] If it is true that sales taxes, transit taxes and particularly *gabelles* increased more than direct taxes, and taking into account the fact that these—*tailles*—were in general borne by those without fiscal privilege, one must conclude that in general terms the system moved towards fiscal injustice. Moreover, it did so with unusual effectiveness. If it is accepted that the revenue tripled, then it came quite close to equalling the growth in the volume of money coined (3.55 from 1501–10 to 1601–10; 4.17 from 1511–20 to 1601–10).[79] Furthermore, there seems to be no doubt that the increase in fiscal pressure was concentrated in the years of the Wars of Religion, especially from 1560 to 1589. In this period both the per capita tax burden and the grain equivalent doubled (Figures 96 and 97).[80] The regional evidence does not suggest any mitigation of the lot of the taxpayer.[81] Although the pressure eased somewhat between 1590 and 1609, it soon returned to its earlier level.

By contrast, the revenue in Castile increased sixfold between 1500 and 1600,

[76] Fortea Pérez (1992), 165–6.

[77] De Tapia (1987), 59–63.

[78] Collins (1988), 49.

[79] Spooner (1972).

[80] Hoffman (1986), 46; ESFDB \rjb\frb004 based on \frd012; Hoffman in Hoffman and Norberg (1994), 238; ESFDB \rjb\frb006 based on \rjb\frd015.

[81] Jacquart (1974), 200–1.

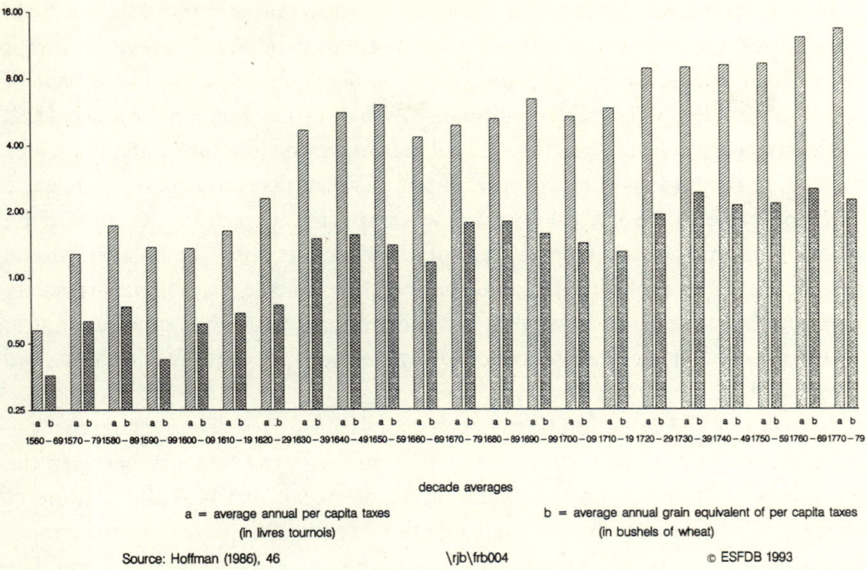

FIG. 96. Per capita royal tax receipts in France, 1560–1779 (expressed in *livres tournois* and in bushels of wheat)

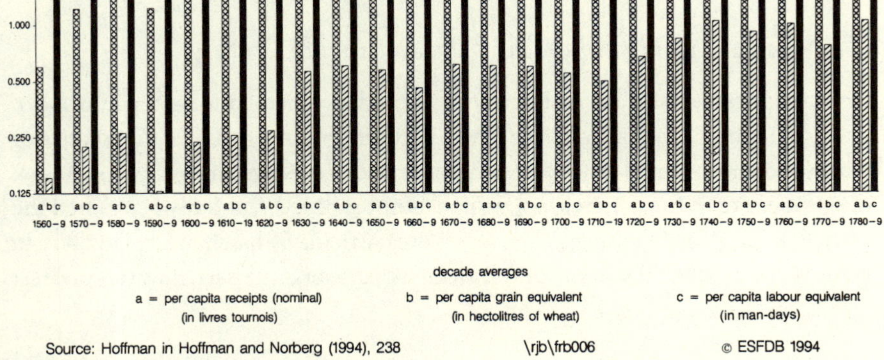

FIG. 97. Per capita royal tax receipts in France, 1560–1789 (expressed in *livres tournois*, hectolitres of wheat and man-days)

while the amount of money in circulation rose from 5 to 90.82 million ducats, that is, it increased eighteenfold. From this it must be inferred that the fiscal system was unable to tax effectively the new creation of wealth. Nevertheless, it is also true that Castile had a unique advantage presented by the arrival of treasure from the Indies. The continual growth of this revenue in the second half of the sixteenth century freed the Castilian taxpayer from a substantially greater burden. In the mid-1550s, the proportion of Castilian taxes to American treasure in the overall balance of royal revenues was respectively 79 and 21 per cent. In the quinquennium 1561–5, the proportion of taxes actually rose (the balance was 88 per cent to 12 per cent); it fluctuated somewhat up to 1580, but fell progressively thereafter, reaching the low point for the century in the last quinquennium, when taxes constituted 74 per cent of total revenue while American treasure had risen to 26 per cent of the total.[82]

In the cases of France and Castile, one cannot automatically conclude that the general fiscal burden was greater or smaller on the basis of the gap between the growth of tax revenue and an index of taxable wealth such as the volume of money coined or the size of the monetary stock. The fiscal systems simply functioned within parameters which dictated the types of wealth which could be taxed and by how much; and also who paid more, who paid less and who paid nothing at all. For instance, it has been stated previously that much urban wealth, or the wealth of the richest citizens, evaded the usual fiscal mechanisms. Similarly, the distribution of the *taille* in France, even in areas of land tax (*taille réelle*), was scarcely a model of efficient administration or fiscal justice. The rich knew by what means they could avoid paying all or part of their contribution. In privileged fiscal systems such as those of Italy, France or Castile, urban wealth had to be tapped by means of indirect mechanisms such as forced loans, the sale of offices and so on.

15.6 *The Fiscal Burden in the Seventeenth Century*

The temporary cessation of large-scale armed conflicts among the European powers (France, England, and the United Provinces), as a result of the treaties or truces of 1598, 1604 and 1609 was without any doubt a stimulus for rulers to slow down the rate of fiscal increase. Castile did not succeed, but Sully restrained the growth of taxation in France. The 1590s were particularly harsh in England but, in spite of the underassessment of the richest taxpayers, the fact that the poorest

[82] The other figures for tax revenue and American treasure are respectively: for 1566–70, 81 and 19 per cent; for 1571–5, 86 and 14 per cent; for 1576–80, 80 and 20 per cent; for 1581–5, 77 and 23 per cent; for 1586–90, 76 and 24 per cent; for 1591–5, 75.5 and 24.5 per cent.

hardly paid anything, that indirect taxation was relatively low in this period, and that there was no fiscal privilege meant that the tax system was 'relatively equitable'.[83] It is noteworthy that Sir Thomas Smith's *De republica Anglorum* (1583) practically ignored fiscal matters. Even so, it has been asserted that 'the Stuarts inherited a fiscal system which was already close to the point of breakdown'.[84]

Both Philip III and Henri IV were confronted with a genuine breakdown. The challenges of restoring the royal Treasury, preparing for new commitments and financing the growing costs were met by the various princes in different ways in accordance with the political framework within which the fiscal system had to operate (Chapter 9.2). One method adopted to raise more revenue and to redistribute the fiscal burden more equitably was to define the limits of the privileged class in a more accurate manner. In France, for instance, the crown undertook systematic *recherches* from the second half of the fifteenth century until the ministry of Colbert. If the overall results are to be judged on the basis of the *élection* of Bayeux, they were disappointing. Those whose status was in doubt were subjected to trial. The highest percentages of convictions—and therefore inclusion in the *taille* rolls—resulting from these *recherches* were 6.2 per cent in 1463 and 6 per cent in 1666, whereas in 1540, 1598 and 1624 convictions were as low as 1.6, 1.4 and 3.2 per cent respectively.[85] Therefore, it can be deduced that even as the fiscal burden became most oppressive in the period between the Wars of Religion and the Fronde—and Normandy was the most heavily taxed province in France—there was no substantial reappraisal of the prevailing legal, and consequently fiscal, status. Yet in the period from 1463 to 1666, the number of noble families almost trebled (it increased by 283 per cent). The failure of these attempts to enlarge the fiscal base is scarcely surprising. Even in the eighteenth century, there was reference to *lois fondamentales* in order to counteract the timid attempts to eliminate fiscal privilege.[86]

In Castile, similar measures were taken against the usurpation of fiscal exemption. As early as 1566, Philip II tried to call a halt to the extension of fiscal privilege to 'servants and friends' of those who already enjoyed exemption. During Olivares' ministry, a thorough inspection was made of doubtful exemptions that supposedly affected whole villages or towns. On most occasions, the Treasury was in the right in its demands, but the urgency of the need for money made it expedient for it to accept an indemnity for the continuation of the exemption, thereby reinforcing any future claim. The procedure bears a resemblance to the purchase of exemptions in Brittany in the 1630s (a procedure in

[83] Palliser (1983), 380. [84] Russell (1990), 166. [85] Wood (1980), 35.
[86] Chaussinand Nogaret (1980), 193.

France known as *affranchissement*) and, just like this process, it 'had the effect of exempting the richest taxpayers at precisely the moment when the king would double the direct tax burden; it reinforced the already overwhelming preponderance of the peasantry on the tax rolls'.[87] Without a significant extension of the social base subject to taxation, the monarchies of *ancien régime* Europe confronted the new challenges of the seventeenth century by increasing the tax burden on those who had always carried it. Depending on the political and constitutional framework within which the fiscal system operated, there were times when the possibility of continuing to exploit the usual body of taxpayers reached its limit. Once this point was reached, an attempt had to be made to break out of the constitutional framework, or the political and military strategy of the prince could be seriously affected.

A period of acute direct fiscal pressure seems to have begun in the principal European monarchies more or less simultaneously. In France, the turning-point appears to be around 1627: from 1620 to 1627 the *taille* had already risen by 20 per cent, but from 1627 to 1633–4 the increase reached 66 per cent.[88] In grain equivalent or per caput, the fiscal burden doubled between the period 1620–9 and 1630–9 and then again in between the 1630s and 1640s.[89] In the kingdom of Naples, the fiscal burden rose from some 3 ducats per hearth in the middle of the sixteenth century to a maximum of 11 in 1638.[90] In Castile, the tax that was primarily responsible for the rise in fiscal pressure during the seventeenth century was the *servicio de millones*. If we are to judge by the quantities demanded by the crown and granted by the *Cortes*, Castilian taxpayers were paying seven times more in the 1650s than in the 1610s and almost nine times more than in the 1590s. A different story is told by the accounts of the sums which actually reached the Treasury from various provinces. In Segovia, for instance, the ratio between the annual minimum (in 1594) and maximum (in 1660) was just over 3. In Seville, perhaps the most important fiscal district in the kingdom, the same ratio was 2.21 for the years in which the most tax (in 1640) and least tax (in 1607) was collected. Why was there such a deficit in the actual collection of taxes and did this imply a covert form of tax relief for those required to pay, or the diversion of funds towards those who administered the tax collecting machinery? The prevailing impression is that in periods of greatest fiscal pressure, the collection of taxes at local level took place without paying too much attention to the original form of taxation (whether direct or indirect). In the final analysis, the objective was to collect by whatever means the largest possible amount through *ad hoc* methods

[87] Collins (1988), 90.
[88] Ibid. 161.
[89] Hoffman (1986), 46.
[90] Calabria (1991), 55.

in each contributing community. In Castile, the *servicios de millones* were collected from 1601 onwards by means of *sisas* (excise taxes), first on wine, later on oil and finally on meat and vinegar. It is not unimportant to find out how this option came to be chosen. When, in 1590, the *Cortes* granted the first *servicio de millones*, the rules for its collection envisaged that in contrast to the traditional *servicios*, this time there would not be exemptions for the nobility and the clergy—after all, it was a question of a tax on wealth without exceptions of any kind. The experiment did not last long. Meanwhile heated discussions were taking place about the nature of fiscal equity and the progressive or regressive character of taxes in general. Opinions not too dissimilar to those which were voiced later in England or in Cameralist thought were beginning to be heard. An indirect tax such as the *sisa* on consumer goods was fair, it was said, in a society characterized by fiscal inequity. There were no exemptions in such a tax, since everyone who consumed had to pay. Those who were in favour argued that 'it affects each person according to their budget because the poor man buys less and the rich man spends a lot'. Others insisted that it would be fairer to tax consumer products which featured on the rich man's shopping list—turkey, partridge, rabbit, mutton and fresh fish. There were those who went even further and warned about its harmful long-term effect: 'although it seems smooth, its smoothness is that of blood-letting, leaving the body to bleed to death'.

Historians nowadays are mostly in agreement about the regressive nature of excises on consumer goods. A German scholar of the nineteenth century, Engel, formulated a proposition that has come to be regarded as a 'law', namely that the richer a society is, the less of the expenditure of its members is allocated to food consumption—and vice versa.[91] However, it is no less true that resorting to the market for the supply of consumer goods was uncommon in *ancien régime* Europe, except, that is, in urban areas. In other words, most of the revenue from the most widely used taxes on consumer goods was expected to come from the urban centres. This is what was understood by those who in 1611 distributed the quotas of the *servicio* of 17.5 million *maravedís*: almost a quarter (23.7 per cent) of the total was assigned to urban Castile, with significant imbalances such as those of Madrid (74 per cent of the total for its region), Seville (37.4 per cent) or Segovia (30 per cent). Clearly, the urban population did not constitute a quarter of the total population of Castile in 1611. No town in Castile had a population the size of Madrid's in the last quarter of the sixteenth century. It was presumed then, and now, that the wealth and economic power of the inhabitants of the cities would allow them to bear more of the fiscal burden than their rural neighbours. Twenty years later, in 1631, the administration decided to investigate the relative burden

[91] Kula (1972), 244.

of the *sisas* or excises. It was found that in the urban centres of the province of Valladolid, the 'typical consumer' was paying 2,036 *maravedís* while a person living in the villages paid 708. In all the territory of the kingdom included in the survey (2,961 localities of very different size, a total of 317,729 households in all), the differences in the annual contribution varied from 1.57 to 3.04 ducats per caput per annum.[92] Castile in 1630 foreshadowed the Dutch situation of the mid-1760s as described in the memorandum published by Moreau de Beaumont: 'Although taxes are extremely high, farmers and other rural folk are in general very well-off, because all of the contributions are collected on consumables. Consumer goods are sold accordingly, and in this manner farmers pay taxes and impositions with the consumers' money.'[93]

Accounts from the province of Seville between 1601 and 1670, or more precisely, the city of Seville's share in the collection of the provincial excise taxes (*sisas de millones*), show that the situation did not vary throughout the period. From a relatively low start (under 50 per cent before 1609), the figure rose dramatically in 1609 itself (to 81.4 per cent of the total) and oscillated thereafter around 70 per cent of the total.[94] What we must now consider is whether urban wealth or economic power could bear such imbalances. An initial approach to the question might come from urban demography. It has been demonstrated that the urban population of Castile suffered a sharp decline during the seventeenth century.[95] The population of Seville, for instance, was reduced by more than half between the end of the sixteenth century and 1655.[96] As a result, the fiscal burden per caput would have increased by a factor of 4.31. However, since this was a tax which applied to those who made use of the market, some were in a superior economic position and could avoid being taxed. Those who lived in the cities and produced their own wine, oil or meat would have no reason to buy at the market. Those who owned farm lands were able to evade the excise. One of the most widespread forms of fraud was to bring into town more wine or oil than was needed for domestic use. The houses of the agricultural landowners, including the clergy, were converted into a seventeenth-century prototype of the 'duty-free' shop!

[92] Sebastián and Vela (1992), 12.

[93] Bonney (1994), 69.

[94] The precise percentages are: 1601: 49.5; 1602: 47.2; 1604: 37.7; 1609: 81.4; 1612: 78.4; 1635: 67.9; 1636: 69.5; 1637: 70.4; 1638: 68.1; 1639: 65.9; 1640: 69.2 (uncertain data); 1643: 64.3; 1644: 65.8; 1666: 72.8 (uncertain data); 1670: 71.7.

[95] Gelabert (1990), 12–14; Ringrose (1990), 65–6.

[96] Domínguez Ortiz (1989), 5. The figures for (a) the number of households; (b) the number of 'persons'; and (c) population estimates at certain dates are as follows: 1588: (a) 25,886; (b) 123,667; (c) 140,000; 1591: (a) 23,166; 1597: (a) 24,301; (c) 150,000; 1638: (a) 20,000; 1655: (b) 55,017; (c) 63,000; 1693: (a) 16,081.

In the countryside, it proved extremely difficult to impose the excise. The peasants tired of repeatedly telling the royal officials that they did not own small taverns or butcheries. The choice of one particular form of indirect taxation was detrimental to the urban consumer's standard of living and also to economic activity in general. But it was perhaps the only thing that could be done, especially considering the fact that from the beginning of the seventeenth century the contribution of the treasure from the Indies, which hitherto had freed the Castilian taxpayer from an excessive burden, was in decline. And this was not the worst. As in the sixteenth century, the Spanish Habsburgs were flooding the European monetary system—against their volition and that of their subjects—with gold and, especially, silver. The market value of silver tended to decline with the passing of time, and the purchasing power of the treasure which arrived from the Indies followed the same downward trend. This situation was tolerable during the second half of the sixteenth century because more silver than ever before arrived from America. However, after the maxima recorded in the years 1596–1600, the steadily smaller quantities of treasure that arrived were able to purchase fewer and fewer goods.[97]

It has been asserted for France that 'the whole burden of the Thirty Years' War was carried at the expense of peasant incomes'.[98] Let us recall some representative figures of the total revenue in France at this time: 39 million *livres* in 1620, 55 million in 1629, 208 million in 1635.[99] The *taille* amounted to 61.5 per cent of total revenue in 1634.[100] Consider as well the fact that 'many towns did not pay the *taille*; indeed, many bourgeois of privileged towns . . . did not pay the *tailles* on their rural property'.[101] If all this is taken into account, it appears that by the mid-1640s the limits of the equation between burden and strength must have been reached, not long after Richelieu (who died on 4 December 1642) had written the text quoted at the beginning of this chapter. Henceforth the weight of the *taille* seems to have been reduced considerably: in the *élection* of Étampes, the *taille* amounted to 138,780 *livres* in 1645, 109,123 in 1651, 78,650 in 1685 and 66,750 *livres* in 1700.[102] Hoffman's calculations also lend support to the view that the period 1650–69 represented a relative relief in comparison to the twenty preceding years (Figures 96 and 97). Some comments on the fiscal burden in seven-

97 Flynn (1982), 142. 98 Bercé (1974), i, 69. 99 Bonney (1981*a*), 304–5.

100 Collins (1988), 234; 61.9 per cent according to Bercé (1974), i, 67.

101 Collins (1988), 90; Temple (1975), 75–6.

102 Although 'en supposant un nombre plues élevé de taillables vers 1640, la différence reste considerable': Jacquart (1974), 619.

teenth-century France have come to be regarded as received wisdom,[103] but they do not consider the worst years of the seventeenth century (according to Hoffman, the 1680s and 1690s). The pauperization of the peasantry from the mid-1630s is evident from the fact that the administration occasionally accepted tax remissions, while non-payment increased notoriously thereafter.

Who, therefore, bore the fiscal burden? Collins suggests that the increase was borne by a 'relatively small minority of the peasantry'. The same author points out two perfectly compatible ways of dealing with the situation. There were those who could continue to pay until a certain limit, beyond which they would abandon their hamlets 'wandering the countryside'; these people therefore constituted a contingent of part-time or part-life taxpayers. Full-time taxpayers were those others who managed to endure the fiscal burden without being overwhelmed.[104] However, in order to be able to survive, they had to be given assistance by their landlords, whose political power at the village level was decisive in protecting them, so that the *élus* and other tax officials would not treat them in the same manner as those who lacked this sort of protection. The landlords were not acting unselfishly: the *taille* competed with the landlords' rents and led to difficulties in collecting them. This reasoning is also applicable to the case of Castile. By the second decade of the seventeenth century, attention was being drawn to the fact that seigneurial estates were relatively more populated than royal lands. Their relative well-being had not arisen 'because Nature has given them more abundant fruits, but because their impositions are diverted to royal lands, where soldiers do not meet resistance against their abuses and taxes do not fall on those able to obtain tax remissions'.[105] It has been demonstrated that in Extremadura the population of the seigneurial estates continued to increase in the sixteenth century when the growth of settlements on royal lands had ceased; and in the seventeenth century the demographic decline was less pronounced in the former areas than in the latter.[106] The survey of 1631 revealed that while the 'typical peasants' of the feudal estates were paying on average 680 *maravedís* per annum, those living on crown lands had had to pay 1,387 *maravedís* per annum. In France it was also the case that 'depopulation

[103] Goubert (1969), 129: 'rarement . . . au-dessous de 5 per cent . . . parfois à 10 per cent' of gross peasant revenue. But for 'la majeure partie des paysans' of the Beauvaisis, the fiscal burden is estimated at 20 per cent upon the gross peasant revenue, a percentage considered 'très raisonnable': Goubert (1960), 180. Another set of calculations: Mousnier (1979–84), i, 733–8. In both cases there are comments such as 'no holding could have met its obligations. And yet the peasants did survive' (Mousnier); or 'et cependant, tous ces paysans qui théoriquement ne pouvaient vivre sur leurs terres, ont vécu' (Goubert).

[104] Collins (1988), 189.

[105] Domínguez Ortiz (1948), 117.

[106] Llopis Agelán (1989).

occurred in those parishes which were most heavily taxed'.[107] The evolution of the *taille* in the *généralité* of Caen (Normandy) and in the *élection* of Paris between 1615 and 1645 shows a striking divergence between the two areas, the former with a rather more upward trend than the latter.[108] The increase of land sales on the part of peasants suffering financial hardship reinforces the image of economic instability as well as the geographical and social mobility of the French peasantry. The purchasers, 'nobles and privileged urbanites', took advantage of their fiscal exemption to attain the position described by Vauban in 1707: 'the exemptions raised the value of the privileged investors' property relative to land held by taxpaying peasants—which presumably dropped in price every time the *taille* was increased'.[109]

15.7 *Conclusion: The Fiscal Burden and the Economy*

What was the impact of taxation on the economy? Did it act as a motor for the economy, generating growth, or did it retard the process of economic development? Our knowledge of the fiscal data of the European countries is rarely sufficient to answer questions of this scope. The English evidence from 1660 until the close of the eighteenth century is of exceptional interest, both in its own right and as a basis for comparison with others, in any attempt to provide an answer.[110] In this period the English fiscal system proved to be truly efficient. The fiscal administration managed to increase substantially the resources at the disposal of successive governments. Some of the vital elements of this process are well known. Firstly, the administrative machinery and its personnel appear to have been 'one of the most professional and efficient bureaucracies available to any government in Europe'.[111] Secondly, and perhaps more importantly, if it is true that English citizens were subject to a heavier fiscal burden for almost a century and a half than their neighbours on the other side of the Channel, we must try to determine what type of taxation produced such extraordinary fruits at a relatively low political cost.

It has been said that the 'government's room for manoeuvre was strictly circumscribed', an issue which introduces a first point of comparison with other countries. The room for manoeuvre was limited not only for English governments; this was a general characteristic of the countries of *ancien régime* Europe. When seventeenth-century France is taken as a paradigm of 'fiscal absolutism', more attention is usually paid to the quantitative aspects and the fiscal exploi-

[107] Dupâquier (1979), 61; Bonney (1992*a*), 169.

[108] Bonney (1992*b*), 119.

[109] Hoffman (1986), 54.

[110] Beckett and Turner (1990), 380.

[111] O'Brien (1988), 28.

tation of particular groups than to the government's inability to collect taxes from those who in reality possessed the most wealth. In other words, a system of direct taxation like that of France, which from 1662 to 1669 provided its government with practically the same proportion of total revenue (approximately 40 per cent) as that of England between 1661 and 1670 (45.1 per cent),[112] might have yielded twice as much if certain social groups had not been completely untouched by the fiscal system. The 'room for manoeuvre' was also restricted in France until the final days of the *ancien régime*, albeit for other reasons.

There seems to be no doubt that the substantial increase in fiscal resources in England between 1660 and the close of the eighteenth century was achieved by getting the most out of a system based on indirect taxation. What is most surprising is that this increase does not appear to have been a consequence of economic growth in the long term, but rather of political and administrative efficiency and the slow but steady extension of the tax base. Nevertheless, there is no doubt that the backdrop for these events was a period of sustained demographic and economic growth. It is tempting to compare the consequences for the economy of a progressive consolidation of a system based on indirect taxation in the generally contrasting situations of England and Castile (with economic and demographic growth on the one hand and general crisis on the other). It has been shown that the progressive importance of indirect taxation in England (which provided 65.4 per cent of the total tax revenue for the period 1791–9) meant that 'the more the country became dependent on excise and customs income ... , the more any surplus income was diverted away from expenditure on industrial consumer goods, that is away from home demand'; and that 'the overall rise in the incidence of taxation was regressive and, in consequence, would have tended to reduce demand'.[113] If this is true in conditions of economic and demographic growth, it is worth trying to evaluate the effects in the radically different context of seventeenth-century Castile.

It is clear that the typical Castilian consumer of this period, subject to growing taxation on consumer goods, had at his disposal progressively less money to buy anything other than foodstuffs, as was true of his English counterpart in the eighteenth century. This 'typical consumer' in most cases would be a city dweller and a wage-earner. The information available about the trend of wages in seventeenth-century Castile is regrettably scarce and poor, but nevertheless it has been the only material available in the last half century for studies of general aspects of the Castilian and Spanish crisis of the seventeenth century. E. J. Hamilton and later J. M. Keynes pointed out that the gap between European prices and wages had favoured the accumulation of capital and provided busi-

[112] Bonney (1991*a*), 229; Beckett and Turner (1990), 380.

[113] Beckett and Turner (1990), 401.

nessmen and employers with the opportunity of obtaining exceptionally high profits. The less pronounced gap in Spain's case meant that profits were not so 'extraordinary': in these terms, 'one of the "classic" explanations for the economic backwardness of the peninsula was formulated'.[114] The revision of the postulates of both Hamilton and Keynes, as is true of most revisionism, has reached the opposite conclusion: real wages also decreased in Spain, in a proportion half-way between that of France and England. However, the data of the alleged Spanish wage-earner that scholars have been using can hardly be indicative of the state of the Castilian job market because they are from Valencia. The behaviour of real wages there (the index stood at 59 in 1591–1600 as against 100 in 1521–30) was rather 'unexpected' for those who made the calculations thirty years ago; they also discovered that the reason for the discrepancies in Hamilton's figures lay in the fact that whereas the nominal wages in his calculations had trebled, theirs merely doubled.[115] The root of the problem was, and still is, not so much in the classes of workers as in the fact that one series is from Valencia and the other also includes data from Andalusia and Castile. Moreover, Hamilton recognized that 'the greatest defect of the composite series (of wages) consists of the abnormally high percentage of professional labour included', that is to say that certain types of wage-earners (gardeners, doormen, stewards) appear in his series with the same wages for twenty years or more.[116] It is also possible to study the evolution of nominal wages according to Hamilton, as well as those for a selection of four types of wage-earners (labourer, journeyman carpenter, master carpenter and master mason) who have in common the circumstances of belonging to Castilian provinces and being non-professionals. In eight of the ten observations, Hamilton's data show slightly higher figures than Gelabert's own calculations.[117] Thus, Gelabert's sample of wage-earners leans towards the most modest class of workers. Both series, nevertheless, indicate that, in effect, nominal wages were not only maintained but even rose during the first half of the seventeenth century. The evolution of real wages depicted by Hamilton shows that, although there were large fluctuations in annual trends, real wages fell below the index level of 100, based on the period 1571–80, in only five years in the period 1601–50. They began the period at index 115.75 (1601–10) and ended at

[114] Nadal (1959), 520.

[115] Phelps Brown and Hopkins (1959), 21.

[116] Hamilton (1970), 270.

[117] Nominal (a) and real (b) wages in Castile, after Hamilton's data and nominal (c) and real (d) wages in Castile after Gelabert's calculations (base 100 = 1621–30). 1601–5: (a) 92.6; (b) 102; (c) 92.2; (d) 102; 1606–10: (a) 98.5; (b) 112; (c) 96.2; (d) 110; 1611–15: (a) 98.7; (b) 119; (c) 98.2; (d) 118; 1616–20: (a) 99; (b) 115; (c) 93.1; (d) 108; 1621–5: (a) 98.2; (b) 109; (c) 94.9; (d) 105; 1626–30: (a) 101.8; (b) 92; (c) 105.1; (d) 95; 1631–5: (a) 106.0; (b) 103; (c) 105.2; (d) 102; 1636–40: (a) 107.5; (b) 100; (c) 103.3; (d) 96; 1641–5: (a) 106.9; (b) 86; (c) 93; (d) 99.7; (d) 87; 1646–50: (a) 108.5; (b) 88; (c) 110.5; (d) 89.

index 100.81 (1641–50), that is to say, with a loss of 13 per cent. Considering the same period (but with the base readjusted to the years 1621–30), real wages fell by 10 per cent in Hamilton's series and by 14.5 per cent in that compiled by Gelabert. The decline in the level of real wages (although it is underestimated because of the use of an unweighted commodity index) was attributed by Hamilton to the variations in prices produced by *vellón* inflation. In any case, those who had work were losing purchasing power during the first half of the seventeenth century. However, it seems evident that in the cities capable of assimilating the greatest number of wage-earners (Segovia, Cuenca, Seville and so on) the population fell sharply between 1600 and 1650. Cuenca, which in 1561 had 58 per cent of its population working in the industrial sector (fundamentally the textile industry), retained only 36.8 per cent in 1707. Sectors which scarcely played a part in the job market were buoyant, however: those dependent on the church increased from 9 per cent to 18.4 per cent, while the proportion of farmers rose from 9.6 per cent to 23.8 per cent.[118]

Uninterrupted growth in nominal wages, such as that which took place in Castile during a century and a half, could have been tolerated by the employers without excessive difficulties as long as they could counterbalance it by raising retail prices, something which could be done in times of great demand, whether at home or in the Americas, as was the case in most of the sixteenth century. In this period, the cities were full of workers, whose real wages according to Hamilton's data hardly changed at all between 1521 and 1600. Around 1600 the scene changed radically. The inertia or slight downward trend in real wages between 1600 and 1650, along with the decline in urban population and in its industrial sector, leads one to believe that very few people were in urban employment, a hypothesis that is reinforced by the parallel increase in the number of city dwellers who were swelling the ranks of the agricultural sector. It also seems probable that if the nominal wage remained stable or decreased relatively little, it was because employers who wanted to retain their employees had to pay them at least the minimum so that they could eat. However, the minimum required was without a doubt very high. In addition to the *vellón* inflation, indirect taxation on consumer goods must have been a very significant contributory factor to the high level of nominal wages. When an urban worker's nominal wage has been deflated by taking into consideration the prices of consumer goods subject to excise tax (meat, wine) as well as those that were not (bread), the result is a much more pronounced reduction in purchasing power. The data for the city of Valladolid shows that the purchasing power of wages dropped by 30 per cent for the middle and upper categories of workers and by

[118] Reher (1990), 27.

almost 50 per cent for the lower ones.[119] Half the price of wine in the years 1657–61, for example, corresponded to the excises that were being charged on it. The excise tax on oil constituted 57 per cent of the price in 1668. By comparing the evolution of the nominal wages of building workers in Madrid and Barcelona between 1737 and 1798, Vilar was able to demonstrate, but not to explain satisfactorily, that even in 1775 wages continued to be higher in Madrid (Castile) than in Barcelona (Catalonia).[120] With indirect taxation pushing up nominal wages it would be difficult for employers to hire workers in times when demand was falling, particularly when there were alternative investments.[121] It is clear that, as a consequence of *vellón* inflation and the indirect taxes which burdened consumer goods, the real wages of Castilian workers were declining steadily—even for the reduced numbers who had managed to retain employment.

In conclusion, a fiscal system based for the most part on indirect taxation seems to be able to work efficiently and provide increasing revenues in times of demographic and economic growth (for example, in sixteenth-century Castile or eighteenth-century England),[122] but it is extremely inefficient and produces tax revenues a great deal below what might be expected under a system of direct taxes. Thus, while fraud must be taken into account when attempting to explain the fall in Castilian tax revenue, another significant contributory factor was the narrowing of the social base of taxation, that is to say, the reduction in the number and strength of the taxpayers. Towards the end of the seventeenth century the Dutch fiscal system, also based for the most part on excise taxes, seems to have reached its 'political ceiling': in order to continue increasing tax revenues during the eighteenth century, it became necessary to institute direct taxation which introduced some elements of fiscal justice and balanced the fiscal system overall.[123] However, this had to be a politicial decision. Similarly, the elimination of fiscal privilege had to be a political decision in France, and the financial consequences of the Glorious Revolution were the result of a political decision in England. In Castile no decision of this sort was taken. Political circumstances dictated the nature of the fiscal systems. Economic conditions created the potential for enhanced tax revenue, but ultimately it was political

[119] Gutiérrez Alonso (1989), 179–81. Purchasing power of daily wages of building workers in Valladolid (1611–20 and 1676–80) calculated in (a) bread (in *cuartales*); (b) meat (in *libras*); (c) wine (in *azumbres*); and (d) nominal wage (in *maravedís*). For the years 1611–20, the figures for a master were (a) 9.6; (b) 8.6; (c) 5.2; (d) 204. The figures for a skilled worker were (a) 8.3; (b) 7.5; (c) 4.5; (d) 176.8. The figures for an unskilled worker were (a) 5.0; (b) 4.5; (c) 3.6; (d) 107.1. For the years 1676–80, the figures for a master were (a) 7.3; (b) 6.1; (c) 6.3; (d) 340. The figures for a skilled worker were (a) 5.7; (b) 4.7; (c) 4.9; (d) 263.5. The figures for an unskilled worker were (a) 3.3; (b) 2.7; (c) 2.8; (d) 156.4.

[120] Vilar (1967), 403.

[121] Fortea Pérez (1981), 460–70; Faccini (1988), 85.

[122] Swiss cities during the 16th cent. provide further evidence: Körner (1980), 98–9.

[123] Fritschy (1990), 68–9.

circumstances which determined whether any particular ruler was able to gain from the increased general wealth of his country. The prevalence of indirect taxation, even in France in the eighteenth century, demonstrates that the unwillingness of taxpayers to concede an efficient, permanent system of direct taxation, let alone a system of direct taxes indexed against inflation, could be neutralized by the state only to the extent of making the taxpayer contribute through prices instead of through taxes.

APPENDIX

The European State Finance Database and the Graphical Presentation of Data

Richard Bonney

Previous generations of fiscal historians have produced interesting research and standard works of reference—we may cite as examples the work of Castillo Pintado on the *asientos* of Phillip II[1] and of Harris on the *assignats* during the French Revolution.[2] The problem with such research is that because the data underlying the author's calculations were not conserved, new work has to be undertaken by subsequent historians to return to the *status quo ante*: no methodological or interpretative advance necessarily occurs in the process, which is inherently wasteful of research time. The group of scholars preparing *Economic Systems and State Finance* decided that this state of affairs was unsatisfactory, and that there should be an attempt to preserve the research materials which informed its conclusions. This idea was the origin of the European State Finance Database (ESFDB), an international collaborative research project for the collection of data in European fiscal history. The data are drawn from the main extant sources of a number of European countries, as the evidence and the existing state of scholarship permit. The aim is to collect the data made available by scholars, whether drawing upon their published or unpublished archival research, or from other published material. The material in the ESFDB will be updated from time to time and other scholars are encouraged to deposit their data. There are no geographical or chronological boundaries to the collection, although version one, a copy of which has been deposited at the Economic and Social Research Council (ESRC) Data Archive at the University of Essex, has concentrated on data within the period *c*.1200 to *c*.1815. One generic database (ARCHIVE @ UK.AC.Essex; generic code 33250) with various subsets has been established,

[1] Castillo Pintado (1963*b*); graph of *asientos* based on Castillo Pintado's figures in Braudel (1973), ii, 694; new research of Gelabert in Bonney (1995).

[2] Harris (1930), still described by Crouzet (1993), 585, as 'essentiel'.

thus facilitating cross-referencing, instead of creating multiple databases which are then difficult to locate.

The existence of the ESFDB has meant that an editorial decision was taken to present all the statistical material for this book in the form of charts and graphs so as not to overawe the non-statistical reader. On the other hand, the specialist reader who may need to refer to the figures on which the graphs and charts are based may do so through the dataset reference: there is a concordance between the ESFDB's filenames and the filenames used by the ESRC Data Archive. There are full explanatory notes and references in the datasets where multiple sources are used (cited in this publication as 'various'). The data deposited at the ESRC Data Archive may be consulted in one or two formats: SAS[3] transport format, which enables the datasets to be transferred onto any operating system, while the user has all the benefits of a widely available and respected statistical program; alternatively, for those who do not use SAS, the data is available in ASCII form with help files partly generated from the SAS datasets.

Because of the prior decision to hold all material in the database within the SAS format, graphical output has been generated using SAS/GRAPH. This is a powerful program, but as with any piece of software it imposes certain constraints on the user, and to some extent these constraints have determined the presentation of the graphs and charts. The dispersed and fragmentary nature of the data of European fiscal history also poses its own difficulties. Sometimes the gaps in the evidence are genuine null values because, for example, no tax was levied in that year; more usually, null values are a result of evidence which has failed to survive or which is unknown. The explanatory notes to the datasets deal with many of these technicalities, but much depends on specialist knowledge and interpretation of the evidence. We resolved at the outset that where we had ourselves collected the data (as against receiving data already collected by others) we would keep as full a record as possible not only of the data captured but also the methods used for any subsequent interpretation (or, as some would have it, 'massaging') of the evidence. These stages would also be carefully distinguished and cross-referenced, so that it would be possible for a scholar coming afresh to the material to work backwards through the data files to arrive at the 'original' data, which would be held on computer in a form which replicated as closely as possible the form of the original statistical evidence. The processes of creating datasets and presenting data in graphical form require choices to be made; such choices are problematic. However, the datasets and graph/bar chart programs provide the evidence of the reasons why certain decisions were made: subsequent scholars who wish to suggest an alternative methodology may do so on

[3] SAS is a trademark of SAS Institute Inc., Cary, NC, USA.

the basis of the figures which we have attempted to gather together for the first time. In general, we have added the keywords 'expressed in' to the caption of the figure in which statistical manipulation or conversion of the data has occurred: for example, in Figure 68, the description 'expressed in *gulden* of money of account and in metric tonnes of silver' implies that a conversion into silver values has taken place. Where the data is held in the money of account, the keyword 'in' alone is used: for example, in Figure 70, the description 'in florins' implies that no statistical manipulation or conversion of the data has occurred.

An international project in data collection, with a central point of deposit at the ESRC Data Archive, can only operate effectively with a mutual respect of colleagues' data. This is why the ESFDB requires all colleagues supplying data, or who consult the resulting Database, to undertake to give full and proper acknowledgement (including specific citation) in any resulting scholarly work or publication to the name of the contributing scholar whose files they have used, including the specific filenames (ESFDB dataset name).[4]

[4] Further enquiries, concerning either the deposit or consultation of materials, may be directed to the Editor of this volume, who is Director of the European State Finance Database at the Department of History, University of Leicester, preferably via e-mail to 'bon@leicester.ac.uk' (from abroad) or 'bon@uk.ac.leicester' (from within the UK).

BIBLIOGRAPHY

Aakjær, S. (ed.), *Kong Valdemars Jordebog*, 3 vols. (Copenhagen, 1926–45).

Aalbers, J., 'Holland's financial problems, 1713–1733, and the wars against Louis XIV', in A. C. Duke and C. A. Tamse (eds.), *Britain and the Netherlands. VI* (The Hague, 1977), 79–93.

Abels, R. P., *Lordship and Military Obligation in Anglo-Saxon England* (London, 1988).

Abu-Lughod, J., *Before European Hegemony: The World System, A.D. 1250–1350* (New York–Oxford, 1989).

Adams, C., *For Good and Evil: The Impact of Taxes on the Course of Civilization* (Lanham, Md., 1993).

Adshead, S. A. M., *Salt and Civilization* (Basingstoke, 1992).

Aegidius Romanus, *De regimine principum* (Augsburg, 1473).

Aerts, E., and Crouzet, F. (eds.), *Economic Effects of the French Revolutionary and Napoleonic Wars* (Proceedings of the Tenth International Economic History Conference, Session B-1; Leuven, 1990).

Aftalion, F., *The French Revolution: An Economic Interpretation*, trans. M. Thom (Cambridge, 1990).

Ahmad, S., 'Adam Smith's four invisible hands', *History of Political Economy*, 22 (1990), 137–44.

Alberigo, G., 'La riforma dei principi', in H. Jedin and P. Prodi (eds.), *Il Concilio di Trento come crocevia della politica europea* (Bologna, 1979).

Albertus Magnus, *Opera omnia* (Paris, 1890–9).

Allen, W. R., 'Modern defenders of Mercantilist theory', *History of Political Economy*, 2 (1970), 381–97.

Alsop, J. D., 'The theory and practice of Tudor taxation', *English Historical Review*, 97 (1982), 1–30.

Alvarotus, Jacobus, *Super feudis* (Lyon, 1522).

Åmark, K., *Sveriges statsfinanser, 1719–1809* (Stockholm, 1961).

Amberg, R., *Die Steuer in der Rechtsphilosophie der Scholastiker: Ein Beitrag zur Beurteilung der Scholastiker in ihren Beziehungen zum Rechts- und Wirtschaftsleben ihrer Zeit* (Berlin–Leipzig, 1909).

Amiet, J. J., 'Die französischen und lombardischen Geldwucherer des Mittelalters, namentlich in der Schweiz', *Jahrbuch für schweizerische Geschichte*, 1–2 (1876–7), 177–255.

Anderson, J. L., 'A measure of the effect of British public finance, 1793–1815', *Economic History Review*, 2nd ser., 27 (1974), 610–19. [1974*a*]

Anderson, M., *Peter the Great* (London, 1978).

Anderson, P., *Lineages of the Absolutist State* (London, 1974). [1974*b*]

Anderson, P., *Passages from Antiquity to Feudalism* (London, 1977).

Andrén, A., 'Städer och kungamakt: en studie i Danmarks politiska geografi före 1230', *Scandia*, 49 (1983), 31–76.

[Anselmus Laudunensis], *Enarrationes in omnes sanctissimi Pauli Apostoli epistolas*, ed. Eucharium Cervicornum (Cologne, 1533).

Antoine, M., *Le dur métier du roi: Études sur la civilisation politique de la France d'ancien régime* (Paris, 1986).

——*Louis XV* (Paris, 1989).

Antonetti, G., 'La crise économique de 1729–1731 à Paris d'après les règlements de faillites', in *Histoire économique et financière de la France: Études et documents. II. 1990* (Comité pour l'histoire économique et financière de la France; Paris, 1990), 35–181.

Appelby, J. O., 'Locke, liberalism and the natural law of money', *Past and Present*, 71 (1976), 43–69.

Aquinas, T., *Summa theologiae*, ed. P. Caramello, 2nd edn, 3 vols. (Turin–Rome, 1952–6).

Ardant, G., *Théorie sociologique de l'impôt*, 2 vols. (Paris, 1965).

——*Histoire de l'impôt*, 2 vols. (Paris, 1971–2).

Aristide, I., *La fortune de Sully* (Paris, 1990).

Arnould, M. A., 'L'impôt direct dans le Tournaisis au début du régime espagnol, 1523–1571', *Recherches sur l'histoire des finances publiques en Belgique. I* (Brussels, 1967).

Artola, M., *La hacienda del antiguo régimen* (Madrid, 1982).

Arup, E., 'Den finansielle side af erhvervelsen af hertugdommerne 1460–87', *Historisk Tidsskrift*, 7 (1902–4), 317–88, 399–489.

——'Leding og ledingsskat i det 13. aarhundrede', *Historisk Tidsskrift*, 8 (1914–15), 141–237.

Ashton, R., 'Revenue farming under the early Stuarts', *Economic History Review*, 2nd ser., 9 (1956), 310–22.

——*The Crown and the Money Market, 1603–40* (Oxford, 1960).

Aspinall, A., and Smith, E. A. (eds.), *English Historical Documents. XI. 1783–1832* (London, 1959).

Aspromourgos, T., 'The life of William Petty in relation to his economics: a tercentenary appreciation', *History of Political Economy*, 20 (1988), 337–56.

Aston, T. H. (ed.), *Crisis in Europe, 1560–1660* (London, 1965).

Atwell, W. S., 'International bullion flows and the Chinese economy, *circa* 1530–1650', *Past and Present*, 95 (1982), 68–90.

Aubin, C., 'Les assignats sous la Révolution française: un exemple d'hyperinflation', *Revue économique*, 42 (1991), 745–62.

Bagge, S., 'Borgerkrig og statsutvikling i Norge i middelalderen', *Historisk Tidsskrift*, 65 (1986), 145–97.

Baker, N., *Government and Contractors: The British Treasury and War Supplies, 1775–1783* (London, 1971).

Baldwin, J. W., 'La décennie décisive: les années 1190–1203 dans le règne de Philippe Auguste', *Revue historique*, 26 (1981), 311–37.

——*The Government of Philip Augustus* (Berkeley, 1986).

Ball, T., Farr, J., and Hanson, R. L. (eds.), *Political Innovation and Conceptual Change* (Cambridge, 1989).

Balle, S., *Statsfinanserne på Christian 3s tid* (Aarhus, 1992).

Banchi pubblici, banchi privati e monti di pietà nell'Europa preindustriale. Amministrazione, tecniche operative e ruoli economici. Atti del convegno, Genova, 1–6 ottobre 1990, 2 vols. continuously paginated (Società ligure di storia patria; Genoa, 1990).

Barber, M., *The Trial of the Templars* (Cambridge, 1978).

Barbiche, B., 'Les commissaires députés pour le "régalement" des tailles en 1598–1599', *Bibliothèque de l'École des Chartes*, 118 (1960), 58–96.

Barbier, J. A., and Klein, H. S., 'Revolutionary wars and public finances: the Madrid Treasury, 1784–1807', *Journal of Economic History*, 41 (1981), 315–39.

Barro, R. J., 'Are government bonds net wealth?', *Journal of Political Economy*, 82 (1974), 1095–117.

Barrow, T. C., *Trade and Empire: The British Customs Service in Colonial America, 1660–1775* (Cambridge, Mass., 1967).

Barthe Porcel, J., 'Los juros: desde el *yuro deheretat* hasta la desparición de las *Cargas de Justicia*, siglos XIII al XX', *Anales de la Universidad de Murcia*, 3 (1948–9), 219–87.

Bartlett, R. P., *Human Capital: The Settlement of Foreigners in Russia, 1762–1804* (Cambridge, 1979).

Bartolus de Saxoferrato, *Commentaria in corpus juris civilis*, in *Consilia* (Lyon, 1535).

Barudio, G., *Das Zeitalter des Absolutismus und der Aufklärung, 1648–1779* (Frankfurt, 1981).

Bates, D., *Normandy before 1066* (London, 1982).

Bauer, C., 'Die Epochen der Papstfinanz: ein Versuch', *Historische Zeitschrift*, 138 (1928), 457–503.

Bayard, F., *Le monde des financiers au xviie siècle* (Paris, 1988).

Beales, D., *Joseph II. I. In the Shadow of Maria Theresa, 1741–1780* (Cambridge, 1987).

——'Was Joseph II an enlightened despot?', in R. Robertson and E. Timms (eds.), *The Austrian Enlightenment and its Aftermath. Austrian Studies. II* (Edinburgh, 1991), 1–21.

Becagli, V., *Un unico territorio gabellabile. La riforma doganale leopoldina. Il dibattito politico, 1767–1781* (Florence, 1983).

Beckett, J. V., 'Land tax or excise: the levying of taxation in seventeenth- and eighteenth-century England', *English Historical Review*, 100 (1985), 285–308.

——and Turner, M., 'Taxation and economic growth in eighteenth-century England', *Economic History Review*, 2nd ser., 43 (1990), 377–403.

Bédarida, F., Crouzet, F., and Johnson, D. (eds.), *De Guillaume le conquérant au Marché commun: Dix siècles d'histoire franco-britannique* (Paris, 1979).

——Crouzet, F., and Johnson, D. (eds.), *Britain and France: Ten Centuries* (Folkestone, 1980).

Beer, A., 'Die Finanzverwaltung Oesterreichs, 1749–1816', *Mitteilungen des Instituts für österreichische Geschichtsforschung*, 15 (1894), 237–366.

Beer, A., *Die Finanzen Oesterreichs im XIX. Jahrhundert* (Vienna, 1973).

Beik, W. H., *Absolutism and Society in Seventeenth-Century France: State Power and Provincial Aristocracy in Languedoc* (Cambridge, 1985).

Benigni, P., 'Oligarchia cittadina e pressione fiscale: il caso di Arezzo nei secoli XVI e XVII', *La fiscalité et ses implications sociales en Italie et en France aux xviie et xviiie siècles* (Collection de l'École française de Rome; Rome, 1980).

Bennett, M., 'Contribution and assessment: financial exactions in the English Civil War, 1642–6', *War and Society*, 4 (1986), 1–9.

Bercé, Y. M., *Histoire des croquants: Étude des soulèvements populaires au xviie siècle dans le sud-ouest de la France* (Paris–Geneva, 1974).

Bérenger, J., *Finances et absolutisme autrichien dans la seconde moitié du xviie siècle* (Paris, 1975).

——'A propos d'un ouvrage récent: les finances de l'Autriche à l'époque baroque, 1650–1740', *Histoire, économie et société*, 3 (1984), 221–45.

Bergeron, L., *Banquiers, négociants et manufacturiers parisiens du Directoire à l'Empire* (Paris–The Hague, 1978). [1978*a*]

——'Le réseau de la finance internationale', in L. Bergeron (ed.), *Histoire économique et sociale du monde. III. Inerties et révolutions, 1730–1840* (Paris, 1978), 119–36. [1978*b*]

Berktay, H., 'Three empires and the societies they governed: Iran, India and the Ottoman empire', *Journal of Peasant Studies*, 18 (1991), 242–63.

Bernard, P. P., *Joseph II and Bavaria: Two Eighteenth-Century Attempts at German Unification* (The Hague, 1965).

Bestmann, Uwe *et al.* (eds.), *Hochfinanz, Wirtschaftsräume, Innovation. Festschrift Wolfgang von Stromer. III* (Trier, 1987).

Bethell, L. (ed.), *The Cambridge History of Latin America. I. Colonial Latin America* (Cambridge, 1984).

Bianchini, L., *Della storia delle finanze del regno di Napoli libri sette*, 3 vols. (Naples, 1834–5).

Bibó, I., *Válogatott tanulmányok. III* (Budapest, 1986).

Biel, G., *Epitome et collectorium ex Occamo circa quatuor sententiarum libros* (Basle, 1508).

Bilbao, L. M., 'Ensayo de reconstrucción histórica de la presión fiscal en Castilla durante el siglo XVI', in E. Fernández de Pinedo (ed.), *Haciendas forales y hacienda real: Homenaje a D. Miguel Artola y D. Felipe Ruiz Martín* (Bilbao, 1990), 37–61.

Binney, J. E. D., *British Public Finance and Administration* (Oxford, 1958).

Biraben, J.-N., *Les hommes et la peste en France et dans les pays européens et méditerranéens*, 2 vols. (Paris, 1975–6).

Bisson, T. N., *Conservation of Coinage: Monetary Exploitation and its Restraint in France, Catalonia, and Aragon, c. A.D. 1000–c. 1225* (Oxford, 1979).

——'Les comptes des domaines au temps de Philippe Auguste', in R.-H. Bautier (ed.), *La France de Philippe Auguste: Le temps des mutations* (Paris, 1982), 521–39.

——*Fiscal Accounts of Catalonia under the Early Count-Kings, 1151–1213* (Berkeley, 1984).

——*Medieval France and her Pyrenean Neighbours: Studies in Early Institutional History* (London, 1989).

Bizzochi, R., 'Politica fiscale e immunità ecclesiastica nella Toscana medicea fra Repubblica e Granducato (secoli XV–XVIII)', in H. Kellenbenz and P. Prodi (eds.), *Fisco, religione, stato nell'età confessionale* (Bologna, 1989), 355–85.

Black, J., *British Foreign Policy in the Age of Walpole* (Edinburgh, 1985).

Blanc, H., *La chambre des blés de Genève, 1628–1798* (Geneva, 1941).

Blanning, T. C. W., *Reform and Revolution in Mainz, 1743–1803* (Cambridge, 1974).

——*Joseph II and Enlightened Despotism* (London, 1978).

——*The French Revolution in Germany: Occupation and Resistance in the Rhineland, 1792–1802* (Oxford, 1983).

——*The Origins of the French Revolutionary Wars* (London–New York, 1986).

Blaug, M., *Economic Theory in Retrospect*, 3rd edn (Cambridge, 1978).

Blickle, P., Rublack, H.-C., and Schulze, W., *Religion, Politics and Social Protest: Three Studies on Early Modern Germany* (London, 1984).

Bloch, M., *Feudal Society*, trans. L. A. Manyon (London, 1962).

Blockmans, W. P., 'Voracious states and obstructing cities: an aspect of state formation in preindustrial Europe', *Theory and Society*, 18 (1989), 733–55.

Blockmans, W., and Genet, J.-P. (eds.), *Visions sur le développement des états européens. Théories et historiographies de l'état moderne. Actes du colloque organisé par la Fondation européenne de la science et l'École française de Rome* (Rome, 1993).

Bluche, F. (ed.), *Dictionnaire du grand siècle* (Paris, 1990).

Bodin, J., *Les six livres de la république* ([1576]; 1583 edn repr. Darmstadt, 1977).

——*The Six Bookes of a Commonweale*, trans. R. Knolles, 1606, ed. K. D. McRae (Cambridge, Mass., 1962).

——*On Sovereignty: Four Chapters from the Six Books of the Commonwealth*, ed. J. H. Franklin (Cambridge, 1992).

Bois, G., *The Crisis of Feudalism: Economy and Society in Eastern Normandy, c.1300–1550* (Cambridge, 1984).

Boisguilbert, P. Le Pesant de, *Le Détail de la France, sous le regne present. Augmenté en cette nouvelle Edition de plusieurs Memoires & Traitez sur la même matiere. Seconde partie. Année 1707. Factum de la France ou moyens tres-faciles de faire recevoir au Roy quatrevingts millions par dessus la capitation* ... ([Paris], 1707).

[Boisguilbert, P. Le Pesant de], *Pierre de Boisguilbert ou la naissance de l'économie politique*, 2 vols. (INED edn, Paris, 1966).

Boislisle, A. M. de (ed.), *Correspondance des contrôleurs-généraux des finances avec les intendants des provinces, 1683–1715*, 3 vols. (Paris, 1874–9).

Bolin, S., 'Tax money and plough money', *Scandinavian Economic History Review*, 2 (1954), 3–21.

Bonney, M. M., 'The English medieval wool and cloth trade: new approaches for the local historian', *The Local Historian*, 22 (1992), 18–40. [1992*c*]

——and Bonney, R. J., *Jean-Roland Malet: Premier historien des finances de la monarchie française* (Comité pour l'histoire économique et financière de la France; Paris, 1993).

Bonney, R. J., *Political Change in France under Richelieu and Mazarin, 1624–1661* (Oxford, 1978).

——'The failure of the French revenue farms, 1600–60', *Economic History Review*, 2nd ser., 32 (1979), 11–32.

——*The King's Debts: Finance and Politics in France, 1589–1661* (Oxford, 1981). [1981*a*]

——'Cardinal Mazarin and the great nobility during the Fronde', *English Historical Review*, 96 (1981), 818–33. [1981*b*]

——*Society and Government in France under Richelieu and Mazarin, 1624–61* (Basingstoke, 1988).

Bonney, R. J., *L'absolutisme* (Paris, 1989).

——'Bodin and the development of the French monarchy', *Transactions of the Royal Historical Society*, 5th ser., 40 (1990), 43–61.

——'Jean-Roland Malet: historian of the finances of the French monarchy', *French History*, 5 (1991), 180–233. [1991*a*]

——*The European Dynastic States, 1494–1660* (Oxford, 1991). [1991*b*]

——'The state and its revenues in *ancien régime* France', *Historical Research*, 65 (1992), 150–76. [1992*a*]

——'Louis XIII, Richelieu and the royal finances', in J. A. Bergin and L. W. B. Brockliss (eds.), *Richelieu and his Age* (Oxford, 1992), 99–133. [1992*b*]

——'*Le secret de leurs familles*: the fiscal and social limits of Louis XIV's *dixième*', *French History*, 7 (1993), 383–416. [1993*a*]

——'Comparative fiscal systems on the eve of modernity: the French enquiry of 1763', in J.-P. Genet and E. Eldhem (eds.), *La genèse de l'État moderne et le cas ottoman. Table-ronde d'Istanbul, 1991* (Varia Turcica, 26; Istanbul, 1994), 61–81.

——'Taxation and the problem of European regions', in M. Prak and A. Mączak (eds.), *The Changing Relationships of European Regions*. [forthcoming]

——(ed.), *The Rise of the Fiscal State in Europe, c.1200–c.1815* (Oxford, forthcoming, 1995). [1995]

Boone, M., 'Triomferend privé-initiatief versus haperend overheidsoptreden? Over pachters van indirecte belastingen in laatmiddeleeuwse steden', *Tijdschrift voor sociale geschiedenis*, 15 (1989), 113–38.

——*Geld en macht: De Gentse stadsfinanciën en de Bourgondische staatsvorming, 1384–1453* (Ghent, 1990).

——'*Plus deuil que joie*. Les ventes de rentes par la ville de Gand pendant la période bourguignonne: entre intérêts privés et finances publiques', *Crédit Communal: bulletin trimestriel*, 176 (1991–2), 3–24.

Bordo, M. D., and Capie, F. (eds.), *Monetary Regimes in Transition* (Cambridge, 1994).

——and White, E. N., 'A tale of two currencies: British and French finance during the Napoleonic War', *Journal of Economic History*, 51 (1991), 303–16.

Bornitz, J., *Aerarium sive Tractatus Politicus de Aerario sacro* . . . (Frankfurt, 1612).

Bosher, J. F., *The Single Duty Project: A Study of the Movement for a French Customs Union in the Eighteenth Century* (London, 1964).

——*French Finances, 1770–1795: From Business to Bureaucracy* (Cambridge, 1970).

Bossenga, G., *The Politics of Privilege: Old Regime and Revolution in Lille* (Cambridge, 1991).

Botero, G., *The Reason of State*, ed. and trans. P. J. and D. P. Waley (London, 1956).

Bottomore, T. *et al.*, *A Dictionary of Marxist Thought* (Oxford, 1983).

Bouwsma, W. J., *A Usable Past: Essays in European Cultural History* (Los Angeles, 1990).

Bowsky, W. M., *The Finances of the Commune of Siena, 1287–1355* (Oxford, 1970).

Boyajian, J. C., *Portuguese Bankers at the Court of Spain, 1626–1650* (New Brunswick, NJ, 1983).

Boyer-Xambeu, M.-T., Deleplace, G., and Gillard, L., *Monnaie privée et pouvoir des princes: L'économie des relations monétaires à la Renaissance* (Paris, 1986).

Braddick, M., 'State formation and social change in modern England: a problem stated and approaches suggested', *Social History*, 16 (1991), 1–18.

Braesch, F., *Finances et monnaie révolutionnaires. I. Les exercices budgétaires 1790 et 1791 d'après les Comptes du Trésor* (Nancy, 1934).

——*Finances et monnaie révolutionnaires. II. Les recettes et les dépenses du Trésor pendant l'année 1789. Le compte rendu au Roi, de mars 1788. Le dernier budget de l'ancien régime* (Paris, 1936). [1936*a*]

——*Finances et monnaie révolutionnaires. V. La livre tournois et le franc de germinal. Essai sur la monnaie métallique* (Paris, 1936). [1936*b*]

Braudel, F., 'Les emprunts de Charles Quint sur la place d'Anvers', *Charles-Quint et son temps: Colloques internationaux du Centre national de la recherche scientifique, Paris, 30 septembre–3 octobre 1958* (Centre national de la recherche scientifique; Paris, 1959), 191–200.

——*The Mediterranean and the Mediterranean World in the Age of Philip II*, trans. S. Reynolds, 2 vols. (Glasgow, 1972–3).

——*Civilization and Capitalism, 15th–18th Century*, trans. S. Reynolds, 3 vols. (London, 1981–4).

——and Labrousse, E. (eds.), *Histoire économique et sociale de la France. II. Des derniers temps de l'âge seigneurial aux préludes de l'âge industriel, 1660–1789* (Paris, 1970).

——and Spooner, F. C., 'Prices in Europe from 1450 to 1750', in E. E. Rich and C. H. Wilson (eds.), *Cambridge Economic History of Europe: The Economy of Expanding Europe in the Sixteenth and Seventeenth Centuries. IV* (Cambridge, 1967), 374–486.

Braun, H.-J., 'Economic theory and policy in Germany, 1750–1800', *Journal of European Economic History*, 4 (1975), 301–22.

Brennan, G., and Buchanan, J. M., *The Power to Tax: Analytical Foundations of a Fiscal Constitution* (Cambridge, 1980).

Brewer, A., 'Petty and Cantillon', *History of Political Economy*, 24 (1992), 711–28. [1992*a*]

——*Richard Cantillon: Pioneer of Economic Theory* (London–New York, 1992). [1992*b*]

Brewer, J., *The Sinews of Power: War, Money and the English State, 1688–1783* (London, 1989).

Bromley, J. S. (ed.), *New Cambridge Modern History. VI. The Rise of Great Britain and Russia, 1688–1715/25* (Cambridge, 1971).

Brooks, C., 'Public finance and political stability: the administration of the land tax, 1688–1720', *Historical Journal*, 17 (1974), 281–300.

Brooks, N., 'The development of military obligations in eighth- and ninth-century England', in P. Clemoes and K. Hughes (eds.), *England before the Conquest: Studies in Primary Sources Presented to D. Whitelock* (Cambridge, 1971), 69–84.

Brown, E. A. R., '*Cessante causa* and the taxes of the last Capetians: the political application of a philosophical maxim', *Speculum*, 15 (1972), 565–87.

——'Taxation and morality in the thirteenth and fourteenth centuries: conscience and political power and the kings of France', *French Historical Studies*, 8 (1973), 1–28.

——'The tyranny of a construct: feudalism and historians of medieval Europe', *American Historical Review*, 79 (1974), 1063–88.

Brown, H. G., 'A discredited regime: the Directory and army contracting', *French History*, 4 (1990), 48–76.

Bruguière, M., *La première restauration et son budget* (Geneva, 1969).

——*Pour une renaissance de l'histoire financière, xviiie–xxe siècles* (Paris, 1991).

Brunner, O., *Land und Herrschaft: Grundfragen der territorialen Verfassungsgeschichte Österreichs im Mittelalter*, 5th edn (Vienna, 1965).

Brunschwig, H., *Enlightenment and Romanticism in Eighteenth-Century Prussia*, trans. F. Jellinek (Chicago–London, 1974).

Buchholz, W., 'Der moderne Steuerstaat: Bedingungen seiner Entstehung und Entwicklung in Mittelalter und Neuzeit', *Sozialwissenschaftliche Informationen*, 19 (1990), 5–15.

Büchi, H., *Finanzen und Finanzpolitik Toskanas im Zeitalter der Aufklärung (1737–1790) im Rahmen der Wirtschaftspolitik* (Berlin, 1915).

Buganov, V., 'Bauernaufstände und Bauernkriege in Ost-, Mittel- und Westeuropa in der Feudalzeit', *Jahrbuch für die Geschichte der sozialistischen Länder Europas*, 21 (1977), 115–30.

Bühler, W., 'Die Entwicklung des Finanzwesens in der freien Reichstadt Überlingen bis zur Mitte des 18. Jahrhunderts', in E. Maschke *et al.* (eds.), *Städtisches Haushalts- und Rechnungswesen* (Sigmaringen, 1977), 158–72.

Buisseret, D. J., *Sully and the Growth of Centralized Government in France, 1598–1610* (London, 1968).

——(ed.), *Monarchs, Ministers and Maps: The Emergence of Cartography as a Tool of Government in Early Modern Europe* (Chicago–London, 1992).

Buist, M. G., *At spes non fracta. Hope & Co., 1770–1815. Merchant Bankers and Diplomats at Work* (The Hague, 1974).

——'The sinews of war: the role of Dutch finance in European politics, c.1750–1815', in A. C. Duke and C. A. Tamse (eds.), *Britain and the Netherlands. VI* (The Hague, 1977), 124–40.

Bulst, N., and Genet, J.-P. (eds.), *La ville, la bourgeoisie et la genèse de l'État moderne, xiie–xviiie siècles* (Paris, 1988).

Burke, P. (ed), *New Cambridge Modern History. XIII. Companion Volume* (Cambridge, 1972).

——*The Fabrication of Louis XIV* (New Haven–London, 1992).

Burleigh, M., *Prussian Society and the German Order: An Aristocratic Corporation in Crisis, c.1410–1466* (Cambridge, 1984).

Büsch, O., *Militärsystem und Sozialleben im alten Preussen, 1713–1807: Die Anfänge der sozialen Militarisierung der preussisch-deutschen Gesellschaft* (Berlin, 1962).

Bush, M. L., 'Tax reform and rebellion in early Tudor England', *History*, 76 (1991), 379–400.

Bushkovitch, P., 'Taxation, tax farming and merchants in sixteenth-century Russia', *Slavic Review*, 37 (1978), 381–98.

Butcher, J., and Dick, H. (eds.), *The Rise and Fall of Revenue Farming: Business Elites and the Emergence of the Modern State in South-East Asia* (Basingstoke, 1993).

Buurman, G. B., 'A comparison of the single tax proposals of Henry George and the Physiocrats', *History of Political Economy*, 23 (1991), 481–96.

Calabria, A., *The Cost of Empire: The Finances of the Kingdom of Naples in the Time of Spanish Rule* (Cambridge, 1991).

Campbell, J., 'Observations on English government from the tenth to the twelfth century', *Transactions of the Royal Historical Society*, 5th ser., 25 (1975), 39–54.

——'Asser's Life of Alfred', in C. Holdsworth and T. P. Wiseman (eds.), *The Inheritance of Historiography, 350–900* (Exeter, 1986), 115–35.

Cantillon, R., *Essai sur la nature du commerce en général*, ed. H. Higgs (London, 1931).

——*Essay de la nature du commerce en général*, ed. T. Tsuda (Tokyo, 1979).

Capra, C., 'Alcuni aspetti del riordinamento tributario in Lombardia nell'età teresiana', *La fiscalité et ses implications sociales en Italie et en France aux xviie et xviiie siècles* (Rome, 1980), 3–16.

——'Le finanze degli stati italiani nel secolo XVIII', *L'Italia alla vigilia della Rivoluzione Francese: Atti del LIV Congresso di storia del Risorgimento Italiano, 1988* (Rome, 1990), 141–73.

Caracciolo, F., *Sud, debiti e gabelle: Gravami, potere e società nel Mezzogiorno in età moderna* (Naples, 1983).

Carafa, Diomede, *De regis et boni principis officio* (Naples, 1668).

Carande, R., *Carlos V y sus banqueros*, 3 vols. (Madrid, 1943–67).

——*Carlos V y sus banqueros. Los caminos del oro y de la plata. Deuda exterior y tesoros ultramarinos* (Madrid, 1967).

——'Gobernantes y gobernados en la hacienda de Castilla, 1536–1556,' *Siete estudios de historia de España* (Barcelona, 1969), 109–42.

——*El crédito de Castilla en el precio de la política imperial, ora in Otros siete estudios de historia de España* (Barcelona, 1978).

Caravale, M., and Caracciolo, A. (eds.), *Lo Stato Pontificio da Martino V a Pio IX* (Turin, 1978).

Caron, P. (ed.), *Tableaux de dépréciation du papier-monnaie* (Paris, 1909).

Caroso, J.-L., 'Economic thought in late eighteenth-century Portugal: Physiocratic and Smithian influence', *History of Political Economy*, 22 (1990), 429–41.

Carr, R., *Spain, 1808–1939* (Oxford, 1975).

Carsten, F. L., *The Origins of Prussia* (Oxford, 1954).

Castillo Pintado, A., 'Los juros de Castilla: apogeo y fin de un instrumento de crédito', *Hispania*, 23 (1963), 43–70. [1963*a*]

——'Dette flottante et dette consolidée en Espagne, 1557–1600', *Annales E.S.C.*, 18 (1963), 745–59. [1963*b*]

——'Mecanismos de base de la hacienda de Felipe IV', *Historia de España. XXV* (Madrid, 1982).

Cazel, F. A., Jr, 'The tax of 1185 in aid of the Holy Land', *Speculum*, 30 (1955), 385–92.

——'The fifteenth of 1225', *Bulletin of the Institute of Historical Research*, 34 (1961), 67–81.

——'Financing the Crusades', in K. M. Setton (ed.), *A History of the Crusades. VI. The Impact of the Crusades on Europe* (Madison, Wis., 1989), 116–49.

Cesarano, F., 'Monetary theory in Ferdinando Galiani's *Della moneta*', *History of Political Economy*, 8 (1976), 380–99.

——'Law and Galiani on money and monetary systems', *History of Political Economy*, 22 (1990), 321–40.

Chabert, A., *Essai sur les mouvements des revenus et de l'activité économique en France de 1798 à 1820* (Paris, 1949).

Chabod, F., *Storia di Milano nell'epoca di Carlo V (Il ducato di Milano e l'impero di Carlo V, 2*; Turin, 1971).

Challis, C. E., *Currency and the Economy in Tudor and Early Stuart England* (Historical Association, New Appreciations in History, 4; London, 1989).

——(ed.), *A New History of the Royal Mint* (Cambridge, 1992).

Chandaman, C. D., *The English Public Revenue, 1660–88* (Oxford, 1975).

Chaunu, H., and Chaunu, P., *Séville et l'Atlantique, 1504–1650* (Paris, 1956).

Chaunu, P., *Séville et l'Atlantique, 1504–1650*, 12 vols. (Paris, 1955–60).

——*Seville et l'Atlantique, xvie–xviie siècle* (Paris, 1977).

Chaunu, P., and Gascon, R., *Histoire économique et sociale de la France. I. De 1450 à 1660. L'État et la ville* (Paris, 1977).

Chaussinand Nogaret, G., 'Le fisc et les privilégiés sous l'ancien régime', *La fiscalité et ses implications sociales en Italie et en France aux xviie et xviiie siècles* (Rome, 1980), 191–206.

Chen, Shao-Kawan, *The System of Taxation in China in the Tsing Dynasty, 1644–1911* (1914; repr. New York, 1970).

Chirot, D. (ed.), *The Origins of Backwardness in Eastern Europe: Economics and Politics from the Middle Ages until the Early Twentieth Century* (Berkeley, 1989).

Christensen, H., *Len og magt i Danmark, 1439–1466* (Aarhus, 1983).

Chroust, A. (ed.), *Briefe und Acten zur Geschichte des Dreißigjährigen Krieges* (Königliche Akademie der Wissenschaften, Kommission für bayerische Landesgeschichte, 9; Munich, 1903).

Church, W. F., *Richelieu and Reason of State* (Princeton, NJ, 1972).

Cipolla, C. M. (ed.), *The Economic Decline of Empires* (London, 1970).

——*Before the Industrial Revolution: European Society and Economy, 1000–1700* (London, 1976).

——*The Monetary Policy of Fourteenth-Century Florence* (Berkeley, 1982).

——*Il governo della moneta a Firenze e a Milano nei secoli XIV–XVI* (Bologna, 1990).

Clamageran, J.-J., *Histoire de l'impôt en France*, 3 vols. (Paris, 1867–76).

Clark, J. G., *La Rochelle and the Atlantic Economy during the Eighteenth Century* (Baltimore–London, 1981).

Clark, P. A. (ed.), *The European Crisis of the 1590s* (London, 1985).

Coats, A. W., 'The interpretation of Mercantilist economics: some historiographical problems', *History of Political Economy*, 5 (1973), 485–95.

Cohn, H. J., *The Government of the Rhine Palatinate in the Fifteenth Century* (Oxford, 1965).

——(ed.), *Government in Reformation Europe, 1520–1560* (London, 1971).

Coleman, D. C. (ed.), *Revisions in Mercantilism* (London, 1969).

Collins, I., *Napoleon and his Parliaments, 1800–1815* (London, 1989).

Collins, J. B., *Fiscal Limits of Absolutism: Direct Taxation in Early Seventeenth-Century France* (Berkeley, 1988).

Collins, R., *Early Medieval Spain: Unity in Diversity, 400–1000* (London, 1983).

Commynes, P. de, *Mémoires*, ed. J. Calmette (Paris, 1925).

Comptes du Trésor, 1296, 1316, 1384, 1477, ed. R. Fawtier (Paris, 1930).

Connelly, O., *Napoleon's Satellite Kingdoms* (New York–London, 1965).

Constable, G., 'The financing of the crusades in the twelfth century', in B. Z. Kedar, H. E.

Meyer, and R. C. Smail (eds.), *Outremer: Studies in the History of the Crusading Kingdom of Jerusalem Presented to Joshua Prawer* (Jerusalem, 1982), 64–88.

Contamine, P., *War in the Middle Ages*, trans. M. Jones (Oxford, 1984).

——(ed.), *War and Competition between States* (Oxford, forthcoming).

Conti, E., *L'imposta diretta a Firenze nel quattrocento, 1427–1494* (Rome, 1984).

Coppola, G., 'Fisco, finanza e religione: lo stato di Milano da Carlo a Federigo', in H. Kellenbenz and P. Prodi (eds.), *Fisco, religione, stato nell'età confessionale* (Bologna, 1989), 293–354.

Corpus juris canonici, ed. Aemilius Friedberg, 2 vols. (Lipsiae, 1879–91).

Cova, A., 'Riforma dell'imposta fondiaria e produzione agricola in Lombardia nella seconda metà del Settecento', *Annali della Facoltà di scienze politiche dell'Università di Milano*, 2 (1982), 597–621.

Coville, A., *Les Cabochiens et l'ordonnance de 1413* (Paris, 1888).

Cozzi, G., Knapton, M., and Scarabello, G., *La Repubblica di Venezia nell'età moderna: Dal 1517 alla fine della Repubblica* (Turin, 1992).

Craeybeckx, J., 'Aperçu sur l'histoire des impôts en Flandre et au Brabant au cours du xvie siècle', *Revue du nord*, 20 (1947), 87–108.

——'La portée fiscale et politique du 100e denier du duc d'Albe', *Recherches sur l'histoire des finances publiques en Belgique. I* (Brussels, 1967).

Craig, G. A., *The Politics of the Prussian Army, 1640–1945* (Oxford, 1955).

Craig, Sir John, *The Mint* (Cambridge, 1953).

Crook, D., 'The later eyres', *English Historical Review*, 97 (1982), 241–68.

Crouzet, F., *De la supériorité de l'Angleterre sur la France: L'économique et l'imaginaire, xviie–xxe siècles* (Paris, 1985).

——*L'économie britannique et le blocus continental, 1806–1813*, 2nd edn, 2 vols. (Paris, 1987).

——*Britain Ascendant: Comparative Studies in Franco-British Economic History* (Cambridge–Paris, 1990).

——*La grande inflation: La monnaie en France de Louis XVI à Napoléon* (Paris, 1993).

Crowley, J. E., 'Neo-mercantilism and *The Wealth of Nations*: British commercial policy after the American Revolution', *Historical Journal*, 33 (1990), 339–60.

Cuenca Esteban, J., 'Ingresos netos del estado español, 1788–1820', *Hacienda pública española*, 69 (1981), 183–208.

Czoernig, C. von, *Statistisches Handbüchlein fur die Oesterreichische Monarchie* (Vienna, 1864).

Dal Pane, L., *La finanza toscana dagli inizi del secolo XVIII alla caduta del Granducato* (Milan, 1965).

Danstrup, J., and Karker, A. (eds.), *Kulturhistorisk Leksikon for Nordisk Middelalder*, 22 vols. (Copenhagen, 1956–78).

Davenant, C., *The Political and Commercial Works*, ed. C. Whitworth, 5 vols. (London, 1771; repr. Farnborough, 1967).

Davies, C. S. L., *Peace, Print and Protestantism, 1450–1558* (St Albans, 1977).

Davis, J. A., 'The Neapolitan army during the *decennio francese*', *Rivista Italiania di Studi Napoleonici*, 25 (1988), 161–77.

Davis, J. R., 'Adam Smith on the providential reconciliation of individual and social interests: is man led by an invisible hand or misled by a sleight of hand?', *History of Political Economy*, 22 (1990), 341–52.

Day, J., *Les douanes de Gênes, 1376–1377*, 2 vols. (Paris, 1963).

——'The great bullion famine of the fifteenth century', *Past and Present*, 79 (1978), 3–54.

——'Moneta metallica e moneta creditizia', in R. Romano and U. Tucci (eds.), *Storia d'Italia. Annali. VI. Economia naturale, economia monetaria* (Turin, 1983), 337–60.

——(ed.), *Études d'histoire monétaire, xii*[e]*–xix*[e] *siècles* (Lille, 1984).

——*The Medieval Market Economy* (Oxford, 1987). [1987*a*]

——'Cinq siècles d'innovation financière', *Journal des Caisses d'Épargne*, 106 (1987), 84–8. [1987*b*]

——'The "General Crisis" and the Great Depression', *Annali della Facoltà di Economia e Commercio della Università di Bari*, new ser., 30 (1991), 31–5.

De Bloch, J., *Les finances de la Russie au xix*[e] *siècle: Historique et statistique*, 2 vols. (Paris, 1899).

Deleule, D., *Hume et la naissance du libéralisme économique* (Paris, 1979).

Delmas, J. (ed.), *Histoire militaire de la France. II. De 1715 à 1871* (Paris, 1992).

De Luca, G. B., *Il principe cristiano pratico* (Rome, 1680).

Delumeau, J., *Vie économique et sociale de Rome dans la seconde moitié du xvi*[e] *siècle*, 2 vols. (Paris, 1957–9).

——'Le progrès de la centralisation dans l'État pontifical au xvie siècle', *Revue historique*, 226 (1961), 399–410.

De Maddalena, A., and Kellenbenz, H. (eds.), *Finanze e ragion di stato in Italia e in Germania nella prima età moderna* (Bologna, 1984).

——(eds.), *La repubblica internazionale del denaro tra XV e XVII secolo* (Bologna, 1986).

Denley, P., and Elam, C., *Florence and Italy: Renaissance Studies in Honour of Nicolai Rubinstein* (London, 1988).

Dent, J., *Crisis in Finance: Crown, Financiers and Society in Seventeenth-Century France* (Newton Abbot, 1973).

Denton, J. H., 'The crisis of 1297 from the Evesham Chronicle', *English Historical Review*, 93 (1978), 560–79.

——*Robert Winchelsey and the Crown, 1294–1313: A Study in the Defence of Ecclesiastical Liberty* (Cambridge, 1980).

Depeyrot, G., Hackens, T., and Moucharte, G. (eds.), *Rythmes de la production monétaire, de l'antiquité à nos jours* (Louvain-La-Neuve, 1987).

De Roover, R., *Gresham on Foreign Exchange: An Essay in Early English Mercantilism with the Text of Sir Thomas Gresham's Memorandum for the Understanding of the Exchange* (Cambridge, Mass., 1949).

——*L'évolution de la lettre de change: xiv*[e]*–xviii*[e] *siècles* (Paris, 1953). [1953*a*]

——'Il trattato di Fra Santi Rucellai sul cambio, il monte comune e il monte delle doti', *Archivio storico italiano*, 111 (1953), 3–41. [1953*b*]

——*Rise and Decline of the Medici Bank, 1397–1494* (Cambridge, Mass., 1963).

——*San Bernardino of Siena and Sant' Antonino of Florence: The Two Great Economic Thinkers of the Middle Ages* (Cambridge, Mass., 1967).

Desaivre, L., *La dîme royale à Niort et à La Rochelle en 1718* (Niort, 1880).

De Schepper, H., 'La organización de la finanzas públicas en los Países Bajos reales, 1480–1700: una reseña', *Cuadernos de investigación histórica* (1984), 7–34.

Descimon, R., 'Paris on the eve of St-Bartholomew: taxation, privilege and social geography', in P. Benedict (ed.), *Cities and Social Change in Early Modern France* (London, 1989), 69–104.

Desmaretz, N., *Mémoire de M. Desmarets sur l'administration des finances, depuis le 20 février de l'année 1708, jusqu'au 1er septembre 1715* (repr. Paris, 1789).

De speculo Regis Edwardi III, ed. J. Moisant (Paris, 1891).

Dessert, D., *Argent, pouvoir et société au grand siècle* (Paris, 1984).

De Vries, J., *The Economy of Europe in an Age of Crisis, 1600–1750* (Cambridge, 1976).

——*European Urbanization, 1500–1800* (London, 1984).

Deyon, P., *Le mercantilisme* (Paris, 1969).

Diaz, F., *Francesco Maria Gianni: Dalla burocrazia alla politica sotto Pietro Leopoldo di Toscana* (Milan–Naples, 1966).

——*I Lorena in Toscana: La Reggenza* (Turin, 1987).

Dickinson, H. T. (ed.), *Britain and the French Revolution, 1789–1815* (Basingstoke, 1989).

Dickson, P. G. M., *The Financial Revolution in England: A Study in the Development of Public Credit, 1688–1756* (London, 1967).

——*Finance and Government under Maria Theresia, 1740–1780*, 2 vols. (Oxford, 1987).

Diefendorf, J., *Businessmen and Politics in the Rhineland, 1789–1834* (Princeton, NJ, 1980).

Dietz, F. C., *English Government Finance, 1484–1558* (Chicago, 1920).

Dittrich, E., *Die deutschen und österreichischen Kameralisten* (Darmstadt, 1974).

Di Vittorio, A., *Finanze e moneta a Ragusa nell'età delle crisi* (Naples, 1983).

Dobson, R. B., *The Peasants' Revolt of 1381* (Basingstoke, 1986).

Dolley, R. H. M., and Metcalf, D. M., 'The reform of the English coinage under Edgar', in R. H. M. Dolley (ed.), *Anglo-Saxon Coins* (London, 1961), 136–68.

Domínguez Ortiz, A., 'La ruina de la aldea castellana', *Revista internacional de sociología*, 24 (1948), 99–124.

——*Politica y hacienda de Felipe IV* (Madrid, 1960).

——'La población de Sevilla a mediados del siglo XVII', *Archivo hispalense*, 72 (1989), 3–15.

Dormans, E. H. M., *Het tekort: Staatsschuld in de tijd der Republiek* (Amsterdam, 1991).

Dorwart, R. A., *The Administrative Reforms of Frederick William I of Prussia* (Cambridge, Mass., 1953).

Doucet, R., 'Les finances anglaises en France à la fin de la Guerre de Cent Ans', *Le Moyen Age*, 2nd ser., 27 (1926), 265–332.

——'Le grand parti de Lyon au xvie siècle', *Revue historique*, 171 (1933), 472–512; 172 (1933), 1–40.

Downing, B. M., *The Military Revolution and Political Change: Origins of Democracy and Autocracy in Early Modern Europe* (Princeton, NJ, 1992).

Doyle, W., 'The price of offices in pre-Revolutionary France', *Historical Journal*, 27 (1984), 831–60.

——*The Oxford History of the French Revolution* (Oxford, 1989).

Dreyfus, F. G., *Sociétés et mentalités à Mayence dans la seconde moitié du dix-huitième siècle* (Paris, 1968).

Dubois, H. (ed.), *Local and International Credit in the Middle Ages and the Sixteenth Century: Papers of the Ninth International Economic History Congress* (Berne, 1986).

Du Boulay, F. R. H., *Germany in the Later Middle Ages* (London, 1983).

Duffy, M., *The Military Revolution and the State, 1500–1800* (Exeter, 1980).

Dufraisse, R., 'L'intégration "hégémoniale" de l'Europe sous Napoléon Ier', *Revue de l'Institut Napoléon*, 142 (1984), 11–41.

Dukes, P., *The Making of Russian Absolutism, 1613–1801* (London–New York, 1982).

Dull, J. R., *The French Navy and American Independence: A Study of Arms and Diplomacy, 1774–1787* (Princeton, NJ, 1975).

Dupâquier, J., *La population rurale du bassin parisien à l'époque de Louis XIV* (Paris, 1979).

——(ed.), *Histoire de la population française*, 4 vols. (Paris, 1988).

Dupont-Ferrier, G., *Études sur les institutions financières de la France à la fin du moyen âge. II. Les finances extraordinaires et leur mécanisme* (Paris, 1933; repr. Geneva, 1976).

Duran, J. A., 'The reform of financial administration in Russia during the reign of Catherine the Great', *Canadian Slavic Studies*, 4 (1970), 485–96.

Durand, G., *États et institutions, xvie–xviiie siècles* (Paris, 1969).

Earle, P. (ed.), *Essays in European Economic History, 1500–1800* (Oxford, 1974).

Edwards, J. G., *The Second Century of the English Parliament* (Oxford, 1979).

Einaudi, L., *La finanza sabauda all'aprirsi del secolo XVIII e durante la guerra di successione spagnola* (Turin, 1908).

——'The theory of imaginary money from Charlemagne to the French Revolution', in F. C. Lane and J. C. Riemersma (eds.), *Enterprise and Secular Change: Readings in Economic History* (Homewood, Ill., 1953), 229–61. [Originally published as 'Teoria della moneta immaginaria nel tempo da Carlomagno alla rivoluzione francese', *Rivista di storia economica*, 1 (1936), 1–35.]

Elliott, J. H., *Imperial Spain, 1469–1716* (London, 1963).

——*The Old World and the New, 1492–1650* (Cambridge, 1970).

——'Self-perception and decline in early seventeenth-century Spain', *Past and Present*, 74 (1977), 41–61.

——*Richelieu and Olivares* (Cambridge, 1984).

——*The Count-Duke of Olivares: The Statesman in an Age of Decline* (New Haven–London, 1986).

——*Spain and its World, 1500–1700* (New Haven–London, 1989).

——'A Europe of composite monarchies', *Past and Present*, 137 (1992), 47–71.

Ellis, G., *Napoleon's Continental Blockade: The Case of Alsace* (Oxford, 1981).

——*The Napoleonic Empire* (Basingstoke, 1991).

Emmanuelli, F.-X. (ed.), *L'intendance de Provence à la fin du xviie siècle: Édition critique des mémoires 'pour l'instruction du duc de Bourgogne'* (Paris, 1980).

Emsley, C., *Napoleonic Europe* (London–New York, 1993).

Endres, A. M., 'The functions of numerical data in the writings of Graunt, Petty and Davenant', *History of Political Economy*, 17 (1985), 245–64.

Engel, P., and Kristó, Gy., *Magyarország története, 1301–1457* (Budapest, 1987).

Erslev, K., *Konge og Lensmand i det sextende Aarhundrede: Studier over Statsomvæltningen i 1536 og dens følger for Kongemagt og Adelsvælde* (Copenhagen, 1879).

——*Valdemarernes Storhedstid* (Copenhagen, 1898).

État, finances et économie pendant la Révolution française: Colloque tenu à Bercy les 12, 13, 14 octobre 1989 à l'occasion du Bicentenaire de la Révolution française (Comité pour l'histoire économique et financière de la France; Paris, 1991).

Evans, R. J. W., and Thomas, T. V. (eds.), *Crown, Church and Estates: Central European Politics in the Sixteenth and Seventeenth Centuries* (New York, 1991).

Evensky, J., 'The evolution of Adam Smith's views of political economy', *History of Political Economy*, 21 (1989), 123–45.

Faccini, L., *La Lombardia fra '600 e '700: Riconversione economica e mutamenti sociali* (Milan, 1988).

Faroqi, S., 'Political activity among Ottoman taxpayers and the problem of sultanic legitimation, 1570–1650', *Journal of the Economic and Social History of the Orient*, 35 (1991), 1–39.

Faure, E., *La disgrâce de Turgot: 12 mai 1776* (Paris, 1961).

——*17 juillet 1720: La banqueroute de Law* (Paris, 1977).

Favier, J., *Un conseiller de Philippe le Bel: Enguerran de Marigny* (Paris, 1963).

——*Les contribuables parisiens à la fin de la guerre de cent ans: Les rôles d'impôt de 1421, 1423 et 1438* (Paris–Geneva, 1970).

——*Philippe le Bel* (Paris, 1978).

——*De l'or et des épices: Naissance de l'homme d'affaires au Moyen Age* (Paris, 1987).

Fayle, C. E., 'The deflection of strategy by commerce in the eighteenth century', *Journal of the Royal United Service Institution*, 60 (1923), 281–90.

Feldbaek, O., *Danmarks Historie. IV. Tiden, 1730–1814* (Copenhagen, 1982).

Feller, R., *Geschichte Berns*, 4 vols. (Berne, 1946–60).

Felloni, G., *Gli investimenti finanziari genovesi in Europa tra il Seicento e la Restaurazione* (Milan, 1971).

——'Distribuzione territoriale della ricchezza e dei carichi fiscali nella repubblica di Genova', in A. Guarducci (ed.), *Prodotto lordo e finanza pubblica, secoli XIII–XIX: Atti della 'Ottava settimana di studi', 3–9 maggio 1976* (Istituto internazionale di storia economica F. Datini, 2nd ser., 8; Florence, 1988), 769–803.

Fisher, J., *The Portugal Trade: A Study of Anglo-Portuguese Commerce, 1700–1770* (London, 1971).

Fleming, R., *Kings and Lords in Conquest England* (Cambridge, 1991).

Flora, P. (ed.), *State, Economy and Society in Western Europe, 1815–1975. A Data Handbook. I. The Growth of Mass Democracies and Welfare States* (Frankfurt, 1983).

Floud, R., and McCloskey, D. (eds.), *The Economic History of Britain since 1700. I. 1700–1860* (Cambridge, 1981).

Flynn, D. O., 'Fiscal crisis and the decline of Spain (Castile)', *Journal of Economic History*, 42 (1982), 139–47.

Foley, V., 'An origin of the *Tableau Économique*', *History of Political Economy*, 5 (1973), 121–50.

Forrest, A., and Jones, P., *Reshaping France: Town, Country and Region during the French Revolution* (Manchester, 1991).

Forsyth, M. G., *Reason and Revolution: The Political Thought of the Abbé Sieyes* (Leicester–New York, 1987).

Fortea Pérez, J. I., *Córdoba en el siglo XVI: las bases demográficas y económicas de una expansión urbana* (Córdoba, 1981).

——*Monarquía y Cortes en la Corona de Castilla: Las ciudades ante la política fiscal de Felipe II* (Salamanca, 1990).

——'The Cortes of Castile and Philip II's fiscal policy', *Parliaments, Estates and Representation*, 11 (1991), 117–38.

——'Los encabezamientos de alcabalas andaluces en la hacienda real de Castilla (1557–1595)', *Poder político e instituciones en la España moderna* (Alicante, 1992), 141–93.

Fortescue, Sir John, *The Governance of England: Otherwise Called The Difference between an Absolute and a Limited Monarchy*, ed. C. Plummer (Oxford, 1885).

Frame, R., *The Political Development of the British Isles, 1100–1400* (Oxford, 1990).

François Quesnay et la Physiocratie, 2 vols. (Institut national d'Études démographiques; Paris, 1958).

Frêche, G., 'Compoix, propriété foncière, fiscalité et démographie historique en pays de taille réelle, xvie–xviiie siècles', *Revue d'histoire moderne et contemporaine*, 18 (1971), 321–53.

——*Toulouse et la région Midi-Pyrénées au siècle des lumières, vers 1670–1789* (Paris, 1974).

Frey, W., *Beiträge zur Finanzgeschichte Zürichs im Mittelalter* (Zurich, 1910).

Friis, A., and Glamann, K., *A History of Prices and Wages in Denmark, 1660–1800*. I (Copenhagen–London, 1958).

Fritschy, W., 'Taxation in Britain, France and the Netherlands in the eighteenth century', *Economic and Social History in the Netherlands*, 2 (1990), 57–79.

Fritz, B., 'Kronans fögderier och län under medeltiden', *Bebyggelseshistorisk Tidsskrift*, 4 (1988), 135–48.

Froumenteau, N. [probably Barnaud, N.], *Le Secret des Finances de France descouvert et desparti en trois livres* (Paris, 1581).

Fryde, E. B., 'Materials for the study of Edward III's credit operations, 1327–48', *Bulletin of the Institute of Historical Research*, 22 (1949), 105–38; 23 (1950), 1–30.

——'Financial resources of Edward I in the Netherlands, 1294–98: main problems and some comparisons with Edward III in 1337–40', *Revue belge de philologie et d'histoire*, 40 (1962), 1168–87.

——'Medieval London as a financial centre: some early dealings in royal tallies of assignment', in A. Vannini Marx (ed.), *Credito, banche e investimenti, secoli XIII–XX* (Istituto internazionale di storia economica F. Datini Prato, 2nd ser., ii, 4; Florence, 1985), 41–8.

Fryde, M. M., and Fryde, E. B., 'Public credit, with special reference to north-west Europe', in M. M. Postan, E. E. Rich, and E. Miller (eds.), *The Cambridge Economic History of Europe. III* (Cambridge, 1963), 430–553.

Fryde, N., *List of Welsh Entries in the Memoranda Rolls, 1282–1343* (Cardiff, 1974).

——*The Tyranny and Fall of Edward II* (Cambridge, 1979).

——'Hochfinanz und Landesgeschichte im deutschen Hochmittelalter', *Blätter für deutsche Landesgeschichte*, 125 (1989), 1–12.

Fügedi, E., 'Mátyás király jövedelme 1475-ben', in G. Barta (ed.), *Mátyás király, 1458–1490* (Budapest, 1990), 41–61.

Fuhrmann, H., *Germany in the High Middle Ages, c.1050–1200* (Cambridge, 1986).

Gabillard, J., 'Le financement des guerres napoléoniennes et la conjoncture du premier Empire', *Revue économique*, 4 (1953), 548–72.

Galasso, G., *Mezzogiorno medievale e moderno* (Turin, 1965).

Galbraith, V. H., *The Making of Domesday Book* (Oxford, 1961).

——*Domesday Book: Its Place in Administrative History* (Oxford, 1974).

Galster, G. (ed), *Danmarks Middelalderlige Regnskaber, I pt.* 1 (Copenhagen, 1944–53).

Ganshof, F. L., *Frankish Institutions under Charlemagne*, trans. B. and M. Lyon (Providence, RI, 1968).

García Sanz, A., *Desarrollo y crisis del Antiguo Régimen en Castilla la Vieja: Economía y sociedad en tierras de Segovia, 1500–1814* (Madrid, 1977).

Garzon Pereja, M., *La hacienda de Carlos II* (Madrid, 1980).

Gascon, R., *Grand commerce et vie urbaine au xvie siècle: Lyon et ses marchands*, 2 vols. (Paris, 1971).

Gayer, A. D., Rostow, W. W., and Schwartz, A. J., *The Growth and Fluctuation of the British Economy, 1790–1850*, 2 vols. (Hassocks, 1975).

Gelabert, J. E., 'Il declino della rete urbana nella Castiglia dei secoli XVI–XVIII', *Cheiron*, 6 (1989–90), 9–46.

——'El impacto de la guerra y del fiscalismo en Castilla', in J. H. Elliott and A. García Sanz (eds.), *La España del Conde Duque de Olivares* (Valladolid, 1990), 555–73.

Genet, J.-P., *Four English Political Tracts of the Later Middle Ages* (London, 1977).

——'Féodalisme et naissance de l'État moderne', *Villes, bonnes villes, cités et capitales: Études d'histoire urbaine, XIIe–XVIIIe siècles, offertes à Bernard Chevalier*, ed. M. Bourin (Tours, 1989).

——(ed.), *L'État moderne: Genèse, bilans et perspectives* (Paris, 1990).

——and Le Mené, M. (eds.), *Genèse de l'État moderne: Prélèvement et redistribution* (Paris, 1987).

Gentil da Silva, J., *Stratégies des affaires à Lisbonne entre 1595 et 1607: Lettres marchandes des Rodriguez d'Evora et Veiga* (Paris, 1956).

——*Desarrollo económico, subsistencia y decadencia en España* (Madrid, 1967).

Gerhard D., *Old Europe: A Study of Continuity, 1100–1800* (New York, 1981).

Gerson, J., *Gersonii opera* (Cologne, 1484).

Gerteis, K., *Die deutschen Städte in der Frühen Neuzeit: Zur Vorgeschichte der 'bürgerlichen Welt'* (Darmstadt, 1986).

Gherardi, R., *Potere e costituzione a Vienna fra Sei e Settecento: Il 'buon ordine' di Luigi Ferdinando Marsili* (Bologna, 1980).

Gilchrist, J., *The Church and Economic Activity in the Middle Ages* (London, 1969).

Gillingham, J., *Richard the Lionheart* (London, 1978).

——' "The most precious jewel in the English Crown": levies of danegeld and heregeld in the early eleventh century', *English Historical Review*, 104 (1989), 373–84.

Gilomen, H.-J., 'Die städtische Schuld Berns und der Basler Rentenmarkt im 15. Jahrhundert', *Basler Zeitschrift für Geschichte und Altertumskunde*, 82 (1982), 5–64.

Ginter, D. E., *A Measure of Wealth: The English Land Tax in Historical Analysis* (London, 1992).

Given-Wilson, C., 'Wealth and credit, public and private: the earls of Arundel, 1306–1397', *English Historical Review*, 106 (1991), 1–26.

Goldsmith, R. W., *Premodern Financial Systems: A Historical Comparative Study* (Cambridge, 1987).

Goodare, J., 'Parliamentary taxation in Scotland, 1560–1603', *Scottish Historical Review*, 68 (1989), 23–52.

Goubert, P., *Beauvais et le Beauvaisis de 1600 à 1730: Contribution à l'histoire sociale de la France du xviie siècle*, 2 vols. (Paris, 1960).

——*L'ancien régime. I. La société* (Paris, 1969).

Governo della Toscana sotto il regno di Sua Maestà il re Leopoldo II, 2nd edn (Florence, 1791).

Grampp, W. D., 'Malthus and his contemporaries', *History of Political Economy*, 6 (1974), 278–304.

Grant, A., *Independence and Nationhood: Scotland, 1306–1469* (London, 1984).

Green, J. A., 'The last century of Danegeld', *English Historical Review*, 96 (1981), 241–58.

——' "Praeclarum et magnificum antiquitatis monumentum": the earliest surviving pipe roll', *Bulletin of the Institute of Historical Research*, 55 (1982), 1–17.

——*The Government of England under Henry I* (Cambridge, 1986).

Green, V. H. H., 'Taxation, Church', in J. R. Strayer (ed.), *Dictionary of the Middle Ages. XI* (New York, 1988), 605–11.

Greengrass, M. (ed.), *Conquest and Coalescence: The Shaping of the State in Early Modern Europe* (London, 1991).

Gresky, R., *Die Finanzen der Welfen im 13. und 14. Jahrhundert* (Hildesheim, 1984).

Grice-Hutchinson, M., *The School of Salamanca: Readings in Spanish Monetary Theory, 1544–1605* (Oxford, 1952).

——*Early Economic Thought in Spain, 1177–1740* (London, 1978).

Griffiths, G., *Representative Government in Western Europe in the Sixteenth Century* (Oxford, 1968).

Groenewegen, P. D. (ed.), *The Economics of A. R. J. Turgot* (The Hague, 1977).

Gross, J.-P., 'Progressive taxation and social justice in eighteenth-century France', *Past and Present*, 140 (1993), 79–126.

Groves, H. M., *Tax Philosophers: Two Hundred Years of Thought in Great Britain and the United States*, ed. D. J. Curran (Madison, Wis., 1974).

Guenée, B., *States and Rulers in Later Medieval Europe*, trans. J. Vale (Oxford, 1985).

Guéry, A., 'Les finances de la monarchie française sous l'ancien régime', *Annales E.S.C.*, 33 (1978), 216–39.

——'Le roi dépensier: le don, la contrainte, et l'origine du système financier de la monarchie française d'ancien régime', *Annales E.S.C.*, 39 (1984), 1241–69.

——'La naissance financière de l'État moderne en France', in J. Bouvier and J.-C. Perrot (eds.), *États, fiscalités, économies: Actes du cinquième congrès de l'association française des historiens économistes, 16–18 juin 1983* (Paris, 1985), 53–62.

——'État, classification sociale et compromis sous Louis XIV: la capitation de 1695', *Annales E.S.C.*, 41 (1986), 1041–60.

Guicciardini, Francesco, 'La decima scalata', *Dialogo e discorsi del reggimento di Firenze*, ed. R. Palmarocchi (*Opere*, ed. V. de Caprariis, vii; Bari, 1932).

——'Dialogo del reggimento di Firenze', *Opere di Francesco Guicciardini*, ed. E. Lugnani Scarano (Turin, 1970).

Gurevich, A. J., *Categories of Medieval Culture* (London, 1985).

Gutiérrez Alonso, A., *Estudio sobre la decadencia de Castilla: La ciudad de Valladolid en el siglo XVII* (Valladolid, 1989).

Habib, I., *The Agrarian System of Mughal India, 1556–1707* (London, 1963).

Hadwin, J. F., 'The last royal tallages', *English Historical Review*, 96 (1981), 344–58.

Hall, C. D., *British Strategy in the Napoleonic War, 1803–15* (Manchester, 1992).

Hall, J. A., *States in History* (Oxford, 1986).

Hall, T. E., 'Thought and practice of enlightened government in French Corsica', *American Historical Review*, 74 (1969), 880–905.

Hallam, E. M., *Capetian France, 987–1328* (London, 1980).

Hallauer, R., *Der Basler Stadtwechsel, 1504–1746: Ein Beitrag zur Geschichte der Staatsbanken* (Basle, 1904).

Hamilton, E. J., *American Treasure and the Price Revolution in Spain, 1501–1650* (New York, 1970).

Hamm, F., *Zur Grundlegung und Geschichte der Steuermoral* (Trier, 1908).

Hammarström, I., *Finansförvaltning och varuhandel, 1504–1540* (Uppsala, 1956).

Hanak, P. (ed.), *The Corvina History of Hungary from the Earliest Times to the Present* (Budapest, 1991).

Hanson, C. A., *Economy and Society in Baroque Portugal, 1668–1703* (London–Basingstoke, 1981).

Hardman, J., *Louis XVI* (New Haven–London, 1993).

Harris, R. D., 'French finances and the American War, 1777–1783', *Journal of Modern History*, 48 (1976), 233–58.

——*Necker: Reform Statesman of the Ancien Régime* (Berkeley, 1979).

——*Necker and the Revolution of 1789* (Lanham, Md., 1986).

Harris, S. E., *The Assignats* (Cambridge, Mass., 1930; repr., New York, 1969).

Harriss, G. L., 'Fictitious loans', *Economic History Review*, 2nd ser., 8 (1955–6), 187–99.

——*King, Parliament and Public Finance in Medieval England to 1369* (Oxford, 1975).

——'Medieval doctrines in the debates of supply, 1610–1629', in K. M. Sharpe (ed.), *Faction and Parliament: Essays on Early Stuart History* (Oxford, 1978), 73–103.

——'Theory and practice in royal taxation: some observations', *English Historical Review*, 97 (1982), 811–19.

——*Cardinal Beaufort: A Study of Lancastrian Ascendancy and Decline* (Oxford, 1988).

Hartley, T. E., *Elizabeth's Parliaments: Queen, Lords and Commons, 1559–1601* (Manchester, 1992).

Hartmann, P. C. (ed.), *Das Steuersystem der europäischen Staaten am Ende des Ancien Regime. Eine offizielle französische Enquete (1763–8). Dokumente, Analyse und Auswertung. England und die Staaten Nord- und Mitteleuropas* (Munich, 1979).

Hartung, J., 'Die direkten Steuern und die Vermögensentwicklung in Augsburg von der Mitte des 16. bis zum 18. Jahrhundert', *Jahrbuch für Gesetzgebung, Verwaltung und Volkswirtschaft im Deutschen Reich*, 20 (1898), 167–209.

Harvey, S. P. J., 'Domesday Book and Anglo-Norman governance', *Transactions of the Royal Historical Society*, 5th ser., 25 (1975), 173–95.

Harvey-Phillips, M. B., 'Malthus' theodicy: the intellectual background to his contribution to political economy', *History of Political Economy*, 16 (1984), 591–608.

Hastrup, K., *Culture and History in Medieval Iceland: An Anthropological Analysis of Structure and Change* (Oxford, 1985).

Hatcher, J., *Plague, Population and the English Economy, 1348–1530* (London, 1977).

Hatton, R. M., *Charles XII of Sweden* (London and Southampton, 1968).

Hauser, H. (ed.), *La vie chère au xvi*[e] *siècle: La response de Jean Bodin à M. de Malestroit, 1568* (Paris, 1932).

Hecksher, E. F., *Mercantilism*, trans. M. Shapiro (London, 1935).

——'Natural and money economy as illustrated from Swedish history in the sixteenth century', in F. C. Lane and J. C. Riemersma (eds.), *Enterprise and Secular Change: Readings in Economic History* (Homewood, Ill., 1953), 206–28. [Originally published in *Journal of Economic and Business History*, 3 (1930–1), 1–29.]

Heers, J., *Gênes au xv*[e] *siècle: Activité économique et problèmes sociaux* (Paris, 1961).

Helleiner, K. F., *The Imperial Loans: A Study in Financial and Diplomatic History* (Oxford, 1965).

Henderson, W. O., *Studies in the Economic Policies of Frederick the Great* (London, 1963).

Hendricks, C. D., 'Charles V and the Cortes of Castile: politics in Renaissance Spain', Ph.D. thesis (Cornell University, 1976).

Henneman, J. B., 'Financing the Hundred Years' War: royal taxation in France in 1340', *Speculum*, 42 (1967), 275–98.

——'The Black Death and royal taxation in France, 1347–1351', *Speculum*, 43 (1968), 405–28. [1968*a*]

——'*Enquêteurs-réformateurs* and fiscal officers in fourteenth-century France', *Traditio*, 24 (1968), 309–49. [1968*b*]

——'Taxation of Italians by the French crown, 1311–1363', *Mediaeval Studies*, 31 (1969), 15–43.

——*Royal Taxation in Fourteenth-Century France: The Development of War Financing, 1322–1356* (Princeton, NJ, 1971).

——*Royal Taxation in Fourteenth-Century France: The Captivity and Ransom of John II, 1356–1370* (Philadelphia, 1976).

——'The military class and the French monarchy in the late Middle Ages', *American Historical Review*, 83 (1978), 946–65.

——'Nobility, privilege and fiscal politics in late Medieval France', *French Historical Studies*, 13 (1983), 1–17.

——'Taxation, French', in J. R. Strayer (ed.), *Dictionary of the Middle Ages. XI* (New York, 1988), 618–25.

Henning, F.-W., *Das vorindustrielle Deutschland, 800 bis 1800* (Paderborn, 1985).

[Henry of Ghent], *Quodlibeta Magistri Henrici Goethals a Gandavo, doctor solemnis* (Paris, 1518).

Heper, M., 'The state and public bureaucracies: a comparative and historical perspective', *Comparative Studies in Society and History*, 27 (1985), 86–110.

Herbin, R., and Rebereau, A., *Le cadastre français* (Paris, 1953).

Herlihy, D., *Pisa in the Early Renaissance* (New Haven, 1958).

——'Direct and indirect taxation in urban finance, ca. 1200–1400', *Finances et comptabilités urbaines du xiiie au xive siècle* (Brussels, 1964), 385–405.

——'Problems of record linkages in Tuscan fiscal records', in E. A. Wrigley (ed.), *Identifying People in the Past* (1972).

——*Cities and Society in Medieval Italy* (London, 1980).

——and Klapisch-Zuber, C., *Les Toscans et leurs familles: Une étude du castasto florentin de 1427* (Paris, 1978).

——and Klapisch-Zuber, C., *Tuscans and their Families: A Study of the Florentine Catasto of 1427* (New Haven–London, 1985).

Hermann, C., 'L'État et l'église', in C. Hermann (ed.), *Le premier âge de l'État en Espagne, 1450–1700* (Paris, 1989), 381–405.

Herr, R., *The Eighteenth-Century Revolution in Spain* (Princeton, NJ, 1969).

——*Rural Change and Royal Finances in Spain at the End of the Old Regime* (Berkeley, 1989).

Hertzberg, E., 'Lén og veizla i Norges sagatid', *Germanistische Abhandlungen zum LXX. Geburtstag Konrad von Maurers* (Göttingen, 1893), 285–331.

Hildebrandt, R., 'Zur Frage der reichsstädtischen Finanzen und Haushaltpolitik seit dem Westfälischen Frieden', in E. Maschke *et al.* (eds.), *Städtisches Haushalts- under Rechnungswesen* (Sigmaringen, 1977), 91–107.

Hiler, D., 'Fiscalité, conjoncture et consommation à Genève au xviiie siècle', *Bulletin du Département d'histoire économique, Université de Genève*, 13 (1982–3), 24–51.

Hill, D. (ed.), *Ethelred the Unready: Papers from the Millenary Conference* (British Archaeological Reports, British ser., 59; Oxford, 1978).

Hilton, R. H., *Bondmen Made Free: Medieval Peasant Movements and the English Rising of 1381* (London, 1973).

——and Aston, T. H., *The English Rising of 1381* (Cambridge, 1984).

Hincker, F., *La Révolution française et l'économie: Décollage ou catastrophe?* (Paris, 1989).

Hinze, O., 'Der preussische Militär- und Beamtenstaat im 18. Jahrhundert', in W. Hubatsch (ed.), *Absolutismus* (Darmstadt, 1988), 45–56.

Hobbes, Thomas, *Leviathan or the Matter, Forme and Power of a Commonwealth Ecclesiasticall and Civil*, ed. M. Oakeshott (Oxford, 1960).

Hocquet, J.-C., *Le sel et le pouvoir de l'an mil à la Révolution française* (Paris, 1985).

——(ed.), *Le roi, le marchand et le sel* (Villeneuve d'Ascq, 1987).

Hoffman, P. T., 'Taxes and agrarian life in early modern France: land sales, 1550–1730', *Journal of Economic History*, 46 (1986), 37–55.

——and Norberg, K. (eds.), *Fiscal Crises, Liberty, and Representative Government, 1450–1789* (Stanford, 1994).

Holl, B., 'Hofkammerpräsident Gundaker Thomas Graf Starhemberg und die österreichischen Finanzpolitik der Barockzeit, 1703–1715', *Archiv für österreichische Geschichte*, 132 (1976), 3–441.

Hollander, S., 'Ricardo and the Corn Laws: a revision', *History of Political Economy*, 9 (1977), 1–47.

——'On Mathus's population principle and social reform', *History of Political Economy*, 18 (1986), 187–235.

——'On Malthus's Physiocratic references', *History of Political Economy*, 24 (1992), 368–80.

Hollister, C. W., 'The origins of the English Treasury', *English Historical Review*, 93 (1978), 262–75.

Holmsen, A., *Norges Historie: Fra de eldste tider til 1660*, 4th edn (Oslo, 1977).

Holt, J. C., 'The loss of Normandy and royal finance', in J. Gillingham and J. C. Holt (eds.), *War and Government in the Middle Ages: Essays in Honour of J. O. Prestwich* (Woodbridge, 1984), 92–105.

——'1086', in J. C. Holt (ed.), *Domesday Studies* (Woodbridge, 1987), 41–64.

Holzmair, E., 'Kriegsfinanzen im Zeitalter Napoleons', *Numismatische Zeitschrift*, 73 (1949), 120–34.

Hóman, B., *Magyar pénztörténet, 1000–1325* (Budapest, 1916).

——*A magyar királyság pénzügyei és gazdaságpolitikája Károly Róbert korában* (Budapest, 1921).

——'La circulazione delle monete d'oro in Ungheria dal X al XIV secolo e la crisi europea dell'oro nel secolo XIV', *Rivista Italiana di numismatica*, 2nd ser., 5 (1922), 109–56.

Hope-Jones, A., *Income Tax in the Napoleonic Wars* (Cambridge, 1939).

Hoppit, J., 'Attitudes to credit in Britain, 1680–1790', *Historical Journal*, 33 (1990), 305–22.

Horrox, R., ed., 'Financial memoranda of the reign of Edward V: Longleat miscellaneous manuscript book II', *Camden Miscellany*, 29 (Camden Society, 4th ser., 34; London, 1987), 197–244.

[Hostiensis], *Summa hostiensis* (Lyon, 1537; repr. Aalen, 1962).

Housley, N. J., *The Later Crusades, 1274–1580* (Oxford, 1992).

Hoyle, R. W. (ed.), *The Estates of the English Crown, 1558–1640* (Cambridge, 1992).

Huang, R., 'Fiscal administration during the Ming dynasty', in C. O. Hucker (ed.), *Chinese Government in Ming Times: Seven Studies* (New York–London, 1969), 73–128.

——*Taxation and Governmental Finance in Sixteenth-Century Ming China* (Cambridge, 1974).

Hubatsch, W., *Frederick the Great of Prussia: Absolutism and Administration*, trans. P. Doran (London, 1975).

Hume, D., *Writings on Economics*, ed. E. Rotwein (Edinburgh, 1955).

Hume, L. J., 'Charles Davenant on financial administration', *History of Political Economy*, 6 (1974), 463–77.

Hüppe, S., *A lengyel alkotmány története* (Budapest, 1894).

Hutchison, T. W., *Before Adam Smith: The Emergence of Political Economy, 1662–1776* (Oxford, 1988).

Ingrao, C. W., *In Quest and Crisis: Emperor Joseph I and the Habsburg Monarchy* (West Lafayette, Ind., 1979).

——*The Hessian Mercenary State: Ideas, Institutions and Reform under Frederick II, 1760–1785* (Cambridge, 1987).

Innocent IV [Sinibaldus Fliscus], *Commentaria super libros quinque Decretalium* (Frankfurt-am-Main, 1570).

Isenmann, E., 'Reichsstadt und Reich an der Wende vom späten Mittelalter zur frühen Neuzeit', in J. Engel (ed.), *Mittel und Wege früher Verfassungspolitik* (Spätmittelalter und frühe Neuzeit, 9; Stuttgart, 1979), 9–223.

——'Reichsfinanzen und Reichssteuern im 15. Jahrhundert', *Zeitschrift für historische Forschung*, 7 (1980), 1–76, 129–218.

——*Die deutsche Stadt im Spätmittelalter, 1250–1500: Stadtgestalt, Recht, Stadtregiment, Kirche, Gesellschaft, Wirtschaft* (Stuttgart, 1988).

Israel, J. I., 'Spanish wool exports and the European economy, 1610–40', *Economic History Review*, 2nd ser., 23 (1980), 193–211.

——*Dutch Primacy in World Trade, 1585–1740* (Oxford, 1989).

Jacquart, J., *La crise rurale en Ile-de-France, 1550–1670* (Paris, 1974).

Jacoud, G., 'La monnaie fiduciaire: d'une émission libérée au privilège de la Banque de France (26 octobre 1795 à 14 avril 1803)', in *Histoire économique et financière de la France: Études et documents. III. 1991* (Comité pour l'histoire économique et financière de la France; Paris, 1991), 87–135.

James, M., 'Pierre-Louis Roederer, Jean-Baptiste Say and the concept of *industrie*', *History of Political Economy*, 9 (1977), 455–75.

Jaubert, A. N., 'The royal castles during the reign of Erik Menved', *Journal of Danish Archaeology*, 7 (1988), 216–24.

Jeannin, P., 'Les comptes du Sund comme source pour la construction d'indices généraux de l'activité économique en Europe, xvie–xviiie siècle', *Revue historique*, 231 (1964), 55–102, 307–40.

Jennings, R. M., and Trout, A. P., *The Tontine: From the Reign of Louis XIV to the French Revolutionary Era* (Homewood, Ill., 1982).

Jeserich, K. G. A., Pohl, H., and von Unruh, G.-C. (eds.), *Deutsche Verwaltungsgeschichte. I* (Stuttgart, 1983).

Jespersen, K. J. V., *Danmarks historie. III* (Copenhagen, 1989).

Johansen, H. C., *Danmarks historie. IX* (Copenhagen, 1985).

John, E., *Orbis Britanniae and Other Studies* (Leicester, 1966).

Johnson, H. C., 'The concept of bureaucracy in Cameralism', *Political Science Quarterly*, 79 (1964), 378–402.

——*Frederick the Great and his Officials* (New Haven–London, 1975).

Jones, D. W., *War and Economy in the Age of William III and Marlborough* (Oxford, 1988). [1988*a*]

Jones, E. L., *The European Miracle: Environments, Economies, and Geopolitics in the History of Europe and Asia*, 2nd edn (Cambridge, 1988). [1988*b*]

Jörberg, L., *A History of Prices in Sweden, 1734–1914*, 2 vols. (Lund, 1972).

Jordan, W. C., *Louis IX and the Challenge of the Crusade* (Princeton, NJ, 1979).

Justi, J. H. G. von, *Staatswirtschaft oder systematische Abhandlung aller oekonomischen und Cameral-Wissenschaften. I*, 2nd edn (Leipzig, 1758).

Kaeuper, R. W., *War, Justice, and Public Order: England and France in the Later Middle Ages* (Oxford, 1988).

Kagan, R. L., *Lucrecia's Dreams: Politics and Prophecy in Sixteenth-Century Spain* (Berkeley, 1990).

Kahan, A., *The Plow, the Hammer and the Knout: An Economic History of Eighteenth-Century Russia*, ed. R. Hellie (Chicago–London, 1985).

Kain, R. J. P., and Baigent, E., *The Cadastral Map in the Service of the State: A History of Property Mapping* (Chicago–London, 1992).

Kaiser, T. E., 'The abbé de Saint-Pierre: public opinion and the reconstitution of the French monarchy', *Journal of Modern History*, 55 (1983), 618–43.

Kallbrunner, J., *Kaiserin Maria Theresias politisches Testament* (Munich, 1952).

Kamen, H., *The War of Succession in Spain, 1700–15* (London, 1969).

——*Spain in the Later Seventeenth Century, 1665–1700* (London–New York, 1980).

——*European Society, 1500–1700* (London, 1984).

Kann, R. A., *A Study in Austrian Intellectual History from Late Baroque to Romanticism* (New York, 1973).

Kantorowicz, E. H., *The King's Two Bodies: A Study in Mediaeval Political Theology* (Princeton, NJ, 1957).

——'Inalienability: a note on canonical practice and the English coronation oath in the thirteenth century', *Selected Studies* (Locust Valley, NY, 1965), 138–50. [1965*a*]

——'Mysteries of state: an absolutist concept and its late mediaeval origins', *Selected Studies* (Locust Valley, NY, 1965), 381–98. [1965*b*]

Kaplan, S. L., *Bread, Politics and Political Economy in the Reign of Louis XV*, 2 vols. (The Hague, 1976).

Kappelhof, A. C. M., *De belastingheffing in de Meierij van Den Bosch gedurende de generaliteitsperiode, 1648–1730* (Tilburg, 1986).

Kehl, P., *Die Steuer in der Lehre der Theologen des Mittelalters: Eine quellengeschichtliche Studie* (Volkswirtschaftliche Studien, 17; Berlin, 1927).

Kellenbenz , H. (ed.), *Fremde Kaufleute auf der iberischen Halbinsel* (Cologne–Vienna, 1970).

——(ed.), *Öffentliche Finanzen und privates Kapital im späten Mittelalter und in der ersten Hälfte des 19. Jahrhunderts* (Forschungen zur Sozial- und Wirtschaftsgeschichte, 16; Stuttgart, 1971).

——'Wirtschaft und Gesellschaft Europas, 1350–1650', in H. Kellenbenz (ed.), *Handbuch der europäischen Wirtschafts- und Sozialgeschichte. III. Europäische Wirtschafts- und Sozialgeschichte vom ausgehenden Mittelalter bis zur Mitte des 17. Jahrhunderts* (Stuttgart, 1986), 331–45.

Kennedy, P., *The Rise and Fall of the Great Powers: Economic Change and Military Conflict from 1500 to 2000* (New York, 1989).

Kennedy, W., *English Taxation, 1640–1799: An Essay on Policy and Opinion* (London, 1913).

Kerhervé, J., *L'État breton aux xive et xve siècles: Le duc, l'argent et les hommes*, 2 vols. (Paris, 1987).

——'Taxation and ducal power in late medieval Brittany', *French History*, 6 (1992), 1–23.

Keynes, G., *A Bibliography of Sir William Petty, FRS* (Oxford, 1971).

Keynes, S., and Lapidge, M., *Alfred the Great: Asser's Life of Alfred and Other Contemporary Sources* (Harmondsworth, 1983).

Khromov, P. A., *Ekonomicheskoe razvitie Rossii, 1800–1917* (Moscow, 1950).

Kieniewicz, S., *History of Poland* (Warsaw, 1968).

Kiesewetter, H., 'Competition for wealth and power: the growing rivalry between industrial Britain and industrial Germany, 1815–1914', *Journal of European Economic History*, 20 (1991), 271–99.

Kindleberger, C. P., *A Financial History of Western Europe* (London, 1984) [1984*a*]

——'Financial institutions and economic development: a comparison of Great Britain and France in the eighteenth and nineteenth centuries', *Explorations in Economic History*, 21 (1984), 103–24. [1984*b*]

——'The economic crisis of 1619 to 1623', *Journal of Economic History*, 51 (1991), 149–75.

King, J. E., 'The origin of the term "political economy"', *Journal of Modern History*, 20 (1948), 230–1.

Kirby, D., *Northern Europe in the Early Modern Period: The Baltic World, 1492–1772* (London–New York, 1990).

Kirshner, J., 'The moral theology of public finance: a study and edition of Nicholas de Anglia's *Quaestio Disputata* on the public debt of Venice', *Archivum Fratrum Praedicatorum*, 40 (1970), 47–72.

Klackenberg, H., *Moneta nostra: Monetarisering i medeltidens Sverige* (Lund, 1992).

Klang, D. M., *Tax Reform in Eighteenth-Century Lombardy* (New York, 1977).

Klein, E., *Von der Reform zur Restauration: Finanzpolitik und Reformgesetzgebung des preussischen Staatskanzlers Karl August von Hardenberg* (Berlin, 1965).

——*Geschichte der öffentlichen Finanzen in Deutschland, 1500–1870* (Wiesbaden, 1974).

Klingenstein, G., 'Revisions of Enlightened Absolutism: "The Austrian monarchy is like no other"', *Historical Journal*, 33 (1990), 155–67.

Klyuchevsky, V., *Peter the Great*, trans. L. Archibald (London, 1965).

Knecht, R. J., *Francis I* (Cambridge, 1982).

Knudsen, J. B., *Justus Möser and the German Enlightenment* (Cambridge, 1986).

Koch, H. W., *A History of Prussia* (London–New York, 1978).

Koenigsberger, H. G., *Politicians and Virtuosi: Essays in Early Modern History* (London, 1986).

——and Mosse, G. L., *Europe in the Sixteenth Century* (London, 1968).

Kohn, H., *Prelude to Nation States: The French and German Experience, 1789–1815* (Princeton, NJ, 1967).

Körner, M., *Solidarités financières suisses au xvi*[e] *siècle: Contribution à l'histoire monétaire, bancaire et financière des cantons suisses et des États voisins* (Lucerne–Lausanne, 1980).

——*Luzerner Staatsfinanzen, 1415–1798* (Lucerne–Stuttgart, 1981).

——'Zum Problem der Währungsvielfalt in der alten Schweiz', in E. van Cauwenberghe *et al.* (eds.), *Minting, Monetary Circulation and Exchange Rates: Eighth International Economic History Congress, 'C' Themes, 7, Budapest, 1982* (Trier, 1984), 219–35.

——'Investissements urbains en Suisse au xvie siècle: répartition sectorielle', in A. Guarducci (ed.), *Investimenti e civiltà urbana, secoli XIII–XVIII* (Prato, 1989), 949–81.

——'Les péages vaudois dans les comptes du Trésorier romand à Berne au xvie siècle', in P.-L. Pelet and J.-F. Poudret (eds.), *La monnaie de sa pièce . . . Hommages à Colin Martin* (Lausanne, 1992), 235–50.

Koser, R., 'Der preussische Staatschatz von 1740 bis 1756', *Forschungen zur brandenburgischen und preussischen Geschichte*, 4 (1891), 529–51.

——'Die preussischen Finanzen im Siebenjährigen Kriege', *Forschungen zur brandenburgischen und preussischen Geschichte*, 13 (1900), 1–47.

——'Die preussischen Finanzen von 1763 bis 1786', *Forschungen zur brandenburgischen und preussischen Geschichte*, 116 (1903), 445–76.

Krüger, K., *Die Einnahmen und Ausgaben der dänischen Rentmeister, 1588–1628: Ein Beitrag zur frühneuzeitlichen Finanzgeschichte* (Marburg, 1970).

——*Finanzstaat Hessen, 1500–1567: Staatsbildung im Übergang vom Domänenstaat zum Steuerstaat* (Marburg, 1980).

——'Gerhard Oestreich und der Finanzstaat: Entstehung und Deutung eines Epochenbegriffs der frühneuzeitlichen Verfassungs- und Sozialgeschichte', *Hessisches Jahrbuch für Landesgeschichte*, 33 (1983), 333–46.

——'Die Staatsfinanzen Dänemarks und Schwedens im 16. Jahrhundert: ein Strukturvergleich', *Zeitschrift für historische Forschung*, 15 (1988), 129–50.

Kouri, E. I., and Scott, T. (eds.), *Politics and Society in Reformation Europe: Essays for Sir Geoffrey Elton on his Sixty-Fifth Birthday* (London, 1987).

Kuczynksi, M., and Meek, R. L. (eds.), *Quesnay's Tableau Économique* (London–New York, 1972).

Kuethe, A. J., and Inglis, G. D., 'Absolutism and enlightened reform: Charles III, the establishment of the *alcabala*, and commercial reorganization in Cuba', *Past and Present*, 109 (1985), 118–43.

Kula, W., *Problemi e metodi di storia economica* (Milan, 1972).

Kunisch, J. (ed.), *Der dynastische Fürstenstaat: Zur Bedeutung von Sukzessionsordnungen für die Entstehung des frühmodernen Staates* (Berlin, 1982).

Ladero Quesada, M. A., 'Les finances royales de Castille à la veille des temps modernes', *Annales E.S.C.*, 25 (1970), 775–83.

——*La hacienda real de Castilla en el siglo XV* (La Laguna, 1973).

——'La hacienda real de Castilla en 1504: rentas y gastos de la Corona', *Historia. Instituciones. Documentos*, 3 (1976), 311–45.

——*El siglo XV en Castilla: Fuentes de renta y política fiscal* (Barcelona, 1982).

——'Cortes de Castilla y León y fiscalidad regia', *Las Cortes de Castilla y León en la edad media. I* (Valladolid, 1988), 289–373.

——'La genèse de l'État dans les royaumes hispaniques médiévaux, 1250–1450', in C. Hermann (ed.), *Le premier âge de l'État en Espagne, 1450–1700* (Paris, 1989), 9–65.

Lane, F. C., *Venice: A Maritime Republic* (Baltimore, 1973).

Lanzinner, M., *Fürst, Räte und Landstände: Die Entstehung der Zentralbehörden in Bayern, 1511–1598* (Göttingen, 1980).

Lapeyre, H., *Simón Ruiz et les 'Asientos' de Philippe II* (Paris, 1953).

La Roncière, C. M. de, 'Indirect taxes or "gabelles" at Florence in the fourteenth century: the evolution of tariffs and problems of collection', in N. Rubinstein (ed.), *Florentine studies: Politics and society in Renaissance Florence* (London, 1968), 140–92.

Law, J., *Oeuvres complètes*, ed. P. Harsin, 3 vols. (Paris, 1934).

Lawson, M. K., '"These stories look true": levels of taxation in the reigns of Aethelred II and Cnut', *English Historical Review*, 104 (1989), 385–406.

Lawson, P., *The East India Company: A History* (London–New York, 1993).

LeDonne, J. P., 'Indirect taxes in Catherine's Russia. I. The Salt Code of 1781', *Jahrbücher für Geschichte Osteuropas*, 23 (1975), 161–90.

——'Indirect taxes in Catherine's Russia. II. The liquor monopoly', *Jahrbücher für Geschichte Osteuropas*, 24 (1976), 173–207.

——*Ruling Russia: Politics and Administration in the Age of Absolutism, 1762–1796* (Princeton, NJ, 1984).

——*Absolutism and Ruling Class: The Formation of the Russian Political Order, 1700–1825* (New York–Oxford, 1991).

Le Flem, J. P., 'Los aspectos económicos de la España moderna', in M. Tunon De Lara (ed.), *Historia de España. V* (Barcelona, 1980), 9–133.

Leigh, A. H., 'John Locke and the quantity theory of money', *History of Political Economy*, 6 (1974), 200–19.

Lemarchand, G., *La fin du féodalisme dans le pays de Caux: Conjoncture économique et démographique et structure sociale dans une région de grande culture de la crise du xviie siècle à la stabilisation de la Révolution, 1640–1795* (Paris, 1989).

Le Roy Ladurie, E., *Les paysans de Languedoc*, 2 vols. (Paris, 1966).

——'Les comptes fantastiques de Gregory King', *Annales E.S.C.*, 23 (1968), 1086–102.

——*The Mind and Method of the Historian*, trans. S. and B. Reynolds (Brighton, 1981).

——*The French Peasantry, 1450–1660* (Aldershot, 1987).

Lesage, C., *Napoléon Ier: Créancier de la Prusse, 1807–1814* (Paris, 1924).

Letwin, W., *The Origins of Scientific Economics: English Economic Thought, 1660–1776* (London, 1963).

Levi, M., 'The predatory theory of rule', *Politics and Society*, 10 (1981), 431–65.

Lévy, C.-F., *Capitalistes et pouvoir au siècle des lumières. II. La monarchie buissonnière, 1718–1723* (The Hague, 1980).

Lewis, P. S., *Later Medieval France: The Polity* (London, 1968).

——*Essays in Later Medieval French History* (London, 1985).

Leyden, Philippus de, *De cura reipublicae et sorte principantis* [1355], ed. R. Fruin and P. C. Molhuijsen (The Hague, 1900).

Leyser, K. J., *Medieval Germany and its Neighbours, 900–1250* (London, 1982).

Liebel, H. P., *Enlightened Bureaucracy versus Enlightened Despotism in Baden, 1750–1792* (Proceedings of the American Philosophical Society, 55; Philadelphia, 1965).

Liebel-Weckowicz, H. P., 'Count Karl v. Zinzendorf and the liberal revolt against Joseph II's economic reforms, 1783–1790', in H.-U. Wehler (ed.), *Sozialgeschichte heute: Festschrift für Hans Rosenberg zum 70. Geburtstag* (Göttingen, 1974), 69–85.

Limm, P., *The Thirty Years' War* (London, 1984).

Lind, G., 'Military and absolutism: the army officers of Denmark–Norway as a social group and political factor, 1660–1848', *Scandinavian Journal of History*, 12 (1987), 221–43.

Lindkvist, T., *Plundring, skatter och den feodala statens framväxt: Organisatoriska tendenser i Sverige under övergången från vikingatid till tidig medeltid* (Uppsala, 1990).

Linehan, P., *The Spanish Church and the Papacy in the Thirteenth Century* (Cambridge, 1971).
Llopis Agelán, E. *et al.*, 'El movimiento de la población extremeña durante el Antiguo Régimen' (unpubd paper delivered to the IV Congreso de la Asociación de Historia Económica, Alicante, 1989).
Lloyd, H. A., *The State, France and the Sixteenth Century* (London, 1980).
[Locke, John] *Locke on Money*, ed. P. H. Kelly, 2 vols. (Oxford, 1991).
Lönnroth, E., *Statsmakt och statsfinans i det medeltida Sverige: Studier över Skatteväsen och länsförvaltning* (Göteborg, 1940).
——'The Baltic Countries', in M. M. Postan, E. E. Rich, and E. Miller (eds.), *Cambridge History of Europe. III. Economic Organization and Policies in the Middle Ages* (Cambridge, 1963), 361–96.
Lot, F., and Fawtier, R., *Le premier budget de la monarchie française: Le compte général de 1202–1203* (Paris, 1932).
——and Fawtier, R., *Histoire des institutions françaises au Moyen Age*, 3 vols. (Paris, 1957–62).
Lovett, A. W., 'Juan de Ovando and the council of finance, 1573–75', *Historical Journal*, 15 (1972), 1–21.
Loyn, H. R., *The Governance of Anglo-Saxon England, 500–1087* (London, 1982).
Loyseau, C., *Cinq livres du droit des offices* (Paris, 1610).
——*A Treatise of Orders and Plain Dignities*, ed. and trans. H. A. Lloyd (Cambridge, 1994).
Lublinskaya, A. D., *French Absolutism: The Crucial Phase, 1620–1629* (Cambridge, 1978).
Lunt, W. E., *Papal Revenues in the Middle Ages*, 2 vols. (New York, 1934).
Lütge, F., *Deutsche Sozial- und Wirtschaftsgeschichte*, 3rd edn (Berlin, 1966).
Lüthy, H., *La banque protestante en France de l'édit de Nantes à la Révolution*, 2 vols. (Paris, 1959–61).
Lynch, J., *Spanish Colonial Administration, 1782–1810: The Intendant System in the Viceroyalty of the Río de la Plata* (London, 1958).
——*Bourbon Spain, 1700–1808* (Oxford, 1989).
Lynn, J. A., 'The growth of the French army during the seventeenth century', *Armed Forces and Society*, 6 (1980), 568–686.
——'How war fed war: the tax of violence and contributions during the *grand siècle*', *Journal of Modern History*, 65 (1993), 286–310.
Lyon, B., and Verhulst, A., *Medieval Finance: A Comparison of Financial Institutions in Northwestern Europe* (Bruges, 1967).
Macartney, C. A., *The Habsburg Empire, 1790–1918* (London, 1968).
McCulloch, J. R., *A Treatise on the Principles and Practical Influence of Taxation and the Funding System*, ed. D. P. O'Brien (Edinburgh–London, 1975).
McCusker, J. J., *Money and Exchange in Europe and America, 1600–1775: A Handbook* (Chapel Hill, NC, 1978).
McFarlane, K. B., 'War, the economy and social change: England and the Hundred Years' War', *Past and Present*, 22 (1962), 3–15.
——*Lancastrian Kings and Lollard Knights* (Oxford, 1972).
Machiavelli, Niccolò, *Istorie fiorentine*, ed. F. Gaeta (Milan, 1962).
——*The Discourses*, ed. B. Crick (Harmondsworth, 1979).
MacKay, A., *Spain in the Middle Ages: From Frontier to Empire, 1000–1500* (London, 1977).

——*Money, Prices and Politics in Fifteenth-Century Castile* (London, 1981).

——'The lesser nobility in the kingdom of Castile', in M. Jones (ed.), *Gentry and Lesser Nobility in Late Medieval Europe* (Gloucester, 1986), 159–80.

——'La Cortes de Castilla y León y la historia monetaria', in *Las Cortes de Castilla y León en la edad media. I* (Valladolid, 1988), 375–426.

Mackesy, P. G., *The War for America, 1775–1783* (London, 1964).

McKitterick, R., *The Frankish Kingdoms under the Carolingians, 751–987* (London, 1983).

McLain, J. J., *The Economic Writings of Du Pont de Nemours* (Newark, Del., 1977).

Mączak, A., 'Money and society in Poland and Lithuania in the sixteenth and seventeenth centuries', *Journal of European Economic History*, 5 (1976), 69–104.

——'The structure of power in the Commonwealth in the sixteenth and seventeenth centuries', in A. Fedorowicz, with M. Bogucka and H. Samsonowicz (eds.), *A Republic of Nobles: Studies in Polish History to 1864* (Cambridge, 1982), 109–34.

Madariaga, I. de, *Russia in the Age of Catherine the Great* (London, 1981).

Maddicott, J. R., *The English Peasantry and the Demands of the Crown, 1294–1341* (Past and Present, supp. 1; London, 1975).

——'Magna Carta and the local community, 1215–1259', *Past and Present*, 102 (1984), 25–65.

——'Trade, industry and the wealth of King Alfred', *Past and Present*, 123 (1989), 3–51.

Magalhães Godinho, V., *Prix et monnaies au Portugal, 1750–1850* (Paris, 1955).

——*L'économie de l'empire portugais au xve et xvie siècles* (Paris, 1969).

Magnusson, L., 'Mercantilism and "reform" mercantilism: the rise of economic discourse in Sweden during the eighteenth century', *History of Political Economy*, 19 (1987), 415–33.

Major, J. R., *Representative Government in Early Modern France* (New Haven–London, 1980).

Mal[l]et, J.-R., *Comptes rendus de l'administration des finances du royaume de France* (London, 1789).

Malthus, T. R., *Principles of Political Economy Considered with a View to their Practical Application*, 2nd edn (London, 1836).

Mann, F. K., 'Die Gerechtigkeit in der Besteuerung', in H. Teschemacher (ed.), *Beiträge zur Finanzwissenschaft: Festgabe für Georg von Schanz. II* (Tübingen, 1928), 112–40.

——*Steuerpolitische Ideale: Vergleichende Studien zur Geschichte der ökonomischen und politischen Ideen und ihres Wirkens in der öffentlichen Meinung, 1600–1935* (Jena, 1937).

Margolin, J.-C. (ed.), *L'avènement des temps modernes* (Paris, 1977).

Marino, J. A., *Pastoral Economics in the Kingdom of Naples* (Baltimore–London, 1988).

Marion, M., *L'impôt sur le revenu au dix-huitième siècle, principalement en Guyenne* (Toulouse, 1901; repr. Geneva, 1976).

——*Les impôts directs sous l'ancien régime, principalement au xviiie siècle* (Paris, 1910).

——*Histoire financière de la France depuis 1715. I. 1715–1789* (Paris, 1914).

——'Le recouvrement des impôts en 1790', *Revue historique*, 121 (1916), 1–47.

——*Histoire financière de la France depuis 1715. II. 1789–1792* (Paris, 1919).

——*Histoire financière de la France depuis 1715. III. 20 septembre 1792 – 4 février 1797* (Paris, 1921).

——*Histoire financière de la France depuis 1715. IV. 1797–1818* (Paris, 1925).

Marion, M., *Histoire financière de la France depuis 1715. V. 1819–1875* (Paris, 1928).

Marks, L. F., 'La crisi finanziaria a Firenze dal 1494 al 1502', *Archivio storico italiano*, 121 (1954), 40–72.

——'The financial oligarchy in Florence under Lorenzo', in E. F. Jacob (ed.), *Italian Renaissance Studies* (London, 1960), 123–47.

Marongiu, A., 'Bodin et le consentement à l'impôt', *Jean Bodin: Actes du Colloque interdisciplinaire d'Angers* (Angers, 1985), 365–73.

Marshall, P. J., *Trade and Conquest: Studies on the Rise of British Dominance in India* (Aldershot–Brookfield, Vt, 1993).

Massaloux, J.-P., *La régie de l'enregistrement et des domaines aux xviiie et xixe siècles: Étude historique* (Geneva, 1989).

Mathias, P., *The Brewing Industry in England, 1700–1830* (Cambridge, 1959).

——and O'Brien, P. K., 'Taxation in Britain and France, 1715–1810: a comparison of the social and economic incidence of taxes collected for the central governments', *Journal of European Economic History*, 5 (1976), 601–50.

——and Pollard, S. (eds.), *The Cambridge Economic History of Europe. VIII. The Industrial Economies: The Development of Economic and Social Policies* (Cambridge, 1989).

Matilla Tascón, A., *La única contribución y el catastro de La Ensenada* (Madrid, 1947).

Matthew, D. J. A., *The Norman Kingdom of Sicily* (Cambridge, 1992).

Matthews, G. T., *The Royal General Farms in Eighteenth-Century France* (New York, 1958).

Mauersberg, H., *Wirtschafts- und Sozialgeschichte zentraleuropäischer Städte in neuerer Zeit dargestellt an den Beispielen von Basel, Frankfurt a. M., Hamburg, Hannover und München* (Göttingen, 1960).

Mauro, F., *Le xvie siècle européen: Aspects économiques* (Paris, 1966).

Maxwell, K., 'The Atlantic in the eighteenth century: a southern perspective on the need to return to the "big picture"', *Transactions of the Royal Historical Society*, 6th ser., 3 (1993), 209–36.

Meek, R. L., *The Economics of Physiocracy: Essays and Translations* (London, 1962).

——(ed.), *Turgot on Progress, Sociology and Economics* (Cambridge, 1973). [1973*a*]

——(ed.), *Precursors of Adam Smith* (London, 1973). [1973*b*]

Mémoires concernant les impositions et droits en Europe: Première partie contenant les droits qui ont lieu dans les Isles Britanniques, les Couronnes du Nord, les États d'Allemagne, ceux d'Italie, d'Espagne et de Portugal, ed. J.-L. Moreau de Beaumont (Paris, 1768).

Mémoires concernant les impositions et droits. Seconde partie. Impositions et droits en France, ed. J.-L. Moreau de Beaumont, ii–iv (1769).

Menjot, D., 'L'établissement du système fiscal étatique en Castille, 1268–1342', *Génesis medieval del estado moderno: Castilla y Navarra, 1250–1370* (Valladolid, 1987), 149–72.

Mensi, F. von, *Die Finanzen Österreichs von 1701 bis 1740* (Vienna, 1890).

Merino, J. P., 'La hacienda de Carlos IV', *Hacienda pública española*, 69 (1981), 139–82.

Merriman, R. B., *The Rise of the Spanish Empire in the Old World and the New*, 4 vols. (New York, 1918–34).

——*Six Contemporaneous Revolutions* (Glasgow, 1937).

Meuvret, J., 'Comment les Français du xviie siècle voyaient l'impôt', *Études d'histoire économique* (Paris, 1971), 295–308.

Meyer, J., *Le poids de l'État* (Paris, 1983).

——*Le despotisme éclairé* (Paris, 1991).

Meyssonnier, S., *La balance et l'horloge: La genèse de la pensée libérale en France au xviiie siècle* (Paris, 1989).

Michaud, C., *L'église et l'argent sous l'ancien régime: Les receveurs généraux du clergé de France aux xvie–xviie siècles* (Paris, 1991).

Mieck, I., *Die Entstehung des modernen Frankreich 1450 bis 1610: Strukturen, Institutionen, Entwicklungen* (Stuttgart, 1982).

Miller, E., 'The economic policies of governments', in M. M. Postan, E. E. Rich, and E. Miller (eds.), *Cambridge Economic History of Europe. III. Economic Organization and Policies in the Middle Ages* (Cambridge, 1963), 281–429.

Miller, J. (ed.), *Absolutism in Seventeenth-Century Europe* (Basingstoke, 1990).

Miller, J. A., 'Politics and urban provisioning crises: bakers, police and *Parlements* in France, 1750–1793', *Journal of Modern History*, 64 (1992), 227–62.

Mills, M. H., 'Exchequer agenda and estimate of revenue, Easter term 1284', *English Historical Review*, 40 (1925), 229–34.

Mirabeau, V. de Riquetti, marquis de, *Théorie de l'impôt avec supplément* [1760, 1766] (repr. Darmstadt, 1972).

Mirri, M., *La lotta politica in Toscana intorno alle riforme annonarie* (Pisa, 1972).

——'La fisiocrazia in Toscana: un tema da riprendere', *Studi di storia medievale e moderna in onore di Ernesto Sestan. II. Età moderna* (Florence, 1980).

Miskimin, H. A., *Money, Prices and Foreign Exchange in Fourteenth-Century France* (New Haven–London, 1963).

——*The Economy of Later Renaissance Europe, 1460–1600* (Cambridge, Mass., 1977).

——*Money and Power in Fifteenth-Century France* (New Haven–London, 1984).

——*Cash, Credit and Crisis in Europe, 1300–1600* (London, 1989).

Mitchell, B. R., *European Historical Statistics, 1750–1975*, 2nd revd. edn (Basingstoke, 1981).

Mitchell, S. K., *Studies in Taxation under John and Henry III* (New Haven, 1914).

——*Taxation in Medieval England* (New Haven, 1951).

Molho, A., *Florentine Public Finances in the Early Renaissance, 1400–1433* (Cambridge, Mass., 1971).

Molinié-Bertrand, A., 'Le clergé dans le royaume de Castille à la fin du xvie siècle: approche cartographique', *Revue d'histoire économique et sociale*, 51 (1973), 6–53.

——'Les "hidalgos" dans le royaume de Castille à la fin du xvie siècle: approche cartographique', *Revue d'histoire économique et sociale*, 52 (1974), 51–82.

Monroe, A. E., *Early Economic Thought: Selections from Economic Literature prior to Adam Smith* (Cambridge, Mass., repr. 1951).

Montesquieu, Charles Louis de Secondat, baron de, *De l'esprit des lois*, ed. G. Truc (Paris, 1961).

——*The Spirit of the Laws*, ed. A. M. Cohler, B. C. Miller, and H. M. Stone (Cambridge, 1989).

Moosvi, S., *The Economy of the Mughal Empire, c.1595: A Statistical Study* (Delhi, 1987).

Morazé, C., 'Finance et despotisme: essai sur les despotes éclairés', *Annales E.S.C.*, 3 (1948), 279–96.

Morineau, M., 'Les mancenilliers de l'Europe', in P. Deyon *et al.* (eds.), *Histoire économique et sociale du monde. II. Les hésitations de la croissance, 1580–1740* (Paris, 1978), 139–62.

——'Budgets de l'État et gestion des finances royales en France au xviiie siècle', *Revue historique*, 264 (1980), 289–336.

——*Incroyables gazettes et fabuleux métaux: Les retours des trésors américains d'après les gazettes hollandaises, xvie–xviiie siècles* (Cambridge–Paris, 1985).

——'Produit brut et finances publiques: analyse factorielle et analyse sectorielle de leurs relations', in A. Guarducci (ed.), *Prodotto lordo e finanza pubblica* (Florence, 1988), 79–105.

——'Monnaie, monnayage, monétisation et monétarisation', in *Histoire économique et financière de la France. Études et documents. II. 1990* (Comité pour l'histoire économique et financière de la France; Paris, 1990), 395–406.

Morrisson, C., 'La place de Forbonnais dans la pensée économique', in C. Morrison and R. Goffin, *Questions financières aux xviiie et xixe siècles* (Paris, 1967).

Mortensen, P., and Rasmussen, B. M. (eds.), *Fra stamme til stat* (Aarhus, 1988–91).

Mosse, G. L., *The Struggle for Sovereignty in England from the Reign of Queen Elizabeth to the Petition of Right* (East Lansing, Mich., 1950).

Mounier, A., *Les faits et la doctrine économiques en Espagne sous Philippe V: Gerónimo de Uztáriz, 1670–1732* (Bordeaux, 1919).

Mousnier , R. É., *Le conseil du roi de Louis XII à la Révolution* (Paris, 1970). [1970*a*]

——*La plume, la faucille et le marteau: Institutions et société en France du moyen âge à la Révolution* (Paris, 1970). [1970*b*]

——*La vénalité des offices sous Henri IV et Louis XIII*, 2nd edn (Paris, 1971).

——*The Institutions of France under the Absolute Monarchy, 1598–1789*, trans. B. Pearce and A. Goldhammer, 2 vols. (Chicago–London, 1979–84).

Mozzarelli, C., *Sovrano, società e amministrazione locale nella Lombardia teresiana, 1749–1758* (Bologna, 1982).

Mueller, R. C., 'I Banchi locali a Venezia nel tardo medioevo', *Studi storici*, 1 (1987), 145–55.

——'Cash, credit and calamity: banking crises in medieval and Renaissance Venice', in M. Steele (ed.), *Financial Crises before 1720* (10th International Economic History Congress, Leuven, 1990; Birmingham, 1990), 39–64.

Müller, K. O., 'Die Finanzwirtschaft in Württemberg unter Herzog Karl Alexander, 1733–1737', *Württembergische Vierteljahrshefte für Landesgeschichte*, 38 (1932), 289–92.

Mun, T., *England's Treasure by Forraign Trade* [1664] (repr. Oxford, 1933).

Munro, J. H. A., *Wool, Cloth, and Gold: The Struggle for Bullion in Anglo-Burgundian Trade, 1340–1478* (Brussels–Toronto, 1972).

Muratori, L. A., *Opere*, ed. G. Falco and F. Forti (Milan–Naples, 1964).

Murphy, A. E., *Richard Cantillon: Entrepreneur and Economist* (Oxford, 1986).

Musgrave, R. A., *Fiscal Systems* (New Haven–London, 1969).

——*Public Finance in a Democratic Society. II. Fiscal Doctrines, Growth and Institutions* (Brighton, 1986).

Musset, L., 'Que peut-on savoir de la fiscalité publique en Normandie à l'époque ducale?', *Revue historique de droit français et étranger*, 4th ser., 38 (1960), 483–4.

Nabholz, H., 'Die Anfänge des Bankwesens in Zürich', *Geld- und Kreditsystem der Schweiz: Festschrift Gottlieb Bachmann* (Zurich, 1944), 105–34.

Nadal, J., 'La revolución de los precios españoles en el siglo XVI', *Hispania*, 19 (1959), 503–29.

Nader, H., *Liberty in Absolutist Spain: The Habsburg Sale of Towns, 1516–1700* (Baltimore–London, 1990).

Nathanson, M. L., *Historisk statistik Fremstilling af Danmarks National og Stats Huusholdning fra Frederik den Fjerdes Tid indtil Nutiden* (Copenhagen, 1836).

Neal, L., *The Rise of Financial Capitalism: International Capital Markets in the Age of Reason* (Cambridge, 1990).

Necker, J., *Sur l'administration de M. Necker par lui-même* (Paris, 1791).

Nelson, J. L., 'The reign of Charles the Bald: a survey', in M. T. Gibson and J. L. Nelson (eds.), *Charles the Bald: Court and Kingdom*, 2nd edn (Aldershot, 1990).

Neumann, F. J., 'Die Steuer nach der Steuerfähigkeit', *Jahrbücher für Nationalökonomie und Statistik*, new ser., 1 (1880), 511–78.

Nolte, P., *Staatsbildung als Gesellschaftsreform: Politische Reformen in Preußen und den süddeutschen Staaten, 1800–1820* (Frankfurt, 1990).

North, M., *Geldumlauf und Wirtschaftskonjunktur im südlichen Ostseeraum an der Wende zur Neuzeit, 1440–1570* (Sigmaringen, 1990).

Nortier, M., and Baldwin, J. W., 'Contributions à l'étude des finances de Philippe Auguste', *Bibliothèque de l'École des Chartes*, 138 (1980), 5–33.

Nye, J. V., 'The myth of free-trade Britain and fortress France: tariffs and trade in the nineteenth century', *Journal of Economic History*, 51 (1991), 23–44.

O'Brien, P. K., 'European economic development: the contribution of the periphery', *Economic History Review*, 2nd ser., 35 (1982), 1–18.

——'The political economy of British taxation, 1660–1815', *Economic History Review*, 2nd ser., 41 (1988), 1–32.

——'The impact of the Revolutionary and Napoleonic wars, 1793–1815, on the long-run growth of the British economy', *Review: A Journal of the Fernand Braudel Centre*, 12 (1989), 335–95.

——'Power with Profit: The State and the Economy, 1688–1815' (inaugural lecture delivered in the University of London, 7 March 1991).

——and Hunt, P. A., 'The rise of a fiscal state in England, 1485–1815', *Historical Research*, 66 (1993), 129–76.

——and Pigman, G. A., 'Free trade, British hegemony and the international economic order in the nineteenth century', *Review of International Studies*, 18 (1992), 89–113.

O'Callaghan, J. F., 'The Cortes and royal taxation during the reign of Alfonso X of Castile', *Traditio*, 27 (1971), 379–98.

——*A History of Medieval Spain* (Ithaca, NY, 1975).

Odén, B., *Kronohandel och finanspolitik, 1560–1595* (Lund, 1966).

——'Naturaskatter och finanspolitik: et finansiellt dilemma', *Scandia*, 33 (1967), 1–18.

Oestreich, G., 'Ständetum und Staatsbildung in Deutschland', in G. Oestreich, *Geist und Gestalt des frühmodernen Staates: Ausgewählte Aufsätze* (Berlin, 1969).

——*Neostoicism and the Early Modern State*, ed. B. Oestreich and H. G. Koenigsberger, trans. D. McLintcock (Cambridge, 1982).

Olsen, M., 'A failure of Enlightened politics in the French Revolution: the Société de 1789', *French History*, 6 (1992), 303–34.

[Oresme, Nicolas], *The De Moneta of Nicholas Oresme and English Mint Documents*, ed. C. Johnson (London–Edinburgh, 1956).

Ormrod, W. M., 'The English government and the Black Death of 1348–49', in W. M. Ormrod (ed.), *England in the Fourteenth Century: Proceedings of the 1985 Harlaxton Symposium* (Woodbridge, 1986), 175–88.

——'The crown and the English economy, 1290–1348', in B. M. S. Campbell (ed.), *Before the Black Death: Studies in the 'Crisis' of the Early Fourteenth Century* (Manchester, 1991), 149–83. [1991*a*]

——'State-building and state finance under Edward I', *Harlaxton Medieval Studies*, 1 (1991), 15–35. [1991*b*]

——'Political theory in practice: the forced loan on English overseas trade of 1317–18', *Historical Research*, 64 (1991), 204–15. [1991c]

——'Royal finance in thirteenth-century England', in P. Coss and S. D. Lloyd (eds.), *Thirteenth-Century England. V. Proceedings of the 1993 Newcastle Conference* (Woodbridge, forthcoming 1995).

Osterloh, K.-H., *Joseph von Sonnenfels und die österreichische Reformbewegung im Zeitalter des aufgeklärten Absolutismus* (Lübeck–Hamburg, 1970).

Otazu, A. (ed.), *Dinero y crédito, siglos xvi al xix* (Madrid, 1978). [1978*a*]

——*La reforma fiscal en la España moderna: El caso de Extremadura* (Madrid, 1978). [1978*b*]

Otruba, G., 'Staatshaushalt und Staatsschuld unter Maria Theresia und Joseph II.', *Österreich im Europa der Aufklärung. Kontinuität und Zäsur in Europa zur Zeit Maria Theresias und Josephs II. Internationales Symposion in Wien, 20–23 Oktober 1980. I* (Vienna, 1985).

Ozanam, D., 'Notas para un estudio de los presupuestos de la monarquía española a mediados del siglo xviii', in A. Otazu (ed.), *Dinero y crédito, siglos xvi al xix* (Madrid, 1978), 49–62.

Palacký, F., *Dějiny národu českeho v Čechách a na Maravě* (Prague, 1907).

Palliser, D. M., *The Age of Elizabeth: England under the Later Tudors, 1547–1603* (London–New York, 1983).

Palmieri, G., *Riflessioni sulla pubblica felicità relativamente al regno di Napoli* (Naples, 1790).

Palmieri, Matteo, *Della vita civile*, ed. F. Battaglia (Bologna, 1944).

——*Della vita civile*, ed. G. Belloni (Istituzione nazionale di studi sul Rinascimento, Studi e testi, 7; Florence, 1982).

——*Ricordi fiscali, 1427–1474, con due appendici relative al 1474–1495*, ed. E. Conti (Istituto storico italiano per il medio evo, Studi storici, 132–5; Rome, 1983).

Parker, D., 'The social foundations of French absolutism, 1610–1630', *Past and Present*, 53 (1971), 67–89.

Parker, N. G., *The Army of Flanders and the Spanish Road, 1567–1659: The Logistics of Spanish Victory and Defeat in the Low Countries' Wars* (Cambridge, 1972).

——'The emergence of modern finance in Europe, 1500–1730', in C. M. Cipolla (ed.), *Fontana Economic History of Europe. II. The Sixteenth and Seventeenth Centuries* (London, 1974), 527–94.

——*Spain and the Netherlands, 1559–1659: Ten Studies* (Glasgow, 1979).

——*The Military Revolution: Military Innovation and the Rise of the West, 1500–1800* (Cambridge, 1988).

——and Smith, L. M. (eds.), *The General Crisis of the Seventeenth Century* (London, 1985).

Parry, G., 'Enlightened government and its critics in eighteenth-century Germany', *Historical Journal*, 6 (1963), 178–92.

Patrologiae cursus completus: Series graecae, ed. J.-P. Migne, 161 vols. (Paris, 1857–66).

——*Series latinae*, ed. J.-P. Migne, 221 vols. (Paris, 1844–65).

Paultre, C., *La 'taille tarifée' de l'abbé de Saint-Pierre et l'administration de la taille* (Paris, 1903).

Peacock, A. T., and Wiseman, J., *The Growth of Public Expenditure in the United Kingdom*, revd. edn (London, 1967).

Perrot, J.-C., *L'âge d'or de la statistique régionale française, an IV–1804* (Paris, 1977).

——*Une histoire intellectuelle de l'économie politique, xviie–xviiie siècle* (Paris, 1992).

——and Woolf, S. J., *State and Statistics in France, 1789–1815* (Chur, 1984).

Perrotta, C., 'Is the Mercantilist theory of the favourable balance of trade really erroneous?', *History of Political Economy*, 23 (1991), 301–35.

Petersen, E. L., 'From domain state to tax state: synthesis and interpretation', *Scandinavian Economic History Review*, 23 (1975), 116–48.

——'War, finance and the growth of absolutism: some aspects of the European integration of seventeenth-century Denmark', in G. Rystad (ed.), *Europe and Scandinavia: Aspects of the Process of Integration in the Seventeenth Century* (Lund, 1983), 33–50.

Peterson, C., *Peter the Great's Administrative and Judicial Reforms: Swedish Antecedents and the Process of Reception* (Stockholm, 1979).

Petran, J., 'Der Höhepunkt der Bewegung der untertänigen Bauern in Böhmen', *Acta Universitatis Carolinae: Philosophica et historica*, 3 (Prague, 1969), 107–40.

Petrarch, *Opera* (Basle, 1554).

[Petty, Sir William], *The Petty Papers: Some Unpublished Writings of Sir William Petty from the Bowood Papers*, ed. the marquis of Lansdowne, 2 vols. (London, 1927).

——*The Economic Writings of Sir William Petty*, ed. C. H. Hull, 2 vols. (1899, repr. New York, 1963).

Peyer, H. C., *Von Handel und Bank im alten Zürich* (Zurich, 1968).

——*Verfassungsgeschichte der alten Schweiz* (Zurich, 1978).

Phelps Brown, E. H., and Hopkins, S. V., 'Builders' wage-rates, prices and population: some further evidence', *Economica*, 101 (1959), 18–38.

——and Hopkins, E. H., 'Seven centuries of the prices of consumables, compared with builders' wage rates', in E. M. Carus-Wilson (ed.), *Essays in Economic History* (London, 1962), ii, 179–96.

Phillips, C. R., *Ciudad real, 1500–1750: Growth, Crisis and Readjustment in the Spanish Economy* (Cambridge, Mass., 1979).

Phillips, W. D., Jr, *Enrique IV and the Crisis of Fifteenth-Century Castile, 1425–1480* (Cambridge, Mass., 1978).

Pichler, J. W., *Necessitas: Ein Element des mittelalterlichen und neuzeitlichen Rechts dargestellt am Beispiel österreichischer Rechtsquellen* (Berlin, 1983).

Pickl, O. (ed.), *Krieg, Militärausgaben und wirtschaftlicher Wandel* (Acts of the 7th International Economic History Congress, Edinburgh 1978; Graz, 1980).

——'Fisco, Chiesa e stato nell'Austria interna all'epoca della Riforma e della Controriforma (XVI–XVII secolo)', in H. Kellenbenz and P. Prodi (eds.), *Fisco, religione, stato nell'età confessionale* (Bologna, 1989), 119–46.

Pieper, R., *Die Preisrevolution in Spanien, 1500–1640: Neuere Forschungsergebnisse* (Wiesbaden, 1985).

——*Die spanischen Kronfinanzen in der zweiten Hälfte des 18. Jahrhunderts (1753–1788): Ökonomische und soziale Auswirkungen* (Vierteljahrschrift für Sozial- und Wirtschaftsgeschichte, supp. 85; Wiesbaden, 1988).

Pinaud, P.-F., 'Guerre et finances de 1792 à 1815: le service de la trésorerie aux armées', *Revue historique*, 283 (1990), 53–69.

——'The settlement of the public debt from the *ancien régime*, 1790–1810', *French History*, 5 (1991), 414–25.

Pinto, I. de, *An Essay on Circulation and Credit in Four Parts and a Letter on the Jealousy of Commerce*, trans. S. Baggs (London, 1774; fac. repr., Farnborough, 1969).

Pipes, R., *Russia under the Old Regime* (New York, 1974).

Po-Chia Hsia, R., *Social Discipline in the Reformation: Central Europe, 1550–1750* (London–New York, 1989).

Pollard, A. J., 'New Monarchy renovated? England, 1461–1509', *Medieval History*, 2 (1992), 78–82.

Popofsky, L. S., 'The crisis over tonnage and poundage in Parliament in 1629', *Past and Present*, 126 (1990), 44–75.

Porchnev, B. F., *Les soulèvements populaires en France de 1623 à 1648* (Paris, 1963).

Post, G., *Studies in Medieval Legal Thought: Public Law and the State* (Princeton, NJ, 1964).

Postan, M. M., 'The costs of the Hundred Years' War', *Past and Present*, 27 (1964), 34–53.

Postel-Vinay, G., 'À la recherche de la révolution économique dans les campagnes, 1789–1815', *Revue économique*, 40 (1989), 1015–45.

Posthumus, N. W., *Inquiry into the History of Prices in Holland. I* (Leiden, 1946).

Potter, D. L., *War and Government in the French Provinces: Picardy, 1470–1560* (Cambridge, 1993).

Poulsen, B., 'Slesvig før delingen i 1490: et bidrag til senmiddelalderens finansforvaltning', *Historisk Tidsskrift*, 90 (1990), 38–63. [1990*a*]

——*Bondens penge: Studier i sønderjyske regnskaber, 1400–1650* (Odense, 1990). [1990*b*]

Powicke, F. M., *Henry III and the Lord Edward: The Community of the Realm in the Thirteenth Century*, 2 vols. (Oxford, 1947).

Prak, M., 'Civil disturbances and urban middle class in the Dutch Republic', *Tijdschrift voor sociale geschiedenis*, 15 (1989), 165–73.

——'Citizen radicalism and democracy in the Dutch Republic', *Theory and Society*, 20 (1991), 73–102.

Prakash, O., *Precious Metals and Commerce: The Dutch East India Company in the Indian Ocean Trade* (Aldershot–Brookfield, Vt, 1994).

Prasch, R. E., 'The ethics of growth in Adam Smith's *Wealth of Nations*', *History of Political Economy*, 23 (1991), 337–51.

Press, V., *Kaiser Karl V., König Ferdinand und die Entstehung der Reichsritterschaft*, 2nd edn (Wiesbaden, 1980).

——'Soziale Folgen des Dreissigjährigen Krieges', in W. Schulze (ed.), *Ständische Gesellschaft und soziale Mobilität* (Munich, 1988), 239–68.

Prestwich, M. C., *War, Politics and Finance under Edward I* (London, 1972).

——'The crown and the currency: the circulation of money in late thirteenth- and early fourteenth-century England', *Numismatic Chronicle*, 142 (1982), 51–65.

——*English Politics in the Thirteenth Century* (London, 1990).

Price, J. L., *Holland and the Dutch Republic in the Seventeenth Century: The Politics of Particularism* (Oxford, 1994).

Price, J. M., *France and the Chesapeake: A History of the French Tobacco Monopoly, 1674–1791, and of its Relationship to the British and American Tobacco Trades*, 2 vols. (Ann Arbor, 1973).

Prodi, P., 'San Carlo Borromeo e le trattative tra Gregorio XIII e Filippo II sulla giurisdizione ecclesiastica', *Rivista di storia de la Chiesa in Italia*, 11 (1957), 195–240.

——*The Papal Prince. One Body and Two Souls. The Papal Monarchy in Early Modern Europe*, trans. S. Haskins (Cambridge, 1987).

——'Introduzione', in H. Kellenbenz and P. Prodi (eds.), *Fisco, religione, stato nell'età confessionale* (Bologna, 1989), 7–20.

Pro Ruiz, J., 'The Cadaster: the struggle against tax fraud in modern Spain, 1715–1982' (unpubd paper delivered to the International Economic History Congress, Leuven, August 1990).

Prosdocimi, L., 'Il progetto di "Riforma dei Principi" al Concilio di Trento (1563)', *Aevum*, 13 (1939), 3–64.

Pugliese, S., *Condizioni economiche e finanziarie della Lombardia nella prima metà del secolo XVIII* (Turin, 1924).

Pulido Bueno, I., *Consumo y fiscalidad en el Reino de Sevilla: El servicio de millones en el siglo XVII* (Seville, 1984).

Quazza, G., *Le riforme in Piemonte nella prima metà del Settecento*, 2 vols. (Modena, 1957).

——*Il problema italiano e l'equilibrio europeo, 1720–1738* (Turin, 1965).

Radding, C. M., 'Royal tax revenues in later fourteenth-century France', *Traditio*, 32 (1976), 361–8.

Raeff, M., *Michael Speransky: Statesman of Imperial Russia, 1772–1839*, revd. edn (The Hague, 1969).

——'The well-ordered police state and the development of modernity in seventeenth- and eighteenth-century Europe: an attempt at a comparative approach', *American Historical Review*, 80 (1975), 1221–43.

——*The Well-Ordered Police State: Social and Institutional Change through Law in the Germanies and Russia, 1600–1800* (New Haven–London, 1983).

Rambaud, J., *Naples sous Joseph Bonaparte, 1806–1808* (Paris, 1911).

Ramsay, J. H., *Lancaster and York: A Century of English History, A.D. 1399–1485*, 2 vols. (Oxford, 1892).

Ranieri, F., *Recht und Gesellschaft im Zeitalter der Rezeption: Eine rechts- und sozialgeschichtliche Analyse der Tätigkeit des Reichskammergerichts im 16. Jahrhundert*, 2 vols. (Cologne–Vienna, 1985).

Rao, A. M., *Il Regno di Napoli nel Settecento* (Naples, 1983).

'Rapport fait au nom du Comité de l'Imposition sur la contribution personnelle imprimé par ordre de l'Assemblée Nationale', *Assemblée Nationale: Procès verbal*, 34 (1790).

Rashid, S. 'Malthus' *Principles* and British economic thought', *History of Political Economy*, 13 (1981), 55–79.

Redlich, F., 'Contributions in the Thirty Years' War', *Economic History Review*, 2nd ser., 12 (1959), 247–54.

Reher, D. S., *Town and Country in Pre-Industrial Spain: Cuenca, 1550–1870* (Cambridge, 1990).

Reinhard, W., 'Finanza pontificia, sistema beneficiale e finanza statale nell'età confessionale', in H. Kellenbenz and P. Prodi (eds.), *Fisco, religione, stato nell'età confessionale* (Bologna, 1989), 459–504.

——(ed.), *Power Elites and State Building in Europe* (Oxford, forthcoming).

Repgen, K. (ed.), *Krieg und Politik, 1618–1648* (Munich, 1988).

Reuter, T., 'Plunder and tribute in the Carolingian Empire', *Transactions of the Royal Historical Society*, 5th ser., 35 (1984), 75–94.

Rey, M., *Le domaine du roi et les finances extraordinaires sous Charles VI, 1388–1413* (Paris, 1965).

[Ricardo, D.], *The Works and Correspondence of David Ricardo*, ed. P. Sraffa and M. H. Dobb, 10 vols. (Cambridge, 1951–5).

Ricca-Salerno, G., *Storia delle dottrine finanziarie in Italia* (Palermo, 1881).

Richard, J. (ed.), *Histoire de la Bourgogne* (Toulouse, 1978).

Richards, J. F., *Power, Administration and Finance in Mughal India* (Aldershot–Brookfield, Vt, 1993).

Richardson, H. G., and Sayles, G. O., 'Irish revenue, 1278–1384', *Proceedings of the Royal Irish Academy*, 62 (1962), Section C, 87–100.

Richelieu, A.-J. du Plessis, Cardinal de, *Testament politique*, ed. L. André (Paris, 1947).

Richet, D., 'Le cours officiel des monnaies étrangères circulant en France au xvie siècle', *Revue historique*, 225 (1961), 359–96.

Ricuperati, G., 'Gli strumenti dell'assolutismo sabaudo: segreterie di stato e consiglio delle finanze nel XVIII secolo', *Rivista storica italiana*, 192 (1990), 796–863.

Riedel, A. F., *Der brandenburgisch-preussische Staatshaushalt in den beiden letzten Jahrhunderten* (Berlin, 1866).

Riley, J. C., *International Government Finance and the Amsterdam Capital Market, 1740–1815* (Cambridge, 1980).

——*Population Thought in the Age of the Demographic Revolution* (Durham, NC, 1985).

——*The Seven Years War and the Old Regime in France: The Economic and Financial Toll* (Princeton, NJ, 1986).

——'French finances, 1727–1768', *Journal of Modern History*, 59 (1987), 209–43.

——and McCusker, J. J., 'Money supply, economic growth and the quantity theory of money: France, 1650–1788', *Explorations in Economic History*, 20 (1983), 274–93.

Ringrose, R., 'Il mutamento dei sistemi urbani: concetti generali e il caso spagnolo', *Cheiron*, 6 (1989–90), 47–74.

Rist, C., *Histoire des doctrines relatives au crédit et à la monnaie depuis John Law jusqu'à nos jours*, 2nd edn (Paris, 1951).

Roberts, C., 'The constitutional significance of the financial settlement of 1690', *Historical Journal*, 20 (1977), 59–76.

Roberts, M., *Gustavus Adolphus: A History of Sweden, 1611–1632*, 2 vols. (London, 1953–8).

——*The Military Revolution: An Inaugural Lecture* (Belfast, 1956).

——*Essays in Swedish History* (Minneapolis, 1967).

——(ed.), *Sweden's Age of Greatness, 1632–1718* (Basingstoke, 1973).

——*The Age of Liberty: Sweden, 1719–1772* (Cambridge, 1986).

Rodríguez-Salgado, M. J., *The Changing Face of Empire: Charles V, Philip II and Habsburg Authority, 1551–1559* (Cambridge, 1988).

Roeck, B., *Eine Stadt in Krieg und Frieden: Studien zur Geschichte der Reichsstadt Augsburg zwischen Kalenderstreit und Parität*, 2 vols. (Göttingen, 1989).

Roederer, Pierre-Louis, *The Spirit of the Revolution of 1789 and Other Writings on the Revolutionary Epoch*, ed. M. G. Forsyth (Aldershot, 1989).

Rogers, A., 'Henry IV, the Commons and taxation', *Mediaeval Studies*, 31 (1969), 44–70.

Root, H. L., *Peasants and King in Burgundy: Agrarian Foundations of French Absolutism* (Berkeley, 1987).

——'Politiques frumentaires et violence collective en Europe au xviiie siècle', *Annales E.S.C.*, 45 (1990), 167–89.

——'Institutions, interest groups and authority in *ancien régime* France', *French History*, 6 (1992), 411–34.

——*La construction de l'État moderne en Europe: La France et l'Angleterre* (Paris, 1994).

Roscoe, W., *The Life of Lorenzo de' Medici. III* (Heidelberg, 1825).

Rose, P. L., *Bodin and the Great God of Nature: The Moral and Religious Universe of a Judaiser* (Geneva, 1980).

Rose, R. B., 'Tax revolt and popular organization in Picardy, 1789–1791', *Past and Present*, 43 (1969), 92–108.

Rosen, J., *Finanzgeschichte Basels im späten Mittelalter* (Stuttgart, 1989).

Rosenberg, H., *Bureaucracy, Aristocracy, and Autocracy: The Prussian Experience, 1660–1815* (Boston, Mass., 1958).

Roseveare, H., *The Treasury, 1660–1870: The Foundations of Control* (London–New York, 1973).

Ross, C., *Edward IV* (London, 1974).

Rousselot de Surgy, J. P., *Encyclopédie Méthodique: Finances*, 3 vols. (Paris, 1784–7).

Rowan, S., 'Imperial taxes and German politics in the fifteenth century: an outline', *Central European History*, 13 (1980), 203–17.

Rowen, H. H., *The King's State: Proprietary Dynasticism in Early Modern France* (New Brunswick, NJ, 1980).

Rozdolski, R., *Die grosse Steuer- und Agrarreform Josefs II.* (Warsaw, 1961).

Ruiz Martín, F., *Lettres marchandes échangées entre Florence et Medina del Campo* (Paris, 1965).

——'Las finanzas españolas durante el reinado de Felipe II', *Hispania*, 28 (1968), 109–73.

Ruiz Martín, F., 'La Banca en España hasta 1782', *El Banco de España: Una historia económica* (Madrid, 1970), 1–196.

——'Crédito y banca, comercio y transportes en la época del capitalismo mercantil', *Actas de las I jornadas de metodología aplicada a las ciencias históricas. III. Historia moderna* (Santiago de Compostela, 1975), 723–49.

——*Las finanzas de la monarquía hispánica en tiempos de Felipe IV, 1621–1665* (Madrid, 1990).

Russell, C. S. R., *The Causes of the English Civil War* (Oxford, 1991).

Russell, P. E., *The English Intervention in Spain and Portugal in the Time of Edward III and Richard II* (Oxford, 1955).

Ryder, A., *The Kingdom of Naples under Alfonso the Magnanimous: The Making of a Modern State* (Oxford, 1976).

Sabine, B. E. V., *A History of Income Tax* (London, 1966).

Salomon, N., *La campagne de Nouvelle Castille à la fin du xvie siècle d'après les Relaciones Topográficas* (Paris, 1964).

Sanchez Bella, I., *La organización financiera de las Indias* (Seville, 1968).

Sander, P., *Die reichsstädtische Haushaltung Nürnbergs dargestellt aufgrund ihres Zustandes von 1431 bis 1440* (Leipzig, 1902).

Sandford, C. T., 'Tax compliance costs, evasion and avoidance', in D. Collard, R. Lecomber, and M. Slater (eds.), *Income Distribution: The Limits to Redistribution* (Bristol, 1980), 150–65.

——Godwin, M., and Hardwick, P., *Administrative and Compliance Costs of Taxation* (Bath, 1989).

Sanz Ayan, C., *Los banqueros de Carlos II* (Valladolid, 1988).

Saul, N. E., *Russia and the Mediterranean, 1797–1807* (Chicago–London, 1970).

Sawyer, P., *När Sverige blev Sverige* (Alingsås, 1991).

Say, J.-B., *Traité d'économie politique* (Paris, 1841).

Schama, S., *Patriots and Liberators: Revolution in the Netherlands, 1780–1813* (London, 1977). [1977*a*]

——'Municipal government and the burden of the poor in South Holland during the Napoleonic wars', in A. C. Duke and C. A. Tamse (eds.), *Britain and the Netherlands. VI* (The Hague, 1977), 94–123. [1977*b*]

Schilling, H., 'Between the territorial state and urban liberty: Lutheranism and Calvinism in the county of Lippe', in R. Po-Chia Hsia (ed.), *The Common People and the Reformation* (Ithaca, NY, 1988), 263–83.

Schlögl, R., *Bauern, Krieg und Staat: Oberbayerische Bauernwirtschaft und frühmoderner Staat im 17. Jahrhundert* (Göttingen, 1988).

Schmelzle, H., *Der Staatshaushalt des Herzogtums Bayern im 18. Jahrhundert* (Stuttgart, 1900).

Schmoller, G., 'Skizze einer Finanzgeschichte von Frankreich, Österreich, England und Preußen, 1500–1900', *Schmollers Jahrbuch für Gesetzgebung, Verwaltung und Volkswirtschaft*, 33 (1909), 1–64.

Schmuki, K., *Steuern und Staatsfinanzen: Die bürgerliche Vermögenssteuer in Schaffhausen im 16. und 17. Jahrhundert* (Zurich, 1986).

Schnapper, B., *Les rentes au xvie siècle: Histoire d'un instrument de crédit* (Paris, 1957).

Schofield, R., 'Taxation and the political limits of the Tudor state', in C. Cross, D. Loades, and J. J. Scarisbrick (eds.), *Law and Government under the Tudors: Essays Presented to Sir Geoffrey Elton* (Cambridge, 1988), 227–55.

Schroeder, P. W., 'The collapse of the second coalition', *Journal of Modern History*, 59 (1987), 244–90.

Schulz, H., *Das System und die Prinzipien der Einkünfte im werdenden Staat der Neuzeit, dargestellt anhand der kameralwissenschaftlichen Literatur, 1600–1835* (Berlin, 1982).

Schulz, U. (ed.), *Mit dem Zehnten fing es an: Eine Kulturgeschichte der Steuer* (Munich, 1986).

Schulze, W., *Reich und Türkengefahr im späten 16. Jahrhundert: Studien zu den politischen und gesellschaftlichen Auswirkungen einer äußeren Bedrohung* (Munich, 1978).

——*Bäuerlicher Widerstand und feudale Herrschaft in der frühen Neuzeit* (Stuttgart–Bad Cannstatt, 1980).

Schumpeter, J. A., *History of Economic Analysis*, ed. E. B. Schumpeter (1954; repr. London, 1967). [1954*a*]

——'The crisis of the tax state', *International Economic Papers*, 4 (New York, 1954), 5–38. [Translation of 'Die Krise des Steuerstaates', *Zeitfragen aus dem Gebiet der Soziologie*, 4 (1918), 1–71.] [1954*b*]

Schürer, K., and Arkell, T. (eds.), *The Interpretation and Use of Document Sources for the Study of Population in the Later Seventeenth Century* (Oxford, 1992).

Scott, H. M. (ed.), *Enlightened Absolutism: Reform and Reformers in Later Eighteenth-Century Europe* (Basingstoke, 1990).

Searle, E., *Predatory Kinship and the Creation of Norman Power, 840–1066* (Berkeley, 1988).

Sebastián, M., and Vela, J., 'Hacienda real y presión fiscal en Castilla a comienzos del reinado de Felipe IV' (unpubd paper delivered to the annual meeting of the Asociación española de historia moderna, Murcia, 1992).

Seidl, C. (ed.), *Lectures on Schumpeterian Economics* (Berlin, 1984).

Seligman, E. R. A., *The Shifting and Incidence of Taxation* (London, 1899).

——*The Income Tax: A Study of the History, Theory and Practice of Income Taxation at Home and Abroad* (New York, 1914).

——*Encyclopaedia of the Social Sciences*, 15 vols. (New York, 1930–4 and repr.)

Seligmann, A., *La première tentative d'émission fiduciaire en France: Étude sur les billets de monnaie du Trésor royal à la fin du règne de Louis XIV, 1701–1718* (Paris, 1925).

Sella, D., and Capra, C. (eds.), *Il ducato di Milano dal 1535 al 1796* (Turin, 1984).

Semmel, B., 'Malthus: "Physiocracy" and the commercial system', *Economic History Review*, 2nd ser., 17 (1964–5), 522–35.

Sen, G., *The Military Origins of Industrialisation and International Trade Rivalry* (London, 1984).

Sharpe, K. M., *The Personal Rule of Charles I* (New Haven–London, 1992).

Sheehan, J. J., *German History, 1770–1866* (Oxford, 1989).

Shehab, F., *Progressive Taxation: A Study in the Development of the Progressive Principle in the British Income Tax* (Oxford, 1953).

Shennan, J. H., *Government and Society in France, 1461–1661* (London, 1969).

Sherwig, J. M., *Guineas and Gunpowder: British Foreign Aid in the Wars with France, 1793–1815* (Cambridge, Mass., 1969).

Shoup, C. S., *Ricardo on Taxation* (New York, 1960).

Sideri, S., *Trade and Power: Informal Colonialism in Anglo-Portuguese Relations* (Rotterdam, 1970).

Sieveking, H., *Studio sulle finanze genovesi nel medioevo e in particolare sulla casa di San Giorgio* (Atti della società di storia ligure, 25, pts. 1–2; Genoa, 1906).

Sigg, O., *Die Entwicklung des Finanzwesens und der Verwaltung Zürichs im ausgehenden 16. und im 17. Jahrhundert* (Zurich, 1971).

Silberling, N. J., 'Financial and monetary policy of Great Britain during the Napoleonic wars', *Quarterly Journal of Economics*, 38 (1924), 214–33, 397–439.

Simon, W. M., *The Failure of the Prussian Reform Movement, 1807–1819* (New York, 1971).

Skinner, Q., *The Foundations of Modern Political Thought. II. The Age of Reformation* (Cambridge, 1978).

Slack, P., *The Impact of Plague in Tudor and Stuart England* (London, 1985).

Small, A. W., *The Cameralists: The Pioneers of German Social Polity* (Chicago, 1909; repr. New York, n.d.).

Smith, A., *An Inquiry into the Nature and Causes of the Wealth of Nations*, ed. R. H. Campbell, A. S. Skinner, and W. B. Todd, 2 vols. (Oxford, 1976).

——*Essays on Philosophical Subjects*, ed. W. P. D. Wightman and J. C. Bryce (Oxford, 1980).

Smith, Sir T., *De republica Anglorum*, ed. M. Dewar (Cambridge, 1982).

Solow, B. L., *Slavery and the Rise of the Atlantic System* (Cambridge, 1991).

Sommer, L., *Die österreichischen Kameralisten in dogmengeschichtlicher Darstellung*, 2 vols. (Vienna, 1920–5).

Sonnenfels, J. von, *Grundsätze aus der Polizey, Handlungs- und Finanzwissenschaft*, 6th edn, 3 vols. (Vienna, 1771–6).

——*Grundsätze aus der Polizey, Handlungs- und Finanzwissenschaft* (Vienna, 1971).

Sonnino, P. (ed.), *The Reign of Louis XIV: Essays in Celebration of Andrew Lossky* (Atlantic Highlands, NJ, 1990).

Speier, H., 'Militarism in the eighteenth century', *Social Research*, 3 (1936), 304–36.

Spengler, J. J., *French Predecessors of Malthus: A Study in Eighteenth-Century Wage and Population Theory* (Durham, NC, 1942).

——'Boisguilbert's economic views *vis-à-vis* those of contemporary *réformateurs*', *History of Political Economy*, 16 (1984), 69–88.

——and Allen, W. R., *Essays in Economic Thought: Aristotle to Marshall* (Chicago, 1960).

Spooner, F. C., *The International Economy and Monetary Movements in France, 1493–1725* (Cambridge, Mass., 1972).

Spufford, P., *Handbook of Medieval Exchange* (London, 1986).

——*Money and its Use in Medieval Europe* (Cambridge, 1989).

Stafford, P., *Unification and Conquest: A Political and Social History of England in the Tenth and Eleventh Centuries* (London, 1989).

Stamp, J., *The Fundamental Principles of Taxation in the Light of Modern Developments* (London, 1921).

Staum, M. S., 'The Institute economists: from Physiocracy to entrepreneurial capitalism', *History of Political Economy*, 19 (1987), 525–50.

Steel, A., *The Receipt of the Exchequer, 1377–1485* (Cambridge, 1954).

Steele, M., 'La real hacienda', *Historia general de España y America. IV* (Madrid, 1986), 143–67.

Steinnes, A., *Gamal Skatteskipnad i Noreg. II.* (Oslo, 1933).

Stenton, F. M., *Anglo-Saxon England*, 3rd edn (Oxford, 1971).

Steuart, Sir J., *An Inquiry into the Principles of Political Oeconomy*, ed. A. S. Skinner, 2 vols. (Edinburgh–London, 1966).

Stigler, G. J., 'Smith's travels on the ship of state', *History of Political Economy*, 3 (1971), 265–77.

Stolleis, M., *Pecunia nervus rerum: Zur Staatsfinanzierung in der frühen Neuzeit* (Frankfurt, 1983).

Stone, L., *The Causes of the English Revolution, 1529–1642* (London, 1972).

——(ed.), *An Imperial State at War: Britain from 1689 to 1815* (London–New York, 1994).

Stow, K. R., *Taxation, Community and State: The Jews and the Fiscal Foundations of the Early Modern Papal State* (Stuttgart, 1982).

Strayer, J. R., *Feudalism* (Princeton, NJ, 1965).

——*On the Medieval Origins of the Modern State* (Princeton, NJ, 1970).

——*Medieval Statecraft and the Perspectives of History* (Princeton, NJ, 1971).

——'The costs and profits of war: the Anglo-French conflict of 1294–1303', in H. A. Miskimin, D. Herlihy, and A. L. Udovitch (eds.), *The Medieval City* (New Haven, 1977), 269–91.

——*The Reign of Philip the Fair* (Princeton, NJ, 1980).

——and Taylor, C. H., *Studies in Early French Taxation* (Westport, 1972).

Strieder, J., 'Finanznot des Staates und Entstehung des neuzeitlichen, kapitalistischen Wirtschaftslebens', *Neue Jahrbücher für Wissenschaft und Jugendbildung*, 8 (1932), 447–63.

Stromer, W. von, *Oberdeutsche Hochfinanz, 1350–1450*, 3 vols. (Vierteljahrschrift für Sozial- und Wirtschaftsgeschichte, 55–7; Wiesbaden, 1970).

Stumpo, E., *Finanza e stato moderno nel Piemonte del Seicento* (Rome, 1979).

Suhm, P. F. (ed.), 'Kong Christian den 2dens Forordninger og aabne Breve Jylland angaaende', *Nye Samlinger til Danske Historie. I* (Copenhagen, 1792).

Sumption, J., *The Hundred Years' War: Trial by Battle* (London, 1990).

Sureda Carrion, J., *La hacienda castellana y los economistas del siglo XVII* (Madrid, 1949).

Sussman, N., 'Missing bullion or missing documents: a revision and reappraisal of French minting statistics, 1385–1415', *Journal of European Economic History*, 19 (1990), 147–62.

Sutherland, D. M. G., *France, 1789–1815: Revolution and Counter-Revolution* (London, 1989).

Sutter Fichtner, P., *Protestantism and Primogeniture in Early Modern History* (New Haven, 1990).

Swanson, D. F., and Trout, A. P., 'Alexander Hamilton's report on the public credit (1790)', *Journal of European Economic History*, 19 (1990), 623–33.

Swedberg, R., *Joseph A. Schumpeter: His Life and Work* (Oxford, 1991).

Symcox, G., *Victor Amadeus II: Absolutism in the Savoyard State, 1675–1730* (London, 1983).

Syrett, D., *Shipping and the American War, 1775–83: A Study of British Transport Organization* (London, 1970).

Szabo, F. A. J., 'Haugwitz, Kaunitz and the structure of government in Austria under Maria Theresia, 1745 to 1761', *Historical Papers: Communications historiques* (Saskatoon, 1979).

Takayama, H., 'The financial and administrative organization of the Norman kingdom of Sicily', *Viator*, 16 (1985), 129–55.

Tallett, F., *War and Society in Early Modern Europe, 1495–1715* (London–New York, 1992).

Tanner, J. R., *Constitutional Documents of the Reign of James I* (Cambridge, 1930).

Tanzi, V., *Public Finance in Developing Countries* (Aldershot, 1991).

Tapia, S. de, 'La documentación fiscal concejil en el siglo XVI: un instrumento imprescindible para la historia social', *Los archivos y la investigación* (Avila, 1988), 49–70.

Tapiès, F. de, *La France et l'Angleterre ou statistique morale et physique comparée à celle de l'Angleterre* (Versailles–Paris, 1845).

Temple, N., 'The control and exploitation of French towns during the *ancien régime*', in R. F. Kierstead (ed.), *State and Society in Seventeenth-Century France* (New York, 1975), 67–93.

TePaske, J. J., and Klein, H. S., 'The seventeenth-century crisis in New Spain: myth or reality?', *Past and Present*, 90 (1981), 116–35.

——and Klein, H. S., with Brown, K. W., *The Royal Treasuries of the Spanish Empire in America*, 3 vols. (Durham, NC, 1982).

Thallóczy, L., *A kamara haszna (lucrum camerae) története kapcsolatban a magyar adóügy és pénzügy fejlődésével* (Budapest, 1879).

't Hart, M., 'Cities and statemaking in the Dutch Republic, 1580–1680', *Theory and Society*, 18 (1989), 663–87.

——'"The devil or the Dutch": Holland's impact on the financial revolution in England, 1643–1694', *Parliaments, Estates and Representation*, 11 (1991), 39–52.

——*The Making of a Bourgeois State: War, Politics and Finance during the Dutch Revolt* (Manchester–New York, 1993).

Théret, B., 'Le système français libéral du xixe siècle: bureaucratie ou capitalisme?', *Histoire économique et financière de la France: Études et documents. III. 1991* (1991), 137–224.

Thomas, G., and Meyer, J., 'The expansion of the state', *Annual Review of Sociology*, 10 (1984), 461–82.

Thomas, P. D. G., *British Politics and the Stamp Act Crisis: The First Phase of the American Revolution, 1763–1767* (Oxford, 1975).

Thomson, S. H., 'Medieval Bohemia', in L. I. Strakhovsky (ed.), *A Handbook of Slavic Studies* (Cambridge, Mass., 1949), 97–101.

Thompson, E. P., 'The moral economy of the English crowd in the eighteenth century', *Past and Present*, 50 (1971), 76–136.

Thompson, I. A. A., *War and Government in Habsburg Spain, 1560–1620* (London, 1976).

——'Crown and *Cortes* in Castile, 1590–1665', *Parliaments, Estates and Representation*, 2 (1982), 29–45.

——'The end of the *Cortes* of Castile', *Parliaments, Estates and Representation*, 4 (1984), 125–33.

Thorpe, L., *Einhard and Notker the Stammerer: Two Lives of Charlemagne* (Harmondsworth, 1969).

Thuillier, G., *La monnaie en France au début du xix*^e^ *siècle* (Geneva, 1983).

Tilly, C. (ed.), *The Formation of Nation States in Western Europe* (Princeton, NJ, 1975).

——*The Contentious French* (Cambridge, Mass., 1986).

——*Coercion, Capital, and European States, A.D. 990–1990* (Oxford, 1990).

Toboso Sánchez, P., *La deuda pública castellana durante el Antiguo Régimen* (Madrid, 1987).

Tocqueville, Alexis de, *L'ancien régime et la Révolution* [1856], ed. J.-P. Mayer (Paris, 1967).

Todd Lowry, S., *The Archaeology of Economic Ideas: The Classical Greek Tradition* (Durham, NC, 1987).

Tollet, D., 'Les Juifs et le trésor royal polonais sous les règnes des Wasa, 1588–1668' (forthcoming in a collection of essays for J. Gierowski).

Touzery, M., 'Arpents, arpentage et arpenteurs dans l'élection de Paris à la fin du xviiie siècle: le cadastre de Bertier de Sauvigny, 1776–1790', *Bulletin de la société historique de la ville de Paris*, 110 (1983), 150–97.

Toye, J. F. J. (ed.), *Taxation and Economic Development* (London, 1978).

Tractatus universi iuris. XII (Venice, 1584).

Tracy, J. D., *A Financial Revolution in the Habsburg Netherlands: Renten and Renteniers in the County of Holland, 1515–1565* (Berkeley, 1985).

——(ed.), *The Rise of Merchant Empires: Long-Distance Trade in the Early Modern World, 1350–1750* (Cambridge, 1990).

——(ed.), *The Political Economy of Merchant Empires* (Cambridge, 1991).

Tribe, K., *Land, Labour and Economic Discourse* (London, 1978).

——'Cameralism and the science of government', *Journal of Modern History*, 56 (1984), 263–84.

——*Governing Economy: The Reformation of German Economic Discourse, 1750–1840* (Cambridge, 1988).

Trusen, W., *Spätmittelalterliche Jurisprudenz und Wirtschaftsethik* (Wiesbaden, 1961).

Tulard, J., 'Der "domaine extraordinaire" als Finanzierunginstrument napoleonischer Expansion', *Geschichte und Gesellschaft (Zeitschrift für historische Sozialwissenschaft*, 6; 1980), 490–9.

——*Le grand empire, 1804–1815* (Paris, 1982).

Tullio, G., 'Smith and Ricardo on the long-run effects of the growth of government expenditure, taxation and debt: is their theory relevant today?', *History of Political Economy*, 21 (1989), 723–36.

Twitchett, D. C., *Financial Administration under the T'ang Dynasty* (Cambridge, 1963).

Ulllmann, W., *Principles of Government and Politics in the Middle Ages* (London, 1961).

Ulloa, M., *La hacienda real de Castilla en el reinado de Felipe II*, 3rd edn (Madrid, 1986).

Ustaríz, G., *The Theory and Practice of Commerce*, trans. J. Kippax (London, 1751).

Vaggi, G., *The Economics of François Quesnay* (Basingstoke, 1987).

Vale, M. G. A., *The Angevin Legacy and the Hundred Years' War, 1250–1340* (Oxford, 1990).

Van Cauwenberghe, E. H. G. (ed.), *Precious Metals, Coinage and the Changes of Monetary Structures in Latin America, Europe and Asia, Late Medieval and Early Modern Times* (Louvain, 1989).

Van Cleve, T. C., *The Emperor Frederick II of Hohenstaufen* (Oxford, 1972).

Van Daal, J., and Heertje, A. (eds.), *Economic Thought in the Netherlands, 1650–1950* (Aldershot, Brookfield, Va., Hong Kong, Singapore, Sydney, 1992).

Van der Wee, H., 'Anvers et les innovations de la technique financière aux xvie et xviie siècles', *Annales E.S.C.*, 22 (1967), 1067–89.

——(ed.), *La banque en occident* (Antwerp, 1991).

Van Zanden, J. L., *The Rise and Decline of Holland's Economy: Merchant Capitalism and the Labour Market* (Manchester–New York, 1993).

Vann, J. A., *The Making of a State: Württemberg, 1593–1793* (Ithaca, NY–London, 1984).

Vannini Marx, A. (ed.), *Credito, banche e investimenti secoli XIII–XX* (Istituto internazionale di storia economica F. Datini Prato, 2nd ser., 4; Florence, 1985).

Vauban, Sébastien le Prestre, Maréchal de, *Projet d'une dixme royale*, ed. J.-F. Pernot (Saint-Léger-Vauban, 1988).

Vaupell, O., 'Oplysninger om Haerens Styrketal og Udgifterne til den i Aarene 1680 til 1896', *Miltaert Tidsskrift*, 27 (1898), 392–402.

Velde, F. R., and Weir, D. R., 'The financial market and government debt policy in France, 1746–1793', *Journal of Economic History*, 52 (1992), 1–39.

Véron de Forbonnais, F., *Recherches et considérations sur les finances de France depuis l'année 1595 jusqu'à l'année 1721*, 2 vols. (Basle, 1758).

Veseth, M., *Mountains of Debt: Crisis and Change in Renaissance Florence, Victorian Britain and Postwar America* (New York–Oxford, 1990).

Vettori, A., *Finanzhaushalt und Wirtschaftsverwaltung Basels, 1689–1798* (Basle, 1984).

Veyrassat, B., *Négociants et fabricants dans l'industrie cotonnière suisse, 1760–1840: Aux origines financières de l'industrialisation* (Lausanne, 1982).

Vigo, G., *Fisco e società nella Lombardia del Cinquecento* (Bologna, 1979).

Vilar, P., 'Réflexions sur la "crise de l'ancien type", "inégalité des récoltes" et "sous-développement"', in *Conjoncture économique, structures sociales: Hommage à Ernest Labrousse* (Paris–The Hague, 1974), 37–58.

——'Slancio urbano e movimento dei salari: il caso de Barcellona nel Settecento', in R. Romano (ed.), *I prezzi in Europa dal XIII secolo a oggi* (Turin, 1967), 375–417.

Vilar Berrogain, J., *Literatura y Economia: La figura satírica del arbitrista en el Siglo de Oro* (Madrid, 1973).

Viljoen, S., *Economic Systems in World History* (London–New York, 1974).

Villain, J., *Le recouvrement des impôts directs sous l'ancien régime* (Paris, 1952).

Villari, R., *La rivolta antispagnola a Napoli: Le origini, 1585–1647* (Bari, 1967).

——*The Revolt of Naples*, trans. J. Newell and J. A. Marino (Oxford, 1993).

Virgoe, R., 'The benevolence of 1481', *English Historical Review*, 104 (1989), 25–45.

Von Eyb, Albrecht, *Spiegel der sitten, in latein genant Speculum morum. Von sunden vnd tugenden dargegen. Von ständen vnd ämptern mancherlay personen* ([1471], Augsburg, 1511).

Von Reumont, A., *Lorenzo de' Medici il Magnifico. I*, 2nd edn (Leipzig, 1883).

Vovelle, M., *The Fall of the French Monarchy, 1787–1792*, trans. S. Burke (Cambridge, 1984).

Wachenhausen, M., *Staatsausgabe und Öffentliches Interesse in den Steuerrechtfertigungslehren des naturrechtlichen Rationalismus* (Berlin, 1972).

Wagner, F., 'Finanzielle Ratschläge aus der Zeit Albrecht Achills', *Forschungen zur deutschen Geschichte*, 25 (1885), 342–53.

Walker, B., *Political Economy*, 2nd edn (New York, 1887).

Walker, G. J., *Spanish Politics and Imperial Trade, 1700–1789* (London–Basingstoke, 1979).

Walker, M., *German Home Towns: Community, State, and General Estate, 1648–1871* (Ithaca, NY–London, 1971).

——'Rights and functions: the social categories of eighteenth-century German jurists and Cameralists', *Journal of Modern History*, 50 (1978), 234–51.

——*Johann Jakob Moser and the Holy Roman Empire of the German Nation* (Chapel Hill, NC, 1981).

Wallerstein, I., *The Modern World-System. I. Capitalist Agriculture and the Origins of the European World-Economy in the Sixteenth Century* (New York, 1974).

——*The Modern World-System. II. Mercantilism and the Consolidation of the European World-Economy, 1600–1750* (New York, 1980).

Walter, F., *Die theresianische Staatsreform von 1749* (Vienna, 1958).

Wangermann, E., *From Joseph II to the Jacobin Trials: Government Policy and Public Opinion in the Habsburg Dominions in the Period of the French Revolution*, 2nd edn (Oxford, 1969).

——*The Austrian Achievement, 1700–1800* (London, 1973).

Waquet, J.-C., *Le grand-duché de Toscane sous les derniers Médicis: Essai sur le système des finances et la stabilité des institutions dans les anciens États italiens* (École française de Rome; Rome, 1990).

Warren, W. L., *Henry II* (London, 1973).

——*King John*, 2nd edn (London, 1978).

Waugh, S. L., *The Lordship of England: Royal Wardships and Marriages in English Society and Politics, 1217–1327* (Princeton, NJ, 1988).

Webber, C., and Wildavsky, A., *A History of Taxation and Expenditure in the Western World* (New York, 1986).

Weir, D. R., 'Tontines, public finance and revolution in France and England, 1688–1789', *Journal of Economic History*, 49 (1989), 95–124.

Weisz, L., 'Der organisierte Kredit in Zürich von der Reformation bis zum Jahre 1835', *Geld- und Kreditsystem der Schweiz: Festschrift Gottlieb Bachmann* (Zurich, 1944), 143–4.

Wernham, R. B. (ed.), *New Cambridge Modern History. III. The Counter-Reformation and the Price Revolution, 1559–1610* (Cambridge, 1971).

Weulersse, G., *Le mouvement physiocratique en France de 1756 à 1770*, 2 vols. (Paris–The Hague, 1910; repr. 1968).

——*La Physiocratie sous les ministères de Turgot et de Necker, 1774–1781* (Paris, 1950).

——*La Physiocratie à la fin du règne de Louis XV, 1770–4* (Paris, 1959).

White, E. N., 'Was there a solution to the *ancien régime*'s financial dilemma?', *Journal of Economic History*, 49 (1989), 545–68.

——'Measuring the French Revolution's inflation: the *Tableaux de dépréciation*', *Histoire et mesure*, 6 (1991), 245–74.

Willard, J. F., *Parliamentary Taxes on Personal Property, 1290 to 1334* (Cambridge, Mass., 1934).

Williams, F., 'Monetary institutions in Agenais from the establishment to the disappearance of the Agen mint', *Journal of European Economic History*, 20 (1991), 569–613.

Wilson, C. H., 'Treasure and trade balances: the Mercantilist problem', in F. C. Lane and J. C. Riemersma (eds.), *Enterprise and Secular Change: Readings in Economic History* (Homewood, Ill., 1953), 337–49. [Originally published in *Economic History Review*, 2nd ser., (1949), 152–61.]

——*England's Apprenticeship, 1603–1763* (London, 1965).

——*Economic History and the Historian: Collected Essays* (London, [1969]).

——and Parker, N. G. (eds.), *An Introduction to the Sources of European Economic History, 1500–1800. I. Western Europe* (London, 1977).

Winter, J. M. (ed.), *War and Economic Development: Essays in Memory of David Joslin* (Cambridge, 1975).

Witt, P.-C., *Wealth and Taxation in Central Europe: The History and Sociology of Public Finance* (Leamington Spa, 1987).

Wittmann, W., *Einführung in die Finanzwissenschaft* (Stuttgart, 1975).

Wolfe, M., 'Jean Bodin on taxes: the sovereignty–taxes paradox', *Political Science Quarterly*, 83 (1968), 268–84.

——*The Fiscal System of Renaissance France* (New Haven, 1972).

Wolffe, B. P., 'Henry VII's land revenues and chamber finance', *English Historical Review*, 311 (1964), 225–54.

——*The Crown Lands, 1461* to *1536: An Aspect of Yorkist and Tudor Government* (London, 1970).

——*The Royal Demesne in English History* (London, 1971).

Wood, J. B., *The Nobility of the Élection of Bayeux, 1463–1666: Continuity through Change* (Princeton, NJ, 1980).

Woolf, S., *Napoleon's Integration of Europe* (London–New York, 1991).

Wrigley, E. A., and Schofield, R. S., *The Population History of England, 1541–1871* (London, 1981).

Zagorin, P., *Rebels and Rulers, 1500–1660*, 2 vols. (Cambridge, 1982).

Zangheri, R., *Catasti e storia della proprietà terriera* (Turin, 1979).

Zaninelli, S., *Il nuovo censo dello stato di Milano dall'editto del 1718 al 1733* (Milan, 1963).

Ziegler, W., *Studien zum Staatshaushalt Bayerns in der zweiten Hälfte des 15. Jahrhunderts: Die regulären Kammereinkünfte des Herzogtums Niederbayern, 1450–1500* (Munich, 1981).

Zwitzer, H. L., *'De Militie van den Staat': Het leger van de Republiek der Verenigde Nederlanden* (Amsterdam, 1991).

LIST OF CONTRIBUTORS

JÁNOS BARTA is Professor of Medieval and Early Modern European History at Kossuth Lajos University, Debrecen (Hungary). His main fields of research are the economic history of central eastern Europe and the rise of Enlightened absolutism in the Habsburg lands and Prussia. He is the author of nine books in Hungarian, including a synthesis of eighteenth-century Hungarian history (1984) and a biography of Maria Theresa (1988).

RICHARD BONNEY is Professor of Modern History at the University of Leicester (UK). His books include *Political Change in France under Richelieu and Mazarin, 1624–1661* (1978); *The King's Debts: Finance and Politics in France, 1589–1661* (1981); and *The European Dynastic States, 1494–1660* (1991). His collected essays are forthcoming in 1995. He is the Founding Editor of the Oxford Journal *French History* and is preparing the Oxford History of Early Modern France.

CARLO CAPRA is Professor of Early Modern History at the Università degli studi di Milano (Italy). His main fields of research are eighteenth-century Italy and the Revolutionary and Napoleonic period. His publications include *La Lombardia Austriaca nell'età delle riforme* (1987). He is working on a history of European bureaucracy from Louis XIV to Napoleon.

JUAN GELABERT is Professor of Early Modern History at the University of Cantabria, Santander (Spain). His main field of research is the social and economic history of Castile in the sixteenth and seventeenth centuries. His publications include *Santiago y la tierra de Santiago de 1500 a 1640* (1982) and *Economia y sociedad: El siglo de oro* (1988).

JEAN-CLAUDE HOCQUET is Directeur de Recherche at the Centre National de la Recherche Scientifique at the Université de Lille III (France). He has researched on the history of salt production and trade, maritime transport, weights and measures and public finance. His publications include: *Le sel et la fortune de Venise*, 2 vols. (1978–9); *Le sel et le pouvoir de l'an mil à la Révolution française* (1985); and *Le roi, le marchand et le sel* (1987).

EBERHARD ISENMANN is Professor of Medieval History at the Ruhr-Universität Bochum (Germany). His publications include *Die deutsche Stadt im Spätmittelalter, 1250–1500: Stadtgestalt, Recht, Stadtregiment, Kirche, Gesellschaft, Wirtschaft* (1988).

MARTIN KÖRNER is Professor of Swiss History at the University of Berne (Switzerland). His main research interest is in monetary, banking and financial, as well as the urban, history of the late Middle Ages and early modern period. His publications include *Solidarités financières suisses au xvie siècle: Contribution à l'histoire monétaire, bancaire et* *financière des cantons suisses et des États voisins* (1980); *Luzerner Staatsfinanzen, 1415–1798* (1981); and *Banken und Versicherungen im Kanton Luzern* (1987).

GIOVANNI MUTO is Professor at the Università degli studi di Napoli Federico II (Italy). His main research areas are financial history and social stratification in Spanish Italy. His publications include *Le finanze pubbliche napoletane tra riforme e restaurazione, 1520–1634* (1980) and *Saggi sul governo dell'economia nel Mezzogiorno spagnolo* (1992).

W. M. ORMROD is Lecturer in History at the University of York (UK) and is a specialist in the political and administrative history of later medieval England. He is the author of numerous articles on government and finance, and has also edited several collections of articles. He is the author of *The Reign of Edward III: Crown and Political Society in England, 1327–1377* (1990), and is currently working on a political biography of Edward III; a volume of essays on the Black Death; and a volume entitled *Political Life in England, 1300–1450*.

BJØRN POULSEN is Archivist and Senior Research Fellow at the Provincial Archives of southern Jutland, Aabenraa (Denmark). He is a specialist on the economic and social history of medieval and early modern Denmark, and has written books and articles on trade, urban history, monetary history and numismatics, agricultural history and salt production. His most recent book is *Bondens penge: Studier i sønderjyske regnskaber, 1400–1650* (1990). He is now working on Danish maritime history in the Middle Ages.

WINFRIED SCHULZE is Professor of Early Modern History at the Ludwig-Maximilians-Universität München (Germany). He has published on German history in the sixteenth century, on German and European peasant rebellions, on the French Revolution, and on German historiography after 1945. His current interests centre on early modern European history.

MARJOLEIN 'T HART is Lecturer in Economic and Social History at the University of Amsterdam (Netherlands). She has published widely on Dutch finances and state formation in the early modern period, including most recently *The Making of a Bourgeois State: War, Politics and Finance during the Dutch Revolt* (1993).

INDEX

Richard Bonney